HTML & Web Design

Tips & Techniques

Kris Jamsa
Konrad King
Andy Anderson

McGraw-Hill/Osborne

New York Chicago San Francisco
Lisbon London Madrid Mexico City Milan
New Delhi San Juan Seoul Singapore Sydney Toronto

McGraw-Hill/Osborne
2600 Tenth Street
Berkeley, California 94710
U.S.A.

To arrange bulk purchase discounts for sales promotions, premiums, or fund-raisers, please contact **McGraw-Hill**/Osborne at the above address. For information on translations or book distributors outside the U.S.A., please see the International Contact Information page immediately following the index of this book.

HTML & Web Design Tips & Techniques

1234567890 DOC DOC 0198765432

ISBN 0-07-219394-8

Publisher	Brandon A. Nordin
Vice President & Associate Publisher	Scott Rogers
Acquisitions Editor	Jim Schachterle
Project Editor	Janet Walden
Acquisitions Coordinator	Tim Madrid
Technical Editors	Charles Hornberger, Wendy Willard
Copy Editor	Darren Meiss
Proofreader	Pat Mannion
Indexer	David Heiret
Computer Designers	Carie Abrew, George Toma Charbak, Tabitha M. Cagan
Illustrators	Michael Mueller, Lyssa Wald
Series Designer	Roberta Steele
Cover Series Design	Greg Scott

This book was composed with Corel VENTURA ™ Publisher.

To Bonnie,
You are, and always will be, the most important part of my life.
–Andy

To my wife Karen,
Thanks for enduring the late hours, solitary meals, missed vacations, and especially for listening to my moans and groans about the writing "process." Your knowing smiles and not so gentle (but needed) "Just Do It!" inspired me to see the project through from concept to completion.
–Konrad

To Stephanie,
Although you have grown up to become a very special woman, you will always be our little girl.
–Dad

About the Authors

Konrad King is an author and computer systems consultant for a wide range of clients. A former Air Force officer, Konrad has worked with mainframes as well as PCs and PC-based networks. He has written and worked with award-winning authors on several books on SQL database design and implementation, Web design, and Microsoft Office software, such as FrontPage and PowerPoint. When not writing, Konrad designs, develops, and maintains Web sites; installs and maintains networks and enterprise software; and develops custom software applications in Visual C++, Visual Basic, DataFlex, and various SQL database platforms. Having worked in the computer field since 1984, Konrad is able to draw from a vast pool of knowledge about what works in the "real world" and what does not.

Andy Anderson is a graphics artist and designer and has worked with Photoshop, Illustrator, and most graphics arts programs for the Web since their release. An author and university professor, Andy is also a sought-after lecturer in the U.S., Canada, and Europe. The remainder of his time is spent developing curriculum and resource materials for various corporations and seminar companies. His clients include designers and trainers from the U.S. government, Boeing, Disneyland, and other Fortune 500 companies.

Kris Jamsa is the author of more than 90 computer books, with cumulative sales of several million copies. Kris holds a bachelor of science degree in computer science from the United States Air Force Academy, a masters degree in computer science from the University of Nevada, Las Vegas, a Ph.D. in computer science with an emphasis in operating systems from Arizona State University, and a masters of business administration from San Diego State University. In 1992, he and his wife, Debbie, founded Jamsa Press, a computer- book publishing company. After expanding the company's presence to 70 countries and 28 languages, they sold Jamsa Press to a larger publishing house. Today, Kris is the founder of Jamsa Media Group, which produces high-quality computer books. He is also very active in analyzing emerging technologies. Kris lives on a ranch in Houston, Texas, with his wife Debbie, their three dogs, and six horses. When he is not in front of his PC, Kris is normally riding and jumping his horse Robin Hood.

Contents at a Glance

Chapter 1   **HTML Basics** . . . . **xxii**

Chapter 2   **HTML Tables** **62**

Chapter 3   **HTML Forms** **112**

Chapter 4   **Cascading Style Sheets (CSS)** **158**

Chapter 5   **XHTML and Emerging Trends** **220**

Chapter 6   **Graphics** **264**

Chapter 7   **Animation, Sound, and Video** **316**

Chapter 8   **JavaScript** **358**

Chapter 9   **Java Applets and ActiveX Objects** **418**

Chapter 10   **PHP4** **464**

Chapter 11   **Active Server Pages (ASP)** **524**

Chapter 12   **Security and Performance** **586**

           Index **637**

Contents

Acknowledgments, xv

Introduction, xv

Chapter 1   **HTML Basics** . . . . **xxii**

Downloading and Installing the Personal Web Server 16

Managing the Personal Web Server and Publishing Your Web Pages 18

Describing Web Page Contents with a Title 21

Identifying Web Documents Using the Document Type Definition 23

Inserting Comments into a Web Document 24

Specifying the Typeface for Web Page Text 26

Controlling the Flow of Text with Paragraph and Line Break Tags 27

Changing the Size of Text Using Heading Level Tags and the Font Tag *size* Attribute 32

Changing the Color of Text in an HTML Document 33

Adding Graphics to a Web Page Using a Basic <img> Tag 35

Changing the Alignment of Text and Graphics 37

Adding a Hypertext Link to a Web Page 40

Enhancing Individual Letters and Words Using Character Formatting Tags 41

Using Symbols and Special Characters in an HTML Document 42

Using Horizontal Rules to Organize Web Content 44

Using Blockquote Tags to Control Left and Right Text Margins 47

Creating Ordered and Unordered Lists 48

Creating Nested Lists 51

Creating Definition Listings 52

Using Preformatted Text Tags to Control the Display of Web Content 54

Displaying a Navigation Menu Within a Web Page Frame 56

Displaying Multiple Web Pages Onscreen at the Same Time 57

Chapter 2	**HTML Tables**	**62**
	Creating a Table with Cells that Span Multiple Columns or Multiple Rows	72
	Working with Table and Cell Border Widths	75
	Working with Table and Cell Border Colors	76
	Working with Background Images and Colors	78
	Determining a Color Attribute's Value	81
	Working with Cell Padding and Cell Spacing	83
	Setting Table Dimensions Using Relative or Absolute Values	84
	Setting Cell Dimensions Using Relative or Absolute Values	85
	Aligning Cell Content Horizontally and Vertically	86
	Aligning a Table on a Web Page	89
	Controlling the Width and Height of a Cell by Inserting a Transparent GIF	89
	Wrapping Text Around an Image	91
	Displaying a Gallery of Thumbnails Within a Table	93
	Creating Bullets and Lists with Tables and Graphics	96
	Creating a Navigation Sidebar Using a Table	97
	Adding Images and Links to Table Cells	98
	Nesting Tables to Control Borders on a Web Page	99
	Approximating an Image Map by Placing Pieces of an Image Within a Table	100
	Slicing a Graphic Image into Table Cells to Create a Quick-Loading Web Graphic	102
	Reducing the Amount of Time a Web Browser Spends Drawing a Table	103
	Simulating Web Page Frames Using a Table	104
	Focusing the Viewer's Attention with Cell Background Colors	107
	Aligning Web Page Content Visually with Visible Table Borders	108
	Controlling Gutter Size and Margin Width of Text on a Web Page	110
Chapter 3	**HTML Forms**	**112**
	Creating a Single-Line Input Field on a Form	119
	Creating a Multiline Input Field on a Form	120
	Validating Text Element Data Prior to Submitting Form Results	122
	Placing Check Boxes on a Form	124
	Placing Radio Buttons on a Form	126
	Validating Radio Button Group Selections Prior to Submitting Form Results	128
	Placing a Drop-Down List (Selection Menu) on a Form	129
	Verifying the Visitor Has Made a Selection List Choice Prior to Submitting Form Results	132
	Changing the Items Available on a Selection List Based on Visitor Supplied Information	134
	Sending All Selection List Values to the Web Server Through a Hidden Field	136
	Adding a Reset Button to a Form	138
	Preventing a Visitor from Clearing Form Elements Accidentally	139
	Adding a Submit Button to a Form	140

Replacing the Standard Submit and Reset Buttons on a Form with Other Graphics Images 141

Sending Form Results by E-Mail Without a CGI Script 143

Controlling the Layout of Form Elements and Text with HTML Tables 145

Creating a Shortcut Key for Form Navigation with a <label> Tag 148

Instructing the Web Browser to Execute a Form Validation Function with the *onClick* Attribute 149

Passing Values to the Web Server Through Hidden Fields 151

Hiding Visitor Input from View Within a Password Element 152

Adding a Generic Button Object to a Form 153

Enabling and Disabling Form Elements on-the-Fly 154

Chapter 4   Cascading Style Sheets (CSS) **158**

Applying Multiple CSS Rules to a Single Selector 170

Selecting a Typeface with the *font-family* Property 172

Specifying the Size of Text with the *font-size* Property 174

Creating Overlapping Text 177

Aligning Web Page Text 179

Controlling Margins and Line Height 181

Displaying Text Within Columns 183

Working with Borders 186

Indenting Paragraphs and Controlling Letter, Word, and Line Spacing 188

Offsetting Text with Initial Caps 189

Customizing the Appearance of Hyperlinks 191

Creating a Drop-Shadow Effect 192

Applying a Border Graphic 194

Positioning Background Images and Watermarks 196

Floating Images and Text 199

Customizing the Appearance of Lists 201

Creating Text and Image Effects with Filters 203

Aligning Labels with Form Elements and Adding Color to Forms 206

Displaying a Gallery of Thumbnails with Captions 209

Controlling the Cursor 212

Layering Web Page Elements 214

Sending Your Style Sheet Through a Validator 216

Chapter 5   XHTML and Emerging Trends **220**

Converting HTML to XHTML Using HTML Tidy 233

Selecting the Correct DOCTYPE for Your Web Page 237

Validating Your Web Page with an XHTML Validator 238

Setting the Text Size on an XHTML Web Page with Keywords 242

Grouping an XHTML Form's Selection List Items with the <optgroup> Tag 245

Adding Color to XHTML Tables with Cascading Style Sheet Rules 247

Embedding Fonts Within an XHTML Web Page with CSS Rules 249

Inserting an XHTML Page Within Another with an Inline Frame 251

Updating Multiple XHTML Page Inline Frames at Once 255

Changing XHTML Page Appearance Based on Media Type 257

Controlling the Way the Web Browser Prints an XHTML Web Page 261

Chapter 6   **Graphics** **264**

Working with Cross-Platform Issues When Creating Graphics Images for the Web 274

Specifying Image Dimensions Within an Image Tag 277

Working with the *alt* Attribute and Text-Only Viewers 278

Creating a Tool Tip by Inserting a *title* Attribute in an Image Tag 281

Compressing Photographs into a JPEG File 283

Saving Clip Art and Text to a GIF-Formatted File 286

Making Images Appear to Load Faster 288

Working with the PNG-8 and PNG-24 File Formats 290

Converting Graphics into Web Images with Image-Editing Programs 291

Creating Web-Friendly Graphics Images on Your Scanner 292

Creating Colorful Horizontal Rules 294

Retrieving a Fast-Loading "Teaser" Image with the *lowsrc* Attribute 296

Ensuring Accurate Color Presentation with the Web-Safe Color Palette 298

Creating Graphical Hyperlink Anchors 300

Creating Tiled Backgrounds from Graphics Images 301

Creating Transparency in a GIF Image 304

Retrieving Full-Size Images after Clicking on Thumbnails 307

Preloading and Caching Images Behind the Scenes 309

Expanding the Web-Safe Color Palette with Dithering Techniques 311

Smoothing the Edges of Text Converted into a Graphic Through Anti-Aliasing 313

Chapter 7   **Animation, Sound, and Video** **316**

Creating a GIF Animation from Scratch 334

Controlling GIF Animation Through Internal Settings 336

Creating a Banner Ad Using GIF Animation 338

Creating Smooth Transitions Between GIF Animation Frames Using Tweening 341

Incorporating a Completed Flash Splash Screen into a Web Site 342

Creating a Flash Movie from Scratch 345

Building Text-Based Animations Using FlaX 348

Broadcasting Streaming Audio and Video 348

Creating Your Own Streaming Media 351

Creating a Page that Features a Web Cam 352

Integrating Video and Audio into a Web Site Using SMIL (Smile) 354

Chapter 8   **JavaScript** **358**

Handling Older Browsers that Do Not Support Scripts 370

Storing Multiple Values in One Variable by Using JavaScript Arrays 371

Letting a Script Make Decisions and Process Accordingly 372
Making Decisions Based on Two or More Conditions 374
Executing Code When a Condition Is Not True 375
Repeating Statements a Specific Number of Times 376
Repeating Statements While a Condition Is True 377
Responding to JavaScript Events 378
Executing JavaScript Statements Within the Body of a Web Page 380
Calling a User-Defined JavaScript Function 382
Calling JavaScript Functions Within an Event Handler 384
Looking Closer at JavaScript Event Handlers 385
Creating an Interactive Navigation Bar with a Mouseover Effect 388
Taking Advantage of the Scripting Object Model Arrays 390
Referring to Web Page Objects by Name Instead of Position Number 392
Leveraging the Contents of the Document Object 393
Taking Advantage of the JavaScript Images Array 396
Exploiting the JavaScript Links Array 398
Changing Web Page Colors Using JavaScript 401
Storing a Cookie on the Visitor's Hard Drive 402
Formatting Cookie Data Using JavaScript 404
Retrieving a Cookie Value from the Cookie File 406
Removing a Cookie from the Cookie File 407
Saving Time and Programming by Using Prewritten (External) Scripts 409
Creating an Animation Using the *onLoad* Event 410
Displaying Self-Changing Banners Using JavaScript 411
Pointing Hyperlinks to New Files On-the-Fly 413
Pre-caching Pictures to Reduce Image Display Time 415
Creating a Scrolling Marquee Using JavaScript 416

Chapter 9   **Java Applets and ActiveX Objects** **418**
Using an Applet to Create a Pop-Up Navigation Menu 437
Using an Applet to Animate a Text String 440
Using an Applet to Display and Print a Calendar for Any Year 442
Using an Applet to Display a Passage at Random from a Text File 443
Using an Applet to Create a Navigation Menu that Runs in Its Own Window 444
Using an Applet to Scroll the Contents of a File Vertically Within a Rectangular Box Onscreen 448
Using an Applet to Animate an Image Along a Sine Wave 450
Editing Java Source Code to Build a Custom Applet 452
Using the Microsoft Chat ActiveX Control to Add Internet Chat to a Web Page 457
Using Only ActiveX Objects with Internet Explorer 460

Chapter 10   **PHP4** **464**
Sending Data from an HTML Form to a PHP Script 484
Using PHP to Parse and Extract Form Results 488

Using PHP to Send an E-Mail Message 491

Determining Whether a Visitor's Web Browser Accepts Cookies 493

Using PHP and a Disk File to Set Up Username/Password Access to a Web Site 496

Preventing Visitors from Linking Directly to Pages on Your Site 498

Using a PHP Session to Establish a Persistent Connection Between a Site Visitor and the Web Server 499

Creating a MySQL Database and Tables 502

Displaying SQL Query Results in an HTML Table on a Web Page 504

Using PHP to Generate a Random Password 507

Using PHP and MySQL to Set Up Username/Password Access to a Web Site 509

Preventing Visitors from Changing Variable Values with URL Arguments 511

Using PHP and MySQL to Track Where Visitors Go on Your Web Site 512

Determining the Visitor's IP Address for Web Page Requests Sent Through a Proxy Server 514

Preventing One Visitor from Assuming Another Visitor's PHP Session Identity 516

Using PHP Functions to Create Web Page Templates 517

Using PHP to Add File Upload Functionality to a Web Page 520

Chapter 11   **Active Server Pages (ASP)** **524**

Controlling the Flow of Content from Web Server to Web Browser Through the HTML Output Stream 539

Preventing the Web Browser from Displaying Stale Active Server Pages 543

Redirecting the Web Browser to Another Web Page 545

Maintaining Variable Values Between HTTP Requests with the Cookies Collection 547

Retrieving Form Results from the ASP Form Collection 550

Retrieving Form Results from the ASP QueryString Collection 553

Retrieving Information from the Server Variables Collection 556

Connecting to a MySQL DBMS Through the MyODBC Driver 559

Setting Up Username/Password Access to a Web Site 562

Starting a Session and Working with Session Variables 565

Executing SQL Queries and Displaying Query Results Sets Within an HTML Table 568

Displaying Banner Ads with the Microsoft Banner Ad Rotator 573

Tracking Microsoft Banner Ad Rotator Impressions and Click-Throughs 576

Handling "Status: 404 Not Found" Errors 580

Chapter 12   **Security and Performance** **586**

Downloading and Installing a Public Key, Digital Signature, and Server ID 600

Creating a Secure Web Page Under IIS 601

Installing a Software-Based Firewall 603

Fine-Tuning a Firewall's Port Assignments 605

Reducing Your Site's Exposure to Viruses 607

Improving Performance and Security by Disabling Printer and File Sharing 610

Using Client Certificates to Restrict User Access 612

Auditing System Events to Detect Intruders 614

Exploiting the NTFS File System 617

Disabling Remote Services 620

Analyzing Your System's Vulnerability 623
Processing Credit Card Data 625
Taking a Close Look at a Web Site's Performance Chain 625
Creating a Web Farm 631
Monitoring Server Performance 631

Index **637**

Acknowledgements

It's nearly impossible to thank everyone who is involved in the process of taking an author's manuscript from concept to book form. Please take a moment and turn to page near the front of the book that lists the Osborne team that brought this book together. This book's quality content is a direct result of their hard work and dedication.

We'd also like to thank this book's technical editors Charles Hornberger and Wendy Willard for their candor and selfless content contributions. Their insights greatly improved the book's quality. And, we'd like to thank Jim Schachterle for his support throughout this project and our project editor, Janet Walden, for pulling together all the pieces.

Introduction

Analysts now estimate that across the Internet, over 100 million domain names are in use (for Internet statistics, visit http://www.nua.com/surveys). With fast DSL and cable-modem connections available to the masses, and with companies offering low-cost Web hosting, tens of millions of users are now creating personal Web sites. Further, with the estimates of online users now exceeding 500 million (and with that number growing at a rate of 7 percent per month!), Web developers must find ways to exploit new technologies to attract and capture the attention of users as they "surf" the Web.

Throughout this book's chapters, you will learn ways to put Web technologies immediately to use on your Web pages. Each chapter presents ways you can quickly integrate a technology, such as dynamic content, security, database access, as well as client-side and server-side processing. You will first learn a technology's fundamentals and the best ways to exploit the technology within your Web pages. Then, you can take advantage of ready-to-use solutions you can simply cut-and-paste into your Web pages. Finally, you will examine behind-the-scenes settings and techniques you can use to unlock your Web site's full potential.

If a fast, state-of-the-art, eye-catching Web site is your goal, this book will help you achieve it.

Who Should Read This Book

Across the Web, millions of users and professional Web developers work with Web pages daily. To simplify their efforts, many Web developers rely on numerous Web development software programs to help them with Web page design. Unfortunately, to exploit new Web technologies *fully* and to drive Web site performance, developers must at some point roll up their sleeves and dig into HTML tags, attributes, Cascading Style Sheet rules, JavaScript, Active Server Pages, PHP, and more.

Despite the vast number of sites that make up the World Wide Web, you would be hard pressed to find a Web developer who would not be happier if his or her site were faster, more secure, or easier to manage. Further, the users who visit sites not only want entertaining and current content, but also want that content to download quickly. Most users assume that the sites that present themselves as secure truly are secure. Regardless of the content you place on a Web site, users expect quality, speed, and security.

This book examines hundreds of ways Web developers can improve their site's performance, security, content, and ease of management. You do not have to be an experienced programmer or network administrator to perform the operations this book presents. Each Tip presents step-by-step instructions you can easily perform, as well as solutions you can cut-and-paste into your Web pages. Within the books chapters, you will learn:

- The HTML fundamentals you must know to create your first Web site, and the steps you must perform to host that site on the Web

- Ways you can use HTML-based tables to organize information you present on a Web page, and how to use tables to arrange text and graphics

- How you can use Cascading Style Sheets to gain full control of text formatting within a Web page and to simplify future updates

- How XHTML differs from HTML, new XHTML capabilities you can exploit within your pages, as well as ways you can migrate your HTML pages to XHTML

- Techniques you can use to better exploit graphics within your Web pages while reducing the time users must wait for images to download

- How to create dynamic Web page content using PHP and Active Server Pages

- Behind-the-scenes operations you can perform to use HTTP and CGI settings to automate solutions that exploit your user's browser type, connection speed, and more

- Ways you can secure your system from hackers and identify potential security holes in your system that malicious users can exploit

- How you can integrate e-commerce solutions and credit card processing into your Web site

- And much more!

What You Need to Perform the Techniques We Present

This book presents a myriad of ways you can improve your Web site's content, performance, security, and ease of management. Within each chapter, you will find operations you can immediately perform on your Web site.

To take advantage of the techniques we present, you do not need high-end software or other graphics arts tools. You simply need to spend five to ten minutes performing the Tip's step-by-step instructions. The Tips will help you download from the Web (for free!) any tools that you will need.

For high-end Web developers and programmers, this book examines ways you can use scripts to access many low-level operations. Each programming language this book presents is built into browsers, servers, or is readily available for download from the Web. If you have not programmed in these languages before, do not worry. Each chapter's introduction will provide the foundation you will need to exploit the language.

What This Book Covers

This book contains 12 chapters. Each chapter examines a specific Web technology, programming language, or design technique. Within each chapter, you will find a thorough discussion of a technology or language followed by Tips you can quickly perform to enhance your Web pages and the overall design and performance of your Web site.

Chapter 1: HTML Basics   To start, this chapter lays the foundation that designers new to Web development need to exploit the techniques they will learn throughout the remainder of the book. Designers will learn how to create HTML pages, how to display pages from files that reside on their own PC, and then how to use a Web server to make their pages available to visitors across the Web.

Chapter 2: HTML Tables   Within a Web page, tables provide designers with a powerful way to organize large amounts of data for display onscreen. Many Web designers also use tables to gain better control over the alignment of text and graphics that appear on a page. A designer might, for example, use tables to flow text around an image. In addition, a Web page may present a table of thumbnail images from which users can select the pictures that they want to download as a larger graphic.

Chapter 3: HTML Forms   Across the Web, millions of sites use forms to interact with visitors. Forms may ask the visitor to provide a wide range of information, such as a shipping address, personal data, or credit card numbers for purchases. In addition, forms let visitors search for specific products, services, or content available at the site, or perhaps elsewhere on the Web. Developers create forms using HTML tags. After the user submits his or her information, the Web server runs a special program (which developers call a *script*) that processes and likely stores the data. In this chapter, you will learn how to create forms using HTML, how to validate the information a user enters using JavaScript, and then how to process the data the user submits.

Chapter 4: Cascading Style Sheets (CSS)   Within a Web page, developers use a wide range of HTML tags to format text, graphics, and links. Using only HTML tags, such <b> for bolding, <i> for italics, and so on, a Web developer can format Web page text as he or she desires. Unfortunately, if the formatting must later be changed, the developer must change numerous tags. Cascading Style Sheets make Web sites much easier to manage. Using Cascading Style Sheets, Web developers can assign font, color, alignment, and many other attributes to the text that appears on a page. If the developer must later change the page appearance, he or she can simply change the style definition and the changes will immediately appear within the styled text. Further, for Web designers looking for high-end designs, Cascading Style Sheets allows precise positioning and even stacking text and graphics to create countless effects.

Chapter 5: XHTML and Emerging Trends   To ensure that your Web pages work and look the way you want them to in the next generation of Web browsers, you must adhere to the World Wide Web Consortium's recommendations. When followed carefully, the "rules" within the XHTML standard prevent you from creating Web pages with improper syntax, missing or proprietary tags, and invalid attributes. By avoiding such bad code, you ensure your Web pages will look great and will work with all standard Web browsers. Moreover, by guaranteeing the correctness of your Web page description (by making it compliant with the XHTML standard), you allow browser manufacturers to omit code designed to "guess" the intentions of malformed HTML. Browsers designed to run on non-PC devices (such as cell phones, palm organizers, onboard computers within cars, and so on) must be small, because these devices have limited memory capacities. This chapter shows you how to run an application (HTML Tidy) which checks your Web page HTML, corrects any errors, and converts your HTML to XHTML. You will also learn how to use online validation programs that check new Web pages you create to ensure they comply with the XHTML standard. Then you will find Tips that show you how to extend the capabilities of the markup language by adding new tags and attributes, as well as Tips that let you detect the user's browser type so your pages display quickly and correctly in browsers running on non-PC devices.

Chapter 6: Graphics   Across the Web, pages make extensive use of graphics. Unfortunately, many sites that offer great visuals lose impatient visitors who are not willing to sit through long download times. In this chapter you will learn techniques, such as caching and preloading, you can use, as well as settings you can fine-tune to reduce image download times. You will also learn about the various graphics file formats and when you should use each. Further, the chapter discusses color palettes and ways you can ensure your content is "Web friendly." Finally, graphics professionals will learn ways to simplify the migration of images to the Web.

Chapter 7: Animation, Sound, and Video   With high-speed cable-modem and DSL connections becoming readily available, many Web sites use animations, background music, and video to capture users' attention. In this chapter, you will learn how to integrate a range of animations, from simple animated graphics to high-end Flash animations. Further, you will learn how to play background music as users view your pages and how to deliver streaming video content on demand. Finally, you will learn how to broadcast audio (just as a Web-based radio station) from your Web site.

Chapter 8: JavaScript   JavaScript is a programming language Web designers can use to automate tasks within a Web page. Web developers place JavaScript statements within the HTML tags that define a Web page. The JavaScript statements may, for example, validate the information the user entered into a form. (The program or script may ensure each field has a value or that the values appear correct and meaningful.) Or, JavaScript statements may perform specific processing as the user performs operations on the page. For example, you might use JavaScript to display a pop-up window that contains help text when a user clicks on a help link. Just as the user's browser displays the contents of an HTML page, the browser also executes the JavaScript statements. In this chapter, you will first learn how to create simple JavaScript applications. Then, you will examine many JavaScript solutions that you can cut-and-paste into your own Web pages.

Chapter 9: Java Applets and ActiveX Objects   For years, programmers have used the Java programming language to create applets that can run on a variety of platforms; meaning, the same Java applet can run under Windows, Linux, and on a Mac. Java applets provide programmers a way to automate tasks without introducing the risk of computer viruses to users who download the applets. Across the Web, there are countless "generic" Java applets you may want to leverage within your own pages. In this chapter, you will learn how to integrate Java applets into your HTML content. Further, the chapter examines how to provide support for ActiveX objects for Windows-based sites. Unlike Java applets, which do not provide security risks to the users that download them, ActiveX objects do not restrict the operations the code can perform. Therefore, it is important that you only integrate ActiveX objects you received from reputable developer sites that contain certificates of authentication. Chapter 9 details the precautions you should take.

Chapter 10: PHP4   PHP is a programming language that developers use to create dynamic (changing) Web page content on-the-fly. Using PHP, for example, you can customize your Web page content based on the information a user provides within a form, or perhaps based on information you glean from a cookie your site previously stored on the user's disk. Across the Web, over 1,000,000 sites use PHP to create dynamic Web pages. Before you can take advantage of PHP, you must download and install a PHP processor on your system. This chapter will walk you through the installation process. Then, you will learn how to create simple PHP-based applications. As discussed, PHP is a programming language and the chapter's introduction will lay the foundation you need to create, test, and debug PHP programs. Then, the Tips section will present several PHP-based solutions you can put to immediate use within your Web pages.

Chapter 11: Active Server Pages (ASP)   Like PHP, Active Server Pages provide a way for Web developers to create on-the-fly content. To create an Active Server Page (a dynamic Web page), you can use a myriad of programming languages that include VBScript, JScript (the Microsoft version of JavaScript), PerlScript, Python, Rexx, and more. This chapter lays the foundation from which you can develop your own Active Server Page solutions. In addition, the chapter's Tips provide solutions to a range of common Web page needs, such as creating and processing cookies, processing forms, interacting with databases, using usernames and passwords to control site access, displaying and tracking banner ads, and more.

Chapter 12: Security and Performance   This year, hackers and computer viruses will cost users and businesses over 12 billion dollars! In this chapter, you will learn steps you should take immediately to protect your site. If you are not currently using a firewall to protect your site (or simply your PC), you will learn how to download, install, and configure a site. You will also learn how your choice of file system (the software the operating system uses to store files and directories on your disk) can affect your ability to protect files (using permissions and encryption). Further, the chapter presents the steps you must perform to create secure transmissions (that exchange packets behind the scenes using encryption), and how to perform credit card transactions. Finally, the chapter looks at ways you can improve your site's performance.

How to Read This Book

Although this book's chapters build on the information presented in preceding chapters, we structured the book so that you can turn to any Tip and find the information you need.

To help you quickly locate the information you need, at the start of each chapter, we have included a list of the specific Tips that chapter presents. If you need more information on a topic, each chapter provides introductory text that will give you a solid foundation.

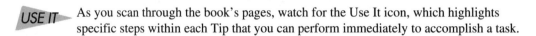 As you scan through the book's pages, watch for the Use It icon, which highlights specific steps within each Tip that you can perform immediately to accomplish a task.

Using This Book's Companion Web Site

Throughout this book's chapters, we will present numerous HTML files, Active Server Pages, JavaScript code, PHP solutions, and much more. In many cases, you can simply cut-and-paste the solutions we present into your own Web pages. All of this book's files are readily available from the McGraw-Hill/Osborne Web site at http://www.osborne.com.

CHAPTER 1

HTML Basics

TIPS IN THIS CHAPTER

▶ Downloading and Installing the Personal Web Server — 16

▶ Managing the Personal Web Server and Publishing Your Web Pages — 18

▶ Describing Web Page Contents with a Title — 21

▶ Identifying Web Documents Using the Document Type Definition — 23

▶ Inserting Comments into a Web Document — 24

▶ Specifying the Typeface for Web Page Text — 26

▶ Controlling the Flow of Text with Paragraph and Line Break Tags — 27

▶ Changing the Size of Text Using Heading Level Tags and the Font Tag *size* Attribute — 32

▶ Changing the Color of Text in an HTML Document — 33

▶ Adding Graphics to a Web Page Using a Basic <img> Tag — 35

▶ Changing the Alignment of Text and Graphics — 37

▶ Adding a Hypertext Link to a Web Page — 40

▶ Enhancing Individual Letters and Words Using Character Formatting Tags — 41

▶ Using Symbols and Special Characters in an HTML Document — 42

▶ Using Horizontal Rules to Organize Web Content — 44

▶ Using Blockquote Tags to Control Left and Right Text Margins — 47

▶ Creating Ordered and Unordered Lists   48

▶ Creating Nested Lists   51

▶ Creating Definition Listings   52

▶ Using Preformatted Text Tags to Control the Display of Web Content   54

▶ Displaying a Navigation Menu Within a Web Page Frame   56

▶ Displaying Multiple Web Pages Onscreen at the Same Time   57

Hypertext Markup Language, or as it is more commonly known, HTML, is the computer language at the heart of the World Wide Web. When you create a Web site, you use HTML to put the text, pictures, animations, and perhaps video and sound onto the individual Web pages that make up the site. In addition, HTML lets you insert hypertext links and interactive buttons that connect your Web pages to other pages on your Web site and on other Web sites around the world. Web design is a creative process, and HTML is simply one of the tools (the page description language) you use to produce Web pages.

HTML is a text markup and not a programming language. In theory, a Web page you create using HTML should be viewable by anyone with a computer, any Web browser, and access to the Internet. In reality, the ability to view all the content on a Web page depends on the capabilities of your Web browser. *Web browsers* are programs that interpret the HTML in Web page documents and display text, pictures, and animations on the visitor's computer screen. Either alone or with the help of other installed programs, browsers also play back any video and sound files you use HTML to insert on a Web page. The latest versions of the two most popular Web browsers, Microsoft's Internet Explorer and Netscape's Netscape Navigator, can display just about anything you can use HTML to put onto a Web page.

For visitors to access Web pages on your Web site, they must first connect to the Internet and start a Web browser. After the Web server sends a Web page to the visitor's computer, the Web browser interprets the HTML in the Web page file and displays the file's contents as text and graphics images in the browser's application window.

Web servers and Web browsers use the HyperText Transport Protocol (HTTP) to communicate. Among other things, the HTTP protocol specifies both the way in which Web browsers and servers send messages and the structure of the messages themselves. A thorough discussion of the various HTTP message types and structures is beyond the scope of this book. However, to design and create even complex Web sites, you need only a basic understanding of the HTTP request and response stream (between Web browser and Web server) illustrated in Figure 1-1.

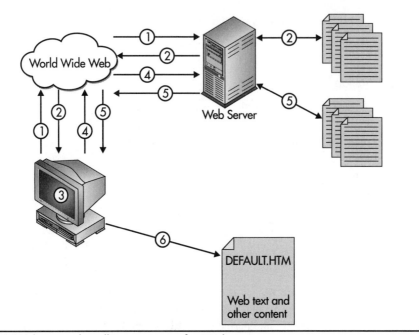

World Wide Web

Web Server

DEFAULT.HTM

Web text and
other content

Figure 1-1   A Web server handling a request for Web content

1. Each time you enter a Web address (such as http://www.NVBizNet.com) into your browser's Address field and press ENTER, the Web browser sends an HTTP request for a file over the Internet to the Web server.

2. After it receives the HTTP request for a file, the Web server retrieves the requested file and sends the Web page to the Web browser.

3. The Web browser analyzes the Web page file to determine if there are any inserted files (such as graphics, animations, sounds, and so on) that the browser needs from the Web server.

4. The Web browser sends multiple HTTP requests (one for each file the browser needs) to the Web server.

5. As the Web server receives the HTTP requests for files, the server finds each file and sends the files (one file per HTTP request) to the Web browser.

6. The Web browser takes the original Web page files, follows the instructions given by the HTML tags in the file to combine the Web page and the inserted file contents into a Web document the browser displays onscreen.

Understanding the Roles of Web Browsers and Web Pages

To keep up with the changing market, and to make the Internet available to all, Microsoft and Netscape have made versions of their Web browsers for all commercially available computer platforms and operating systems. Because the Web browser must interpret the HTML code in order to display the Web page onscreen, the brand and version of browser used by visitors to your Web site determine which features in HTML will work for them. In short, the version of the browser used determines what the visitor will see onscreen. Therefore, using HTML's latest, most advanced features and page formatting capabilities in your Web page design does not guarantee that everyone viewing the page will be able to see everything that HTML lets you put on the page.

When you design a Web page, keep in mind that not all your site visitors will be using the latest version of Internet Explorer or Netscape Navigator. Stick with the basic HTML you will learn in this chapter for the majority of the content you place on your Web pages. Then, use some of HTML's more advanced features to add pizzazz and keep site visitors coming back for another look. By combining basic and advanced HTML capabilities on the same page, you make it possible for everyone to access the important information you want to publish and for those with the latest browsers to have a truly memorable experience.

A Web page consists of a series of HTML instructions that you can enter into a file using any text editor. As mentioned previously, Web browsers such as Netscape Navigator and Internet Explorer follow the instructions in the text document you create to display the Web page content onscreen. (Web page *content* is the text, graphics, and other things [such as video and sound] that you use HTML to place on a Web page.)

If you think creating a Web page document is easy, you are right. In fact, Web site creation began with the simplest of intentions. The original HTML standard described an uncomplicated, easy-to-learn language that let you create text-only documents, which were viewable by anyone who had access to the Internet. Although the HTML standards committee, the World Wide Web Consortium (or W3C), has added many new instructions (called *tags* and *attributes*) to the HTML language, you can still create even the most feature-rich Web page by typing simple HTML commands into a document you create with a text editor (such as Windows Notepad). You can visit the W3C's Web site at http://www.w3.org/ for a complete description of various Internet technologies including HTTP, HTML, Extensible Hypertext Markup Language (XHTML), Extensible Markup Language (XML), Cascading Style Sheets (CSS), and so on.

Now that you know what a Web page is and (in general terms) how to create one, let's take a quick look at some Web page HTML. If you do not have a permanent (that is, always-on) connection to the Internet, establish a dial-up connection through your ISP. Next, start your Web browser and display your favorite Web page by entering the URL (Uniform Resource Locator; that is, the Web page address) into your Web browser's Address field. For example, you might type http://www.Osborne.com in the browser's Address field. Then, press ENTER.

The Web browser, in turn, will send an HTTP request to the Web server for the Web page whose address you entered. After the Web server responds by sending the Web page to your browser, the browser will display the page onscreen and request any embedded objects (such as graphics images) inserted on the page. After your browser has retrieved and displayed all the page content, select View | Source to display the HTML used to describe the page. (If you are using Netscape Navigator, select View | Page Source.) Internet Explorer, in turn, will use Windows Notepad to display the Web page HTML, whereas Netscape Navigator simply displays the HTML statements in a new window onscreen. Do not worry about what the individual HTML statements mean; you will learn all about them as you read this book. For now, the important point to remember is that you can view the source of any Web page.

HTML Container Tags

Essentially, a Web page is a text file that contains instructions in the form of HTML codes (called tags) and attributes. The tags are the commands the Web browser later follows to format the text and insert the graphics images you want on the Web page. Some, but not all, HTML commands require both a start and an end tag. Those that do are called *container* tags, because the instruction in the start tag applies to everything the Web page contains between the start tag and the end tag.

Each HTML command (that is, each HTML tag) starts with a less-than sign (<) followed by the tag's name and any attributes, and ends with a greater-than sign (>). To create an end tag for a start tag, you insert a forward slash (/) in front of the tag's name. Thus, a start tag has the form <tagname [attributes]> and an end tag has the form </tagname>. The tag's name tells the Web browser the tag's purpose; the attributes (if any) that follow the tagname give the Web browser additional information the browser needs to carry out the tag's instructions.

For example, the following code illustrates how the start and end paragraph tags (<p> </p>) enclose, or *contain*, a section of text. In this example, the <p> tag instructs the Web browser to display the text up to the </p> tag using the default formatting rules:

```
<p> This is an example of paragraph text. </p>
```

If you want the browser to display the paragraph text using a specific font and color, you would add attributes that specified such things as the color, typeface, size, and so on to a <font> tag that follows the <p> tag and precedes the text whose look you want to specify. (You will learn about attributes after you read more about tags in the next two sections.)

HTML Section Tags

To organize the various parts of the HTML that describes a Web page, you use a set of *section* tags. The types of HTML tags in each section of the Web page definition have a specific purpose:

- **<html> </html>**   These occur at the start and end of an HTML document. As such, start and end HTML tags enclose all the other HTML tags you use to describe the Web page.

- **<head> </head>**   Start and end header tags immediately follow the start HTML tags (<html>) and denote the Web page header. You can use tags in the Web page header to include such information as the name of the author and the date the author created the page. In addition, you insert tags with information that describes your page so that Web search engines can add references to your page to their search indexes. Of the HTML tags and information you place in the header section, the visitor's browser displays only the Web page title. You insert the Web page title in the header section between start and end title tags (<title></title>), as shown in the code sample that follows this list of section tags.

- **<body> </body>**   Start and end body tags immediately follow the Web page header section and denote the Web page body. The body section of the Web page contains the tags that tell the Web browser what to display onscreen and how you want it to look.

The following code illustrates the correct placement of the HTML section tags:

```
<html>
<head>
  <title> The Web Page's Title </title>
</head>
<body>
  Text content and body tags inserted here
</body>
</html>
```

Note that you can write HTML tags as all uppercase, all lowercase, or a combination of the two, because Web browsers are currently case-insensitive. However, standards such as the XHTML and XML specification require that you use lowercase tags—even if Web browsers continue to support both lower and uppercase tags for a time. As such, write all your HTML tags and attributes in lowercase. That way, as Web browsers force Web designers to comply with newer standards, the Web browsers will still render correctly the Web pages you create now.

HTML Empty Tags

In addition to container tags (refer to "HTML Container Tags" earlier in this chapter), HTML uses a second type of tag called an *empty* tag. Whereas container tags enclose page content, such as a line of text within a start and end tag, empty tags do not require an end tag. Think of an empty tag as a single command or statement such as "go here" or "do this." For example, the following HTML code uses the line break tag (<br>) to instruct the Web browser to drop down to the next line before displaying the next item on the page (in this example, a second line of text):

```
<html>
<head>
  <title> Example of the line break tag </title>
</head>
<body>
  <p> This text is displayed on line one <br>
      This text is displayed on line two </p>
</body>
</html>
```

Creating a Web Page

HTML text documents are actually quite simple to create. To create an HTML document, you open a text-editing program and then type in the HTML code. After you have entered the HTML statements, you save your document as a text file with an .htm or .html extension. For example, start your favorite text editor (such as Windows Notepad) now, and enter the following HTML:

```
<html>
<head>
  <title>Example of a Simple HTML Document</title>
```

```
</head>
<body>
  <p>HELLO WORLD! Here I am.</p>
</body>
</html>
```

Now, save your work to a Web page file (that is, a file with an .htm or .html extension) on your hard drive. Because you will likely download from the Osborne Web site or enter into your text editor and save many of the Web pages you encounter throughout this book, create a folder (such as C:\HTMLExamples) in which to store the Web pages. Then, save the code you entered for this example as TestPage.htm in the folder you create.

To take your first Web page for a test drive, start your Web browser, and type **File://** followed by the drive letter and pathname of your Web page into the browser's Address field. For example, if you saved the Web page in this example as TestPage.htm in the C:\HTMLExamples folder, type **File://c:/HTMLExamples/TestPage.htm** into the browser's Address field. Then, press ENTER. Your Web browser, in turn, will display the Web page shown in Figure 1-2. That is all there is to it! You are now officially a Web page author.

Controlling the Format of Text

In standard word processing, a paragraph defines a group of sentences. Typically, a blank line or an indented first word identifies the start of a new paragraph. For example, each paragraph in this book

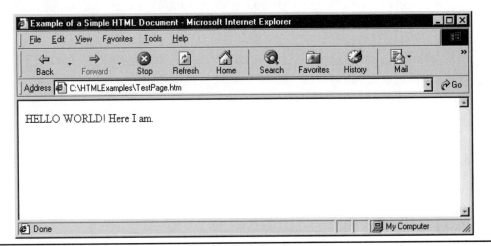

Figure 1-2   Simple Web page displayed by Internet Explorer

begins with the first line indented. The indented first line (or blank line) is a visual cue that lets the reader know another paragraph is starting.

When you insert text into a Web page, the </p> tag controls the end of text and the subsequent beginning of the next paragraph. The </p> tag instructs the Web browser to move down one line, insert a blank line, and then to begin the next paragraph on the line below the blank line for the text following the </p> tag.

In this following code, the start and end paragraph tags (<p></p>) mark the beginning and end of each paragraph, as shown in Figure 1-3.

```
<html>
<head>
  <title>Welcome to Lots of Text </title>
</head>
<body>
  <p>The text between the two paragraph tags defines a single
  paragraph. Paragraphs contain one or more sentences</p>
  <p>The next paragraph starts here with a blank line inserted
  between the two paragraphs</p>
</body>
</html>
```

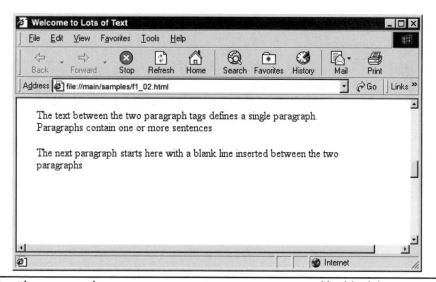

Figure 1-3   The paragraph tags organize text into groups separated by blank lines

HTML also has several text formatting tags you can use to change the appearance of text, usually for emphasis. To apply a formatting style, place the format's start tag at the beginning of the text you want to style. The following list describes three of the most common formatting tags.

- **<b></b>**   Text placed between the Bold tags is displayed in **bold** font.
- **<i></i>**   Text placed between the Italic tags is displayed in *italic* font.
- **<u></u>**   Text placed between the Underline tags is displayed with an <u>underline</u>.

The following HTML code displays text in the bold, italic, and underlined style, as shown in Figure 1-4.

```
<html>
<head>
  <title> Welcome to Basic Font Styles </title>
</head>
<body>
  <b>This text displays bold</b><br>
  <i>This text displays in italic</i><br>
  <u>This text displays underlined</u><br>
</body>
</html>
```

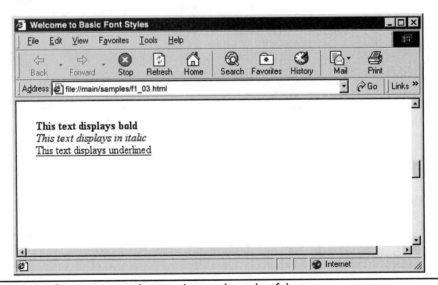

Figure 1-4   HTML formatting tags let you change the style of the text

HTML Attributes

You insert one or more *attributes* in an HTML tag to give the Web browser additional information about the way in which the browser is to carry out the tag's instruction. For example, a <font> tag tells the Web browser you want to change the appearance of the text that follows the tag. The *color* and *face* attributes that follow the tag's name in the following code tell the browser the color (red) and typeface (Helvetica) that the browser is to use in order to change the appearance of the text that follows the tag:

```
<p> <font color="red" face="helvetica">
   This text is red, Helvetica text. </font> </p>
```

Attributes, which you always insert after the tag's name in either start tags or empty tags, consist of three components: the attribute's name, followed by the equal sign (=), followed by the attribute's value enclosed in quotes—either double ("") or single ('').

▶ *NOTE*

By the way, the Web browser ignores any spaces you place on either side of the equal sign (=) between an attribute and the attribute's quoted value. As such, you will see some Web documents with no spaces (as shown by the HTML statement in the preceding example) and some documents with spaces on either one or both sides of the equal (=) sign. When writing your HTML tags, select whichever looks best to you; just be consistent.

The Web browser will continue to apply the attribute(s) you specify within a start tag until the browser reads the associated end tag. In this example, the Web browser will continue to make text look as specified by the *color* and *font* attributes in the <font> tag until the browser encounters the </font> tag in the Web page HTML. Figure 1-5 illustrates the components of an HTML tag with two attributes.

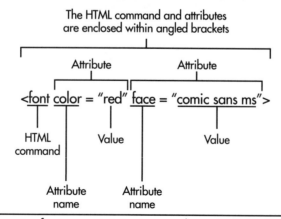

Figure 1-5   The components of a tag containing two attributes

Working with Fonts

Unless you specify otherwise in the Web page HTML, visitors to your Web site view page text using their default typeface, style, color, and character size. The visitor's Web browser controls the default settings for the text displayed onscreen by the browser. Using the start and end font tags (<font> </font>), you control how text looks when displayed by the visitor's Web browser. Note that the font tag is *deprecated*, which means that future versions of the Web browsers that conform to the latest HTML standard may no longer support, and therefore ignore, the <font> tag and its attributes. Although you can use attributes within the <font> tag to affect the appearance of text, you can achieve the same effects (and more) by creating CSS rules as you will learn to do in Chapter 4.

The following attributes you can place within the start font tag instruct the Web browser how to display the text in the Web document:

- **<font color="color">**   The *color* attribute defines the color of the text. Color values can be names (such as "red", "green", "yellow", "blue", and so on) or hexadecimal triplets (such as #FF0000, #008000, #FFFF00, #0000FF, and so on) that represent the amount of red, green, and blue the Web browser is to mix to produce the color of text you want.

- **<font size="##">**   The *size* attribute defines the size of the text (relative to a base font size) using values from –7 to 7. The lower the value, the smaller the size of the font.

- **<font face="font name">**   The *face* attribute defines the name of the font's typeface (Times New Roman, Helvetica, and Arial are a few examples of typefaces found on most computer systems). If the font defined in the *face* attribute is not available on the visitor's computer, the Web browser ignores the *face* attribute and substitutes the browser's default typeface.

The Web browser controls the default values for color, size, and typeface. To return text to the browser's default values, place a </font> tag at the end of the text whose appearance you changed with attributes in a <font> tag. The following code instructs the Web browser to display the text in red using the Helvetica typeface, and then returns to displaying text (following the </font> tag) using the browser's default text characteristics:

```
<html>
<head>
  <title>Font Color Example </title>
</head>
<body>
  <font color="#ff0000" face="helvetica">
  <p> This is red text in Helvetica</p> </font>
  <p>This is normal text</p>
</body>
</html>
```

Assigning the Same Set of Attributes to Multiple Page Elements

When you want to assign the same set of attributes to several adjacent Web page elements at once, enclose the elements you want to affect with start and end division tags (<div></div>). Say, for example, that you want to center two lines of text and a graphic image between the left and right margins on the Web page. Rather than add the *align* attribute to each of the three HTML tags, place a <div> tag before the first element and a </div> tag after the end of the last element, as shown in the following code:

```
<div align="center">
  <p> This text is centered ABOVE the picture.</p>
  <img src="image.jpg">
  <p> This text is centered BELOW the picture. </p>
</div>
```

The <div> tag lets you assign one or more formatting attributes to a group of HTML tags. The </div> tag instructs the Web browser to again use the default values for attributes specified in the <div> tag.

Creating Web Pages Using Text Editors, Word Processors, and Web Layout Applications

Creating an "exceptional" Web page requires good design technique and a thorough understanding of HTML tags and attributes. Setting the concepts of "good" and "bad" page design aside, making a Web page boils down to one thing, creating a document (that is, a text file) that contains the HTML code necessary to tell the Web browser to display what you want onscreen. Although this chapter discusses the ins and outs of basic HTML code, it is a good idea to familiarize yourself with the programs available for creating text documents in which you write and store your Web page HTML.

A Web page is nothing more than a text document that contains all of the text content and HTML (tags and attributes) the Web browser needs to display the information you want onscreen. As such, you do not need a specialized program to generate a Web page. You need only a general knowledge of HTML and a program that lets you save a text-only file. Three types of programs let you create HTML documents: text editors, word processors, and HTML layout programs (such as Dreamweaver and FrontPage). All three have their advantages and, in some cases, disadvantages.

Text Editors

A text editor is the simplest (and perhaps easiest to use) of the three types of programs that let you create a text document. A text editor is a no-frills application that lets you enter text into the computer and save what you type to a file on the hard drive or on a floppy disk. On a Windows computer, Microsoft supplies a text editor called Notepad, and on the Macintosh, the text editor is called SimpleText.

Typically, text editors do not have a spell check module or advanced formatting tools, such as style sheets and paragraph rules. Text editors do however let you type information onto an electronic sheet of paper and save what you type to a file. The major disadvantage of using a text editor to create a Web page is that text editors provide little help in writing tags that conform to HTML syntax rules. You type the HTML; the text editor records the text. However, the text editor will not alert you to misspelled words or HTML syntax errors. The advantage in using a text editor to create a Web page is that text editors force you to learn the HTML more quickly, because they provide no crutch on which you can lean. Figure 1-6 shows an HTML document written using Microsoft Notepad.

After you type your HTML into Notepad, select File | Save and enter a filename to save your Web page to disk. Be sure to give your filename an .htm or .html (and not the default .txt) extension.

Word Processors

The two most popular word processors on the market are Microsoft Word and Corel WordPerfect. Word processors give you an advantage over simple text editors in that you can call the word processor to spell check what you type. However, unless you use a spell check module designed to check

Figure 1-6   Notepad lets you create an HTML document

HTML, you will spend a lot of time instructing the word processor to ignore the spelling of HTML tags, because most tag names are only abbreviations and not correctly spelled words in English.

If your word processor does not have an HTML spell check module, you can instruct the application to *learn* new words. For example, the word processor will mark the image tag <img> as being a misspelled word. However, when you instruct the word processor to learn that the character string "<img>" is spelled correctly, the word processor will accept subsequent occurrences of it in the document as spelled correctly. A word of caution, make sure that the HTML tag you type is syntactically correct before you click the spell check program's learn button.

Thus, a word processor has two advantages. First, you can tell the word processor to check the spelling of words and tags you enter into your Web page HTML; and second, you still have to learn HTML quickly because must you still type the HTML you want the browser to execute into the document.

When you save the file, *be sure to use the word processor's "save as" function to save the document as a text-only file.* Word processors do something that text editors do not; they insert special codes into a document. These embedded codes can affect how the Web browser interprets the document and worst case, can prevent the Web browser from displaying your Web page at all, or even cause the browser to crash. Because HTML documents do not require embedded text formatting codes, tell the word processor to save your HTML file using the text-only option.

Web Layout Applications

Web layout applications let you create Web pages in much the same way as page layout applications such as PageMaker and QuarkXPress let you lay out and print a paper document. Although dozens of Web layout applications are on the market, the three most popular programs for creating Web pages are Adobe's GoLive, Macromedia's Dreamweaver, and Microsoft's FrontPage.

When you use a Web layout program such as GoLive, you open a new document, and begin typing text and dragging graphics onto the blank layout window. As you add text and graphics to the Web page, the program generates the HTML code for you. The advantage of using a Web layout program is that you see how the page will look in a Web browser as you create the page. Figure 1-7 shows a Web page under construction in GoLive.

The disadvantage in using Web layout programs is that they do the entire HTML coding for you. Although that may seem like a good thing, you never get a chance to learn any HTML, and therefore you may never advance beyond what the layout program is capable of doing. Suppose, for example, you want to add a specific feature to your Web page and the layout program does not have a button to make it happen. That means you are stuck because you do not know how to code the feature yourself. In addition, Web layout programs are not perfect. Sometimes they generate additional HTML code that is not necessary to your Web page. If you do not know HTML, you cannot make a decision as to what you need and what you should remove.

If you are new to Web design, it is a good idea to start by using a simple text editor or word processor. After you understand HTML, move on to a Web layout program such as Dreamweaver or GoLive. If you understand HTML, using a Web layout program gives you the best of both worlds. The Web layout program generates all the HTML code quickly and on the fly, while at any time letting you stop and modify the code to fit your specific needs.

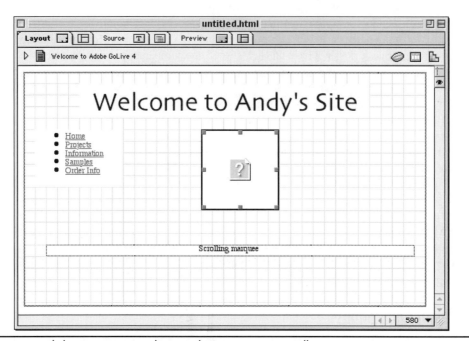

Figure 1-7 Web layout programs let you design a page visually

Working with Relative vs. Absolute Pathnames for Files

When you create a new Web site, you will have to move the Web content (that is, the HTML documents, graphics, animation, sound, and other support files) from your development computer to the Web server. If your Web pages contain links to pages stored in the same or related folders (such as a subfolder or parent folder), you can save yourself considerable time and work by using relative pathnames when referencing files in the Web page HTML tags.

When a site visitor clicks on a hypertext link, the Web browser uses the pathname given by the hyperlink's *href* attribute to locate the file the browser is to retrieve. When specifying the location of a file, you can use either an *absolute* or a *relative* pathname. Suppose, for example, that you have a graphics file named clock.jpg located in the folder named Folder_B, and that Folder_B, in turn, is located within a folder named Folder_A, as illustrated in Figure 1-8.

A relative path consists of the folder names the browser needs to navigate to get to the file starting at the location of the Web page with the hyperlink that references the external file. For example, if clock.jpg is located in the Folder_B (as shown in Figure 1-8), and the Web page that references clock.jpg is located in Folder_A, the relative pathname for clock.jpg in the current Web page is Folder_B/clock.jpg. In other words, the current folder contains Folder_B, which in turn, contains the file clock.jpg. The following <img> tag uses a *src* attribute with a relative pathname.

```
<img src="Folder_A/clock.jpg">
```

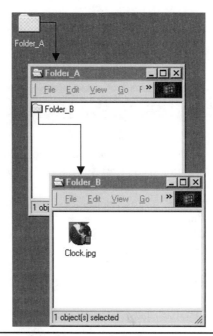

Figure 1-8   The folder hierarchy of the file named clock.jpg

A relative pathname instructs the Web browser to start looking for the file within the folder that contains the current HTML document. Say for example that the HTML document that contains the image in the <img> tag in the preceding example is located in a folder named idx_folder. The relative pathname in the *src* attribute then implies the folder named Folder_A is located within the idx_folder.

Absolute paths, on the other hand, locate a file by starting at the top level of the folder hierarchy and moving downward through all the intervening folders to reach the file—without regard to the location of the current Web document. Absolute paths always begin with a slash (/) to differentiate them from relative paths.

Suppose, for example, that clock.jpg is located on the D drive in the folder named Folder_B, which is located within the folder named Folder_A. To specify an absolute pathname, you must tell the browser where to look for the file starting with the drive on which the folder with the file is located. The following code shows the absolute pathname for clock.jpg in the current example:

```
<img src="/D:Folder_A/Folder_B/clock.jpg">
```

Using absolute pathnames makes moving Web site files from a local drive to a Web server or from one Web server to another difficult. For example, to use relative pathnames successfully, you need only create on the Web server a main folder for the site and then place all the documents and support files into subfolders within the main folder—as they are on your development machine. The relative pathnames will be as valid on the Web server as they are on your system—even if the remainder of the Web server's folder hierarchy is nothing like yours. Conversely, if you use absolute addresses, the Web server must have exactly the same folder hierarchy as that found on your development system in order for the Web server to be able to find the files referenced in hyperlinks within your Web pages.

Downloading and Installing the Personal Web Server

As you learned earlier in this chapter, you can display within your Web browser the Web pages you create and save to a local or network drive—without first connecting to the Internet or a Web server. Simply enter the pathname of the .html (Web page) file as File://<*.html file pathname>* into the Web browser's Address field. Thus, if you save a Web page name TestPage.htm in the MyWebs folder at the root (that is, top) folder on your C drive, you can display the page in your Web browser by entering **File://C:/MyWebs/TestPage.htm**.

To make your Web pages available to others across the Internet, you must have a Web server. Further, as you will learn in Chapters 10, 11, and 12, a Web server is also required if you want to execute server-side scripts (programs that the server runs on the behalf of your Web page). If you are using one of the Windows operating systems (Windows 95, 98, Me, NT, or XP) you can install the Personal Web Server (PWS) on your personal PC or network workstation free of charge. After you install the PWS and establish an Internet connection, other users on the Web can view the Web pages you publish on your system. In addition, you can use the PWS to test Web pages that submit form results and pages with server-side scripts, such as those embedded in PHP and Active Server Pages (which you will learn about in Chapters 10 and 11, respectively).

USE IT   If you have a Windows 98 CD, insert the CD in your CD-ROM drive and skip the download-procedure discussion that follows; you will find the PWS in the \Add-Ons\ PWS\ folder on the Windows 98 CD. Otherwise, you must install the PWS from the Windows NT 4 Option Pack, which you can download from the Microsoft's Web site on the Internet by performing the following steps:

1. If you do not have a permanent (that is, always-on) connection to the Internet, use your modem to establish a dial-up connection through your ISP.

2. Start your Web browser, and type the following URL into the browser's Address field: **http://www.microsoft.com/msdownload/ntoptionpack/askwiz.asp** and press ENTER.

3. Within the Windows NT Option Pack Web page, click the Option 1 hyperlink. Your browser, in turn, will display the Download Step 2 Web page, which lets you select the operating system for which you want to download the NT 4 Option Pack download program.

4. Within the Download Step 2 page, use the drop-down menu on the Web page to select your operating system. Unless you are installing the PWS on an NT Workstation or NT Server, select the Windows 95 option. For NT Workstation, select the NT Workstation option and for NT Server install the Internet Information Server (IIS) instead of the PWS. Then, click Next. Your Web browser, in turn, will display the Download Step 3 Web page.

5. Within the Download Step 3 page, click the download.exe link near the bottom right-hand corner of the Web page. Windows, in turn, will display the File Download dialog box.

6. Within the File Download dialog box, click the Save This Program To Disk radio button and then click OK. Windows, in turn, will display the Save As dialog box.

7. Within the Save As dialog box, use the drop-down list button to the right of the Save In field to select the folder in which you want to save the download.exe program file. For example, you might use the drop-down list button to navigate to the C:\My Download Files folder. Then, click Save.

8. Within Windows, use the Explorer to navigate to the folder in which you saved download.exe. Run the application. Download.exe, in turn, will display the Windows NT 4.0 Option Pack license agreement.

9. Read the terms of the agreement. Then, click Yes to continue with the installation. The download program, in turn, will display a Download Options dialog box.

10. Within the Download Options dialog box, click the Download Only radio button and then click Next button. The download program, in turn, will display the Language and CPU/Operating System Options screen.

11. Within the Language and CPU/Operating System screen, select the Language and CPU/ Operating System, and then click Next. The download program, in turn, will display the Installation Options screen.

12. Within the Installation Options screen, click the Full Installation radio button and then click Next. The download program, in turn, will display the Save In Folder screen.

13. Within the Save In Folder screen, enter the folder in which you want the download program to store the NT 4 Option pack's files. (For example, you might enter C:\PWSSetupFiles into the Save In Folder field.) Then, click Next. The download program, in turn, will display the Download Location dialog box with a list of sites from which you can download the NT 4 Option Pack.

14. Within the Download Location dialog box, select the download site nearest your geographical location (if more than one site is on the list). Then, click Next. The download program will present you with the download site's Security Certificate. Click Yes to accept the certificate and complete the NT 4 Option Pack download.

After you complete Step 14, the download program will retrieve the NT 4 Option Pack from the location you selected and store the NT 4 Option Pack files within the folder you entered in Step 13.

Before you can start the PWS, you must install the application on your computer. Whether you downloaded the NT 4 Option Pack or are using your Windows 98 CD, perform the following steps to complete the PWS installation:

1. Execute setup.exe either within the Windows 98 CD-ROM (**x:\Add-Ons\PWS\Setup.exe**, where *x* is the letter of your CD-ROM drive) or within the folder you entered in Step 13 of the preceding download procedure.

2. On the setup program's initial installation screen, click Next. Setup.exe, in turn, will display the PWS End User License Agreement. Read the agreement and then click Accept to continue with the installation. The setup program, in turn, will display either the Installation Options dialog box or the Select Components Dialog box. (Which dialog box the program displays is not important and depends on whether you are upgrading an older version [or reinstalling the current version] of PWS or if you are installing the Web server for the first time.)

3. Within the Installation Options or the Select Components dialog box, click Next to accept the default installation options.

After you complete Step 3, the setup program will finish installing the PWS software and prompt you to restart the computer. While restarting your computer, Windows will load and start the PWS for you. As such, when you next see your Windows desktop, look in the system tray at the right-hand side of the Windows status bar and you will see the icon for the PWS. The following Tip will show you how to manage the Web server and teach you how to publish your Web pages on the company intranet and/or the Internet itself.

Managing the Personal Web Server and Publishing Your Web Pages

After successfully installing the Personal Web Server (PWS), as you learned to do in the preceding Tip, you have to work out how to stop and start the Web server and determine the location of the server's home directory. The tool you will use for this purpose is Personal Web Manager, which you can open in different ways depending on your particular operating system.

USE IT The easiest way to start the Personal Web Manager is to double-click the program's icon in the Windows system tray (on the right-hand end of the Windows status bar). Or, on a Windows 98 system, select Start | Programs | Microsoft Personal Web Server and then choose Personal Web Manager.

After you start the application, the Personal Web Manager will display the program's Main screen, which contains the name of your Web server and the server's home directory, similar to that shown in Figure 1-9.

The Web manager displays the name of your Web server in blue text near the top of the page. Anyone working at your computer or using another workstation on your local area network can use the Web server name to view Web pages on your PWS. (You can change the name of your Web server simply by changing the name of your PC on the Identification tab of the Control Panel, Network Properties dialog box.) The Main screen of the Personal Web Manager also shows you the PWS's root folder in blue text just beneath the name of your Web server.

Knowing the name of the Web server and the home directory, you are ready to publish your Web pages. Suppose, for example, that your computer's name (and hence your PWS's name) is konrad, and the server's home directory is C:\WebShare\wwwroot. If you place a Web page such as TestPage .htm, for example, into the C:\WebShare\wwwroot folder on your computer, you (and anyone using a

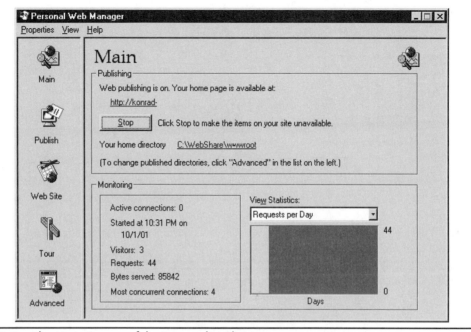

Figure 1-9   The Main Screen of the Personal Web Manager program

workstation connected to your local area network) can display the Web page by typing **http://konrad/ TestPage.htm** into the Web browser's Address field and then pressing ENTER.

Now, suppose you create a folder beneath your Web server's home (root) directory, say HTDocs, and then place inside the folder a Web page, such as TestPage2.htm. The pathname of TestPage2.htm would be c:\WebShare\wwwroot\htdocs\TestPage2.htm. However, using a browser, you would display the page by typing into the browser's Address field the URL **http://konrad/htdocs/TestPage2.htm** and then pressing ENTER.

In addition to browsers running on workstations attached to your local area network, you can let computers anywhere in the world access your Web pages on the Internet. To do this, you will have to connect your computer to the Internet and give those who want to visit your IP address. Bear in mind that unless your ISP assigns to you a permanent IP address (normally at a monthly fee), your PWS may have a different IP address assigned to it each time you connect your computer (and the Web server) to the Internet.

If your ISP has not assigned your computer a static IP address, you can find out your current IP address by executing ipconfig.exe. Ipconfig.exe runs under the MS-DOS command shell. To start an MS-DOS session, select Start | Run. Windows, in turn, will display the Run dialog box. Within the Run dialog box, type **command.com** into the Open field. Then, press ENTER or click OK. At the MS-DOS command prompt type **ipconfig.exe** and then press ENTER. The ipconfig application, in turn, will list your computer's IP address directly above the Subnet Mask, as shown in Figure 1-10.

(You can run the Windows version of ipconfig.exe by selecting Start | Run and typing **winipcfg.exe** into the Open field of the Run dialog box.) After you know the computer's IP address, substitute the

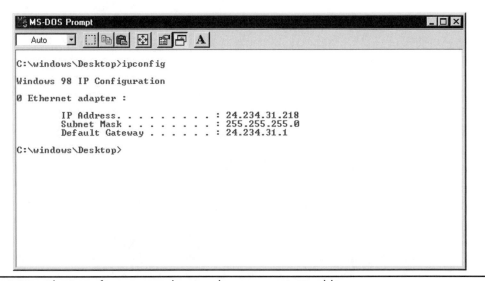

Figure 1-10   The ipconfig program showing the computer's IP address

IP address for the Web server name to access the server's Web pages on the Internet. For example, given a PC with an IP address of 24.234.31.218, to display the Web pages in the preceding example across the Internet, you would use either of the following:

```
http://24.234.31.218/TestPage.htm
http://24.234.31.218/HTDocs/TestPage2.htm
```

After you determine the computer's IP address, you can give this address to others. Bear in mind, however, that unless your ISP allocates a static, permanent IP address to your computer, the IP address will change each time you disconnect from and reconnect to the Internet. Moreover, the IP address might change without your knowledge, even if you have a permanent (that is, always-on) Internet connection. When your Web server's IP address changes, those trying to view your Web pages using the old IP address will no longer be able to do so—even though the PWS is running and your computer is connected to the Internet.

The solution is to contact your ISP and ask for a static IP address. At present, your ISP cannot assign your computer a static IP address if you are connecting to the Internet through a dial-up connection on a standard phone line—you need an ISDN, DSL, or cable modem Internet connection. After you receive your static IP address, you must enter the address into the TCP/IP Properties dialog box on your computer. To do so, perform the following steps:

1. Select Start | Settings and then choose Control Panel. Windows, in turn, will open the Control Panel.

2. Within the Control Panel window, double-click the Network icon. Windows, in turn, will display the Network dialog box.

3. Within the Configuration tab of the Network dialog box, click TCP/IP to select the protocol. (If you are working on a Windows NT machine, you will find the TCP/IP protocol on the Protocols tab of the Network dialog box instead.) Then, click Properties. Windows, in turn, will display the TCP/IP Properties dialog box.

4. Within the Address tab of the TCP/IP Properties dialog box, click the Specify An IP Address radio button. Then, enter the IP address and Subnet mask given to you by your ISP.

After you complete Step 4, click OK at the bottom of the TCP/IP Properties Dialog box and then click OK at the bottom of the Network dialog box. Windows will then update your system settings and prompt you to reset your computer. After your computer resets and you again connect your computer to the Internet, the PWS will be accessible at the same (static) IP address on a permanent basis.

Once your computer has a static IP address, you can then purchase a domain name, either through your ISP or from a domain name registrar such as VeriSign (http://www.NetSol.com). After you purchase a domain name, such as MyWebServerName.com for example, ask your ISP to associate your domain name with your static IP address in the ISP's Domain Name Server (DNS). With the domain name pointing in place, visitors throughout the Internet will be able to view the Web pages on your PWS by using either your IP address (as shown previously) or by addressing the Web server with your domain name as either of the following:

```
http://www.MyWebServerName.com/TestPage.htm
http://www.MyWebServerName.com/HTDocs/TestPage2.htm
```

If you have a dial-up connection to the Internet or would rather not pay for a static IP address and use one of your computers as a Web server, you can have your ISP host your Web site for you. Many ISP's offer 5–10MB (or more) of Web space as part of your monthly fee for Internet access. Contact your ISP or a domain name registrar (such as VeriSign) for information on the Web-site hosting options they offer. If you have your ISP or another company host your site, you will simply copy the Web pages you want to publish to your site's folder hierarchy on the host company's hard drive instead of the PWS's root folder (and root subfolders) on your hard drive.

Note that after you install the PWS, Windows automatically starts the Web server each time you restart your computer. To stop the Web server, click the Stop button below the Web server name in the upper half of the Main section of the Personal Web Manager. (After you stop the PWS, the server will remain halted until you manually restart the Web server—even if you restart your computer in the interim.) To restart the PWS, click the Start button that replaced the Stop button on which you clicked to stop the Web server. (You can also stop or pause the PWS by selecting Properties | Stop Service or Properties | Pause Service, and then restart the Web server by selecting Properties | Start Service or Properties | Continue Service.)

Describing Web Page Contents with a Title

As you surf the Web, your browser displays the title of each Web page you view within the browser's title bar (across the top of the browser application window). The Web page title gives the name and describes, in a few words, the purpose of the Web page, as shown in Figure 1-11.

This is a
Web page
title

Figure 1-11   The title of a Web page appears in the title bar section of the browser window

USE IT   To create a Web page title, insert the title's text between start and end title tags (<title>
</title>) in the header section of the Web page HTML, as shown in the following code:

```
<html>
<head>
  <title>Welcome to Andy's Photoshop Book - Welcome Page</title>
</head>
<body>
  ... Content the Web browser displays goes here ...
</body>
</html>
```

Each Web page title should describe the contents of the page to your site visitors. Every time a
visitor glances at the application window's title bar, the page title should remind him or her of the
name and purpose of the Web page currently displayed by the browser. On a Web site containing
many pages, page titles act as road signs.

However, titles do more that remind visitors of their current location on your Web site. Titles are
also used for the following:

- Web browsers use title text when a visitor bookmarks a page, that is, when the visitor adds a Web page to the list of Favorites in Internet Explorer or to the list of Bookmarks in Netscape Navigator. Using a title like Home Page does not help to identify your site among the other bookmarks on the visitor's system.

- Spiders (automated Web search programs) use title text when listing your Web page on search engines. Again, a title like Home Page does not provide useful information. Use descriptive wording in your titles—words visitors might enter into the search field for a search engine when trying to find your Web site.

- Title text helps you, the Web author, manage and control large multipage sites. Think of a title as a heading that identifies the page. If your Web site contains fifteen pages, the titles help you to locate quickly the page with which you want to work. For example, a real estate site might use the title to indicate pages with Houses for Rent, or Houses for Sale.

In addition to these roles, the W3C considers a Web page without a title as invalid or illegal. The term "illegal" as used here does not mean that someone will arrest you for creating pages without titles. However, the use of titles helps all Web authors create standardized pages, and someday, when titles become a required part of a Web page, your Web content will already comply with the new standard.

Identifying Web Documents Using the Document Type Definition

One of the best ways to learn HTML tricks and techniques is to view the HTML statements used in Web pages you encounter as you surf the Web. To view the HTML source code for a Web page, select View | Source from within your browser. (If you are using Netscape Navigator, select View | Page Source.) As you examine Web pages, you will find that many HTML documents have a document type tag (<!doctype>) at the start of the Web page.

USE IT The Document Type Definition (DTD) identifies the version of HTML used to create the Web page. This information is important to Web browsers, HTML validation programs, and to other software programs used for Web design and layout. To validate an existing HTML document go to http://validator.w3c.org. The HTML validation program checks the organization and syntax of the Web document based on the information supplied within the DTD. When the declaration indicates that the document adheres to a strict version of HTML 4.01, the validator judges the Web page based on the HTML 4.01 standard and generates a report with the results of the examination.

In the future, knowing the version of HTML used to create a page will help Web browsers and other programs display Web pages with greater accuracy. In fact, the W3C considers a Web page created with HTML version 4 as invalid unless the HTML document starts with a DTD. The DTD goes at the top of the HTML document before the <html> tag. The following shows the correct format for a typical DTD:

```
<!doctype html public "version name" "url">
```

- **html**   Identifies the code as a version of the HTML.
- **public**   Identifies the language as accessible by the public.
- *version name*   Identifies the complete name for the specific version of HTML. For example, the complete name for HTML 4.0 is -//W3C//DTD HTML 4.01 Transitional//EN.
- *url*   Indicates where on the World Wide Web a public definition of the HTML code resides, such as www.w3.org/TR/html4/loose.dtd.

A valid DTD for a Web page described using HTML version 4.01 would be as follows:

```
<!doctype html public "-//W3C//DTD HTML 4.01 Transitional//EN"
  "www.w3.org/TR/html4/loose.dtd">
```

The *loose.dtd* option in the previous code declares that the document may include all the elements allowed in the HTML 4 "strict" standard, additional presentation description attributes, and may include deprecated elements. Conversely, using *strict.dtd* in the DTD would declare that the document strictly adheres to the HTML 4 standard. The strict version of HTML 4.01 emphasizes the structure of the HTML document over the presentation of the page within the Web browser. This does not mean that strict version of HTML 4.01 downplays the presentation of the Web page; it simply focuses on the structure of the HTML markup code. Deprecated tags and elements such as frames and link targets are not allowed in HTML strict. A third Document Type Definition, *frameset.dtd*, is used when validating HTML documents containing frames.

Currently, neither Netscape Navigator nor Internet Explorer require that you include a DTD before the start of your Web page HTML, that is, before the start HTML tag (<html>) at the top of your Web document. However, you should include one at the start of any Web page you code using HTML version 4.0 or later. The W3C is giving you a hint here. What is optional today may be required in the near future. Therefore, stay ahead of the game and use the DTD in all your Web pages now. (In the interest of conserving space and reducing the complexity of example code, we omit the Document Type Definition in the examples shown in this book.)

Inserting Comments into a Web Document

HTML comments are a way to remind you and anyone who works on your HTML documents of what exactly you were thinking when you created a particular Web page. You can use comments to explain specific portions of a document. You can also use comments to insert personal information like your name, address, and phone number in the Web page HTML, so anyone interested in obtaining your services as a Web designer will know how to contact you.

In addition, you might use comments to temporarily hide some of the Web document's HTML statements from the Web browser. Suppose, for example, you want to add a section of HTML code to an existing document, but you do not want the browser to display the new content until management gives permission to proceed. Placing HTML comment tags (<!-- -->) around the statements you want to hide instructs the Web browser to ignore the statements until you remove you comment tags.

USE IT To create a comment, enclose the informational text (or the HTML statements you want to *comment out*) within the start and end comment tags, such as <! –– *comment* ––>. Placing a begin comment tag before each line of text or HTML statement is not necessary; the Web browser will ignore anything it finds after the start comment tag and before the next end comment tag. For example, the following code shows three lines of comments inserted within the Web page header section:

```
<head>
  <title> A document containing comments </title>
  <! -- Author          Andy Anderson
        Company         One-of-a-Kind Productions, Inc.
        Contact Info    316 333 4444 -- >
</head>
```

Although the Web browser does not display the information you place between start and end comment tags onscreen, a site visitor can still read the comments by instructing the Web browser to display the Web page HTML. The browser, in turn, will display the source code (including comments) for the HTML document in a separate document window.

Besides using comments to identify personal information, you can use comments in a training environment to help explain the purpose of specific HTML tags and attributes to your students. In addition, you might use comments to prevent the display of embedded scripts onscreen when the Web browser does not support the script tag, as shown in the following code:

```
<html>
<head>
  <script language="JavaScript">
<!--
  function displayIt()
  {
   alert("This JavaScript function displays this text in the browser window!")
   return;
  }
//-->
  </script>
</head>
<body>
  ... Web Page Content the Browser is to Display Goes Here ...
</body>
</html>
```

Without the comment tags around the JavaScript function definition in this example, Web browsers that do not support the script tag may ignore the tag and display the JavaScript code as text onscreen. Conversely browsers supporting scripts ignore the HTML comment tags because scripts use // and /* */ to denote comments.

Specifying the Typeface for Web Page Text

When displaying Web page text, a Web browser uses the browser's default typeface and font size, unless you specify a size and typeface within the Web page HTML. Controlling the size and appearance of text is important, because the way text looks sets the mood for the page. Understand that typography does not end with the words themselves; the presentation is equally important. For example, designers use typeface and size to indicate the importance of certain text passages, which is why headlines are larger and often in a different typeface than body text.

The typeface you choose conveys mood and creates the atmosphere in which the visitor reads the message. Using the wrong typeface confuses the reader, because the content "feels" out of place. For example, several studies (one conducted by Yale) indicate that serif typefaces convey a more serious mood than sans (that is, without) serif typefaces. Therefore, you would use a typeface like Helvetica or Times New Roman for a formal document and a typeface like Comic Sans or Arial for a less serious or more casual message, as the examples show here:

Serif fonts, such as Helvetica generate a more formal look to the text.
Use serif fonts to convey a more serious mood to the document.

On the other hand, using a San Serif font such as Comic Sans
generates a more casual look to the document.

USE IT To change the typeface of a font, enclose the text between the start and end font tags in the form:

```
<font face="typeface">
 ... Web page text displayed using the specified typeface ...
</font>
```

The *face* attribute tells the Web browser which typeface to use when displaying Web page text onscreen. For example, the start font tag <font> instructs the Web browser to display text following the tag using the Helvetica typeface until the browser encounters a </font> tag:

```
<font face="helvetica"> This text displays in Helvetica </font>
```

When the browser reads a </font> tag in the Web page HTML, the browser reverts to displaying Web page text in the browser's default typeface.

Thus, the *face* attribute instructs the Web browser to search the host computer for a specific typeface (such as Helvetica in this example). The Web browser will use the typeface when displaying text placed between the start and end font tags (<font></font>). However, if the visitor has not installed on his or her computer the typeface you specify in the <font> tag, the Web browser will use the browser's default typeface instead.

Understand the site visitor can select the browser's default typeface by working with the Web browser's preferences. For example, to change the default typeface in Internet Explorer 5, select Tools | Internet Options. Then, click the Fonts button. Internet Explorer, in turn, will display the Fonts dialog box, on which you can select the browser's default Web page (and view source) font. (Internet Explorer refers to the typeface selection as the "font.") The default typeface tells the visitor's Web browser what character style to use when the Web document does not specify a typeface or when the visitor's computer does not have the typeface specified.

In addition to specifying a *primary* typeface, the *face* attribute lets you select a second, third, or even a fourth typeface. Say, for example, you want your document text displayed using the Helvetica typeface. However, if Helvetica is not available, Georgia is an acceptable substitute. The following code illustrates how you can specify an alternative typeface to use if the primary typeface is unavailable on the visitor's computer:

```
<font face="helvetica, georgia">
  The primary typeface is Helvetica. The browser will use the
  Georgia typeface if Helvetica is not available.
</font>
```

The *face* attribute instructs the Web browser to display the text between the start and end font tags (<font></font>) using the Helvetica typeface, and if Helvetica is not available, use the Georgia typeface instead. If neither the primary nor any of the alternative typefaces are available, the Web browser will use its default typeface.

When specifying fonts, use lowercase font names because then the system will look for the font name in both lowercase and uppercase. By contrast, if you use uppercase names, and the visitor's system has the font installed in lowercase, the Web browser will not find the desired font.

Controlling the Flow of Text with Paragraph and Line Break Tags

When you place unformatted text on a Web page, the width of the browser's application window controls the number of words the browser displays on each line onscreen. Unformatted text is simply text entered into an HTML document between the start and end body tags (<body> </body>), such as that shown in the following code:

```
<html>
<head>
  <title> Example of unformatted text </title>
</head>
<body>
  When you insert unformatted text
  into an HTML document. It does not matter
  how the text appears within the
  HTML document because the Web browser
  does not recognize the carriage return or
  enter key as a valid
  formatting tool.
</body>
</html>
```

Web browsers ignore the carriage return and line feed characters you insert into the Web page HTML by pressing ENTER to move down to the next line when typing. By default, Web browsers define the length of each line to be the width of the Web browser application window and not the number of characters on each line in the Web page HTML. The following illustrates how the Web browser sets the length of each line of unformatted text in the preceding HTML to the width of the browser's application window.

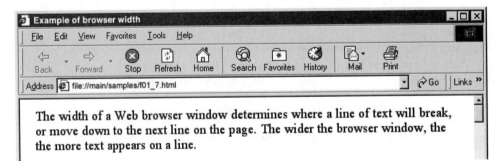

USE IT   To group lines of text into paragraphs and to control the last word on each line, HTML provides the start and end paragraph tags (<p></p>) and the <br> tag. When it encounters a <p> tag, the Web browser moves to the next line onscreen, inserts a blank line, and then displays the text that follows the <p> tag on the next line below the blank line. Therefore, to group related sentences into "blocks" of paragraph text, place a <p> tag before the first word in the paragraph and a </p> tag after the last. For example, if the Web page HTML has three lines of text, each enclosed by start and end paragraph tags (<p></p>), the Web browser will display the text as three paragraphs with a blank line between each line of text.

Unlike the <p> tag, the <br> tag has no end tag. After the Web browser encounters a <br> tag in the Web page HTML, the browser moves down to the next line onscreen before displaying additional text. Thus, you can use either the <br> tag or the <p> tag to tell the Web browser to move to a new line before displaying more text. When you only want to move to the next line, use the <br> tag; when you want to move to the next line and insert a blank line between the current line of text and the next, use the <p> tag in the Web page HTML.

The text in the following HTML describes the effect of the <p> tag and the <br> tag and how the text will appear in a Web browser as shown in Figure 1-12:

```
<html>
<head>
  <title> Example of formatted text </title>
</head>
<body>
  <p>When you insert formatted text
     into an HTML document.</p>
  <p>The placement of the paragraph and line break tags
     within the HTML document<br>
     determines the line breaks for the text.</p>
  <p>The paragraph tags leave a blank line between lines
     of text</p>
  and the line break tags break the text without inserting<br>
  an additional blank line.
</body>
</html>
```

Formatting tags (such as the <p> tag and the <br> tag) determine where a line of text ends in the browser's application window. In word-processing terms, the <br> tag inserts a hard return, and the <p> tag inserts two hard returns on the page.

The Web browser (like a word processor) executes a soft return to break the text at the right-hand margin on each page. Remember, in a Web document the right-hand side of the browser's application window represents the right-hand margin of the Web page. As such, you can use formatting tags to specify the last word on a line, but the Web browser will still insert soft returns as necessary to make each line of text fit within the width of the browser's application window.

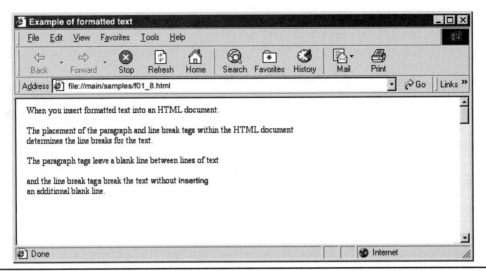

Figure 1-12   The text formats in the Web browser window based on the use of the paragraph and break tags

Although, as previously stated, the width of the browser window controls the width of a line of text, there are occasions where you will not want the browser to break the line of text. In that case, insert a no break space ( ) between the words you want the browser to display together on the same line. Say for example you create a subheading for a paragraph of text and you want the heading to remain on one line. To force the browser to keep the words on one line, insert the no break space between the words of the subheading, as shown here:

```
<html>
<head>
  <title>Example of using a no break space</title>
</head>
<body>
  <font size="7">A Message from Abraham Lincoln</font>
  <p>This country, with its institutions belongs
     to the people who inhabit it.</p>
  <p>Whenever they shall grow weary of the existing
     government, they can execute their constitutional
     right of amending it, or their constitutional
     right to dismember it or overthrow it.</p>
```

```
<cite>Abraham Lincoln</cite>
</body>
</html>
```

In this example, the no break space inserted between "Abraham" and "Lincoln" prevents the Web browser from splitting the president's name onto two lines. If the browser does not have enough space remaining on the current line to display *both* the first and last name together, the browser will display both names on the next line onscreen, as shown in Figure 1-13.

If there were only a space (as opposed to a no break space) between the first and last names, in this example, the browser would have displayed the first name on one line and the last name on the next.

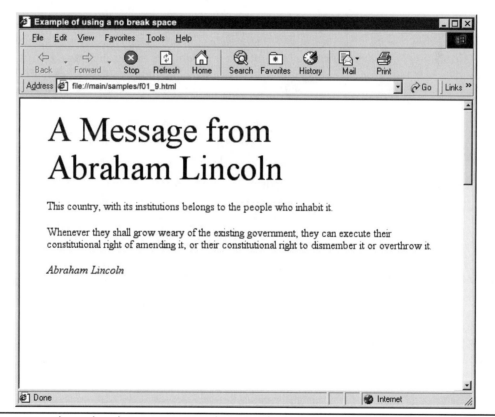

Figure 1-13   The no break space prevents the name from displaying on two lines

Changing the Size of Text Using Heading Level Tags and the Font Tag *size* Attribute

When you create a Web document without specifying the font size, the Web browser displays the text using the browser's default text size. The default values that browsers use for the size of characters vary, but on average run between 12 and 14 points, or approximately the point size of the text in this book.

To insert and control the size of heading text on a Web page, enclose the heading text within start and end heading level tags (<h1> ... </h1> to <h6> ... </h6>). The number that follows the letter "h" in a start heading tag specifies the size of the heading text in relative terms. When using the heading tags, the lower the number that follows the "h," the larger the heading will be onscreen.

USE IT   To use heading tags to specify the size of text on a page, place the text between the start and end heading tags. When a Web browser encounters an end heading tag in the Web page HTML, the browser automatically places the text following the end heading tag on the next line, and reverts to using the browser's default font size. The following illustrates the six heading level sizes you can specify using the start heading tag by showing how the text in each heading size appears in the browser application Window.

Heading 1
Heading 2
Heading 3
Heading 4
Heading 5
Heading 6

A second way to change the size of text in an HTML document is to use the *size* attribute in the <font> tag in the form <font size="*n*"> (where *n* is a number from 1 to 7). When you use the *size* attribute, the larger the value, the greater the size of the text—the opposite of the heading tags in which increasing the size of *n* decreases the size of the letters.

To set the text using the *size* attribute, place the text between the start and end font tags (<font></font>). The following illustrates the HTML code for the font tag using the *size* attribute, and shows how the text in each size will appear in the Web browser's application window.

Font Size 1

Font Size 2

Font Size 3

Font Size 4

Font Size 5

Font Size 6

Font Size 7

Both the start heading tag and the *size* attribute in the <font> tag let you specify the size of text; the start heading tag also tells the Web browser to display the text in boldface.

Bear in mind that the resolution of the visitor's monitor affects the size of text displayed within the Web browser's application window. Text on a monitor running at a resolution of 1024×768 pixels appears smaller than the same "size" text on a monitor using a lower resolution such as 800×600 pixels. Moreover, different platforms may also display text in different sizes even at the same resolution. The Mac, for example, displays text about two point sizes smaller than text displayed at the same resolution on an Intel-based machine.

The W3C deprecated the font tag and its attributes in the HTML 4 standard. As such, future version releases of HTML-compliant Web browsers may no longer support the font tag. A better way to control text formatting is to use CSSs, which you will learn about in Chapter 4 of this book.

Changing the Color of Text in an HTML Document

If you do not specify the color of text on a page, a Web browser will display the text in the browser's default text color, usually black. If you want to change the color of a word or a group of words, use the *color* attribute in the <font> tag to tell the Web browser what color to use.

USE IT Suppose, for example, that you want to change the color of one sentence in a paragraph of text. Insert a <font> tag with a *color* attribute in the form <font color="*color*"> just before the beginning of the text whose color you want to change. The *color* attribute instructs the browser to display the text following the tag in the specified color. Later in the text, insert a </font> tag at the point where you want to Web browser to start using the browser's default text color again.

For example, the *color* attribute in the <font> tag after the first sentence in the following HTML tells the Web browser to display the second sentence in red, as shown here:

To change the color of the text in the next sentence. Insert the FONT tag with the color attribute at the begining and end of the line. **The color changes and then reverts back to a default color of black.**

Then, the </font> tag, after the end of the second sentence, tells the Web browser to stop using red, which causes the Web browser to use the default text color again when displaying the remaining Web page text:

```
<html>
<head>
   <title>Changing the color of text </title>
</head>
<body>
   <p> To change the color of the text in the next sentence.
      <font color="red"> Insert the FONT tag with the color
```

```
        attribute at the beginning and end of the line.</font>
        The color changes and then reverts back to a default
        color of black.</p>
</body>
</html>
```

You can specify the value of the *color* attribute either by name or by number. As you saw in the preceding example, you can use color names such as red, green, blue, and so on. Or, you can use the hexadecimal triplet that represents a color. For example, the hexadecimal triplet for red is #FF0000. Therefore, you can tell the browser to start displaying text in red with either <font color="red"> or <font color = "#FF0000">.

When you specify a color as a hexadecimal triplet, the numbers in the triplet represent the amount of red, green, and blue the browser is to "mix" to create the color you want. For example, the color black has a hexadecimal triplet value of "#000000". Each two-digit number in the triplet represents the amount of one of the three primary colors red, green, and blue the browser is to use to create the composite color. Thus, for black (#000000), the browser is to mix "00" red, "00" green, and "00" blue. Conversely, to create the color white, the browser must use the maximum amount of red, green, and blue. Hence, the hexadecimal triplet for white is "#FFFFFF".

In the print world, there are few limitations on the range of colors available to enhance brochures and magazine advertisements. Most computers too have video cards capable of displaying thousands, if not millions, of colors. Both Macintosh and Windows-based computers have a color lookup table that instructs the monitor how to display color. When you assign a color using a hexadecimal value, the Web browser works with the video card's lookup table; if the color is available in the table, then the system will display the color correctly onscreen. If the lookup table does not contain the correct color, the system creates the color by mixing (dithering) existing color pixels together to produce a visual equivalent of the requested color.

Many years ago, when video cards were only capable of displaying a maximum of 256 colors, deciding which colors to use was an easier job (fewer colors) but more restricting. To complicate matters, computer operating systems reserved some of these colors for their visual interface (that is, for use in displaying the system's desktop). Because the Windows and Macintosh operating systems choose a different set of colors for their visual interface (40 colors) that leaves 216 colors (256 − 40 = 216) that are displayed the same way in Macintosh and Windows Web browsers.

Today, you have a greater range of color from which to choose when creating a Web page, because video cards in both Macintosh and Windows computers can display millions of colors. However, you still create each color as a combination of red, green, and blue values (a triplet). For a complete listing of browser-safe colors that shows both the color names and corresponding hexadecimal triplet values, visit http://www.htmlhelp.com/cgi-bin/color.cgi.

Although most visitors will leave the browser's default text color set to black, some may have selected another default text color. As such, it is a good idea to specify the color you want the browser to use when displaying your Web page text, even if the color you want is black. Do not assume that all your visitors use black as the browser's default text color. In Chapter 4 of this book, you will learn how to set the color of all text on a page with a few CSS rules.

Adding Graphics to a Web Page Using a Basic <img> Tag

Visiting Web sites without encountering pages that contain pictures and drawings is virtually impossible. Graphics images help to explain complicated procedures or actions that would be difficult to describe using text alone. In addition, most visitors to your Web site feel intimidated when they see a Web page with nothing but text. Inserting an occasional graphic into a long body of the text gives visitors a break from reading, and if used correctly, helps explain the text. Suppose, for example, you want to create a Web page that explains the steps necessary to change the ink cartridge on an Epson 1520 inkjet printer. A few well-designed illustrations would explain the process better than several paragraphs of text.

In addition, site visitors have the option to change the default typeface used to display text on a Web page by working with the browser's preferences. That means that the Web page text will look different to a visitor using the Arial typeface as the browser default than the text looks in your Web browser that defaults to the Helvetica typeface. Although this is frustrating, you learned how to prevent this change in typeface by specifying the font the browser is to use rather than leaving the typeface selection as the browser default. The real problem with typeface selection comes into play when you use a specialized or custom typeface, such as those often used to write the company name in a logo. Remember, if the specified typeface is not available on the visitor's computer, the Web browser will display the text using the browser's default font.

Say, for example, your site has a logo whose text is written in the Skia typeface. If you type the logo on the Web page as text and the visitor's system does not have the Skia typeface installed, the visitor's Web browser will substitute the browser's default typeface, which will change the entire look of the logo. Fortunately, you can preserve the exact appearance of a logo (or other text) by converting the text into a graphics image (using an image-editing program like Photoshop). If you insert a picture of the text on the Web page, the text will look the same in all Web browsers—even those on systems without the typeface you use to create the text. When you convert text to a graphics image, the visitor's settings that control font usage have no effect on the text in the picture, as shown in Figure 1-14.

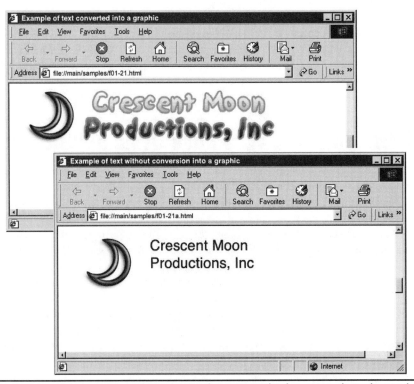

Figure 1-14   Logos with text converted into a graphic image display correctly in the Web browser

USE IT   The <img> tag lets you place a graphics image (whether of converted text or a picture or drawing), on a Web page. A typical <img> tag contains a single *src* attribute, which tells the Web browser the pathname of the graphics file. Therefore, most of your image tags will be of the form <img src=" *path/filename*">. Note the value of the *src* attribute contains both the path and filename of the graphics file. For example, the following code instructs the Web browser to retrieve and display the picture in the file named photo.jpg stored in the *images* folder on the Web server.

```
<img src="images/photo.jpg" width="300 height="155">
```

Proper HTML coding requires that you place all <img> tags between the start and end body tags (<body></body>) that enclose the Web page content the browser displays onscreen. The following simple HTML code, when processed by a Web browser will display the graphics image house.jpg:

```
<html>
  <head><title>Image of a House</title>
</head>
<body>
  <center><img src="house.jpg" width="400" height="175"></center>
</body>
</html>
```

In addition to placing a simple image tag within an HTML document, you have several attributes that control the image within the browser window:

- *alt*   The *alt* attribute supplies alternate text for browsers that do not display graphics or for browsers where the user has turned off the display of graphics. Alternate text is also used by browsers as a tool tip (the text displays in a box near the mouse pointer, when the mouse hovers over the image) and by reader programs for the visually impaired.

  ```
  <img src="images/photo.jpg" alt="Photo of Florida Sunset">
  ```

- *height* and *width*   The *width* and *height* attributes define the size of the image displayed within the browser window. Always specify the *width* and *height* attributes in your image tags so the browser can display the remainder of your Web page text while waiting for images to download. When you specify the *width* and *height* attributes in an <img> tag, the browser reserves space for the images, even if they load slowly, and the document text will flow around where the images are supposed to go.

  ```
  <img src="images/photo.jpg" width="200" height="55">
  ```

- *border*   The *border* attribute gives the pixel-width of the border the Web browser is to draw around an image. If you use an image as the anchor for a hyperlink, the browser will draw a border around the picture. As such, drawing a border around pictures may make the visitor think the picture is a hyperlink. Therefore, it is recommended that you set the *border* attribute to zero (0).

  ```
  <img src="images/photo.jpg" width="200" height="55" border="0">
  ```

Working with graphics as well as using animations and video clips on a Web page is discussed in detail in Chapters 6 and 7.

 NOTE

Images are an indispensable part of a Web page. However, Web pages with many graphics take longer to download and display than Web pages with only text. Take care not to overload your Web pages with too many graphics. A picture may be worth a thousand words, but if your Web page takes too long to load, no one will wait around to see the message.

Changing the Alignment of Text and Graphics

Because most Web pages have both graphics images and text, aligning graphics and text within the browser application window is a basic element of Web page design. By default, the Web browser will display objects in the HTML document in the order in which the browser finds them. Moreover, the browser places the objects one after another onscreen from left to right, top to bottom.

Suppose, for example, that you want the browser to display an image above a line of text that describes the image. If you simply place an <img> tag in the HTML document and then type the line of text, the browser will display the text next to (that is, to the right of) and not below the image. Remember, the Web browser displays the items in the HTML document onscreen one after another moving from left to right. The browser puts an item at the left-hand margin of a new line only when the browser reaches the right-hand margin of the current line on the page.

The following code shows the order of the graphic and text elements. The <p> tag instructs the browser to display the text that follows the image on the line below the image onscreen:

```
<html>
<head>
  <title> Example of text and graphic placement </title>
</head>
<body>
  <img src="flower.jpg">
  <p> The illustrated flowers grow wild on the
  flat plains of Kansas </p>
</body>
</html>
```

Placing the <img> tag in the HTML document ahead of the text tells the Web browser to display the picture before the browser displays the text. Inserting the <p> tag between the image and the text tells the Web browser to display a line break (that is, to move to the next line on the page) and insert a blank line after displaying the image and before displaying the text that follows the image in the Web page HTML. Figure 1-15 shows how a Web browser will display the image in relation to the text in this example.

Figure 1-15   Without alignment, text and graphics move to the left side of the browser window

Notice that inserting the <p> tag correctly aligns the graphics image and text vertically. However, you may also want the browser to center both the picture and the text between the left and right-hand margins of the Web page. HTML provides the start and end center tags (<center></center>) to let you work with the horizontal alignment of objects on the Web page. Understand that although the center alignment tags are still used, they are deprecated tags, which means Web browsers may no longer support them at some point in the future. The preferred method of aligning text and graphics is with rules in a CSS, which you will learn about in Chapter 4.

USE IT By default, the Web browser aligns the first object on each line flush with the left-hand margin on the Web page. As such, you would use the <center> tag to change the default alignment and thereby change the horizontal position of an object on a line or group of lines. The start and end center tags (<center></center>)in the following HTML tell the Web browser to center the graphics image and text (enclosed within the tags) between the left and right margins of the Web page, as shown in Figure 1-16:

```
<html>
<head>
  <title> Example of text and graphic placement </title>
</head>
<body>
  <center><img src="flower.jpg">
    <p>The illustrated flowers
    grow wild on the flat plains of Kansas</p>
  </center>
</body>
</html>
```

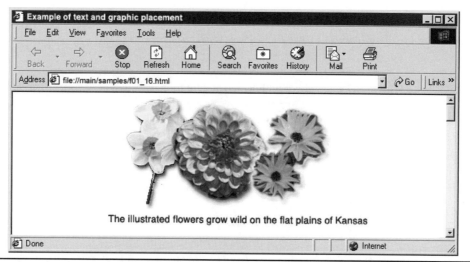

Figure 1-16 The start and end center tags instruct the Web browser to display the graphic and text elements centered between the left and right Web page margins

Adding a Hypertext Link to a Web Page

Web pages have a distinct advantage over paper documents: Web pages, unlike paper documents, can have hypertext links to other pages, either on the same Web site or on other sites. Rather than turning pages as they would when reading a book, site visitors click on hypertext links to move from page to page (or site to site). A *hypertext link* is a single word or a group of words upon which a visitor clicks to instruct the Web browser to retrieve a Web page (or other file) from the Web server.

To a site visitor, a typical hypertext link appears on the Web page as underlined text. Normally, the Web browser uses one color (such as blue) to represent hypertext links to Web pages not yet visited, and another color (such as purple) for links to pages the browser recently retrieved.

USE IT   To create a hypertext link, place a set of start and end anchor tags (<a></a>) around the text on which the visitor is to click to activate the link. (*Hypertext* is the text between the start and end anchor tags.) Then, set the *href* attribute in the <a> to the pathname of the file the browser is to retrieve when the visitor clicks on the hypertext. For example, the words "Click here to move to the next page" in the following HTML statement are the "hypertext" in a hypertext link, and the Web browser will underline the words on the Web page:

```
<a href="info.htm">Click here to move to the next page.</a>
```

When the visitor clicks on the underlined words (or between them) in this example, the Web browser will load the Web page in the file named info.htm. Notice that you place the *href* attribute within the <a> tag and the hypertext itself outside the <a> tag between the start and end anchor tags (<a></a>).

To create a hyperlink to a Web page on another Web site, include the site's URL along with the Web page filename in the *href* attribute. For example, the following code creates a hypertext link to the index page (that is, the home page) at www.anywhere.com:

```
<a href="http://www.anywhere.com/index.html">
  Click here to go to Anywhere.com</a>
```

When the site visitor clicks anywhere within "Click here to go to Anywhere.com" (that is, anywhere on hyperlink's anchor text), the Web browser will retrieve (and display) the homepage document (index.html) from the www.anywhere.com Web site. Thus, in this example, the value of the *href* attribute (href ="http://www.anywhere.com/index.html") creates a hypertext link between a Web page on your site and the index.html (homepage) document on the www.anywhere.com Web site. Note that you can also create a hyperlink to a Web site's homepage by supplying only the site's URL (without the index page filename) in the *href* attribute as:

```
<a href="http://www.anywhere.com">
  Click here to go to Anywhere.com</a>
```

In addition to using hypertext links to move from document to document, or site to site, you can use hypertext links to let the visitor download files from the Web site. For example, the following code tells the Web browser to download an image file named corvette.zip when visitors click on either of the words in "Click here":

```
<a href="http://www.home.com/cars/corvette.zip">
  Click here</a> to download a photo of my new Corvette.
```

The *href* attribute tells the Web browser to retrieve the picture of the Corvette (corvette.zip) from the cars folder on the www.home.com Web site.

You can make your Web pages interactive and user-friendly by adding hypertext links that let visitors download files and navigate the pages on your site or onto other sites. When you create hypertext links, make sure the hypertext or the text that precedes or follows the hyperlink explains, in easy-to-understand wording, exactly what will occur when a visitor clicks on the text to activate the hyperlink.

In addition, because most Web surfers associate underlined text with hypertext links, avoid the use of the start and end underline tags (<u></u>) to emphasize text within a Web document. To emphasize a word or group of words within a Web document choose styles such as bold, italic, or change the typeface, color, or size of the text.

Enhancing Individual Letters and Words Using Character Formatting Tags

When you want the Web browser to display text on a Web page, you simply type the text you want displayed between the start and end body tags (<body></body>) of the Web page HTML. As the Web browser reads the HTML document, the browser displays any text it finds onscreen. To tell the browser how you want the text to look, enclose the text between a pair of formatting tags. (HTML provides tags you can use to instruct the browser to apply such formatting options as bold, italic, and strikethrough.) You need to understand that Web browsers do not recognize normal formatting codes embedded in documents by word processors like Microsoft Word.

 Suppose, for example, that you want specific words in your Web document to appear in boldface. To boldface a letter, word, or group of words, enclose the desired text between start and end bold tags (<b></b>) such as those shown around the word "bold" in the following:

```
The last word in this sentence is <b>bold</b>
```

Character formatting tags are container tags, meaning they require both a start and an end tag. The Web browser will apply the formatting instruction to all the text within the "container," that is to all the text between the start and end formatting tags. In this example, the start and end bold tags (<bold> </bold>) that enclose the word "bold" instruct the Web browser to display the word in boldface type as **bold**. As mentioned previously, you can use character formatting tags to specify the appearance of several sentences (or even paragraphs), groups of words, individual words, or even a single letter within a word. For example, when the browser displays the text in the following HTML, only the letter "B" in the word "Bold" will display in boldface.

```
The first letter is <b>B</b>old
```

In addition to the start and end bold tags (<b></b>), you can use the following tags to enhance the look of text on a Web page:

- **<cite> </cite>**   The citation tags emphasize text, usually in italics.
- **<code> </code>**   The code tag sets the enclosed text in a monospace font such as Courier to set off the text. Use the code tags to identify a piece of HTML code within a training document.
- **<del> </del>**   The deleted text tags mark text as deleted by striking through the text. For example, use the deleted tags to mark through information in a legal document.
- **<q> </q>**   The quotation tags surround the enclosed text with quotation marks.
- ****   The subscript tags create a subscript, or display the text slightly lower than the surrounding text.
- ****   The superscript tags create a superscript, or display the text slightly higher than the surrounding text.
- **<em> </em>**   The emphasis tags highlight text by changing the enclosed words into italic font.
- **<strong> </strong>**   The strong tags highlight text by bolding and italicizing the enclosed words.
- **<i> </i>**   The italic tags highlight text by italicizing the enclosed words.
- **<u> </u>**   The underline tags highlight text by underlining the enclosed words. This tag is deprecated.

You can use formatting tags singularly or in combination. The following example combines the start and end bold tags (<b></b>) and the start and end superscript tags (<super></super>) to make the word "super" stand out on the page.

```
Character formatting tags are a <super><b>super</b></super> way
to grab the attention of a visitor to your Web page.
```

Although character formatting tags visually changes text within the browser window, a more efficient way to change text styles and adhere to the W3C recommendations is to use CSS rules.

Using Symbols and Special Characters in an HTML Document

Placing ordinary text on a Web page is as simple as creating an HTML document and entering the text between the document's HTML tags. A Web browser has no trouble reading and displaying letters (A–Z, a–z) and numbers (0–9) it finds in the HTML document. There are, however, certain special characters and symbols that text-editor applications let you type into the document, but the Web browser will not display on the Web page. Fortunately, HTML provides a text notation you can use to tell the Web browser to display certain commonly used special characters and lets you enter a numerical code for the rest.

USE IT   Say, for example, you create a Web page, and you want to display a copyright symbol (©) to indicate that certain items on the page and perhaps the overall design are protected under United States copyright laws. To get the Web browser to display the copyright symbol, you must enter the specific numeric value that represents the symbol. In a computer, each letter, number, and symbol is stored as a unique numeric value known as the character's ASCII code. To display a symbol such as the copyright on a Web page, you enter the symbol's unique value (that is, its ASCII code) into the Web page HTML.

For example, the numeric value of the copyright symbol is 169. To instruct the Web browser to display the character represented by the ASCII value 169, precede the character value with an ampersand (&) pound sign (#) combination and place a semicolon (;) after the code. Thus, to tell the Web browser to display the copyright symbol on the Web page, you would enter © into the Web page HTML. For the more commonly used symbols, HTML simplifies the process by letting you use a text code as opposed to a number to represent the symbol. For example, the character notation for the copyright symbol is ©.

The following code illustrates the use of the copyright symbol in an HTML document. To display a special character, the &#*xxx*; (where *xxx* represents the ASCII value of the special character) informs the browser which special character to display within the Web document onscreen. Figure 1-17 shows the results of using a Web browser to display the following HTML:

```
<html>
<head>
  <title> Copyright example </title>
</head>
<body>
  <p>The copyright symbol &#169; indicates the
  product falls under the protective umbrella
  of copyright as defined by the United States.</p>
</body>
</html>
```

▶ **NOTE**

For a listing of special character codes and their corresponding values, visit http://www.htmlhelp.com/reference/charset/.

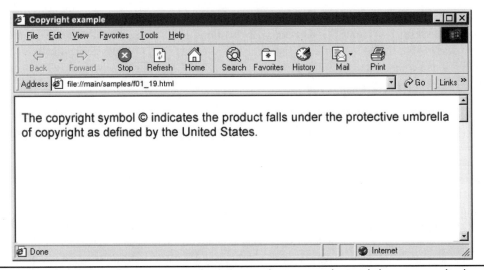

Figure 1-17   The ASCII value © in the HTML code instructs the Web browser to display a copyright symbol in the text

Using Horizontal Rules to Organize Web Content

When you create a Web page, organizing the page content into groups of related information is important. For example, you might organize the contents of a Web page that deals with vehicle sales into sections on cars, trucks, and vans. Or, you might organize the page by separating rental vehicle data from information about cars available for lease or direct sale.

One way to organize a Web page is to use horizontal rules (that is, horizontal lines) to separate different types of content. Suppose, for example, that you create a Web page to display research data, and you want to separate the research results from the footnotes. To create a horizontal rule that separates the research text from the footnotes, use the <hr> tag. The <hr> tags in the following HTML instruct the Web browser to place ruled lines horizontally (that is, left to right) across the browser's application window, as shown in Figure 1-18.

```
<html>
<head>
  <title>Use of the Horizontal Rule</title>
</head>
<body>
  <center>
    <h2>Using ImageReady to Slice an Image</h2>
  </center>
```

```
<p>When you slice an image . . . remainder of text</p>
<p>Slicing an image has . . . remainder of text </p>
<p>Treat each individual . . . remainder of text </p>
<p>However, it is just as . . . remainder of text </p>
<p>You can accomplish this . . . remainder of text </p>
<hr width="75%">
<hr width="50%">
<h3>Footnotes</h3>
<cite>1001 Photoshop Tips: Andy Anderson 2001</cite>
<hr align="left" noshade size="2" width="25">
<cite>Web Design &amp; HTML: Konrad King, Andy Anderson</cite>
</body>
</html>
```

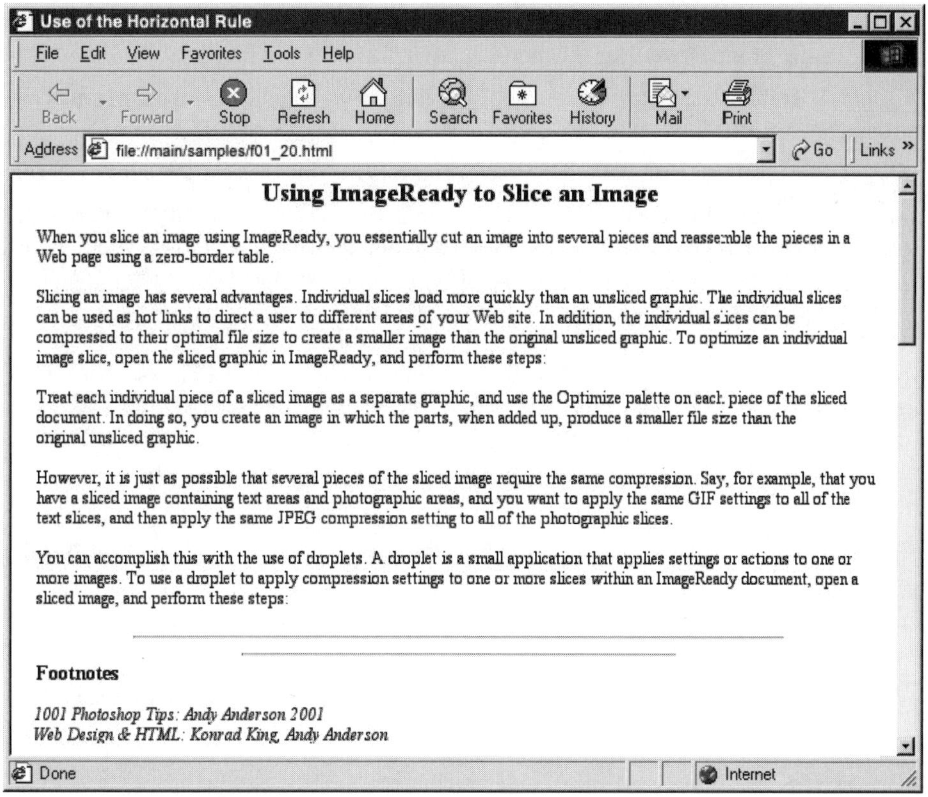

Figure 1-18   A Web page that contains body text and footnotes

In addition to creating a horizontal rule using the <hr> tag, you can create attractive rules by using graphics images. The following illustrates the use of the picture of a line in place of a horizontal rule drawn by the Web browser.

Footnotes

1001 Photoshop Tips: Andy Anderson 2001
Web Design & HTML: Konrad King, Andy Anderson

You can use the following attributes to control the appearance of a horizontal rule:

- *align*   The *align* attribute instructs the Web browser to align the horizontal rule to the right, left, or center of the browser application window.

- *noshade*   The *noshade* attribute instructs the Web browser to display the horizontal line without shading the line.

- *size*   The *size* attribute (measured in pixels) controls the thickness of the horizontal rule.

- *width*   The *width* attribute defines the length of the line. You can specify the horizontal rule's width either in pixels or as a percentage of the browser application window's width. For example, if you set the width to 50 percent (width="50%"), the browser will draw a horizontal rule with a length equal to half the width of the browser window.

If you place a horizontal rule in a table cell or within a position box, the browser uses the *width* and *align* attributes to set the length and horizontal position of the line relative to the vertical sides of the cell or position box (and not relative to the width of the Web page as a whole). The following illustrates the horizontal rule tag using various width, size, and alignment options.

Normal horizontal rule

No shade

Width changed

Height changed

Left
Center
Right

Using Blockquote Tags to Control Left and Right Text Margins

One of the more difficult things to accomplish in HTML is controlling the distance between text and the left and right text margins of a Web document. By default, the Web browser adjusts the left and right-hand page margins (that is, the width of the Web page) such that the page fits within the width of the browser's application window. (The alternative would be to allow a portion of the Web page to extend "beneath" the right-hand side of the application window and provide a horizontal scrollbar the visitor could use to display content that falls outside the viewable area within the application window.)

Of course, Web authors understand that Web browsers will shift text content from one line to the next as necessary. As such, developers create Web pages using a variety of text formatting/positioning options such as CSS or placing text into the cells of an HTML table. Without specific formatting instructions, the Web browser will place the first character of text right next to the left-hand margin and will wrap (move down to the next line) only when the browser reaches the right-hand margin on the Web page. Remember, the width of the browser application window on the visitor's computer determines the distance between the left and right-hand margins on a Web page. Moreover, the browser wraps text to the next line when the browser encounters the right-hand side the application window. A *blockquote* formats text by indenting, or increasing the margins on the right and left sides of the blockquoted text. As such, using blockquotes to indent a portion of text document makes text stand out and thereby helps to organize the content on the page.

USE IT   For example, the following HTML defines a Web page with a title followed by two paragraphs of blockquote style text, as shown in Figure 1-19:

```
<html>
<head>
  <title>Example of the Blockquote tag</title>
</head>
<body>
  <p>This is regular text</p>
  <blockquote>The text in this paragraph is
    blockquoted. Notice how the text indents
    on the left side of the page, and wraps
    when it encounters the right margin
  </blockquote>
  <p>This is more regular text; see what happens
  when the regular text reaches a margin.</p>
  <blockquote>The text in this paragraph
    is blockquoted. Notice how the text
    indents on the left side of the page,
    and wraps when it encounters the right
    margin
  </blockquote>
</body>
</html>
```

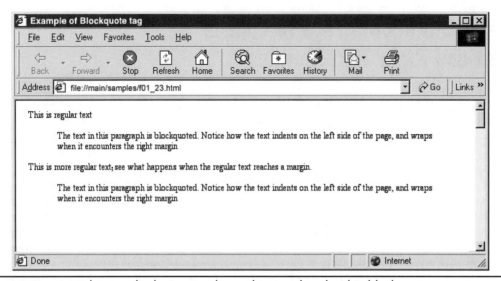

Figure 1-19   A Web page displaying regular and text enclosed within blockquotes

Creating Ordered and Unordered Lists

Previously in this chapter, you learned several ways in which to lay out content on a Web page. Ordered and unordered lists provide yet another tool you can use to organize related text into groups of either bulleted or numbered items in a list. Lists are very useful because they provide information in a structured format. Ordered lists use an alphabetical or numerical system to organize Web content, and unordered lists use symbols, or bullets, to identify each item in the list. Figure 1-20 shows a Web page—with an ordered and unordered list.

USE IT   Use ordered, or numbered, lists to create step-by-step instructions, where the order of the elements in the list is important. The following HTML code describes the ordered list shown in Figure 1-20.

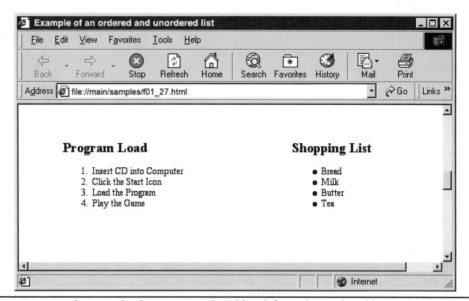

Figure 1-20   A Web page displaying an ordered list (left) and unordered list (right)

```
<html>
<head>
  <title>Example of ordered list</title>
</head>
<body>
  <h2>Program Load</h2>
  <ol>
    <li>Insert CD into Computer</li>
    <li>Click the Start Icon</li>
    <li>Load the Program</li>
    <li>Play the Game<</li>
  </ol>
</body>
</html>
```

As shown in this example, to denote an ordered list within the Web page HTML, place the list's items between start and end ordered list tags (<ol></ol>). Then, to add items to the list, place the text for each item between start and end list item tags (<li></li>).

By default, the Web browser will display an Arabic numeral (1, 2, 3, 4…) before each item in the list—with the first item numbered 1. If you wish to use letters or roman numerals instead, insert a *type* attribute in the start ordered list tag as follows:

- **<ol type="1">**   Displays items using Arabic numerals (default)
- **<ol type="a">**   Displays items using lowercase letters
- **<ol type="A">**   Displays items using uppercase letters
- **<ol type="i">**   Displays items using lowercase roman numerals
- **<ol type="I">**   Displays items using uppercase roman numerals

To begin an ordered list at a number other than "1" (or alphabetically with a letter other than "a") insert a *start* attribute with a value other than "1" in the <ol> tag. For example, an ordered list that starts with the following <ol> tag would begin the list with the letter "e", because "e" is the fifth letter of the alphabet:

```
<ol type="a" start="5">
```

Similarly, if you assign a "1" to the *type* attribute in order to indicate the browser is to place an Arabic numeral before each item in the list, the browser would start the list with the first list item numbered 5.

Unordered lists let you create groups of text items where the order of the items in the list is not important, such as in a shopping list. The following HTML code will create the unordered list shown previously in Figure 1-20:

```
<html>
<head>
  <title>Example of unordered list</title>
</head>
<body>
  <h2>Shopping List</h2>
  <ul>
    <li>Bread</li>
    <li>Milk</li>
    <li>Butter</li>
    <li>Tea<</li>
  </ul>
</body>
</html>
```

To denote an unordered list within the Web page HTML, place the list's items between start and end unordered list tags (<ul></ul>). As is the case with an ordered list, you add items to an unordered list by placing the text for each item between start and end list tags (<li></li>).

By default, the Web browser will display a solid black dot (●) as the bullet character before each item in the unordered list. If you want the browser to use a different bullet character, use the *type* attribute in the <ul> tag to select the bullet symbol as follows:

- **<ul type="disc">**   Displays items using a solid black dot (default)
- **<ul type="square">**   Displays items using a black outlined square
- **<ul type="circle">**   Displays items using a black outlined dot (that is, an unfilled circle)

Creating Nested Lists

In the preceding Tip, you learned the how to create ordered and unordered lists. You can also create an ordered or unordered list within another list; that is, you can create a *nested* list. You might use a nested list to display a set of actions that are important to a specific step in the outer list, as shown here:

Program Load

1. Insert CD into Computer
2. Click the Start Icon
3. Load the Program
      a. Double-click the game icon
      b. Enter serial number
      c. Click the Finish button
4. Play the Game

USE IT   Step 3 of the list shown requires more explanation than a simple, "Load the Program" statement. Therefore, you might insert a nested list to describe the steps necessary to load the program. The following HTML code describes the insertion of the nested list shown previously:

```
<html>
<head>
  <title>Example of Ordered List</title>
</head>
<body>
  <h2>Program Load</h2>
  <ol>
    <li>Insert CD into Computer</li>
    <li>Click the Start Icon</li>
```

```
    <li>Load the Program</li>
      <ol type="a">
        <li>Double-click the game icon</li>
        <li>Enter serial number</li>
        <li>Click the Finish button</li>
      </ol>
    <li>Play the Game<</li>
  </ol>
</body>
</html>
```

In this example, the nested list is an ordered list defined by start and end ordered list tags (<ol> </ol>). The ordered list is *nested*, because the start and end ordered list tags (<ol></ol>) occur within (that is, are nested in) an outer set of start and end ordered list tags(<ol></ol>). (The text phrases between the start and end list item tags [<li></li>] appear onscreen as the items in each list [both outer and nested]).

Although the coding of a nested list may appear complicated, you follow the same rules when creating a nested list as when creating the outer list. Define the nested list between a set of start and end ordered list tags (<ol></ol>) or between a set of start and end unordered list tags (<ul></ul>). Then add items to the nested list by inserting text between sets of start and end list item tags (<li> </li>) you inserted after the definition for a list item in the outer list. Keep in mind that you can nest both ordered lists and unordered lists in an outer list (which may be an ordered list or an unordered list).

◣ Creating Definition Listings

Earlier in this chapter, you learned how to create ordered and unordered lists and how to nest one list within another. In addition to items arranged in bulleted lists and numbered lists, HTML also lets you create a definition list. As its name implies, a *definition list* is a list of terms, each followed by a definition. The Web browser indents each definition on the next line below the term being defined, as shown in Figure 1-21.

A definition list is the only type of list that does not identify the individual list items using the start and end list item tags (<li></li>). Instead, the definition list uses two new tags:

- **<dt></dt>**   Start and end definition term tags denote the term to be described or defined. (The start and end definition term tags are similar in function to the start and end list item tags used to denote individual items in ordered and unordered lists.)

- **<dd></dd>**   The start and end definition description tags denote one or more paragraphs of indented descriptive text.

USE IT   To create a definition list within the Web page HTML, insert the terms and definitions between start and end definition list tags (<dl></dl>). For example, the following HTML will create a two-term definition list as shown previously:

```html
<html>
<head>
  <title>Example of a Definition List</title>
</head>
<body>
  <center><h2>Basic HTML</h2></center>
  <dl>
    <dt><b>Basic HTML Tags</b> </dt>
      <dd>HTML tags are commands used by a Web browser to
          display information in a browser window.
          HTML tags are accepted by both Mac and Win versions
          of the standard browser applications.</dd>
    <dt><b>The Importance of the Title Tag </b> </dt>
      <dd>The title tag represents the description
          of a Web page to visitors to your Web site.
          The title to a Web page appears in the title
          bar of the Web browser window.</dd>
  </dl>
</body>
</html>
```

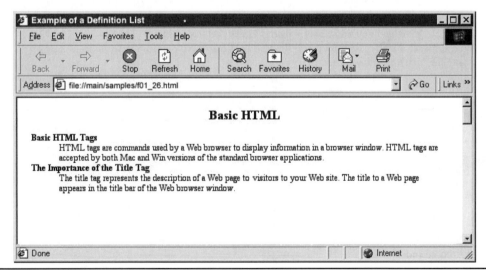

Figure 1-21   A definition list with two items and descriptions

Using Preformatted Text Tags to Control the Display of Web Content

Previously, in this chapter, you learned how to change the appearance of text by using formatting tags. For example, if you want the browser to display a word in boldface, you enclose the word within start and end boldface tags (<b></b>) in the Web page HTML. Similarly, to move text down one or more lines, you insert one or more <br> tags. Thus, when creating a Web page, you often use one set of HTML tags to control how the text looks, and another set of tags to control the layout of the text on the page. Unfortunately, when the Web browser displays the text, the browser ignores multiple spaces and new lines you may have entered in the HTML document to space or align page content, as shown in Figure 1-22.

You can, however use the start and end preformatted text tags (<pre></pre>) to combine both format and layout functions in a single set of HTML tags. The start and end preformatted text tags

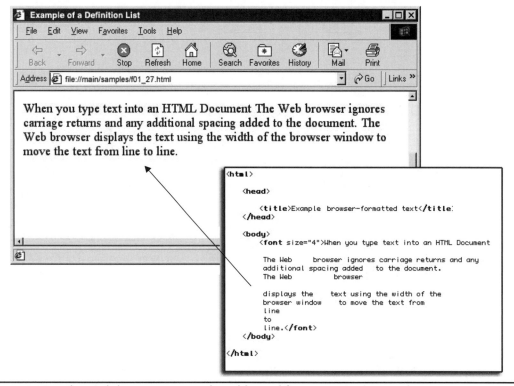

Figure 1-22   The Web browser ignores the additional formatting (spaces and carriage returns) entered into the body of the HTML document

(<pre></pre>) tell the Web browser to use a fixed pitch font and to display onscreen all the spaces, and new lines, the browser finds within the preformatted text in the Web page HTML. (To avoid misaligned paragraph text in the browser window, uses spaces and not the TAB key to line things up, because not all browsers interpret the TAB key the same way.)

USE IT   You might use preformatted text to display such things as program listings and recipes. Figure 1-23, for example, shows a Web page with preformatted text.

Normally, you use preformatted text when you want to control the length of each line of text and the spacing of the words within a line. Unfortunately, you cannot use <img> tags to insert pictures, or <object> tags to insert ActiveX controls or Java applets within preformatted text. Although the start and end preformatted text tags (<pre></pre>) let you control the placement of text, you must use HTML tables or CSS rules to control the location of elements other than text.

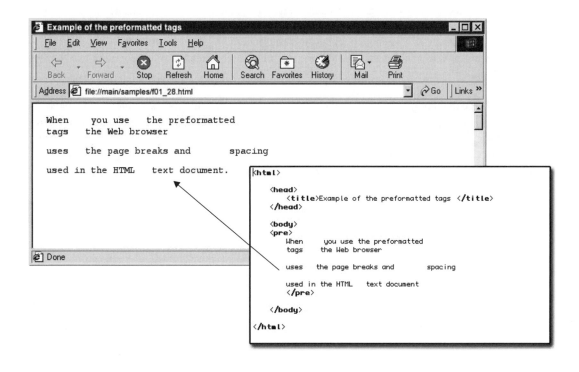

Figure 1-23   The preformatted tags control the line breaks within a Web document without the use of HTML formatting tags

Displaying a Navigation Menu Within a Web Page Frame

You use HTML frames when you want to display more than one Web page in a single application window. Because the Web browser maintains a separate URL for each frame, the browser can load a new Web page into any of the frames without changing the contents of the others. One of the most common uses of a framed Web page is to display a Web site's navigation menu while the visitor moves from page to page on the site. A typical navigation menu consists of graphics in the form of buttons or simply hypertext links that connect to all the pages in a Web site. A well-designed navigation menu guides the user through the twists and turns of a site like a road map.

An important consideration when designing a navigation menu is where on the Web page to place the menu. Most Web pages place the navigation menu horizontally across the top, or vertically down the left side of the application window. Whatever placement you choose, be consistent. If you place the navigation menu vertically down the left side of the site's index page (that is, the site's homepage), place the menu in the same place on the site's remaining pages. Consistent placement helps the user feel comfortable with navigation, and comfortable visitors will spend more time exploring your site. On a marketing site, increased visitor comfort with the site's navigation translates into increased sales, and on information sites, visitors will remember more and be more likely to return to the site for more information.

Frames give you way of keeping a navigation menu in view at all times while the visitor travels around the pages on your Web site. Suppose, for example, that you create a Web page with two frames, such as that shown in Figure 1-24.

USE IT   Place the navigation menu in the thin, 100-pixel rectangular frame along the left-hand side of the page and display new Web pages in the larger frame on the right. Because the frame with the navigation bar remains in place along the left side of the browser application window as the browser loads selected Web pages into the frame on the right, the visitor never loses sight of the road map of your site. The following code creates the framed Web page shown in Figure 1-24:

```
<html>
<head>
  <title>Welcome to Product Review</title>
</head>
<frameset cols="100,400,*">
  <frame src="n_nav.html" name="left">
  <frame src="h_main.html" name="right">
</frameset>
</html>
```

As you can see from the code in this example, the frameset page does not include the HTML from all the Web pages displayed onscreen together. The frameset Web page simply instructs the Web browser to display Web pages in the frames defined by the start frameset tag (<frameset>).

In this example, the frameset page instructs the Web browser to display the HTML documents n_nav.html, and h_main.html (the site's navigation menu and index page, respectively) within two frames onscreen. The Web browser loads the n_nav.html document into the first frame of 100 pixels

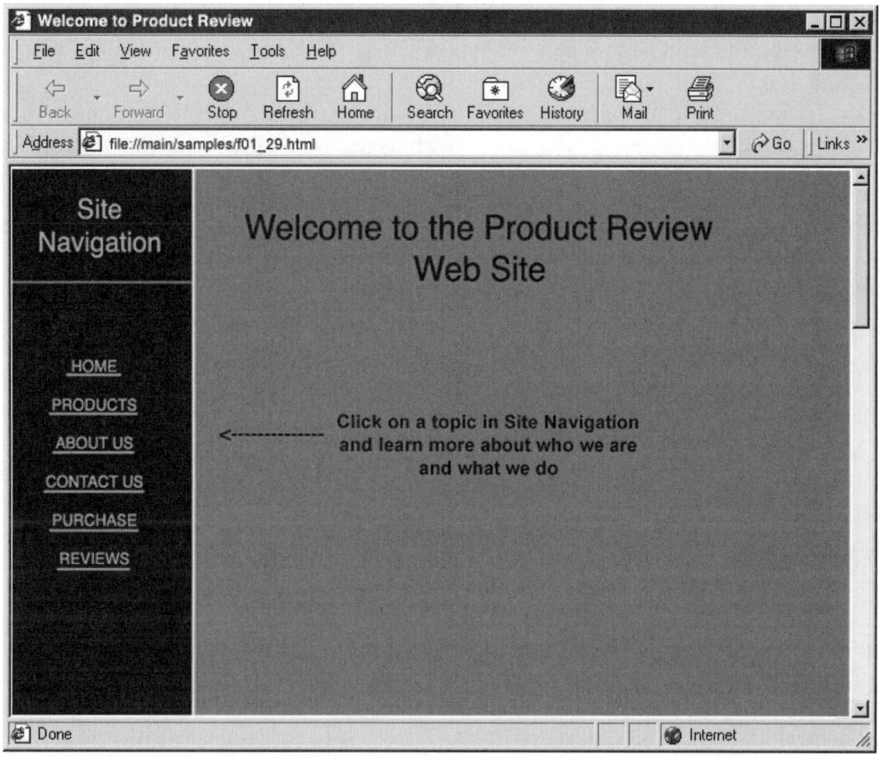

Figure 1-24 The document window contains two frames that hold the navigation menu and the site information

in width and the h_main.html document into the second frame of 400 pixels in width. HTML tags used to define Web pages loaded into frames perform exactly as they do when a Web browser displays one of the pages at a time. Frames simply arrange multiple Web pages within a single document window.

Displaying Multiple Web Pages Onscreen at the Same Time

Frames provide a way to have a Web browser display multiple Web pages onscreen at the same time. A typical Web page that contains frames might have two frames—one frame in which to display a navigation bar and a second in which to display a Web page with content you want the visitor to view. When the visitor clicks on a button or hyperlink on the navigation bar in one frame, the Web browser loads and displays a Web page in the second content frame.

USE IT   To create a Web page with frames, you need at least three Web pages. First, you need the two or more Web pages you want to display onscreen at the same time. (If you have only one Web page to display, there is no reason to split the browser's application window into frames.) Second, you need a frameset page whose job it is to tell the Web browser the size and number of frames as well as the names of the Web page to display in each frame.

Suppose, for example, that you have a Web page with a navigation bar that you have stored in a file named n_menu.html. Moreover, you have a Web page with company information that you have saved to a file named opendoc.html. You could use a frames page such as that defined by the following HTML to display both pages (n_menu.html and opendoc.html) onscreen at once:

```
<!doctype html public "-//W3C//DTD HTML 4.01 Frameset//EN"
        "http://www.w3.org/TR/html4/frameset.dtd">
<html>
<head>
  <title> Example of a frame document </title>
</head>
<frameset cols="80,400">
  <frame name="menu" src="n_menu.html">
  <frame name="content" src="opendoc.html">
</frameset>
</html>
```

Notice that in the HTML document containing the frames, the start and end frameset tags (<frameset></frameset>) replace the start and end body tags (<body></body>) you see in a Web page without frames. This is because the frames page has no "body" or "content" to display. The sole purpose of the frames page is to divide the browser's application window into frames (like picture frames), and to give the Web browser the pathname or URL of the Web page to display in each of the frames.

In this example, the *cols* attribute in the <frameset> tag tells the Web browser to draw two frames and to make the first frame 80 pixels wide and the second 400 pixels wide. Thus, the *cols* attribute tells the Web browser not only the number of frames to draw (by the number of column widths listed in the attribute's value) but also the pixel-width of each frame. (For example, if you have three fames, the *cols* attribute would have three values and appear as cols="*n,n,n*"; if you have four frames, the *cols* attribute would have four values and appear as: cols="*n,n,n,n*", and so on.)

The *src* attribute in a frame's <frame> tag tells the Web browser the name of the Web page to display within the frame when the browser initially loads the frames page. In the current example, the Web browser will load n_menu.html into the first frame (named menu) and opendoc.htm into the second frame (named content), as shown in Figure 1-25.

When the site visitor clicks on a hyperlink in the menu frame, the *target* attribute in the <a> tag tells the Web browser into which frame to load the Web page given by the <a> tag's *href* attribute. For example, the following hyperlink tells the Web browser to display the document aboutus.html in the frame named content when the visitor clicks anywhere within the "About us" hypertext link:

```
<a href="aboutus.html" target="content">About Us</a>
```

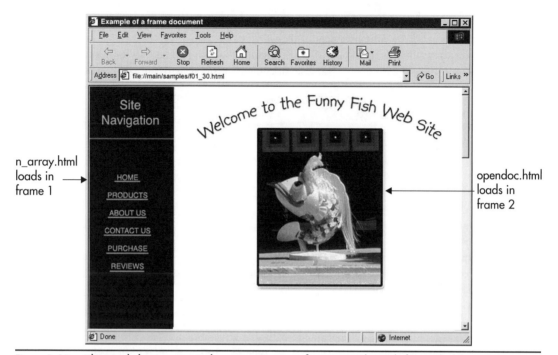

n_array.html loads in frame 1

opendoc.html loads in frame 2

Figure 1-25   The Web browser window contains two frames, with each frame holding a separate HTML document

Thus, when the visitor clicks on the "About Us" hypertext link, the Web browser will replace the document (opendoc.html, from the previous example) displayed in the target frame (content) with aboutus.html (named by the *href* attribute in this example). If a hyperlink's <a> tag has no *target* attribute, the browser will load the hyperlinked document into the frame used to display the Web page whose hyperlink the visitor activated. For example, the following HTML will cause the Web browser to replace n_menu.html with aboutus.html in the menu frame (given that "About Us" is a hypertext link on the menu bar displayed within the menu frame):

```
<a href="aboutus.html">About Us</a>
```

Similarly, when the visitor clicks on a hyperlink in the content frame, the hyperlink will have either a *target* attribute that tells the browser to load the linked page into the content frame, or no *target* attribute, in which case the browser will load the linked page into the content frame anyway. By displaying linked pages the browser retrieves within the content frame, you can leave the navigation menu (in the menu frame) onscreen at all times.

Web page frames provide an excellent way to organize your Web site. However, because framed Web documents require the browser to load and display three or more Web pages, it takes the Web browser longer to display a Web page with frames than one without. Moreover, not all Web browsers support frames. Those that do not support frames will display neither the Web pages in the frames nor the frames defined by the frameset page.

To handle browsers that do not support frames, include the start and end no frames tags (<noframes></noframes>) within your frameset document, as illustrated in the following code:

```
<!doctype html public "-//W3C//DTD HTML 4.01 Frameset//EN"
         "http://www.w3.org/TR/html4/frameset.dtd">
<html>
<head>
  <title>A frameset document with NOFRAMES</title>
</head>
<frameset cols="80,400">
<frame name="menu" src="n_menu.html">
  <frame name="content" src="opendoc.html">
  <noframes>
    <a href="main-noframes.html">Click to view
      a non-frame based version of the document.</a>
  </noframes>
</frameset>
</html>
```

If the Web browser does not support frames, the hypertext link appears within the browser window, instructing the user to click on the link to load a non-framed version of the Web page.

CHAPTER 2

HTML Tables

TIPS IN THIS CHAPTER

▶ Creating a Table with Cells that Span Multiple Columns or Multiple Rows   72

▶ Working with Table and Cell Border Widths   75

▶ Working with Table and Cell Border Colors   76

▶ Working with Background Images and Colors   78

▶ Determining a Color Attribute's Value   81

▶ Working with Cell Padding and Cell Spacing   83

▶ Setting Table Dimensions Using Relative or Absolute Values   84

▶ Setting Cell Dimensions Using Relative or Absolute Values   85

▶ Aligning Cell Content Horizontally and Vertically   86

▶ Aligning a Table on a Web Page   89

▶ Controlling the Width and Height of a Cell by Inserting a Transparent GIF   89

▶ Wrapping Text Around an Image   91

▶ Displaying a Gallery of Thumbnails Within a Table   93

▶ Creating Bullets and Lists with Tables and Graphics   96

▶ Creating a Navigation Sidebar Using a Table   97

▶ Adding Images and Links to Table Cells   98

▶ Nesting Tables to Control Borders on a Web Page   99

▶ Approximating an Image Map by Placing Pieces of an Image Within a Table   100

▶ Slicing a Graphic Image into Table Cells to Create a Quick Loading Web Graphic   102

▶ Reducing the Amount of Time a Web Browser Spends Drawing a Table   103

▶ Simulating Web Page Frames Using a Table   104

▶ Focusing the Viewer's Attention with Cell Background Colors   107

▶ Aligning Web Page Content Visually with Visible Table Borders   108

▶ Controlling Gutter Size and Margin Width of Text on a Web Page   110

HTML tables provide the Web designer with two valuable tools—a tool to place text and numerical information in a tabular form and a way to position objects on a Web page precisely. Although you will occasionally use tables to display tabular data, the true power of tables lies in their utility as a page layout tool. HTML tables let you lay out Web pages in ways that were difficult if not impossible to do prior to the introduction of tables with the release of HTML 3 in 1995. In fact, using tables for page layout has become so widespread that the World Wide Web Consortium (W3C) has worked hard to standardize the way in which browsers across multiple platforms render tables. As a result, today's Web designers can use tables and be sure of consistent performance and display of information in all but the oldest Web browsers.

When you work with tables, the most obvious use for a table is to display text and numeric information in columnar form. Say, for example, that you want to display a listing of all the executives within a company and their corresponding office phone numbers. You would create a two-column table with the individual cells in the left column containing the names of the executives. The corresponding cells in the right column contain the executive's office phone number. As shown in Figure 2-1, you might increase the information the table provides, by adding a third column that contains e-mail address, and a fourth, fifth, and sixth column for address, city, and state.

Because the cells in the table read from left to right, the table orders the information you place in its cells in an easy-to-read format, and distills the complexity of the information into a user-friendly spreadsheet format.

The second (and perhaps most important) application of tables is to place Web content (that is, text, numbers, graphics images, or blank space) into individual table cells, and then control the design of the Web page by placing the cells into organized rows and columns. In fact, for many designers, creating a structured Web page starts with drawing a row and column matrix (in other words, a table) that fits

Name	Phone Number	E-mail Address	Street Address	City	State
Konrad King	702-361-0141	kki@NVBizNet.com	765 E. Eldorado Lane	Las Vegas	NV
Karen King	702-222-3333	karen@NVBizNet.com	765 E. Eldorado Lane	Las Vegas	NV
Sam Spade	789-333-4444	spades@DiggerMail.com	77 Sunset Strip	High Town	OH
Walter Winchell	658-444-5555	winchellw@eatDoughnuts.com	587 Anystreet Way	Island City	HI
Kris Duncan	458-555-6666	duncan@eatDoughnuts.com	658 High Street	Austin	TX
Fred Berry	458-666-7777	fred@firemail.com	875 Western Ave.	Houston	TX

Figure 2-1   Table used to display numeric and text data in tabular form

the width and height of the entire page. The designer then lays out the Web page by placing the page content into the table's row and column cell structure at the location where the designer wants each element (or object) to appear on the Web page.

Suppose, for example, that you want to place a graphic element in the upper-right corner of a Web page. All that is required to do so is to create a table with a cell in the upper-right corner of the page, and then place the graphics image into that cell. Similarly, if you want to place text in the lower-right corner of the page, simply make sure the table's structure creates a cell where you want the text to appear and then place the text you want into the cell.

When the Web browser, in turn, displays the Web page with the table, the dimensions of the table and its cells hold the graphics image(s) and text in position on the page. Because each cell in a table can hold any Web page object at a specific spot on the Web page, you can use tables to control the placement of everything from simple text to interactive graphics buttons and background images. Figure 2-2, for example, shows a Web page in which a table with zero-width cell borders provides an invisible grid of cells that hold the page content in place.

Saying that the introduction of HTML tables completely changed the way in which Web designers create Web pages would not be an exaggeration.

▶ **NOTE**

Due to the complexity and amount of HTML required to create extensive page layout tables, you may want to use one of the Web design tools, such as Dreamweaver or GoLive. These programs not only generate well-written and efficient HTML code but they can also save you hours of time by letting you use the mouse pointer to "draw" the table you want onscreen.

In addition to using tables to place graphics and text on a Web page, you can also use tables to group a set of navigation buttons along the top, bottom, or sides of a page. Using a table to organize navigation buttons into an ordered pattern at the same relative location on each page makes the site

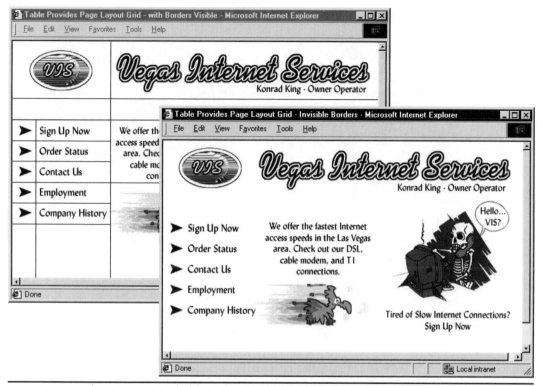

Figure 2-2   Web page content held in place within the cells of a table

easier to navigate. Moreover, by painting groups of cells with different background colors you can create a visually organized Web page.

Suppose, for example, that you create a column of navigation buttons along the left side of a Web page. Use the same background color for each of the table's cells that hold the navigation buttons, as shown in Figure 2-3.

Then, by using a contrasting color for the backgrounds of the remaining cells in the table, you will draw the visitor's eyes to the group of cells that are the site's navigation menu—thereby making it easier for the visitor to find the buttons necessary to move from page to page on the site. Moreover, by using the same background color for the navigation button cells on all Web pages, you give the visitor a visual cue as to where to look for help with navigating to specific pages of interest on the site. In general, using background color to group table cells that perform a single function creates a visually pleasing, visitor-friendly Web site.

Tables also provide an excellent way to divide a single graphics image into multiple parts to approximate an image map on Web browsers that do not support image maps. *Image maps* are graphics images subdivided into clickable regions. Depending on a site's purpose and tone, you might use an image map as a unique navigation tool. Suppose, for example, that you create a historical Web site for your family. The graphics image on the index page might be that of a large tree with extended

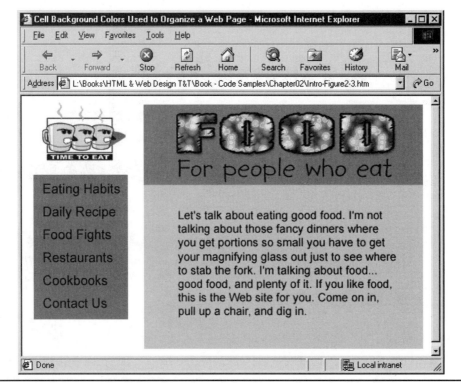

Figure 2-3 Web page with table cell background colors used to organize content

branches, with each branch of the (family) tree named after a particular branch of your family. By dividing the picture of the tree into separate pieces and then placing each part into a separate cell in a table such that each cell holds a branch of the tree, you can turn each branch of the tree into a "hotspot," such as those you find on an image map. After you do this, the visitor will be able to click on a branch on the tree to access information about a particular set of relatives. Although the visitor sees a complete tree with extending branches, in reality the graphics image on the Web page is broken and divided into separate pieces and then reassembled into a single image using an HTML table.

Oddly enough, most Web designers that use tables as a design tool do not consider the actual coding of the tables to be the most difficult part. Instead, it is visualizing the Web page broken into a table format of rows and columns of cells that they find difficult. For example, in the previous paragraph, a tree with extending branches creates the image map for an historical Web site. However, if you want to create an image map of the United States, you need only to look at a map of the country to see that dividing the United States among the cells of an HTML table will not work, simply because the borders of the individual states do not form perfect rectangles. Sketching the Web page on paper and then dividing the images and text into the framework of horizontal and vertical lines is a quick way to ensure that a design is workable. In other words, the sketch (or *storyboard*) will show you if you can divide the objects on a Web page into the individual cells of the brick-like structure of an HTML table. Always analyze the project before doing the actual coding.

Understanding the HTML Tags that Create a Table

The HTML tables you use to display content on a Web page, like the tables you see in printed materials (books, magazines, newspapers, and so on), consist of columns of data arranged in rows. Not surprisingly then, the basic HTML tags used to create a table tell the Web browser which part of an HTML file to include in the table and group individual data items in that part of the file into rows of cells:

- **<table></table>**   Alert the Web browser that it is to treat the text between the start and end tags as a table

- **<tr></tr>** (table row)   Alert the Web browser that it is to put the data items and perhaps headings between the start and end tags on a single, new row in the table

- **<td></td>** (table data)   Alert the Web browser that the HTML tags, attributes, and text (if any) between the start and end tags is content (in other words, the data) that the Web browser is to display in a table column

For example, you would write the following HTML code to have a Web browser display the simple three-column, two-row table shown here:

```
<table border="1">
   <tr><td>1</td>
       <td>2</td>
       <td>3</td></tr>
   <tr><td>4</td>
       <td>5</td>
       <td>6</td></tr>
</table>
```

As mentioned in the bulleted list that precedes the table's HTML, the start and end table tags (<table></table>) at the beginning and end of the code tell the Web browser that the HTML code and other text between the tags describes a table. (Ignore the *border* attribute for now; we discuss this attribute in the next section of this chapter.) Each pair of the start and end table row tags (<tr></tr>) tell the Web browser to display the content between them on the same, new (horizontal) row in the table. Meanwhile, each pair of start and end table data tags (<td></td>) defines each of the table's cells, and the content between them tells the Web browser what to place in the cell.

Thus, to create the two-column, three-row table shown next, you would use three sets of start and end table row tags (<tr></tr>) and two sets of start and end table data tags (<td></td>) per row (six sets in total) as shown here:

```
<table border="1">
  <tr><td>A</td>
      <td>B</td></tr>
  <tr><td>C</td>
      <td>D</td></tr>
  <tr><td>E</td>
      <td>F</td></tr>
</table>
```

As was the case in the previous example, the first line of code in the current example contains a <table> tag, which tells the Web browser all subsequent HTML code the browser reads until it has processed the </table> tag is part of an HTML table definition.

The second line of code reads like this:

```
<tr><td>A</td>
```

Each time the Web browser reads a <tr> tag within a table definition, the browser knows to move to a new row in the table. The <td> tag that follows the <tr> tag, meanwhile, tells the browser to put everything it sees prior to the </td> tag into a single cell within the table. Therefore, in the current example, the first <td> tag tells the Web browser to place an "A" into the first cell on the left in the new table row the browser starts after processing the <tr> tag that precedes the <td> tag.

The third line of code in the table HTML for the current example reads like this:

```
<td>B</td></tr>
```

Because there is no <tr> tag in front of the second <td> tag in the code, the Web browser puts everything between the second pair of start and end table data tags (<td></td>) ("B", in the current example), into the second cell (to the right) in the first row of the table. (If there were a third pair of start and end table data tags [<td></td>] prior to the </tr> tag, the Web browser would place everything between those tags into the third cell [to the right] in the first row of the table, and so on.) The </tr> tag tells the Web browser: "That's it. There are no more cells in the current row," at which point the browser expects to see either a new <tr> tag, or a </table> tag. In the current example, the <tr><td></td><td></td></tr> pattern repeats twice more (thus telling the browser to create two more rows of two cells [or columns] each), before the </table> tag signals the end of the HTML table's definition in the last row of code.

Adding Borders, Headings, and a Caption

When you want to use an HTML table to display tabular data (instead of using a table as a page layout tool, as you will learn how to do later in this chapter), you may want to draw borders around the table and around each of its cells and include a caption (or title) that summarizes the table's data. Moreover, most tabular data includes a row and/or column of headings that tells the viewer the meaning of (or relationship among) the items in the same column or row. Figure 2-4, for example, shows a table with visible borders, headings, and a caption.

HTML provides a *border* attribute you can use to tell the Web browser to display a border around a table and around each of its cells. Moreover, you can use start and end caption tags

Tags and Attributes Used to Create a Table

HTML Tag/Attribute	Description
<TABLE></TABLE>	Start and end of table definition
<TR>	New table row
<TD></TD>	Start and end table data item definition
border	Pixel width of the borders around the perimeter of the table and its cells
<CAPTION></CAPTION>	Start and end table caption text
<TH></TH>	Start and end table heading text

Figure 2-4   A table used to display information in a tabular format

(<caption></caption>) to specify the table's title (or caption), and start and end table heading tags (<th></th>) to tell the Web browser to format a cell's content as a heading:

- *border*   Attribute in a <table> tag that tells the Web browser the number of pixels wide to draw the border around the perimeter of the table and each of the table's cells
- **<caption> </caption>**   Alert the Web browser that it is to style the text between the start and end tags as a caption (most browsers use a boldface font)
- **<th></th>** (table heading)   Alert the Web browser that the text between the start and end tags is to be formatted as heading text (most browsers use a boldface font)

The table heading and caption tags are extremely helpful for the visually impaired, because browsers designed for blind users will speak differently to differentiate the table caption and table headings from the table data. In addition, you might include a *summary* attribute within the <table> tag to provide a longer description of the table's purpose for the benefit of visitors using speech- or Braille-based browsers.

To display a table with borders, a title, and headings such as that shown in Figure 2-4, you would first change the table's <table> tag to include a *border* attribute to which you assign the pixel width of the table's border. For example, to draw one-pixel wide borders (such as those shown around the table and its cells shown in Figure 2-4), you would code the table's <table> tag as follows:

```
<table border="1">
```

Then, to give the table a title (or caption), you would insert start and end caption tags (<caption></caption>) in the table definition immediately after the <table> tag. Thus, the first line of code (with only a <table> tag) in the previous example becomes the following two lines of code that tell the Web browser to draw a table with both one-pixel-wide borders and a caption:

```
<table border="1">
  <caption>Tags and Attributes Used to Create a Table</caption>
```

Note that newer HTML specifications (starting with the HTML 4.01 standard) state that the caption element, if present, *must* immediately follow the opening <table> tag.

Next, to put a heading at the top of each of the table's columns, insert start and end table heading tags (<th></th>) that enclose "heading" text after the <tr> tag that starts the row in which you want the heading(s) to appear. For example, to add a heading atop each column in a two-column table, you would write the following:

```
<table border="1" >
  <caption>Tags and Attributes Used to Create a Table</caption>
  <tr><th>HTML Tag</th>
      <th>Description</th></tr>
```

To add a column of headings instead of the row of headings, add one set of start and end table heading tags (<th></th>) that enclose heading text to each row of data items designated by the table's start and end table row tags (<tr></tr>). For example, the following HTML with two sets of start and end table heading tags (<th></th>) following a single <tr> tag tells the Web browser to create a table with two headings in different columns of the *same* row in the table:

```
<table border="1" >
  <caption>Headings in a Row</caption>
  <tr><th>Heading 1</th>
      <th>Heading 2</th></tr>
  <tr><td>Row 1, Item 1</td>
      <td>Row 1, Item 2</td></tr>
  <tr><td>Row 2, Item 1</td>
      <td>Row 2, Item 2</td></tr>
</table>
```

Conversely, the following HTML with a single set of start and end table heading tags (<th></th>) after each <tr> tag tells the Web browser to create a table with the same two headings, but to place the headings in the same column on *different* rows in the table:

```
<table border="1" >
  <caption>Headings in a Column</caption>
  <tr><th>Heading 1</th>
      <td>Row 1, Item 1</td>
      <td>Row 1, Item 2</td></tr>
  <tr><th>Heading 2</th>
      <td>Row 2, Item 1</td>
      <td>Row 2, Item 2</td></tr>
</table>
```

Figure 2-5 shows the tables produced by table definitions in the two preceding examples side-by-side, so you can compare the appearance of a table with its headings across a row to a table with its headings down a column.

Headings in a Row

Heading 1	**Heading 2**
Row 1, Item 1	Row 1, Item 2
Row 2, Item 1	Row 2, Item 2

Headings in a Column

Heading 1	Row 1, Item 1	Row 1, Item 2
Heading 2	Row 2, Item 1	Row 2, Item 2

Figure 2-5 Table headings can be in rows (as on the left) or in columns (as on the right)

Using a Table for Page Layout

When using an HTML table to display tabular data, you can let the data in the table dictate the dimensions of the table's cells and therefore the dimensions of the table itself. However, to use an HTML table as a "grid" of cells that let you position graphics images and text at specific locations on a Web page, you need to do two things. First, you need to "hide" the table's borders. Second, you need to control the dimensions of the table and the dimensions of the cells within the table.

You already know how to make a table's borders invisible—simply omit the *border* attribute from the table's <table> tag. Or, if you prefer to make the "invisible" (in other words, the zero-pixel width) borders an explicit instead of an implicit setting, write the <table> tag as follows:

```
<table border="0">
```

If you do not specify the width and height of a table's cells, the Web browser changes their dimensions according to the data you put into them. The browser will set the width of each column to the width of the widest object in one of the column's cells. Similarly, the Web browser will set the height of each row to the height of the "tallest" object in the row. The minimum height and width of a cell with a graphics images are the dimensions of the graphics image. The minimum width for a cell with only text data is the number of characters in the longest word or number, and the minimum height is the height of the tallest character.

Creating a Table with Cells that Span Multiple Columns or Multiple Rows

Previously in this chapter, you learned how to use the start and end table heading tags (<th></th>) and start and end table data tags (<td></td>) to create cells in a table. You also learned how to set the *width* and *height* attributes in a <th> tag or a <td> tag to specify a cell's dimensions. If you define the cells in a table without using the *cellspan* attribute or the *rowspan* attribute, all cells in a row will have the same height, and all cells in a column will have the same width, such as the cells in the table shown in Figure 2-6.

Sometimes, however, you want cells that span multiple rows and/or multiple columns, such as three of the cells shown in Figure 2-7. HTML provides two attributes (*colspan* and *rowspan*) you can use to specify the width and/or height of a cell as a number of columns and/or rows of adjacent cells.

USE IT   To specify a cell that spans multiple rows, such as the second cell from the top in the first column of Figure 2-7, set the *rowspan* attribute in the cell's <td> tag or <th> tag. For the current example, in which the cell spans two rows, you would write the cell's definition as follows:

```
<td rowspan="2">Row 1 & 2, Col 1</td>
```

Column 1	Column 2	Column 3	Column 4
Row 1, Col 1	Row 1, Col 2	Row 1, col 3	Row 1, col 4
Row 2, Col 1	Row 2, Col 2	Row 2, col 3	Row 2, col 4
Row 3, Col 1	Row 3, Col 2	Row 3, col 3	Row 3, col 4
Row 4, Col 1	Row 4, Col 2	Row 4, col 3	Row 4, col 4

Figure 2-6 A table in which all cells in a row have the same height and all cells in a column have the same width

If the cell spanned three rows, you would set the value of the *rowspan* attribute to "3", and so on. One important thing to remember is that if you set the *rowspan* attribute for a cell to "2", you must type one less set of <td></td> tags between the next set of start and end table row tags (<tr></tr>) in the

Column 1	Column 2	Column 3	Column 4
Row 1 & 2, Col 1	Row 1, Col 2	Row 1 & 2, Col 3 & 4	
	Row 2, Col 2		
Row 3, Col 1	Row 3, Col 2	Row 3, Col 3	Row 3, Col 4
Row 4, Col 1	Row 4, Col 2 & 3		Row 4, Col 4

Figure 2-7 A table with cells of variable widths and heights within a single row or column

table definition, because the "next" row has one less column. For example, row 2 in the following 3-row, 2-column table has only one set of start and end table data tags (<td></td>) because the first cell from row 1 extends into the second row:

```
<table>
<tr><td rowspan=2>r1&2,c1</td><td>r1,c2</td></tr>
<tr><!--- no cell needed -->  <td>r2,c2</td></tr>
<tr><td>r3,c1</td>            <td>r3,c2</td></tr>
</table>
```

Similarly, if you want to create a cell that spans multiple columns, such as the second cell from the left in the bottom row of the table in Figure 2-7, set the *colspan* attribute in the cell's <td> tag or <th> tag. For the current example, in which the cell spans two columns, you would write the cell's definition as follows:

```
<td colspan="2">Row 4, Col 2 & 3</td>
```

If the cell spanned three columns, you would set the value of the *colspan* attribute to "3", and so on. Remember, if you set the *colspan* attribute for a cell to "2", you must type one less set of <td></td> tags or <td></td> tags between the start and end table row tags (<tr></tr>) for the current row, because the row has one less than the normal number of cells (or columns). For example, row 2 in the following 3-row, 3-column table has only two sets of start and end table data tags (<td></td>) because the first cell in the row is two cells wide:

```
<table>
<tr><td>r1,c1</td><td>r1,c2</td><td>r1,c3</td></tr>
<tr><td colspan=2>r2,c1&2</td>  <td>r2,c2</td></tr>
<tr><td>r3,c1</td><td>r3,c2</td><td>r3,c3</td></tr>
</table>
```

Finally, you can create a cell that spans both multiple rows and multiple columns, such as that shown by the second cell from the top on the right side of the table in Figure 2-7, by setting both the *rowspan* and *colspan* attributes in the cell's <td> tag or <th> tag. For the current example, in which the cell spans two rows and two columns, you would write the cell's definition as follows:

```
<td rowspan="2" colspan="2">Row 1 & 2, Col 3 & 4</td>
```

Perhaps the easiest way to lay out a table with cells that span multiple columns and/or rows is to draw the table on paper and then type its definition into your text editor. If you add descriptive text such as that shown in the cells of the table in Figure 2-7, you can easily correct errors in the table's definition. (One such error that numbering the cells will let you find and easily correct is typing too many sets of <td></td> tags between the start and end table row tags [<tr></tr>] for the row below the one in which you created a cell that spans two rows.)

Working with Table and Cell Border Widths

A *border* is a visible line around the perimeter of a table and around each of the cells within the table. Unlike table and cell backgrounds, which are independent, table and cell borders are related. As you will learn in the next Tip, you can set table border and cell border colors independently. However, if you set the table's border width to one or more pixels, the Web browser will also draw a border around each of the table's cells. Conversely, if you set the table's *border* attribute to zero, the Web browser neither draws a border around the outside of the table nor around the perimeters of any of the cells within the table.

The following illustration shows two tables. The table on the left has no borders because the *border* attribute in its <table> tag is set to "0". Meanwhile, the table on the right in the figure has a one-pixel border around the perimeter of the table and around each of its cells, because the *border* attribute in its <table> tag is set to "1".

Note that the HTML standard refers to the border around a table as the table's *frame* and to the border around individual cells within the table as *rules*. Setting the *bordercolor* and/or *border* attribute within the <table> tag affects both the table frame and its cell rules. For example, setting *border="0"* implies *frame="void"* and *rules="none"*—which in effect, makes all borders within and around the table invisible. When you examine Cascading Style Sheets (CSS) in Chapter 4, you will see that newer Web browsers let you control cell attributes separately from those of the table overall. As such, you will learn how to create CSS rules (not to be confused with table cell rules, which are lines) that let you specify the width and color of a table's frame independently of the rules (that is, borders) around the table's cells.

USE IT   Earlier in this chapter you learned how to draw a one-pixel border around a table and the cells within the table by setting the *border* attribute in the table's <table> tag as follows:

```
<table border="1">
```

To increase the width of the table's border, simply increase the number of pixels assigned to the *border* attribute in the table's <table> tag. For example, to draw a 10-pixel border around a table, such as that shown next, set the *border* attribute's value to "10" within a <table> tag that reads as follows:

```
<table border="10">
```

Please take note of two interesting things about the effect of changing the value of the *border* attribute. First, although the width of the border around the perimeter of the table increases as you increase the value assigned to the *border* attribute, each of the borders around the cells within the table, meanwhile, remains one pixel in width. No matter how wide you make the border around the table, most Web browsers will draw a one-pixel-wide border around each of the cells in the table—unless you set the *border* attribute's value to zero, in which case neither the table nor its cells will have borders. Second, by default, Web browsers draw both table and cell borders using two colors, in an attempt to give the table (and its cells) a three-dimensional look. If using the default, gray border, the Web browser will draw the left and top sides of table using light-gray and the bottom and right side of the table as dark gray. The Web browser also uses two colors—although they're not easy to see, given their usual one-pixel width—when drawing the borders around the cells within the table. The left side and top of each cell is dark gray, while the bottom and right side of the cell is light-gray. You can learn how to set the table and cell borders to something other than the default, gray colors by reading the next Tip.

Working with Table and Cell Border Colors

As you learned previously, a *border* is a visible line around the perimeter of a table and around each of the cells within the table. Table and cell borders have two attributes you can set—width (which you worked with in the preceding Tip) and color. To adjust the colors of cell and table borders, insert a *bordercolor* attribute in the table's <table> tag. For example, to have the Web browser draw a 10-pixel-wide navy (dark) blue border around the table and a one-pixel-wide navy (dark) blue border around each of its cells, set the *bordercolor* attribute in the table's <table> tag as follows:

```
<table bordercolor="#00008B">
```

Unfortunately, the *bordercolor* attribute's setting does not have the same effect in all Web browsers. Setting the *bordercolor* attribute to "#00008B", for example, will cause Netscape Navigator to draw the table and cell borders using two colors—two sides light blue and two sides dark blue. Internet Explorer, meanwhile, supports two additional attributes to control border colors: *bordercolorlight* and *bordercolordark*. If you specify only a *bordercolor* setting, Internet Explorer will draw the table and cell borders using a single color—navy (dark) blue, in the current example. (In Chapter 4, which discusses CSSs, you will learn how to create CSS rules that let you control attributes of the frame [that is, the border around the table] independently of the attributes of the borders around the table's cells.)

USE IT   If you want Internet Explorer to use two different colors for a table's borders, you must either omit the *bordercolor* attribute from the <table> tag (so the Web browser will use the default light-gray/dark-gray borders), or specify *bordercolorlight* and *bordercolordark* settings in the <table> tag. For example, Internet Explorer will ignore the *bordercolor* setting in the following

<table> tag and use the values assigned to the *bordercolorlight* and *bordercolordark* attributes to draw the top and left sides of the table's border using blue and the bottom and right sides of the table's border using navy (dark) blue:

```
<table border="10" bordercolor="#00008B"
        bordercolorlight="#0000FF" bordercolordark=" #00008B">
```

The *bordercolorlight* and *bordercolordark* attribute settings in the preceding code also tell Internet Explorer to draw the top and left sides of the border around each cell using navy (dark) blue and the bottom and right sides of the border in blue.

 NOTE

By including both bordercolor *and* bordercolorlight/bordercolordark *attributes in the <table> tag, you can display two-color borders in both Internet Explorer and Netscape Navigator. Internet Explorer will ignore the* bordercolor *attribute setting, and will use the* bordercolorlight *and* bordercolordark *settings. Netscape Navigator, meanwhile, will ignore the* bordercolorlight *and* bordercolordark *attributes and use the* bordercolor *attribute to set the table and cell border colors.*

If your site's visitors use Internet Explorer version 5 and later or Netscape Navigator version 6.1 and later, you can use the *style* attribute to specify the color of each side of a table and its cells independently. For example, use a *style* attribute in the <table> tag as shown here to color the top and left sides of a table dark blue while coloring the bottom and right sides of the table light blue:

```
<table border="10" style="border-top-color:#0000FF;
  border-left-color:#0000FF; border-bottom-color:#00008B;
  border-right-color:#00008B">
```

Although the *style* attribute in this example sets the top and left sides to one color and the bottom and right sides of the table to another color, you can set each of the four *border-color* properties within the style attribute to different colors. To set all four sides of the table to the same color, set the *border-color* property to the color you want as follows:

```
<table border="10" style="border-color:#006400">
```

Just as you insert a *style* attribute in the <table> tag to work with the colors of a table's sides, you insert a *style* within a <td> tag to exert the same control over the colors used for the sides of a cell. For example, to color the sides of a cell red, blue, green, and magenta, you might use the setting for the *style* attribute in a <td> tag:

```
<td style="border-left-color:#FF0000; border-top-color:#0000FF;
  border-right-color:#008000; border-bottom-color:#FF00FF">
```

Similarly, to set all four sides of a cell to the same color, such as red for example, use the *border-color* property as follows:

```
<td style="border-color:#FF0000">
```

Bear in mind that using the *border-color* property to set all four sides of a table or all four sides of a cell to the same color actually gets you two colors. For table borders, both Internet Explorer and Netscape Navigator set the top and left sides of the table to the color you specify and the bottom and right sides of the table to a darker version of the same color. Similarly, when you use *border-color* to set the sides of a cell to a single color, both browsers display the bottom and right sides of the cell to the color you specify and the top and left sides of the cell to a darker version of the same color.

Working with Background Images and Colors

The value you assign to the *bordercolor* attribute in the <table> tag changes the color of the border around the table and the borders around the cells within the table—with the exception of those cells whose <td> tags include *bordercolor* settings of their own. Therefore, if you want the Web browser to draw a green border around a particular cell within the table—without regard to the color of the borders around other cells in the table or around the table itself—add a *bordercolor* attribute to the cell's <td> tag. For example, to tell a Web browser to draw a green border around a cell you would write the cell's <td> tag as follows:

```
<td bordercolor="#008000">
```

For Internet Explorer in particular, you might specify a cell's border colors as follows to draw the cell using green along the top and left sides and a lime (light) green along the bottom and right sides of the cell:

```
<td bordercolorlight="#00FF00" bordercolordark="#008000">
```

▶ NOTE

Although all Web browsers support the use of the bordercolor *attribute in the <table> tag, many do not support the use of* bordercolor, bordercolorlight, *and* bordercolordark *attributes in <td> tags. Therefore, design your tables under the assumption that many of your Web site's visitors will see the border around every cell in the same color(s) as the border around the perimeter of the table itself.*

Because background images and colors are "attributes" of a table or of a cell within a table, you specify them (like the *border* attribute) as part of an HTML tag. (Web page elements, such as tables, rows, data, and so on, have HTML tags of their own, whereas attribute settings are always found within HTML tags.) Because both a table and each of its cells have a background, which you can set independently, perhaps the easiest way to understand the interaction between the table background and the background of each of its cells is to think of them as layered. Figure 2-8, for example, shows four tables. The two tables at the top of the Figure show a table with a background color and a table with a background image. The two tables at the bottom of the figure show what happens when you tell the Web browser to draw some of the table's cells with a background color or background image.

A table background is a rectangular object that lies on top of the Web page like a mat within a picture frame. The individual rectangular-shaped data areas within the table—defined by start and end table data tags (<td></td>)— are called *cells*. A table lies on top of the Web page background; each of the table's cells is a rectangular object that lies on top of the table's background. The content you place within a cell (by placing text and/or HTML tags *between* the cell's start and end table data tags [<td></td>]), in turn, lies on top of the cell's background.

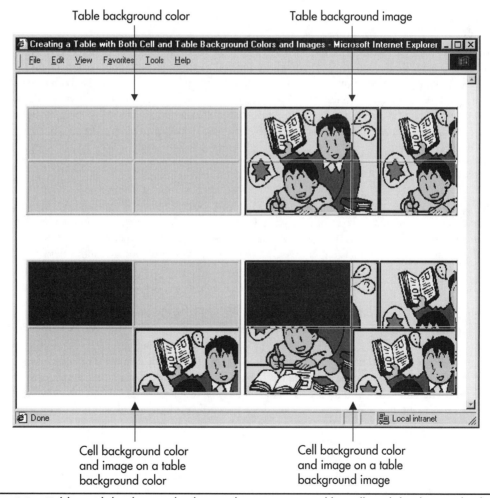

Figure 2-8   Tables with background colors and images covered by cells with background colors and images

USE IT When you specify a table's background color by setting the *bgcolor* attribute in the table's <table> tag, the Web browser will "paint" the color assigned to the attribute onto the table's otherwise transparent background. For example, setting the *bgcolor* attribute to the hexadecimal value "#0000FF" in the following <table> tag tells the Web browser to paint the table background blue:

```
<table border="1" bgcolor="#0000FF">
```

Similarly, if you set the *background* attribute in the <table> tag, the Web browser will use the graphics file assigned to the attribute as "wallpaper" to cover the table's background. For example, the *background* setting in the following code tells the Web browser to cover the table background with the picture in the file named picture1.gif stored in the Web site's images subfolder:

```
<table border="1" background="images/picture.GIF">
```

Because each of the table's cells, like the table itself, has a background, you specify a cell's background color or background image as an attribute within the cell's <td> tag. Therefore, independent of the background image or color (if any) that you specified for the table, you can tell the Web browser to paint a cell's background with a color by assigning the color's value as a hexadecimal number to the *bgcolor* attribute in the cell's <td> tag. For example, the hexadecimal value "#00008B" assigned to the *bgcolor* attribute in the following <td> tag tells the Web browser to paint the cell's background navy (dark) blue:

```
<td bgcolor="#00008B">
```

Similarly, if you set the *background* attribute in a cell's <td> tag, the Web browser will use the picture in the file assigned to the attribute as "wallpaper" to cover the cell's background. For example, the *background* setting in the following <td> tag tells the Web browser to cover the cell's background with the graphics image in the file picture1.gif stored in the Web site's images subfolder:

```
<td background="images/picture.gif">
```

Although HTML syntax does not prevent you from doing so, it does not make sense to specify both a background color and a background image for the same table or cell. If you specify both, whichever appears last in the <table> tag "wins"—sort of like wallpapering a painted wall, or painting over wallpaper. Whatever is applied to the background last (in other words, the layer on top) is what the viewer sees. Because they are "layered", a cell's background color or background image will obscure the table's background color or image. Conversely, if a cell's <td> tag has neither a *background* attribute nor a *bgcolor* attribute, the Web browser will draw the cell's background as if it were a transparent pane of glass laying atop the table's background. Consequently, you will see the table background "through" the cell's transparent background.

Similarly, because the table's background sits on top of the Web page background, the table's background image or color obscures the color or picture used as the Web page background. Conversely, if you set neither the *background* attribute nor the *bgcolor* attribute in the table's <table> tag, the Web browser will draw the table's background as if it were a transparent pane of glass lying on top of the Web page background. As a result, you will see the Web page background "through" the table's transparent background. By the way, although it would be a "cool" effect, if you specify neither a color nor an image for the Web page background, you will not see the inside of your monitor. Instead, the Web browser will set the background color of the Web page to either gray or white—depending on the browser's default settings.

Although currently supported by Web browsers, the HTML standard does not allow you to use the *background* attribute with either the <table> or <td> tag. Moreover, the *bgcolor* attribute—deprecated since HTML 4.01—is officially illegal in the XHTML 1.0 standard. To specify the background image for a table or cell, current HTML (and XHTML) standards require that you use the CSS *background-image* property. For example, to specify an image you want the browser to use as the table background, insert a *style* attribute within the <table> tag as follows:

```
<table border="1"
  style="background-image:url(images/picture.GIF)">
```

Similarly, to specify the background image for a cell, use a *style* attribute in the <td> tag to set the *background-image* property as shown here:

```
<td style="background-image:url(images/picture.GIF)">
```

The CSS *background-color* property lets you select the background color for the table background and/or the background color of any of its cells. For example, to set the table's background to aqua, you would set the *background-color* property in the <table> tag as shown here:

```
<table border="1" style="background-color:#00FFFF">
```

Similarly, to set the background color for a table cell to dark blue, for example, use the *style* attribute to set the *background-color* property within the <td> tag as follows:

```
<td style="background-color:#00008B">
```

Determining a Color Attribute's Value

Whenever you use one of the color selection attributes such as *bordercolor*, *bgcolor*, *bordercolorlight*, *bordercolordark*, and so on in an HTML tag to set an element's color, you specify the color you want as a hexadecimal number. For example, to create a table with a light yellow background, you would set the *bgcolor* attribute in the table's <table> tag as follows:

```
<table bgcolor="#FFFFE0">
```

Similarly, to draw a dark blue border around the perimeter of a table and around each of the cells within the table, you would set the *bordercolor* attribute in the table's <table> tag as follows:

```
<table bordercolor="#00008B">
```

The attribute value that tells the Web browser what color to use when drawing a Web page element or painting a background color is called a *hexadecimal (base 16) red-green-blue triplet*. In other words, the one large hexadecimal number is actually three separate hexadecimal values (hence the term "triplet" in its name). These values tell the browser "how much" red, green, and blue to mix in order to create the color you want the browser to use when drawing the element or painting the background.

When creating a color, each of the three primary colors (red, green, blue) can have a value from 0–255 (inclusive), where "0" means none and 255 is the maximum amount. Therefore, in the second example in the current Tip in which the *bordercolor* attribute in the <table> tag sets the table borders to dark blue, the "#00008B" *bordercolor* setting tells the Web browser to create the border color by mixing 0 red with 0 green and 139 blue. (A hexadecimal value of 8B equals a decimal value of 139.) Thus, the Web browser creates the shade of dark blue you specified by mixing no red, with no green, and just over half the maximum amount of blue.

USE IT To determine the hexadecimal red-green-blue triplet for the color you want the Web browser to use, visit http://www.htmlhelp.com/cgi-bin/color.cgi, or check the font or background color menu in your favorite image editor. Most graphics programs will provide the RGB (that is, the red, green, blue) values used to create the color you select from a palette of color swatches or mix on a "custom colors" screen within the application. Or, if you use the Microsoft Office suite of programs, click the drop-down list button to the right of the Font Color button on the standard toolbar in Microsoft PowerPoint or Microsoft Word. Then, click More Colors at the bottom of the drop-down menu. The Office application, in turn, will display a Colors dialog box similar to that shown in Figure 2-9.

If the Custom tab's contents are not visible, click the Custom tab on the Colors dialog box. To "mix" a custom color, click on the color you want in the color palette at the top of the Custom tab and then on the color saturation slide-bar to the right of the palette. Each time you create a color, the dialog box will show you the color in the color swatch in the lower-right corner of the dialog box 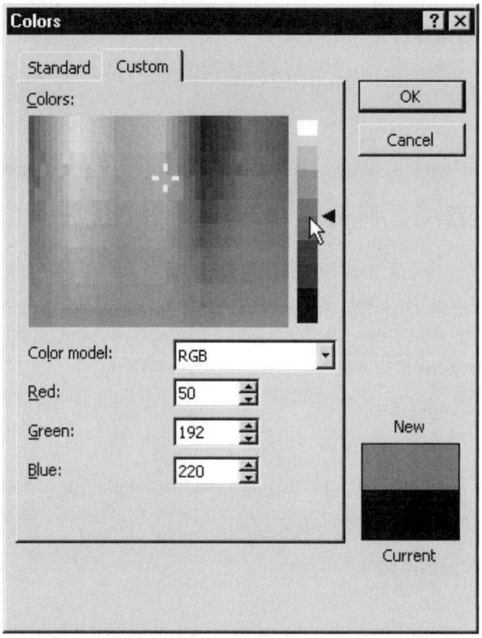

Figure 2-9 The Custom tab of the Microsoft Word Colors dialog box

and the color's RGB value in the Red, Green, and Blue fields. If the RGB values are decimal and not hexadecimal numbers, you must convert each one to its hexadecimal equivalent. Then, combine the three hexadecimal RGB values into a single hexadecimal triplet as "#RRGGBB" (where RR, GG, and BB are the hexadecimal red, green, and blue values of the color you mixed).

▶ *NOTE*

You can view a list of hexadecimal triplets at http://www.htmlhelp.com/cgi-bin/color.cgi. In addition, you will find a slightly longer list of hexadecimal triplets and an example of the color each represents at http://www.hypersolutions.org/pages/rgbhex.html.

Working with Cell Padding and Cell Spacing

Whereas cell *padding* tells the Web browser the number of pixels of blank space to leave between the sides of a cell and its contents, cell *spacing* tells the Web browser the amount of blank space to leave between cells and between the border around a table and its cells. Figure 2-10 illustrates the difference between cell padding and cell spacing.

Because *cellspacing* and *cellpadding* affect the overall placement of cells within a table, you set both attributes in the table's <table> tag. By default, both *cellspacing* and *cellpadding* have a value greater than zero (0). For example, if you omit both attributes from the <table> tag, Internet Explorer will leave a two-pixel space between each cell and between the table's borders and its cells. Thus, Internet Explorer's default *cellspacing* is two (2). Similarly, with *cellpadding* unset, Internet Explorer will leave a one-pixel space between each cell's border and its contents.

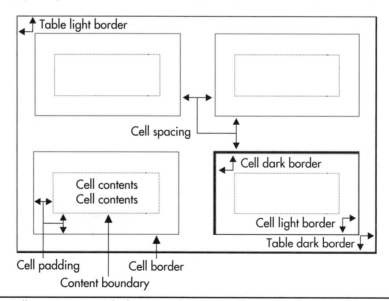

Figure 2-10 Cell spacing controls the space between cells, and cell padding controls the space between a cell's border and its content

USE IT   To increase the blank space between cells in a table, set the *cellspacing* attribute in the
table's <table> tag to a value greater than one (1). For example, setting the *cellspacing*
attribute to ten (10) in the following code tells the Web browser to leave a 10-pixel blank space between
each of the table's cells and between the table's border and its cells:

```
<table border="1" cellspacing="10">
```

Similarly, if you want to increase the blank space between the sides of a cell and its contents, set
the value of the *cellpadding* attribute accordingly. (In the current example, the Web browser will still
leave only a one-pixel space between the border of a cell and its contents because the <table> tag has
no *cellpadding* attribute.) To have the Web browser leave a five-pixel blank space between the sides
of a cell (that is, the border around a cell) and its contents, for example, write the preceding <table>
tag as follows:

```
<table border="1" cellspacing="10" cellpadding="5">
```

Although the <table> tag in this example has both *cellspacing* and *cellpadding* attributes, you do
not have to set one to set the other. Just keep in mind that most Web browsers will use a default value
of one (1) or two (2) pixels for either attribute or for both attributes if you do not explicitly set the
attribute's value in the <table> tag.

Setting Table Dimensions Using Relative or Absolute Values

To control a table's dimensions, add a *width* and/or a *height* attribute to the table's <table> tag. You
can specify table dimensions either in relative terms (using percentages) or in absolute terms (using
pixel counts).

USE IT   For example, to draw the table using the Web browser's entire application window, write
the table's <table> tag as follows:

```
<table width="100%" height="100%">
```

The Web browser, in turn, will change the dimensions of the table (and its cells) as necessary to
take up the entire application window. In other words, the Web browser will make the table (and its
cells) larger if the Web site visitor expands the size of the browser's application window, and will
make the table (and its cells) smaller when the site visitor reduces the window's size.
    If you do not want the Web browser to change the dimensions of a table based on the size of the
application window, set the table's height and width to a fixed number of pixels. For example, to have
the Web browser draw a table 764 pixels wide by 558 pixels tall each time, write the <table> tag
as follows:

```
<table width="764" height="558">
```

By dropping the percent sign (%) from an attribute's value setting, you tell the Web browser to
use the value as a number of pixels and not a percentage. When you specify the table's dimensions
using absolute values (in other words, when you specify the table's width and height as a number of

pixels), the Web browser will change neither the table's dimensions, nor the dimensions of its cells when the site visitor changes the size of the Web browser's application window. For example, given a screen resolution of 800×600 and a table width and height of 764×558, if the Web site visitor reduces the height of the Web browser's application window, only a portion of the table will be visible onscreen. The Web browser, in turn, will add a vertical scrollbar to the application window, so that the site visitor can scroll the offscreen portion of the table into view. (Similarly, if the visitor reduces the width of the application window, Windows will display a horizontal scrollbar to allow the visitor to scroll screen contents horizontally.) Conversely, if the site visitor increases the screen resolution to 1024×768, for example, the table's size will remain constant, and the Web browser will display white space in its application window, below and to the right of the table.

When setting the *width* and *height* attributes in a <table> tag, keep in mind that you are really setting only the table's minimum dimensions. The content you place in a table's cells will determine the table's actual dimensions. Suppose, for example, that you specify a 764×558 table, with two rows of two cells each. If you place a 450×350 pixel picture into each of the cells in the first row, the Web browser will automatically expand the table's width to 900 pixels to accommodate the width of the data in the table—that is, the two pictures in the first row. If you then add a 450×350 pixel graphics image to either of the cells in the table's second row, the Web browser will increase the table's height to 700 pixels to accommodate the height of the two pictures in the table's column.

Setting Cell Dimensions Using Relative or Absolute Values

In addition to (or instead of) specifying a table's dimensions by setting the table's *height* and *width* attributes in the <table> tag, you can create a table of a specific height and width by specifying the dimensions of the table's cells.

 For example, if you want to create an 800×600 table with two rows of four columns each, you can specify each cell as 200×300 pixels by writing the <td> tag for each cell as follows:

```
<td width="200" height="300">
```

(To specify the dimensions of a cell with heading data, set the *width* and *height* attributes in the heading cell's <th> tag.)

▶ *NOTE*

If you specify a table's width by setting the width *attribute in the table's <table> tag, make sure that the width of the cells in each row add up to exactly the width of the table to avoid browser-specific "strange" behavior. Each browser handles malformed tables in its own way. Therefore, if you want to control the way your table looks in every browser, do not write table HTML in which the table's dimensions conflict with the dimensions of its cells.*

Rather than set a cell's dimensions to a fixed number of pixels, you can tell the Web browser to draw each cell as a percentage of the table's overall width and height. Suppose, for example, that you want the Web browser to draw a table that fills the application window and has three equal-width columns. You would write the table's HTML as follows with both a relative width (set by the value of the *width* attribute in the <table> tag) and relative width columns (set by the value of the *width* attributes in the <th> tags and <td> tags):

```
<table width="100%">
   <tr><th width="33%" >Heading 1</th>
       <th width="33%" >Heading 2</th>
       <th width="33%" >Heading 3</th></tr>
   <tr><td width="33%" >Column 1 Data</td>
       <td width="33%" >Column 2 Data</td>
       <td width="33%" >Column 3 Data</td></tr>
</table>
```

Or, if you want to specify a table with a fixed width and two columns that take up 80 percent of the table's width and one that takes up 20 percent of the width, you would write the table's HTML as follows:

```
<table width="600">
   <tr><th width="40%" >Heading 1</th>
       <th width="40%" >Heading 2</th>
       <th width="20%" >Heading 3</th></tr>
   <tr><td width="40%" >Column 1 Data</td>
       <td width="40%" >Column 2 Data</td>
       <td width="20%" >Column 3 Data</td></tr>
</table>
```

If you specify the widths of the table's cells as percentages of the table's width, make sure that the sum of the widths specified in the <th> tags (if any) and in the <td> tags for a single row does not exceed 100 percent. Should the sum of the percentages be less than 100 percent, the Web browser will split the remainder evenly among the cells in the row.

When specifying cell (or table) dimensions, you can specify a width without specifying a height, or vice versa. However, if you are specifying the dimensions of a cell as a percentage of the table's width, make sure you set the table's width as a number of pixels or as a percentage of the Web browser's application window by setting the *width* attribute in the table's <table> tag. Similarly, if you specify the height of the cells in the table as a percentage of the table's overall height, be sure you set the table's height as well. To specify the table's height, set the *height* attribute in the table's <table> tag to either a number of pixels or a percentage of the browser application window's height.

Aligning Cell Content Horizontally and Vertically

If a cell is wider than its contents, the Web browser will, by default, align the content in the cell flush with the cell's left side.

  To change the default horizontal (that is, left-to-right) alignment of a cell's content, add an *align* attribute to the cell's <td> tag. The *align* attribute has three possible settings:

- *left*   Align the content flush against the left side of the cell
- *right*   Align the content flush against the right side of the cell
- *center*   Center the content between the left and right sides of the cell

Figure 2-11 shows the way in which Internet Explorer will render a table defined by the following HTML with each of the *align* attribute value settings used in the table cell <td> tags:

```
<table border="1" width="100%" height="100%">
  <tr><th width="33%">Alignment - Center</th>
      <th width="33%">Alignment - Left</th>
      <th width="33%">Alignment - Right</th></tr>
  <tr><td width="33%" align="center">Center</td>
      <td width="33%" align="left">Left</td>
      <td width="33%" align="right">Right</td></tr>
</table>
```

When a cell is taller than then height of its content, the Web browser will by default, center the content vertically between the top and bottom of the cell. To change the default vertical (that is, top-to-bottom) alignment of a cell's content, add a *valign* attribute to the cell's <td> tag. The *valign* attribute has four possible settings:

- *top*   Display the content such that it starts flush with the top of the cell.
- *middle*   Center the content vertically between the top and bottom of the cell.
- *baseline*   In Netscape Navigator, display the content such that it ends flush with the bottom of the cell. In Internet Explorer, the "baseline" setting changes only the vertical position of text in a cell if the cell includes both a text and an image. The "baseline" setting causes Internet Explorer to position text such that it ends flush with the bottom edge of a picture. If the cell has no picture, Internet Explorer will ignore the *valign* attribute's "baseline" setting and start text content flush with the top of the cell.
- *bottom*   Display content such that it ends flush with the bottom of the cell.

Figure 2-12 shows the way in which Netscape Navigator will render a table defined by the following HTML with each of the possible *valign* attribute value settings used in the table cell <td> tags:

```
<table border="1" width="100%" height="100%">
  <tr><th width="25%">Vertical Alignment - Top</th>
      <th width="25%">Vertical Alignment - Middle</th>
      <th width="25%">Vertical Alignment - Baseline</th>
      <th width="25%">Vertical Alignment - Bottom</th></tr>
  <tr><td width="25%" valign="top">Top</td>
      <td width="25%" valign="middle">Middle</td>
      <td width="25%" valign="baseline">Baseline</td>
      <td width="25%" valign="bottom">Bottom</td></tr>
</table>
```

Alignment - Center	Alignment - Left	Alignment - Right
Center	Left	Right

Figure 2-11   Table showing the effects of the three horizontal alignment settings

Vertical Alignment - Top	Vertical Alignment - Middle	Vertical Alignment - Baseline	Vertical Alignment - Bottom
Top	Middle	Baseline	Bottom

Figure 2-12   Table showing the effects of the four vertical alignment settings

Aligning a Table on a Web Page

In a previous Tip in this chapter, you learned how to align content in a cell along the cell's left side, right side, or centered within the cell. As long as the cell's content is narrower than the width of the cell itself, you can use the value of the *align* attribute in the cell's <td> tag to position the cell's content horizontally within the cell. Similarly, if you create a table that is narrower than the width of the Web page on which it is displayed, you can use the *align* attribute to position the entire table horizontally on the page.

USE IT By default, a Web browser will render a table flush with the left side of a Web page. To change a table's alignment, enclose the table definition between a set of start and end division tags (<div></div>). Then, set the *align* attribute within the <div> tag to "left", "right", or "center"— depending on how you want the table aligned relative to the left and right sides of the Web page.

For example, to have the Web browser display a table flush with the right side of a Web page (instead of the default, which is the left side), enclose the table's definition within start and end division tags (<div></div>). Then set the *align* attribute in the <div> tag to "right", such as that shown in the first line of the following Web page HTML:

```
<div align="right">
  <table border="1" width="50%" height="50%">
    <tr><th width="50%">Heading 1</th>
        <th width="50%">Heading 2</th></tr>
    <tr><td width="50%">Row 1 - Column 1</td>
        <td width="50%">Row 1 - Column 2</td></tr>
    <tr><td width="50%">Row 2 - Column 1</td>
        <td width="50%">Row 2 - Column 2</td></tr>
  </table>
</div>
```

If you write a <table> tag that includes a *width* attribute set to "100%" or with a pixel value greater than the pixel width of the browser's application window, the Web browser will ignore the setting of the *align* attribute within the <div> tag in the enclosing start and end division tags (<div></div>).

Controlling the Width and Height of a Cell by Inserting a Transparent GIF

While drawing a table, a Web browser will expand the size of the cells (and the table overall) as necessary to accommodate their contents. Suppose, for example, that you create a cell with a <td> tag that has no *width* or *height* attribute. If you place a 150×100–pixel graphics image in the cell, the Web browser will automatically draw the cell with a width of 150 pixels and a height of 100 pixels so the picture will fit into it. Similarly, if you insert the same 150×100–pixel image into a cell defined with a 50-pixel width and height, for example, the Web browser will expand the cell from its defined 50×50–pixel dimensions to accommodate the graphics image.

You can take advantage of the browser's cell-resizing behavior by placing a one-pixel transparent GIF (graphics image) in a cell and telling the Web browser to stretch the picture to a desired height and/or width. The Web browser, in turn, will stretch the graphics image and expand the dimensions of the cell to the size of the stretched GIF. Expanding the cell to the dimensions of the transparent image in the cell will cause the browser to insert a precise amount of blank space between cells to the left and right of the cell with the GIF and/or between those cells directly above and/or below it.

A *transparent GIF* is an "invisible" graphics image you can use either with or without a table to affect the positions of objects on a Web page. The site visitor will not see the transparent GIF on the computer screen, because the Web browser displays the GIF as if it were a pane of clear glass lying on the cell (or Web page) background. Although the visitor can "see right through" the transparent GIF, the graphics image still takes up space in the cell. As a result, the Web browser will make the cell large enough to hold it.

Suppose, for example, that you create a Web page with a 100-pixel-wide menu down the left side of the page, and you want to separate the menu from the remaining content (to its right) with 20 pixels of blank space, similar to that shown in Figure 2-13.

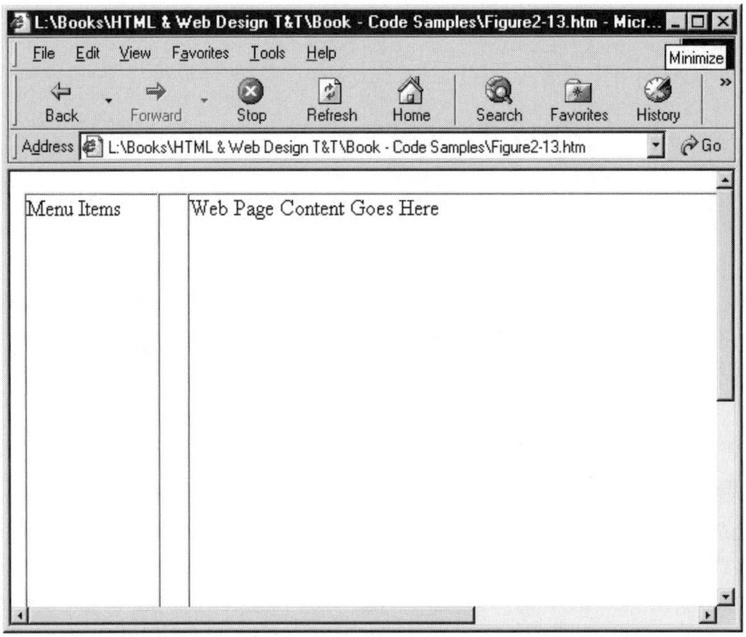

Figure 2-13   A Web page with a 100-pixel menu bar along the left side separated by 20 pixels of blank space from the page content on the right

USE IT You can use the following code to create a three-column table in which a 20-pixel-wide blank cell (with the stretched, transparent GIF) separates the content in the left cell from the content in the right cell:

```
<table border="1" width="767" height="554"
       cellspacing="0" cellpadding="0">
  <tr><td valign="top" width="100">Menu Items</td>
      <td><img height="1" width="20" src="images/spacing.gif"></td>
      <td valign="top" width="647">
         Web Page Content Goes Here</td></tr>
</table>
```

In the current example, the <img> tag that follows the second <td> tag (in the third line) tells the Web browser to place the transparent GIF stored in the file spacing.gif into the second cell in the table. The *width* attribute in the <img> tag tells the Web browser to "stretch" the 1×1–pixel image such that it appears 20 pixels wide in the cell.

The reason you would use a transparent GIF—instead of setting the *width* attribute in the cell's <td> tag to the number of pixels of blank space you want and then leaving the cell blank—is because Web browsers handle empty table cells differently. For example, although Internet Explorer shows the cell background color in blank cells, Netscape Navigator does not—showing the table or Web page background color instead. Moreover, some browsers ignore the *height* and/or *width* attribute settings in the <td> tag for empty cells and draw the cells such that they are only as tall as the tallest nonempty cell in the row and as wide as the widest nonempty cell in the column. Finally, neither Netscape Navigator nor Internet Explorer will draw the left and top borders on a cell that has no content— even if the table's border attribute has a value of one or more. However, if you put a one-pixel GIF, stretched to the dimensions you want, into a table cell, all Web browsers will render the "blank" cell in the same way—with the dimensions of the GIF, the cell's specified background color, and borders (if any)—because although the cell appears blank, it is not empty.

▶ NOTE

You will learn how to create transparent GIF files in the chapter on graphics later in this book. For now, you can use the one-pixel transparent GIF in the file spacing.gif, which you can download from this book's Web site at http://www.osborne.com.

Wrapping Text Around an Image

When you consider the initial design of a Web page, an issue of primary importance is the layout of the document. A well-designed Web page contains text and graphics arranged in an organized, easy-to-understand format. Moreover, the organization of the page helps the reader's eyes move smoothly from graphics images to associated text, and back again.

USE IT   Say, for example, that you create a Web page containing three images. Each image requires a small paragraph of information that describes the object and the item's sales price. By placing the graphics images, descriptive text, and the sales price into a table, you can tell the Web browser to display text information to the right of each image and the sales price below the picture, as shown here:

The following HTML statements will create the table shown previously, in which the first image appears in row 1, column 1; with its associated description (next to the picture) in row 1, column 2; and sales price (below the picture) in row 2, column 1. (Row 3, columns 1 and 2 were added to create additional space between items, descriptions, and prices.)

```
<table border="4" cellpadding="0" cellspacing="2">
<tr><td width="72" align="center"><img height="32" width="32"
      src="image_1.jpg"></td>
    <td>Insert Description</td></tr>
<tr><td width="72" align="center">Insert Price</td>
    <td></td></tr>
<tr><td width="72"></td>
```

```
   <td></td></tr>
<tr><td width="72" align="center"><img height="32" width="32"
      src=" image_2.jpg "></td>
   <td>Insert Description</td></tr>
<tr><td width="72" align="center">Insert Price</td>
   <td></td></tr>
<tr><td WIDTH="72"></td>
   <td></td></tr>
<tr><td width="72" align="center"><img height="32" width="32"
      src=" image_3.jpg "></td>
   <td>Insert Description</td></tr>
<tr><td width="72" align="center">Insert Price</td>
   <td></td></tr>
<tr><td width="72"></td>
   <td></td></tr>
</table>
```

Using a table to control the flow of text and graphics creates a visually pleasing Web page. In addition, because text-heavy Web pages are smaller than Web pages containing an overabundance of graphics images, using text in the description and selling price cells, as opposed to converting the text into a graphic, creates a smaller document and therefore a faster-loading Web page.

Displaying a Gallery of Thumbnails Within a Table

The display of graphics is a part of life on the World Wide Web. Say, for example, that you own a real-estate company and need to display photographs of the various homes you market. You want site visitors to have the option of selecting a full-size image by first opening a Web page that contains a thumbnail graphic of each available home. When the visitor clicks one of the thumbnails, the Web browser loads a page containing the full-size image.

Using a table to display thumbnails serves two purposes: It organizes the images into concise rows and columns, and it gives the visitor the option of selecting and viewing individual images with a simple point and click of the mouse. In addition, downloading graphics takes time, and Web site visitors typically do not like to wait. Organizing the thumbnails into a table on a separate page lets the Web site visitors choose exactly what they want to view, as shown in Figure 2-14.

USE IT To use a table to display a group of thumbnail images, create a table with a separate cell for each thumbnail. To link a thumbnail to its corresponding full-size image, insert an <a> tag and *href* attribute in each cell that contains a thumbnail image. The <a> tag creates a link from the thumbnail to the full-size image. For example, the following code links the thumbnail image home_1.jpg to the Web page containing the full-size image (page_1.htm):

```
<a href="page_1.htm"><img src="home_1.jpg"></a>
```

Figure 2-14 The Web page displays a thumbnail for each full-size graphic

When a Web site visitor clicks a thumbnail, the Web browser loads the Web page containing a full-size image. The <a> tag and *href* attribute in the following code link the thumbnail (specified by the *src* attribute in the <img> tag) to its corresponding full-size image, and creates the Web page displayed in Figure 2-14:

```
<table border="4" cellpadding="0" cellspacing="2"
      width="137" bgcolor="#ffccff">
<tr><td align="center" valign="middle"> <a href="page_1.htm">
      <img src="home_1.jpg"></a></td>
    <td align="center" valign="middle"> <a href="page_2.htm">
      <img src="home_2.jpg"></a></td>
    <td align="center" valign="middle"> <a href="page_3.htm">
      <img src="home_3.jpg"></a></td>
    <td align="center" valign="middle"> <a href="page_4.htm">
```

```
        <img src="home_4.jpg"></a></td></tr>
</table>
```

Once the Web browser displays the thumbnail page, the visitor need only click a thumbnail to display the full-size image. For example, clicking the thumbnail in the upper-left corner of Figure 2-14 will cause the Web browser to display the full-size image shown in Figure 2-15.

Because a thumbnail is a smaller version of the full-size image, use naming conventions that link the thumbnail to the original image. If, for example, you create and save an image with the name home_1.jpg, name the corresponding thumbnail home_1s.jpg. Creating associative file names helps you identify the files quickly, because the names will display alphabetically in a standard file listing.

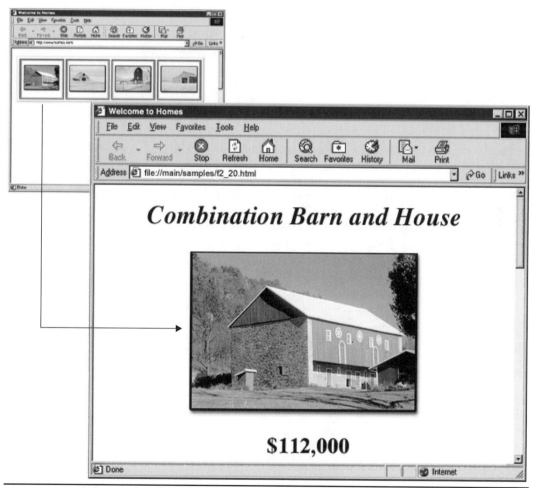

Figure 2-15   Clicking a thumbnail loads the full-size image

Creating Bullets and Lists with Tables and Graphics

Web designers have always been able to create lists with a square or round bullet preceding each item in the list. Unfortunately, creating a standard bulleted (or to use the HTML term, *unordered*) list restricts the Web designer to placing one of a limited number of bullet symbols next to each item in a list. For example, the following code will generate the bulleted list shown next:

```
<ul>
  <li>List item 1 </li>
  <li>List item 2 </li>
  <li>List item 3 </li>
</ul>
```

The start and end unordered list tags (<ul></ul>) identify the beginning and end of the bulleted list, and the <li> tag identifies an item in the list.

- List item 1
- List item 2
- List item 3

On the other hand, tables let you use customized bullets by inserting the graphic of the bullet into a table cell. Typically, a table used in the creation of a bulleted list contains two columns. The first column holds the customized graphic used for the bullet, and the second column contains the text describing the list item. A standard two-column table creates lists using eye-catching graphics as the individual bullet symbols, such as those shown here:

➡	Locust Trees
➡	Wild Oak Trees
➡	Paper Birch Trees

USE IT   Say, for example, that you create a list containing three items, and you want to use the image of an arrow as the bullet for each of the list items. The following illustrates the coding required to create the bulleted list shown previously:

```
<table border="4" cellpadding="0" cellspacing="2" width="137">
  <tr><td><img height="32" width="32" src="arrow.gif"></td>
      <td>List Item 1</td></tr>
  <tr><td><img height="32" width="32" src="arrow.gif"></td>
      <td>List Item 2</td></tr>
  <tr><td><img height="32" width="32" src="arrow.gif"></td>
      <td>List Item 3</td></tr>
</table>
```

Because table cells can hold any kind of graphic, experiment by substituting common bullet graphics with something out of the ordinary. For example, if you create a bulleted list on the steps necessary to grow roses, substitute a standard bullet symbol with a graphic image of a red rose.

Creating a Navigation Sidebar Using a Table

When you design a multipage Web site, you need to make the navigation of the site easy for your visitors. In the previous Tip, you learned how to create a bulleted list using the individual cells within a table. Tables also provide an excellent way to create an organized navigation bar.

USE IT   A *sidebar* is a simple form of a navigation bar. Typically, a sidebar consists of a list of words displayed on the left side of the Web page. Each word is actually a link to another Web page on the site. When you use a table to generate a sidebar, each cell in the table contains the individual elements of the sidebar. The following code listing creates the navigation sidebar shown in Figure 2-16:

```
<table border="0" cellpadding="0" cellspacing="2" width="96">
  <tr><td><a href="home.htm">Home</a></td></tr>
  <tr><td><a href="samples.htm">Samples</a></td></tr>
  <tr><td><a href="aboutus.htm">About Us</a></td></tr>
  <tr><td><a href="contactus.htm">Contact Us</a></td></tr>
  <tr><td><a href="purchase.htm">Purchase</a></td></tr>
</table>
```

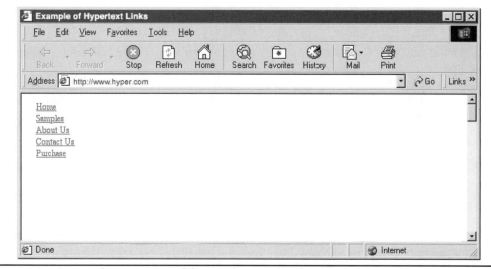

Figure 2-16   A typical navigation sidebar enclosed within a table

For consistency, always place the navigation sidebar in the same location on each of the site's Web pages. This makes it easier for your visitors to locate and use the site's navigation system. The two most common areas to place navigation are as a sidebar, vertically along the left side of the Web page (as this Tip illustrates), or as a horizontal bar across the top of the page.

Adding Images and Links to Table Cells

Each cell in a table is an individual controllable element in which you can place text, graphics, or a combination of both text and graphics. To add a cell to a table, insert a set of start and end table data tags (<td></td>) such as those shown in the following code, between the table's start and end table tags (<table></table>):

```
<table>
  <tr>
    <td> insert cell data here </td>
  </tr>
</table>
```

USE IT   To place a graphics image in a cell, insert an <img> tag, such as the following, between the cell's start and end table data tags (<td></td>):

```
<table>
  <tr>
    <td> <img src="image.jpg" ></td>
  </tr>
</table>
```

The *src* attribute in the <img> tag tells the Web browser the filename of the graphics image it is to display in the table cell. Therefore, in the current example, the Web browser will display the picture in image.jpg.

To convert the graphics image in a table cell to a hyperlink, enclose the <img> tag with a set of start and end anchor tags (<a></a>). For example, the following code converts the picture in the table (from the previous example) into a hyperlink:

```
<table>
  <tr>
    <td><a href="info.htm"><img src="image.jpg"></a></td>
  </tr>
</table>
```

When processing the HTML in the current example, the Web browser displays the picture from the file image.jpg when it draws the table initially. If the site visitor then clicks the picture, the Web browser will display the contents of the file assigned to the <a> tag's *href* attribute. Therefore, in the current example, the Web browser will display the contents of the file info.htm when the site visitor clicks the picture in the table.

Nesting Tables to Control Borders on a Web Page

When you create a Web page without tables, the Web browser displays the Web page elements it finds in the file one after another starting in the upper-left corner of the browser's application window. The browser places a default amount of space between the first page element and the left edge of the application window. Unfortunately, not all Web browsers (and not even all versions of the same Web browser) use the same default spacing values, which creates a problem when you design a Web page that calls for precise placement of graphics and text.

USE IT Suppose, for example, that you create a Web page containing three graphic images that require specific spacing from the left border of the Web page. To control the border of a complicated Web page, create a table and insert a second table with the three graphic elements into a cell in the second column of the first table. Placing a table into a cell within another table is called *nesting*. When you *nest* tables together, it creates an organized layout, and gives you greater control over the individual elements within a complicated Web page.

The following code illustrates the nesting of a table containing three graphics into the cell of another table:

```
<table border="2" cellpadding="0" cellspacing="2">
   <tr><td width ="30"></td>
       <td width ="32"></td>
       <td width ="30"></td></tr>
   <tr><td width ="30"> <img src="trans.gif" width="30"></td>
       <td width ="32" align="center">
<! -- The nested table begins here... -- >
<table border="4" cellpadding="0" cellspacing="2">
<tr><td width ="32"><img src="image_1.jpg"></td></tr>
<tr><td width ="32"><img src="image_2.jpg"></td></tr>
<tr><td width ="32"><img src="image_3.jpg"></td></tr>
</table></td>
<! -- The nested table ends here... -- >
       <td width="30"> <img src="trans.gif" width="30">
       </td></tr>
   <tr><td width ="30"></td>
       <td width ="32"></td>
       <td width ="30"></td></tr>
</table>
```

In the current example, the second column of the table contains the nested table, and the first column of the outer table has a fixed width of 30 pixels. As a result, when the Web browser loads the Web page, the first column in the table pushes the nested table 30 pixels to the right of the left edge of the browser's application window, as shown in Figure 2-17.

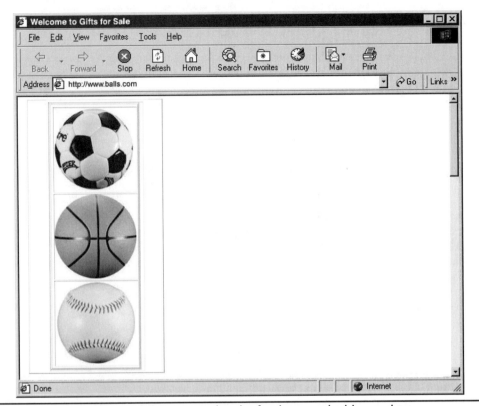

Figure 2-17   The table successfully creates a border for the nested table graphics

Approximating an Image Map by Placing Pieces of an Image Within a Table

Image maps are an excellent way to help visitors navigate a Web site. An image map is like a group of clickable buttons all combined into a single graphic. When visitors to your site move the mouse pointer over the image map, the internal coding of the image map lets them click specific areas of the graphic, called *hotspots*. Hotspots are invisible borders surrounding specific portions of an image. For example, an image map of the United States would have a hotspot defining the dimensions of each state. When a site visitor clicks the state of Kansas, the hotspot defining Kansas might load a Web page with the current weather in Kansas, or it might send them to a Web site describing the history of Kansas. Image maps help visitors visually navigate through a complicated Web site.

The problem with image maps is that they are complicated to code and not all versions of Web browsers support image maps. To overcome this problem, use a table to create the flexibility of an image map. To get the table's cells to function like hotspots on an image map, divide the image into rectangular pieces and place each piece in a separate cell in the table. Then, to each cell, add an <a>

tag with an *href* attribute that tells the Web browser what action to take when the visitor clicks the graphics image you placed in the cell.

USE IT In the following code, when the visitor clicks the graphic file named home.gif, the Web browser links to and opens the Web page titled home.htm:

```
<a href="home.htm"> <img height="20" width ="80" src="home.gif"></a>
```

When correctly designed and placed in the cells of a table with zero width (that is, invisible) borders, the Web browser will display the pieces of the picture next to each other, such that the visitor sees them as a single graphics image.

The following code creates the navigation bar shown in Figure 2-18:

```
<table border="0" cellpadding="0" cellspacing="0" width="327">
  <tr height="20">
    <td width="80" height="20"><a href="home.htm">
      <img height="20" width ="80" src="home.gif"></a></td>
    <td width="80" height="20"><a href="samples.htm">
      <img height="20" width="80" src="samples.gif"></a></td>
    <td width="80" height="20"><a href="aboutus.htm">
      <img height="20" width="80" src="aboutus.gif"></a></td>
    <td width="80" height="20"><a href="contact.htm">
      <img height="20" width="80" src="contact.gif"></a></td>
    <td width="80" height="20"><a href="resource.htm">
      <img height="20" width="80" src="resource.gif"></a></td>
  </tr>
</table>
```

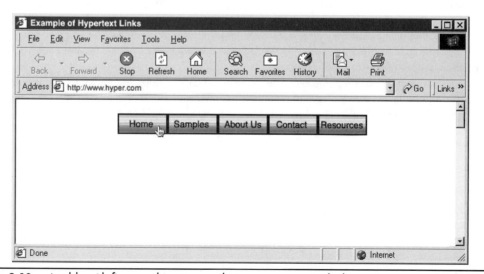

Figure 2-18 A table with five graphics images that appear as a single, larger image on a Web page

Slicing a Graphic Image into Table Cells to Create a Quick Loading Web Graphic

In the previous Tip, you learned how to create an image map by combining separate graphic elements within a table. Tables also let you assemble graphic images to create the appearance of a single graphic. Dividing a picture into pieces and placing the pieces into separate table cells allow the Web browser to retrieve and display the image faster than it could if the picture were a single, large file. The speed savings depends on the colors within the sliced images. Slices containing fewer colors, such as a bright blue sky, create smaller file sizes than slices that contain more colors.

USE IT   Say, for example, that you have a large graphic on a Web page, and the large file size of the image creates an unacceptably long download time for the page. The image in question is a landscape photograph containing large areas of solid blue sky, named big_sky.jpg.

If you divide the large graphics image into pieces and save each of these pieces in a separate JPEG-formatted file on disk, you can take advantage of the relationship between file size and image color depth. When you save a graphics image in the JPEG format, your graphics program selects a compression method based on the amount of color contained in the image. However, no matter the compression method used, the more color in the picture, the larger the size of the JPEG file the graphics program creates.

If you divide a large graphics image into pieces, the graphics program can select a different compression method for different parts or *slices* of the image. The program will save those slices with less color in smaller-size JPEG files, and those slices with more color in larger-size JPEG files (see Figure 2-19). However, given a picture with varying amounts of colors in different parts of the image, the sum of the sizes of the sliced JPEG files will be less than the number of bytes required to store the picture in a single JPEG file. Therefore, the Web browser will be able to load and display all of the file slices faster than it could load the single file, because the browser has to retrieve less data from the file server. Remember, when you put the slices (that is, the pieces) of a picture into the cells of a table with zero-width (invisible) borders, the table holds the pieces next to each other (without a space in between) such that they appear as a single, larger image.

When the table loads the image onto the Web page, it loads faster because the browser has less information to download from the server.

Slicing an image requires a graphic-editing program such as Adobe ImageReady 3.0. It is the only program currently on the market that will automatically slice a photographic image, optimize each slice according to the image's available colors, and save the sliced images into a separate folder.

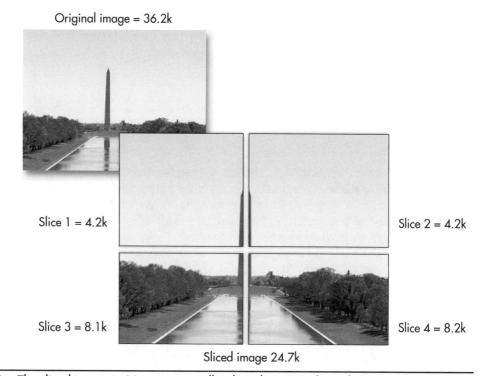

Original image = 36.2k

Slice 1 = 4.2k

Slice 2 = 4.2k

Slice 3 = 8.1k

Slice 4 = 8.2k

Sliced image 24.7k

Figure 2-19 The sliced image is 32 percent smaller than the original graphic

Reducing the Amount of Time a Web Browser Spends Drawing a Table

Although tables are an excellent way to control and display the contents of a Web document, like any other Web element they take time to download. In the previous Tip, you leaned how to speed up the loading of a graphic image by slicing the image into separate pieces and reassembling the pieces. Although slicing an image enhances its download speed, the browser must also create and load the table. When you create a table, the less complicated the table structure, the faster the table loads.

USE IT   To make a table load faster, provide the dimension of graphics images you insert within table cells. In the following code, a graphic image named image.jpg loads into a table cell that the browser makes the same width and height as the image:

```
<table>
  <tr>
    <td><img width="58" height="12" src="image.jpg"></td>
  </tr>
</table>
```

When you omit the width and height attribute settings from an <img> tag, the browser must base the cell's height and width on the dimensions of the picture it is to place in the cell. As a result, it will take longer for the Web browser to draw the table onscreen, because it must download the graphics image to determine the cell's dimensions. If you provide explicit image dimensions for all graphics images, the Web browser can draw the table, display any text in the table's cells, and then go back and download and insert the slower loading graphics images into the table. Because the browser can retrieve and display text content quickly, the site visitor can read the table's text content while waiting for the browser to retrieve and display the larger, slower-loading images in the table.

▶ **NOTE**

When specifying image dimensions, make sure the width *and* height *attribute values match the actual width and height of the image the browser is to place within the cell. If the height and/or width you specify differ from the image dimensions, the Web browser will stretch (or squash) the image to match the* height *and* width *attribute values. As a result, the image displayed may be distorted.*

Simulating Web Page Frames Using a Table

Web designers spend a lot of time organizing the information contained on a Web page. A well-designed Web page contains information grouped into definable areas. As you design and create Web sites, you will spend a great deal of time organizing content on each of the site's Web pages. A well-designed Web page has its content grouped into definable areas. For example, many sites have pages on which a group of headings (or a banner) appears across the top of the page, a navigation bar is available down one of the sides or across the bottom, and the actual content appears below the headings and either to the right of or above the navigation bar.

A Web site with well-organized Web pages creates a pleasing environment that invites the visitor to enter the site and spend some time exploring its content. One way to organize the content on a Web page is to use *frames*, which divide a Web page into several windows, called a *frameset*, with each window capable of displaying a separate Web document. A typical framed Web page, such as that shown in Figure 2-20, has three frames.

The first frame runs left-to-right across the top of the page and contains heading information, such as company name and address. The second frame contains the navigation system and runs the left side of the page, from under the heading frame to the bottom of the page. The third frame contains organized areas of text and graphics.

The visible border
defines the frames

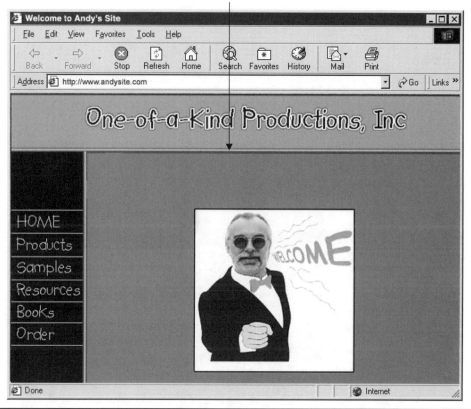

Figure 2-20 A typical Web page divided into frames

Although frames provide an excellent tool for organizing information on a Web page, they have two major flaws. First, frames are not fully supported by all Web browsers, and second, it takes longer for a Web browser to load a framed Web page because the browser must load and display a separate Web document in each of the frames on the page.

USE IT Although tables do not let you load multiple Web documents into a single browser application window, you can use tables to create the visual look of the organization provided by framed Web pages. For example, the following code creates a table that gives a Web page the organized look of a framed page, as shown in Figure 2-21:

```
<table border="4" cellpadding="0" cellspacing="2"
   width="600">
  <tr height="25">
    <td height="25" colspan="2" bgcolor="#9900ff">
      <center><font color="white">THIS IS THE HEADING AREA
```

```
      </font></center>
    </td> </tr>
  <tr height="300">
    <td width="100" height="300" bgcolor="#cc0000">
      <center><font color="white">This area holds
        </font>
        <p><font color="white">the navigation</font></p>
        <p><font color="white">array</font>
      </center></td>
    <td width="400" height="300" bgcolor="black">
      <center><font color="white">
        This area holds the Web page content</font></center>
    </td>
  </tr>
</table>
```

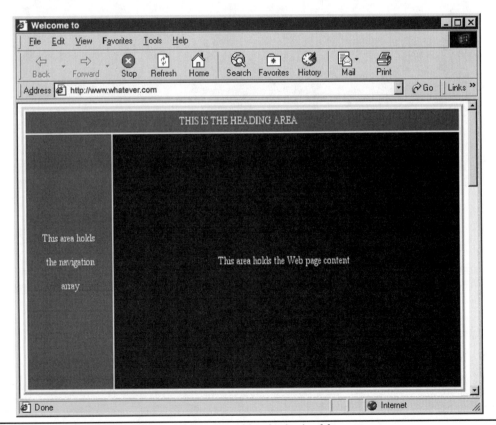

Figure 2-21   A Web page using a table to simulate the look of frames

By using a different background color for each division (red, blue, and black, in the current example), you can make each of the divisions appear independent like the frames in a framed Web page.

Focusing the Viewer's Attention with Cell Background Colors

In this chapter, you learned that the primary uses for tables in a Web document are to display tabular data, to organize and place content at specific locations, to create image maps, and to reduce the time it takes the Web browser to download graphics images. You can also use tables to attract the attention of site visitors and thereby draw their eyes to specific areas on a Web page. Color is a strong element you can use to grab a visitor's attention. In the previous Tip, you worked with background color to create groups of table cells that divide the Web page into regions by purpose.

USE IT Now, suppose that you create a text-heavy document and you want the visitor to pay particular attention to one specific paragraph. Create a multicell table and place the Web page text in one of the table's cells. Then color the cell to the left of the "important" paragraph and perhaps even include some descriptive text in the colored cell, such as that shown in Figure 2-22.

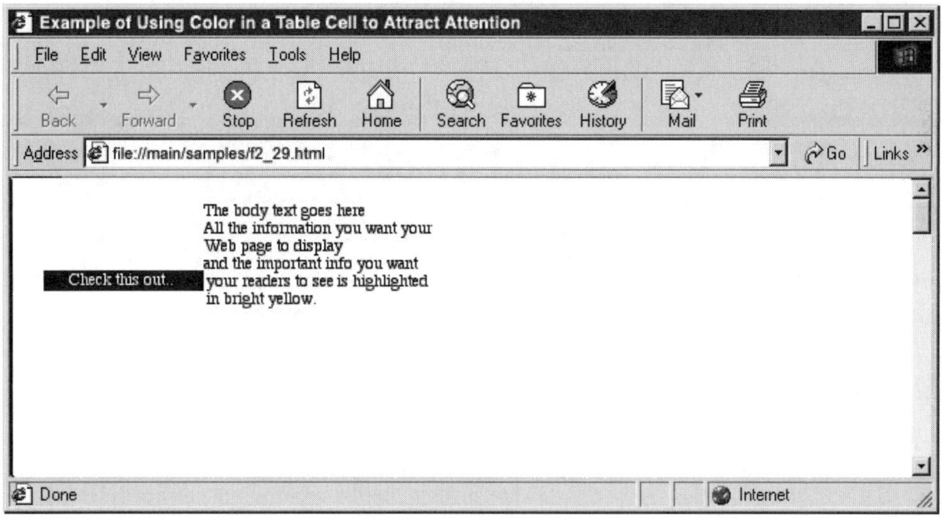

Figure 2-22   A table with a colored cell that draws the eye to a specific area of the Web page

The following code creates the Web document shown in Figure 2-22:

```
<table border="0" cellpadding="0" cellspacing="2" width="317"
       bgcolor="black">
  <tr>
    <td width="89" height="20">
      <img src="trans.gif" height="20"></td>
    <td rowspan="3" valign="top"><font color="white">
      The body text goes here<br>
      All the information you want your <br>
      Web page to display <br>
      and the important info you want <br>
      your readers to see is highlighted<br>
      in bright yellow.</font></td></tr>
  <tr>
    <td width="89" align="center" bgcolor="yellow">
      Check this out..</td></tr>
  <tr><td width="89"> </td></tr>
</table>
```

Changing the background color of the table cell containing the words *Check this out* to yellow (by setting the *bgcolor* attribute in the cell's <td> tag to "yellow") draws the visitor's attention to the cell and emphasizes a portion of the text in the adjacent cell.

Aligning Web Page Content Visually with Visible Table Borders

When you use a table to align graphics and text, you create an organized layout to the page, help the visitor's eyes move through the document, and increase the attractiveness of the page layout.

USE IT Suppose, for example, that you want to create a Web page that contains photographs of your employees along with their names, positions in the company, and mailing addresses. To organize the information, create a single column table with four rows, such as that shown next:

Row 1 contains the employee's name; row 2 holds the employee's photograph; row three holds their position in the company; and row 4 holds their mailing address. Not only does using a table help to organize the information on the Web page, but using the *border* attribute helps to further define the outer border of the table and separates the table from other graphics and text on the Web page.

The following code creates the table shown previously:

```
<table border="6" cellpadding="0" cellspacing="2" width="175">
  <tr>
    <td width="175" height = "30" align="center">
    James Markin
    </td></tr>
  <tr height="90">
    <td width="175" height="90" align="center" valign="middle">
      <img height="67" width="92" src="employee_1.jpg">
    </td></tr>
  <tr>
    <td width="175" height = "30" align="center">
    Senior Designer
    </td></tr>
```

```
<tr>
  <td width="175" height="93" align="center" valign="middle">
    <font size="4">Riven Productions</font>
    <br><font size="4">433 Spaeder Street</font>
    <br><font size="4">Hollywood, CA 23435</font>
  </td></tr>
</table>
```

When you turn off the *border* attribute (*border* = *"0"*), the table cells merge, creating a solid look to the separate cells in the table. Using the *border* attribute visually divides the information into definable blocks of information that are easy to read.

Controlling Gutter Size and Margin Width of Text on a Web Page

When you create documents using programs such as Microsoft Word, the word processor lets you control the outside margins along the sides of each page and the gutter space between columns of text. Unfortunately, HTML does not give you this same type of control over the placement of text on a Web page. However, by placing text content in a table, you can simulate the outside margin and gutter control available in a word processor.

Say, for example, that you want to create a Web page that when displayed by a Web browser resembles a two-column word processor document with appropriate gutter spacing between the columns of text, as shown in Figure 2-23.

USE IT   In the table shown in Figure 2-23, the first and last columns of the table control the space allocated to the left and right margins. Meanwhile, the third column controls the amount of gutter space the browser will leave between the two columns of text. Finally, the second and fourth columns hold the document text.

The following code will generate the table displayed in Figure 2-23 (notice that the table actually contains five cells):

```
<table border="0" cellpadding="0" cellspacing="2" width="600">
<! -- Column controlling left margin  -- >
  <tr height="250">
    <td width="20" >
      <img src="trans.gif" width="20"></td>
    <td width="200" valign="top">
      <center><font size="5"><b> Heading Inserted Here</b>
        </font></center>
      <p>Body Text Inserted Here.</p>
      <p>Body Text Inserted Here.</p></td>
<! -- Column controlling gutter space  -- >
    <td width="15" >
```

```
   <img src="trans.gif" width="15"></td>
<td width="200" valign="top">
   <center><font size="5"><b>Heading Inserted Here</b>
      </font></center>
   <p> Body Text Inserted Here.</p>
   <p> Body Text Inserted Here.</p></td>
<! -- Column controlling right margin   -- >
   <td width="20">
      <img src="trans.gif" width="20"></td></tr>
</table>
```

Placing text into a table lets you organize and control how the text displays inside a Web browser window, and well-organized text is easier to read and understand. In addition, not all browsers display empty table cells correctly. Therefore, to ensure that the table displays as intended, insert a transparent GIF into the margin and gutter table cells and set the *width* attribute within the <img> tag to the width of the gutter or margin you want.

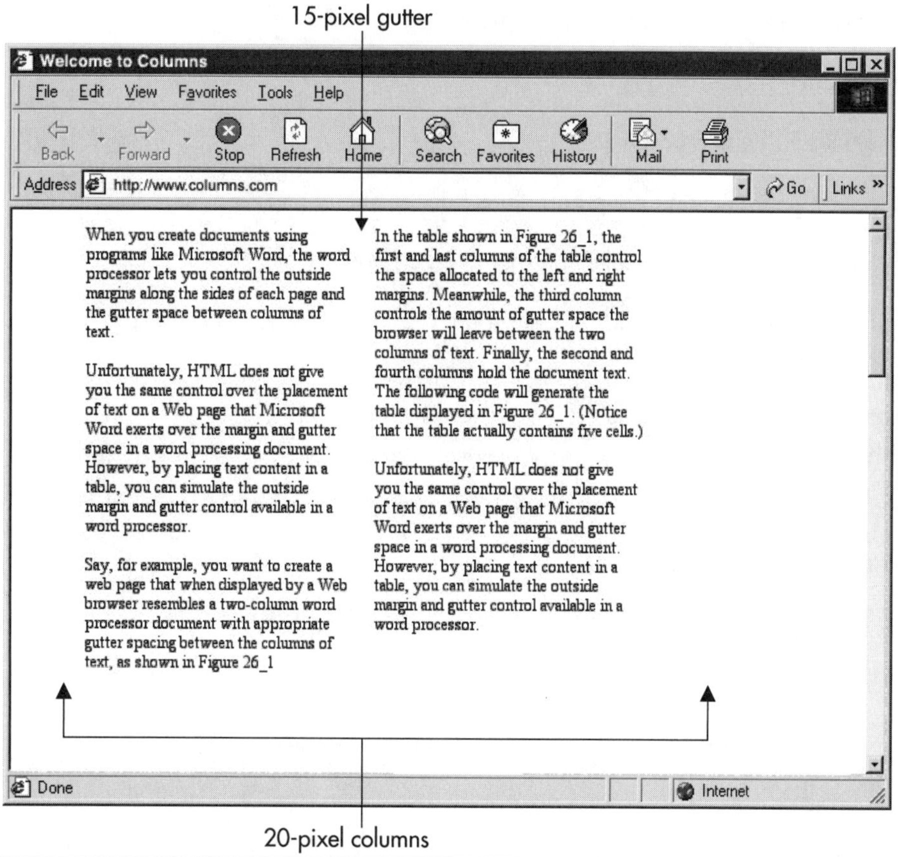

15-pixel gutter

20-pixel columns

Figure 2-23   A two-column text document displayed using a table

CHAPTER 3

HTML Forms

TIPS IN THIS CHAPTER

▶ Creating a Single-Line Input Field on a Form   119

▶ Creating a Multiline Input Field on a Form   120

▶ Validating Text Element Data Prior to Submitting Form Results   122

▶ Placing Check Boxes on a Form   124

▶ Placing Radio Buttons on a Form   126

▶ Validating Radio Button Group Selections Prior to Submitting Form Results   128

▶ Placing a Drop-Down List (Selection Menu) on a Form   129

▶ Verifying the Visitor Has Made a Selection List Choice Prior to Submitting
Form Results   132

▶ Changing the Items Available on a Selection List Based on
Visitor Supplied Information   134

▶ Sending All Selection List Values to the Web Server Through a Hidden Field   136

▶ Adding a Reset Button to a Form   138

▶ Preventing a Visitor from Clearing Form Elements Accidentally   139

▶ Adding a Submit Button to a Form   140

▶ Replacing the Standard Submit and Reset Buttons on a Form with Other
Graphics Images   141

▶ Sending Form Results by E-Mail Without a CGI Script   143

▶ Controlling the Layout of Form Elements and Text with HTML Tables   145

▶ Creating a Shortcut Key for Form Navigation with a <label> Tag   148

▶ Instructing the Web Browser to Execute a Form Validation Function with the *onClick* Attribute   149

▶ Passing Values to the Web Server Through Hidden Fields   151

▶ Hiding Visitor Input from View Within a Password Element   152

▶ Adding a Generic Button Object to a Form   153

▶ Enabling and Disabling Form Elements on-the-Fly   154

I f you have spent any time visiting Web sites on the Internet, chances are good that you have filled out many Web-based forms. In fact, you probably work with forms (such as search engines or login screens) every time you surf the Web. Although the majority of Web pages consist of text, images, and hyperlinks, which let you retrieve information, almost all Web sites have at least one form that lets you send information back to the Web site's operator. A form might be as simple as a login screen where you provide your username and password for access to the site, or as complex as the user interfaces on Hotmail, E*Trade, eBay, Yahoo, and such. Figure 3-1, for example, shows the account setup form and login form at http://www.hotmail.com.

From a designer's viewpoint, forms let you establish a dialog with your site's visitors. Instead of using text and pictures to *send* information, forms let you use text boxes, check boxes, radio buttons, and selection menus to *retrieve* information.

To process the responses (that is, the form results) you receive from the site visitor, you will normally use some type of script running on the Web server and possibly a script the browser runs before submitting the information the visitor entered into the form. You will learn how to implement such scripts later in this chapter. For now, understand that the scripts that process the form results normally serve two purposes. First, either the Web server or (preferably) the Web browser might run a script that validates the form's data, that is, a script that makes sure the visitor filled out all "required" fields and that the data provided in the form is valid. Second, either the Web server will run a script that processes the form results itself, or the script may place the form results into a file and forward them to another program for further processing. (Some programmers refer to the form results that the browser submits to the Web server as the *form data set*.)

Although they vary greatly in appearance, all forms have several elements in common. Forms consist of one or more labeled input fields, check boxes, radio buttons, or drop-down menus Web

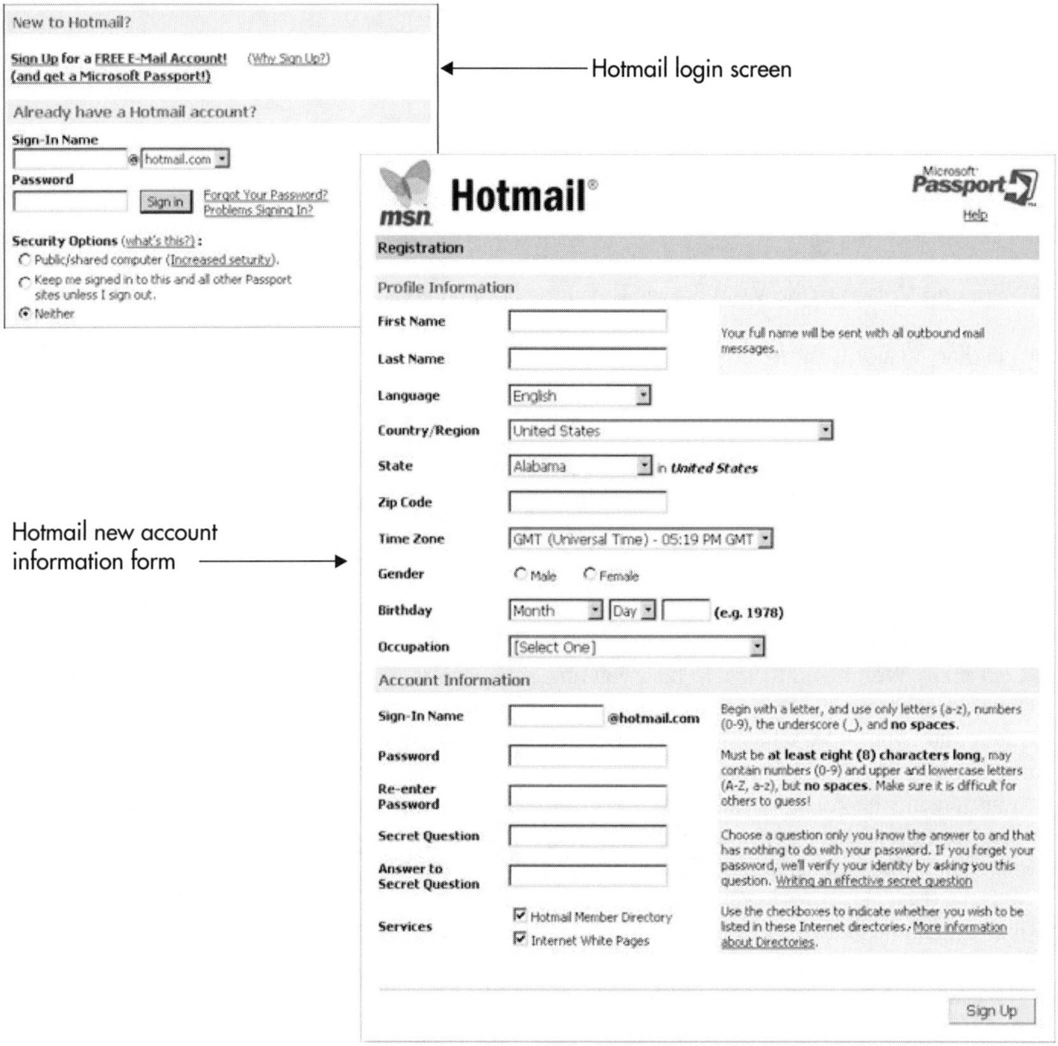

Figure 3-1 Examples of forms found at http://www.hotmail.com

site visitors use to enter information. All forms also have a Submit button on which a visitor clicks to send the form results to the Web server. Most forms (especially those with many input fields) also have a Reset button on which a visitor can click to clear all previously entered responses and start over. Beyond these basic items (labeled input fields and two special-purpose pushbuttons), you can include anything on a form that you can directly on the Web page (with the exception that one form cannot contain a second form). As you will learn in this chapter, an HTML form—like an HTML table—is a "container" that holds Web page objects. However, unlike an HTML table (which is designed to send information to the site visitor), a form's purpose is to retrieve responses from the visitor.

Understanding HTML Forms Processing

The most difficult thing to understand about HTML forms processing is "what happens where." When a visitor views a Web page that does not contain a form, the server simply responds to the browser's requests for the Web page and the individual items the page contains, such as graphics and animations. For example, when someone "visits" a Web site, the visitor's browser requests a Web page from the Web server. After the server returns the HTML page, the browser examines the HTML statements and begins to display the page. When the browser encounters tags that require more data from the server, such as an <img> tag that specifies a graphic, the browser requests the server to send the corresponding file. As shown in Figure 3-2, the server and browser continue this "request/ response" interaction until the browser has retrieved all the files the browser needs to display the Web page content.

After the Web server sends the HTML document (including any referenced graphics images, animations, sound files, or video clips as requested by the Web browser), the Web server's job is done. It is up to the Web browser to display the Web page text and graphics and to play back any sound files or movie clips available on the page. When the visitor clicks one of hyperlinks on the Web page, the browser sends another request for a Web page to the Web server, which, in turn, sends the requested document (and support files as the files are requested) to the Web browser for the browser to process and display.

When working with a Web page that contains a form, the browser and server perform the previous two-way conversation to download the page and its contents (which includes the form). After the visitor fills in the form's entries and clicks Submit, the browser sends the form results back to the server, which must then process the results in some way. Normally, the server will process the form results by running a specific script. Depending on the script's purpose, the script, for example, might place the user's data into a database, might use the information to start an e-commerce transaction, or, in the case of a form at a search-engine site such as Yahoo, use the form's contents to search the server database for a list of related links. As you will learn later, within the HTML entries that create the form, the designer specifies the program the server runs after the visitor submits the form results.

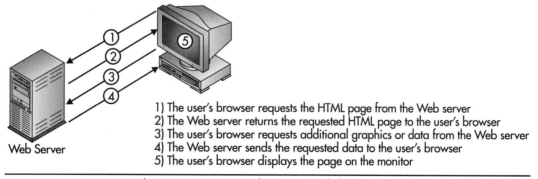

1) The user's browser requests the HTML page from the Web server
2) The Web server returns the requested HTML page to the user's browser
3) The user's browser requests additional graphics or data from the Web server
4) The Web server sends the requested data to the user's browser
5) The user's browser displays the page on the monitor

Web Server

Figure 3-2   HTTP request/response interaction between Web browser and Web server

Normally, behind the scenes, when the visitor clicks Submit, the browser will run a script that resides within the same HTML file as the form. The script verifies that the visitor filled out the form completely and may check the "correctness" of some of the responses. Then, the browser will package up the information and send it to the Web server, telling the server the name of the application the server should run to process the form results. Figure 3-3 shows the split of work performed during forms processing by the Web browser and the Web server.

In summary, after the Web server sends the Web page with the form to the Web browser, the server goes on about its business—as the server does after sending any other Web page (with or without forms) to a Web browser. The Web browser takes care of accepting the visitor's input into the form's text fields and mouse click selections on the form's radio buttons, check boxes, and selection lists. When the visitor has finished filling out the form, the Web browser must again communicate with the Web server to send the information entered on the form to the Web server for processing. The Web server, in turn, runs a specific script to process the form results and sends a message to

1) The Web server sends the form to the visitor's Web browser
2) The Web browser displays the form, which the visitor, in turn, fills out
3) The visitor clicks the Submit button to send the data to the Web server
4) The Web server passes the form data (called the form results) to the CGI script
5) The CGI script that processes the form results may format the data and sent it on to an application
    program for processing
6) The CGI script creates a confirmation message and sends it to the Web server
7) The Web server sends the confirmation message to the Web browser for display

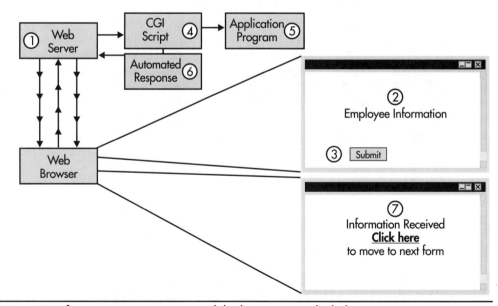

Figure 3-3   HTML forms processing events and the locations at which they occur

the Web browser confirming the receipt of form results and often the success or failure of
form data processing.

Understanding the Tags and Attributes Used to Create a Form

As mentioned previously in this chapter, in addition to text fields, radio buttons, and check boxes
used to prompt visitors for input, you can include pushbuttons, text, graphics images, and other Web
page objects on a form. The HTML start and end form tags (<form></form>) tell the Web browser
which portion of an HTML file to include in the form. Remember, a Web page form is a "container"
not unlike an HTML table. You use a set of start and end table tags (<table></table>) to enclose the
content you want the Web browser to place within a table. Similarly, you use a set of start and end
form tags (<form></form>) to tell the Web browser which part of the Web page content is part of
a form. The main difference between forms and tables is that the browser simply displays the data
within an HTML table, but the Web browser not only displays a form, but also accepts input into
the form's elements and sends the form results to the Web server for processing. (Moreover, you
can place multiple tables and multiple forms on a single Web page; however, although you can nest
one table within another, you cannot nest forms.)

For example, as you read the text in this chapter you will learn how to replace the following
placeholders for input fields and pushbuttons between a set of start and end form tags (<form></form>)
to create forms that let you collect the information you want from your site visitors:

```
<form name="ExampleForm"
      action="http://www.NVBizNet2.com/_scripts/_pl/FrmScrpt.CGI"
      method="POST" title="Form ToolTip"
      enctype="application/x-www-form-urlencoded">
  <p>Form input fields & misc. pushbuttons</p>
  <p>Form RESET and SUBMIT pushbuttons</p>
</form>
```

As shown in the current example, <form> tags typically include the following attributes:

- *action*   The uniform resource locator (URL) or Web address to which the Web browser sends
  the visitor's form responses after the visitor clicks the form's Submit button. For example, to
  send the form results (that is, the information entered and selections made on a form) as an
  e-mail message, you might set the value of the *action* attribute to a text string consisting of
  the keyword *mailto:* and an e-mail address. Similarly, to forward the form results to a program
  for further processing, set the value of the *action* attribute to the URL of the script responsible for
  sending the form results on their way.

- *enctype*   Tells the Web browser the encoding method to use for passing form data to
  the CGI script on the server. Normally, you will set the value of the *enctype* attribute
  to "application/x-www-form-urlencoded".

- *id*   Used to give the form a unique name by which you can refer to the form in a script. If you do not "name" the form (by providing an *id* or a *name* attribute value), you must refer to the form by number. For example, in JavaScript, you would refer to the first form on the Web page as document.forms[0], the second form as document.forms[1], the third form as document.forms[2], and so on. Conversely, if you give each form on the Web page a unique ID, your script could refer to the form as document.*formID* (or simply as *formID*).

- *method*   Specifies the way in which the browser is to send the form results to the URL specified in the *action* attribute. The value of the *method* attribute will be either POST or GET. If you set the value of *method* to GET, the Web browser sends the form data to the Web server at the end of the URL given by the *action* attribute in the <form> tag. Conversely, if you set the value of the *method* attribute to POST, the Web browser sends the form data to the Web server in a separate HTTP message. According to HTML standards, you should use the GET method when the form is idempotent, that is, when the script processing the form makes no changes to data stored on the Web server. For example, forms used to search a database would use the GET method. Conversely, if processing form results causes side effects, such as changing the data stored in a DBMS, for example, you should use the POST method.

▶ **NOTE**

Never use the GET method to submit form results from a form that asks for a password. If you do so, you will expose the password the visitor enters as part of a URL stored in several locations including the Web browser's history file and the Web server's log file.

- *name*   Text string you can use to refer to the form by name in a script included within the Web page HTML. If you do not "name" the form (by providing a *name* or *id* attribute value), you must refer to the form by number. For example, if you give each form on the Web page a name or unique ID, your script could refer to the form as document.formname (or document.formID).

- *onReset*   The name of a function (that is, a script within the Web page HTML) the Web browser is to execute if the visitor clicks the form's Reset button. The function will return a value of either True or False. If the function returns True, the Web browser will remove the visitor's input and reset the form's elements to their original, default values. Conversely, if the function returns a value of False, the Web browser will not reset the form field values.

- *onSubmit*   The name of a function (that is, a script within the Web page HTML) the Web browser is to execute when the visitor clicks the form's Submit button. Normally you use an *onSubmit* function to validate form results prior to sending them to the Web server for processing. If the function returns a value of False, the Web browser will not send the form results to the Web server. Conversely, if the function returns a value of True, the Web browser sends the form results on to the Web server for processing by the CGI script or other program named in the *action* attribute in the <form> tag.

- *target*   The name of the window in which you want the Web browser to display the form's confirmation page.

- *title*   Text (such as the name or description of the form) you want the Web browser to display when the site visitor lets the mouse pointer hover over any one spot within the form for several seconds.

The first seven Tips, which follow this introduction to HTML forms, will show you how to create text input fields, check boxes, radio buttons, selection menus, Reset buttons, and Submit buttons on forms. A few of the remaining Tips will then explore the attributes available for use in the <form> tag in depth. For now, the important thing to understand is that you place the objects you want on the form (that is, you place the form's elements on the form) by inserting the HTML tag(s) for each element between the form's start and end form tags(<form></form>). Moreover, every form must have some type of a "submit" button that, when clicked, tells the Web browser to send the form results (that is, the form's data) to a URL specified by the *action* attribute in the form's <form> tag.

Creating a Single-Line Input Field on a Form

When you want the site visitor to enter a short string of text, insert an <input> tag with its *type* attribute set to "text" within the form.

USE IT   For example, the two <input> tags in the following code create the First Name and Last Name fields shown on the form in Figure 3-4.

```
<form name="ExampleForm">
<p>First Name: <input type="text" name="FirstName" size="15">
   Last Name: <input type="text" name="LastName" size="20"></p>
<p>[Form RESET and SUBMIT pushbuttons go here]</p>
</form>
```

Notice that the text label to the left of each of the two single-line text fields on the form are not a part of the <input> tag. Each single-line text <input> tag does, however, have the following attributes:

- *type*   Set to "text" to let the Web browser know that the form element is a single-line text box.
- *id*   Used to assign a name to the input field. You can use the value of the *id* attribute to work with the contents of the input field within a script embedded in the Web page HTML. Note that each *id* you use within the Web page HTML must be unique, that is, no two *id* values can be the same within a single page.

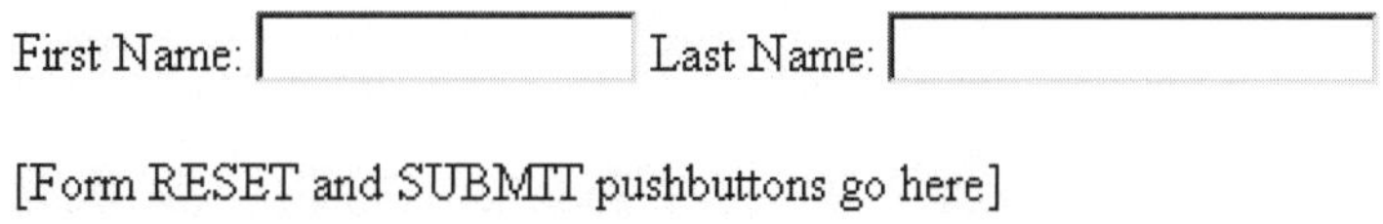

First Name: [   ]   Last Name: [   ]

[Form RESET and SUBMIT pushbuttons go here]

Figure 3-4   A form with two single-line text input fields

- *name*   Used to identify the input field. You can use the value of the *name* attribute to refer to the value in the input field within a script running at the Web browser, and the browser passes the field's name along with the field's value to the Web server when the visitor clicks the form's Submit button.

- *size*   The width, in characters, of the text box.

- *value*   Tells the Web browser to place the text you assign to the attribute into the input field when the browser first draws the form.

- *maxlength*   The maximum number of characters the visitor can type into the input field.

- *readonly*   When present, the field can receive the focus. However, the visitor cannot change the value in the input field.

- *disabled*   When present, the field cannot receive the focus, nor can the visitor change the input field's value. Moreover, the browser does not submit the field's name or value to the Web server with the form results.

- *tabindex*   Used to set the tabbing order in which form elements receive the focus. By assigning ascending values to the *tabindex* attribute within the tag for each form element, you can tell the browser where to move the cursor (that is, the focus). Each time the visitor presses TAB, the browser will move the focus to the form element with the next highest *tabindex*.

- *accesskey*   The key the user can press while holding down the ALT key (or the COMMAND or CONTROL key on a Macintosh system) to move to (that is, give the focus to) the input field.

The <input> tags in the current example tell the Web browser to place two single-line text boxes (named "FirstName" and "LastName") on a form named ExampleForm. The FirstName text box is 15 characters in length; the LastName text box has a length of 20 characters.

When entering text into a single-line text box, the site visitor can enter any number of text characters into the field. However, the Web browser will display only the number of characters given by the <input> tag's *size* attribute onscreen at once. In the current example, if the visitor enters a 20-character first name, because the input field is only 15 characters wide, only 15 characters of the first name are visible at a time. (If you want to limit the number of characters the visitor can enter, add a *maxlength* attribute set to the maximum acceptable string length to the <input> tag.)

Creating a Multiline Input Field on a Form

When you want the site visitor to enter several lines of text, insert a set of start and end text area tags (<textarea></textarea>) between the form's start and end tags (<form></form>).

USE IT   For example, to insert the multiline text box shown below the first and last name fields in Figure 3-5, add the start and end text area tags (<textarea></textarea>) shown after the <input> tags in the following code that defines a form:

```
<form name="ExampleForm">
<p>First Name: <input type="text" name="FirstName" size="15">
   Last Name: <input type="text" name="LastName" size="20"></p>
<p>Message: <textarea name="TextMessage" rows="5" cols="60">
          </textarea></p>
<p>[Form RESET and SUBMIT pushbuttons go here]</p>
</form>
```

As was the case with the label next to the single-line text fields in the preceding example, the text ("Message:") to the left of the multiline text field is not a part of the field's <textarea> tag. A multiline text input tag does, however, have the following attributes:

- *rows*   The number of rows of text you want the Web browser to display inside the multiline text box at once onscreen.

- *cols*   The number of characters you want the text box to display on each line of the multiline text box.

- *id*   Used to assign a name to the input field. You can use the value of the *id* attribute to work with the contents of the input field within a script embedded in the Web page HTML.

- *name*   A name used to identify the input field. You can use the value of the name field to refer to the value in the input field within a script executed by the Web browser. The browser normally passes the field's name along with the field's contents to the Web server when the visitor clicks Submit.

The <textarea> tag in the current example tells the Web browser to place a multiline text box (named "TextMessage") on a form named "ExampleForm". Moreover, the Web browser is to display up to 5 rows of text with up to 60 characters per row onscreen at once.

When typing text into a multiline text box, the site visitor can enter any number of characters into the form element. However, at any one time, the Web browser will display only the number of characters given by multiplying the value of the <textarea> tag's *row* attribute by the value of

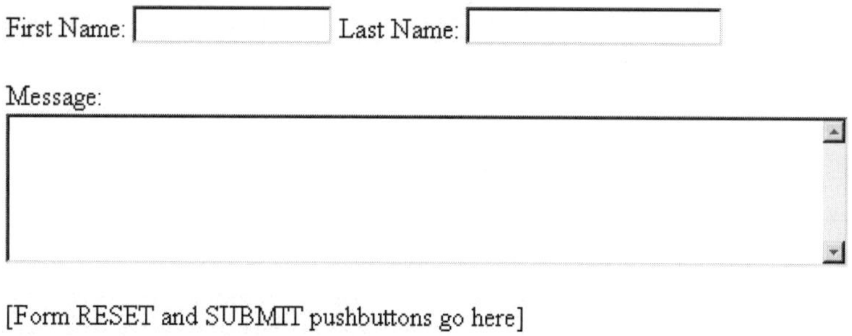

First Name: [   ]   Last Name: [   ]

Message:

[   ]

[Form RESET and SUBMIT pushbuttons go here]

Figure 3-5   A form with a multiline text input field

its *cols* attribute. Thus, in the current example, the Web browser will display up to 300 characters (5 rows×60 characters/row) of text onscreen in the text box.

The value of the *row* attribute in the <textarea> tag affects the height of the text box, and the value of the *cols* attribute in the tag affects the input field's width. However, the combination of the *rows* and *cols* values determines only the size of the text area onscreen (and therefore, the number of characters the browser can display in the text box at the same time). The product of *rows* × *cols* does not limit the total number of characters the visitor can type into the field.

Unlike form elements that use an <input> tag with a *type* attribute set to the specific type of input the element is to accept, you use a set of start and end text area tags (<textarea></textarea>) to insert a multiline text input element on a form. Although you control the dimensions of the text area with attributes within the <textarea> tag, the tag has no *value* attribute you can use to specify a default, initial value. If you want the Web browser to display default text within the text area, specify the text you want between the start and end text area tags(<textarea></textarea>). For example, if you want to prompt the visitor to start a message entered into a text area with "Attention Customer Service:", you might write the text area definition with the form HTML as follows:

```
<p>Message: <textarea name="TextMessage" rows="5" cols="60">
            Attention Customer Service:</textarea></p>
```

Validating Text Element Data Prior to Submitting Form Results

Validating a single-line or multiline text field prior to submitting form results to the Web server typically involves making sure the visitor has entered something into the field. Suppose, for example, that your Web page HTML included the following form definition that asks the site visitor to enter a name and an e-mail address:

```
<form name="ExampleForm"
      action="http://NVBizNet2.com/_scripts/_pl/FrmScrpt.CGI"
      method="POST"
      enctype="application/x-www-form-urlencoded">
  First Name:
    <input type="text" name="FirstName" id="FN" size="15"><br>
  Last Name:
    <input type="text" name="LastName" id="LN" size="20"><br>
  E-mail: <input type="text" name="Email" id="EM" size="30"><br>
  <p><input type="submit" value="Submit">
     <input type="reset"></p>
</form>
```

USE IT   To make sure that the visitor does not skip over the e-mail field without entering something into it, insert a JavaScript script that "validates" the form's text field enclosed within a set of start and end script tags (<script></script>) in the Web page HTML. Although you can place scripts anywhere in the Web page definition, place your form validation functions right after the start Web page <body> tag at the beginning of the Web page HTML. (Placing all your scripts in the same area of the Web page HTML makes them easier to find when you want to see the code behind references to the scripts in the Web page HTML tags.). Thus, to make sure the visitor enters something into the e-mail text field in the current example, your Web page HTML will start something like this:

```
<html><body>
<script language="JavaScript">
<!--
  function ValidateForm(Form)
  {
   if (Form.Email.value == "")
     {
       alert("Please enter a value for the \"E-mail\" field.");
       Form.Email.focus();
       return(false);
     }
   else return(true);
  }
// -->
</script>
```

The start and end comment tags (<!-- and -->) that enclose the JavaScript have no effect on the script in Web browsers that are able to read and execute JavaScript. However, the start and end comment tags prevent Web browsers that do not support scripting languages from displaying the JavaScript code onscreen with other Web page text content.

The first line in the JavaScript defines the *ValidateForm* function, so you can refer to it (that is, call it as a function that returns a value) elsewhere in the Web page HTML. The second and third lines of code check the value of the form field named Email and display the Alert message box shown here, if the Email text field is blank when the Web browser executes the script.

If the Email field is blank, the fourth and fifth lines in the JavaScript (which follow the ALERT method) tell the Web browser to move the cursor (that is, the form's focus) to the "Email" text input field and return a value of False to the HTML tag that "called" the function.

To have the Web browser execute the *ValidateForm()* function when the visitor clicks Submit, add the *onSubmit* attribute to the form's <form> tag such that the tag reads as follows:

```
<form name="ExampleForm" onSubmit="return ValidateForm(ExampleForm)"
      action="http://NVBizNet2.com/_scripts/_pl/FrmScrpt.CGI"
      method="POST"
      enctype="application/x-www-form-urlencoded">
```

Make sure you do not omit the "return" that precedes the *ValidateForm()* function call; otherwise, the Web browser will still submit the form results to the Web server even if the *ValidateForm()* function returns a value of False, which indicates that there is a problem with the form results.

When written correctly (as in the current example), the *onSubmit* attribute tells the Web browser to execute a JavaScript function to validate the form results after the visitor clicks Submit. If the function returns True, the Web browser will submit the form results to the URL specified by the *method* attribute in the <form> tag. Conversely, if the JavaScript function returns a value of False, the Web browser will return to form data entry, placing the cursor in the form element specified by the focus method in the JavaScript.

Placing Check Boxes on a Form

When you want the Web site visitor to choose one or more items from a list by clicking a check mark into the check box next to each item the visitor wants to select, insert an <input> tag on the form with the *type* attribute set to "checkbox" for each item on the list.

USE IT For example, to insert the seven check boxes shown below the multiline text box in Figure 3-6, add the <input> tags shown after the end </textarea> tag in the following form definition:

```
<form name="ExampleForm">
<p>First Name: <input type="text" name="FirstName" size="15">
   Last Name: <input type="text" name="LastName" size="20"></p>
<p>Message: <textarea name="TextMessage" rows="5" cols="60">
           </textarea></p>
<p>Areas of Interest:<br>
  O.S.: <input type="checkbox" name="Win98" value="ON">Windows 98
        <input type="checkbox" name="WinXp" value="ON">Windows XP
        <input type="checkbox" name="WinNT" value="ON">Windows NT <br>
  Hardware: <input type="checkbox" name="DT" value="ON">Desktop
            <input type="checkbox" name="LT" value="ON">Laptop
            <input type="checkbox" name="PDA" value="ON">PDA
```

```
            <input type="checkbox" name="Prtr" value="ON">Printers
            <input type="checkbox" name="Mon" value="ON">Monitors </p>
<p>[Form RESET and SUBMIT pushbuttons go here]</p>
</form>
```

As is the case with other form elements, the text labels before and/or after the check boxes on a form are not a part of the element's HTML. The <input> tag for each check box does, however, have the following attributes:

- *type*   Set to "checkbox" to let the Web browser know that the form element is a check box.

- *id*   Used to assign a unique name to a check box. You can use the value of the *id* attribute to refer to the "checked" status of a specific check box in a script embedded in the Web page HTML.

- *name*   A name used to identify each check box. You can use the value of the *name* attribute to refer to the "checked" status of a specific check box in a script executed by the Web browser. Moreover, the Web browser will pass the value of the *name* attribute as the "name" portion of the name/value to the Web server if the site visitor checks the check box. If the site visitor clears the check box, the Web browser does not pass the name of the check box and its associated value (that is, the setting of the check box's *value* attribute) to the Web server.

- *value*   Text string passed to the Web server as the "value" portion of the name/value. The Web browser sends only the name/value pair for each "check marked" (that is, selected) check box to the Web server when the visitor clicks Submit.

- *checked*   When set to True (as in *checked="true"*), the Web browser will check mark the check box (that is, show the check box as "selected") when the browser draws the form. By default, the checked attribute is False (that is, the check box is unchecked), so you do not have to include *checked="false"* in the <input> tag for a check box you do not want selected (that is, check marked) initially.

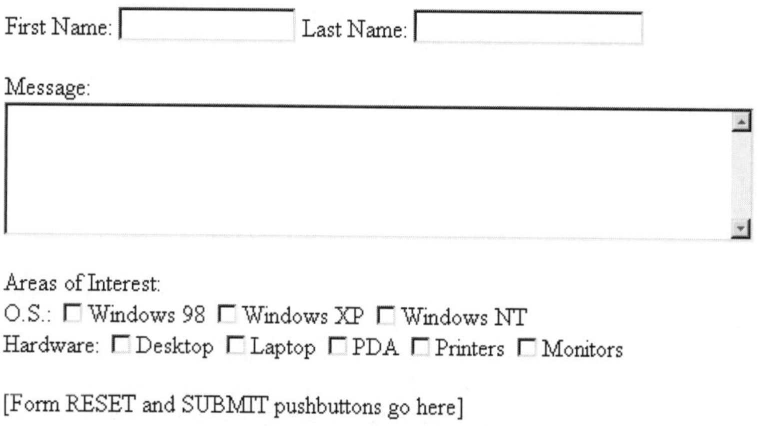

Figure 3-6   A form with seven check boxes below a multiline text input field

The <input> tags with the *type* attribute set to "checkbox" in the current example tell the Web browser to place seven check boxes on a form named ExampleForm. The Web browser takes care of toggling the contents of each check box such that when a visitor clicks an empty check box, the Web browser selects the form element by putting a check mark into the check box. Conversely, when the site visitor clicks a selected check box (one which already contains a check mark) the Web browser deselects the form element by removing the check mark and thereby clearing the check box.

Placing Radio Buttons on a Form

When you want the Web site visitor to choose only a single item from a list of items, create the list on the form by inserting a <input> tag with the *type* attribute set to "radio" for each item in the list.

USE IT For example, to insert the Yes and No radio buttons shown at the bottom of the form in Figure 3-7, add the <input> tags shown in the third and fourth lines from the bottom in the following form definition:

```
<form name="ExampleForm">
<p>First Name: <input type="text" name="FirstName" size="15">
   Last Name: <input type="text" name="LastName" size="20"></p>
<p>Message: <textarea name="TextMessage" rows="5" cols="60">
            </textarea></p>
<p>Areas of Interest:<br>
  O.S.:
     <input type="checkbox" name="Win98" value="ON">Windows 98
     <input type="checkbox" name="WinXp" value="ON">Windows XP
     <input type="checkbox" name="WinNT" value="ON">Windows NT
     <br>
  Hardware:
     <input type="checkbox" name="DT" value="ON">Desktop
     <input type="checkbox" name="LT" value="ON">Laptop
     <input type="checkbox" name="PDA" value="ON">PDA
     <input type="checkbox" name="Prtr" value="ON">Printers
     <input type="checkbox" name="Mon" value="ON">Monitors </p>
<p>May we give your e-mail address to others?
  <input type="radio" value="Yes" name="ShareEmail">Yes
  <input type="radio" value="No" checked name="ShareEmail">No
</p>
<p>[Form RESET and SUBMIT pushbuttons go here]</p>
</form>
```

As is the case with the labels on other form elements, the text before and/or after the radio buttons on a form are not a part of the radio button HTML. The <input> tag for each radio button does however have the following attributes:

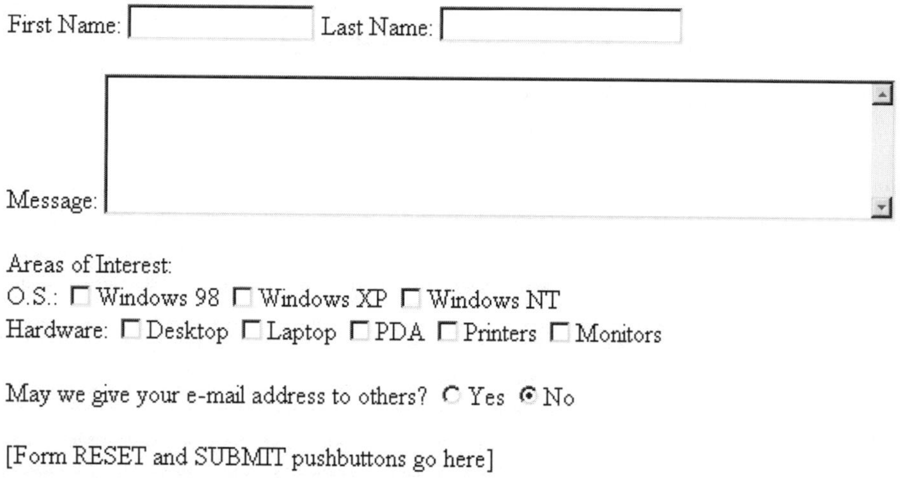

First Name: [   ]   Last Name: [   ]

Message: [   ]

Areas of Interest:
O.S.: ☐ Windows 98 ☐ Windows XP ☐ Windows NT
Hardware: ☐ Desktop ☐ Laptop ☐ PDA ☐ Printers ☐ Monitors

May we give your e-mail address to others? ○ Yes ● No

[Form RESET and SUBMIT pushbuttons go here]

Figure 3-7   A form with Yes/No radio buttons

- *type*   Set to "radio" to let the Web browser know that the form element is a radio button.

- *id*   Used to assign a unique name to a radio button. You can use the value of the *id* attribute to refer to the selected status of a specific radio button in a script embedded in the Web page HTML.

- *name*   A name used to identify a group of radio buttons. The Web browser passes the name of the button group and the value of the selected radio button's *value* attribute as a name/value pair to the Web browser when the visitor clicks Submit. If the visitor does not select one of the radio buttons in the button group (as defined by the name given to the radio buttons in the group), the Web browser will not pass a name/value pair for the group to the Web server.

- *value*   Text string passed to the Web server as the "value" portion of the name/value pair if the site visitor clicks the radio button to select it. The Web browser sends only the *name* and *value* (that is, the name/value pair) of the one selected radio button in each button group to the Web server when the visitor clicks Submit.

- *checked*   By including the *checked* attribute in the <input> tag for a radio button, you tell the Web browser to select the radio button when it draws the form (and each time the site visitor clicks Reset). In the current example, the third-to-last line of code tells the Web browser to select the No radio button in the ShareEmail button group.

The <input> tags with the *type* attribute set to "radio" in the current example tell the Web browser to place two radio buttons in the button group ShareEmail on a form named ExampleForm. The Web browser makes sure that the site visitor selects only one of the radio buttons in a button group. (The Web browser considers all the radio buttons with the same value for the *name* attribute to be in the same button group.) When the visitor clicks a radio button in a button group, the Web browser clears the button group's previous selection (if any), and puts a black dot in the radio button the visitor clicked to make that radio button the button group's selected item. (Unlike a check marked check box, clicking a currently selected radio button does not clear the selection.)

Validating Radio Button Group Selections Prior to Submitting Form Results

The Web browser allows the Web site visitor to select only a single radio button from any group of radio buttons with the same *name* attribute value. As such, you need not use JavaScript to test for multiple radio button selections within a single radio button group. However, the Web browser does not force the site visitor to select at least one of the radio buttons in any button group. As such, you must write a validation function that checks the number of radio buttons selected in each button group that you do not want the visitor to skip.

Suppose, for example, that your form includes the two groups of radio buttons shown in Figure 3-8.

USE IT If each of the radio buttons in the first group has its *name* attribute set to "Contact_Ok", and each of the buttons in the second group has its *name* attribute set to "User_Count", you can use the following JavaScript to ensure that the visitor selects one radio button from each of the two radio button groups:

```
<html><body>
<script language="JavaScript">
<!--
  function ValidateForm(Form)
  {
   function countSelections(buttonGroup)
   {
    for (i = 0;  i < buttonGroup.length;  i++)
      {
       if (buttonGroup[i].checked) return (true);
      }
     return (false);
   }
//** Other form validation statements **

   if (!countSelections(Form.Contact_Ok))
     {
      alert("Please select either \"Yes\" or \"No\" from the" +
            " \"Contact\" options.");
      return (false);
     }
   if (!countSelections(Form.User_Count))
     {
      alert("Please select one of the \"User Count\" options.");
      return (false);
     }
   return(true);
  }
// -->
</script>
```

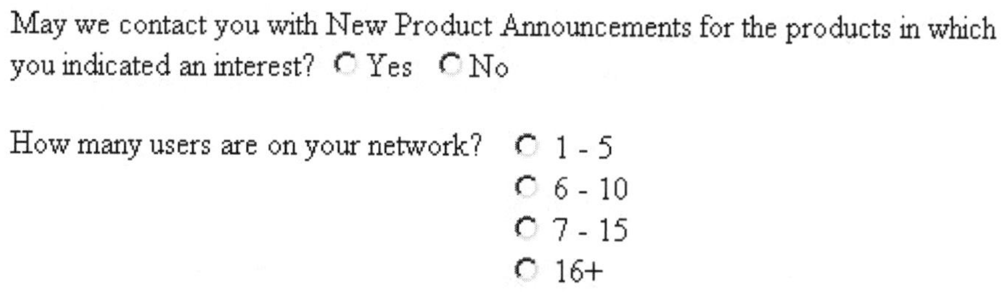

May we contact you with New Product Announcements for the products in which you indicated an interest? ○ Yes ○ No

How many users are on your network? ○ 1 - 5
　　　　　　　　　　　　　　　　　　 ○ 6 - 10
　　　　　　　　　　　　　　　　　　 ○ 7 - 15
　　　　　　　　　　　　　　　　　　 ○ 16+

Figure 3-8　Two groups of radio buttons from a form on a Web page

Notice that each button group has a *length* property that you can use to "step through" the group button array—checking the value of the *checked* property for each button in the group. By passing first the Contact_Ok button group and then the User_Count button group to the *countSelections()* function, you can use the same code to check for a selection in each of the two radio button groups— even though each button group has a different number of buttons. The *checked* property value of the selected radio button in each button group is True. Therefore, the *countSelections()* function will return True for any button group passed to it in which at least one radio button was selected. For any button groups in which the visitor failed to make a selection (or said another way, for any radio button groups the user skipped, the function will return False). The *ValidateForm()* function (which called the *countSelections()* function), in turn, will return a value returned by the *countSelections()* function to the calling *onSubmit* attribute in the <form> tag.

As you learned in the preceding Tip, to have the Web browser execute the form validation function when the visitor clicks Submit, add the *onSubmit* attribute to the form's <form> tag, such that it reads something like this:

```
<form name="ExampleForm" onSubmit="return ValidateForm (ExampleForm)"
      action="http://NVBizNet2.com/_scripts/_pl/FrmScrpt.CGI"
      method="POST"
      enctype="application/x-www-form-urlencoded">
```

Make sure you do not omit the *return* that precedes the *ValidateForm()* function call; otherwise, the Web browser will still submit the form results to the Web server, even if the *ValidateForm()* function returns a value of False to indicate that a problem occurred with the form's data. When written correctly (as in the current example), the *onSubmit* attribute tells the Web browser to execute a JavaScript function to validate the form results after the site visitor clicks Submit. If the function returns True, the Web browser will submit the form results to the URL specified as the value of the *method* attribute in the <form> tag. Otherwise, the Web browser will return to form data entry.

Placing a Drop-Down List (Selection Menu) on a Form

To allow Web site visitors to choose one or more items from a drop-down list, place a selection menu on the form by inserting the menu options between a set of start and end select tags (<select></select>).

USE IT   For example, to create the selection menu (or drop-down list) shown at the bottom of the form in Figure 3-9, add the start and end select tags (<select></select>) and start and end option tags (<option></option>) shown near the end of the following form definition:

```
<form name="ExampleForm">
<p>First Name: <input type="text" name="FirstName" size="15">
   Last Name: <input type="text" name="LastName" size="20"></p>
<p>Message: <textarea name="TextMessage" rows="5" cols="60">
            </textarea></p>
<p>Areas of Interest:<br>
   O.S.: <input type="checkbox" name="Win98" value="ON">Windows 98
         <input type="checkbox" name="WinXp" value="ON">Windows XP
         <input type="checkbox" name="WinNT" value="ON">Windows NT <br>
   Hardware: <input type="checkbox" name="DT" value="ON">Desktop
             <input type="checkbox" name="LT" value="ON">Laptop
             <input type="checkbox" name="PDA" value="ON">PDA
             <input type="checkbox" name="Prtr" value="ON">Printers
             <input type="checkbox" name="Mon" value="ON">Monitors </p>
<p>May we give your e-mail address to others?
   <input type="radio" value="Yes" name="ShareEmail">Yes
   <input type="radio" value="No" checked name="ShareEmail">No</p>
<p>Select Highest Level of Authority:<br>
   <select size="1" name="PurchaseInvolvement">
     <option value="MPD">Make Purchase Decision</option>
     <option value="SV">Select Vendor</option>
     <option value="SP">Select Product</option>
     <option value="SR">Specify Requirements</option>
     <option value="AN">Assess Needs</option>
   </select></p>
<p>[Form RESET and SUBMIT pushbuttons go here]</p>
</form>
```

Once again, the text title (or label) that describes the purpose of the drop-down menu (Select The Highest Level Of Authority, in the current example) is not a part of the selection list HTML. The drop-down list's <select> tag has the following attributes:

- *size*   The number of menu items (or options) visible onscreen at one time. In the current example (with *size="1"*), the form shows only a single item until the site visitor clicks the drop-down list button to the right of the selection menu. If you set the *size* attribute to a value greater than one (1), the Web browser will display the drop-down list as a list of items (with a scrollbar, if needed) instead of as a single item with a drop-down list button.

- *id*   Used to assign a unique name to a drop-down list element. You can use the value of the *id* attribute to refer to the selected status of the items on the selection list within scripts embedded on the Web page.

- *name*   A name used to identify the drop-down list element on the form. You can use the value of the *name* attribute to refer to the selected status of items in the selection (or drop-down) list within a script executed by the Web browser. Moreover, the Web browser will pass to the Web server the value of the *name* attribute as the "name" portion of the name/value pair for each list item the site visitor selects.

- *multiple*   If the *multiple* attribute is present in the drop-down list element's <select> tag, the Web browser will let the site visitor select more than one item from the drop-down list. Otherwise, the Web browser will ensure that the visitor selects only a single item by "deselecting" the previous item selected (if any) when the site visitor clicks a new item on the list.

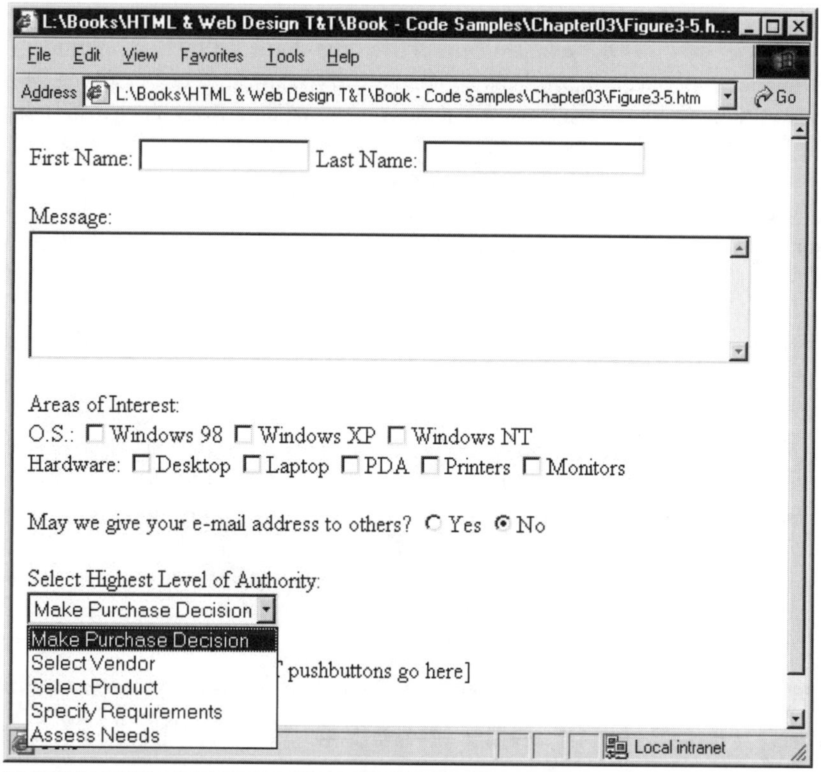

Figure 3-9   A form with a drop-down list (selection menu)

To add the list items to a drop-down list, enclose each item text between start and end option (<option></option>) tags between the list's start and end selection list tags (<select></select>). Each <option> tag may have the following attributes:

- *value*   Text string passed to the Web server as the "value" portion of the name/value pair if the site visitor clicks the item in the drop-down menu (or selection list) to select it. The Web browser sends only the *name* (of the drop-down list) and (option) *value* (that is, the name/value pair) of the selected list items (or options) to the Web server when the visitor clicks Submit. If the <option> tag has no *value* attribute, the Web browser will send to the Web server the selection item text (found between the start and end option tags [<option></option>]) as the "value" portion of the name/value pair.

- *selected*   By including the *selected* attribute in the <option> tag for an item on the drop-down list, you tell the Web browser to select the item when it draws the selection list and each time the visitor clicks Reset.

The Web browser indicates the selected item(s) in a drop-down list by highlighting it (or them). If the <select> tag does not have a *multiple* attribute, the site visitor can select only one item from the drop-down list. When the visitor is allowed to choose only one item from the selection list, the Web browser will clear the previous selection (if any) when the visitor clicks a new selection.

To allow the site visitor to select more than one item from the drop-down list, include the *multiple* attribute in the drop-down list's <select> tag. Moreover, if you want your site visitors to select more than one item from a drop-down list, be sure to prompt them to make multiple selections with text such as "select all that apply" and "hold down the CTRL key as you click list items to make multiple selections". (Even if you allow multiple selections, the Web browser will deselect previous selections, if any, if the site visitor clicks a drop-down list item without holding down the CTRL key.)

▶ **NOTE**

If you want the visitor to make at least one selection from drop-down list (that is, from the selection menu), be sure to include a blank selection (option) as the first item in the list. That way, if the visitor makes no selection from the list, the form results will have a blank value within the name/value pair for the selection list that the Web browser sends to the Web server. If you do not include a blank item at the beginning of the list, the form results will appear as if the visitor selected the first item on the list—even if the visitor made no selections. See the next Tip for details.

Verifying the Visitor Has Made a Selection List Choice Prior to Submitting Form Results

Validating visitor selections from a selection (or drop-down) menu is similar to verifying that the visitor has made at least one selection from a radio button group (which you learned about in the preceding Tip). To tell the Web browser to let the visitor make only a single selection from the menu, omit the *multiple* attribute from the <select> tag. Conversely, you can tell the browser to allow the

visitor to make multiple selections by including the *multiple* attribute in the form element's
<select> tag. Therefore, as was the case with the radio button group, you can let the Web browser
limit the number of selections the visitor can make from the selection menu. As such, you need only
validate that the user makes at least one choice.

USE IT   If you want the visitor to select at least one of the items on a selection list, make the first
item in the list read something like "-- Select One --" or "- Select At Least One -" to
prompt the visitor to make a selection from the list. Then, prevent the visitor from selecting the first
item (because it is a prompt and not a "real" menu choice). The following JavaScript, for example,
will check a selection list named Company_Type to make sure that the site visitor selected at least
one of the items on the list (other than the first item, which is item zero [0]):

```
<html><body>
<script language="JavaScript">
<!--
  function ValidateForm(Form)
  {
//** Other form validation statements **

   if (Form.Company_Type.options[0].selected)
     {
       alert("The first \"Company Type\" option is not " +
             "a valid selection. Please choose one of " +
             "the other options.");
       Form.Company_Type.focus();
       return (false);
     }

   if (Form.Company_Type.selectedIndex < 1)
     {
       alert("Please select one of the \"Company Type\" "+
             "options.");
       Form.Company_Type.focus();
       return (false);
     }
   return(true);
  }
// -->
</script>
```

The selection list's *selectedIndex* property contains an index of the item(s) the visitor selected
from the drop-down menu. To prevent the visitor from selecting the first item in the list, you must
make sure that the first item (that is, the item with index zero [0]) was not selected, and *then* check
to see if at least one of the other items on the list (with index value of one [1] or more) was.

As you learned in the two previous Tips, to have the Web browser execute the form validation function when the visitor clicks Submit, add an *onSubmit* attribute to the form's <form> tag, such that it reads something like this:

```
<form name="ExampleForm" onSubmit="return ValidateForm(ExampleForm)"
      action="http://NVBizNet2.com/_scripts/_pl/FrmScrpt.CGI"
      method="POST"
      enctype="application/x-www-form-urlencoded">
```

Make sure you do not omit the *return* that precedes the *ValidateForm( )* function call. Otherwise the Web browser will still submit the form results to the Web server, even if the *ValidateForm( )* function returns a value of False to indicate it has found a problem with the form results. When written correctly (as in the current example), the *onSubmit* attribute tells the Web browser to execute a JavaScript function to validate the form results after the site visitor clicks Submit. If the function returns True, the Web browser will submit the form results to the URL specified by the value of the *method* attribute in the <form> tag. Otherwise, the Web browser will return to form data entry, placing the cursor in the form element specified by the focus method in the JavaScript.

Changing the Items Available on a Selection List Based on Visitor Supplied Information

Earlier in this chapter, you learned that a selection list is a menu from which the site visitor can select either one or several choices depending on whether or not you included the *multiple* attribute in the selection list's <select> tag. (If you insert the *multiple* attribute in the tag, the Web browser will let the site visitor select more than one item from the menu.) Although you must specify whether the visitor can make multiple selections from the menu within the selection list's definition, you can change the selections available on the menu at any time—even after the browser has drawn the selection list onscreen.

Suppose, for example, that you have a form such as the one shown in Figure 3-10, which asks site visitors to enter the names of family members and then to select the name of the oldest person on the list.

USE IT   In the current example, the selection menu (shown above the Submit and Reset buttons in Figure 3-10) has only a single item, the prompt "-- Family Member Names --". To have the Web browser add another item (that is, the name of another family member) to the selection list, program a generic form button object to call a JavaScript function that adds an item to the list, with code similar to the following:

```
<input type="button" value="Add Name to List"
       onClick="addToList(ExampleForm)"></p>
```

Next, define the JavaScript *addToList( )* function that the Web browser will call when the visitor clicks the Add Name To List button by inserting the following JavaScript after the <body> tag in the

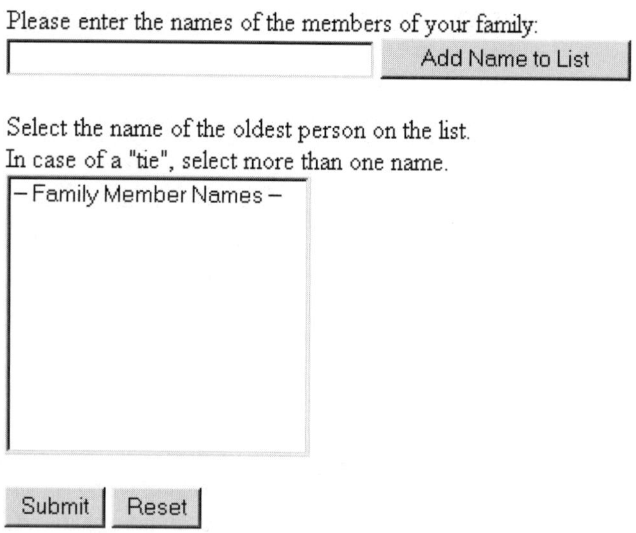

Please enter the names of the members of your family:

[   ] [Add Name to List]

Select the name of the oldest person on the list.
In case of a "tie", select more than one name.

```
- Family Member Names -




```

[Submit] [Reset]

Figure 3-10   A form in which data entered into a text field changes the items on a selection list

Web page HTML. (The function name and button label value you use will depend on the function you want the Web browser to perform when the visitor clicks the button.)

```
<script language="JavaScript">
<!--
  function addToList(Form)
  {
   var NextItem = Form.OldestFamilyMember.length;
   var NewName  = Form.MemberName.value;

//Make sure the name wasn't left blank
   if (NewName == "")
     {
      alert("Please enter a name first!");
      return;
     }
//Add a new "option" (i.e. item) to the selection list
   if (Form.OldestFamilyMember.options[0].value == "PromptText")
     NextItem = 0;
//the comma (,) in the '",' appended to the NewName parameter
//in the Option() constructor adds a comma separator between
//quoted items in the options list
   Form.OldestFamilyMember.options[NextItem] =
     new Option(NewName, '"'+NewName+'",', 0, 0);
//Clear the name entry form element
```

```
    Form.MemberName.value = "";
    Form.MemberName.focus();
    return;
  }
// -->
</script>
```

After checking to make sure the visitor entered "something" into the text field for the family member name, the *addToList()* function adds a new item to the selection list by using the following syntax:

```
SelectListName.options[NextItemIndex] =
  new Option(OptionText, OptionValue, SelectedByDefault,
            SelectedWhenAdded);
```

In the current example, both the *SelectedByDefault* and *SelectedWhenAdded* parameters in the *new Option()* function call are set to zero (0). As such, new items added to the selection list are unselected by default, and the Web browser does not automatically select an item as the visitor adds it to the selection list. If you want the Web browser to select each item as the visitor adds it to the menu, set the value of the *SelectedWhenAdded* parameter to one (1).

Sending All Selection List Values to the Web Server Through a Hidden Field

In the preceding Tip, you learned how to use the JavaScript *new* operator to add additional options (that is, items) to a selection list in response to the site visitor's inputs into a text field on the form. However, when the visitor clicks Submit, the Web browser sends only the values of the selection list's selected items to the Web server as part of the form results. Normally, this is exactly what you want the Web browser to do—send only the values of item(s) the visitor selected, because you already have a list of all the items in the list.

However, when you ask a site visitor to add items to a selection list, you want the Web browser to send not only the values of the menu's selected items, but also the values of all the unselected items as well. Otherwise, there is no reason to ask the visitor to add the items to the selection list in the first place. You could just have the visitor enter the values the visitor would select from the item list into a text field or a text area.

Suppose, for example, that you ask site visitors to enter the makes and models of their favorite cars and then to select the cars they have actually owned from the selection list. For marketing purposes, you would want the list of all the types of cars each visitor might be interesting in purchasing in the future based on the visitor's favorite car make and model list. Similarly, in the example used in the preceding Tip, you wanted the list of the names of all the visitor's relatives. Otherwise, you would have simply asked the visitor to enter the names of the oldest relatives into a single-line or multiline text field.

To retrieve the values of both the selected and unselected items on a selection list, let the browser's default behavior add the list of selected items to the form results. Then, use a JavaScript function to store the values of all the menu items in a hidden field before you let the Web browser send the form results to the Web server. (Although the Web browser does not display onscreen the values in a form's hidden fields, it does send their names and values to the Web server along with the other form data after the visitor clicks Submit.)

USE IT   For example, to have the Web browser send to the Web server all the names of relatives that the visitor added to the selection list in the preceding Tip, insert the following JavaScript between the start and end body tags (<body></body>) in the Web page HTML:

```
<script language="JavaScript">
<!--
//other JavaScript functions (if any)

  function prepFormResults(Form)
  {
//statements to validate form results (if any)
//return false; if invalid data found

  var itemList = "";
  for (var i = 0; i < Form.OldestFamilyMember.length; i++)
  {itemList = itemList +
               Form.OldestFamilyMember.options[i].value;
  Form.RelativeNameList.value = itemList;
  }
  return;
  }
//other JavaScript functions (if any)

// -->
</script>
```

The *prepFormResults()* function in the current example assumes that the form's definition includes the following hidden field definition into which it can place the concatenated string of item values from the selection list:

```
<input type="hidden" name="RelativeNameList" value="">
```

The function also assumes that the form's <form> tag includes an *onSubmit* attribute which names the *prepFormResults()* function as the function the Web browser is to call before sending form results to the Web server after the visitor clicks Submit. (You need the Web browser to execute the *prepFormResults()* function before submitting the form results, so the function can place the values of the items on the selection menu into the form's hidden field: *RelativeNameList.*)

Adding a Reset Button to a Form

Most forms include a Reset button on which the site visitor can click to return all form elements (text input fields, check boxes, radio buttons, drop-down list selections) to their initial values.

USE IT For example, to place a Reset button on a form (such as the Reset button shown near the lower-left corner of the form in Figure 3-11), insert the following <input> tag with its *type* attribute set to "reset" between the form's start and end form tags (<form></form>) wherever you want a Reset button to appear:

```
<input type="reset">
```

If you want the form's Reset button to have a label other than the word "Reset", simply include the text you want on the label as the attribute's value in the Reset button's <input> tag. For example, to label the Reset button "Clear Form", specify the button's <input> tag as follows:

```
<input type="reset" value="Clear Form">
```

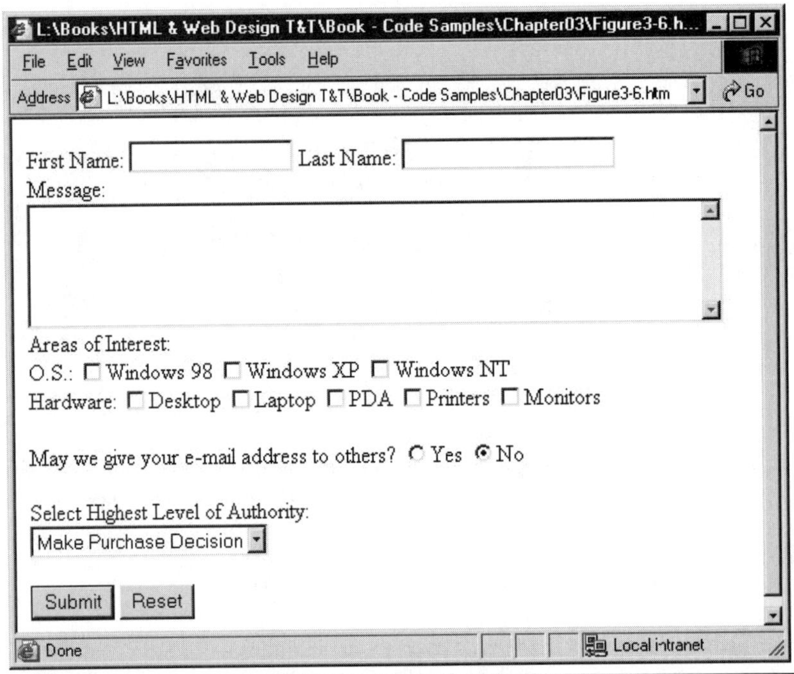

Figure 3-11   A form with a Submit button and a Reset button

Although the Web browser returns all form elements to their initial values and selected states when the site visitor clicks the Reset button, the browser does not move the cursor (or focus) to the first element on the form. As a result, the site visitor must scroll the screen contents to the start of the form and position the cursor within the form's first element to start over after clicking Reset. If you have a form that spans more than one Web page, you may want to display a text message that tells the user how to get back to the start of the form. Or, you may want to move the cursor to the start of the form yourself by having the Web browser execute an *onReset* script after the site visitor clicks Reset. (The next Tip shows you how to insert an *onReset* attribute in the form's <form> tag so that the Web browser will execute an *onReset* script when the visitor clicks Reset.)

Preventing a Visitor from Clearing Form Elements Accidentally

When a site visitor clicks a form's Reset button, you want the Web browser to clear all visitor input and reset all form elements to their original, default values. Fortunately, Web browsers "know" what they are supposed to do in response to a mouse click on a form's Reset button, so you need not write a script that performs the default "reset form" behavior. However, if your form has many elements, or if the visitor entered a large amount of text data into multiline text fields, you may want to make your form more user-friendly by prompting the site visitor to confirm a form reset before actually letting Web browser clear the form.

USE IT Like the *onSubmit* attribute that tells the Web browser to execute a script before performing the normal, default action of submitting form results to the Web server, the *onReset* attribute tells the Web browser to execute a script before "resetting" the elements in a form. For example, the *onReset* attribute in the following form definition tells the Web server to execute the JavaScript function *PreResetProc()* when the site visitor clicks Reset:

```
<form name="ExampleForm"
  onReset="return PreResetProc(ExampleForm)"
  onSubmit="return ValidateForm(ExampleForm)"
  action="http://NVBizNet2.com/_scripts/_pl/FrmScrpt.CGI"
  method="POST"
  enctype="application/x-www-form-urlencoded">
```

The JavaScript function, in turn, can do any type of pre-reset processing you want it to do—including replacing the standard "clear all form elements" reset with a reset that clears only some of the form's fields. Like the *onSubmit* attribute, the *onReset* attribute tells the Web browser to call a JavaScript function. Then, if the function returns a False, the Web browser will not execute the standard form reset. Conversely, if the *onReset* function returns True, the Web browser will execute the standard "clear all form elements" reset.

For example, the following JavaScript used with a form defined by the preceding <form> tag will display the confirmation dialog box shown here:

```
<html><body>
<script language="JavaScript">
<!--
   function PreResetProc(Form)
   {
    if (confirm("Are you sure you want to clear the form's " +
               "fields?"))
      {
//*** Other Pre-Reset processing (if any) ***

       Form.FirstName.focus();
       return (true);
      }
    else
      {
       Form.FirstName.focus();
       return (false);
      }
   }
// -->
</script>
```

If the visitor clicks Cancel, the confirm method and the *PreResetProc()* function, in turn, will return a value of False and the Web browser will not execute its standard form reset action. Conversely, if the Web site visitor clicks OK, the confirm method and the *PreResetProc()* function, in turn, will return a value of True, and the Web browser will reset all form elements to their original, default values.

Adding a Submit Button to a Form

Asking your Web site visitors to fill out a form serves no purpose unless you also provide them with a way to transmit the information they enter and selections they make to you or to a script on the Web server for processing. When the site visitor clicks Submit, the Web browser sends the form results (that is, the name/value pairs for text boxes and selected radio buttons, check boxes, and selection list items selected) to the Web server. The Web server, in turn, passes the form results to the program (or script) named in the <form> tag's *action* attribute, which you learned about at the beginning of this chapter.

USE IT   To insert a Submit button on a form, insert the following code between the form's start and end form tags (<form></form>) wherever you want the button to appear:

```
<input type="submit" value="Submit" name="B1">
```

The Submit button has the following attributes:

- *value*   The text you want the browser to place on the Submit button as a label. In the current example, the Web browser will label the Submit button with the text "Submit" (as shown previously in Figure 3-11). If you omit the *value* attribute, the Web browser will provide the Submit button with a browser-specific, default label. (Both Internet Explorer and Netscape Navigator, for example, label the Submit button with the text "Submit Query" if you omit the *value* attribute.)

- *name*   You can use the *name* attribute to associate a name with the Submit button. If you want the Web browser to include in the form results it sends to the Web server a name/value pair with the Submit button's name and value (that is, its text label), set both the *name* and *value* attributes in the button's <input> tag.

If the form's <form> tag has an *onSubmit* attribute, the Web browser will execute the script named by the attribute before sending the form results to the Web server. Typically, you will use the *onSubmit* attribute to tell the Web browser to execute a function that validates the information entered into the form elements. If the form results are valid, the validation function will return a value of True, and the Web browser will send the form results to the Web server. Conversely, if the script finds that the information entered by the site visitor violates one or more of the form's data validity rules (as programmed into the validation function), the script will alert the site visitor to the error(s) and return a value of False. The Web browser, in turn, will not send the form results to the Web server, so the site visitor can correct the values entered into the form elements before attempting to submit the form results again. (Within the Tips titled, "Validating Text Element Data Prior to Submitting Form Results," "Validating Radio Button Group Selections Prior to Submitting Form Results," and "Preventing a Visitor from Clearing Form Elements Accidentally," you will find information that shows you how to add the *onSubmit* attribute to the form's <form> tag so that the Web browser will execute a script prior to submitting form results to the Web server after the visitor clicks Submit.)

Replacing the Standard Submit and Reset Buttons on a Form with Other Graphics Images

Every form has a Submit button on which the visitor must click to send the form results (that is, the information entered and selections made on the form) to the URL given by the value of the *action* attribute in the form's <form> tag. Most forms also have a Reset button the visitor can use to clear information entered on the form and reset its elements to their original, default values. When a Web browser encounters the following <input> tags in your Web page HTML, it draws the standard Submit and Reset buttons (shown here) on the form:

```
  Submit  |  Reset
```

```
<input type="submit" value="Submit"> <input type="reset">
```

USE IT   You can use a graphics image in place of a standard form button by replacing the button's <input> tag with a hyperlink. For example, to replace the standard Submit button with a graphics image that performs the same function, you would use the following anchor tag syntax in place of the button's <input> tag:

```
<a href="#" onClick="document.formname.submit();return false">
   <img src="SubmitButtonGraphic.GIF"></a>
```

Thus, to use the graphics image in a file named submit.gif as the submit button on a form whose *name* attribute is set to "ExampleForm", you would replace the standard Submit button's <input> tag with the following:

```
<a href="#" onClick="document.ExampleForm.submit();return false">
   <img src="Submit.GIF"></a>
```

Setting the *href* attribute in the hyperlink's <a> tag to a pound sign (#) prevents the Web browser from moving to an offscreen section of the current Web page by pointing the hyperlink to a nonexistent (null) bookmark. After all, you do not want the Web browser to follow a hyperlink to an actual bookmark or to another URL when the site visitor clicks the hyperlink's graphics submit button (specified by the *src* attribute in the hyperlink's <img> tag). Instead, you want the Web browser to execute the JavaScript form submit method as specified by the *onClick* attribute in the hyperlink's <a> tag.

Similarly, if you want to replace a form's standard Reset button with a graphics image, replace the button's <input> tag in the form definition with the hyperlink syntax:

```
<a href="#" onClick="document.formname.reset();return false">
   <img src="ResetButtonGraphic.GIF"></a>
```

Notice that the hyperlink for the graphics Reset button tells the Web browser to execute the JavaScript form reset method (instead of the JavaScript form submit method linked to the graphics Submit button in the preceding example). Therefore, if the form's *name* attribute value is "ExampleForm", and the filename of the reset button graphic is reset.gif, you would code the form's graphics image reset button as follows:

```
<a href="#" onClick="document.ExampleForm.reset();return false">
   <img src="Reset.GIF"></a>
```

▶ **NOTE**

When you replace a form's standard Reset button with a hyperlinked graphics image that performs the same function, the Web browser will still execute the JavaScript function specified by the onReset *attribute in the <form> tag before clearing the form's elements. However, if you replace the form's standard Submit button, the Web browser will no longer execute the function specified by the* onSubmit *function. The next Tip shows you how to get the Web browser to execute a script prior to sending form results to a Web server—even after you replace the standard Submit button.*

Sending Form Results by E-Mail Without a CGI Script

As mentioned previously in this chapter, *form results* are the name/value pairs the Web browser sends to the address (that is, the URL) set by the *action* attribute in the form's <form> tag when the visitor clicks Submit. Each name/value pair consists of the *name* of the form element followed by its *value*. Perhaps the easiest way to understand what the Web browser sends when it submits form results to the Web server is to tell the Web browser to use its e-mail setup to send form results to an e-mail address.

USE IT For example, the action attribute in the <form> tag in the first line of the following form definition tells the Web browser to send the form results as an e-mail message to kki@NVBizNet.com. (To send form results in an e-mail message to yourself, substitute your e-mail address for kki@NVBizNet.com.)

```
<form name="MailToForm" action="mailto:kki@NVBizNet.com"
      method="POST" title="MailTo Test" enctype="text/plain">
<p>First Name: <input type="text" name="FirstName" size="15">
   Last Name: <input type="text" name="LastName" size="20"><br>
   E-Mail: <input type="text" name="E-MailAddr" size="20"></p>
Areas of Interest:<br>
  O.S.: <input type="checkbox" name="Win98" value="ON">Windows 98
        <input type="checkbox" name="WinXp" value="ON">Windows XP
        <input type="checkbox" name="WinNT" value="ON">Windows NT <br>
<p>May we give our your e-mail address to others?
  <input type="radio" value="Yes" name="ShareEmail">Yes
  <input type="radio" value="No" checked name="ShareEmail">No</p>
<p><input type="submit" value="Submit">
  <input type="reset"></p>
</form>
```

If the site visitor fills out the form generated by the preceding code, shown in Figure 3-12, and then clicks Submit, the Web browser will send the following form results by e-mail to the address that follows *mailto:* in the form's *action* attribute setting:

Figure 3-12   A form with information to be sent by e-mail

```
FirstName=Konrad
LastName=King
E-Mail Addr=Konrad@NVBizNet.com
WinXp=ON
ShareEmail=Yes
```

Notice that the form results include form element names separated by an equals sign (=) from the value the visitor entered or selected. The "text/plain" setting of the *enctype* attribute (in the second line of the form definition) told the Web browser to format the form results in this manner. Had the form definition contained the default *application/x-www-form-urlencoded* encoding, the Web browser would have sent the form results as a single line of comma-delimited text with an ampersand (&) separating each form element's name from its value. However, regardless of the encoding type, the important thing to understand is that the Web browser sends form results as name/value pairs. While form results include all text box names (whether they contain any data or not), the Web browser sends only the name/value pair for each check box, radio button, or selection list item selected when the visitor clicks Submit.

Bear in mind that using *mailto:* in the *action* attribute does not work in all browsers. In order to send form results by e-mail in the manner described here, the visitor's system must have an e-mail program installed and configured properly. However, *mailto:* gives you a quick way to test your forms by sending the form results as plain text to your own e-mail address. Using *mailto:*, you can submit a form (to yourself via e-mail) without involving your ISP or a CGI script on the Web server. In Chapter 10 on PHP and Chapter 11 on ASP, you will learn how to process form results at the Web server. By using a Web server–based script, you can send form results by e-mail (through SMTP [mail] server)—even if the visitor does not have an e-mail program installed.

Controlling the Layout of Form Elements and Text with HTML Tables

The example code for forms given thus far in this chapter makes no attempt to lay out forms elements other than to separate them with paragraph (<p>) and line break (<br>) tags. Sometimes, however, you may have a group of check boxes or radio buttons you want to align vertically to make the form more visually appealing. Similarly, when you create a survey form, you may want all the text along the left side of a form and all the "answers" in a column down the right side. Fortunately, you can both use tables within a form and enclose an entire form within the cells of a table.

Suppose, for example, that you have a multiline text box such as the one shown in Figure 3-13, whose label appears along the lower-left corner (as is the default when placing text in the same paragraph as a form element or a graphics image).

USE IT   To move the label, "Message:" in the current example, to the upper-left corner of the form element, place the label and the form element in a two-column table such as that defined by the following:

```
<table border="0" cellspacing="0" width="100%" id="TextboxTable"
       cellpadding="0" height="63">
 <tr>
   <td width="10%" valign="top" height="63">Message: </td>
   <td width="90%" height="63">
     <textarea name="TextMessage" rows="5" cols="60"></textarea>
   </td>
 </tr>
</table>
```

Separate the text label from the form element by placing each in its own table cell, so that you can align the label text independent of the text box (form element). Insert the label in the table's left cell and the text box in the right cell. Then, tell the Web browser to display the text at the top of the left cell by setting the cell's *valign* attribute in its (<td>) tag to "top". Next, set the *height* attribute for

Figure 3-13   A label that precedes a form element in its default position at the element's lower-left corner

each of the two <td> tags to the pixel-height of the multiline text box. When you are done, the Web browser will draw the label next to the upper-left corner of the text box, as shown in Figure 3-14.

USE IT   In addition to aligning labels with form elements, you can also use one or more tables in a form to visually group form elements. Suppose for example that you want to line up the check boxes below the text box shown in Figure 3-14. Because each of the check boxes has a single-line label, you can place both the check box and its label in the same table cell. (If a check box has a multiline label, you would put the check box and label in separate cells so that you could place the check box where you want it in relation to its label—like you did the "Message:" label next to the multiline text box earlier in this Tip.) If you place the check boxes shown in Figure 3-14 into a multicolumn, multirow table as follows, you can create the arrangement of check boxes shown below the text box in Figure 3-15:

```
<p>Areas of Interest:<br>
<table border="0" cellpadding="0" cellspacing="0" width="573"
      id="CheckboxTable">
<tr><td width="43"  align="left" valign="top">O.S.:</td>
   <td width="109" align="left" valign="top">
     <input type="checkbox" name="Win98" value="CHECKED">
     Windows 98</td>
   <td width="117" align="left" valign="top">
     <input type="checkbox" name="WinME" value="CHECKED">
     Windows ME</td>
   <td width="115" align="left" valign="top">
     <input type="checkbox" name="WinNT" value="CHECKED">
     Windows NT </td>
```

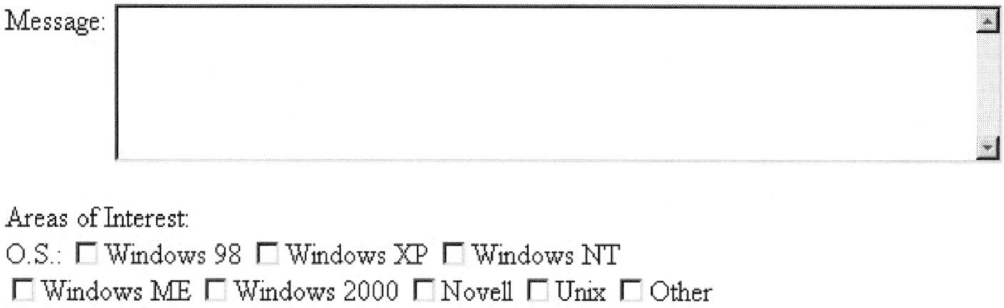

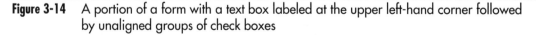

Figure 3-14   A portion of a form with a text box labeled at the upper left-hand corner followed by unaligned groups of check boxes

```
      <td width="189" align="left" valign="top">
        <input type="checkbox" name="Win2000" value="CHECKED">
        Windows 2000</td></tr>
<tr><td width="43" height="30" align="left" valign="top">
       </td>
      <td width="109" height="30" align="left" valign="top">
        <input type="checkbox" name="WinXP" value="CHECKED">
        Windows XP </td>
      <td width="117" height="30" align="left" valign="top">
        <input type="checkbox" name="Novell" value="CHECKED">
        Novell</td>
      <td width="115" height="30" align="left" valign="top">
        <input type="checkbox" name="UNIX" value="CHECKED">
        Unix </td>
      <td width="189" height="30" align="left" valign="top">
        <input type="checkbox" name="OtherOS" value="CHECKED">
          Other</td>
</tr></table></p>
```

Notice that tables used to lay out forms hold form elements and text in position while remaining invisible themselves. While creating the form, you may want to set the *border* attribute in the form's <table> tags to one (1), so you can see the "grid" of cells that make up the table. Then, after you have things aligned as you want, set the *border* attributes to zero (0) to make the gridlines disappear. 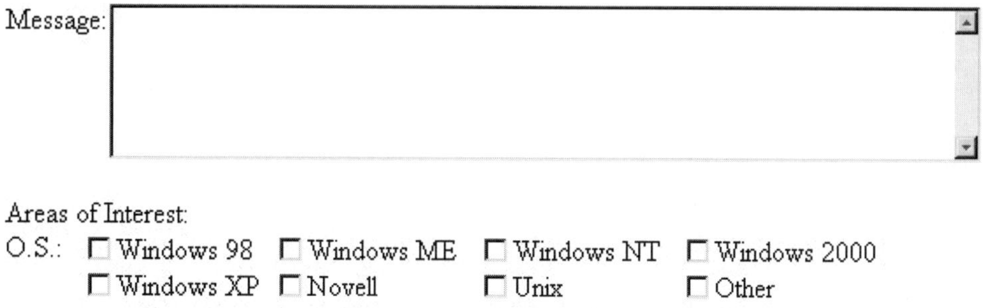

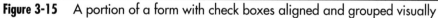

Figure 3-15   A portion of a form with check boxes aligned and grouped visually

Creating a Shortcut Key for Form Navigation with a <label> Tag

In the introduction at the beginning of this chapter and in the preceding tips, the "label" next to the form elements was like any other text on a Web page. Although you can place plain text next to a form element to serve as a label that lets site visitors know the purpose of the text box, radio button, or check box, the visitor cannot use the letters in the plain text labels to move around on the form, place a check mark in a check box, or select a radio button. To use text as shortcuts for navigation and form element selection, you must enclose each text label within a set of start and end label tags (<label></label>).

USE IT For example, to create the form element labels shown in Figure 3-16, enclose the text next to each input field within start and end label tags (<label></label>) as follows:

```
<label for="FN" accesskey="F"><u>F</u>irst Name: </label>
  <input type="text" name="FirstName" id="FN" size="15"><br>
<label for="LN" accesskey="L"><u>L</u>ast Name: </label>
  <input type="text" name="LastName" id="LN" size="20"><br>
<label for="EM" accesskey="E"><u>E</u>-mail: </label>
  <input type="text" name="Email" id="EM" size="30"><br>
<table border="0" cellspacing="0" width="563" cellpadding="0">
  <tr><td width="62" valign="top" height="63">
      <label accesskey="M" for="TM">
        <u>M</u>essage: </label></td>
    <td width="501" height="63">
      <textarea id="TM" name="TextMessage" rows="5" cols="60">
      </textarea></td></tr>
</table>
```

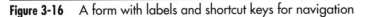

Figure 3-16   A form with labels and shortcut keys for navigation

Each of the <label> tags has two important attributes:

- *for*   The value of the *for* attribute in the <label> tag must match the *id* value of the form element to which you want to link the label.
- *accesskey*   The shortcut key the visitor can use to move to the text box (if the label is linked to a text box), to select a radio button (if the label is linked to a radio button), or to check or clear a check box (if the label is linked to a check box). To use the shortcut key, the visitor must hold down the ALT key while pressing the *accesskey* value.

The *accesskey* value need not appear in the label text (that is, the text enclosed between the start and end label tags) nor does it modify the text in any way. However, to use the shortcut key, the visitor needs to know what it is. As such, use one of the letters in the label text as the *accesskey* attribute's value and underline the letter (or number) you use to provide the site visitor with a visual cue. Notice that the start and end underline tags (<u></u>) in the current example tell the Web browser to underline the shortcut key value in each of the text labels. As a result, using labels to navigate to or select elements on a form becomes similar to making selections from Windows application menus with shortcut keys.

▶ *NOTE*

Although form element labels (defined by placing text between start and end text label tags[<label></label>]) are a part of the HTML 4 standard, only Internet Explorer 4.0 (and later) and Netscape 6.0 (and later) currently support them. Web browsers that do not support the tags will still display the "label" text they enclose. However, visitors using browsers without label support will not be able to use the accesskey *values to navigate the form or make form element selections.*

Instructing the Web Browser to Execute a Form Validation Function with the *onClick* Attribute

In previous Tips in this chapter, you learned how to use the *onSubmit* attribute in the <form> tag to tell the Web browser to execute a data validation function prior to sending form results to the URL named in the <form> tag's *action* attribute. Unfortunately, if you replace the form's standard Submit button with a graphics image hyperlinked to the JavaScript form submit method, the Web browser will no longer execute the script specified by the *onSubmit* attribute before sending the form results to the Web server.

USE IT   To have the Web browser execute a script prior to sending form results when using a graphics image as the form's Submit button, set the value of the *onClick* attribute in the hyperlink anchored on the graphics image to the name of the form validation function instead of the JavaScript form submit method. Then, if the validation function determines that the form results are valid, have the script execute the JavaScript form submit method. Otherwise, code the script to return to form data entry, so the visitor can correct the problems(s) with the form results. The validation function would be in the following form:

```
<script language="JavaScript">
<!--
  function validateAndSubmit(Form)
  {
//**** Form Results Validation Statements which set     ****
//**** the Boolean "Form_Results_Valid" TRUE if results ****
//**** valid or FALSE if not                            ****
    if (Form_Results_Valid)
      {
       Form.submit();
      }
    else
      {
//**** Alert the visitor to errors ****
       return;
      }
  }
// -->
</script>
```

(In the first *if* statement, the Form_Results_Valid is only a placeholder to indicate that if the form results are valid, you would do the "form submit," otherwise you would alert the visitor to the error and return.) The *onClick* attribute in the hyperlink anchored on the graphics image used as a Submit button, in turn, would reference the form validation function instead of the JavaScript form submit method, as follows:

```
<a href="#" onClick="validateAndSubmit(ExampleForm);return false">
    <img src="SubmitButtonGraphic.gif"></a>
```

(In this example, ExampleForm is the name of the form whose form results the site visitor wants to submit, and SubmitButtonGraphic.gif is the filename of the graphics image used as the form's Submit button.)

If you are using standard buttons (and not graphics images in place of buttons) on your form, you can still use the *onClick* attribute in the button definition to tell the Web browser to execute a script that first validates and then submits the form's data. Simply replace the form's standard Submit button (created with an <input> tag whose *type* attribute is set to "submit"), with a form button object defined as follows:

```
<input type="button" value="Submit"
    onClick="validateAndSubmit(ExampleForm)">
```

Passing Values to the Web Server Through Hidden Fields

A *hidden* field, as its name implies, is a form element that—though part of a form's definition—is not visible to the person filling out the form. You can use hidden fields to pass name/value pairs to the Web server in addition to the information entered by the site visitor. For example, the following HTML will tell the Web browser to display the form shown here:

Username: [   ]
Password: [   ]

[Submit] [Reset]

```
<form name="ExampleForm" method="POST"
      action="http://NVBizNet2.com/_scripts/_pl/FrmScrpt.CGI"
      enctype="application/x-www-form-urlencoded">
  Username:
    <input type="text" name="Username" id="UN" size="20"><br>
  Password:
    <input type="text" name="Password" id="PW" size="20"><br>
  <p><input type="button" value="Submit"
            onClick="validateAndSubmit(ExampleForm)">
    <input type="button" value="Reset"
            onClick="resetForm(ExampleForm)"></p>

  <input type="hidden" name="LoginAttempts" value="0">
  <input type="hidden" name="LoginDateTime">
  <input type="hidden" name="ExampleFor"
         value="HTML & Web Design Tips & Techniques">
</form>
```

Notice that the three input fields at the end of the form definition in the current example have a *type* attribute value of "hidden" and are not visible onscreen (as shown previously). Although the Web browser does not display the form's three hidden fields, the browser does send the name/value pair for each of the fields to the Web server along with the remaining (visible) form results, as shown in Figure 3-17.

USE IT You can set a hidden field's value by including a *value* attribute setting in the field's <input> tag as shown by the first and third hidden fields in the current example:

```
<input type="hidden" name="LoginAttempts" value="0">
<input type="hidden" name="ExampleFor"
       value="HTML & Web Design Tips & Techniques">
```

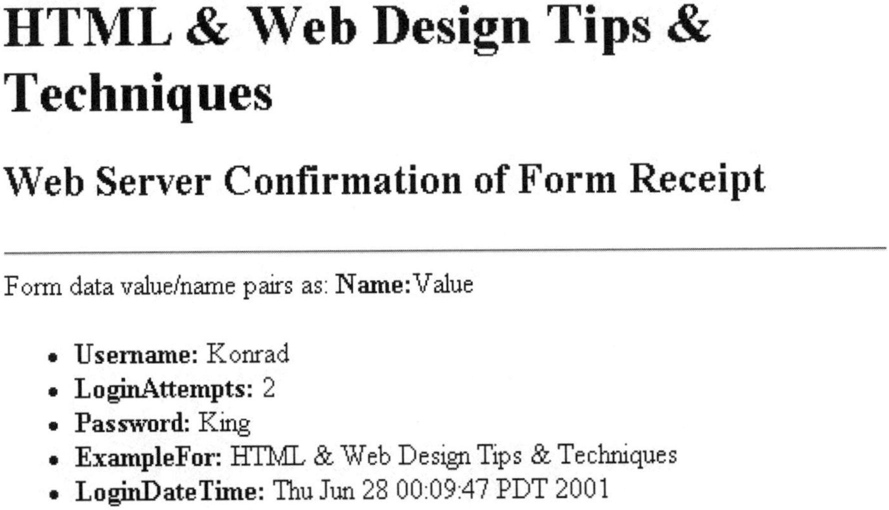

HTML & Web Design Tips & Techniques

Web Server Confirmation of Form Receipt

Form data value/name pairs as: **Name:** Value

- **Username:** Konrad
- **LoginAttempts:** 2
- **Password:** King
- **ExampleFor:** HTML & Web Design Tips & Techniques
- **LoginDateTime:** Thu Jun 28 00:09:47 PDT 2001

Figure 3-17   Form results sent to the Web server after entering "Konrad" into the Username field and "King" into the Password field

Whether you assign a value to the hidden field initially or not, you can also assign a value to hidden fields in a JavaScript function. For example, the *validateAndSubmit()* function executed when the site visitor clicks Submit in the current example includes the following lines:

```
ExampleForm.LoginAttempts.value++;
ExampleForm.LoginDateTime.value = new Date();
```

The first line of code increments the value in the hidden field named LoginAttempts, and the second line assigns the current date and time to the hidden field LoginDateTime.

Hiding Visitor Input from View Within a Password Element

A password field is a variation of a single-line text field. Unlike hidden fields (which you learned about in the preceding Tip), the Web browser will display a password field onscreen. However, the Web browser will not display any text the visitor types into the field. Instead, the browser obscures the text from view by displaying an asterisk (*) for each character the site visitor enters. You would use a password field on a form whenever you do not want someone looking over the visitor's shoulder at the computer screen to see what the visitor is typing. Typically, you use password fields on forms wherever you ask for a password or other security code to login to a Web site or to an account on a Web site. Some of the more security-conscious sites even create the field that asks for a username or an account number as a "password" type field so that anything entered into the field is hidden from view.

USE IT To create a password field, insert an <input> tag such as the following on the form where you want the password field to appear:

```
<input type="password" name="Password" id="PW" size="20">
```

The value of the *type* attribute sets the password field apart from normal single-line text fields (which, as you know, have a *type* attribute value of "text"). By setting the <input> tag's *type* attribute to "password", you tell the Web browser to obscure anything entered into the field. (Although set to "Password", "PW", and "20" in the current example, you can set the password field's *name, id,* and *size* attributes to any desired value.)

▶ **NOTE**

Although the Web browser hides the information in a password field from sight by displaying asterisks (*), the browser does not encrypt the field's contents. As such, if you transmit the data entered into password fields unencrypted across a nonsecure connection, someone with the correct knowledge could intercept the (plain-text) password data and use it for some malicious purpose.

You will learn how to use login forms (with username [single-line text] and password fields) to log in to online databases in Chapters 10, 11, and 12. Moreover, Chapter 12's coverage of e-commerce will show you how to establish a secure connection with a Web server and how to encrypt your form results (including the data in a password field) so that unauthorized people will not be able to view it. For now, the important thing to understand is that a password field lets you hide visitor data input into a single-line text field from view.

Adding a Generic Button Object to a Form

In previous Tips, you learned how to insert Submit and Reset buttons on a form. Because almost all forms have both Submit and Reset buttons, browsers that support forms "know" what to do when the visitor clicks either of the two buttons. For example, Web browsers with forms support will send form results to the URL named by the *action* attribute in the form's <form> tag when the visitor clicks Submit (unless, of course, you change the Submit button's default behavior with an *onSubmit* attribute setting in the form's <form> tag). Similarly, Web browsers will clear data entered into all form objects and reset the form's elements to their initial, default values when the visitor clicks Reset unless you change the Reset button's default behavior with an *onReset* attribute setting in the form's <form> tag).

To create either a Reset button or a Submit button on a form, insert an <input> tag with a *type* attribute set to the type of button you want (that is, *type="reset"* for a Reset button and *type="submit"* for a Submit button). In addition to Reset and Submit buttons, you can use the

<input> tag to create a third type of button object whose function is not predefined. Typically, you will use this third, generic button type to tell the Web browser to execute a script of some kind when the visitor clicks the button.

USE IT Given the syntax used to create Reset and Submit buttons, it will come as no surprise that you can create a "generic" button on a form by inserting an <input> tag similar to the following anywhere between the form's start and end form tags (<form></form>):

```
<input type="button" value="ButtonLabel" onClick="scriptName">
```

The "button" value of the *type* attribute tells the Web browser it is to draw a button on the form. After drawing the button, the browser uses the text assigned to the *value* attribute in the <input> tag as a label on top of the button. (Be sure the text string you assign to the *value* attribute tells the site visitor what clicking the button will do.) When the visitor clicks the button, the Web browser will execute the script specified by the value of the *onClick* attribute in the button's <input> tag.

You can use generic button objects on a form to execute scripts that do such things as calculate the sum of other form elements, display text messages, load a new Web page into a frame or window, or to add items to a selection list. In short, the function of a generic button you add to a form is limited only by your imagination and the methods available in the scripting language you use.

Enabling and Disabling Form Elements on-the-Fly

Sometimes item selections on a form are mutually exclusive. For example, if you ask the site visitor "Are you currently married?", and the visitor clicks the No radio button in answer to the question, you do not want the visitor to enter a name into the Spouse text field as well. Similarly, if you have a group of check boxes in which the visitor is to click all that apply, and the visitor checks the check box labeled None or None Of The Above, you want to prevent the visitor from selecting any of the other check boxes in the group. Each form element has a *disabled* attribute that you can use to either allow or prevent the site visitor from making any changes to the element.

▶ **NOTE**

Some older browsers may not support the disabled *attribute. As such, your validation function must check to make sure that the visitor has entered only valid data into the form results—even if you have a script that sets the status of certain input fields to "disabled".*

USE IT Suppose, for example, that you use the form shown in Figure 3-18 to get the visitor's marital status. By executing the following JavaScript function, you can have the Web browser gray out the prompt for the visitor to enter the spouse's name and prevent the site visitor from modifying or even clicking the cursor (that is, the form's focus) into the text field.

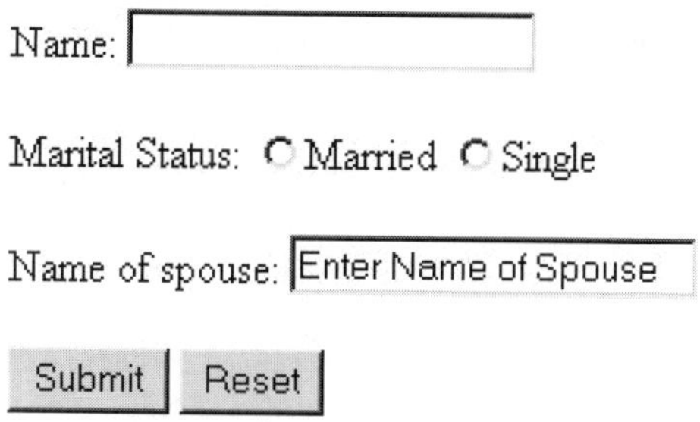

Figure 3-18   A form with radio buttons that control the *disabled* attribute status of a text field

```
function disableSpouseName(Form, status)
{
 if (status) Form.SpouseName.value = "Enter Name of Spouse";
 Form.SpouseName.disabled = status;
 return;
}
```

To tell the Web browser when to execute the function, code the form's MaritalStatus radio buttons as follows:

```
<p>Marital Status:
  <input type="radio" name="MaritalStatus" value="Married"
    onClick="disableSpouseName(ExampleForm, false)">Married
  <input type="radio" name="MaritalStatus" value="Single"
    onClick="disableSpouseName(ExampleForm, true)">Single</p>
```

The *onClick* attribute in the <input> tag for each radio button tells the Web browser to execute the *disableSpouseName()* function when the visitor clicks either radio button. By passing either True or False to the *disableSpouseName()* function, the Web browser either enables or disables the SpouseName field (labeled Name Of Spouse in Figure 3-18). For example, if the visitor clicks the Married radio button, the Web browser passes the value False to the *disableSpouseName()* function. The function, in turn, sets the *disabled* attribute of the form's SpouseName element to False, which enables the element, so that the visitor can enter the name of the spouse into the text field. Conversely, if the visitor clicks the Single radio button, the Web browser passes the value True to the *disableSpouseName()* function. The function, in turn, sets the *disabled* attribute of the form's SpouseName element to True, which disables the element to prevent the visitor from entering the name of a spouse into the text field.

You can disable any of the form's elements, including any buttons on the form. For example, if you want to disable the form's Submit button initially, you would define it as follows:

```
<input disabled type="Submit" name="Submit" value="Submit">
```

Then, to enable the Submit button while the visitor fills out the form, have the Web browser execute a JavaScript function that includes the following statement:

```
FormName.Submit.disabled=false;
```

In short, you can disable any form element by executing a JavaScript statement with the following syntax:

```
FormName.ElementName.disabled=true;
```

Conversely, you can enable any form element by executing a similar JavaScript statement that sets the *disabled* attribute to False.

▶ *NOTE*
_____

If you use a JavaScript statement to change the status of an element's disabled *attribute, the Web browser's standard "reset" function will not change the element's status back to the original default. Therefore, if you disable a form element that was initially enabled, you must use an* onReset *attribute in the form's <form> tag to have the Web browser execute a function that changes the element's disabled status back to False when the visitor clicks Reset.*
_____

CHAPTER 4

Cascading Style Sheets (CSS)

TIPS IN THIS CHAPTER

▶ Applying Multiple CSS Rules to a Single Selector   170

▶ Selecting a Typeface with the *font-family* Property   172

▶ Specifying the Size of Text with the *font-size* Property   174

▶ Creating Overlapping Text   177

▶ Aligning Web Page Text   179

▶ Controlling Margins and Line Height   181

▶ Displaying Text Within Columns   183

▶ Working with Borders   186

▶ Indenting Paragraphs and Controlling Letter, Word, and Line Spacing   188

▶ Offsetting Text with Initial Caps   189

▶ Customizing the Appearance of Hyperlinks   191

▶ Creating a Drop-Shadow Effect   192

▶ Applying a Border Graphic   194

▶ Positioning Background Images and Watermarks   196

▶ Floating Images and Text   199

▶ Customizing the Appearance of Lists   201

▶ Creating Text and Image Effects with Filters   203

▶ Aligning Labels with Form Elements and Adding Color to Forms   206

▶ Displaying a Gallery of Thumbnails with Captions   209

▶ Controlling the Cursor   212

▶ Layering Web Page Elements   214

▶ Sending Your Style Sheet Through a Validator   216

One of the recurring challenges you have when creating Web pages is positioning elements exactly where you want them to appear on each page. A Web page has no internal x-y coordinate system to which you can refer when inserting text, images, and other objects. In Chapter 2 of this book, you learned how to use an HTML table to create a grid of cells that hold your Web page elements in place. Unfortunately, using invisible tables for page layout complicates your Web page HTML by adding tags (at least two for each row and column in the table). Moreover, hidden tables make your Web page harder to maintain. Suppose, for example, that you want to add a picture or some text at a specific location on the page. To do so often requires that you recode all or a portion of the layout table to get a new cell into place where you want the additional content to go.

A Cascading Style Sheet (CSS) is a set of specifications (called *rules*) that give you complete control over the layout of your Web page and the appearance of its content. You can use CSS rules to select a background color, graphics image, or watermark to display behind other content. In addition, the CSS *position* property eliminates the need for hidden page layout tables by letting you tell the Web browser exactly where to place each element on the page. Finally, with CSS rules you can specify the typeface and control the size, color, and appearance of text. In addition to using plain, boldface, and italics, you can add drop shadows and create other special effects—without converting character data into slower loading graphics images.

Although you can add a style sheet to a Web document several different ways, perhaps the easiest is to insert the style sheet rules within the Web page header as shown here:

```
<html>
<head>
  <style type="text/css">
    ... style sheet rules ...
  </style>
</head>
<body>
  ... Web page elements/content ...
</body>
</html>
```

Although the name is long, the "Cascading Style Sheet" is simply a set of statements between the start and end style tags (<style></style>) near the start of the preceding HTML. When the Web browser reads the HTML document, the browser applies the rules (that is, the formatting and positioning statements) it finds within the style sheet to Web page elements within the body section

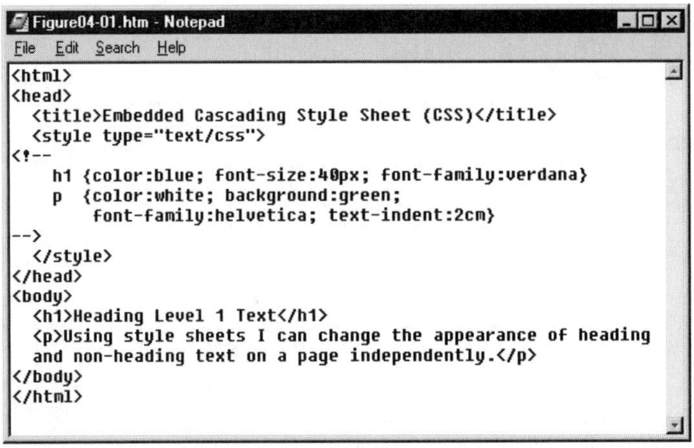

```
Figure04-01.htm - Notepad
File  Edit  Search  Help
<html>
<head>
  <title>Embedded Cascading Style Sheet (CSS)</title>
  <style type="text/css">
<!--
    h1 {color:blue; font-size:40px; font-family:verdana}
    p  {color:white; background:green;
        font-family:helvetica; text-indent:2cm}
-->
  </style>
</head>
<body>
  <h1>Heading Level 1 Text</h1>
  <p>Using style sheets I can change the appearance of heading
  and non-heading text on a page independently.</p>
</body>
</html>
```

Figure 4-1   A Web page with an embedded Cascading Style Sheet

of the page. Figure 4-1 shows a simple style sheet with two rules that instruct the Web browser how to style the two elements within the Web page body.

In addition to positioning page elements and formatting text, CSS rules let you control the space between characters, words, lines, and paragraphs. Moreover, using style sheet rules, you can specify the width of Web page margins, the width of the borders around sections of text and other elements, and the alignment of "floating" text and objects (such as graphics images) inserted within text elements. Figure 4-2, for example, shows how Internet Explorer implements the following style sheet rules that float an image to the left of surrounding text:

```
<head>
  <style type="text/css">
<!--
    p {margin-left:5em; margin-right:5em; text-align:justify}
    img {float:left; border-width:25px; border-color:white}
-->
</head>
```

Note CSS rules in this example both indent the text that surrounds the image away from the left- and right-hand sides of the Web page and create a white border between the text and the sides of the image.

When CSS entered the scene in late 1996, style sheets promised to enhance and ease the Web page design process by giving designers the following:

- Precise control over layout, fonts, colors, backgrounds, and other typographical effects.

- A way to change the appearance and formatting of an unlimited number of Web pages by changing just one document—the style sheet.

- The ability to create eye-catching pages using less code, which in turn, leads to smaller Web pages that the Web browser can download and display more quickly.

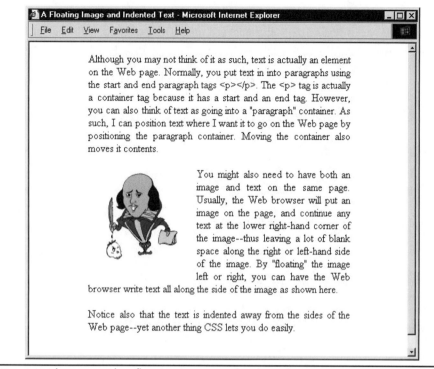

Figure 4-2   A Web page with a floating image and indented text

Despite its lukewarm reception (as a competitor to the then "hot" Dynamic HTML, DHTML), CSS is starting to make good on its promises as both Netscape and Microsoft Web browsers support more and more of the capability defined in the CSS specification.

Separating Content from Appearance

HTML (as originally envisioned) was not designed to control the appearance of a Web page. HTML was supposed to let authors specify the elements to include on the page and let the Web browser decide how the content actually appeared onscreen. Remember, HTML was developed to let anyone with a computer, a Web browser, and a connection to the Internet display any HTML document— regardless of the video card capabilities or monitor resolutions.

However, as developers expanded Web page content to include multicolor text of various typefaces and sizes, graphics images, pictures, and animations, designers were less and less willing to let the browser dictate how the Web page would look. Before CSS, designers had to use HTML tables for page layout and insert transparent (spacer) GIFs throughout the Web page content to control margins and the space between objects on a page. In addition, through HTML formatting tags and attributes within the <font> tag and the <body> tag, Web designers gained some control over the appearance of the page text and background.

Style sheets, meanwhile, let you write layout and formatting instructions within the Web page header section or in an external file apart from the HTML used to specify page content. Moreover, rather than using tables and graphics for layout, CSS rules are simple text statements that let you position and format one or several page elements at a time. Thus, working with content separately from appearance makes your Web pages easier to maintain and faster to update. Suppose, for example, you want to change the typeface used on the pages throughout an entire Web site. Without style sheets, you need to edit (or add) one or more <font> tags on every page. By placing the typeface specification within a CSS document linked to each page, you need only change a single CSS rule to use a new typeface throughout the pages on a Web site.

Creating a Style Sheet

To create a style sheet, simply write one or more CSS rules between start and end style tags (<style></style>) within the header section of the Web page HTML. (You will learn how to create style sheets as external documents later in this chapter.) For example, start your favorite text editor (such as Windows Notepad) and enter the following HTML:

```
<html>
<head>
  <title>Embedded Cascading Style Sheet (CSS)</title>
  <style type="text/css">
    h1 {color:blue; font-size:40px; font-family:verdana}
    p  {color:white; background:green; font-family:helvetica;
        text-indent:2cm}
  </style>
</head>
<body>
  <h1>Heading Level 1 Text</h1>
  <p>Using style sheets I can change the appearance of heading
  and non-heading text on a page independently.</p>
</body>
</html>
```

In this example, the code between the start and end style tags defines the style sheet. For now, do not worry about the individual statements (called rules) within the style sheet—you will learn about CSS syntax in a moment. Simply save your Web page to an HTML file (such as CSS_Test1.htm). Next, open the HTML document in your Web browser to display a page similar to that shown in Figure 4-3.

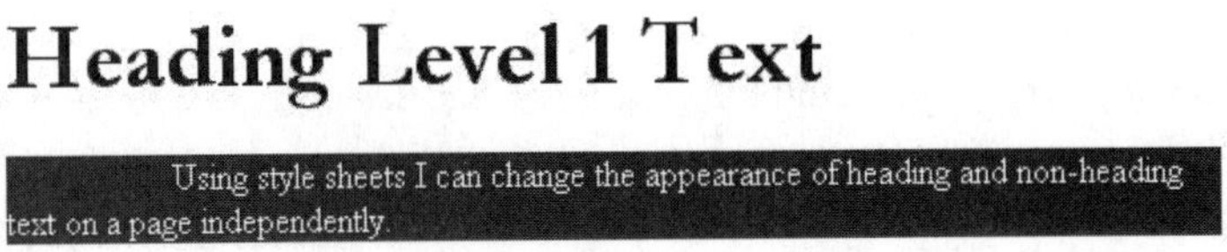

Figure 4-3   Web page with a style sheet that formats heading and paragraph text

Understanding CSS Terminology

A style sheet consists of one or more rules. A style sheet *rule* is simply a formatting or positioning instruction the Web browser will apply to a specific type of HTML element. The style sheet in the preceding example consists of two rules. The first rule instructs the Web browser to display text enclosed within start and end level-1 heading tags (<h1></h1>) using the Verdana typeface and blue characters that are 40 pixels in size:

```
h1 {color:blue; font-size:40px; font-family:verdana}
```

The second CSS rule instructs the Web browser to indent by two centimeters the first line of text enclosed within start and end paragraph tags (<p></p>) and to display the text using the Helvetica typeface with green letters on a white background:

```
p {color:white; background:green; font-family:helvetica;
   text-indent:2cm}
```

The following simple CSS rule consists of a "selector" (h1) that specifies the HTML element to which the rule will apply and a rule that tells the browser to display the element in blue:

```
h1 {color:blue}
```

CSS statements always take the form of *selector {rule}*. Within the braces that follow the selector, you can place one or more rules, which you separate with a semicolon. The previous rule tells the Web browser to display in blue all text between start and end level-1 heading tags (<h1></h1>). The *selector* (*h1*, in this example) is the HTML tag to which the browser is to apply the rule; the *declaration* (*color:blue*, in this example) is the position or formatting instruction the Web browser is to apply. A declaration, similar to a rule, consists of two parts: a *property* (such as *color*) and a *value* (such as *blue*).

As you saw from the two rules in the preceding example, you can group multiple declarations within the braces following the selector(s) in a CSS rule. Simply insert a semicolon (;) between each pair or declarations. Figure 4-4, for example, points out the individual parts of the first, multideclaration rule from the style sheet on the Web page shown previously in Figure 4-3.

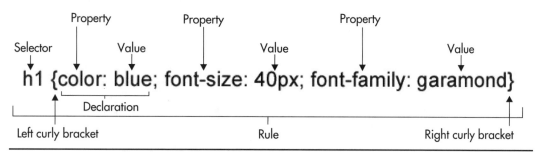

Figure 4-4   A CSS rule with a single selector and three declarations

You can use any HTML tag as a selector and a single rule may have more than one selector. For example, to direct the Web browser to apply the same CSS rule to level-2 heading, paragraph, and unordered list text you might write a rule such as this:

```
h2, p, ul {color:green; font-family:arial}
```

This rule tells the Web browser to display all level-2 heading, paragraph, and unordered list text in green using the Arial typeface. Note any HTML tag is fair game as a selector. As such, you can apply CSS rules to images (by using the *img* selector) and tables (by using the *table* selector).

For example, start your favorite text editor (such as Windows Notepad) and enter the following HTML:

```
<html>
<head>
  <title>CSS Rule Used to Style a Table</title>
  <style type="text/css">
    table {background:green; color:white; font-size:20px;
           position:absolute; left:150px; top:200px}
  </style>
</head>
<body>
  <h1>Table with White Text and a Green Background</h1>
  <table border="5">
    <tr><td>Row 1, Column 1</td>
        <td>Row 1, Column 2</td></tr>
    <tr><td>Row 2, Column 1</td>
        <td>Row 2, Column 2</td></tr>
  </table>
</body>
</html>
```

As you learned at the start of this section, the code between the start and end style tags (<style></style>) defines the style sheet. The *table* selector tells the Web browser to apply the style sheet rule to tables inserted on the page. Therefore, the Web browser will create the table in this example with a green background and white text that is 20 pixels in size. Moreover, the Web browser will place the table 150 pixels to the right of the left margin and 200 pixels below the top of the Web page. Now, save your Web page to a HTM file (such as *CSS_Test2.htm*) and then open the HTML document in your Web browser to display a page similar to that shown in Figure 4-5.

Understanding Inheritance

As you add text elements to a Web page, you often insert one element within another. For example, when you boldface text, such as the words *boldface text* in the following, you are actually inserting a boldface element into a paragraph element:

```
<p>You insert one element within another whenever you enclose
   text within one set of container tags within text between
```

```
another set of start and end tags. For example, this
<b>boldface text</b> is a boldface element inserted within
a paragraph element.</p>
```

When the Web browser styles an inserted element, the browser applies first the formatting instructions associated with the outer (enclosing) element and then the specific styles (if any) associated with the element itself.

In CSS terms, an element contained within another is a *child* and the enclosing element is its *parent*. Thus, in the previous example, the paragraph text that surrounds the boldface element (boldface text) is the parent, and the boldface element itself is the child. If you enclose one type of page element within another, the Web browser applies the parent's (that is, the enclosing element's) CSS rule to the child (that is, to the enclosed element).

Suppose, for example, that you have a style sheet with the CSS rules shown here:

```
p {color:blue}
b {color:red}
```

Given the following HTML, the Web browser will display in blue the text *All text in* and in red the text *boldface will be red--including boldface italics*:

```
<p>All text in <b>boldface will be red--including boldface
   <i>italics</i>.</b></p>
```

The boldface element (that is, the text enclosed within start and end boldface tags) is a child of the paragraph text element. The italic element, in turn, is a child of the boldface element, because the italic

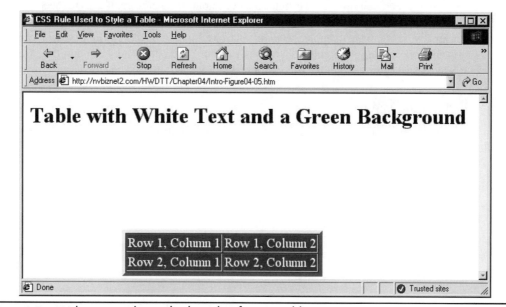

Figure 4-5 Web page with a style sheet that formats tables

element's start and end tags are enclosed within the boldface element's start and end tags. Because the style sheet in this example has no rule for italics elements, the Web browser applies the parent element's rule—that is, the boldface (*b*) selector's rule—to the child element. Thus, the Web browser will display the italic text in red.

If the style sheet in this example had only the rule for the paragraph selector (*p*), the Web browser would display all text in blue. First, the parent/child relationship between the boldface and paragraph element would dictate that the boldface (child) element would inherit the paragraph (parent) element's rule—"display the text in blue." Then, the parent/child relationship between the italic (child) element and the boldface (parent) element would cause the italic (child) element to inherit the boldface (parent) element's rule.

Adding CSS Styles to a Web Page

Before the Web browser will apply CSS rules to format or position elements on a Web page, you must include the CSS rules within the Web page HTML. You can use four different methods to add CSS styles to the Web page HTML:

- Embed a style sheet
- Link to an external style sheet
- Import an external style sheet
- Add styles inline within HTML tags

When you embed a style sheet, the Web browser will apply the style sheet's rules to the elements only on the page in which you inserted the style sheet declaration. Therefore, if a style sheet's rules are unique to a particular Web page, embed the style sheet within the header section of the Web page HTML. Conversely, if you want to apply the same style sheet to two or more Web pages, store the style sheet in an external file (preferably with a .css extension) and either link or import the external style sheet, as you will learn to do in the following sections.

Embedding a Style Sheet

When you *embed* a style sheet, you insert the style sheet's rules between start and end style tags (<style></style>) within the Web page header section:

```
<head>
  <title>Embedded Cascading Style Sheet (CSS)</title>
  <style type="text/css">
<!--
    h1 {color:blue; font-size:40px; font-family:verdana}
    p  {color:white; background:green; font-family:helvetica;
        text-indent:2cm}
-->
  </style>
</head>
```

The *type* attribute in the <style> tag tells the Web browser the type of style sheet to expect.

Normally, browsers that do not support CSS will ignore all code between the start and end style tags when the <style> tag has a *type* attribute set to "text/css". Unfortunately, some older browsers do not recognize start and end style tags. Although these browsers will ignore the HTML tags they do not understand, they will display the contents of the style sheet as body text (instead of applying the sheet's rules to the body elements). To prevent older browsers from displaying style sheets onscreen, enclose the style sheet rules within an HTML comment block, that is between HTML start and end comment tags (<!-- -->). Web browsers that support style sheets will ignore the comment tags and still apply the style sheet rules.

Linking to an External Style Sheet

External style sheets are ideal for when you want to apply the same set of rules to elements on two or more Web pages. In fact, if you link an external style sheet to all the pages on a Web site, you can change CSS rules within a single file and affect the look of elements on pages throughout the site. Moreover, most Web browsers cache external style sheets, thus avoiding the delay in displaying pages while downloading the same style sheet file multiple times.

As its name implies, you can use a <link> tag to link an external style sheet to an HTML document. Instead of typing CSS rules into a style sheet in the header section within every page, you can point the site's HTML documents to a style sheet file. Then, when you change a property such as a typeface, size, or color within the external style sheet file, all your pages will reflect the change instantly.

To link to an external style sheet, insert a <link> tag such as the following in the header of your section of your Web page:

```
<head>
  <title>Linked Cascading Style Sheet (CSS)</title>
  <link rel=stylesheet href="styles.css" type="text/css">
</head>
```

Note that you do not enclose the <link> tag between a set of start and end style tags (<style></style>). In this example, the <link> tag tells the Web browser to use the CSS formatting rules in the file named styles.css. The *type* attribute identifies the file as a text file with CSS information, and the *href* attribute tells the Web browser the name, and if necessary, the path of the file with the style sheet definitions the browser is to open. If the Web browser is unable to locate the external style sheet file (specified by the *href* attribute in the <link> tag), the browser will use the browser's default settings as defined by the browser's preferences.

In addition to a *type* attribute the Web browser can use to avoid downloading style sheet types the Web browser does not support, you can include a *media* attribute to specify the medium or media to which the style sheet's rules apply. By reading the *media* attribute's value (within the <link> tag), the Web browser can selectively download style sheet files applicable only to the media the browser is using. For example, the Web browser can avoid downloading the following style sheet applicable to "tv" (that is, television) when displaying HTML documents on a standard computer screen:

```
<link rel=stylesheet href="WebTv.css" type="text/css"
    media="tv">
```

The available *media* attribute values are as follows:

all	For all output devices
aural	For speech synthesizers
braille	For presentation on tactile feedback devices
embossed	For braille printers
handheld	For small devices such as PDAs (which usually have monochrome screens, bitmapped graphics, and limited bandwidth)
print	For output to a printer
projection	For output to a projection device
screen	For nonpaged computer screens (the default)
tty	For teletype devices (using a fixed-pitch font)
tv	For television screens

Within the external style sheet file (such as *styles.css* for example), define the rules as follows:

```
h1 {color:blue; font-size:40px; font-family:verdana}
p  {color:white; background:green; font-family:helvetica;
    text-indent:1cm}
body {background:#ADD8E6; color:maroon}
```

Notice the absence of all HTML tags within the external style sheet. An external style sheet file should consist solely of CSS rules. Thus, external style sheets contain the same formatting rules as internal (that is, embedded) style sheets. However, you do not enclose the rules in an external style sheet file within start and end style tags or include any HTML tags at all.

Importing an External Style Sheet

Importing an external style sheet is similar to linking, which you learned about in the preceding section. The difference is that you can combine importing with other methods, whereas linking must stand alone. For example, although the header section in the preceding example can contain multiple link statements (to link multiple external style sheets), it cannot also contain embedded rules. Conversely, the following Web page header contains not only an *import* statement, but also embedded CSS rules that style level-two headings and restyle body text on the Web page:

```
<head>
  <title>Imported Cascading Style Sheet (CSS)</title>
  <style type="text/css">
<!--
    @import url(styles.css);
    h2   {color:purple; font-size:30px; font-family:helvetica}
```

```
   body {color:black}
-->
  </style>
</head>
```

In this example, the *@import* statement instructs the Web browser to retrieve the CSS rules within the styles.css file to which the browser adds the embedded rules that follow the *@import* statement. (If a style sheet header includes both *@import* statements and embedded rules, the *@import* statements must precede the CSS rule declarations.) If the rules in the imported style sheet(s) and the rule(s) embedded within the Web page are conflicting, the embedded rules win. For example, styles.css in the preceding example includes the following rule:

```
body {background:#ADD8E6; color:maroon}
```

However, the embedded rule for the *body* selector overrides the text color declaration and the Web browser will display Web page body text in black instead of maroon.

Unlike linked external style sheet files, which the browser can choose to download based on the value of the *type* or *media* attribute within the <link> tag, the Web browser *must* download all imported style sheet files. However, you can use *@import* statements to import multiple external style sheet files and override rules within those by embedding CSS rules within the Web page header.

Applying Styles Inline Within HTML Tags

You can apply a set of CSS formatting rules to a single Web page (by embedding an internal style sheet) or to all the pages on a Web site (by linking or importing the same external style sheet to each of the site's HTML documents). At times, however, you may want to apply a formatting instruction to a specific Web page element only (such as a single paragraph or heading) without creating a universal CSS rule for all elements of the same type.

Suppose, for example, that you want to indent a single level-2 heading 1.5 inches, and display the heading color as white text on a blue background. To specify a CSS formatting rule that applies only to a single tag, use the *style* attribute to specify the rule within the tag as <*tagname* style="*CSS Declarations*">. Thus, in this example, you would insert the CSS rule in the <h2> tag as shown here:

```
<html>
<head>
  <title>Inline Styles</title>
</head>
<body>
  <h2 style="text-indent:1.5 in; background:blue; color:white">
    This heading text is white against a blue background,
    indented 1.5 inches.</h2>
  <h2> This is a standard heading tag. </h2>
</body>
</html>
```

Thus, you use the *style* attribute in an HTML tag to specify the CSS formatting rule for the tag. In this example, the CSS rule applies only to the text of the level-2 heading in whose tag you inserted the *style* attribute with the CSS rule. As such, the browser again applies the browser's default level-2 formatting to the level-2 heading that follows the one to which you applied a CSS rule.

In short, using the *style* attribute to apply an inline style to a single HTML tag gives you precise formatting control of the text that follows the tag. The downside to using inline styles is that you must insert the same code within the Web page element's HTML tag each time you want the browser to apply the style. Moreover, changing a single inline style affects only one element on a Web page. For example, if you have three paragraphs with inline styles, you must make the same change three times (once in each <p> tag) if you want to change the text color in all three paragraphs from black to green.

Applying Multiple CSS Rules to a Single Selector

CSS rules make changing the format of text on a Web site's page easy. Using CSS, you can adjust the style for a given HTML tag by modifying a single CSS rule. Sometimes, however, you want to format a particular Web page element (such as paragraph text) differently in various parts of your Web pages. If you create multiple rules for the same selector (*p*, in this case), the browser will use the selector rule that appears last in the CSS. For example, the second rule in the following style sheet overrides the first:

```
<style type="text/css">
  p {color:red; font-size:18pt}
  p {color:black; font-size:12pt}
</style>
```

As a result, all paragraph text will be black, 12-point type.

To apply more than one CSS rule to an element, you must define a unique named class for each rule. After you define a class, you can apply its formatting to an element by placing the *class* attribute in the element's HTML tag as follows:

```
<p class="YourCSSClassName">
```

USE IT   Suppose, for example, that you want to create a *class* for critical text and another *class* for regular text. To create two classes of CSS rules, you add rules similar to the following to the style sheet:

```
<head>
  <title>CSS Class Declarations</title>
  <style type="text/css">
<!--
  p.critical {color:red; font-size:18pt; font-weight:bold}
  p.regular  {color:black; font-size:12pt}
```

```
-->
  </style>
</head>
```

You can use any name you like for a CSS class. However, be sure to insert a period (.) between the selector (for the HTML tag) and the class name in each CSS rule definition.

After reading the preceding style definition, the Web browser will have two classes of paragraph text styles at its disposal: *p.critical* and *p.regular*. The paragraphs you style as *p.critical* will have red, boldface, 18-point text. Likewise, paragraphs you style as *p.regular* will have black, 12-point text. The following code illustrates how you would use CSS classes to style paragraph text on a Web page:

```
<html>
<head>
  <title>Example: Using Class Selectors</title>
  <style type="text/css">
<!--
    p.critical {color:red; font-size:18pt; font-weight:bold}
    p.normal   {color:black; font-size:12 pt}
-->
  </style>
</head>
<body>
  <p class="critical"> This is red, 18 point, bold face </p>
  <p class="normal"> This is black 12 point text </p>
</body>
</html>
```

The Web browser will use the browser's default settings for any formatting options not specified by a CSS definition within the style sheet. For example, because the CSS rules in the preceding code did not specify a specific typeface, such as Arial or Helvetica, the browser will use its default typeface. Figure 4-6 shows how a Web page described by the preceding HTML will appear in a Web browser.

To make CSS class definitions more flexible, drop the selector from the class declaration. For example, as defined in the style sheet embedded within the header section of the preceding Web page HTML, "critical" and "normal" class rules are available only for use within <p> tags. Because the style sheet rules attach both classes to the paragraph (*p*) selector, you cannot apply the "critical" class to heading text with an HTML statement such as this:

```
<h1 class="critical">This is a critical heading</h1>
```

Given the class definitions in the HTML that produced Figure 4-6, the browser will display the level-1 heading in the browser's default level-1 heading style, because the "critical" class is undefined for level-1 headings.

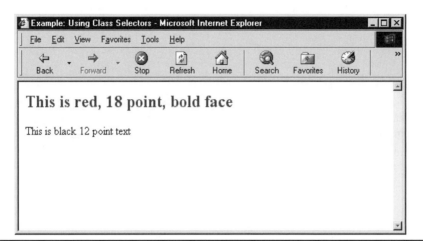

Figure 4-6   Class selectors let you quickly change the formatting of browser text

However, if you drop the selector reference from the class definition as follows, you can use the class name to style any tag within the body of a Web page:

```
<head>
  <title>Example: Using Unattached Class Selectors</title>
  <style type="text/css">
<!--
    .critical {color:red; font-size:18pt; font-weight:bold}
    .normal   {color:black; font-size:12 pt}
-->
  </style>
</head>
```

Note that the "unattached" class name in each definition starts with a period (.) and has no selector for an HTML tag. Now, the following statements cause the Web browser to display the first level-1 heading in red, 18-point, boldface, and the second level-1 heading as black 12-point text:

```
<h1 class="critical">This is a CRITICAL level-1 heading</h1>
<h1 class="normal">This is a normal level-1 heading</h1>
```

Therefore, if you define a CSS class without a selector, you can use the class to style any Web page element. Conversely, if you define a class attached to a particular selector, you can use the class to style only the HTML tag associated with that selector.

Selecting a Typeface with the *font-family* Property

Whether you select Times New Roman, Century Schoolbook, or Matisse ITC, the typeface the browser uses to display text content sets the mood for your Web page. Rather than leave it up to your site visitors to select the typeface (by setting the browser's default font to whatever they like), you should give your site the look you want. Fortunately, CSS rules make it easy to specify the typeface the Web browser is to use when displaying text on pages throughout your Web site.

USE IT   To specify the typeface you want the Web browser to use, add the *font-family* property declaration to a CSS rule. Suppose, for example, you want to create a Web page on which the browser displays all paragraph text in the Helvetica typeface. To create a CSS rule that links the Helvetica typeface to the <p> tag, use the paragraph selector (*p*) and a CSS *font-family* property declaration, as shown in the following code:

```
<head>
  <title>Selecting the Font-Family (i.e Typeface)</title>
  <style type="text/css">
<!--
    p {font-family:helvetica}
-->
  </style>
</head>
```

In this case, the CSS rule for the paragraph tag selector (*p*) tells the Web browser to display all text that follows a <p> tag using the Helvetica typeface. The *font-family* property setting between the curly braces ({ }) is the part of the CSS style declaration that tells the Web browser which font to use.

Instead of selecting a single font, you can create a CSS rule that specifies multiple typefaces. By specifying multiple typeface selections, you give the Web browser alternate choices in case the primary typeface you select is not installed on the visitor's computer. Bear in mind that if the visitor's system does not have the typeface(s) you specify, the Web browser will display the Web page text using the browser's default typeface. To reduce the chances of selecting a typeface unavailable on the visitor's system (and ending up with the browser's default font as a result), create the CSS rule with an alternate font selection (such as Times New Roman) and perhaps a third choice (such as Courier). (No theoretical limit exists as to the number of font choices you can include in a CSS font-family declaration.)

To create a CSS declaration with alternate fonts from which you want the browser to choose, list the font selections one after another in a CSS rule, such as that shown between the start and end style tags in the following:

```
<html>
<head>
  <title> Example of changing typeface </title>
  <style type="text/css">
    p {font-family:helvetica,"times new roman",courier}
  </style>
</head>
<body>
  <h1> Standard H1 heading </h1>
  <p> The Web browser displays text enclosed by the
```

```
        paragraph tags in Helvetica. If Helvetica is
        not available, the CSS declaration instructs
        the Web browser to locate Times New Roman,
        or finally Courier.</p>
    <p> If all three fonts are unavailable, the Web browser
        ignores the CSS declaration and substitutes the
        browser's default typeface.</p>
</body>
</html>
```

In this example, the *font-family* property instructs the Web browser to use Helvetica to display any text that follows a <p> tag. If Helvetica is not available on the visitor's computer, the Web browser searches for Times New Roman. Then, if Times New Roman is not available, the browser will look for Courier. If all the listed typefaces are unavailable, the Web browser substitutes the default typeface as defined by the Web browser's preference settings.

Specifying the Size of Text with the *font-size* Property

When working with the character size of Web page text, you typically have two goals. First, you want to make sure the text is large enough for the visitor to read comfortably. Second, you want the ability to vary the size of the headings and specific words or phrases for emphasis. Because different Web browsers (and even different versions of a particular brand of browser) often have different character size defaults, you must specify the font size of Web page text if you want Web browsers to display your content at a particular size.

Font size is especially important when a Web page has a lot of text. If you set the size too small, the strain of trying to read the text will frustrate visitors and cause them to leave without reading all the material. Conversely, unusually large characters are a distraction that might cause visitors to miss important information your Web page is trying to convey.

The CSS *font-size* property lets you specify the size of your Web page text. Moreover, writing the CSS rules that control text size within an external style sheet makes it easy to experiment with various *font-size* values until you determine the size that works best for your site. Remember, by making a single change to a CSS rule within an external style sheet linked to the site's pages, you can change the size of the text on all the pages across the site.

USE IT   Whereas the *size* attribute within a <font> tag lets you choose only 1 of 14 size settings (1 thru 7 and −1 thru −7), expressed as points, pixels, and ems, the CSS *font-size* property puts an infinite number of character sizes at your disposal. Print designers are most familiar with expressing character size in terms of a point value. On paper, a *point* is 1/72 of an inch. Therefore, a 12-point print has characters 1/6 of an inch tall and 72-point printed text has characters one inch tall. Unfortunately, on a monitor, text of a given point-value is not always the same size when displayed by browsers running at different screen resolutions.

To specify the size of text in terms of point size, append the letters *pt* to a numeric value that follows the *font-size* property as follows:

```
p {font-size:12pt}
b {font-size:18pt}
```

After reading the CSS rules in this example, the Web browser will display paragraph text at 12 points (about the size of the text in this book) and boldface text at 18 points.

Often, Web designers work in terms of pixels. Whereas the medium for print designers is paper, Web designers most often work with computer screens. Because screen resolution, the location of objects, and the size of screen images are normally given in pixels, it is no surprise that Web designers would choose pixels to specify character size as well. One advantage pixels have over point size measures is that a pixel will be the same size when displayed at a given screen resolution on the same size monitor screen—even on different hardware and software platforms. Moreover, expressing both image and text size in terms of pixels makes it easier to keep text and images a uniform size throughout a site's pages.

To specify the size of text in terms of pixels, append the letters *px* to a numeric value that follows the *font-size* property as follows:

```
body, p {font-size:10px}
```

Note that as a general rule, legible text is at least nine pixels in size.

Another way to set font size is to express the size of an element in terms of the point size of a parent element. You establish a parent/child relationship between Web elements by enclosing one Web element within another. The outer element is the parent and the enclosed (inner) element is the child. For example, the HTML citation element in the following code is a child of the paragraph element whose start and end tags enclose it:

```
<p>All text that occurs between a set of start and end
paragraph tags is part of a paragraph element. <cite>This
citation element is a child of the paragraph element whose
start and end tags enclose it.</cite> When you use one
HTML element within another, the inner element is the child,
and the outer element is the parent.</p>
```

Ems let you express the size of a Web page element in terms of the point size of its parent. At a given point size, an em is the width of the letter *M* in the current typeface. Therefore, if your style sheet has the following rules, the size of any citation text within a paragraph element will be 1.5 times as large as its parent text:

```
cite {font-size:1.5em}
p {font-size:12pt}
```

If you applied the CSS rules in this example to the paragraph and citation text in the previous example, the Web browser would display the (parent) paragraph text as 12-point and the citation text as 18-point, or 1.5 times the size of the 12-point parent text.

Figure 4-7 shows the effect of using the following style sheet to style the four text elements (paragraph, boldface, list item, and citation) on the Web page:

```
<head>
  <title>Setting Text Size with Points, Ems, and Pixels</title>
  <style type="text/css">
    b {font-size:18pt}
    cite {font-size:1.5em}
    li {font-size:30px}
    p {font-family:helvetica, "times new roman", courier;
      font-size:12pt}
  </style>
</head>
```

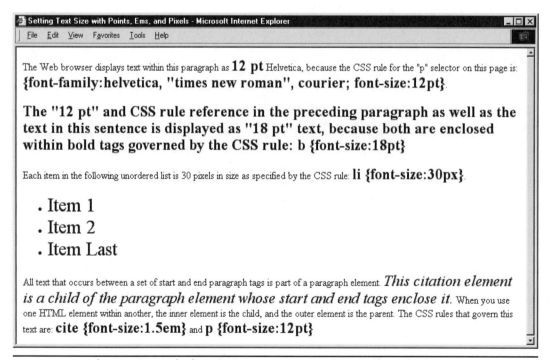

Figure 4-7　Web page text with character set using points, ems, and pixels

Creating Overlapping Text

You can add a little pizzazz to a Web page of hyperlinks by using CSS rules to style and position the hyperlink text to look something like that shown in Figure 4-8. (Although not underlined, each of the text elements in Figure 4-8 is a hyperlink.)

CSS positioning statements let you overlap Web page elements (such as text, images, and other displayed objects). *What's New with Cascading Style Sheets?* appears "behind" the four other hyperlinks in this example, because CSS rules instructed the Web browser to place additional text in space already occupied by other text. As long as you vary the typeface, size, and color of the hyperlink text enough, your visitors will still know where to click to follow each link. In addition, you can make the overlapping hypertext links easier to use by changing the mouse pointer and/or the hyperlink text style as the visitor moves the mouse pointer over each link. (Other Tips in this chapter show you how to change the mouse pointer and the appearance of hypertext when the mouse pointer hovers over a hyperlink.)

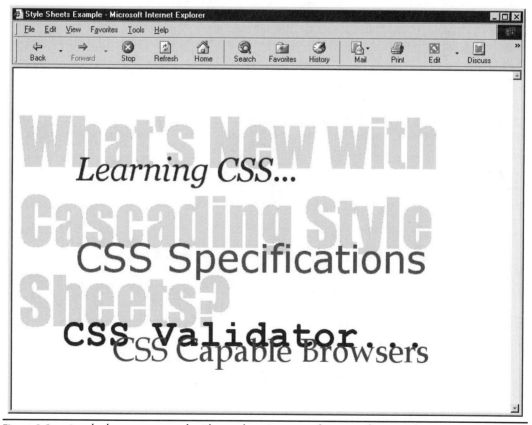

Figure 4-8   A splash page created with overlapping text of various fonts and sizes

The CSS *position* property specifies where the browser is to place an element on the Web page. *Absolute* positioning lets you place an object relative to the left-hand side and top of the page. Meanwhile, *relative* positioning lets you specify an element's location relative to where the object would normally appear. For example, if the Web page HTML has two <img> tags, one after another, the Web browser will normally draw the second image immediately to the right (and right up against) the first. Using relative positioning, you can insert a space between the two pictures as follows:

```
<img src="image1.jpg">
<img style="position:relative; left:20px" src="image2.jpg">
```

The CSS rule in the second <img> tag tells the browser to shift the element (image2.jpg) 20 pixels to the right of its normal position.

USE IT   To overlap objects on a page, use absolute positioning. You could shift one element on top of another by specifying a negative relative position. However, using absolute positioning to place objects at specific locations on the page is a simpler way to achieve the same result. For example, when applied to an object on the page, the following CSS rule instructs the Web browser to place the object 50 pixels down from the top and 10 pixels away from the left-hand side of the page:

```
.link1 {position:absolute; top:50px; left:10px}
```

You can use any of the CSS length units, such as points (pt), inches (in), centimeters (cm), and so on, to specify an element's position. For example, to position a text element using units based on the size of the characters, use ems as shown in the following rule:

```
.link2 {color: #400040;
        font-size:50px; font-style:italic;
        font-family:georgia, serif;
        position:absolute; top:2.5em; left:2em}
```

In this example, the absolute position *top:2.5em* and *left:2em* tells the Web browser to place the element 125 pixels from the top and 100 pixels from the left of the Web page. (The em value in this case is 50px as specified by the *font-size* property.)

After you write the CSS rules that position your objects, you must instruct the Web browser to apply the rules to specific elements within the Web page body. To position two hyperlinks using the CSS classes defined in the previous examples (*link1* and *link2*), insert code such as the following in the Web page HTML:

```
<p><a class="link1"
    href="Figure04-01b.htm">What's New with<br>
    Cascading Style Sheets?</a></p>
<p><a class="link2" href="Figure04-01c.htm">Learning CSS...</a>
</p>
```

The *class* attribute tells the Web browser which of the CSS rules to apply to the element (in this case, the hypertext displayed onscreen).

The start and end paragraph tags (<p></p>) shown in the example affect only the position of the text when the visitor's browser does not have CSS support. If a Web browser cannot follow the style sheet's rules, the paragraph tags cause the browser to insert a blank line between each hyperlink. Enclosing positioned elements within a paragraph or placing a <br> tag between them is not required. Bear in mind, however, that if the Web browser does not support CSS, the positioned elements will appear one after another on the page otherwise.

Aligning Web Page Text

A word processor such as MS-Word or WordPerfect gives you four ways to align paragraph text. As shown in Figure 4-9, you can align text such that each line starts at the left-hand margin, ends at the right-hand margin, is centered, or ends flush with both the left- and right-hand margins.

The first three alignment options (left, right, and center) are nothing new to HTML. After all, the *align* attribute lets you center text within or place it flush with the left- or right-hand margins of the Web page or a table cell. However, the *align* attribute has no "justify" value that lets you format lines of text as shown in the fourth paragraph in Figure 4-9. Fortunately, the CSS *text-align* property

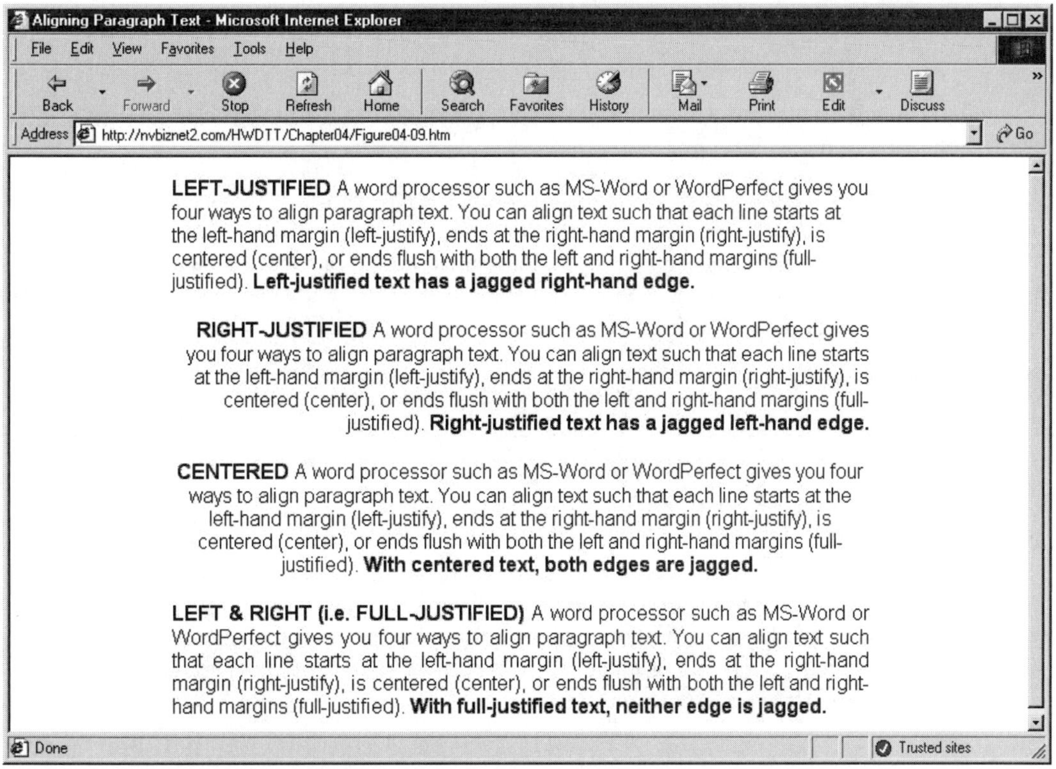

Figure 4-9   Paragraphs of text aligned left, aligned right, centered, and justified

provides a "justify" option you can use to format text such that each line (except the last) begins and ends flush with both left- and right-hand margins.

USE IT To take advantage of the four CSS text alignment options, create the following four unattached rule classes in your style sheet:

```
.left {text-align:left}
.right {text-align:right}
.center {text-align:center}
.justify {text-align:justify}
```

Note that you do not have to create style sheet rules to use the CSS *text-align* property. However, if you define the CSS classes shown here, you can specify an element's alignment as *class=className* within the element's tag rather than typing *style=alignmentRule*, which is a few more keystrokes in length.

After defining the rule classes you need, you can use the *class* attribute in your HTML tags to align text within any container element on the page. Thus, you are not limited to aligning text within paragraph containers. In addition, you can align text within the Web page body, all text within table's cells or within specific cells or rows of cells, and text you use as labels next to form elements. For example, to apply full justification to all Web page text, set the *text-align* property within the <body> tag as follows:

```
<body class="justify">
```

Similarly, to left-justify text within individual paragraphs, add the *class* attribute to the <p> tag as shown here:

```
<p class="left">
```

Bear in mind that child elements—that is, elements enclosed within other elements—inherit the parent element's CSS property values. Thus, the *class* attribute in the following <body> tag (the parent) affects the alignment of the text within all the paragraph (child) elements:

```
<body class="justify">
   <p>Paragraph 1 text will be full-justified</p>
   <p>Paragraph 2 text will be full-justified</p>
   <p>Paragraph 3 text will be full-justified</p>
   <p>Paragraph 4 text will be full-justified</p>
</body>
```

You can, however, override any of the property values in CSS rules passed from parent to child by applying a new CSS rule to the child element. For example, to change the alignment of text within the paragraphs shown in the preceding example, add a *class* or *style* attribute to the start tags of the elements whose alignment you want to change:

```
<body class="justify">
  <p class="left">Paragraph 1 text will be left-justified</p>
  <p>Paragraph 2 text will be full-justified</p>
  <p style="text-align:right">
     Paragraph 3 text will be right-justified</p>
  <p>Paragraph 4 text will be full-justified</p>
</body>
```

Controlling Margins and Line Height

When working with Web page text, you often want to leave some space between the text and the left- and right-hand sides of the browser's application window. Margins make pages with lots of text less daunting by providing a blank space in which visitors can rest their eyes. In addition, you can use margins to place text into newspaper-like columns or to exaggerate the separation between paragraphs, as shown in Figure 4-10.

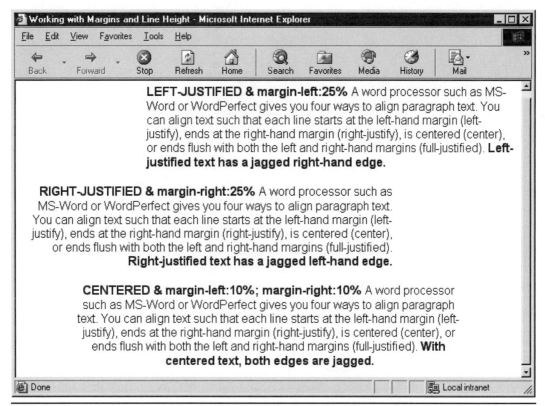

Figure 4-10   Using margin widths to separate text into bursts of information

Prior to CSS rules that set margin properties and give you precise control over the space around Web page elements, you had to use HTML tables to position your text. To indent text away from the sides of the Web page, for example, you might place the text within a three-column table. By placing page text into the center column, you could create margins by leaving the table's two outer columns blank and set to the width of the blank space you wanted to leave between the text and the left- and right-hand sides of the Web page.

USE IT   CSS margin properties give you precise control over the space the browser leaves between an element and the sides of the page or between adjacent elements within the page. You can choose among four margin properties: *margin-left*, *margin-right*, *margin-top*, and *margin-bottom*. Each property names the element's side along which the property will create a space. For example, to create a 40-pixel margin between objects on the page and the left- and right-hand sides of the browser application window, add the following CSS rule to your style sheet:

```
body {margin-left:40px; margin-right:40px}
```

To control the left and right margins between a group of paragraphs and the sides of the Web page, enclose the paragraphs within a set of start and end division tags (<div></div>). Then, apply a CSS rule to the <div> tag as shown here:

```
<body>
  <p>This browser does not indent this paragraph<p>
  <div style="margin-left:10%; margin-right:10%">
    <p>This browser WILL indent this paragraph with a margin
       10% the width of the application window.</p>
    <p>The browser WILL indent this paragraph the same width
       as the preceding one. The CSS rule in the division tag
       governs both paragraphs.
  </div>
  <p>This browser does not indent this paragraph<p>
</body>
```

Note that you can use any of the CSS length units (px, pt, em, in, mm, cm, and so on) to specify a margin-width. In this example, the CSS rule in the <div> tag instructs the browser to leave a margin 10 percent the width of the browser's application window between the paragraph text and both the left- and right-hand sides of the Web page.

Use the CSS *margin-top* and *margin-bottom* properties to control the space above and below an element, respectively. For example, if you want to leave the space of two blank lines between paragraphs, you might style the paragraph selector (*p*) in your style sheet as follows:

```
p {margin-bottom:2em}
```

To leave 1.5 times the normal space between two paragraphs, style the <p> tag of the paragraph you want to affect rather than the paragraph selector (*p*) in a style sheet. For example, you might add a rule such as the following to leave an additional half-line of space between the current paragraph and the one that precedes it:

```
<p style="margin-top:1.5em">
```

If you want to control the space between lines of text within a paragraph, as opposed to the space between two paragraphs, use the CSS *line-height* property. The default line-height is 1em. As such, the Web browser inserts the same amount of space between the lines within the following two paragraphs:

```
<body>
  <p>This is the first line in paragraph 1<br>
     This is the second line in the first paragraph</P>
  <p style="line-height:1em">
     This is the first line in paragraph 2<br>
     This is the second line in the second paragraph</p>
</body>
```

To double-space (that is, to place a blank line between) lines of text within a particular paragraph, set the paragraph's line-height to 2em with a CSS rule such as this:

```
<p style="line-height:2em">
```

Displaying Text Within Columns

You can use the CSS *width* property to lay out a Web page in newspaper-like columns. A newspaper layout works well when you must provide a lot of text or want to present information on diverse topics on a single Web page. The visitor feels comfortable because the layout is familiar—most everyone has read a printed newspaper or magazine. Moreover, vertical columns separate the page full of text into manageable chunks. As a result, a visitor is not overwhelmed with a screen of wall-to-wall words—even if there are no pictures within the columns on the page. Finally, by providing appropriate headings at the top of each column, you can summarize portions of the content to let visitors quickly zero-in on items of interest.

 USE IT   To break your Web page into columns, place the content you want the browser to display in each column within a division (container) element (that is, between a set of start and end division tags [<div></div>]). Then, use CSS classes to set the width of each column and the alignment of the text content within the column. For example, to create a three-column layout such as that shown in Figure 4-11, add the following CSS class definitions to your style sheet:

```
.left {text-align:justify;
       border-color:black; border-style:solid;
       border-left-width:1px; border-bottom-width:1px;
       width:33%}

.middle {text-align:justify;
         border-color:black; border-style:solid;
         border-right-width:1px; border-left-width:1px;
```

```
      border-bottom-width:1px;
      width:34%}
.right {text-align:justify;
      border-color:black; border-style:solid;
      border-right-width:1px; border-bottom-width:1px;
      width:33%}
```

Then, style the three division containers, which hold the column content, as follows:

```
<div class="left">
  <center><h1>Column 1</h1></center>
  ... left-hand column content ...
</div>
<div class="middle">
  <center><h1>Column 2</h1></center>
  ... middle column content ...
</div><div class="right">
  <center><h1>Column 3</h1></center>
  ... right-hand column content ...
</div>
```

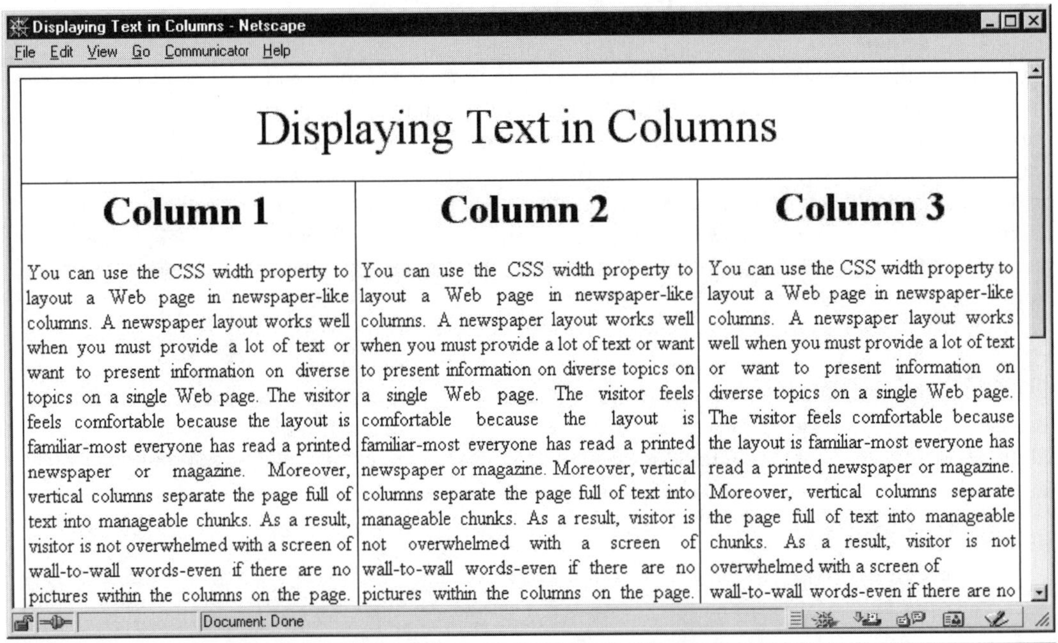

Figure 4-11   A Web page with three columns of text below a banner

In the preceding Tip, you learned how to use the four margin properties to insert a blank space between an element and the sides of the Web page. CSS also provides *padding* properties, which let you create a margin between an object and the sides of its container. In this example, the page has three division containers, each of which holds the content displayed in one of the three Web page columns. To leave a blank space between the column (text) content and the left- and right-hand sides of a container, insert the following declarations within each of the three style sheet classes (*.left, .middle,* and *.right*):

```
padding-left:10px; padding-right:10px;
```

The preceding *padding* property declarations instruct the Web browser to leave a 10-pixel blank space between the content and the left- and right-hand sides of the container, as shown in Figure 4-12.

(In addition to the CSS *padding-left* and *padding-right* properties, you can set *padding-top* and *padding-bottom* to insert blank space between content and the top and bottom of the container.)

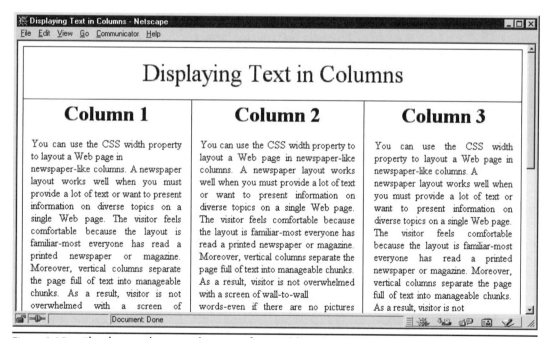

Figure 4-12 The three-column Web page after padding the column contents

Working with Borders

Designers use borders to separate images from surrounding text, to mark headings, and to make important or otherwise special passages stand out from other text on a Web page. The CSS *border* properties let you control the width, style, and color of each side in a border around an object independently. Prior to CSS, you placed objects within HTML tables and set the table *border* attribute to the pixel-width of the border you wanted the browser to draw. Unfortunately, few browsers let you control the color or style of the borders.

USE IT   CSS lets you draw a border around any object or container element on a Web page. As such, you can draw borders around pictures, headings, paragraphs, text within start and end span tags (<span></span>), elements and objects within start and end division tags (<div></div>), and so on. To draw a border around level-1 headings, for example, you might write a CSS rule such as the following:

```
h1 {border:solid 3px black}
```

The first property value, *solid*, specifies the border's line style, the second sets the *border-width* to three pixels, and the third makes the border black. If you write a CSS rule that gives values for the *border* property, the Web browser will make all four sides of the border look the same.

To work with the appearance of each side in a border independently, specify *border-style*, *border-width*, and *border-color* values for all four sides. For example, you could write the "shorthand" form of the border rule in the previous example as follows:

```
h1 {border-top-style:solid;
    border-left-style:solid;
    border-right-style:solid:
    border-bottom-style:solid:
    border-top-width:3px;
    border-left-width:3px;
    border-right-width:3px;
    border-bottom-width:3px;
    border-top-color:black;
    border-left-color:black;
    border-right-color:black;
    border-bottom-color:black}
```

Fortunately, CSS syntax lets you combine explicit and implicit (shorthand) *border* property declarations. For example, if you want a solid, gold border you could write the CSS rule as follows:

```
h1 {border-style:solid;
    border-color:#FFD700;
    border-top-width:1px;
```

```
border-left-width:1px;
border-right-width:2px;
border-bottom-width:2px}
```

Similarly, to specify a .5 inch, blue, double-line border you would write the CSS rule as follows:

```
h1 {border-style:double;
    border-color:blue;
    border-width:.5in}
```

Note, as shown in the preceding examples, that you can specify the *border-color* by name or as hexadecimal triplets, and the *border-width* in any CSS unit of measure (in, cm, pt, px, and so on).

Figure 4-13 shows a 12-pixel, lightgreen border around a level-1 heading in each of the nine available border styles. (The *border-style* "none" tells the browser to ignore the border properties and draw no border.)

Bear in mind that you must set the *border-width* to at least three pixels to see the effect of some border styles. For example, if you select the *border-style* "double", the Web browser needs one pixel to display each of the border's two lines and one pixel to put a space between the lines.

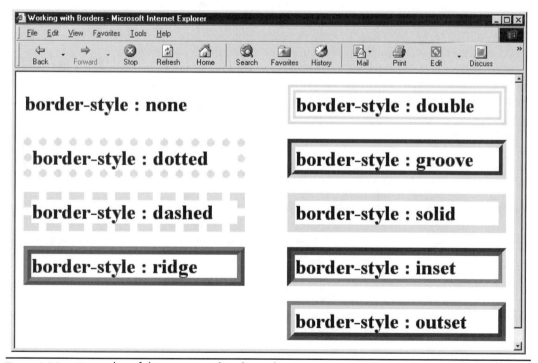

Figure 4-13   Examples of the nine CSS border styles

Indenting Paragraphs and Controlling Letter, Word, and Line Spacing

In addition to tools for positioning objects precisely, designers have long desired more typographical control over Web page text. Layout tables and transparent (spacer) GIF images give you some control over where the browser puts things onscreen. However, they do not make it easy to adjust the spacing between words and lines of text or to indent the first word in each paragraph. Fortunately, CSS rules give you all the control you want.

 USE IT   To indent the first letter in each paragraph of text, for example, create a rule such as the following:

```
p {text-indent:2em}
```

Although you can use any CSS units of measure (pt, px, in, cm, and so on), you will find it most convenient to use ems when indenting paragraph text. The rule in this example will indent the first word approximately five letters, and will continue to do so even if you increase (or decrease) the font-size of the text. Remember, 1em equals the current point-size of the text. Thus, as the font-size changes, so does the size of an em (and the width of the text-indent). If you specify the indentation by using a fixed length unit (such as pixels or points), you must adjust the text-indent value whenever you change the font-size to indent the first word the same number of characters.

Given the names of the properties, it will come as no great surprise that *letter-spacing* lets you control the space between letters; *word-spacing* lets you control the space between words; and (you guessed it) *line-height* lets you control the space between lines. (Actually, I would have guessed *line-spacing*; however, word processors use the term *line height*, so CSS uses the same term to keep things simple.) As was the case with the *text-indent* property, you can use any of the CSS length units to specify the letter, word, and line spacing you want. Bear in mind, when adjusting word and letter spacing, the browser *adds* the length you specify to what it would normally use. Therefore, to *add* 5 pixels of space between letters of text in a level-1 heading, you might write:

```
<h1 style="letter-spacing:5px">Letter Spaced Wide</h1>
```

Similarly, to add a 1-pica space between words in citations, you might write a CSS rule such as this:

```
cite {word-spacing:1pc}
```

As mentioned previously, the *line-height* property lets you control the vertical spacing between lines of text. Not to complicate matters, but the common term for the space between lines is *leading*. Thus, the *line-height* property lets you control leading. You can specify the line-height in any of three ways: by number, by CSS length unit, or by percentage. The Web browser adds the value you specify for *line-height* before each line of text.

When you specify *line-height* by number or by percentage, the Web browser uses the font size to determine the leading. Thus, if you write the following rule, the browser will insert a 25-point space between lines of boldface text:

```
b {font-size:10pt; line-height:2.5}
```

The browser multiplies the *font-size* (10-point) by the *line-height* value (2.5) to get the leading (25). Similarly, you can write the same rule using a percentage:

```
b {font-size:10pt; line-height:250%}
```

As before, the Web browser will set the *line-height* to 25 points, because 250 percent of the current *font-size* (10) is 25. Note that you do not have to include a *font-size* declaration within the rule. When you specify *line-height* as a number or as a percentage, the browser always multiplies the current font size by the *line-height* value to get the leading.

To specify the leading as a CSS length unit, simply include the length unit you want to use as part of the *line-height* value. For example, to create a CSS class you can use to double-space text, add the following rule to your style sheet:

```
.double_space {line-height:2em}
```

Similarly, to have the browser leave a 12-point space before each line of text in a paragraph, you might write an in-line style such as this:

```
<p style="line-height:12pt">
```

Note that if the *line-height* you specify is less than the font size, your lines of text will overlap. For example, if the font size in the preceding example were 24-point, the lines of text in the paragraph would overlap. To be specific, the letters in each line would start halfway down the letters in the preceding line, because the 12-point leading is one-half the size of the 24-point font-size.

Offsetting Text with Initial Caps

Publishers often apply a special style to the first letter of articles in magazines or chapters in books to add a touch of spice to an otherwise plain page of text. When used sparingly, changing the appearance of the character that leads off a passage or section of text catches the reader's eye and makes him or her more likely to read. In addition, if you have a multicolumn layout or a page with lots of text, you might apply a special style to the first letter of each paragraph that starts a new topic to help the visitor move from idea to idea on the page.

 USE IT To set off an initial cap, make the letter 120 to 150 percent larger than the surrounding text. Thus, you might create a CSS class named *icap* with the following:

```
<head>
  <style type="text/css">
<!--
    .icap {font-size:150%}
-->
  </style>
</head>
```

Once defined, you can use *icap* as the *class* attribute's value in the HTML <span> element to apply the class rules as follows:

```
<body>
  <p><span class="icap">T</span>his is an example of ...</p>
  <p><span class="icap">T</span>ext in this paragraph...</p>
  <p style="font-size:2em">
     <span class="icap">I</span>f you had used pixels or...</p>
</body>
```

Figure 4-14 shows a Web page in which *icap* (as defined here) is applied to the first letter in each of three paragraphs.

In addition to increasing its size, you can make your initial cap stand out more by varying its typeface, color, or the color of the background behind the character. When selecting a typeface, use one that you would not normally use for text (such as Comic) or perhaps the same typeface used in your headings. For example, you might enhance the *icap* class defined in the previous example as follows:

```
.icap {font-size:150%; font-family:"comic sans ms", impact}
```

When applied, the *icap* class shown here will increase the size of the styled letter to 1.5 times the size of the surrounding text and use the Comic Sans MS typeface. If Comic Sans MS is not available on the visitor's system, the browser will use Impact instead. (If Impact too is unavailable, the browser will use the current default font; however, the initial cap will still stand out due to its increased size.)

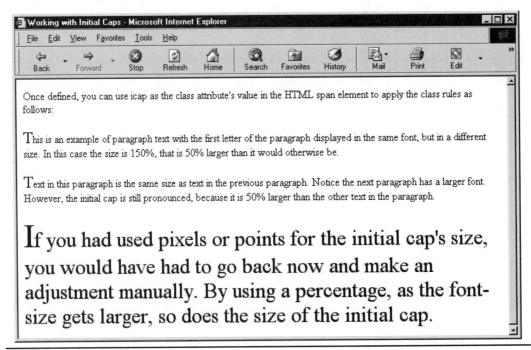

Figure 4-14   Paragraphs with initial caps

Customizing the Appearance of Hyperlinks

If you do nothing special to the anchor (that is, the hyperlink) element in your Web page HTML, Web browsers underline your hyperlink text and typically use one color (such as blue) to display unvisited links and a different color (such as magenta) for links previously visited. CSS gives you a choice. You can continue to let the visitor's browser dictate the appearance of your hypertext, or you can take control of the way your hyperlinks look. For example, you can write CSS rules that change the text color, apply a background color, or even remove the underline if you like. Moreover, you can vary the styles of different types of links on the page. For example, you might leave unchanged the Web page background behind hypertext links embedded within other content. However, for hyperlinks on the site's navigation menu, you might apply a different background color or image to make the menu items more visible. You can even write a CSS rules to create a hover (mouseover) effect, which changes the hypertext's appearance when the visitor moves the mouse pointer over a hyperlink.

USE IT   To customize the appearance of your hyperlinks, add rules that specify the properties of one, some, or all the anchor element's four pseudo-classes:

a:link	Unvisited
a:visited	Visited; meaning that the Web browser history list has an entry pointing to the hyperlink's target (that is, the URL specified by the hyperlink's *href* attribute).
a:hover	The visitor's mouse pointer is over the hyperlink.
a:active	The mouse pointer is over the hyperlink, and the visitor is in the process of depressing or releasing the left mouse button (or the right mouse button for left-handed mice).

For example, to set the color of unvisited links to dark green and visited links to magenta, you would add the following CSS rules to your style sheet:

```
a:link {color:darkgreen}
a:visited {color:magenta}
```

If you decide to remove the underline from your hypertext, you should also take steps to make the hyperlinks stand out in some other way. For example, you might change the hypertext typeface or make its background color different from that used in the Web page background. Whatever you do, you will likely want to apply the same treatment to all classes of hyperlinks. To do so, drop the pseudo-class reference from the CSS rule to style all classes of anchor text as shown here:

```
a {text-decoration:none; background-color:yellow}
```

In this example, setting the *text-decoration* to "none" removes the underline from the hypertext, and the *background-color* value "highlights" the hyperlink anchor text in yellow. Note that Web browsers will apply the declarations in a rule for the anchor element (*a*) to all hyperlink pseudo-classes. Thus, given the preceding CSS rule, each hypertext link on the Web page will have a yellow background and will not be underlined.

To add a little pizzazz to your hyperlinks, use the "hover" pseudo-class to change the appearance of the anchor text when a visitor moves the mouse over a hyperlink. You can use any text formatting properties you like for the mouseover effect. Thus, if you want to display the hypertext at 1.5 times the current font-size, in italics, and with a cyan background, add the following CSS rule to the style sheet:

```
a:hover {font-size:1.5em; font-style:italic;
         background-color:cyan}
```

As a final step in customizing the hypertext on your site, you may want to make it easy for visitors to distinguish links that will take them to another part of your site from those that will take them to another Web site. Similarly, suppose your site has a public and a members-only area. You can help nonmembers avoid clicking links that bring up a password prompt by making links to members-only pages look different from those to pages anyone can view. To accomplish all this styling, assign each of the hyperlink types to a class that makes the hyperlink text look the way you want.

For example, suppose you want all hyperlinks to other (that is, external) Web sites to be light green with a purple background and not underlined. Moreover, you want only the external hyperlinks to change to white text (on the already purple background) when the mouse moves across them. No problem. Add the following CSS rules to your style sheet:

```
a.external {color:lightgreen; background-color:purple;
            text-decoration:none}
a.external:hover {color:white; font-style:bold}
```

Next, apply the *external* class to hyperlinks that target other Web sites, as shown here:

```
<a class="external" href="www.NVBizNet2.com">
  Link to another site</a>
```

Now, suppose you later decide that you want to change the appearance of all external hypertext links or the *hover* property of those links. Nothing could be simpler. You need only change the property values within one or both of the style sheet rules as desired to change the appearance of all external links throughout your site. Such is the power of CSS.

Creating a Drop-Shadow Effect

Although the Internet has gone through many changes, one thing has remained the same—downloading and displaying an image (even a small one) takes longer than retrieving and displaying a page full of text. Of course, nothing is suspicious about this. Files with graphics images are larger than HTML documents, and therefore take longer to send across the Net.

When you want to create a three-dimensional effect by adding a drop-shadow to banner text, you might guess that you must first convert the text to an image and then apply the shadow effect. However, a graphics image of the banner text has a much larger file size than the number of bytes needed to store even two copies of the text. Therefore, to minimize download time, use only text for the banner rather than a picture of it. By using CSS positioning statements and ordinary text, you can create a banner.

To create a text banner with a drop shadow (such as the one shown in Figure 4-15), you need two text elements—one for the banner and one for the shadow. In your style sheet, insert a rule you can use to style and position the banner element and a second rule you can use to style and position the drop-shadow text. Although the banner element can be any color you want, use a shade of gray or black for the drop shadow.

USE IT   Let's start by creating a CSS class such as the following, which makes the banner text look the way you want and positions the banner on the Web page:

```
.banner {position:absolute; top:7px; left:1px
         font-size:100px;
         font-family:"arial black", impact Helvetica, verdana;
         color:red}
```

Figure 4-15   A text banner with a drop-shadow

Next, add a drop shadow class, which uses the same font-size and typeface as the *banner* class, to the style sheet. As shown here, specify *top* and *left* values that will position the *shadow* class element slightly below and to the right of the position specified within the *banner* class:

```
.shadow {position:absolute; top:15px; left:7px
        font-size:100px;
        font-family:"arial black" impact Helvetica verdana;
        color:gray}
```

In this example, the browser will place text styled as *banner* seven pixels down from the top and one pixel away from the left-hand side of the page. Meanwhile, the browser will place text styled as *shadow* fifteen pixels down and seven pixels away from the left-hand side of the page.

Finally, apply the *banner* and *shadow* classes you defined within the style sheet to two identical text elements in separate division containers, as shown here:

```
<body>
   <div class="banner">HTML & Web Design</div>
   <div class="shadow">HTML & Web Design</div>
</body>
```

Experiment with the *top* and *left* values in the *shadow* class until you get the shadow effect you want.

Applying a Border Graphic

Whether you are creating a business or a personal Web site, add a distinctive border or side panel along the left-hand side on each of the site's pages. By adding a decoration, you make a Web page less intimidating. As a result, your visitor feels comfortable and stays longer, especially on pages with few pictures and lots of text. In addition, a border provides a visual clue that lets visitors know if they are still on your site. When the border disappears or changes radically, visitors know a hyperlink has taken them elsewhere on the Web. Finally, on Web sites with several large sections or departments, use a slightly different border for pages in each section to help visitors keep track of where they are on the site.

USE IT Style sheets make it easy to create a border and to change its appearance throughout the site's pages from time to time. Typically, a border consists of a small, rectangular image or tile that the Web browser displays repeatedly in the Web page background. Not surprisingly then, you control a border with the CSS *background-image* property. In the center of the Web page shown in Figure 4-16, for example, is the tile used to create the side panel that runs down the left-hand side of the page.

The first step in creating a border is to make or download a small GIF image the Web browser can repeat to create a border. Use an image editing program such as Photoshop to create your own border tile, or use a tile from the Microsoft Office clip art gallery or from such Web sites as the

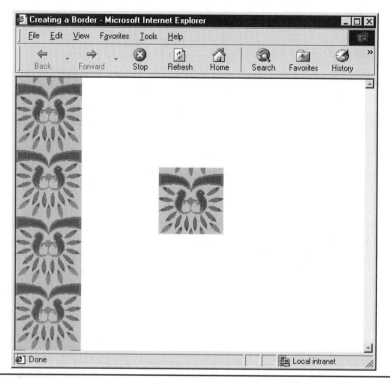

Figure 4-16 Web page with a border tile and a side panel, or border along the left-hand side of the Web page

Microsoft Design Gallery Live (at http://dgl.microsoft.com). After you have the tile you want, store the image in a folder (such as images) on your site. Next, create a style sheet rule such as the following:

```
body {background-image:URL(images/TileFilename.gif);
     background-repeat:repeat-y}
```

In this example, the *background-image* property gives the relative pathname of the file with the graphics image you want the Web browser to display. The *background-repeat* property tells the Web browser to repeat, or tile, the image vertically. Because no *background-position* was specified, the browser will tile the image along the left-hand border of the Web page. Note that you will replace *images/TileFilename.gif* used in this example with the relative address and filename of your own border tile.

To keep your Web site fresh, you may want to change your page borders periodically. Fortunately, CSS makes the job simple. Create or download a new border title and save it to a file in your site's images folder. Then, replace the pathname between the parentheses that follow *URL* in the previous rule with the pathname of the file with the new border tile graphic.

If you have a site with sections and you want to distinguish them from one another by using a different border for each one, create a body selector (*b*) class for each section. Thus, your style sheet will have rules something like the following:

```
body.main {background-image:URL(images/TileFilename1.gif);
           background-repeat:repeat-y}
body.products {background-image:URL(images/TileFilename2.gif);
           background-repeat:repeat-y}
body.custService {background-image:URL(images/TileFilename3.gif);
           background-repeat:repeat-y}
body.employmentOps {background-image:URL(images/TileFilename4.gif);
           background-repeat:repeat-y}
```

To change the border for any section's pages, simply update the URL of the border tile graphic specified within the section's body selector (*b*) class. Of course, when you create multiple body selector (*b*) classes, you must apply the appropriate class to the <body> tag within the Web page document. For example, the <body> tag for each of the Web pages in the site's Employment Opportunity section would look like this:

```
<body class="employmentOps">
```

Positioning Background Images and Watermarks

These days, few Web sites have pages with only black text against a white background. To give their Web sites a distinctive look and feel, designers normally apply at least a background color or add a Web page border or side panel (as shown in the preceding Tip). If a solid-color background does not give your Web pages the look you want, use style sheet rules to create a textured background or perhaps display the company logo as a watermark.

USE IT   The first step in creating a textured background is to either create or download a small GIF image (the texture tile) you want the Web browser to repeat on each Web page background. Use an image-editing program such as Photoshop to create an image about 50 pixels square, or use a tile from the Microsoft Office clip art gallery or from sites like the Microsoft Design Gallery Live (at http://dgl.microsoft.com). After you have the tile you want, store the image in a folder (such as *images*) on your site. Next, create a style sheet rule such as the following:

```
body {background-image:url(images/marbleTile.gif)}
```

The Web browser will tile (that is, display repeatedly) the graphics image in the file specified within the parentheses () following *url* in the *background-image* declaration. In this example, the Web browser will fill the Web page background with the texture in marbleTile.gif, as shown in Figure 4-17. To create the textured background for your Web pages, replace *images/marbleTile.gif* with the relative address and filename in which you stored your background tile.

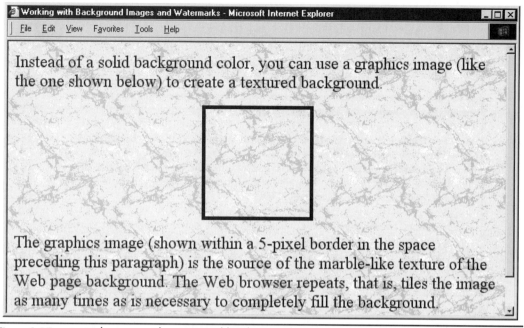

Figure 4-17   A Web page with a textured background

A watermark is similar to a textured background in that a watermark is a graphics image you want the Web browser to display behind other content. However, rather than tile the watermark graphic to fill the Web page background, you want the Web browser to display the picture only once. Moreover, you want the watermark to remain in one place as the visitor scrolls through the page content in the foreground. Fortunately, CSS provides background properties that let you position a single copy of the watermark graphic in the page background and keep it stationary.

Unlike the 50-pixel-square tile you used to create a textured background, the watermark graphic must be a regular-size picture. For example, if want to use your company logo as the watermark, make the logo graphic the size you want it to appear in the Web page background, as shown in Figure 4-18.

To insert a watermark at the center of the Web page background, add the following rule to your style sheet:

```
body {background-image:url(images/LightBulb.gif);
      background-repeat:no-repeat;
      background-position:center;
      background-attachment:fixed}
```

As was the case with the textured background in the previous example, the *background-image* property specifies the name of the graphics file the Web browser is to display. In this example, the Web browser will display the image in LightBulb.gif. For your style sheet rule, replace *images/LightBulb.gif* with the relative address and filename of the watermark you want to use. The *background-repeat* setting

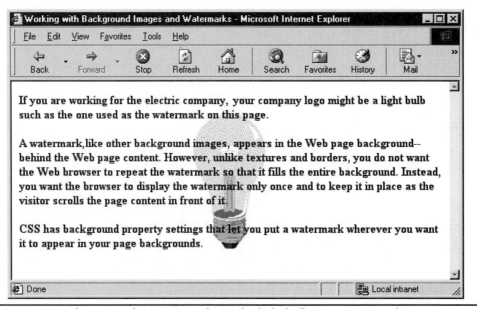

Figure 4-18   A Web page with a company logo (the light bulb) as a watermark

of *no-repeat* tells the Web browser to display the graphics image only once. Meanwhile, the *background-position* property tells the Web browser where to place the image, and the *fixed* specification for *background-attachment* keeps the watermark stationary.

You are not limited to placing a watermark in the center of the page background. CSS syntax gives you three ways in which to specify where you want the watermark to go: by keyword, by length values, and by percentage values. To position by keyword, the valid position values are top, bottom, left, right, and (as you saw previously) center. Thus, to place a watermark (or for that matter, any graphics image) at the lower right-hand corner of the Web page background, set the *background-position* property as follows:

```
background-position:bottom right;
```

Length values give you precise control over where the Web browser will place the watermark. You can use any CSS length unit to specify the distance away from the left-hand side and from the top of the page you want the browser to display the graphics image. For example, to display the image 70 pixels in (away) from the left-hand side of the page and 100 pixels down from the top, you would write the *background-position* declaration as follows:

```
background-position:70px 100px;
```

Note that you specify the distance away from the left-hand side first, followed by the distance down from the top of the Web page.

Percentage values used to position a background image are similar in function to length units. However, instead of specifying an exact location for the left-hand side and top of the image, you specify the distance the image is to be away from the sides of the application window as a percentage of the window's dimensions. For example, to start the background image 25 percent of the way toward the right-hand side of the application window and 50 percent of the way toward the bottom of window, declare the *background-position* as follows:

```
background-position:25% 75%;
```

Note that as you change the dimensions of the browser's application window, the position of the watermark will change to keep the top and left-hand sides of the image at the same percentage length away from the sides of the application window.

Floating Images and Text

Most Web pages have both images and text. Although the old adage about a picture being worth a thousand words may be true, pictures have not yet replaced words on the Web. In fact, a page with nothing but pictures is just as daunting to the site visitor as a page with only text. As such, when creating a Web site, a large part of your page layout work will involve getting text to flow around your images. In the past, you had only the *align* attribute, which, when used within an <img> tag, instructed the Web browser to flow text along the left- or right-hand side of a picture. Nowadays, you can use the CSS *float* property that lets you flow text not only alongside images, but also next to other Web page elements, as shown in Figure 4-19.

USE IT   When you apply the CSS *float* property to an element, you take the element out of the normal flow and "float" the element to the left or right of the elements that follow it within the Web page HTML. Suppose, for example, that the Web page HTML contains an <img> tag followed by paragraph text. During the "normal" flow, the Web browser would place the picture inserted by the image onto the Web page and then move to the left margin of the line below the picture before displaying the text. To have the Web browser "float" the image to the left of the paragraph text (as shown at the top of Figure 4-19), add the *float* property to the <img> tag, as shown here:

```
<img style="float:left" border="0" src="Programmer.gif"
     width="146" height="148">
```

Similarly, to have the paragraph text appear to the left of an image, instruct the Web browser to float the image to the right of the subsequent elements in the HTML document as follows:

```
<img style="float:right" border="0"
     src="images/Shakespeare.gif" width="110" height="132">
```

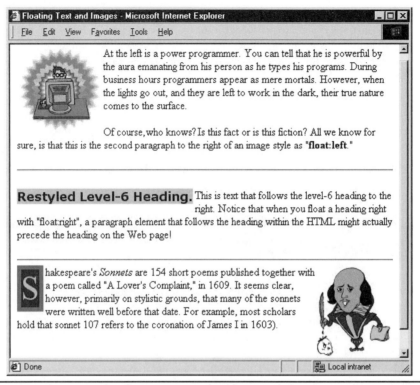

Figure 4-19 A Web page with a floating image, heading, and character within a span container

As mentioned previously, you can use the *float* attribute with other Web page elements in addition to images. For example, to restyle a level-6 heading tag so that it floats to the left of paragraph text (as shown at the center of Figure 4-19), add the following rule to your style sheet:

```
h6 {float:left}
```

In fact, you can float any container element or object you put into a container. Suppose for example, that you want to create a fancy initial cap such as the *S* that starts the last paragraph near the bottom of Figure 4-19. First, create a CSS class such as the following in your style sheet:

```
.fancyLetter {float:left; font-size:3em; font-style:bold;
              color:yellow; background-color:blue;
              border-style:solid; border-width:6px;
              border-color:gray}
```

Then, place the letter you want to style within a span (container) element as follows:

```
<span class="fancyLetter">S</span>hakespeare's <i>Sonnets</i>
are 154 short poems published together with a poem called...
```

Customizing the Appearance of Lists

HTML provides two types of lists: ordered (numbered) and unordered (bulleted). You use an ordered list when the arrangement (that is, the order) of the items in the list is important. For example, you would use an ordered list to show the steps in a procedure, such as cooking instructions in a recipe or a list of top ten song titles (in order by units sold). Conversely, to list the items used in a recipe or the names of books written by an author, you would use an unordered list. Both types of lists are simple in form: the list-item marker (a number, letter, graphics image, or bullet character) followed by the list item. However, you can use CSS rules to work with the appearance of a list so that it fits in with the overall look of the Web page on which the list appears.

USE IT Use the CSS *list-style-type* property to specify the appearance of the list-item markers that precede the items in a list. The valid *list-style-type* values are as follows:

disk	A filled black circle (such as the bullet character that follows the items in this list)
circle	An open circle
square	A filled black square
decimal	1, 2, 3, 4, 5, and so on
decimal-leading-zero	01, 02, …, 98, 99; or 001, 002, …, 099, 100; and so on
lower-roman	i, ii, iii, iv, v, and so on
upper-roman	I, II, III, IV, V, and so on
lower-greek	Traditional Greek numbering (symbols for: alpha, beta, gamma, and so on)
lower-alpha	a, b, c, d, e, and so on
lower-latin	a, b, c, d, e, and so on
upper-alpha	A, B, C, D, E, and so on
upper-latin	A, B, C, D, E, and so on
hebrew	Traditional Hebrew numbering
armenian	Traditional Armenian numbering
georgian	Georgian numbering (an, ban, gan, …, he, tan, in, in-an)
cjk-ideographic	Plain ideographic numbers
hirgana	a, i, u, e, o, ka, ki, and so on
katana	A, I, U, E, O, KA, KI, and so on
hiragana-iroha	i, ro, ha, ni, ho, he, to, and so on
katakana-iroha	I, RO, HA, NI, HO, HE, TO, and so on
none	No bullet character, just a blank
inherit	Use the parent element's list style

To apply a style to the item-markers in a list, use a *style* attribute within the start list tag. For example, to use uppercase roman numerals for the items in a numbered (that is, ordered) list, write the <ol> tag as follows:

```
<ol style="list-style-type:upper-roman">
```

Similarly, to use a square for the bullet that precedes each item in an unordered list, write the <ul> tag as:

```
<ul style="list-style-type:square>
```

When working with an unordered list, you can use the *list-style-image* property to specify a graphics image to replace the standard (disk, circle, and square) list-item markers. For example, the following <ul> tag instructs the Web browser to use the graphics image in FancyDot.gif as the unordered list's bullet character:

```
<ul style="list-style-image:url(images/FancyDot.gif)">
```

Finally, use the *list-style-position* property to control the position of the list-item marker in relation to the list-item text. You can assign one of two values to *list-style-position*: inside and outside. Set the property to outside when you want the browser to place the list-item marker outside the list-item text. As shown by the first and third lists in Figure 4-20, when set to outside, all list-item text appears to the right of the list-item marker—even when the text for an item takes more than one line.

Conversely, set the *list-style-position* to inside as shown here, when you want the browser to make the list-item marker a part of the list-item text:

```
<ul style="list-style-type:square; list-style-position:inside">
```

The *list-style-type* of the second list in Figure 4-20 is set to *inside*. Notice how the bullets (the graphics dots) in the second list line up with the first letter of the list items in the first and third lists. The reason for the shift to the right is that the Web browser rendered the list-item marker *inside* (that is, as part of) each list-item.

Although the examples in this Tip show that you can style lists inline, take advantage of the site-wide formatting power that style sheets provide. Rather than format unordered and ordered lists individually, decide on a look that works best for your site. Then, write CSS rules that make all lists of each type look the same. For example, if you like the look that the *inside list-style-position* value gives your list, and you want to use FancyDot.gif as bullets, write the following rule within your style sheet:

```
ul {list-style:url(images/FancyDot.gif) inside}
```

Note that CSS syntax lets you use shorthand when writing rules. When the values declared in a rule are unique to a specific property, the Web browser applies the value to the property automatically. The shorthand used in this example is equivalent to writing the same CSS rule as follows:

```
ul {list-style-image:url(images/FancyDot.gif);
    list-style-position:inside}
```

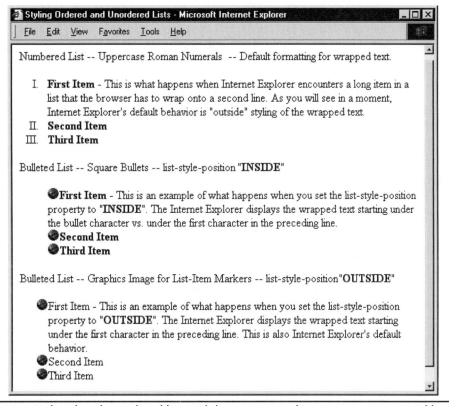

Figure 4-20   Ordered and unordered lists with long item text that wraps onto a second line

Creating Text and Image Effects with Filters

When you create special effects with text instead of using a graphics image that shows the effect, the Web browser can retrieve and display your Web page more quickly. Unfortunately, some Web browsers do not yet support CSS. As a result, when you use features such as absolute positioning, some visitors will not see the special effect you are trying to create. In fact, depending on the CSS properties used to produce the effect, some visitors may see a portion of your Web page as a mishmash of text. In short, CSS code tricks do not degrade well in browsers without support for some of the properties exploited to create a special effect.

Microsoft enhanced CSS by adding filter properties that let Internet Explorer (version 4 and up) work with both text and image elements to produce interesting effects. Web browsers unable to apply the filter specified (as an in-line style or within a style sheet) will simply display the element in its original form. As a result, although your page will not pack the punch you want, visitors using browsers without filter support will still be able to see your page content.

USE IT To create an effect using a *filter* property, apply the *filter* as you would any other CSS style. For example, to create a hyperlink with the glow effect shown in Figure 4-21, use an inline style similar to this:

```
<a style="filter:glow(); width:100%;
   font-size:30pt; text-decoration:none"
   href="http://www.NVBizNet.com">Glow</a>
```

▶ *NOTE*

Filters will not work (that is, they will not produce their defined special effect), if you do not set the element's width *property. For graphics elements, set the* width *equal to the actual width of the image; for text elements, set the width to 100% or to the actual width of the text element.*

Figure 4-21 Web page with text showing the effect of various filters

The available *filter* properties are as follows:

alpha	Lets you make an element partially or fully transparent
blur	Blurs an element as if it were moving at high speed
chroma	Makes the specified color within an element transparent
fliph	Flips an element horizontally
flipv	Flips an element vertically
glow	Makes an element glow by adding a radiance around its outside edges
gray	Renders an element black and white using a gray scale to represent the element's original colors
invert	Renders an element in its reverse color and brightness values
light	Projects a light source on an element
mask	Renders an element with the specified background color and transparent foreground color
shadow	Renders the element with a shadow
dropshadow	Renders the element with a drop-shadow
wave	Renders the element with a wave by creating a sine wave distortion along the element's x-axis
xray	Renders the element in black and white with reverse color and brightness values

Table 4-1 shows the syntax of the filter declaration you must add within an inline style statement or CSS rule in a style sheet. Remember, in order for the *filter* property to have any effect on an element, you must also set the element's width.

Property	Values	Syntax
alpha	opacity level: 0–100 (0 = transparent, 100 = opaque) *finishopacity* level: 0–100 (0 = transparent, 100 = opaque) *style*: 0 = uniform, 1 = linear, 2 = radial, 3 = rectangular *startx*: x-coordinate for start of opacity gradient *starty*: y-coordinate for start of opacity gradient *finishx*: x-coordinate for finish of opacity gradient, *finishy*: y-coordinate for finish of opacity gradient	*filter:alpha(opacity=0,* *finishopacity=75, style=2,* *startx=0, starty=0,* *finishx=140, finishy=270)*
blur	add: true = add original object to blurred object *direction*: direction of motion causing the blur; 0–315 in 45-degree increments *strength*: integer representing the "depth" of the motion blur	*filter:blur(add=true, direction=45,* *strength=5)*

Table 4-1   Filter Properties, Values, and Declaration Syntax

Property	Values	Syntax
chroma	color: color to make transparent; #rrggbb triplet	*filter:chroma(color=#FFFFFF)*
dropshadow	color: shadow color; #rrggbb triplet *offx*: horizontal shadow offset *offy*: vertical shadow offset *positive*: true = create shadow for nontransparent pixels, false = create shadow for transparent pixels	*filter:dropshadow(color=#6699CC, offx=5, offy=5, positive=true)*
fliph		*filter:fliph*
flipv		*filter:flipv*
glow	color: color for glow; #rrggbb triplet *strength*: glow intensity 0–100	*filter:glow(color=#6699CC, strength=5)*
gray		*filter:gray*
invert		*filter:invert*
mask	color: mask color; #rrggbb triplet	*filter:mask(color=#FFFFE0)*
shadow	color: shadow color; #rrggbb triplet *direction*: direction shadow is cast; 0–315 in 45-degree increments	*filter:shadow(color=ff0000, direction=90)*
wave	add: true add original object to filtered object *freq*: integer number of waves in distortion *lightstrength*: strength of light on the wave effect as a percentage *phase*: angular offset of wave as a percentage of 360 degrees *strength*: integer intensity of wave effect	*filter:wave(add=true, freq=1, lightstrength=3, phase=0, strength=5)*
xray		*filter:xray*

Table 4-1　Filter Properties, Values, and Declaration Syntax *(continued)*

Aligning Labels with Form Elements and Adding Color to Forms

As you learned in Chapter 3 of this book, forms let your site visitors send information to you, search a database, or send data of some kind to an application or script running at the Web server. Forms consist mainly of rectangular text input areas, checkboxes, radio buttons, and a couple of pushbuttons (used to submit the form results or reset the form's input elements). In general, a form's input elements and pushbuttons look the same from one form to the next.

Using CSS rules, you can add a splash of color that attracts attention to a form. By using a distinctive color for the blank space that surrounds form elements, you let visitors see at a glance just how many fields the form contains. Moreover, by applying a CSS rule that highlights the text labels next to required fields, you can let visitors knows which input they must fill out before submitting the form's data to the Web server for processing. Hidden behind the scenes, CSS also provides an alternate tool you can use to lay out (that is, to position) the text labels, input elements, and pushbuttons on a form.

USE IT   To give your form a background color that sets it off from other content on a page, place the form's elements into a division container, as shown here:

```
<div style="width:475px; background-color:#FFFFE0;
   border:limegreen 1px solid; padding:5px">
  <form>
    ... Form Elements & Label Text ...
  </form>
</div>
```

In this example, the <div> tag defines a 475-pixel-wide area, which will hold the form's elements. Although the division's width is fixed (at 475 pixels, in this example), the space required by the form's elements and their placement within the form determine the length of the form's (and therefore the division's) rectangular area on the page.

In place of HTML table rows and cells, use <div> and <span> elements to position elements and labels next to the elements on the form. To style form elements you place within division and span containers, create the following three classes in your style sheet:

```
div.row {clear:both; padding-top:5px; font-size:12pt}
div.row {clear:both; padding-top:12px}
div.row span.label{float:left; width:110px; text-align:right}
div.row span.element {float:right; width:375px; text-algin:left}
```

When applied, the *float* property in the *span.label* class and the one in the *span.element* class tell the Web browser where to place elements within the current container. Styling text elements (that is, labels) using the *span.label* class floats the text to the left of other objects within the current division container. Conversely, the *span.element* class applied to a form element floats the element to the right of other container objects.

Use the *div.row*, *span.label*, and *span.element* classes defined in the preceding example to style the <div> and <span> tags that contain the form's labels and input elements as follows to create the form shown in Figure 4-22:

```
<body>
  <div style="width:475px; background-color:#FFFFE0;
     border:limegreen 1px solid; padding:5px>"

  <form>
    <div class="row">
      <span class="label">First Name:</span>
      <span class="element"><input type="text" size="30">
    </span></div>
    <div class="row">
```

```
  <span class="label">Last Name:</span>
  <span class="element"><input type="text" size="30">
</span></div>
<div class="row">
  <span class="label">E-Mail Address:</span>
  <span class="element"><input type="text" size="30">
</span></div>
<div class="row">
  <span class="label">Comments:</span>
  <span class="element">
    <textarea cols="40" rows="10"></textarea></span>
  <p> </p>
</div>

<div class="row">
  <br>  <input type="submit" value="Submit">
    <input type="reset" value="Reset"><br> 
</div>
</form>

</div>
</body>
```

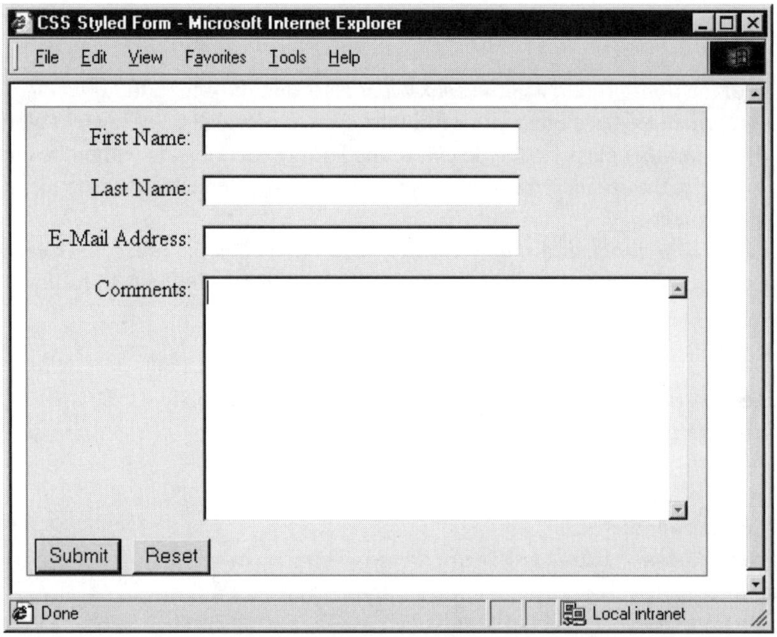

Figure 4-22   Form with input elements and text labels styled by CSS classes

Now, suppose that you want to indicate form elements the visitor must complete prior to submitting the form (that is, you want to denote required fields). Create a CSS class such as the *span.reqLabel* class shown here:

```
div.row span.reqLabel{float:left; width:114px; text-align:right;
        color:red; font-weight:bold; background-color:yellow}
```

Then, use the *class* attribute to style each span element using the *span.reqLabel* class. Be sure to include—somewhere near the form's Submit button—text that lets the visitor know what red, boldface labels mean.

By the way, the 475-pixel *width* assigned to the preceding form's <div> container is not an arbitrary value. The form used in this Tip requires 475 pixels to display at the left side of the form, *E-mail address:* in boldface (not shown in Figure 4-22) and the text area flush against the right-hand side at the bottom of the form. To determine the widths of the division tags your form needs, change the *span.label* and *span.element* classes to display a dashed border around each division, as shown here:

```
div.row span.label{float:left; width:110px; text-align:right;
        border:1px dotted}
div.row span.element {float:right; width:345px;
        text-algin:left; border:1px dotted}
```

Displaying the dashed border around divisions makes it easy to see the effects of changing the division's *width* within the *span.label* and *span.element* declarations. Reduce the width of each division container class until the dashed border just surrounds the label or input element within the division. Next, reduce the *width* of the form's enclosing division container until the border around the form lies just outside the borders of the division containers that hold the form's elements. Be sure to remove the *border* property declaration from the *span.label* and *span.element* class declarations before you publish the Web page with the form to the Web site.

Displaying a Gallery of Thumbnails with Captions

As you already know, a thumbnail is a smaller version of a full-size image. Thumbnails take significantly less time to download and display than their corresponding full-size images. As the size of an image displayed onscreen increases, so does the file size of the graphics file in which the image is stored. The larger the file size, the longer it takes the browser to download and display an image.

You use thumbnails in place of full-size images when visitors are likely to view only some of the images in a collection and to display more images onscreen at once. Although you could use hypertext links alone to cut down the Web page display time even more, thumbnails at least let the visitor see what full-size images look like. Suppose for example, that you create a Web site for a realtor who has full-screen, digital pictures of each house currently under contract. Rather than make visitors wait to download all the full-screen images of houses in the realtor's inventory, display each picture as a thumbnail about one-tenth the size of the original picture. You can then display ten pictures within the space and time required to display a single full-screen image. When the site visitor sees the thumbnail with a description of interest, the visitor will click the thumbnail to retrieve and display a full-screen picture of the house.

If you use an HTML table to lay out the thumbnails and captions, the browser cannot vary the number of thumbnails displayed in a row, based solely on the size of the application window. If you create a table with ten columns, for example, the browser must display all ten thumbnails horizontally—even when only five thumbnails at a time fit horizontally within the left- and right-hand sides of the application window. As a result, the ten-column table will force the visitor to scroll horizontally to see additional images within each row. Using CSS, you can let the Web browser vary the number of thumbnails displayed in any row based on the width of the browser application window. Thus, the requirements of our variable-width thumbnail gallery are relatively straightforward. Within the HTML document, write the code that inserts an image followed by a <br> tag and a text description that the browser centers below the image.

USE IT   To let the browser determine the number of images it will place horizontally across the page, place each image (and its caption) within a separate <div> container and float each <div> container to the left. In addition, style the paragraph element within each <div> container such that the Web browser will center the paragraph text between the left- and right-hand sides of the container, as shown here:

```
div.fLeft {float:left; padding-left:5px; padding-right:5px}
div.fLeft p {text-align:center}
```

The first rule creates a *fLeft* class you can apply to a <div> container to float a container (and its contents) to the left of the element that follows it within the Web page HTML. Whenever there is not enough room to display the next <div> container within the application window on the current line, the Web browser will move to the line below the current <div> containers, and display the next container flush with the left-hand side of the page. The second rule tells the browser to center paragraph text between the left- and right-hand sides of <div> containers styled using the *fLeft* class.

Thus, the code to display variable numbers of thumbnails and captions becomes this:

```
<body>
  <div class="fLeft">
    <a href="images/house1.JPG">
     <img src="house1_sm.JPG" width="100" height="100" border=0
       alt="house 1"<br></a><p>Description /<br>Caption 1
       <br> </p>
  </div>
  <div class="fLeft">
    <a href="images/house2.JPG">
     <img src="house2_sm.JPG" width="100" height="100" border=0
       alt="house 2"<br></a><p>Description /<br>Caption 2
       <br> </p>
  </div>
  <div class="fLeft">
```

```
      <a href="images/house3.JPG">
       <img src="house3_sm.JPG" width="100" height="100" border=0
         alt="house 3"<br></a><p>Description /<br>Caption 3
         <br> </p>
   </div>
   <div class="fLeft">
     <a href="images/house4.JPG">
       <img src="house4_sm.JPG" width="100" height="100" border=0
         alt="house 4"<br></a><p>Description /<br>Caption 4
         <br> </p>
   </div>
</body>
```

To work properly, the code in this example requires that each caption contain the same number of lines, and the length of each line must be no wider than the thumbnail below which the caption is to appear. If one or more lines within the caption are wider than the image, the Web browser will still center the caption text relative to the sides of the container. However, the image will appear to the left and not centered above the text. Use *padding-left* and *padding-right* declarations within the *div.fLeft* class definition to add blank space between the sides of the image and the left- and right-hand walls of the <div> container as shown in Figure 4-23.

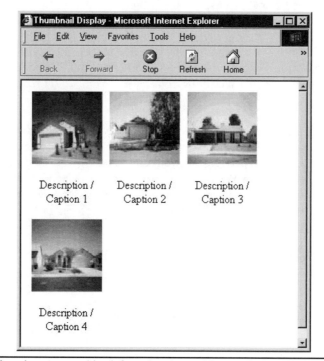

Figure 4-23   Thumbnails separated by left and right padding with centered captions

Center the picture within the container by using width padding between the image and the left-and right-hand sides of the <div> container. The Web browser will then center the text below the picture—given that the total width of the image plus the blank padding on either side of the image is greater than the length of each line within the caption.

Controlling the Cursor

In addition to specifying the appearance of the text on a Web page, you can create CSS rules that instruct the Web browser to display a specific mouse pointer. Normally, you let the Web browser select the cursor automatically based on the type of content currently under the mouse pointer. For example, when the visitor moves the mouse over a hyperlink, the Web browser changes the default mouse pointer (the arrow) into a hand. Changing the cursor from the default arrow to something else lets the visitor know that there is something special about the text or image under the mouse pointer.

At times, however, the Web browser fails to change the cursor even though the HTML contains a hidden feature the visitor may find useful. For example, you can include the *title* attribute in many HTML tags. The *title* attribute, when present, instructs the Web browser to display a tool tip when the mouse pointer hovers over an element whose tag contains the attribute. Suppose for example, that your Web page contained the following HTML:

```
<acronym title="HTML & Web Design Tips and Techniques">
HTWDTT</acronym> provides great tips you can use to exploit Web
technologies.
```

If the site visitor hovers the mouse pointer over *HWDTT* in *HTWDTT provides great tips you can use to exploit Web technologies*, the Web browser displays the tool tip *HTML & Web Design Tips and Techniques* after a few seconds.

USE IT   Unfortunately, Web browsers do nothing to alert site visitors to the availability of a tool tip defined by an HTML tag's *title* attribute. To provide a visual clue that there is "something" hidden from view within the Web page HTML, you can use the CSS *cursor* property to display the help cursor (typically, a question mark), when the visitor moves the mouse over a Web page element. For example, to change the mouse pointer to the question (?) mark whenever the visitor moves the mouse over an <acronym>, <abbr>, or user-defined *help* class element, include the following declarations in your style sheet:

```
abbr, acronym, .help {border-bottom:1px dotted black;
                       cursor:help}
```

The CSS rule in this example actually provides two visual cues, as shown in Figure 4-24.

By underlining text—with a dotted and *not* a solid underline—you show the site visitor the abbreviations, acronyms, and help text throughout the Web page. (Wherever the visitor sees text

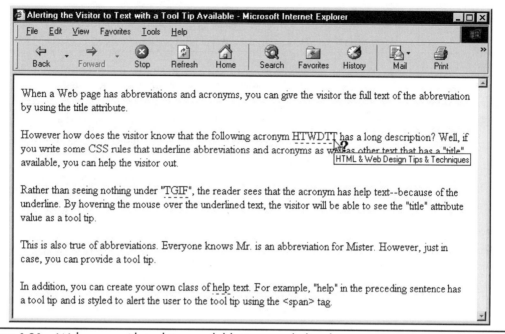

When a Web page has abbreviations and acronyms, you can give the visitor the full text of the abbreviation by using the title attribute.

However how does the visitor know that the following acronym HTWDTT has a long description? Well, if you write some CSS rules that underline abbreviations and acronyms as well as other text that has a "title" available, you can help the visitor out.

[HTML & Web Design Tips & Techniques]

Rather than seeing nothing under "TGIF", the reader sees that the acronym has help text--because of the underline. By hovering the mouse over the underlined text, the visitor will be able to see the "title" attribute value as a tool tip.

This is also true of abbreviations. Everyone knows Mr. is an abbreviation for Mister. However, just in case, you can provide a tool tip.

In addition, you can create your own class of help text. For example, "help" in the preceding sentence has a tool tip and is styled to alert the user to the tool tip using the <span> tag.

Figure 4-24 Web page with tool tip–available items underlined

underlined with black dots, he or she knows that more information is available.) Moreover, to prevent the visitor from confusing the "help available" underlined text with hypertext links, the rule instructs the Web browser to display the help cursor (the question mark) as the visitor moves across text with *title* information available.

Now, suppose that you rewrite the code in the previous example as follows:

```
<acronym title="HTML & Web Design Tips and Techniques">
HTWDTT</acronym> provides great tips you can use to exploit
<span class="help" title="tables, forms, CSS, ASP, Graphics">
Web technologies</span>.
```

The Web browser will then place a broken (dotted) line beneath both *HWDTT* and *Web technologies* to let the visitor know that more information is available. As the visitor moves the mouse pointer over either text element, the Web browser changes the default mouse pointer to a question mark. In addition, if the visitor lets the question mark mouse pointer hover in place for a few seconds, the Web browser will display the tool tip defined by the *title* attribute within the element's tag in the Web page HTML.

Table 4-2 gives the available *cursor* property values and a description of each cursor (that is, mouse pointer) type you can specify.

Cursor Value	Description
auto	The cursor displayed depends on the context.
crosshair	A simple crosshair cursor.
default	The Web browser's default cursor, usually an arrow.
hand	A hand, normally displayed when the mouse pointer is over a clickable region within an image or over a hypertext link.
move	Four-headed arrow, which indicates that the item can be moved.
e-resize, ne-resize, nw-resize, n-resize, se-resize, sw-resize, s-resize, w-resize	Resize cursor, indicating you are changing the size of the item. The resize cursor is typically an arrow that points in the direction indicated: e=east, arrow points right; s=south, arrow points down; nw=northwest, arrow points diagonally, up and to the left, and so on.
text	I-beam cursor for selecting text or positioning the insertion point.
wait	The wait cursor, typically an hourglass.
help	The help cursor, typically the question mark.

Table 4-2   The Available CSS Cursor Types

Layering Web Page Elements

When positioning elements on a Web page, you normally work in two dimensions. For example, to position a form 75 pixels away from the left-hand side and 50 pixels from the top of the page, you would use a <form> tag similar to the following:

```
<form style="position:absolute; left:75; top:50">
```

Of course, your <form> tag will have additional attributes, such as *action* and *method* (to name just two), which tell the browser where to send the form results and how to package them, respectively. However, the point to understand here is that CSS rules let you use absolute and relative positioning to place any container element (and thereby the element(s) within the container) where you want the content to appear on the Web page. With absolute positioning, you specify the distance the browser is to place the element away from the left-hand side and top of the Web page. Similarly, relative positioning means that the position you specify is relative to an element's natural position in the document's flow. (An element's "natural position" is its location on the page absent CSS positioning instructions.)

In reality, when you specify an element's position in two-dimensions, the Web browser adds a third dimension (depth) behind the scenes. Suppose, for example, your HTML has the following statements in the order shown here:

```
<h2 style="position:absolute; top:110px; left:75px;
  background-color:yellow; border:solid 2px; font-size:25pt">
  This is heading level-2 text</h2>
<h1 style="position:absolute; top:100px; left:50px;
  background-color:yellow; border:solid 2px; font-size:35pt">
This is heading level-1 text</h1>
```

You will see only the level-1 heading on the Web page. The Web browser does not "forget" to place the level-2 heading on the page. Quite the contrary, the browser first places the level-2 heading 100 pixels from the top and 50 pixels away from the left-hand side of the Web page. Then, the Web browser places the level-1 heading on top of the level-2 heading. Thus, when a CSS style tells the browser to place an element where other content already exists on the Web page, the browser layers the new content in front of what's already there—unless you adjust the first element's *z-index* value.

The CSS *z-index* property lets you select the layer in which the Web browser will place a Web page element. When writing HTML statements, things can get a bit messy if you locate elements on a page using CSS positioning properties while at the same time relying on the statement order to determine whether an element overlaps or is overlapped by another.

USE IT The third dimension, controlled by the *z-index* property, involves specifying an element's location on an axis perpendicular to the Web page. The lower the *z-index*, the closer the element is to the page surface. Conversely, the higher the *z-index*, the further the object's layer is away from the page. Thus, if you add the following *z-index* declarations to the HTML from the previous example, the Web browser will display the level-2 heading in front of the level-1 heading as shown in Figure 4-25:

```
<h2 style="position:absolute; top:110px; left:75px; z-index:2;
  background-color:yellow; border:solid 2px; font-size:25pt">
  This is heading level-2 text</h2>
<h1 style="position:absolute; top:100px; left:50px; z-index:1;
  background-color:yellow; border:solid 2px; font-size:35pt">
This is heading level-1 text</h1>
```

The z-index of the first element is higher than the z-index of the second. As a result the Web browser will display the first element (the level-2 heading) in a layer above (that is, in front of) the second element (the level-1 heading).

▶ **NOTE**

Although z-index values can be negative, zero, or positive, use only zero and positive values. Some versions of Web browsers incorrectly position elements with a negative z-index in front of objects with a positive z-index. Remember, the z-index is a relative measure. Therefore, you can place one element behind another by specifying a lower (and not necessarily a negative) z-index.

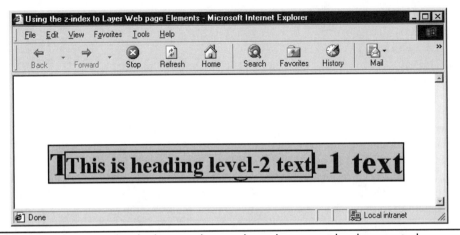

Figure 4-25 An element with a higher z-index overlaps elements with a lower z-index

Sending Your Style Sheet Through a Validator

Sending your style sheet through a CSS validator is like having a teacher check your CSS design homework before you receive a final grade from your site visitors. In addition to checking for errors (such as invalid properties or property values), the CSS validator at http://jigsaw.w3.org/css-validator/ also offers suggestions for improvement. For example, if you send the following external style sheet to the W3C committee's CSS validator, you will receive back a report such as the one shown in Figure 4-26:

```
h1 {color:blue; font-size:40px; font-family:garamond}
p  {color:white; background:green; font-family:helvetica;
    text-indent:1cm}
body {background:#ADD8E6; color:maroon}
```

The "Errors" section of the report shows you what you must fix; the "Warnings" section shows you rules that—although correct—could be improved, and gives you suggestions for improvement; the "Valid CSS Informations" section at the end of the report shows you what you did right.

 USE IT Using the W3C CSS validator is a simple process. Bear in mind that the validator will check only the CSS rules in external (linked) style sheets. Therefore, if you embedded a style sheet in the Web page header section, you must copy the rules to an external file, which you can then send to the validator. To validate a style sheet, perform the following steps:

1. If you do not have a permanent (always-on) connection to the Internet, establish a dial-up connection through your ISP.

2. Start your Web browser, type **http://jigsaw.w3.org/css-validator/** into the browser's Address field, and press ENTER. Your Web browser, in turn, will display the W3C CSS Validation Service screen.

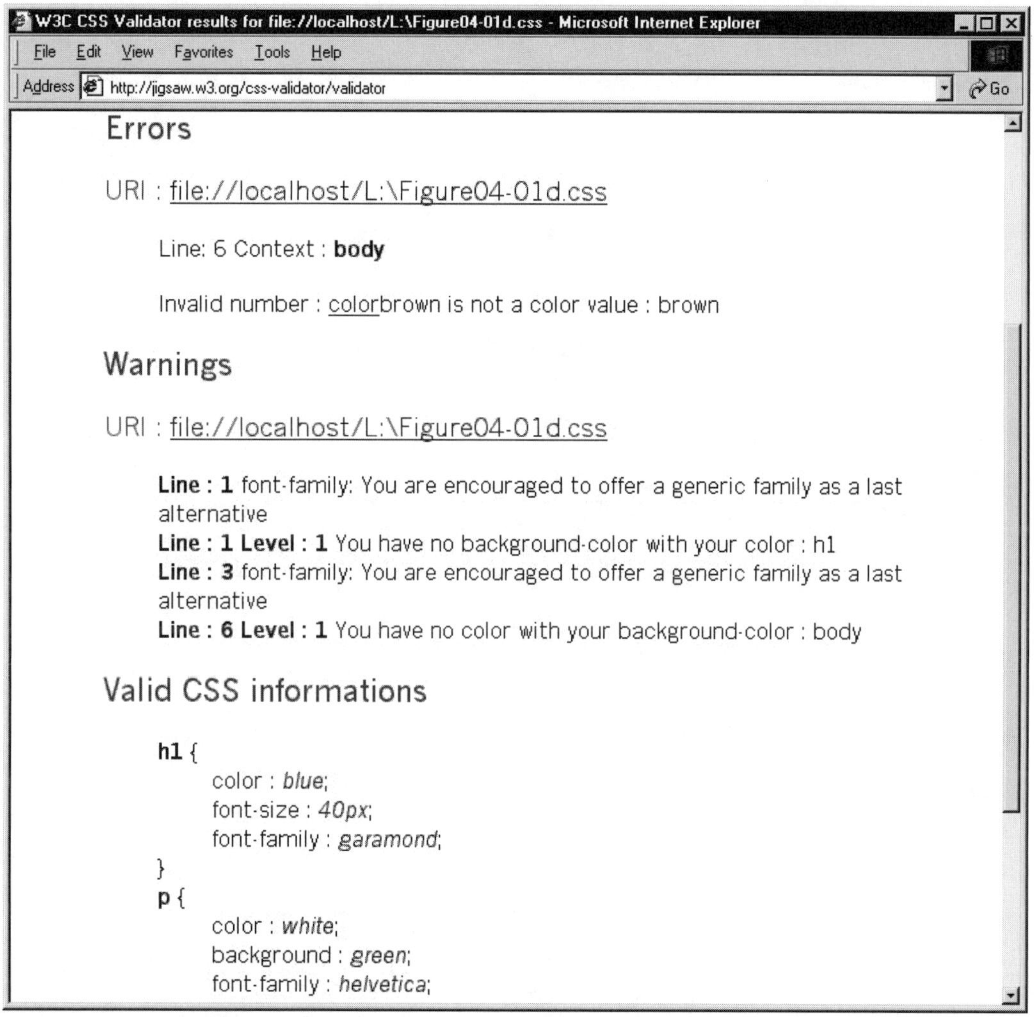

Figure 4-26 CSS validation report from the W3C CSS validator

3. To send a style sheet file to the validator, click the Validate Your Cascading Style Sheet Source File By Upload hypertext link. The Web server, in turn, will display the Validator screen shown in Figure 4-27.

4. Into the Upload A CSS Source File field, enter the full pathname of the external CSS file you want to validate. Rather than enter the pathname, you can click BROWSE and navigate to the file instead.

5. Select the Warnings level, Profile (CSS version), and Medium (all, aural, Braille, handheld, and so on). If you are validating a style sheet intended for use on a Web page to be displayed by a Web browser running on a PC or Macintosh system, accept the default selections.

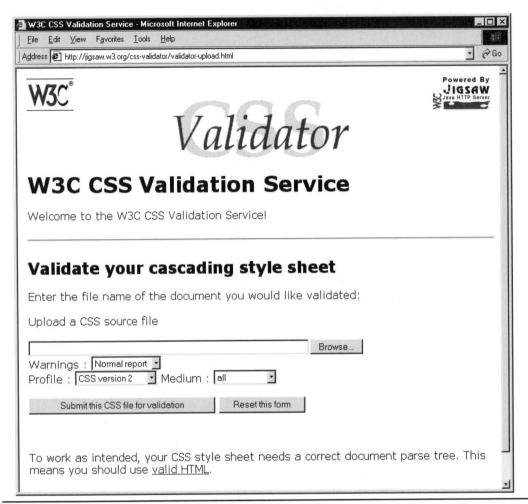

Figure 4-27 The validator options selection screen

6. Click Submit This CSS File For Validation. The Web browser, in turn, will send the file whose name you entered in Step 4, and issue the validation report similar to the one you saw at the beginning of this Tip (in Figure 4-26) in a matter of seconds.

Although you can submit entire style sheets or individual CSS rules for validation by using several different methods, get into the habit of creating and sending only external style sheet files to the validator. First, by placing CSS rules in linked external style sheets, you are more likely to take advantage of the true power of CSS to give the pages across large Web sites a consistent look and feel. Second, by submitting a file with only CSS rules, you don't have to worry about someone viewing server-side scripts you may have embedded within the Web page—some of which might reveal sensitive information about your site.

CHAPTER 5

XHTML and Emerging Trends

TIPS IN THIS CHAPTER

▶ Converting HTML to XHTML Using HTML Tidy — 233

▶ Selecting the Correct DOCTYPE for Your Web Page — 237

▶ Validating Your Web Page with an XHTML Validator — 238

▶ Setting the Text Size on an XHTML Web Page with Keywords — 242

▶ Grouping an XHTML Form's Selection List Items with the <optgroup> Tag — 245

▶ Adding Color to XHTML Tables with Cascading Style Sheet Rules — 247

▶ Embedding Fonts Within an XHTML Web Page with CSS Rules — 249

▶ Inserting an XHTML Page Within Another with an Inline Frame — 251

▶ Updating Multiple XHTML Page Inline Frames at Once — 255

▶ Changing XHTML Page Appearance Based on Media Type — 257

▶ Controlling the Way the Web Browser Prints an XHTML Web Page — 261

In Chapter 1, we introduced you to Hypertext Markup Language (HTML) and the World Wide Web. You learned that Web browsers request HTML documents (that is, Web pages) from Web servers. After a Web server receives an HTTP request for a Web page, the server sends the document over the Internet to the Web browser that requested it. The Web browser, in turn, opens the HTML document and follows the markup instructions written within the file. The markup instructions are HTML tags and attributes that tell the Web browser where to place text and objects onscreen and how the text in the foreground and the background on which objects sit is supposed to look.

As you use the Tips throughout this book to create your own Web pages, you may say to yourself, "Hey, this stuff is easy," and you would be correct. Creating a Web page requires no special programming software or knowledge—all you need is a text editor and an understanding of HTML. Ironically, the very ease with which one can create Web pages has also been the Web's greatest source of difficulty. Having thousands and thousands of people authoring Web pages has made it impossible to get everyone to write HTML the same way. Forget trying to get thousands or even hundreds of people to accept a specific way of doing something creative when the two manufacturers of the most popular Web browsers cannot agree on something as simple as a single tag that lets designers add background music to a Web page.

Moreover, neither Netscape nor Microsoft forces authors to either write proper HTML (according to the World Wide Web Consortium [W3C] recommendations) or have their browsers display nothing at all. Instead, Netscape Navigator, Internet Explorer, and most other Web browsers try to "guess" what the author meant by improperly written HTML. As a result, browsers have grown in size as manufacturers added the code necessary to handle the many different (but incorrect) ways to write the HTML that describes a Web page. The additional code has not only made the browser applications larger but has also introduced bugs, which sometimes cause even correctly written HTML to behave differently from one browser to the next.

To address design problems caused by improper coding practices and overly lenient Web browsers, the World Wide Web Consortium (W3C) rewrote HTML 4.01 as an Extensible Markup Language (XML) application. Hence the new specification's name (XML + HTML = XHTML). By applying the rigorous element and syntax definitions within XML to the previously, more loosely defined HTML specification, the W3C hopes that browser manufacturers will force authors to write proper XHTML code. An XML parser, for example, is under no obligation to (and in fact, should not) render improperly written XML elements. Distributing Web browsers that display only correctly written XHTML will get everyone to structure Web documents properly and let manufacturers reduce the lines of code (and as a result, the number of bugs) within their Web browsers.

Although XHTML sports the name of a "new" recommendation from the W3C, it adds no new features to what's already available within HTML 4.01. What XHTML does is try to prevent authors from writing improperly formed HTML by applying the rigorous rules of XML to HTML. If you have looked at XML in the past and given it up as way too complex for use in encoding simple Web pages, don't worry. You can create XHTML 1.0–compliant Web pages without knowing anything about XML. To write XHTML you use the same HTML tags, attributes, and Cascading Style Sheets with which you are already familiar. If you do understand a little about XML, however, you will realize the true promise of XHTML's future.

In addition to imposing some "new" rules on encoding HTML (which we will discuss in a moment), XHTML is both extensible (hence the *X* in XHTML) and modular. *Extensible* means that XHTML lets both manufacturers and (for the first time) authors extend and expand HTML by adding new tags. *Modular* means that manufacturers can reduce the size of their browsers by eliminating the code for XHTML elements not required for their platforms. A soon to be released recommendation from the W3C will specify exactly which tags belong to which XHTML subsets (or modules) and provide a formal mechanism for adding new modules to extend the language and for removing existing modules to eliminate unneeded elements.

Understanding the Requirements for Creating Valid XHTML Documents

First, understand that XHTML is HTML 4 written as an XML application. What this means is that a W3C committee met and looked at each tag (or element) within HTML 4 and determined how to define that element using XML. As a result, from a Web author's standpoint, the code within an XHTML Web page file looks almost exactly like the code for the same Web page in an HTML 4 file. You use the same tags and attributes in both with a couple of exceptions.

Within the XHTML document you will see a space and forward slash " /" used to close noncontainer (that is, empty) tags such as <br> and <hr>, which become <br /> and <hr /> when written as XHTML. In addition, sometime in the future (but not right now) an XHTML file will have all its embedded scripts, comments, and style sheets contained within CDATA sections, which we will discuss after we go over XHTML's current "rules of the road" for Web page markup on the information superhighway.

Your first reaction to XHTML may be, to paraphrase the military officer in the movie "The Treasure of the Sierra Madre," "Rules! Rules! We don't need no stinking rules!" Of course, "intellectual freedom" and the "rules are meant to be broken" attitude are at the very cornerstones of life on the Internet. The Web was never intended to be some large library of documents where you had to follow certain rules or have specific equipment to check files out for viewing. The whole idea was (and is) to create a means by which anyone with access to the Internet can display anything publicly available regardless of his or her operating system, Web browser, or computer platform.

The new rules XHTML asks Web browsers to impose on designers have nothing to do with content. XHTML simply tries to get everyone to write tags the same way, so that every Web browser can properly draw the page it receives without having to "guess" at the author's intentions. Viewed this way, XHTML's rules actually give you more control and may serve to increase your audience and available tools. If everyone conforms to the standard, manufacturers can spend less time getting their browsers to display malformed HTML correctly and more time making browsers smaller, faster, and able to display the next "new" killer multimedia object you want to include on a Web page.

In total, XHTML's new requirements are not daunting. In fact, as we discuss each rule in detail within the remainder of this section, you may find you have been following most of them all along. After discussing XHTML rules, we take an in-depth look at the Document Type Definition (DTD)— what it is and what it means to the future of XHTML. However, if you are concerned more with the "here and now" than with the XHTML in your future, you can skip right to the Tip "Selecting the Correct DOCTYPE for Your Web Page," which explains how to select the correct DTD for your Web page.

Then, as long as you adhere to the following rules, you'll be writing proper XHTML in no time:

- XHTML documents must be well-formed.

- Elements must nest and not overlap.

- All element and attribute names must be written in lowercase.

- Open container tags must be closed, and each empty tag must have a terminator.

- XHTML documents must start with a DOCTYPE declaration.

- All attributes must have values enclosed within quotes.

- XHTML documents must have a <title> element within the header section.

XHTML Documents Must Be Well-Formed

With the exception of a frameset page, a well-formed XHTML document has an <html> root element that contains two embedded, non-overlapping sections ("header" and "body") as shown here:

```
<html>
  <head>...</head>
  <body>...</body>
</html>
```

The header section (between <head> and </head> section tags) must begin immediately after the <html> tag. In addition, the header section must end (with an </head> tag) before the body section (between <body> and </body> section tags) begins. XHTML frameset documents too must be well-formed. Within a frameset document, however, you replace the "body" section with the "frames" section as follows:

```
<html>
  <head>...</head>
  <frameset cols="100,400,*">
    <frame src="FramedPage1.html" name="left">
    <frame src="FramedPade2.html" name="right">
  </frameset>
</html>
```

If you read Chapter 1, you are already familiar with XHTML section tags—they are the same <html>, <head>, and <body> tags you studied in Chapter 1. In short, you use section tags to organize the Web page XHTML into two containers ("head" and "body"), which you put within a third, the "html" container. Each container (or section) serves a different purpose, as described here:

- **<html></html>**   The "html" container, as its name implies, encloses all the XHTML entities, attributes, scripts, and style sheets the Web browser may process while rendering the Web page. Place the opening <html> tag immediately after the DOCTYPE description at the start of the

XHTML file and the closing </html> tag at the very end of the file. Nothing should follow the </html> tag.

- **<head></head>**   The Web browser loads the contents of the Web page "header" section into memory for possible use later (in the case of scripts and CSS rules), but does not display the content it finds as part of the Web page itself. The Web page header starts with an opening <head> tag (immediately after the <html> tag at the top of the file) and ends with a closing </head> tag. In addition to style sheets and client-side scripts, you can insert tags in the Web page header to include such information as the name of the Web page author, the date he or she created the page, and keywords that search engines should use when indexing the Web page to make it easier for visitors to find. In addition, XHTML requires that you include a <title> element within every Web page header. Of all the HTML tags and information you place within the Web page header, the Web browser displays only the text you enclose within start and end title tags (<title></title>) onscreen. Typically, the Web browser displays the Web page title within the title bar along the top of the browser's application window.

- **<body></body>**   The Web page "body" container immediately follows the Web page header section and contains all the elements you want the browser to display on the Web page. Start the Web page body section by placing an opening <body> tag immediately after the header section's closing </head> tag and end the body section with a closing </body> tag immediately before the enclosing "html" container's closing </html> tag.

The following code illustrates the correct placement of the XHTML section tags and the minimum tags required to define a valid XHTML document:

```
<!DOCTYPE html PUBLIC "-//W3C//DTD XHTML 1.0 Transitional//EN"
  "DTD/xhtml1-transitional.dtd">
<html>
<head><title>My First Valid XHTML Web Page</title></head>
<body bgcolor="white">
  <!-- Content the browser is to display goes here. -->
</body>
</html>
```

Note that all element and attribute names must be lowercase. Whereas you could use all lowercase, uppercase, or a combination of lowercase and uppercase names when describing an HTML Web page, XHTML is case-sensitive and requires that you use all lowercase names. However, although you must write attribute names in lowercase, you can write attribute values as uppercase and/or lowercase—just make sure to enclose every attribute's value within quotes.

Elements Must Nest and Not Overlap

Most Web browsers don't care if you overlap elements by writing code such as the following, in which the <b> tag starts within a paragraph element and ends outside it:

```
<p>The following word is written in boldface: <b>bold</p></b>
```

Technically, overlapping tags is illegal (albeit widely tolerated by Web browsers) in HTML as well. However, as mentioned previously, XHTML documents must be well-formed. As such, one day (soon) Web browsers will enforce the XHTML standard and will not "guess" what is meant when the XHTML statement syntax is wrong. If you always write your closing element (and section) tags in reverse of the order in which you wrote the opening tags, your elements (and sections) will not overlap. Thus, you would rewrite the statement in this example as follows:

```
<p>The following word is written in boldface: <b>bold</b></p>
```

All Element and Attribute Names Must Be Written in Lowercase

HTML (unlike XHTML) is case "insensitive," meaning that <BODY> is the same as <body> within an HTML document. As a result, many authors try to make the code within their Web page files more readable by writing element names in all capital letters to set HTML tags off from text content and attributes (written in lowercase). Thus, a typical HTML document might look like the following:

```
<HTML>
<HEAD><TITLE>My Web Page Title</TITLE></HEAD>
<BODY bgcolor="lightyellow">
  <P>This is written in the <I>default</I> color</P>
  <P><FONT color="red">This is written in <B>red</B></FONT></P>
  <P>Finished up with the default color</P>
</BODY>
</HTML>
```

Unfortunately, although easy to pick out, none of the tags used in this example are valid in XHTML.

When a Web browser encounters a tag within an XHTML document (or an HTML document, for that matter), the browser looks up the tag within the DTD. As you will learn from the discussion of DTDs that follows this look at XHTML rules, a DTD has a list of all language elements (or tags) as well as a list of which attributes are valid or required for each tag. If you misspell a tag's name (for example, if you spell <body> as <boddy>) the browser will not find the element within the DTD and will therefore ignore it and move on to the next tag in the Web document.

Because XHTML is case-sensitive and the XHTML DTD contains element names in lowercase, you must write XHTML tags in lowercase. Otherwise, the Web browser will not find the tags you use within the XHTML DTD and will ignore the undefined tag, and in the case of container tags, the content within the container as well. In other words, the XHTML DTD has an entry for the <table> tag but not for the <TABLE> tag. Meaning, if the browser reads the <TABLE> tag, which is not defined within the DTD, the browser will ignore the tag and move on to the next without displaying the table or its contents.

Although you must write attributes names in lowercase as well, you can write attribute values in either upper- or lowercase. The following three lines, for example, are equivalent:

```
<body bgcolor="lightyellow">
<body bgcolor="LightYellow">
<body bgcolor="LIGHTYELLOW">
```

Open Container Tags Must Be Closed, and Each Empty Tag Must Have a Terminator

Web page elements that have both an open and a close tag are "container" elements because they enclose or *contain* text content, images, or other objects the browser displays onscreen. For example, the following code illustrates how the start and end paragraph tags (<p></p>) enclose, or contain a section of text:

```
<p>This is text within a "paragraph" container.</p>
```

When you insert a "paragraph" container (as defined by begin and end paragraph tags) within the Web page HTML, the Web browser displays the container's contents (that is, the paragraph text) onscreen.

Because the Web browser inserts a blank line (and moves to the left margin) when it encounters the start of a new paragraph container (that is, a <p> tag), many authors have used <p> tags as "paragraph marks" to separate paragraphs as shown here:

```
This is the first paragraph.<p>
This is the second paragraph.<p>
This is the third paragraph.
```

This practice is not valid in XHTML. You must close each paragraph container that you open (with a <p> tag) by inserting a closing </p> tag within the Web page XHTML. The requirement to close open containers extends to all container tags, such as list (<ul></ul>, <ol></ol>), list item (<li></li>), table (<table></table>, form (<form></form>) tags, and so on.

Omitting closing tags for container elements (like for the three paragraph elements in the previous example) was syntactically incorrect in HTML as well. (Even though Web browsers let you get away with doing so.) However, unlike HTML, XHTML requires that you close noncontainer (or "empty") tags as well. Thus, in HTML you could correctly rewrite the code from the last example as follows:

```
This is the first section of text.<br><br>
This is the second section of text.<br><br>
This is the third section of text.
```

In XHTML, however, you must terminate empty <br> tags with a forward slash ("/") separated from the element name by a space as shown here:

```
This is the first section of text.<br /><br />
This is the second section of text.<br /><br />
```

The requirement to close empty tags also extends to image (<img />), frame (<frame />), meta data (<meta />), option (<option />), parameter (<param />) tags, and so on.

You can also use the XHTML empty tag terminator as shorthand to close container tags that happen to be empty. For example, you might insert the following <applet> tag within the Web page XHTML to instruct the Web browser to run the Java applet *MyApplet.class*:

```
<applet code="MyApplet.class" width="200" height="200"></applet>
```

Although <applet> is a container tag, in this case, it contains no content to display in browsers that do not support applets. You would insert content for browsers without applet support within the container, that is, between the <applet> tag and the closing </applet> tag. Because the <applet> container tag is empty (that is, there is no content between the <applet> and </applet> tags), you can replace the closing </applet> tag with the XHTML empty tag terminator with the <applet> tag as shown here:

```
<applet code="javaApplet.class" width="200" height="200" />
```

The same holds true for all container tags. If a container is empty (that is, when there is no content after the container's start tag and before its end tag) you can close the container with a space and forward slash (" /") at the end of the container's start tag.

All Attributes Must Have Values Enclosed Within Quotes

You will find plenty of tags within HTML documents where the author assigned numeric (and sometimes single-word text) values to attributes without enclosing the value in quotes. For example, you might see the following <table> tag used to start the definition for a table that has "invisible" (that is, zero-width) borders:

```
<table border=0>
```

Though the preceding example is a valid HTML statement, XHTML requires that you enclose all attribute values within quotes—both numeric and text. Therefore, to begin a page layout table (with zero-width borders) in XHTML you would write:

```
<table border="0">
```

In addition to enclosing attribute values within quotes, XHTML also requires that all attributes have a value. HTML let you use a shortcut called *attribute minimization* when using attribute that have only one possible value. When allowed, attribute minimization lets you omit the attribute's value and specify only its name within the HTML tag. For example, to insert a check box on a form, you write an <input> tag whose *type* attribute is set to "checkbox", such as that shown here:

```
<input type="checkbox" name="Win98" value="ON">
```

If you wanted the browser to place a check mark into the check box when it draws the check box on the form, HTML lets you write the <input> tag as follows:

```
<input type="checkbox" name="Win98" value="ON" checked>
```

Because the *checked* attribute has only one possible value ("checked"), the Web browser knows what to do when it encounters the attribute within the tag. XHTML, however, requires that you state each attribute's value explicitly (and within quotes)—even when only one value is possible. Thus, in this example you would write the <input> tag for the initially checked (that is, selected) check box as follows:

```
<input type="checkbox" name="Win98" value="ON" checked="checked">
```

XHTML Documents Must Start with a DOCTYPE Declaration

To save time typing, Web page authors typically omit the DOCTYPE declaration from the beginning of HTML documents. Each Web browser has a DTD built into its code. The DTD is like the legend on a roadmap in that the DTD tells the browser how to read the HTML tags (and now XHTML tags) and attributes that describe the Web page.

Because every browser has a built-in DTD, there was no need in the past to identify a file in which the browser could find the definitions of the HTML tags and attributes it found within the Web page HTML. Regardless of the DTD specified within the DOCTYPE declaration, the browser always checked its internal DTD to determine what each tag (and attribute) it encountered was telling it to do. Thus, when designers took advantage of new attributes or tags available in HTML version 4.01, for example, visitors with Web browsers that contained the HTML 3.0 DTD would ignore the "new" tags or attributes as undefined.

The DOCTYPE declaration, now required by XHTML, lets designers specify the DTD file that has the definitions of all the tags and attributes used within the XHTML document. Thus, a browser can retrieve a Web document and read the DOCTYPE declaration at its start to determine the DTD the browser must have to understand all the tags and attributes used to describe the page. If after checking its internal code the browser determines its built-in DTD is not the one the Web page requires, the browser can retrieve the DTD it needs from the URL of the DTD specified within the DOCTYPE declaration.

As such, browsers of the future will be able to support the latest version of XHTML immediately—without manufacturers having to release a new version of the browser. The Web designer will simply use the DOCTYPE declaration to point the browser to the DTD for the version of XHTML used to create the Web page. If the particular DTD required to display a page is built-into the browser already—great; the browser will simply use its internal DTD to display the page as always. Conversely, if the DOCTYPE declaration calls for a DTD other than one built-in, the browser simply retrieves from the URL given within the <!DOCTYPE> element the DTD required to display the Web page correctly.

To be valid, an XHTML document must begin with a DOCTYPE declaration, such as the one shown within the first two lines of the following Web page XHTML:

```
<!DOCTYPE html PUBLIC "-//W3C//DTD XHTML 1.0 Transitional//EN"
    "http://www.w3.org/TR/xhtml1/DTD/xhtml1-transitional.dtd">
<html xmlns="http://www.w3.org/1999/xhtml">
<head><title>My Web Page Title</title></head>
<body>
  <!-- Page content goes here. -->
</body>
</html>
```

Although the <!DOCTYPE> element is split onto two lines for formatting purposes here, you can write it on a single line within your XHTML document. Whether on one line or several, the <!DOCTYPE> element must come immediately before the <html> tag at the start of the Web page definition. Later in this chapter, the Tip "Selecting the Correct DOCTYPE for Your Web Page" will explain how to write a DOCTYPE declaration that specifies the correct DTD for your Web page. For now, let's review the components of a <!DOCTYPE> element, so that you will know how to write one of your own when the time comes.

The items within the <!DOCTYPE> element in this example are as follows:

- *html*   Indicates that the document's root element is the <html> tag.
- *PUBLIC*   Indicates the <!DOCTYPE> element has a formal public identifier (FPI), which follows the keyword *PUBLIC*. If you create a DTD of your own, you would replace *PUBLIC* with *SYSTEM* and omit the FPI (described next).
- **"-//W3C//DTD XHTML 1.0 Transitional//EN"**   The FPI of the DTD needed to read the Web page XHTML. The FPI identifies a specific DTD, and the Web browser compares the FPI to the ID of its internal DTD. If the two match, the browser uses its internal DTD. Conversely, if the ID of the browser's built-in DTD is different, the browser retrieves the DTD from the URL that follows the FPI. Note that the FPI, when present, is a quoted string that begins with a dash (-).
- **"http://www.w3.org/TR/xhtml1/DTD/xhtml1-transitional.dtd"**   The Web address, enclosed within quotes, where the browser can retrieve the document's DTD, which defines and gives the syntax for all entities and attributes used within the XHTML document.

XHTML Documents Must Have a <title> Element Within the Header Section

The Web page <title> element is not new to XHTML. In fact, though optional in the past, and required by XHTML, the <title> element has been around since HTML 2.0. As you surf the Web, your browser displays the title of each Web page it displays within the title bar across the top of the browser application window. The Web page title gives the name and describes, in a few words, the purpose of the Web page.

To create a Web page title, insert the title's text between start and end title tags (<title></title>) within the Web page header section, as shown in the following code:

```
<html>
<head>
  <title>Konrad's Page of XHTML Tips and Techniques</title>
</head>
<body>
  ... Content the Web browser displays goes here ...
</body>
</html>
```

Use the Web page title to describe the contents of the page to your site visitors. That way, each time the visitor glances at the browser application window's title bar, the page title will remind him or her of the name and purpose of the Web page currently displayed by the browser.

In addition to reminding visitors of their current location within your Web site, titles are also used for the following:

- Web browsers use title text when a visitor bookmarks a page for future reference. Specifically, the Web browser adds the text within the <title> element to the list of favorites in Internet Explorer or to the list of bookmarks in Netscape Navigator when the visitor selects Favorites |

Add to Favorites (in Explorer) or Bookmarks | Add Bookmark (in Navigator) from the browser's Standard toolbar.

- Spiders (automated Web search programs) use title text when listing your Web page on search engines.

- Titles let visitors keep track of where they are in a multisection Web site. For example, on a site about Web design, you might group all pages about markup languages within an "HTML" section, those about PHP, JavaScript, and ASP in a "Scripting" section, and those about animation, video, and sound within a "Multimedia" section. By starting the Web page title of the Web pages in each section with the section's name, you make it easy for a visitor to remember where they were on the site when they come across a page to which they want to return later.

Understanding What Else You Must Know About XHTML

With an understanding of the few, simple rules detailed in the preceding section, you are ready to start creating XHTML documents. As such, you could skip the next section and move right to the Tips, which start by showing you a tool (HTML Tidy) you can use to convert existing HTML documents to XHTML with a few mouse clicks. Of course, given that you used proper coding practices to create the HTML documents initially, your new XHTML code will look much like the current HTML. In fact, often the only difference you will see between HTML and XHTML is that previously unterminated empty (noncontainer) tags now have a space–forward slash (" /") terminator (as explained by the rule "Open container tags must be closed and each empty tag must have a terminator" in the preceding section).

In other words, if you are familiar with HTML, for the most part, you already know XHTML as well. Rather than repeat the same tags and attributes you saw in Chapter 1 by presenting them as "new" material under the guise of XHTML, we refer you to Chapter 1 to learn all about HTML tags, attributes, and how to create a Web page.

While reading the Tips within this chapter, bear in mind that the tags presented are a part of the HTML 4.01 standard. However, many Web browsers did not support them. For example, though a part of the HTML 4.0 (and 4.01) specification, most browsers did not support the <iframe> tag (presented in the Tip "Inserting an XHTML Page Within Another with an Inline Frame"). In addition, Cascading Style Sheet (CSS) support, though around for several years, is only now supported reasonably well in Internet Explorer 5.5 (and later) and Netscape Navigator 6.1 (and later). Thus, although "technically" not "XHTML only," the Tips presented here show advanced uses for several HTML elements and CSS rules not available in older Web browsers. However, as browsers become XHTML-compliant, the majority (if not all) will support the techniques you will learn within this chapter's Tips.

Whenever you exploit advanced features, make sure you know your audience. Check the sites like http://www.w3schools.com to see what browsers and hardware capabilities are seeing widespread use throughout the Web. For example, you will find Web browser usage statistics at http://www.w3schools.com/browsers/browsers_stats.asp. After you determine which browser(s) your target audience is likely using, determine capabilities available within specific Web browsers (both by version and type), at such sites as http://www.Webreview.com. For example, the chart at http://www.webreview.com/browsers/browsers.shtml shows exactly which browsers (by version and platform) support frames, java applets, JavaScript, and more. Although it should go without saying, use only elements and CSS techniques supported within the Web browsers used by the majority of your site's visitors.

Using the CDATA Section to Hide Scripts and Style Sheets

When you embed style sheets or scripts within HTML documents, you typically "hide" them from browsers without CSS or script support by enclosing them within comment tags. For example, the following HTML shows an embedded style sheet within the Web page header, and an embedded script within the Web page body:

```
<!DOCTYPE html PUBLIC "-//W3C//DTD XHTML 1.0 Strict//EN"
    "http://www.w3.org/TR/xhtml1/DTD/xhtml1-strict.dtd">
<html>
<head>
  <title>Embedding Style Sheets and Scripts</title>
  <style type="text/css">
<!-- ** embedded style sheet **
  body {background-color:lightyellow}
  p {color:blue; font-face:arial; font-weight:bold}
-->
  </style>
</head>
<body>
  <script type="text/JavaScript">
<!-- ** embedded script **
  If 5 < 10
    document.write ("<p>5 is still less than 10!!!</p>");
-->
  </script>
<!-- this is a comment!  -->
  <p>This is where Web page text belongs.</p>
</body>
</html>
```

Currently, both Netscape Navigator 6.2 and Internet Explorer 6 will display the preceding Web page correctly. Moreover, the W3C validator (at http://validator.w3.org/) validates the page without errors as well. However, future versions of XHTML-compliant browsers may not display the Web page correctly. According to the XHTML 1.0 specification, XML parsers (all the latest version Web browsers will one day be XML parsers) may silently remove the contents of comments. As such, though the browser supports style sheets and scripts, it may simply not "see" them because it ignores all comments (including those within <style> and <script> elements).

Unfortunately, you cannot simply drop the comment tags from around the style sheet or script, because then the parser (that is, the Web browser) will parse symbols such as "<," "&," "--," and "]]>" within the style sheet or script as part of the page markup. The browser would treat the less-than sign (<) in the following *If* statement, for example, as the start of a tag and expect a valid element name to follow:

```
If 5 < 10
  document.write ("<p>5 is still less than 10!!!</p>");
```

So, if you cannot use a comment tag and you cannot go without one, what can you do?

The answer is you can either use external style sheets and scripts or put your embedded sheets and scripts into CDATA sections. CDATA stands for "character data," which the browser should treat like a character literal (that is, like a text string) when parsing the Web document. As such, CDATA is not an XHTML tag per se (hence the uppercase). Instead, CDATA delimits a section or group of statements the browser must treat differently.

For example, rather than embed the script in the previous example within the Web page header, write the CSS rules within the style sheet in an external file such as styles.css, and then write the style sheet within the Web page header as:

```
<style>
  <link type="text/css" rel=stylesheet href="styles.css" />
</style>
```

Similarly, to use an external script file, place the script near the end of the previous example into a file named MyScript.js for example. Then, replace the <script> element with the following:

```
<script type="text/JavaScript" src="../scripts/MyScript.js" />
```

If you want to keep style sheets and scripts embedded within the XHTML document, define them within CDATA sections. There is nothing sinister or complicated about the CDATA section. The only problem is that it is not yet supported by many Web browsers. However, as mentioned, all Web browsers will one day be XML parsers. As such, you will one day use CDATA sections in place of comment blocks to hide style sheets and scripts, which is why we are discussing the CDATA block now.

You begin a CDATA block the same way you start a DOCTYPE declaration—with a less-than sign followed by an exclamation point ("<!") as shown here:

```
<![CDATA[If 5 < 10
   method.write ("<p>5 is still less than 10!!!</p>");]]>
```

Note that you enclose both the CDATA section and the contents of the section (the JavaScript in this example) within brackets ("[" and "]"). When the XML parser encounters "<![DATA" in the Web page XHTML, it knows to ignore everything as "escaped" character data until it encounters the "]]>" that ends the character data declaration.

Converting HTML to XHTML Using HTML Tidy

Just because something is easy to do does not mean it will be done correctly. You will undoubtedly find this to be true when, as a Web page designer, you must fix yet another Web page with badly formed HTML that does not conform to the W3C standard. The beauty of the Web is that anyone with a text editor can create a Web page. Unfortunately, Web browsers (such as Netscape Navigator and Internet Explorer) let novice authors get away with sloppy coding such as missing "end" tags, unquoted attribute values, malformed tables, and so on. Moreover, both Netscape and Microsoft add fuel to the fire by "extending" HTML with their own proprietary tags. Fortunately, XHTML, like "the new sheriff in town," is going to tame the wild, wild Web by forcing Web authors (and Web browsers) to comply with the "law"—the XHTML standard.

If you are like most designers, who must work under constant scheduling pressures, the last thing you want to do is spend a lot of time correcting other people's code—especially when you could be creating the next "killer" site that brings you fame and glory instead. However, for those times when you must clean up some code or want to make sure your latest creation complies with the XHTML standard, HTML Tidy is the tool you need. Unlike HTML validation programs (such as the one at http://validator.w3.org/), HTML Tidy not only tells you what's wrong but also fixes most problems it finds. For example, the program will fix missing and mismatched tags such as those found in the following malformed HTML:

```
<i><h1>Level 1 heading in italics</i>
<p>First paragraph with <b>bold, important text.
<p>Second paragraph with additional bold text.
```

HTML Tidy corrects the code in this example, so that it reads as follows:

```
<h1><i>Level 1 heading in italics</i></h1>
<p>First paragraph with <b>bold, important text.</b></p>
<p><b>second paragraph with additional bold text.</b></p>
```

 Before you can use HTML Tidy the first time, you must download a copy of the program by performing the following steps:

1. If you do not have a permanent, always-on Internet connection, use your modem to establish a dial-up connection through your ISP.

2. Enter **http://www.w3.org/People/Raggett/tidy/#download** into your Web browser's Address field and press ENTER. Your Web browser, in turn, will display the portion of the HTML Tidy home page shown in Figure 5-1.

3. Find the HTML Tidy executable for your operating system. The HTML Tidy home page has hyperlinks you can use to retrieve HTML Tidy for Windows, UnixWare, Linux, OS/2, Solaris, FreeBSD, and several other operating systems. (In addition, you can download the HTML Tidy source code, written in C, and compile your own executable.) For Windows (95/98/NT/2000/XP), download HTML Tidy with a Windows front-end by clicking on the TidyGUI hyperlink. Your Web browser, in turn, will retrieve the Web page at http://perso.wanadoo.fr/ablavier/TidyGUI/.

4. Page down to the "Download and Installation" section near the bottom of the Web page (or type **http://perso.wanadoo.fr/ablavier/TidyGUI/#download** into the browser Address field and press ENTER).

5. Click the TidyGUI-exe.zip hyperlink. Your Web browser, in turn, will display a File Download dialog box. (The specific dialog box you see depends on your browser and its version.)

6. Select the dialog box option to save the ZIP file to disk. For example, within the Internet Explorer 6 File Download dialog box, click Save. Your browser, in turn, will display a Save As dialog box. (Again, the specific dialog box you see will depend on your browser.)

7. Use the drop-down list button to the right of the Save In field to navigate to the folder in which you want to save the ZIP file. For example, you might save the file within C:\WebTools. Next, click Save. The Web browser, in turn, will download and save TidyGUI-exe.zip in the folder you selected.

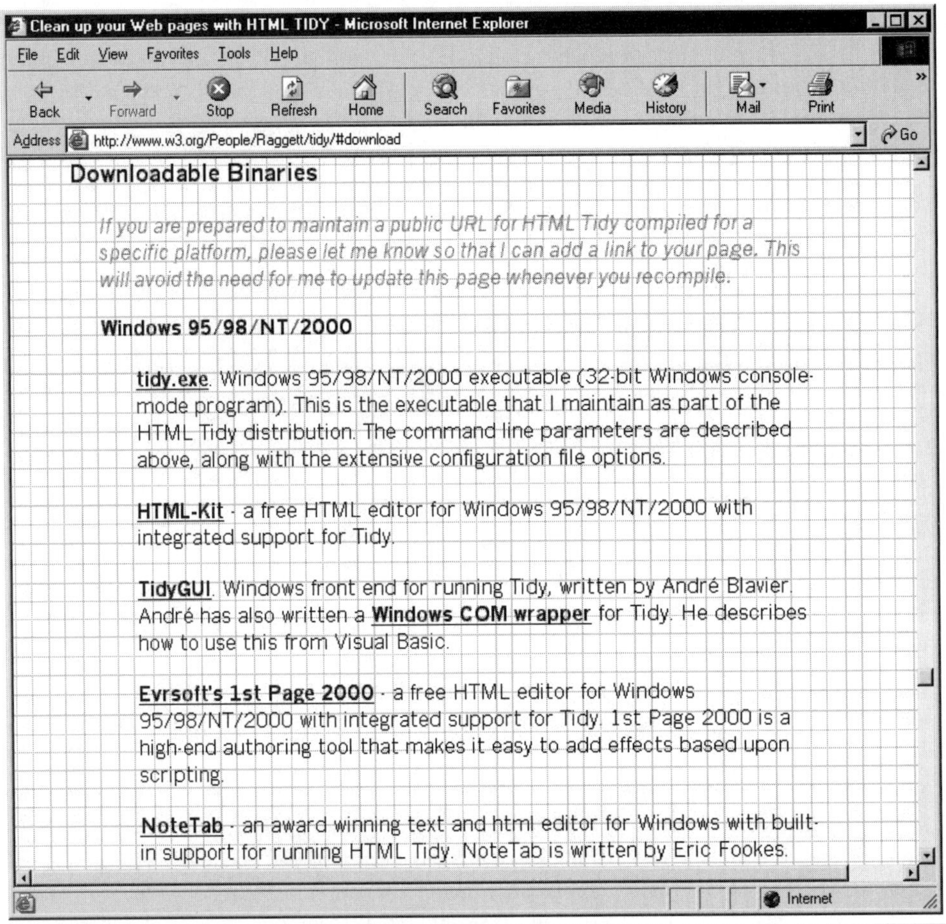

Figure 5-1   The download section of the HTML Tidy home page

After you complete Step 7, extract TidyGUI.exe within the folder in which you stored the ZIP file. To convert an HTML document to XHTML with TidyGUI, perform the following steps:

1. Select Start | Run. Windows, in turn, will display the Run dialog box.

2. Into the Open field within the Run dialog box, enter TidyGUI's full pathname. For example, if you saved TidyGUI.exe within the C:\WebTools folder in the previous procedure, type **C:\WebTools\TidyGUI.exe**. Then, click OK. Windows, in turn, will start TidyGUI, displaying the TidyGUI main screen shown here:.

3. By default, TidyGUI will validate and correct the HTML within a file but will not change the document's type. (In other words, if you supply TidyGUI an HTML document, the program will output an HTML document.) To have TidyGUI convert HTML into XHTML, change the default configuration by clicking Configuration. HTML Tidy, in turn, will display the Tidy Configuration dialog box shown here:

4. Click the XML tab and then click a check mark into the Output As XHTML checkbox.

5. Click Apply and then click the close button (the "X") in the upper-right corner of the Tidy Configuration dialog box. TidyGUI, in turn, will close the Tidy Configuration dialog box, so that you can work with the program's main screen (see Step 2).

6. Into the Source file field at the top of the TidyGUI main screen, enter the pathname of the HTML document you want to convert to XHTML. Then, click the Tidy! button below the Source File field. TidyGUI, in turn, will display general comments and advice about the source file's code within the top pane on the TidyGUI main screen and any warnings about code you should change within the bottom pane.

7. To store the generated XHTML to a disk file, click the Show Output button on the TidyGUI main screen. TidyGUI, in turn, will display the XHTML within a Tidy Output dialog box such as this:

8. Click Save As in the upper-left corner of the Tidy Output dialog box. TidyGUI, in turn, will display the Save As dialog box you can use to store the XHTML document the program produced in a disk file.

After you complete Step 8, click the close button (the "X") in the upper-right corner of the Tidy Output dialog box to close the dialog box and return to the TidyGUI main screen. Then, repeat Steps 6–8 for each Web document you want to convert from HTML to XHTML.

In addition to converting HTML to XHTML, you can also use TidyGUI (or the MS-DOS HTML Tidy) to validate and correct HTML, XHTML, and even XML documents. If you want to validate and correct errors within a document without changing its type, simply skip Steps 3–5 in the previous procedure (or clear the Output As XHTML check box in Step 4). Without one of the XML tab's check boxes checked, TidyGUI will generate an output file of the same type as the input (or source) document.

HTML Tidy has about 50 configuration options you can use to control the way the program validates and/or converts your Web document. For example, by setting the doctype option to Strict, and setting the output-xhtml option and clean option to "yes", you can tell HTML Tidy (and TidyGUI) to generate an XHTML document that adheres to the XHTML 1.0 "strict" DTD. The "clean" attribute tells HTML Tidy to replace presentational attributes and tags with CSS rules as required by the XHTML "strict" DTD. For a thorough description of each configuration option, refer to the Using A Configuration File section of the HTML Tidy home page at http://www.w3.org/People/Raggett/tidy/#config.

Selecting the Correct DOCTYPE for Your Web Page

Technically, every Web document should begin with a DOCTYPE declaration that tells the Web browser the type of code to expect within the file. However, most designers omit the DOCTYPE from the start of the Web page HTML. This works because browsers "assume" that the Web page file contains HTML (tags, attributes, and text content) and follow the file's instructions to display page content onscreen.

Unlike the HTML versions that precede it, the XHTML specification requires that you include a DOCTYPE before the Web page "root" element (that is, before the <html> tag) as shown here:

```
<!DOCTYPE html PUBLIC "-//W3C//DTD XHTML 1.0 Strict//EN"
  "http://www.w3.org/TR/xhtml1/DTD/xhtml1-strict.dtd">
<html xmlns="http://www.w3.org/1999/xhtml">
<head>
  <title>XHTML Document with a doctype declaration</title>
</head>
<body>
  <p>Web page content.</p>
</body>
</html>
```

The "html" which follows the keyword DOCTYPE in this example tells the Web browser the file contains HTML. (More specifically, it says the document's "root" element is the <html> tag.) Following the keyword *PUBLIC* within the DOCTYPE is a literal (that is, a quoted string) called the "formal public identifier," or FPI. The FPI identifies the Web document's DTD, which in this case is the Strict version of the W3C XHTML specification, version 1.0. The *EN* indicates that the specification named by the FPI is in English. Finally, the DOCTYPE gives the URL (within quotes) where the Web browser can retrieve the DTD (http://www.w3.org/TR/xhtml1/DTD/xhtml1-strict.dtd, in this example).

A DTD is the file that contains all the markup rules and lists all the character entities and elements you can use within the Web page HTML. In "language" terms, the DTD contains all the special symbols, words, and syntax (or rules) that govern the ways in which you can combine the words into sentences to describe a Web page. By specifying that a Web document is "strictly" compliant with the XHTML 1.0 standard, for example, you tell the Web browser to hold the Web page HTML to the standard as given within the DTD. Therefore, the Web browser will treat as text content any tags or attributes within the Web page file not defined within the DTD. Moreover, the browser will not display any malformed elements (such as paragraphs with a <p> tag and no terminating </p>) it encounters.

Currently, three XHTML document types exist: Strict, Transitional, and Frameset. Use the Strict DTD, as shown here, for Web documents that have no deprecated (that is, obsolete) elements or attributes and within which you use CSS rules to handle all appearance-related issues (such as color, typeface, font size, and so on):

```
<!DOCTYPE html PUBLIC "-//W3C//DTD XHTML 1.0 Strict//EN"
    "http://www.w3.org/TR/xhtml1/DTD/xhtml1-strict.dtd">
```

A Web page file that starts with the DOCTYPE in this example cannot use any tags or attributes marked "DEPRECATED" within HTML 4.0 specification. Because they are not defined within the XHTML version 1.0 Strict DTD (http://www.w3.org/TR/xhtml1/DTD/xhtml1-strict.dtd), the Web browser simply ignores any deprecated tags or attributes it finds within the document.

When a Web page uses obsolete (deprecated) tags and/or attributes, use the Transitional XHTML DTD as follows:

```
<!DOCTYPE html PUBLIC "-//W3C//DTD XHTML 1.0 Transitional//EN"
    "http://www.w3.org/TR/xhtml1/DTD/xhtml1-transitional.dtd">
```

If your site must support visitors that use older Web browsers without CSS support, you must use the Transitional DTD, because you use (now obsolete) HTML tags and attributes (such as <center>, <font>, *align*, *color*, *face*, and so on) to control the appearance of content.

Finally, for Web pages on which you use HTML frames to divide the browser application window so that you can display multiple Web pages onscreen at once, use the Frameset DTD shown here:

```
<!DOCTYPE html PUBLIC "-//W3C//DTD XHTML 1.0 Frameset//EN"
    "http://www.w3.org/TR/xhtml1/DTD/xhtml1-frameset.dtd">
```

In addition to elements and attributes relating to frames, the Frameset DTD includes the attributes and elements found in the Transitional DTD.

Although you can still use deprecated tags when you select the Transitional or the Frameset DTD, you should avoid doing so. The W3C has removed all deprecated tags from the (soon to be released) XHTML 1.1 specification. As such, eliminating these tags from your XHTML pages now will save you a lot of work later. Please refer to http://www.w3.org/TR/html4/index/elements.html for a list of deprecated tags. There you will find a table with all HTML 4.01 (and by extension XHTML 1.0) elements (tags) presented in table form. Note that the Depr. column contains a "D" to indicate those deprecated tags you should avoid using in all your XHTML pages now (and work to remove from your existing HTML pages as well).

Validating Your Web Page with an XHTML Validator

In the past, both Netscape Navigator and Internet Explorer have been very forgiving when it comes to malformed HTML. If you forgot an </body> tag, for example, the browsers would still display your

Web page. Similarly, if you forgot to enclose tag attributes in quotes, the browsers still used the attribute values when rendering content. Moreover, both browsers even did their best to display content within improperly nested tags, such as those shown here:

```
<p><h2><center>Example: <b>Improper</b> Nesting.</h2></center>
What you open first, you must close <b>last</p></b>.
```

In this example, the start and end center tags (<center></center>) should enclose the start and end level-two heading tags (<h2></h2>) and the </p> tag should follow the </b> after the word *last*.

Forcing the browser to handle code that does not conform to an HTML standard (as defined by a W3C specification) does not come without cost. Browsers applications have swollen in size as Netscape and Microsoft add code to figure out what malformed HTML intends to describe—and to handle proprietary tags and attributes each company supplied to "enhance" HTML. Larger browser applications load and run more slowly; more code means more bugs (which cause errant browser behavior and system lockups); and using proprietary tags and attributes means that a Web page that looks fine in one browser may look bad or may not even display in another. The XHTML standard attempts to provide at least a partial solution to these Web design headaches.

When you indicate that a Web page is XHTML-compliant, Web browsers know that they can find all tags, attributes, and syntax used by the Web document within the DTD. (To be XHTML-compliant, the Web page HTML must include a DOCTYPE declaration that specifies the DTD at the beginning of the Web page file.) Anything not within the DTD browsers will either display as text or simply ignore. This includes malformed HTML, such as that shown at the beginning of this Tip. If your DOCTYPE declaration indicates that the Web page is compliant with the XHTML 1.0 Strict DTD, for example, the browser should hold you to that declaration and ignore HTML whose syntax does not conform to that specified within the DTD. Currently, Netscape Navigator 6 and Internet Explorer 6 still display malformed HTML—even when the DOCTYPE specifies XHTML 1.0 Strict DTD. However, to ensure that your Web pages work the way you want them to in the next generation of browsers, make sure you follow the W3C's recommendations.

USE IT   After you create a Web page, use the HTML Validation service at http://validator.w3.org/ to see if your XHTML complies with the W3C standard for your document type. To use the validation service, perform the following steps:

1. If you do not have a permanent (always-on) connection to the Internet, use your modem to establish a dial-up connection through your ISP.

2. After you start your Web browser, type **http://validator.w3.org/** into the browser's Address field and then press ENTER. Your Web browser, in turn, will display the W3C HTML Validation Service screen shown in Figure 5-2.

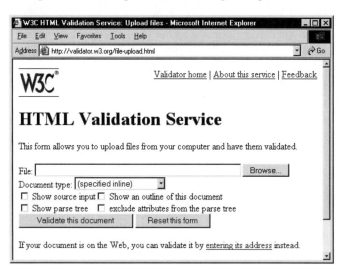

Figure 5-2 The W3C HTML Validation Service Web page

3. To validate a page you have not yet published to the Web server, click the Upload Files hyperlink near the bottom of the page. Your Web browser, in turn, will retrieve the Web page with the file upload form at http://validator.w3.org/file-upload.html, as shown here:

4. Type the full pathname of the XHTML document into the File field at the top of the upload form. Or, use the Browse button to the right of the File field to navigate to and select the file you want to validate on a local or network drive.

5. Click the Validate This Document button at the bottom of the form.

After you complete Step 5, your Web browser will send the Web page you entered (or selected) in Step 4 to the W3C Web site. The site's validation program will check the XHTML document and send to your Web browser a results page similar to that shown in Figure 5-3.

Review the document type shown to the right of the Document Type label near the center of the information block at the top of the results page to make sure you used the correct DOCTYPE declaration within your Web page XHTML. For example, the results shown in Figure 5-3 indicate that the Web page ShowMe.htm was validated against the XHTML 1.0 Strict DTD.

Below the document information block, the validation program lists any warnings and errors. Note that your XHTML document is valid (that is, complies with the standard) only when there are no errors. As such, if you see errors, correct them within your Web document and repeat the validation procedure. (The validation program not only lists errors but also offers suggestions on corrections you must make to bring the code into compliance.)

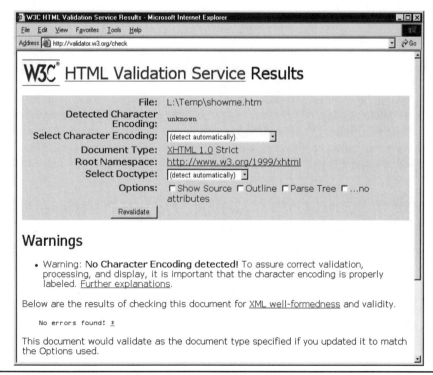

Figure 5-3   The W3C HTML Validation Service results page

In addition to validating Web documents stored in files on local or network drives, you can also validate any Web page already published to a Web server. To do so, perform Steps 1 and 2 in the previous procedure. Then, in place of Steps 3 and 4, type the URL of the Web page you want to validate into the Address field near the middle of the W3C HTML Validation Page (shown previously in Figure 5-2). Next, click the Validate This Page button just above the Upload Files hyperlink on the W3C HTML Validation Service Web page. Rather than accepting a file sent by your Web browser, the validation program will then retrieve the Web page at the Web address you specified and produce a validation report similar to that you saw in Figure 5-3.

As you develop new Web pages, validate each page before you publish it to the Web server. However, if you previously published pages and want to see if they comply with an XHTML (or HTML) standard, you might use the in-place validation option.

Setting the Text Size on an XHTML Web Page with Keywords

When specifying the size of Web page text, you typically have two goals: make the text large enough for visitors to read comfortably and vary the size of specific words or phrases for emphasis. Text size is especially important when a Web page has a lot of text. If the text size is too small, the strain of reading page content frustrates visitors and may result in their leaving without reading all the content. Conversely, if you make the text unusually large, it may distract visitors and cause them to miss important information you are trying to convey. The concept of changing text size for emphasis has been employed for a long time. Prior to Cascading Style Sheets (which you learned about in Chapter 4), you used the *size* attribute within the <font> tag to select the relative size for the text on a Web page. Setting *size* to seven (7), the largest setting, for example, makes text characters a little more than 2.5 times the size of the middle size of four (4). Using CSS rules, you can specify text size using units of measure such as pixels, points, inches, centimeters, and so on. In addition to these units, CSS lets you specify text size through the seven keywords shown in the "Keyword" column of Table 5-1. Although not

Keyword	IE 5.5 Size	IE 6 and Netscape Navigator (NN) 6.1 Size	NN 4.7 Size
xx-small	<font size="1"> 10 pixels	9 pixels	9 pixels
x-small	<font size="2"> 13 pixels	<font size="1"> 10 pixels	<font size="1"> 11 pixels
Small	<font size="3"> 16 pixels	<font size="2"> 13 pixels	<font size="2"> 14 pixels
Medium	<font size="4"> 18 pixels	<font size="3"> 16 pixels	<font size="3"> 16 pixels

Table 5-1 Size Keywords and Text Size for IE 5.5, IE 6.0, NN 4.7, and NN 6.1

Keyword	IE 5.5 Size	IE 6 and Netscape Navigator (NN) 6.1 Size	NN 4.7 Size
Large	<font size="5"> 23 pixels	<font size="4"> 18 pixels	<font size="4"> 24 pixels
x-large	<font size="6"> 32 pixels	<font size="5"> 23 pixels	<font size="5"> 36 pixels
xx-large	<font size="7"> 48 pixels	<font size="6"> 32 pixels	<font size="6"> 54 pixels

Table 5-1 Size Keywords and Text Size for IE 5.5, IE 6.0, NN 4.7, and NN 6.1 *(continued)*

new to XHTML, using keywords to specify text size gives you an easy way to make older HTML pages—which set text size using the *size* attribute within the now deprecated <font> tag—compliant with the XHTML Strict standard. (Though Transitional XHTML lets you use deprecated tags [like <font>], browsers adhering to future version of XHTML standard will apply the Strict standard, which includes no deprecated tags.)

When you use a keyword to specify text size, the Web browser brand and its version determine the actual size that the text appears onscreen. As shown in the preceding table, Internet Explorer version 5 displays "medium" text at 18-pixels, whereas Internet Explorer version 6 and Netscape Navigator (versions 5 and 6) display "medium" text at 16 pixels. Figure 5-4 shows the size of text for each of the seven keywords as displayed by Internet Explorer 6.

USE IT To set the text size using a keyword, set the *font-size* property to a keyword value within a CSS rule or inline within an HTML container tag. For example, the following code shows how to use the *style* attribute to set the *font-size* property inline:

```
<p style="font-size: xx-small">xx-small text<br />
 <span style="font-size: x-small">x-small text</span><br />
 <span style="font-size: small">small text</span><br />
 <span style="font-size: medium">medium text</span><br />
 <span style="font-size: large">large text</span><br />
 <span style="font-size: x-large">x-large text</span><br />
 <span style="font-size: xx-large">xx-large text</span></p>
```

To set the size of all text content on a page to a keyword size, insert a rule such as the following in a CSS within the Web page header section as shown here:

```
<!DOCTYPE html PUBLIC "-//W3C//DTD XHTML 1.0 Transitional//EN"
    "http://www.w3.org/TR/xhtml1/DTD/xhtml1-transitional.dtd">
<html xmlns="http://www.w3.org/1999/xhtml">
<head>
  <title>Text Size Keywords</title>
  <style type="text/css">
```

```
    body {font-size:large}
</style>
</head>
<body bgcolor="#ADD8E6">
  <!-- Web Page Content -->
</body>
</html>
```

After you set the text size using one of the seven size keywords, you can change it using the relative keywords *smaller* and *larger*. As its name implies, applying the keyword *smaller* tells the Web browser to reduce the text size down one notch on the keyword scale. Similarly, applying the keyword *larger* tells the browser to increase text size up one notch. Thus, given the Web page described by the preceding code in which all body text is *large*, you might write the following HTML within the Web page body to emphasize certain words:

```
<p>To emphasize a word you might make it <span style="font-size:larger">
larger</span>.
  Make a word <span style="font-size:smaller">smaller</span> also draws the
visitor's attention.</p>
```

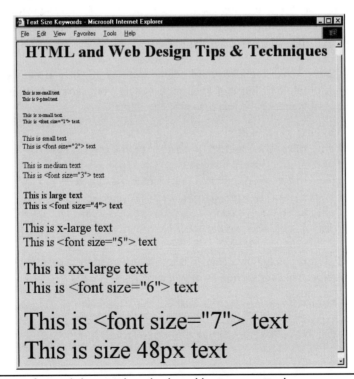

Figure 5-4   Text size for each keyword as displayed by Internet Explorer

In this example, the Web browser will display the word *larger* as *x-large* text (stepping up one notch from *large* in the keyword sale) and the word *smaller* as *medium* text (one step down from *large*).

Grouping an XHTML Form's Selection List Items with the <optgroup> Tag

A selection list on an XHTML (and HTML) form presents a list of items within a scrollable area. You may use a selection list in place of check boxes to save space onscreen—especially when you have a large number of items from which the visitor is to make his or her selections. (A selection list, unlike a set of check boxes, also lets you specify whether a visitor may select only one or multiple items.) In Chapter 3 on HTML forms, you learned how to create a selection list by inserting a <select> element similar to the following between the form's start and end form tags (<form></form>):

```
<select size="10" name="AreasOfInterest" multiple="Yes">
  <option value="Win98">Windows 98</option>
  <option value="WinXp">Windows XP</option>
  <option value="WinNT">Windows NT</option>
  <option value="DT">Desktop</option>
  <option value="LT">Laptop</option>
  <option value="PDA">PDA</option>
  <option value="Prtr">Printers</option>
  <option value="Mon">Monitors</option>
</select>
```

The text between each pair of start and end option tags (<option></option>) represents an item on the list, as shown here:

USE IT   The <optgroup> element lets you group selection list items logically. If a selection list
contains many items or if the list has groups of related items (as is the case in the preceding
example), use the <optgroup> tag to add a "heading" at the start of each item group as shown here:

```
Operating Systems
  Windows 98
  Windows XP
  Windows NT
Hardware
  Desktop
```

Groups of related choices are easier for the visitors to remember and grasp than a single long
(and possibly diverse) list of options. To break a selection list into groups of items, as shown in
this example, insert <optgroup> tags within the selection list's options as follows:

```
<select size="10" name="AreasOfInterest" multiple="Yes">
  <optgroup label="Operating Systems">
    <option value="Win98">Windows 98</option>
    <option value="WinXp">Windows XP</option>
    <option value="WinNT">Windows NT</option>
  </optgroup>
  <optgroup> label="Hardware">
    <option value="DT">Desktop</option>
    <option value="LT">Laptop</option>
    <option value="PDA">PDA</option>
    <option value="Prtr">Printers</option>
    <option value="Mon">Monitors</option>
  </optgroup>
</select>
```

Note that each option group is described by a set of start and end option group tags (<optgroup></
optgroup>). The <optgroup> tag's *label* attribute gives the text the Web browser displays onscreen as
the option group heading.

As of this writing, you cannot nest option groups to create subgroups. However, the HTML 4.01
specification indicates that future versions of HTML (and now XHTML) may allow nested groups to
let authors create a multilevel hierarchy of selection list choices.

Adding Color to XHTML Tables with Cascading Style Sheet Rules

You typically use XHTML tables for two purposes: to position elements on a Web page and to display tabular data. As you learned in Chapter 4, you can use CSS rules to position Web page objects precisely. Therefore, as more and more browsers provide CSS support, you will no longer need tables for page layout one day. Not only does CSS make tables less important for page layout, CSS also enhances an XHTML table's ability to display data in tabular form. Using CSS rules and <thead>, <tfoot>, and <tbody> tags you can color and format each section ("header," "footer," and "body") within a table to set its data apart.

Note that <thead>, <tfoot>, and <tbody> tags are not unique to XHTML. After all, as mentioned in this chapter's introduction, XHTML is nothing more than HTML 4.01 rewritten as an XML application. As such, you will find all XHTML tags in HTML 4.01 as well. We present these "table" tags here, however, rather than in the Chapter 2 (which covers HTML tables), because older versions of Web browsers do not support them. For example, prior to version 6.1, Netscape Navigator did not support the <thead>, <tfoot>, and <tbody> tags. Thus, one of the additional benefits of moving from HTML to XHTML is that XHTML-compliant Web browsers will support all the tags available within HTML 4.01 standard—the last version of the "HTML" standard the W3C will produce. (Future HTML specifications will be released as XHTML 1.0, 1.1, and so on.)

USE IT To create a table with a header, footer, and body, first use the standard <tr> and <td> tags to describe the table's rows and columns. Then, insert the <thead>, <tfoot>, and <tbody> tags within the table's start and end table tags (<table></table>) as shown here:

```
<table cellspacing="0">
  <thead><tr><td>Header C1</td><td>Header C2</td></tr></thead>
  <tfoot><tr><td>Footer C1</td><td>Footer C2</td></tr></tfoot>
  <tbody>
    <tr><td>Body R1,C1</td><td>Body R1,C2</td></tr>
    <tr><td>Body R2,C1</td><td>Body R2,C2</td></tr>
    <tr><td>Body R3,C1</td><td>Body R3,C2</td></tr>
  </tbody>
</table>
```

The table in this example has a single-row, two-column header and footer, and a body section with three rows and two columns. You can put as many rows as you want into the table's header or footer, and a table's header can have more rows than its footer, and vice versa. Simply insert an additional set of open and close table row tags (<tr></tr>) within the table footer or header definition for each row that you want to insert in either section. Both the table header and footer must, however, be the same width as the table body. Moreover, if your table has a footer (as defined within <tfoot> and </tfoot> tags), the footer definition must appear after the table header definition (if any) and immediately before the <tbody> tag that begins the table's body.

After you create your table, you can apply CSS rules such as the following to style each of the three sections within the table independently, as shown in Figure 5-5:

```
<style type="text/css">
  td {border-style:solid; border-width:1px 1px;
     border-color:black; padding-left:10px; padding-right:10px}
  thead {color:black; background:lightgreen; font-weight:bold;
        text-align:center}
  tfoot {color:white; background:blue; font-weight:bold;
        text-align:center}
  tbody {text-align:right; background:lightblue}
</style>
```

Although the table header and footer must span the table's width, neither section must have the same number of columns as the table's body. In fact, you normally want a single-cell header and footer with one or more rows regardless of the number of cells within the table body. When you want a single cell in one row to span multiple cells in subsequent rows, set the *colspan* attribute within the cell's <td> tag to the number of columns the cell is to span. For example, to create a single-cell header and footer for the two-column table defined earlier in this Tip, replace the table's header and footer declarations with the following:

```
<thead><tr><td colspan="2">Header</td></tr></thead>
<tfoot><tr><td colspan="2">Footer</td></tr></tfoot>
```

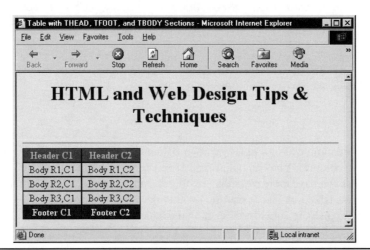

Figure 5-5   An XHTML table with CSS rule–styled header, body, and footer sections

In addition to suggesting that you use CSS rules to style different sections of a table, the HTML specification states that Web browsers may one day scroll the rows within the table body between a stationary table header and footer rows. Moreover, browsers may also reproduce the table header and footer above and below table body rows for tables that span multiple pages when printed. Unfortunately, as of this writing, neither Netscape Navigator nor Internet Explorer supports either of these features.

As a final note, do not confuse table heading cells (as defined by the <th> tags) with the table header section. A table may have both heading cells and a header section. For example, to create a row of heading cells below the table header, add a set of <tr><td></td></tr> tags within the table body. (Each set of <th></th> tags adds a heading column to the row in which it is defined.) If you define a row of heading cells as the first row within the table body, you can use a CSS rule such as the following to create a table with headings below the header section as shown in Figure 5-6:

```
th {text-align:center; background:white}
```

Embedding Fonts Within an XHTML Web Page with CSS Rules

As you create XHTML Web pages, you will rely increasingly on CSS when describing the appearance of Web page text to the Web browser displaying your XHTML Web page. In fact, the <font> tag, long used to specify how text should look, deprecated in HTML 4.01 and XHTML 1.0, is no longer present within the XHTML 1.1 specification. Fortunately, CSS provides the *font-family* property you

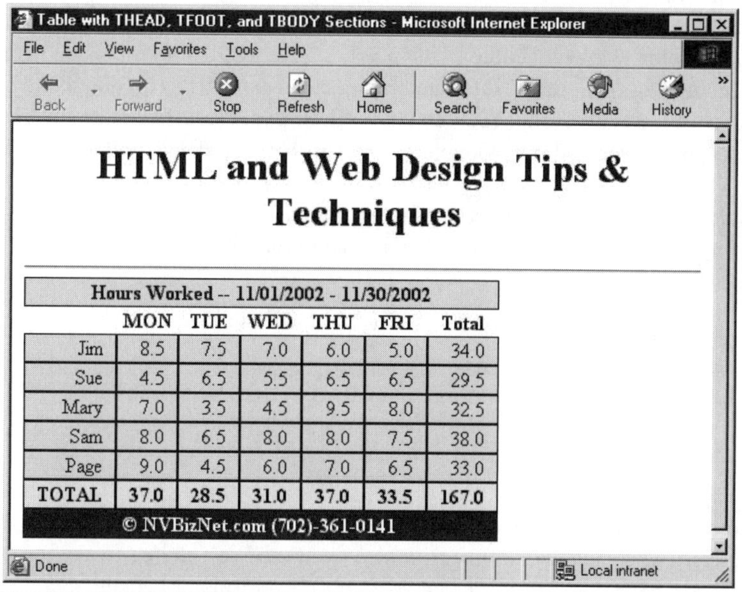

Figure 5-6   An XHTML table with both a header section and a row of heading cells

can use in place of the <font> tag to specify the typeface on your HTML pages you created in the past and on future XHTML Web pages you create.

By using the CSS *font-family* property, you can tell the Web browser to display text in a specific typeface. For example, you might use the following CSS rule to tell the Web browser to display level-two headings on the Web page using the typeface Comic Sans MS:

```
<head>
  <style>
    h2 {font-family: "comic sans ms"}
  </style>
</head>
```

When you use the *font-family* property to select a specific typeface in a CSS rule, you assume that the font is available on the visitor's computer. If the font is not available, the Web browser will substitute a default font (as defined by the browser's preferences). To overcome this problem, CSS (Level 2) lets the browser download the fonts from your Web server when a CSS rule calls for a font not available on the visitor's system. Although this capability is relatively new, it offers the promise of creating Web pages using nonstandard (custom) fonts, which Web browsers will display by downloading the fonts from the Web server as necessary. As a result, you can design a Web page with the knowledge that your visitors will see text in the typeface you selected (rather than in the browser's default typeface).

Keep in mind that the Web browser must download from the Web server any embedded fonts in addition to the other elements on the Web page (such as graphics, animations, and so on). Moreover, some Web browsers require that font files be in a specific format or the browser will not download them. For example, Internet Explorer will download only fonts saved in Embedded Object Type (EOT) formatted files. (You can learn about EOT files and download a free tool that lets you create and save Internet Explorer downloadable fonts in a EOT file by visiting http://www.microsoft.com/typography/web/embedding/weft2/.) Netscape Navigator, meanwhile, can download fonts stored in Portable Font Resource (PFR) files (developed by Bitstream Inc). (For more information about generating Netscape Navigator-downloadable fonts as PFR files, visit http://devedge.netscape.com/.)

USE IT   To download fonts with an XHTML document, specify the font to download in a CSS @*font-face* declaration, such as that shown in the following style sheet:

```
<head>
  <style>
    @font-face {font-family:"new geneva";
      src:url(http://www.MyServer.com/fonts/geneva1.eot)}
  </style>
</head>
```

The @*font-face* declaration instructs the Web browser to download the file specified by *font-family* property (New Geneva, in this example) from the Web address specified by the *src* property (http://www.MyServer.com/fonts/geneva1.eot). To format text using a downloaded font, specify the font's name in a CSS rule exactly as you would any other font. For example, the following style sheet tells the Web browser to use the New Geneva typeface for paragraph text:

```
<head>
  <style>
    @font-face {font-family:"new geneva";
      src:url(http://www.MyServer.com/fonts/geneva1.eot)}
    p {font-family:"new geneva", courier;
      color       :blue}
  </style>
</head>
```

In this example, the first statement in the style sheet tells the Web browser to download the file named geneva1.eot from the fonts folder on the Web server at http://www.MyServer.com. The Web browser, in turn, downloads the font file and assigns it the name *new geneva*. The next statement tells the Web browser to use the downloaded typeface to format paragraph text (that is, text that follows a <p> tag). If the Web browser cannot or will not download the font you specified (using the @*font-face* declaration), the browser will use the alternate typeface (if any) you specified within the CSS rule (Courier, in this example). If neither font is available, the Web browser will use its default font.

The Web browser stores font files (in this example, the file geneva1.eot) within the browser's Temporary Internet Files folder on the visitor's computer. As such, the browser need not download previously downloaded font files each time the visitor returns to the same Web page. When available, the browser retrieves font files from its Internet files cache (on the visitor's hard drive), so that the Web page loads faster on subsequent visits.

Bear in mind that you cannot simply copy EOT and PFR files downloaded by your Web browser to the Fonts folder on your hard drive and start using them on Web pages you create. Fonts, like other intellectual property, have copyrights. Each EOT and PFR file you create (or pay someone else to create for you) has a built-in security model. Web browsers will only display a downloaded font when the font is referenced from a document root specified by the font file's author. Therefore, if you use WEFT, for example, to create a font, you can specify that the font is only to be used on Web pages from http://www.YourDomain.com. If some other Web page author embeds the font file within a Web page he (or she) places on http://www.HisDomain.com, the Web browser retrieving the page will see that the document root (http://www.HisDomain.com) does not match the document root within the downloaded font file (http://www.YourDomain.com). As a result, the Web browser will use its default typeface (rather than your copyrighted typeface) to style the text content.

Inserting an XHTML Page Within Another with an Inline Frame

To display multiple Web pages onscreen at the same time, you use frames. In Chapter 1, you learned how to create frames using <frame> and <frameset> tags. When you divide the Web browser's application window into multiple parts (that is, into frames) with a <frameset> tag, the browser can display a different Web page within each frame. Then, while the frames remain stationary onscreen, the visitor can scroll the page in each frame independently to view page content that does not fit within the frame.

In the past, frames have been an issue with Web designers. Part of the problem was that many authors simply did not understand how to code frameset pages properly. However, even when properly written, many older browsers had no frames support, so designers were constantly writing two sets of pages for many Web sites—one with "frames" documents and one without. Fortunately, XHTML represents the evolution of HTML from being a combination page description/content formatting language to a structural markup language (which most would argue was its original purpose).

In the future, using CSS rules to format text content and exploiting CSS positioning capabilities to handle page layout issues will let Web browser manufacturers concentrate on enhancing their software to handle more complex structures (such as frames). Relieving Web authors of the burden to create two Web pages (one with frames and one without) each time they create a framed page will likely make framed XHTML pages more prevalent than framed HTML pages. In addition, XHTML-compliant Web browsers will support the inline frame tag (<iframe>), which lets you insert one Web page within another as easily as the <img> tag lets you place a picture on a Web page.

When you want to display one Web page within another without dividing the application window into frames, you use an <iframe> tag to embed an inline frame into the page. The scrollable frame that the <iframe> tag generates creates an inline frame that "sits" on the Web page with other objects (such as XHTML tables, graphics images, java applets, and so on) inserted on the page. Like the content within a <frame> tag, the visitor can scroll the Web page displayed within an inline frame to view page content that extends beyond the frame's borders. However, unlike frames created with a <frameset> tag, the inline frame an <iframe> tag creates remains attached to a specific location on the Web page. Therefore, while a frameset's frames remain stationary, an inline frame moves as the visitor scrolls the document with the embedded <iframe> tag.

USE IT   To place an inline frame on a Web page, insert an <inline> tag, such as that shown within the following Web page HTML, where you want the rectangular frame to appear:

```
<iframe src="WebPageURL">
  <!-- alternate content for browsers which do not support
       the <iframe> tag -->
</iframe>
```

Replace *WebPageURL* in this example with the Web address (that is, the URL) of the Web page you want the browser to display within the inline frame.

Suppose for example, you want to simulate "scrollable tables" in which the visitor can scroll the data within the table's body between a stationary table header and footer. Rather than create a single table, create three tables: one with the table header, a second with the table footer, and the third with the table body. Insert the table header and footer onto the Web page as you would any other table. However, insert the table body into a second Web page, which you display between the "header" and "footer" tables on the first page as shown here:

```
<body>
<!-- Web page content before the composite "table" -->
<!-- "Header" Table -->
  <table cellspacing="0" width="525">
    <tr><td colspan="7" class="header">
        Hours Worked -- 11/01/2002 - 11/30/2002</td></tr>
    <tr><th width="80"> </th><th>MON</th><th>TUE</th>
        <th>WED</th><th>THU</th><th>FRI</th><th>Total</th></tr>
  </table>
<!-- The scrollable "table" body within an in-line frame -->
  <iframe src="HoursWorked.htm" width="525"
    height="100" scrolling="auto">
    <p>**The hours table data should be displayed here!**</p>
  </iframe>
<!-- "Footer" Table -->
  <table cellspacing="0" width="525">
    <tr><td class="footer">&copy; NVBizNet.com (702)-361-0141
        </td></tr>
  </table>
<body>
```

In this example, the *src* attribute in the <iframe> tag tells the Web browser to display the Web page HoursWorked.htm within the inline frame. (HoursWorked.htm is a Web page with a single week of hours-worked information displayed in tabular form.) The <iframe> tag's *width* and *height* attributes instruct the Web browser to make the inline frame 525 pixels wide by 100 pixels tall. Finally, setting the *scrolling* attribute to "auto" instructs the Web browser to insert *both* vertical and horizontal scrollbars when the content on the Web page displayed within the frame is either wider or taller than the frame as shown in Figure 5-7.

As you can see from the preceding example, you insert an inline frame on a Web page much like you insert a graphics image—only you use a set of start and end inline frame tags (<inline></inline>) to insert an inline frame rather than the <img> tag you use to insert an image. Inline frames—like images—take up space on a Web page. To position the frame precisely on the page, insert its <iframe> tag into a cell within a page layout table (as you learned to do with text, graphics images, and other objects in Chapter 2) or use CSS positioning rules (which you learned about in Chapter 4).

You can let a site visitor click a hypertext link to change the Web page displayed within an inline frame. However, to do this you must name the frame. To assign a name to an inline frame, use the <inline> tag's *name* attribute, as shown here:

```
<iframe src="HoursWorked.htm" width="525"
  height="100" scrolling="auto" name="HoursTableFrame">
  <p>**The hours table data should be displayed here!**</p>
</iframe>
```

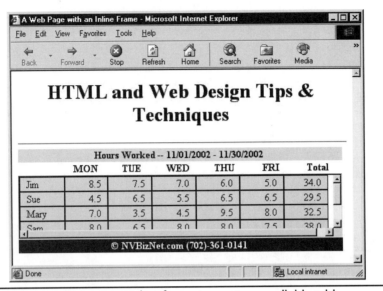

Figure 5-7 A Web page that uses an inline frame to create a scrollable table

The *name* attribute in this example sets the name of the inline frame to "HoursTableFrame." As such, you can instruct the Web browser to display the page a hyperlink retrieves within the inline frame by assigning "HoursTableFrame" to the hyperlink's *target* attribute as follows:

```
<a href="HourswWorkedJan02Wk1.html" target="HoursTableFrame">
  Employee hours 01/07/02 - 01/11/02</a>
<a href="HourswWorkedJan02Wk2.html" target="HoursTableFrame">
  Employee hours 01/14/02 - 01/18/02</a>
<a href="HourswWorkedJan02Wk3.html" target="HoursTableFrame">
  Employee hours 01/21/02 - 01/25/02</a>
<!-- Links to pages with additional hours worked tables -->
```

When clicked, each of the hyperlinks in this example will retrieve a Web page and display the page content within the inline frame "HoursTableFrame". Thus, in this example, the visitor can select the week of hours worked—data the browser displays as a "scrollable table" within an inline frame.

Both Netscape Navigator 6.1 (and later) and Internet Explorer 5.5 (and later) support the <iframe> tag. For additional browsers with inline frames support, check the <iframe> tag information available at http://www.htmlcompendium.org/Menus/0framefy.htm, where you will find a list of HTML and XHTML elements and which browsers support what elements and attributes.

Updating Multiple XHTML Page Inline Frames at Once

Frames let you display two or more Web pages within the browser application window at the same time. For example, in Chapter 1, you used frames to display three Web pages onscreen: a banner or logo in a frame along the top of the screen; a menu within a frame down the screen's left side; and a content page (initially, the site's home page) in a frame to the right of the menu. The preceding Tip showed you how to insert an inline frame within an XHTML Web page as you would a graphics image. Like other objects visible on the Web page, you position inline frames with CSS positioning rules (which you learned about in Chapter 4) or by inserting the inline frames within table cells located where you want the content within the frames to appear.

If you want to float text along the side and bottom of an inline frame, you need only insert an *align* attribute within the frame's <iframe> tag, as shown here:

```
<body>
<!-- Content that precedes the inline frame -->
  <p>
    <iframe width=200 height=200 src="RoastPic.htm"
     align="right"></iframe>
<!-- Text content which flows along the frame's left-hand
     side—the inline frame is aligned "right." -->
  </p>
<!-- additional page content -->
</body>
```

In this example, Web page content within the same paragraph (container) as the inline frame flows along the frame's left side. Setting the <iframe> tag's *align* attribute to "right" instructs the browser to display the 200-pixel by 200-pixel frame flush with the right-hand side of its container, which in this case, is the Web page body. To float text along an inline frame's right side, set the *align* attribute within its <iframe> tag to "left."

Suppose, for example, that you have an unordered (that is, bulleted) list of recipe titles and want to display a picture of the "finished" product to the right of the list whenever a visitor clicks on a recipe title within the list. You might use code similar to the following to describe the Web page body:

```
<body>
  <p>
    <iframe name="FoodPictureFrame" width=250 height=250
     src="RoastPic.htm" align="right" scrolling="no"></iframe>

    <ul><li><a href="RoastPic.htm" target="FoodPictureFrame">
        Yankee Pot Roast</a></li>
      <li><a href="DuckPic.htm" target="FoodPictureFrame">
        Roast Duck</li>
```

```
      <li><a href="ChickenPic.htm" target="FoodPictureFrame">
         Chicken Kiev</li>
      </ul>
  </p>
<!-- additional page content -->
</body>
```

Note that each item in the bulleted list is a hypertext link whose *target* attribute tells the Web browser to display the Web page retrieved (by clicking the hyperlink) within the same inline frame, "FoodPictureFrame". As such, each time a visitor clicks a recipe within the bulleted list, the Web browser retrieves the Web page with the picture of the cooked item and displays the page within the inline frame to the right of the list.

Now, suppose that you also want to display cooking instructions in an inline frame below the bulleted list. (By putting the food recipe within a frame, you can let the visitor scroll through long recipes while at the same time keeping the item list and picture visible onscreen.) To be useful, the cooking instructions within the inline frame below the item list must tell how to prepare the meal displayed within the inline frame ("FoodPictureFrame") to the right of the list. As such, when a visitor clicks a list item, the browser must update the content in two frames—the frame that shows the meal and the frame that shows the recipe.

USE IT To change the content of both frames when a visitor clicks on a hypertext link, you need only add a bit of JavaScript to each hyperlink <a> tag. (Chapter 8 presents JavaScript in detail. However, you need not refer to that chapter before you write the JavaScript you need now.) By clicking on a hyperlink, a site visitor triggers the hyperlink's *onClick* event. Within the hyperlink's <a> tag, then, you can tell the Web browser to execute one or more JavaScript statements whenever the browser detects a mouse click on the link. Thus, to change the contents in two inline frames at once, you might change the code shown previously to the following:

```
<body>
  <iframe name="FoodPictureFrame" width=250 height=250
    src="RoastPic.htm" align="right" scrolling="no"
    hspace="0" vspace="0"></iframe>

  <ul><li><a href="RoastPic.htm" target="FoodPictureFrame"
      onClick="window.RecipeFrame.location='RoastRecipe.htm'">
         Yankee Pot Roast</a></li>
    <li><a href="DuckPic.htm" target="FoodPictureFrame"
      onClick="window.RecipeFrame.location='DuckRecipe.htm'">
         Roast Duck</li>
    <li><a href="ChickenPic.htm" target="FoodPictureFrame"
      onClick="window.RecipeFrame.location='ChickenRecipe.htm'">
         Chicken Kiev</li>
    </ul>

  <div style="position:relative; top:175px">
```

```
    Recipe:<br />
        <iframe name="RecipeFrame" src="RoastRecipe.htm"
          width="100%" height="100" scrolling="auto"></iframe>
  </div>
</body>
```

Each <a> tag in this example now has a JavaScript statement that tells the Web browser to load a Web page into the inline frame named "RecipeFrame" (defined within the division container at the bottom of the page). For example, clicking on the first hypertext link, Yankee Pot Roast, triggers the *onClick* event within the hyperlink's <a> tag. The Web browser, in turn, executes the JavaScript statement tied to the *onClick* event, which instructs the browser to load the Web page RoastRecipe.htm into the inline frame "RecipeFrame". After executing the JavaScript statement, the browser loads the Web page given by the <a> tag's *href* attribute (RoastPic.htm) into the inline frame named by its *target* attribute ("FoodPictureFrame").

Thus, the code in this example loads two Web pages—one as instructed by the hypertext link and the other as instructed within the JavaScript statement (triggered by the <a> tag's *onClick* event). Although, the JavaScript in this example only loads a single Web page, you can load multiple pages by adding additional statements within the quoted string that follows *onClick=*. Simply separate the statements you want the browser to execute with a semicolon (;), as shown here:

```
onClick="window.InlineFrameName.location='WebPageURL';
         window.InlineFrameName.location='WebPageURL';
         window.InlineFrameName.location='WebPageURL';"
```

In each of the three statements in this example, you would replace *InlineFrameName* with the name of the inline frame into which you want the Web browser to load the Web page, whose Web address you type in place of *WebPageURL* at the end of the statement.

Changing XHTML Page Appearance Based on Media Type

Until recently, you could design Web pages knowing that site visitors would display your creations on a monitor attached to a PC. Although screen resolutions vary, standard 15- and 17-inch monitors give you plenty of room to display the graphics and animations needed to spice up a page and drive home the message in its text content. These days, in addition to desktop or laptop computer screens, visitors view Web pages on their televisions, cell phones, personal digital assistants (PDAs), and other wireless devices. What complicates matters for you, the designer, is that each type of non-PC device differs in physical size, layout, and the way in which the visitor interacts with the device while surfing the Web. Therefore, when creating a page with text content intended for both wired (PC) and wireless visitors, you must vary the content's appearance (and perhaps the page layout) based on the media used to display it.

For example, an article on a Web page with a 36pt heading and 18pt type may fit comfortably on a single 17-inch computer screen. However, after retrieving the page on a PDA (such as a Palm Pilot or Handspring Visor), a visitor might see only the heading and a few sentences of content. Because paging through multiple screens while reading distracts the visitor, you want to fit as much text on a single screen as possible. Therefore, you want the PDA's Web browser to display headings and text using a 12pt character size, for example. To set the headings off from regular text, you might display the headings in boldface.

Before CSS rules with *media* attributes, you had to create multiple Web pages to display even the same content using different text styles. Imagine the time and expense involved in creating and managing multiple copies of every Web page on a large news site that might generate several hundred (and perhaps over a thousand) new Web pages each day. Not to mention the added load on the Web server due to the server taking time to determine the visitor's media type so it could select the correct Web page format to send for each HTTP request.

USE IT Fortunately, CSS lets you write rules that tell the visitor's browser how to style the content based on the browser's display type. For example, to display a Web page with 36pt headings and 18pt type on a computer screen while displaying the same page in 12pt type on a handheld (PDA) device, you can include style sheets such as the following within your Web documents:

```
<head>
  <style type="text/css" media="screen">
<!--
    h1 {font-size:36pt; text-align:center; font-weight:bold}
    body {font-size:18pt}
-->
  </style>
  <style type="text/css" media="handheld">
<!--
    h1 {font-size:12pt; font-weight:bold}
    body {font-size:12pt}
-->
  </style>
</head>
```

Note that each of the two style sheets in this example has a *media* attribute. The media type descriptor assigned to the *media* attribute in the first style sheet is "screen," and the media type descriptor for the second style sheet is "handheld." This means that a Web browser will apply the CSS rules within the first style sheet only when the browser is running on a device (such as a PC) whose media type (that is, display type) is "screen." Similarly, a Web browser running on a PDA (that is, on a handheld device such as a PocketPC) will one day "know" its *media* type is "handheld" and will therefore apply the CSS rules within the second style sheet.

Unfortunately, none of the microbrowsers on handheld devices today are as sophisticated as those on PCs. The Palm OS, for example, supports only HTML 3.2, and cellular phone Web browsers use Handheld Device Markup Language (HDML), Wireless Device Markup Language (WML), or a very limited subset of HTML. However, when accepted, the soon-to-be-released module-based XHTML (XHTML version 1.1) will let manufacturers create Web browsers with only the subset of XHTML necessary to display Web content based on device type. In fact, the W3C released XHTML Basic in December 2000 exactly with this in mind. By removing from XHTML the tags that mobile phones,

PDAs, pagers, and set-top boxes could not physically support, the W3C gave manufacturers a smaller DTD they could embed within their browsers. (The smaller the DTD, the less device memory the browser consumes and the less processing power it requires.)

Typically, a handheld device does not connect directly to the Internet. Instead, the handheld communicates with a proxy server, which in turn, retrieves a Web page from the Web server and passes a filtered version of the Web page HTML back to the wireless device for display. Proxy servers, which are currently using older versions of HTML, will soon switch to XHTML and become more "intelligent." Rather than simply filter and pass HTML codes to handheld devices, as they do now, proxy servers will download the appropriate style sheets (based on the media type of the device they are feeding) and apply the CSS rules to the Web content before they pass the formatted content on to the wireless device. Thus, although a cellular phone's Web browser may not support XHTML or CSS, the proxy server that sends Web content to the Web browser will. By including the media descriptor within your style sheets now, you make your Web pages ready for display on non-PC platforms in the future.

CSS Level 1 identifies two media types: "screen" and "print." CSS Level 2 has ten media type descriptors (shown in Table 5-2) that represent target devices for XHTML content.

Interestingly, the CSS (Level 2) standard notes that due to rapidly changing technology, you should not consider the media type list within the standard (as shown here) as definitive of all media types. However, Web page authors (like you) should not rely on media type names not yet defined within the CSS standard. Meaning: Check the latest revision of the CSS standard periodically; the list of media types will grow as manufacturers provide Web access (and Web browsers) on more and more of the devices we use daily.

Although the example at the beginning of this Tip shows how you embed a separate style sheet for each media type, you can use the CSS @*media* rule to specify rules for multiple media types within a

Media Type Descriptor	Apply Style Sheet Rules to
"all"	All device types
"aural"	Speech synthesizers
"Braille"	Braille and tactile feedback devices
"embossed"	Paginated Braille printers
"handheld"	Handheld devices (such as PDAs and cell phones)
"print"	Paginated media (such as the printed page) or printed pages onscreen (such as a "print preview")
"projection"	Projectors, and printing to film slides and transparencies
"screen"	Color computer screens
"tty"	Devices with fixed-pitch character grids, such as teletype machines
"tv"	Television-type devices (low resolution, color, limited scrollability, sound capable)

Table 5-2   CSS Level 2 Media Type Descriptors

single style sheet. For example, you can specify rules for handheld, print, and screen devices within the same style sheet, as shown here:

```
<head>
  <style type="text/css">
<!--
    @media screen, print {
      h1 {font-size:36pt; text-align:center; font-weight:bold}
      body {font-size:18pt} }
    @media handheld {
      h1 {font-size:12pt; font-weight:bold}
      body {font-size:12pt} }
-->
  </style>
</head>
```

Note that each @*media* rule specifies its target media type(s) (separated by commas) followed by a set of rules (within curly braces). Thus, in this example, a PC-based browser (whose media type is "screen") will apply the two CSS rules within the first @*media* rule, whereas the proxy sever for a Web browser running on a PDA will apply the two CSS rules within the second @*media* rule.

Rather than embed style sheets (especially those intended for specific media types) within your XHTML documents, consider linking to style sheets stored as files external to the Web page. By using an @*import* command with syntax, as shown here, you can reduce the amount of code the browser retrieves:

```
@import (<style sheet URL>) <media type list>;
```

Suppose, for example, that you stored the CSS rules in the previous example within two external files (SmallDisplay.css and NormalDisplay.css) within the /StyleSheets folder on your Web site. If you include the following code within the Web page HTML, the visitor's Web browser will retrieve only the external style sheet file whose media type(s) the browser supports:

```
@import (/StyleSheets/NormalDisplay.css) screen, print;
@import (/StyleSheets/SmallDisplay.css) handheld;
```

Thus, the proxy server for browsers running on a cell phone will retrieve only SmallDisplay.css, whereas the PC-based browser will retrieve only NormalDisplay.css, because they do not support the "handheld" media type. Note that if a handheld device (such as a PDA) has print capability, its proxy server will download both external style sheets.

Controlling the Way the Web Browser Prints an XHTML Web Page

If you have a long Web page and you think that your visitors will want it, you can use a CSS rule to control the page breaks on the printed output. There is no practical limit as to the length of a single Web page when viewed onscreen. The browser lets the site visitor scroll through the Web documents without visible page breaks. Each piece of paper, however, has a finite length. As such, the Web browser must eject a page after printing to the last printable line on the page.

Unfortunately, the Web browser may overrun the physical page break when printing the content on a large (long) Web page. If the browser attempts to print all the way to the bottom edge of a page on a laser printer, for example, the visitor will not be able to see the content "printed" in the nonprintable margin at the bottom of one page and top of the next. Moreover, if your Web page has pictures, the browser may print part of a picture on one page and the rest on another. Finally, if the visitor has a dot matrix printer, the browser may print a line of text on the perforation between pages only to have the text become unreadable when the visitor separates the individual pages of the continuous form computer paper. Fortunately, you can use a CSS rule to ensure that browsers print your Web pages with page breaks where you want them.

USE IT Say, for example, that you create a long Web page, and you want to make sure that Web browsers print the content on the page with page breaks between paragraphs and either before or after (but not within) the graphics images on the page. You can use the CSS *page-break-after* and *page-break-before* properties to tell the Web browser to eject a page and continue printing on the next page where you want each page break to occur within your Web page HTML. Table 5-3 describes the instructions the Web browser receives based on each value available for the *page-break-after* and *page-break-before* properties.

For example, the following CSS rule tells the Web browser to eject a page before printing each level-one heading:

```
h1 {page-break-before: always}
```

Value	*page-break-before*	*page-break-after*
"auto"	Neither force nor prevent a page break before the element.	Neither force nor prevent a page break after the element.
"always"	Force a page break before the element.	Force a page break after the element.
"avoid"	Override the *page-break-before* "always" setting for the current element and do not force a page break before the element.	Override the *page-break-after* "always" setting for the current element and do not force a page break after the element.

Table 5-3   CSS *page-break-before* and *page-break-after* Options for Paginating Printed Output

Value	page-break-before	page-break-after
"left"	Force the number of page breaks necessary for the element to appear on a left-hand (that is, an odd-numbered) page.	Force the number of page breaks necessary after printing the element such that the content printed immediately after the element appears on a left-hand (that is, an odd-numbered) page.
"right"	Force the number of page breaks necessary for the element to appear on a left-hand (that is, an even-numbered) page.	Force the number of page breaks necessary after printing the element such that the content printed immediately after the element appears on a right-hand (that is, even-numbered) page.

Table 5-3   CSS *page-break-before* and *page-break-after* Options for Paginating Printed Output (*continued*)

After adding the preceding rule to a CSS in the Web page header, you can use the rule to control page breaks in printouts by inserting level-one headings wherever you want a page break to occur, as shown here:

```
<html>
<head>
  <style>
    h1   {page-break-before:always}
  </style>
</head>
<body>
  <h1 style="page-break-before:auto"> This heading defines the
      start of the document </h1>
  <p> This represents text on page 1... </p>
  <h1> This heading starts a new page </h1>
  <p> This represents text on page 2... </p>
  <h1 style="page-break-before:avoid">
      No page break before this heading</h1>
  <p> This represents additional text on page 2... </p>
  <h1> This heading starts a new page </h1>
  <p> This represents text on page 3... </p>
<body>
</html>
```

To avoid printing a blank page at the beginning of the document, the Web page in this example has an in-line style within the first <h1> tag that sets the *page-break-before* property for the element to "auto." Setting the *page-break-before* property to "auto" tells the Web browser to neither avoid nor force a page break before the element. Note too that the *page-break-before property* is set to "avoid" within the third <h1> tag. This tells the Web browser not to force a page break before the element, which means that the third level-1 heading prints on the same page with the second level-1 heading (if physically possible).

Thus, by assigning *page-break-before* (or *page-break-after*) property values to elements within a style sheet in the Web page header, you control whether the browser ejects a page prior to printing a particular type of element. To gain additional control over pagination, you can override existing CSS rules by inserting in-line styles within tags that insert elements on the page. Often you will omit style sheet rules altogether and use only inline styles to control pagination. For example, if you want to make sure that a graphics image or an XHTML table starts at the top of a printed page (so that the picture or tabular data is not split onto two pages), you would simply use inline styles, such as the following:

```
<img style="page-break-before:always">
<table style="page-break-before:always">
```

Remember that in addition to controlling pagination, you can also use CSS rules to control the character size and typeface used to print a Web page. As such, you can make the Web page printout look much different than it appears onscreen. Within the previous Tip, "Changing XHTML Page Appearance Based on Media Type," you learned how to create style sheet rules for specific media types. For example, to print the Web page text content using only the Courier typeface, you would include the following *@media* rule within a style sheet in the Web page header:

```
@media print {body {font-face:courier}}
```

Although the *@media* rule in this example applies to all body text, you can write "print" media rules for the browser to apply to individual Web page elements.

CHAPTER 6

Graphics

TIPS IN THIS CHAPTER

▶ Working with Cross-Platform Issues When Creating Graphics Images for the Web   274

▶ Specifying Image Dimensions Within an Image Tag   277

▶ Working with the *alt* Attribute and Text-Only Viewers   278

▶ Creating a Tool Tip by Inserting a *title* Attribute in an Image Tag   281

▶ Compressing Photographs into a JPEG File   283

▶ Saving Clip Art and Text to a GIF-Formatted File   286

▶ Making Images Appear to Load Faster   288

▶ Working with the PNG-8 and PNG-24 File Formats   290

▶ Converting Graphics into Web Images with Image-Editing Programs   291

▶ Creating Web-Friendly Graphics Images on Your Scanner   292

▶ Creating Colorful Horizontal Rules   294

▶ Retrieving a Fast-Loading "Teaser" Image with the *lowsrc* Attribute   296

▶ Ensuring Accurate Color Presentation with the Web-Safe Color Palette   298

▶ Creating Graphical Hyperlink Anchors   300

▶ Creating Tiled Backgrounds from Graphics Images   301

▶ Creating Transparency in a GIF Image   304

▶ Retrieving Full-Size Images after Clicking on Thumbnails   307

▶ Preloading and Caching Images Behind the Scenes   309

▶ Expanding the Web-Safe Color Palette with Dithering Techniques   311

▶ Smoothing the Edges of Text Converted into a Graphic Through Anti-Aliasing   313

To most Internet users, the Web is and has always been a visual medium. However, in the beginning, graphics were foreign to the World Wide Web. In fact, graphics images were more than rare—Web designers did not use them. Computers were slow, Internet connections were slow, and when people "surfed" the Web, the best they could expect was white text slowly appearing against a green or black monitor background. It was a dark, boring time for Internet users. Fortunately, those days are long gone.

Today, Web pages with graphics images abound, and the Internet (the electronic roadway that transports information) has become faster and faster. To compare the speed at which information travels across the Internet today, as opposed to ten years ago, would be like comparing a Model-T Ford to a Ferrari. In other words, today's Internet is a lot faster. Moreover, computers running the latest Web browsers, such as Internet Explorer and Netscape Navigator, process and load Web pages faster than ever before.

All this is important because graphics files are larger than text files and require more time to move across the Internet and onto a visitor's computer. Back in the days when a 2400 baud modem was the standard Internet connection, no one was willing to wait the minutes (and perhaps hours) it would have taken to download even a single graphics image. In addition, fewer applications were available to create the graphics and compress them into smaller files. Developing the hardware and software necessary to make graphics a reality on the Internet would take time.

Understanding a Graphics Role in Web Design

You place graphics onto a Web page for the same reasons you include pictures in a brochure or magazine—to help the readers gain a better understanding of what you are trying to say. The goal is to have graphics complement the written text. For example, a Web site designed to promote a major university like the University of California at Berkeley would show images of the campus, classrooms, and possibly the professors and other university staff. Visitors to the Web site would not only read about the benefits of attending the university, but they would also be able to see the campus. By viewing Web pages such as the one in Figure 6-1, visitors gain a thorough understanding of what life at Berkeley is like.

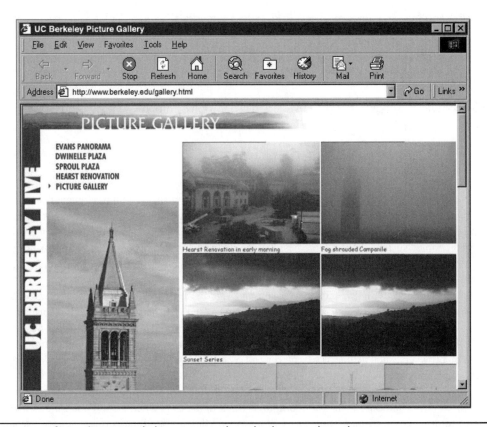

Figure 6-1   Life on the UC Berkeley campus, described in words and pictures

Text alone cannot convey as much information as text combined with a few well-chosen images. When you use descriptive text, however well-written, you must rely on the reader's imagination to construct an image of what you are describing. Conversely, when you use text and add pictures for emphasis, your readers can see exactly what you have in mind.

Unfortunately, when adding illustrations to your Web pages, like with anything else, you can have too much of a good thing. In Figure 6-1, a few well-placed images and descriptive text gives visitors a slice of life at the university. However, a picture of every dormitory room, and images of every building and classroom is too much information. Before you add graphics to a Web page, ask yourself what images best illustrate what you are trying to say. If the goal of the Web site is to attract new students, then choose images that would best achieve that goal.

As you create a Web site, never forget your responsibilities as a designer. Do not give your visitors too much information on a single page or too many choices all at once. It is up to you to decide what your visitors see and when they see it. If you give visitors too much data at one time, you run the risk of causing information overload, which may result in visitors making the wrong choices or reaching the wrong conclusions. (You will learn more about striking a balance between Web images and text later in this chapter in "Balancing Text and Graphics on a Web Page".)

Creating Web Graphics

When you add images to your Web page, you have several choices as to where to get the graphics. You can purchase CDs with ready-made images, or you can download Web graphics from Web sites that sell graphics (such as http://www.photosphere.com or http://creative.gettyimages.com). Another option is to use a digital or film camera to take photographs. You can then save the digital camera's images to disk or use a scanner to scan previously printed photos into files on your computer. Finally, you can create digital clip art and illustrations by using design applications, such as Adobe Photoshop and ImageReady.

Unless you purchase ready-made graphics, you will need one or more programs to help you process and prepare the images for use on the Internet. Not only will graphics applications save you time preparing images, but they also give you control over the image content. Say, for example, that you have a picture of yourself and three friends taken at the Grand Canyon, and you want to focus attention on the people in the picture and not the scenery. To accomplish this, you might open the image in Photoshop (or another image-editing program) and *crop* (cut out) the areas of the image you do not want people to see. Cropping an image directs the visitor's eyes to exactly what you want the visitor to see by removing unwanted portions of the picture, as shown in Figure 6-2.

Figure 6-2   Cropping an image helps to focus the viewer's eyes on the details of the image and avoids unnecessary distraction

Understanding Image File Formats

When a visitor retrieves a Web page that has pictures, the total size of the image files determines how long it will take the Web browser to download and display the page. If your graphics files are too large, site visitors may lose patience and move on to other, faster-loading Web sites. Fortunately, different compression schemes are available to reduce the size of graphics files. Some of the schemes use lossy compression; others are lossless. A *lossy* compression scheme reduces graphics file size by removing color data. Conversely, *lossless* compression reduces the size of a file by compressing large blocks of the same color. Although some of the color information is actually lost during lossy compression, with lossless compression, all the color information remains in the file—the Web browser simply decompresses the color data to redisplay the compressed blocks of color.

The final stage of image preparation involves selecting a file format to use when saving the picture to a disk file. The three most common file formats for Web graphics are JPEG (pronounced "j-peg;" it uses a lossy compression scheme developed by Joint Photographic Experts Group), Graphic Interchange Format (GIF), and Portable Network Graphic (PNG). Both GIF and PNG file formats use a lossless compression scheme to reduce file size. The smaller the graphics file's size, the faster the Web browser can download and display the picture on the Web page. Therefore, compressing graphics files reduces the long wait times normally associated with Web pages that have large images. Of the three formats, the JPEG format is used primarily for photographs, whereas the GIF format is most often used for clip art, illustrations, and drawings.

Using the JPEG format reduces the file size of images containing a lot of color (such as photographs) by removing (lossy) certain colors and then using the remaining colors in a dithering, or pixel-color-mixing scheme that fools the eye into seeing colors that are no longer in the picture. Although a JPEG image could contain a maximum of 16.7 million colors, the compression process removes most of those colors to achieve significant file size reductions.

Whereas a JPEG-formatted file can hold millions of colors, a GIF file can house a maximum of only 256. The GIF format reduces a compression scheme called Run Length Encoding (RLE) to compress large solid areas of color (such as those found in clip art). For example, suppose an image has a solid block of blue color running left to right across the width of the image. When you save the file, the GIF compression scheme records the coordinates of the blue block and removes the block of color from the file. When the Web browser opens the previously saved GIF image, the browser uses the coordinates and run length to re-create the block of color within the image. The technique of recording the coordinates of solid color areas creates GIF files with very small file sizes. Because the saved size of a GIF file image depends on the colors in the image, graphics that contain few colors compress down to small file sizes.

The PNG format uses a combination of the GIF and JPEG compression schemes. The PNG format comes in two flavors: PNG-8 and PNG-24. The PNG-8 format can work only with graphics that have a maximum of 256 colors. Therefore, the PNG-8 format closely resembles the GIF file format. In addition, PNG-8 uses an RLE compression method similar to GIF compression. Using the PNG-8 format on a clip art image produces small file sizes similar to those of the GIF format. The PNG-24 format can handle images with millions of colors, and is used to minimize the size of photographic image files. However, because the PNG format does not remove pixels of color like the JPEG format does, saving a photograph using the PNG-24 format often creates files with an unacceptably large size for use on a Web page.

When selecting a graphics file format, you must ensure that the majority of (and hopefully all) your site visitors can open the graphics files you insert on your Web pages. Although almost all Web browsers can decompress and display GIF- and JPEG-formatted files, the same does not hold true for PNG graphics. (Some Web surfers using older browsers may not be able to display PNG-formatted images.) Therefore, before selecting a graphics file format, make sure you know your audience and the capabilities of the Web browsers your visitors will most likely be using.

▶ **NOTE**

Netscape Navigator and Internet Explorer have provided limited support for PNG-formatted graphics files since 1997. However, for full support of the PNG format, including image transparency, PNG images are best viewed using Internet Explorer versions 5 and up and Netscape Navigator versions 6 and higher.

Placing Web Graphics into a Web Page

Placing images into a Web page requires a graphics image file and the HTML <img> tag. For example, the following <img> tag instructs the Web browser to load and display a graphics file named image.jpg:

```
<img src="image.jpg">
```

Within the <img> tag, the *src* attribute tells the Web browser the source of the graphics image (that is, the name of the file) the browser is to display.

▶ **NOTE**

*To make your image tag compliant with XHTML, the tag must have an end tag or the start tag must end with />. For example, <img src="image1.jpg" /> (include a space before the trailing / and > of empty elements), or <img src="image1.jpg"> **</img>**.*

To insert pictures onto a Web page, create an <img> tag for each picture between the start and end body tags (<body></body>). The Web browser will display images on the Web page in the order in which the <img> tags appear with the HTML document. For example, the following code tells the Web browser to display two graphics images:

```
<html>
<head><title>Example of three image tags</title></head>
<body>
  <img src="image1.jpg" />
  <img src="image2.jpg" />
</body>
</html>
```

In this example, the Web browser will try to display the images left-to-right across the application window. If the width of the browser window is not wide enough to accommodate the horizontal placement of the images, the browser will places the images vertically down the Web browser window.

Dealing with Internet Access Speeds

Another important consideration when including graphics on a Web page is the time delay incurred downloading the image files. Although Internet connection options such as Digital Subscriber Lines (DSL) and cable modems let you send large amounts of data across the Internet in a short amount of time, not everyone has access to a high-speed Internet connection. Whenever you add additional graphics to a Web page, you increase the amount of time required to completely download the page and its content from the Web server.

If visitors to your Web page have a slow, 28.8-baud connection to the Internet, the browser will need about fifteen to twenty seconds to download 40KB to 50KB of data. For most Web surfers, thirty seconds is the maximum they are willing to wait for their browsers to display your page content. Therefore, keep the file size of each of the site's Web pages small to ensure that your visitors will wait for the browser to display all the page content rather than clicking a hyperlink to go elsewhere on the Web. Remember, your visitors will have no more patience when surfing the Web than you do.

To get an accurate file size, right-click the picture's filename, and select Properties from the pop-up menu. (On a Macintosh, CONTROL-click on the filename and then choose Get Info.) The file size in the Properties dialog box (Macintosh: the file size in parentheses in the Get Info dialog box) is an accurate measurement of the graphic file's real size, as shown in Figure 6-3.

Graphics are an indispensable part of the Internet. However, if large graphics files cause visitors to leave your site rather than wait for the images to download, the graphics are not doing you any good. Remember, graphics are a means to an end and not an end in of themselves.

Copyright Issues When Dealing with Web Graphics

No discussion of Web graphics would be complete without mentioning copyright laws. Although copyright laws vary from country to country, if you are an American citizen, you must follow the copyright laws passed by the United States Congress.

U.S. copyright laws protect the rights of people who create new products (inventors) and the intellectual property that belongs to the writers and artists. For example, the text in this book falls under standard U.S. copyright laws that make it illegal for anyone to copy the information contained in these pages (intellectual property) and resell or distribute the copied passages without the express, written permission of the publisher.

In addition to text, graphics and artwork fall under the protection of U.S. copyright laws, and that includes graphics and artwork displayed on Web pages. Just because an image appears on the Internet and you can download and save that image to a file on your hard drive, does not mean that you can use that image without violating copyright laws. The birth of the Internet did not change U.S. copyright laws, it just made the rules harder to enforce.

If you plan to copy images from one site and use them on another, never take anything for granted. In many cases, you will find on the Web page a disclaimer that says images on the page are not to be

Windows operating system

Macintosh operating system

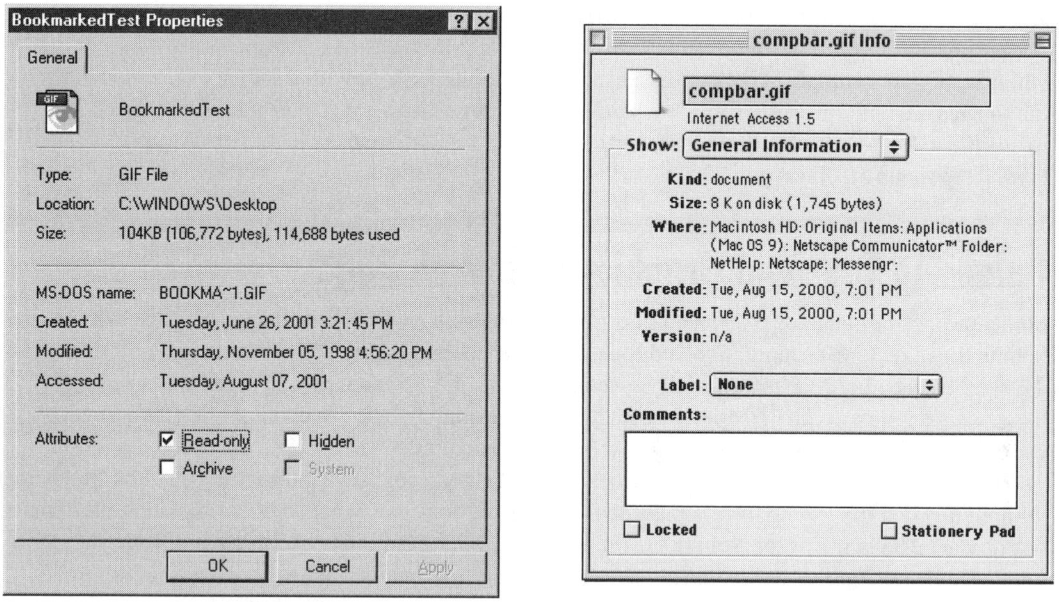

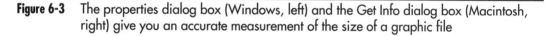

Figure 6-3 The properties dialog box (Windows, left) and the Get Info dialog box (Macintosh, right) give you an accurate measurement of the size of a graphic file

copied and used without the author's permission. However, whether you see a disclaimer or not, always e-mail or write the author before you use an image. Explain exactly what you want to do with the author's pictures and ask for his or her permission to use the pictures. If the author says "no," do not use the images. Conversely, if the author agrees to let you use his or her material, try to get the permission in writing. For example, send to the author a letter that explains what you plan to do with the images, and leave a place for the author's signature. (The standard term for this type of document is a "release form".) When you write a release form, be specific as to how you intend to use the images. The author is probably not going to sign a generic release that does not state what you intend to do with the images.

Some authors will specify the number of times you can use their images or the condition in which you are to display their pictures. For example, when you purchase clip art or photographs from a commercial dealer or Web site, the site's owner(s) may let you use the images as you see fit with certain exceptions, such as prohibitions against using the pictures on Web sites that deal with pornographic material or hate group literature. Always read the release form carefully, and if you are unsure as to the terms of the release, ask the copyright holder for clarification.

Many Web sites offer free clip art; however, they often limit its use to personal Web sites, as opposed to business-related sites. If you use clip art from sources such as Microsoft Office clip art gallery or from such Web sites as the Microsoft Design Gallery Live (at http://dgl.microsoft.com), check the usage license carefully.

Finally, always enclose a self-addressed, stamped envelope the grantor can use to return the signed release form to you. Remember, you are the one asking permission of the author, so make the process as easy as possible. The bottom line—never assume you can use something you did not create. Always ask permission first. If the author says "no," do not use the images. If the author says "yes," get the authorization in writing and be specific as to what you intend to do with the images. Remember, the images are not your property. They belong to someone else—even after you get permission to use them. Respect the intellectual properties of others, as you would want others to respect your ownership rights on things you create.

Balancing Text and Graphics on a Web Page

Sometimes words alone are not enough to convey a message. However, creating a Web page that includes both text and pictures is more involved than randomly inserting graphics on the page. You must strike a proper balance between information presented as text and information conveyed through images. True, a single picture can sometimes provide more meaning than ten Web pages of text. However, even the most meaningful images require a bit of explanation.

For example, most sports enthusiasts would immediately recognize a photograph of Mark McGwire without any text describing the great baseball player. If, however, you add a text box under the image with "Mark McGwire, of the St Louis Cardinals, hitting his 62nd home run breaking Roger Maris' long-held record," you turn the image into a historical photograph. The text conveys an important historical date, and when combined with the image, the two create a snapshot in time and generate a more powerful message than either one alone.

Always choose photographs that support the associated text. For example, replacing the photograph of the city of Paris and the Eiffel Tower with a photo of Wichita, Kansas would be absurd. However, many Web designers insert images on a page without a clear idea of how the images relate to the Web page text.

In addition to balancing text and graphics, if the Web page contains more than one image, choose one of the images as the "main" picture that conveys the theme of the Web page. Place the "theme" image in a prominent position on the page. Web pages that contain a dominant image, such as the one shown at the top of Figure 6-4, help readers focus their eyes. Conversely, Web pages with multiple pictures and no dominant (theme) image can appear confusing to visitors, as shown in the bottom image of Figure 6-4.

Color is an excellent tool you can use to attract visitor attention. Color images grab attention better than black and white, and the good news is that displaying a color image on a Web page does not cost any more than using a black and white picture. The same is not true when using color in print media, where printing in color can cost hundreds, if not thousands of dollars more than printing in black and white.

A trick you can use to focus visitor attention on specific pictures on a page is to use a combination of color and black and whites images. Use a color-dominant image on a page where other (less important) images are black and white. Because people are naturally drawn to view the color picture first, you can focus your visitors' eyes on the picture that conveys the gist of your message when they first view the Web page and then have the visitors move on to view other pictures that further drive your point home.

In addition, when you insert images on a Web page, avoid placing them in the middle with text running down either side. Instead, place images along the left or right side of the page with the text flowing along the opposite side. Placing an image in the middle of a column of text, as in Figure 6-5,

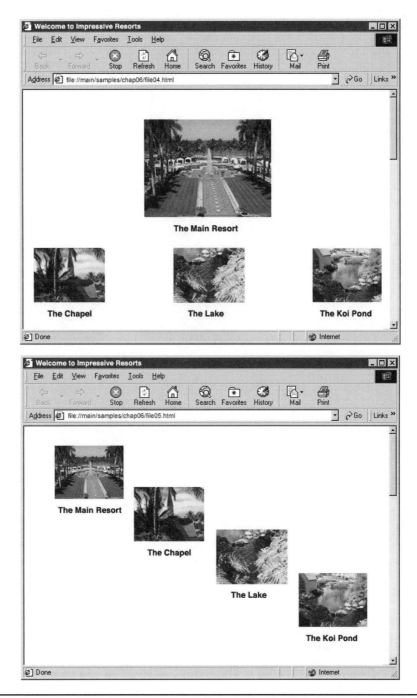

Figure 6-4   Web pages with a dominant image help to focus the attention of visitors (top), but Web pages without a dominant image lack focus (bottom)

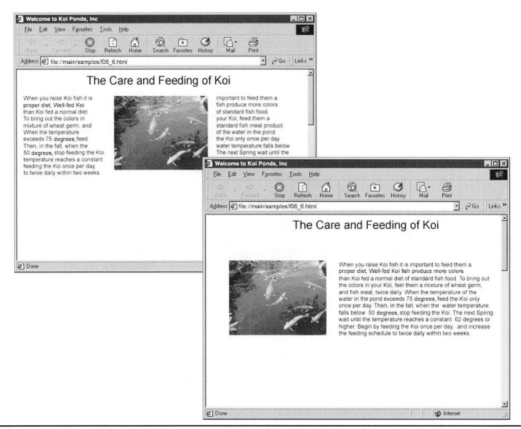

Figure 6-5   The text flowing down the right side of the page is easier to read

forces the reader's eyes to skip back and forth over the graphic. Not only does this confuse visitors, but it also causes undue eyestrain.

Combining text and images on a Web page is not at all difficult. Doing so is a matter of choosing meaningful pictures and then following a few simple rules. Always choose images that relate to the text. If the text does not fit the image, either change the image or rewrite the text. If a picture is worth a thousand words, a picture combined with some well-written text can convey volumes of information quickly and in a small space on the Web page.

Working with Cross-Platform Issues When Creating Graphics Images for the Web

After you insert a graphics image on a Web page, the way the image appears on the visitor's monitor involves many factors. One of these factors is the visitor's operating system. An image displayed by a Macintosh computer looks different when displayed on a Windows system, as shown in Figure 6-6.

An image displayed on a Windows machine

The same image displayed on a Macintosh machine

Figure 6-6   Displaying grayscale images on a Macintosh and Windows computer causes a shift in the brightness of the image

When displaying a picture, the Web browser reads and displays the contents of the graphics image file one pixel at a time. The browser determines the color it is to display onscreen by finding each pixel's color value in the system's color lookup table (CLUT). Thus, the CLUT determines the colors the Web browser will display when interpreting the contents of the graphics file. Unfortunately, the Windows and Macintosh operating systems use different color lookup tables, which is why you see a shift in the colors when a browser displays the same image on one operating system versus the other.

Another issue is the shift in gamma between Windows and Macintosh monitors. The gamma of the monitor defines the midpoint between light and dark. Macintosh monitors average a 1.8 gamma and Windows monitors average a 2.2 gamma. The difference in gamma between the two operating systems translates into images that appear 15 to 20 percent darker when created on a Macintosh and displayed on a Windows computer. Said another way, images appear 15 to 20 percent lighter when created on a Windows system and displayed on a Macintosh.

USE IT   A solution that resolves both the color-shift and gamma issues is to create one image for the Macintosh and a second image for Windows computers. However, in many cases, you do not know who will be viewing your images and what operating system they will be using. Therefore, view your images using the color table and gamma of both the Macintosh and Windows operating systems. Doing so will point out potential problems and let you correct them before you publish the image on the Web site.

To view an image using the color table and gamma of another operating system, you have two choices. You could purchase both a Macintosh and a Windows computer system and then open and view your graphics images in Web browsers on both systems. Or, a more practical method is to use an image-editing program that lets you view images as they appear in both operating systems. For example, Adobe Photoshop version 5.5 or higher lets you view Web graphics using the Windows or Macintosh color lookup table and gamma. Simply open the image in Photoshop, select View | Proof Setup, and choose Macintosh RGB or Windows RGB, depending on your current operating system, as shown in Figure 6-7.

If you use Photoshop for Windows and you choose Macintosh RGB, the visible image shifts into the color table and gamma of a Macintosh monitor. Conversely, if you work in Photoshop for Macintosh and you choose Windows RGB, the visible image shifts into the color table and gamma of a Windows monitor.

If you find that the image is not satisfactory when viewed under the Windows or under the Macintosh operating system, use an image-editing program (such as Photoshop, ImageReady, and so on) to adjust the picture's colors and brightness. Continue to make changes until the picture's appearance is acceptable under both operating systems.

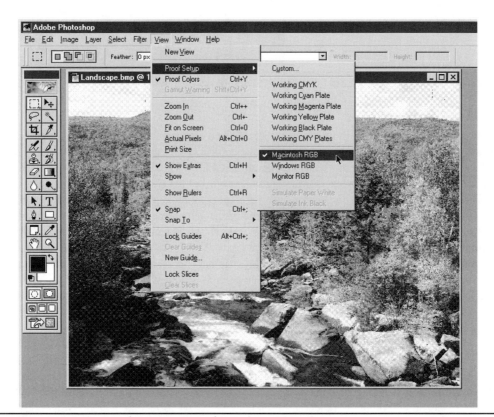

Figure 6-7   Using the Proof Setup option of Windows RGB alerts you to any potential cross-platform problems

Specifying Image Dimensions Within an Image Tag

At the start of this chapter, you learned that the <img> tag instructs the Web browser to load and display a graphics file on the Web page. For example, the following HTML shows an <img> tag in which the *src* attribute instructs the Web browser to retrieve and display the picture stored in the file landscape.jpg, using a width of 200 pixels and a height of 80 pixels:

```
<img src="landscape.jpg" width="200" height="80" />
```

USE IT When adding the *width* and *height* attributes to an <img> tag, you need to understand how the Web browser uses the attribute values you specify. The *width* and *height* attributes define the graphic's dimensions onscreen, which may be different from the actual height and width of the picture in the graphics file. Say, for example, that the picture in landscape.jpg has an actual size of 200 pixels by 80 pixels. Then, inserting the image tag in the preceding example in the Web page HTML tells the Web browser to display the image at 100 percent of the picture's actual size (200×80). However, if by accident you reverse the settings, so the *width* attribute is 80 and the *height* is 200, the image will appear distorted, as shown in Figure 6-8.

Correct width and height

Graphic with width and height attributes reversed ⟶

Figure 6-8 Reversing the width and height attributes creates a distorted image in the browser window

Although changing *width* and *height* attributes may seem like a practical approach to getting an image to fit within an area on a Web page, you should not use this approach on photographs. The *width* and *height* attributes should reflect the exact dimensions of the image in the file. If a photographic image is too large to fit where you want it to on a Web page, open the original image file in an image-editing application such as Photoshop and resize the image to fit on the Web page.

When *width* and *height* attributes in an <img> tag match the actual dimensions of the image in the graphics file, the Web browser does not have to spend time resizing the image. If a browser must resize an image, the browser will add pixels to make the image larger or remove pixels to reduce the size of the image. Unfortunately, forcing the browser to resize an image increases the amount of time required to display the image, and consequently, the remainder of the Web page. Moreover, image-editing programs such as Photoshop do a better "quality" job than Web browsers when resizing an image. This is especially evident when you use *width* and *height* attributes to increase the dimensions of a picture—the image will appear grainy and blurred. Therefore, if you care about the quality of an image, set the *width* and *height* attributes to reflect the actual dimensions of the image in the file.

The most important reason for using the *width* and *height* attributes in each <img> tag is to make it possible for the browser to accurately position text or other Web content around the picture. When you omit *width* and *height* attributes, the Web browser cannot accurately place images and text onscreen until after the browser downloads images completely. As a result, one of two things will happen:

- The browser may load and display the Web page text. Then, after the browser downloads the graphics images, the browser will reload the page and place the text and images where they belong.

- The browser will not display the Web page text until the browser downloads all the graphics images on the page. As a result, your visitors will see only a blank screen while waiting for the browser to finishing retrieving image file contents from the Web server.

Because image files are larger and therefore load more slowly than the Web page text, not specifying the dimensions of the image in each of your <img> tags often keeps the browser from displaying text onscreen. Remember, you must hold your visitors' attention while they wait for the browser to download and display your pictures. If visitors get bored, due to staring at a blank screen, for example, they will go elsewhere. When you supply *width* and *height* attributes in your <img> tags, the Web browser reserves space for each picture and continues to load and display text while waiting for the images to download. As a result, your site visitors can see and read your text content while they wait for the browser to finish downloading and displaying images on the Web page. By getting the browser to display the Web page text quickly, you give the visitor something to read while the browser downloads the graphics and visitors may not notice the time it takes to display the pictures onscreen.

Working with the *alt* Attribute and Text-Only Viewers

The alternate text attribute (*alt*) is an important addition to an <img> tag. When you use the *alt* attribute, it instructs the Web browser to display a text string before downloading a graphics image. In addition, the Web browser will continue to display the alternate text (specified by the *alt* attribute) if the browser cannot download and display the graphics image for some reason. For example, the following HTML tells the Web browser to display text that describes the contents of the picture the visitor would have seen, if the browser is unable to download and display image1.jpg.

 To use the *alt* attribute in the <img> tag, insert a *src* attribute such as that shown in the following example:

```
<html>
<head><title>Example of alternate text</title></head>
<body>
  <img src="image1.jpg" width="100" height="50"
       alt="A picture of James Elliott,
            The founder of InGen, Inc.">
</body>
</html>
```

A Web browser will display the alternate text ("A picture of James Elliott, The founder of InGen, Inc.", in this example) when visitors display the Web page using a browser with graphics turned off, or if the visitors are using a text-only browser. Although the majority of Web surfers today use browsers capable of displaying graphics, alternate text gives those with text-only browsers a sense of what the images are supposed to convey.

If the browser is unable to retrieve and display the picture, the alternate text will remain onscreen in the image placeholder.

When a visitor to your Web site sets his or her browser not to load graphics images, the browser draws a box onscreen wherever you inserted an image tag in the Web page. The browser then displays the alternate text in the image placeholder (that is, in the empty box where the picture would normally go) as shown in Figure 6-9.

Remember, add *width* and *height* that specify the picture's dimensions to each image tag you insert in the Web page HTML. Otherwise, the Web browser will not be able to draw a box of the proper size while downloading or in place of the graphics image. (An image placeholder with the proper dimensions will keep the surrounding text content arranged the way you designed it on the Web page—even if the browser does not display the image itself for some reason.)

Keep the alternate text short and to the point. Say, for example, that you use an image in place of the bullet symbol next to each item in an unordered (that is, bulleted) list. You might use the following <img> tag to display a bullet graphic (in the file red.gif) onscreen:

```
<img src="red.gif" width="10" height="10" alt="This is a red bullet">
```

The alternate text, "This is a red bullet" would take up more space than the original graphics image. Moreover, because the *width* and *height* attributes tell the browser to reserve a 10 by 10 pixel area for the bullet, there is not enough room to display the alternate text, as shown here:

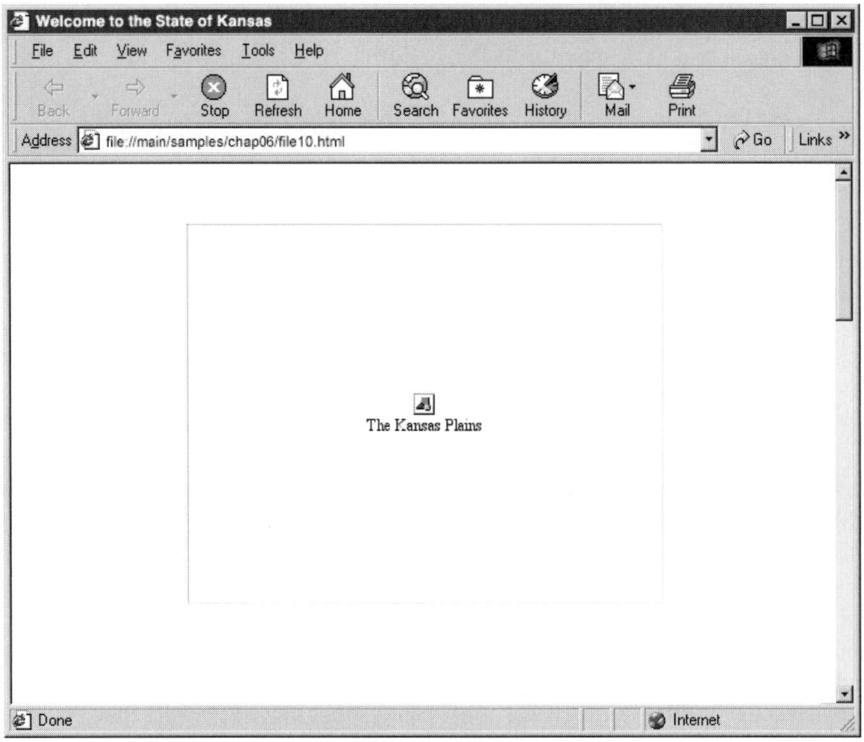

Figure 6-9 The *alt* attribute replaces the image with text

Thus, when displaying small graphics images or when displaying nonessential graphics (such as background tiles and graphical horizontal lines), keep the text short or use an *alt* attribute with a null string such as the one at the end of the following <img> tag:

```
<img src="red.gif" width="10" height="10" alt="">
```

Text-reading programs for the visually impaired use the *alt* attribute (with or without text) to identify each picture for the visually impaired. When visually impaired visitors to your Web site open the Web page, a text-reader program, such as *Jaws*, reads the body text and alternate text in each image tag to the visitor. Therefore, keep alternate text short and to the point, and make sure that the text reflects the meaning of the graphic. The alternate text for redundant graphics images, such as bullets, should be one word, such as *bullet*, or left blank. When a text-reader program encounters an *alt* attribute with a null string, the program ignores the image and continues reading the body text displayed in the Web browser window.

The World Wide Web Consortium (W3C) considers the use of *alt* so important that the standards body has made it a required element of a properly formed <img> tag. Therefore, not only is omitting an *alt* attribute in all your <img> tags considered bad coding, but doing so also makes your <img> tag malformed according to the W3C standard.

Sometimes, as you saw in the previous illustration, the placeholder for an image is too small to let you describe the image with an alternate text string (assigned to the *alt* attribute). If you need more room, such as when you want to describe a map, a graph, or other complex image, use the *longdesc* attribute to supplement the *alt* attribute. The value of the *longdesc* attribute points the user to a separate HTML file that contains the full description of the image. Say, for example, that you create a business organizational chart and use the following <img> tag to insert the picture of the chart (in business.gif) onscreen:

```
<img src="business.gif" alt="Business Organizational Chart"
    longdesc="chart.html">
```

The HTML document (chart.html) identified in the *longdesc* attribute contains a detailed plain-text description of all the data in the business.gif image. When visitors to your Web site move over a graphic containing a *longdesc* attribute, the Web browser opens a window containing the information in the HTML document (in this example, chart.html). The chart.html document is a text-only document.

Unfortunately, many Web browsers do not yet support the *longdesc* attribute. As such, providing a separate hypertext link to the file with the text description is a good idea (in addition to adding the *longdesc* attribute to the <img> tag).

Creating a Tool Tip by Inserting a *title* Attribute in an Image Tag

You can use the *title* attribute within an <img> tag to describe (in words) a graphics image to your visitors in the form of a tool tip. The HTML 4.0 specifications state that using the *title* attribute as a tool tip is appropriate.

USE IT   To create the text, insert the *title* attribute within an image tag as follows:

```
<img src="landscape.jpg" width="200" height="80"
    alt="The Kansas Plains" title="Come visit Kansas today">
```

When a visitor moves the mouse pointer over an image for a few seconds, the browser will display the text assigned to the *title* attribute as a tool tip next to the mouse pointer. Figure 6-10 illustrates how Internet Explorer displays the image and title specified in the preceding <img> tag.

Because tool tip text remains onscreen for only a few seconds, make the text short or your visitors will not be able to read the entire title before it disappears. Moreover, some Web browsers do not handle titles with long text strings correctly. Some browsers will not wrap the long text from one line to the next. Other browsers have a maximum length for the tool tip box and truncate the text to fit the width of the box. Unlike the *alt* attribute, the *title* attribute is relatively new and many Web browsers do not yet support it. Fortunately, the *title* attribute works in Internet Explorer version 4 and higher, and it is fully supported in Netscape version 6 and higher.

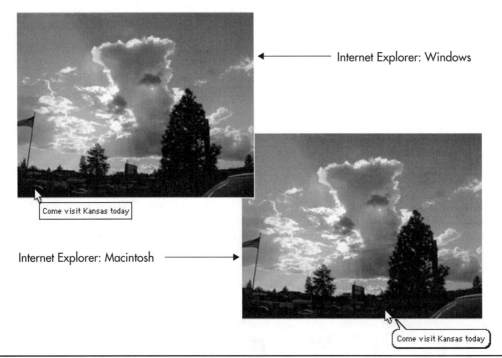

Internet Explorer: Windows

Internet Explorer: Macintosh

Figure 6-10 The title attribute displays the title text in a tool tip format in Windows, and as a balloon on a Macintosh

Do not confuse the *title* attribute with the start and end title tags (<title></title>). The *title* attribute defines text as a tool tip, whereas you insert the start and end title tags in the header section of an HTML document to specify text the browser is to display in the title bar of the browser's application window. For example, Figure 6-11 shows the results of displaying the following HTML with both a <title> tag and an <img> tag with a *title* attribute in a Web browser application window:

```
<html>
<head>
  <title>This is the title of a Web page</title>
</head>
<body>
  <center>
    <img src="landscape.jpg"
         width="200" height="80"
         alt="The Kansas Plains"
         title="Come visit Kansas today">
  </center>
</body>
</html>
```

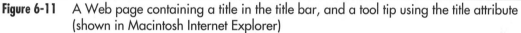

Figure 6-11   A Web page containing a title in the title bar, and a tool tip using the title attribute (shown in Macintosh Internet Explorer)

Compressing Photographs into a JPEG File

The members of the Joint Photographic Experts Group created the JPEG format (pronounced "j-peg") to handle the unique problems associated with displaying images on the Internet. The major problem with sending photographic images across the Internet is the large file size of each picture. Uncompressed graphics files are commonly larger than 1MB. As such, a Web browser connected to the Internet through a 28.8-baud modem would take several minutes to download and display a single picture. As you can see, trying to retrieve Web pages with pictures that have large file sizes could cause a major problem.

The JPEG format solves this problem by significantly reducing the file size of photographic images. It accomplishes file size reduction by selectively removing colors from the image and replacing the missing color information by mixing the remaining colors in a *dither pattern*. A dither pattern uses two or more of the remaining colors within the graphics image, to produce a third color. The dithering process lets the program saving the image save three colors using two pixels instead of three, which reduces the size of the image file. By reducing the number of pixels, files saved using the JPEG format have much smaller file sizes. In fact, JPEG images commonly have file sizes that are 1/100th the size of the original file.

Using color reduction to save a graphics file in the JPEG format is called *lossy compression*, which is compression by loss of information. Remember, when you apply the JPEG compression scheme to a photographic image, the information removed cannot be recovered. Therefore, you should always make a copy of the original image, and save the *copy* to a new filename using the JPEG format. That way you have the original image with all its color information for use later and the compressed file (with a significantly smaller file size) to use on your Web pages.

Because the JPEG format removes pixels from the original image, the compression scheme reduces the picture's visual quality. Designers consider loss of picture quality an inescapable part of life on the Internet and attempt to balance the loss of quality with the speed of the download. The image in Figure 6-12 was saved with a 30-percent compression level (more on compression levels in "Converting Graphics into Web Images with Image-Editing Programs," later in this chapter).

Because the JPEG compression format removes colors from the original image based on a specific set of instructions, you cannot create a JPEG image using a Web-safe palette. In addition, images saved in the JPEG format must use the RGB (red, green, and blue) color space, not grayscale (shades of gray) or CMYK (cyan, magenta, yellow, and black). Finally, the JPEG format gives you the option of saving the image using a progressive or nonprogressive mode. The *progressive mode* loads the file in three passes. This gives the appearance of a blurred image that slowly gets clearer as more information is loaded. The *nonprogressive mode* loads the image in one pass, from top to bottom. The advantage of the progressive mode is not that it loads the final image faster, but that viewers have something to entertain them, rather than seeing the image slowly load from the top to the bottom, as shown in Figure 6-13.

Original image

JPEG image

Figure 6-12   The JPEG format reduces file size and image quality

First pass

Second pass

Final pass

Figure 6-13   The progressive method of loading a JPEG file keeps the viewer entertained as the image loads

USE IT   Before you save photographic images in the JPEG format, here are a few tips for making the file size even smaller:

- **Soft tonal qualities**   JPEG images compress smaller when they contain soft shifts of color. Sharpening an image is counterproductive when the image is compressed using the JPEG format.

- **Additional blurring**   Although blurring is not the best way to handle photographic images, applying a soft blur to background areas before saving the file in the JPEG format creates a smaller file size.

- **Decreased saturation**   Although not always effective, decreasing the saturation, or intensity, of the colors in a photographic image can create smaller file sizes.

- **Reduced image contrast**   Reducing the contrast in an image (similar to blurring) usually creates smaller file sizes.

- **Weighted optimization**   If you own Photoshop 6.0, you can use weighted optimization to control the compression of an image. Weighted optimization lets you use 8-bit alpha channels to set image optimization on a per-pixel basis and smoothly vary compression settings across a graphics image. Weighted optimization lets you generate higher compression in areas of an image like a blue sky, and less compression in areas of the same image that contain details.

When you display photographs on a Web page, you have to strike a balance between the quality of the image and the wait time needed to download large high-resolution pictures. The JPEG format helps you maintain that balance.

Saving Clip Art and Text to a GIF-Formatted File

The GIF (Graphics Interchange Format), as mentioned earlier, is another format you can use to compress graphics files intended for display on the Internet. The GIF format works best on clip art, text, logos, and images that contain many sharp edges and few colors—just the opposite of the types of images for which the JPEG format provides the best compression.

When you save a color graphics image using the GIF format, the conversion process reduces the number of bits allowed to describe the color of each pixel in the file from 24 bits to 8 bits. Consequently, GIF compression reduces the maximum number of colors in a file from 16.7 million to 256. (There are only 256 possible combinations for each of the 8 bits of information available to describe the color of each pixel in a GIF file.) If the original color image contains more than 256 colors, the GIF format retains a representative sample of the major color areas in the original image's color table and uses that sample to create the GIF image. Because photographs typically contain thousands, if not millions, of colors, trying to save photographs in a GIF file will produce unacceptable visual results (see Figure 6-14), as well as creating images with huge file sizes.

The GIF format makes image files smaller both by reducing the number of bits used to describe each color in the file and by compressing the bits that remain using the RLE (Run Length Encoding) technique. RLE is a compression scheme most suitable for compressing large areas of solid color. The GIF format identifies large blocks of solid color and records the location of the areas. When the file is saved, the solid blocks of color are removed from the image and replaced by the coordinates, or location, of the original color. When the Web browser loads the file, it replaces the solid blocks of color using the prerecorded coordinates. Because clip art, logos, and text contain large areas of the same color, the GIF format is ideal for compressing these types of image files.

Images saved in the GIF format use the RGB (red, green, and blue) color space with 256 colors or less, not CMYK (cyan, magenta, yellow, and black). In addition, the GIF format gives you the option of saving the image using an interlaced or noninterlaced mode. The *interlaced mode* loads the file in three separate passes. This gives the appearance of a blurred image that slowly gets clearer as more image information is loaded. The *noninterlaced mode* loads the image in one pass, from the top to bottom. The advantage of the interlaced mode is not that it loads the final image faster, but that the viewers have something to entertain them, rather than seeing the image slowly load from the top to the bottom, as shown in Figure 6-15.

Original image

GIF image

Figure 6-14   The GIF format applied to a photograph creates a block or stepped appearance to the soft area of the image

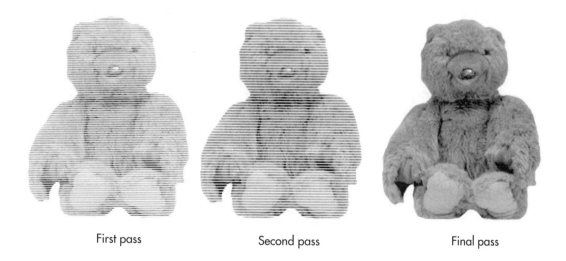

First pass   Second pass   Final pass

Figure 6-15   The interlaced method of loading a GIF file keeps the viewer entertained as the image loads

USE IT   The following are some tricks and considerations that will help you to produce a file with the smallest possible size when saving a graphics in the GIF format:

- **Solid areas of color**   GIF images compress smaller when the image contains large solid areas of color; areas of a GIF image that contain shifting colors will not compress as well.

- **Number of colors**   Using fewer colors produces smaller files. The number of colors in the image determines the size of a GIF image. If a GIF image contains four colors, it compresses significantly smaller than an image containing 20 colors. The less color, the smaller the file size, and the faster the file downloads.

- **Reduced dithering**   Dithering is a process whereby the computer uses two colors to produce a third color. Dithering creates a file with more colors and makes it difficult for the GIF format to compress the image.

Making Images Appear to Load Faster

The reason for using the progressive or interlaced option is not to decrease the amount of time it takes to load a Web image. The primary purpose is to give visitors to your Web site something to look at while they wait for the browser to finish downloading your graphics images.

You use the progressive and interlaced options to instruct the Web browser how to load a graphics file. Absent both options, the Web browser loads the file from the top to bottom. Consequently, visitors to your Web site see the images appear onscreen one scan-line (that is, one horizontal row of pixels) at a time.

When you use the progressive or interlaced options with a JPEG or GIF graphic file, the Web browser loads the image in three passes. (Some programs allow you to choose the number of passes.) In the first pass, the browser loads every third scan line, then the next third, and finally completes the image by loading the final third set of scan lines.

Say, for example, that the large file sizes for the graphics on your Web site are causing the images to load slowly. If you do not save the files using the progressive or interlaced option, the visitor sees a box appear onscreen and the image slowly paints itself into the box from the top to the bottom. Visitors have no idea what the image is until the browser has finished downloading it. As a result, your visitors may get bored and either stop the browser from loading the graphics or worse yet, move to another Web site.

When you use the progressive or interlaced option, the Web browser quickly loads one third of the image. Although the image is blurry, the visitors can get a general idea of the picture's content. Now, if they stop the browser from continuing to download graphics on the Web page, at least they see a blurred representation of the image instead of only half a picture. (Of course, you hope that seeing the complete, albeit blurred, images on the Web page will keep your visitors interested enough to wait for the browser to finish downloading the pictures entirely.)

USE IT   To use the progressive or interlaced option, you must open the graphic file in an image-editing application, and save the file using the Progressive option for files stored in the JPEG format and the Interlaced option for files stored in the GIF format. For example, if you use

Adobe Photoshop, open the image in Photoshop and select File | Save For Web. Then, select progressive (for JPEG-formatted files) or interlaced (for GIF-formatted files), as shown in Figure 6-16.

Remember that when you create a Web page, it is not about buttons and HTML code. Moreover, most visitors to your Web site will never examine your HTML code. The most important consideration during the design phase is figuring out how to keep your visitors entertained and informed. Using the progressive and interlace options helps keeps visitors where you want them.

▶ **NOTE**

When you use an image-editing program to save a picture as a JPEG or a GIF file, you have the option of using the Progressive option for the JPEG format and the Interlaced option for the GIF format. Understand that the Progressive and Interlaced options are not a function of the HTML code. Rather, they are options selected when you save the file.

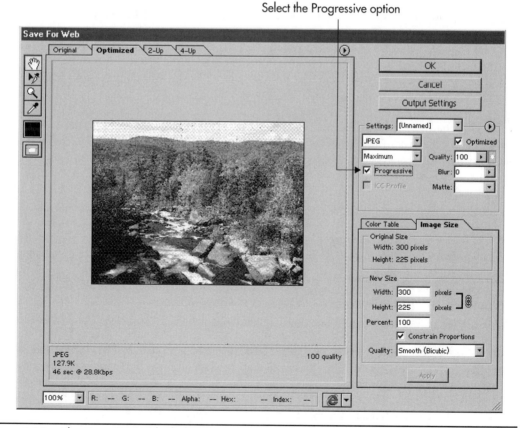

Figure 6-16   The Save For Web dialog box in Photoshop lets you select the Progressive (JPEG) or Interlaced (GIF) option when saving the file

Working with the PNG-8 and PNG-24 File Formats

The PNG (Portable Network Graphic) format is the latest addition to the list of image file formats. The PNG-8 and PNG-24 formats are two of the newest and the most versatile of the formats used to compress graphics files for the Internet. A third PNG format, the PNG-32, gives more control over image color; however, the PNG-8 and PNG-24 are the two most widely used of the PNG formats.

For the Web, PNG really has three main advantages over GIF:

- **Alpha channels**   Variable transparency
- **Gamma correction**   Cross-platform control of image brightness
- **Two-dimensional interlacing**   A method of progressive display

PNG also compresses better than GIF in almost every case, but the difference is generally only around 5 to 25 percent, not a large enough factor to encourage Web designers to switch on that basis alone.

By performing compression similar to the GIF format, the PNG-8 format reduces the colors in the original image to a maximum of 256. In addition, the PNG-8 format uses RLE (Run Length Encoding) compression to reduce the size of the file (as was described in "Saving Clip Art and Text to a GIF-Formatted File" earlier in this chapter). Conversely, the PNG-24 format is capable of saving photographic images in the same way as the JPEG format with one exception: The PNG-24 format does not reduce file size by removing color from the image. It is, therefore, a lossless file compression method.

USE IT   You can use the PNG-8 format to reduce the file size in clip art, logos, and text by compressing large, flat areas of color. Like the GIF format, the PNG format uses lossless compression techniques. (Remember, the JPEG format performs lossy compression by removing some of the original file's color data.) Lossless compression means that the PNG-24 format reduces the picture's file size without losing any of the original color data. In addition, the PNG-8 and PNG-24 formats use RLE compression (like the GIF format) to reduce the size of the file without reducing the quality of the image, as shown in Figure 6-17.

Although PNG is an excellent file format, it does have two major problems. First, because the PNG-24 format does not remove color information from the file, it cannot compress graphics files to as small a size as the JPEG format. (Remember, you are trying to reduce the file size of the image as much as possible, without giving up too much image quality, because Web browsers can download and display smaller files faster than larger files.) Therefore, for the present, the JPEG format is the format to use when saving photographic images for use on a Web page.

The second problem, and perhaps the most important, is that the PNG-8 and PNG-24 formats have only recently received *full* support from the most-used browsers—Netscape Navigator 6 and Internet Explorer 5. Although earlier versions of Explorer and Navigator supported the PNG format, that support was limited to the display of the PNG-formatted graphic. Support for variable transparency and two-dimensional interlacing was sporadic. As of this writing, some polls suggest up to 20 percent of Web visitors do not have the latest versions of Navigator or Explorer, and therefore are incapable of viewing PNG-formatted images. Keep this in mind when using the PNG format.

Original image (233k)

PNG image (166k)

Figure 6-17 The PNG format reduces file size without sacrificing image quality

Converting Graphics into Web Images with Image-Editing Programs

In order to save images for use on the Internet, you must use one of three formats: JPEG, GIF, ir PNG. In truth, Web page image file formats are actually compression schemes, designed to reduce the file size of a graphics image. File size is an important consideration when saving graphics files because the larger the file size, the longer it takes the Web browser to download and display the graphics image, and visitors to your Web site do not want to wait.

Understand that file compression is not a function of HTML code. When you use an <img> tag such as the following to instruct the Web browser to load and display a graphic file, the <img> tag does not determine the compression format of the file:

```
<img src="photo.jpg" width="60" height="150" />
```

In this example, an image-editing program compressed the graphics image using the JPEG format and then saved the compressed picture in the file named photo.jpg. The *src* attribute in the <img> tag (*src="photo.jpg"*) does not make the file a JPEG-compressed image. Instead, the *src* attribute just identifies a graphic file previously saved in the JPEG format.

USE IT To save files in the JPEG, GIF, or PNG format then, you will need an image-editing program. Two of the most popular commercial image-editing programs on the market are Adobe Photoshop and Macromedia Fireworks. In addition to commercially produced programs, many image-editing programs are available on the Internet. On sites such as http://www.shareware.com and http://www.tucows.com you will find a number of downloadable shareware and freeware image-editing applications.

Say, for example, that you have an RGB graphics image and you want to use that image on a Web page, but the file size is too large (over 1MB). If you have Photoshop, you can open the image and select File | Save For Web. Photoshop, in turn, will display the Save For Web dialog box.

All image-editing programs that let you save files in the JPEG format let you control the quality of the image. The quality option is a value from 0 to 100 percent (or 1 to 10). If you select 100 percent, the image-editing program tries to reduce the size of the image file while at the same time removing the minimum possible amount of color information. Incrementally lowering the image quality percentage (down to a value of zero) instructs the image-editing program to remove more and more color to produce a graphics image file that is smaller and smaller. Figure 6-18 shows the difference between JPEG images saved with quality values of 100, 60, and 20 percent.

In short, the lower the quality percentage you select, the smaller the file size and the poorer the visual quality of the image when displayed by a Web browser. What you need to do is strike a balance between quality and file size. On average, the best quality-versus-file-size setting for photographic images is around 30 percent. However, the percentage that works best often depends on the image. Always try to reduce the quality option to its lowest value without sacrificing too much of the quality of the original image.

Creating Web-Friendly Graphics Images on Your Scanner

This chapter discusses creating and working with graphics images and preparing them for display on a Web page. However, in order to prepare and save Web images, they must first be loaded onto your computer. One of the most overlooked areas of Web design is how you go about scanning the images you want to use on your Web pages.

A scanner takes a photograph and divides the image into small pieces called samples. The number of samples (or pixels) per linear inch the scanner saves becomes the resolution of the scanned image. Each one of those pixels represents a piece (that is, a dot) of color in the image. Therefore, if you optically scan an image at a higher resolution, the image contains more pixels and therefore, more information. The problem is that the higher the scan resolution, the larger the file size. A 5 by 5 RGB image scanned at an optical resolution of 72 spi (samples per inch) produces a file with a size of 380KB (the number of pixels in the saved image determines the size of the image file). If you scan the same picture at an optical resolution of 300 spi, you produce an image with more dots (pixels) and a file size of 6.4MB. The problem is that while the picture looks clearer (due to its higher resolution), at 6.4 million bytes, the image file will take too long to download if you insert the picture on a Web page.

The W3C sets the average resolution of a Web graphic to 72 ppi (for 72 pixels per linear inch) to match the number of pixels in a linear inch on an average computer monitor. However, that does not mean that you should scan all images intended for display on a Web page at 72 spi.

Best: 100% compression

Medium: 60% compression

Low: 20% compression

Figure 6-18   The quality value in a JPEG-compressed image controls the visual quality of the image

USE IT   If the image you want to display on a Web page is in perfect condition and is the exact width and height you need, scan the image at a resolution of 72 spi and save the picture to a file using either the JPEG or GIF format. Unfortunately, some pictures you want to use will not be in perfect condition and may not have the exact dimensions you need. When you run into an image that requires restoration or color touchup work or when you need to change the picture's original width and height, scan the image at a higher optical resolution, and before saving the image, reduce the resolution to 72 spi.

When you scan a photograph at a higher resolution, image-editing programs such as Adobe Photoshop have more information (more pixels) available to correct the problems associated with the image (dust and scratches or areas of discoloration). When you increase the dimensions of a scanned image, you force the image-editing program to insert more pixels into the image and to color the new pixels based on an average of the surrounding pixel color values.

Because images scanned at lower resolutions do not have many pixels, the image will blur quickly as you increase the picture's dimensions. Conversely, if you scan the picture at a higher resolution, the file contains more information (pixels). Therefore, the image appears clearer when you increase the dimensions of the image.

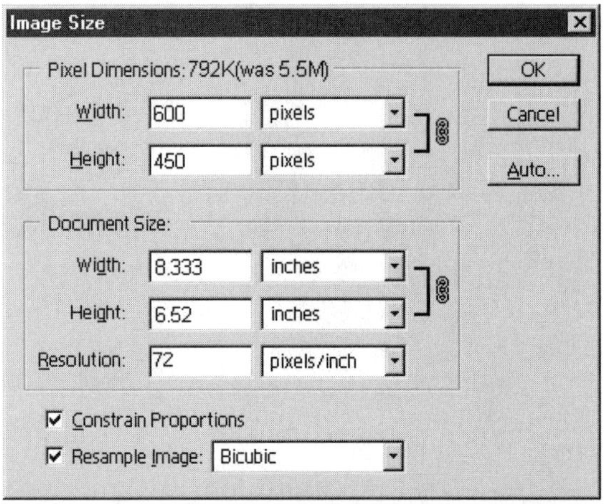

Figure 6-19   The Image Size dialog box in Photoshop lets you modify the resolution of the scanned image

After you finish editing the image, you can reduce the size of the graphics file by saving the file at the W3C standard of 72 ppi. In addition, save the image using either the JPEG or GIF file format to further compress the data and reduce the file size. For example, to change the resolution of a graphic in Photoshop, select Image | Image Size, change the resolution option to 72, and then click OK, as shown in Figure 6-19 (above).

▶ *NOTE*

Use the term spi *when referring to the resolution of the picture as you scan the image. Use the term* ppi *when referring to the resolution of the image after you use an image-editing program to change the picture's resolution, and save the file.*

Creating Colorful Horizontal Rules

Graphics displayed on a Web page serve all types of purposes; they attract attention, create a visual picture for your visitors, and support the written text on the Web page. However, in addition to using images to convey information, you can also use graphics to help organize the content on a Web page.

For example, you can create horizontal rules (that is, draw horizontal lines) to organize text or groups of images on a Web page by inserting horizontal rule tags (<hr>) as shown in the following HTML:

```
<html>
<head>
  <title>Example of Horizontal Lines</title>
</head>
```

```
<body>
  <p>This line of text is separated from the next
    line by a horizontal rule line</p>
  <hr>
  <p>This line of text is separated from the text
    above by a horizontal rule line</p>
</body>
</html>
```

In this example, the <hr> tag creates a visible break between the two lines of text, as shown in Figure 6-20.

However, although you can use them to divide a Web page into sections, horizontal rules lack pizzazz. To add some zing to your Web pages, substitute colorful graphics for the functional (albeit boring), standard horizontal rules.

USE IT   Suppose, for example, that you use an image editing and creation program such as Photoshop to create a 600-pixel-wide by 5-pixel-high graphic of a horizontal line. After saving the graphics image as a small GIF file (line.gif) of only about 645 bytes, you can use the image of the horizontal line in place of the horizontal rules used in the previous code as follows:

```
<html>
<head>
  <title>Example of Horizontal Lines</title>
</head>
<body>
  <p>This line of text is separated from the next
    line by a horizontal rule line</p>
  <p align="center">
    <img src="line.gif" width="800" height="5">
  </p>
  <p>This line of text is separated from the text
    above by a horizontal rule line</p>
</body>
</html>
```

Figure 6-20   The horizontal rule separates and organizes areas of a Web page

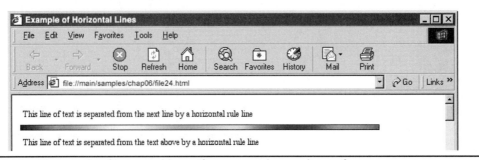

Figure 6-21   The graphic file named line.gif separates the two lines of text

In this example, the start and end paragraph tags ( ) center the graphic file line.gif within the browser application window and place a colorful horizontal line between the two lines of text, as shown in Figure 6-21 (above).

▶ **NOTE**

The appearance of graphics images you can use for horizontal rules is limited only by your imagination. As such, dress up your Web pages by creating and inserting colorful graphics that not only organize the material on the Web page, but also are attractive and eye-catching.

Retrieving a Fast-Loading "Teaser" Image with the *lowsrc* Attribute

The amount of time it takes to load and display an image you insert on a Web page depends on the picture's file size and the speed of the visitor's Internet connection. Images with larger file sizes take longer to load and display than small graphics files. Ideally, you want to use good-looking images that the Web browser can download and display quickly. Unfortunately, some images you want to use are neither small nor fast-loading.

Say, for example, that you want to display a landscape. For visual impact and picture quality, you need to use a large 600-pixel-wide by 300-pixel-tall image. After reading the Tips in this chapter, you decide to save the image to a file using the JPEG format to make the picture's file size as small as possible. However, after you save the image, you see that the picture's file size is still over 200KB. As such, visitors to your Web site that connect to the Internet at a 28.8-baud connection speed will have to wait over 30 seconds for their Web browsers to download and display the landscape.

To give visitors something look at while they are waiting for the browser to display the large image, use an image-editing program to create a low-resolution copy of the original picture. Then, use the *lowsrc* attribute in the <img> tag to tell Web browsers to retrieve and display the faster-loading (smaller file size), low-resolution image before downloading the original image as follows:

```
<img src="land.jpg" lowsrc="landlow.jpg"
     width="600" height="300">
```

The graphics file specified by the *lowsrc* attribute (landlow.jpg) is a low-resolution copy of the original image (land.jpg). When the Web browser encounters the <img> tag in this example, the browser loads the image by the *lowsrc* attribute first and then loads the original image named by the *src* attribute.

Because the *lowsrc* image (landlow.jpg) has a smaller file size than the original image (land.jpg), the browser can quickly download and display landlow.jpg. As such, visitors will be able to view a low-resolution version of the landscape while the browser downloads the original, high-resolution picture. After retrieving the higher resolution image, the browser displays that image over the low-resolution image specified by the *lowsrc* attribute. Therefore, the visitor looking at the low-resolution image will see it apparently go from blurred to crystal clarity—as if by magic.

USE IT As previously stated, the main reason for using the *lowsrc* attribute is to display a low-resolution (faster-loading) image. However, instead of using the *lowsrc* attribute to load and display a low-resolution copy of the same image, why not create a bit of excitement by using a single <img> tag to load two different images (see Figure 6-22)?

In the preceding example, you used an image-editing program to create a low-resolution copy of the original image, that is, of the landscape. However, instead of making a copy of the image, try using a completely different picture. You can set the *lowsrc* attribute to the filename of any image

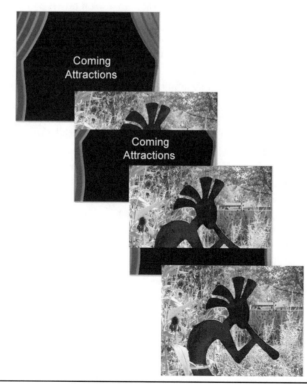

Figure 6-22 The *lowsrc* image of curtains loads first

and not just to a copy of the original. The following example shows how you can use an <img> tag to load an image of curtains with the words "Coming Attractions" between the curtains while waiting for the Web browser to download and displays the picture in photo.jpg:

```
<img src="photo.jpg" lowsrc="curtains.jpg" width="600" height="300">
```

Thus, when the visitor retrieves the Web page, the visitor sees a set of curtains (in the file curtains.jpg), which is later replaced by the image specified by the *src* attribute (photo.jpg), as shown in Figure 6-22.

The trick in selecting a "good" low-resolution (quick-loading) image is to pick a picture that attracts the attention of your Web site's visitors. That way, the visitors will stay until the browser downloads the larger (slow-loading) image(s), rather than becoming impatient and moving on to another Web site.

Ensuring Accurate Color Presentation with the Web-Safe Color Palette

One of the greatest challenges you will face when creating artwork for a Web page is to use Web-safe colors. The *Web-safe color pallette* consists of 216 colors that Web browsers can reproduce accurately, both in a Windows and a Macintosh environment.

Most visitors to your Web site are not Web designers, and many of them have older systems with video cards that support a maximum of 256 colors. In contrast, you may create Web pages on a computer with a video card capable of displaying millions, if not billions of colors. Therefore, it is easy for you to create artwork that looks great on your system but looks grainy and washed out on a system with less color capability.

Say, for example, that you create an image containing thousands or even millions of colors. Because your monitor and video card are capable of displaying that many colors, the image looks great. However, when a visitor using a system that supports only 256 (or thousands) of colors accesses your Web site, the Web browser must map the colors in your image to a smaller number of colors in the color palette on the visitor's system. Consequently, the browser will shift the colors in your image to the closet matching available color on the visitor's system.

When you design graphics for the Internet, two things may happen if you use colors outside the Web-safe color palette. First, older monitors and video cards able to display only 256 colors will shift the colors in your image, making the artwork appear washed out. Second, some systems will "dither" the image colors. Dithering is a process by which an older system begins to mix existing colors in an effort to reproduce colors outside the hardware's displayable range of colors. Dithering makes solid color areas appear with a pattern, as shown in Figure 6-23.

USE IT To ensure that artwork has only Web-safe colors, open the image in an image-editing program and index the colors in the image. When you *index* an illustration, you instruct the image-editing program to shift the colors into those colors available in the Web-safe palette. For

Web-safe color palette   Non–Web-safe color palette

Figure 6-23 Designing images using colors outside the Web-safe color palette causes unwanted dithering

example, to convert the colors of an image into the Web-safe color palette using Adobe Photoshop, perform these steps:

1. Open the image.
2. Select Image | Mode | Indexed Color.
3. After Photoshop displays the Indexed Color dialog box, choose Web from the Palette drop-down menu and click OK, as shown in Figure 6-24.

A better way to save a GIF image is with Photoshop 5.5 and higher, using the Save For Web option. To save a graphics image using Save For Web, open the image in Photoshop and select File | Save For Web. Photoshop opens the Save For Web dialog box and lets you choose how you want to save the file. Not only does the Save For Web feature let you save a GIF image in the Web-safe color palette, it also lets you lock certain colors and remove others from the image's color palette.

Although computers shipped for the last several years have had the ability to display more than 256 colors, avoid creating Web page artwork in the GIF format with colors outside the Web-safe color palette, if possible. By doing so, you reduce the chances that some of your visitors will see a poor-quality image. As with all Web design work, the use of the Web-safe color palette is dependent

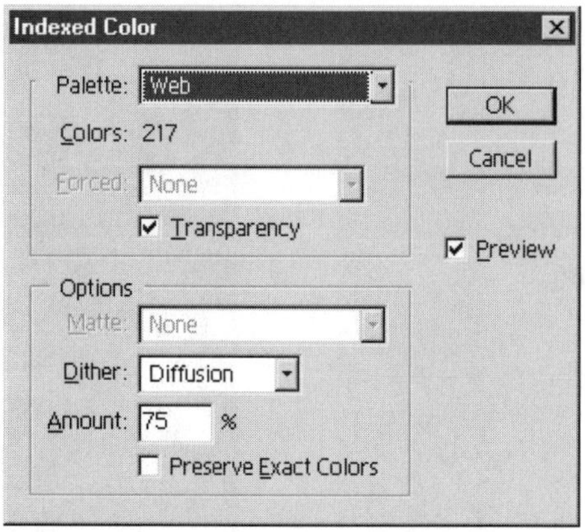

Figure 6-24   The Indexed Color dialog box controls the color space of the active Photoshop document

upon your target audience. If, through research, you discover that your target audience uses older computer hardware, use the Web-safe color palette.

Creating Graphical Hyperlink Anchors

One of the easiest ways to let visitors move from page to page on your Web site is to provide hypertext links to other pages on each of your site's Web pages. As described in Chapter 1, you create a hypertext link by inserting the "link text" (that is, the text on which the visitor clicks to follow the hyperlink to another page) between start and end anchor tags (<a></a>) in the Web page HTML.

Graphics links serve a variety of purposes. Visitors use links to move from page to page and Web site to Web site with the click of a button. You can also use graphic links to let visitors download graphics images and other files, or you can use them to start an e-mail program so the visitor can send an e-mail message. Clickable graphics (that is, text defined as a link) is a common feature on most Web pages. In fact, most visitors to your Web site know exactly what happens when they click on a graphic link. They may not know how to write the HTML code that creates the link; however, they have an idea of what will happen when they click the link's image. Creating graphics links is the easiest and most common way to make your Web pages interactive.

USE IT   In addition to using text as a hypertext link, you can use graphics images. Say, for example, that you want to give visitors a way to send you an e-mail message. You could create a hypertext link. However, instead of using text between the hyperlink's start and end anchor tags (<a></a>), you can insert a graphics image, such as a picture of a mailbox, as follows:

```
<a href="mailto:andy@andy.com"><img src="mailbox.gif"
       border="0"
       width="15" height="20"></a>
```

Figure 6-25   The mailbox icon is a clickable link

In this example, the <img> tag replaces the text used to anchor the hyperlink in the preceding example. Because the start and end anchor tags (<a></a>) enclose the <img> tag, the image inserted by the <img> tag (the picture of a mailbox in the file mailbox.gif, in this example) becomes the clickable link, as shown in Figure 6-25 (above).

Notice the addition of the *border* attribute to the <img> tag. When you use a graphics image as a hypertext link, the Web browser will draw a border around the image—just as the browser draws a line under hyperlink text. To instruct the Web browser not to draw a border around the image, set the *border* attribute to zero within the <img> tag.

When you use a graphics image as a clickable link, make sure the picture illustrates what happens when visitors click the image. For example, you might use a mailbox for a link that sends e-mail, an illustration of a home for a link that returns to the site's home page, or a question mark for a link that displays a Web page with on-line help. In addition, providing descriptive text as a part of the icon is always a good idea. That way, a visitor to your Web site has a combination of text and graphics to identify the purpose of the icon.

Creating Tiled Backgrounds from Graphics Images

The background on a Web page is often a repeating pattern based on the image from a single graphics file. Typically, you use a small, square image that the browser then repeats by putting the square (or tile) next to itself over and over again to fill the background of the Web page. Thus, graphics files used in Web page backgrounds create a repeating pattern similar to the ceramic tiles on a floor, with each tile sitting next to another tile. On an HTML page, the width and height of the graphic file represents the size of a tile. The *background* attribute in the start <body> tag instructs the Web browser to fill the browser's application window with the tiles.

USE IT   To create a Web page background, select the appropriate image file and assign the file's name to the *background* attribute within the start <body> tag as shown in the fifth line in the following code:

```
<html>
<head>
  <title>Example of a background</title>
</head>
<body background="fleur.gif">
  <center>This is an example of a tiled background</center>
</body>
</html>
```

In this example, the Web browser will use the image in fleur.gif as the pattern (or tile) to repeat in the background of the Web page.

When filling the background with a graphics image, the Web browser begins by placing a copy of the image in the upper left-hand corner of the application window. Then, the browser makes copies of the image and places each copy to the right of the previous one. When the Web browser encounters the right-hand border of the Web page, the browser moves down to the next line and creates another series of images. The browser repeats this process until it has filled the entire background with the pattern. Because the browser loads the graphics file with the image only once, the background fills quickly.

Using background images is an excellent way to spice up an otherwise mundane Web page. Unfortunately, the Web page background can become a distraction if used incorrectly. For example, many Web sites use a company logo as the background image. However, if the background contains bright, solid colors, the visitor will have a difficult time reading the text and viewing the other content on the Web page. Therefore, if you want to use a logo as a Web page background, use an image-editing program to soften the logo's colors first. Figure 6-26 shows both the wrong way and the correct way to use a logo as a background image.

Web page backgrounds are often rather plain. However, you can use simple graphics images to generate some interesting and eye-catching backgrounds. For example, you can create a small background graphic that visually separates the areas with different types of content on a Web page. Figure 6-27 shows two Web pages that have unique background images.

The graphics shown as backgrounds in Figure 6-27 were created with an image-editing program. Each background tile used in the image on the left is a 50-pixel-tall by 800-pixel-wide graphics image. Web designers call these types of images *spaghetti graphics*, because they are long and thin. In this example, the first 200 pixels of the image are gray and the remaining 600 pixels are white. When the browser uses the image in the Web page background, the Web browser lays the tiles (that is, the copies of the graphics image) one below the other, creating a seamless background that divides the Web page into two areas.

▶ *NOTE*

Because the background graphic is 800 pixels wide, visitors viewing the Web page with a browser set to a width greater than 800 pixels will see a second gray bar on the right side of the browser window.

Figure 6-26   The background logo on the left is too strong, making it hard to read the information on the Web page

Similarly, the image used to create the background for the other Web page in Figure 6-27 is 50 pixels tall by 800 pixels wide. The left 200 pixels of the image are light gray and have a "drop shadow" effect. The remaining 600 pixels are lighter gray. As a result, the background has a three-dimensional appearance. In this example, both graphics files create two visible sections on the Web page. You could use the left side of the Web page to hold hypertext links to other pages in your site while using the right side of the page to display the content you want the visitor to read.

Graphics images used as backgrounds can draw attention and add life to an otherwise drab page. Remember, however, that the background is just that, a background. Visitors to your Web site want information, and strong-colored backgrounds can easily become a distraction. Make sure the graphics you use for your backgrounds are eye-catching but not distracting.

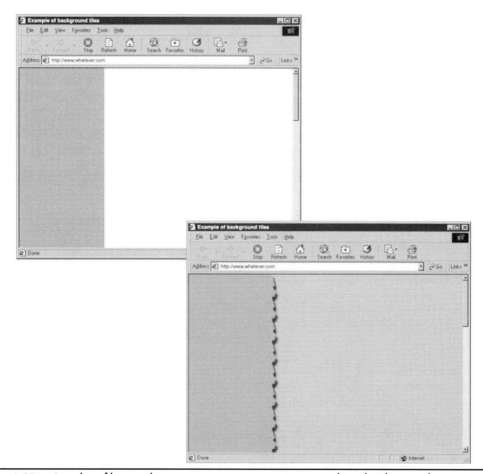

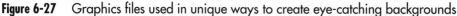

Figure 6-27   Graphics files used in unique ways to create eye-catching backgrounds

Creating Transparency in a GIF Image

When you create and save artwork, the image appears within a square or rectangular container (called a *bounding box*). Unfortunately, you may sometimes want the image to appear in something other than a bounding box.

The GIF file format supports transparency (or masking) in selected portions of a graphics image. In effect, transparency lets what is "behind" the image (usually the Web page background) show through the GIF itself. You can use the transparency effect to remove the "big ugly white box" that otherwise surrounds a piece of artwork, as shown in Figure 6-28.

A GIF image can have a maximum of 256 different colors. However, one of the frustrating things about generating transparency in a GIF image is that the GIF format only supports single color transparency. That is, you can select only one of the eight bits used to describe the color of each pixel

Figure 6-28   Transparency lets the background on a Web page show through the GIF image

in a GIF file as being transparent. In contrast, image-editing programs such as Photoshop and newer Web file formats such as PNG support 8-bit transparency, that is, the ability to make one or all of the colors in the file transparent.

You use an image-editing program to create the transparency in a GIF image. Say, for example, that you have a graphics image and you want to make the background of the image transparent (such as the white background surrounding a graphics image as in Figure 6-28). You can open the graphic in an image-editing program and make the artwork's background (that is, the part you want to make transparent) a single color that is not used elsewhere in the graphic. Then, when you save the GIF image, you would instruct the image-editing program to set the transparency bit for the color you selected. As a result, the portion(s) of the image with the color you selected as transparent will "disappear" from view when a Web browser displays the graphic on a Web page.

An easier way to create transparency is to use Photoshop 5.5 or higher, performing the following steps:

1. Open the image.

2. Make sure that you can see the tablecloth pattern (indicating transparency) in the areas you want to make transparent, and select File | Save For Web.

3. Select the GIF format and check the Transparency option, as shown in Figure 6-29.

Select the
Transparency
option

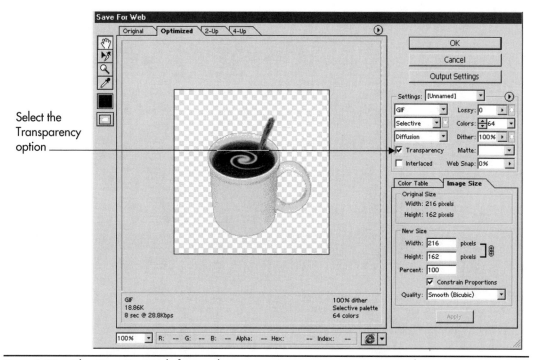

Figure 6-29   The Save For Web feature lets you create transparent areas within a GIF image

You need to remember that when you define a color as transparent, all areas of the image that contain that color become transparent as well. Therefore, the color you choose for the background (the transparent color) should be unique to the background on the image. In addition, because the GIF format lets you choose only one color for transparency, the edges of an image tend to have a sharp, rather than soft appearance. Therefore, graphics images containing soft edges (like the soft edges of an image containing a drop shadow) do not work well when saved in the GIF format.

USE IT   When you create a transparent GIF, you need to understand that transparency is not a function of HTML. You use an image-editing program to select the transparent color and save the transparency effect within the image file. For example, to create a transparent GIF file in Adobe ImageReady, open the image, and then select and erase the areas of the image you want to be transparent when a Web browser displays the image. Although a transparent pixel does not (technically) have a color when displayed onscreen, making one of the colors transparent in a GIF file limits the total number of visible colors in your artwork to 255 (instead of 256). In Photoshop, after you erase all the areas of the image you want to make transparent, select File | Save For Web to save the edit image to a file. When a Web browser displays the image, the erased areas of the image become transparent.

Image-editing and Web-page-creation programs (such as FrontPage) provide different methods for creating a transparency in a GIF. For example, FrontPage lets you select the transparent color by clicking the color in the image with an eyedropper tool. Photoshop, on the other hand, lets you create a transparent GIF using a channel mask. The important thing to understand is that you create the transparency in a GIF by selecting a single color in an image-editing program, and the Web browser will treat every pixel of that color as transparent when the browser displays the image on the Web page.

Retrieving Full-Size Images after Clicking on Thumbnails

The Tips in this chapter have centered on inserting graphics images on a Web page. Moreover, you learned that images you place on a Web page should have small file sizes, so that the Web browser can download and display the images quickly. To get the small image file size you need, you normally save the image using a compression scheme such as the GIF, JPEG, or PNG file format. Although these formats reduce the file size of graphics images, they do so by sacrificing some image quality.

For example, the JPEG format can compress a graphic file to 1/100th of the file's original size. Although the JPEG compressed image may look good in the browser's application window, the picture will often appear grainy when printed. Because the JPEG format reduces file size by removing color from the original image, the JPEG-formatted image may not contain enough color information to print correctly. Moreover, you often save Web graphics at resolution of 72 ppi to match the resolution of a typical computer monitor. However, printers require higher resolutions (typically 300 dpi [dots per inch] or higher). For these two reasons, concentrate on making images on a Web page look as good as possible when displayed on the visitor's screen, and provide visitors with a second image (at a higher resolution) that they can print on paper.

Say, for example, that you want to provide visitors to your Web site the ability to download and print a graphics image. You could insert the full-size image on the Web page, and instruct the visitors to right-click the graphic and select Copy Image from the pop-up menu. However, inserting the full-size, high-resolution image on a Web page means that the Web browser will have to download a picture with a huge file size, which will take a long time—especially for those visitors that just want to view the page without downloading and printing the picture.

A more practical method would be to create thumbnails (that is, small, low-resolution images), and convert the images into links, an example of which is shown in Figure 6-30. After a visitor clicks a thumbnail, the hyperlink's *href* attribute tells the Web browser to download the graphics image file to the visitor's computer.

USE IT To create a thumbnail of a full-size image, open the image in an image-editing program and create a low-resolution copy of the original image. Say, for example, that you have a series of full-size pictures of landscapes, and you want to let visitors download and print these images. One at a time, open the image files (named land1.tif and land2.tif, in this example) in an image-editing program. Create and save a low-resolution copy of the image to another file (landlw1.jpg and landlw2.jpg, in this example). Then, place the low-resolution images (that is, the thumbnails) on the Web page as shown by the <img> tags in the following HTML:

```
<html>
<head>
  <title>Example of downloadable image</title>
</head>
<body>
```

```
<center>
  <font size="5">Click on a graphic image to
                download a full-size version
  </font><br>
  <a href="file:http://www.andy.com/images/land1.tif">
  <img src="landlw1.jpg"
      border="0"
      width="50" height="25"></a>
  <br>
  <a href="file:http://www.andy.com/images/land2.tif">
  <img src="landlw2.jpg"
      border="0"
      width="50" height="25"></a>
</center>
</body>
</html>
```

In this example, the two *href* attributes point to full-size images (land1.tif and land2.tif) located in a folder named Images at the Web site http://www.andy.com. The *src* attributes in the image tags instruct

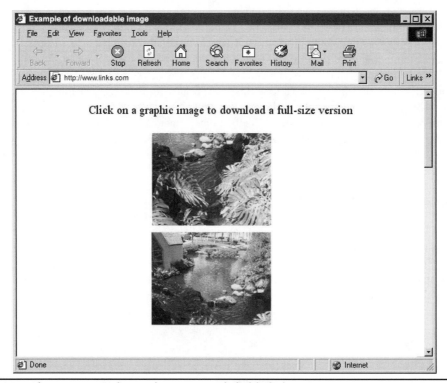

Figure 6-30   The images on this Web page are clickable links

the Web browser to download and display the thumbnails of the larger, high-resolution images, as shown in Figure 6-30.

By placing each thumbnail's <img> tag between a set of start and end anchor tags (<a></a>), you turn the thumbnails (landlw1.jpg and landlw2.jpg, in this example) into hyperlinks. When the visitor clicks a thumbnail, the *file:* that precedes the URL in the *href* attribute in the hyperlink's <a> tag instructs the Web browser to download the picture rather than display the image onscreen.

Preloading and Caching Images Behind the Scenes

Although the W3C works hard to standardize the way you create a Web site, Web designers have little tricks they use when creating Web pages. Specifically, designers spend a lot of time and effort trying to make Web pages containing many graphics load quickly.

When a Web browser downloads the images on a Web page, the browser places a copy of the image into an image cache on the visitor's hard drive. When a Web browser needs to display an image, the browser first checks for the image in the visitor's image cache folder. If the image is not in the cache folder, the Web browser attempts to download the image from the Web site (and stores a copy of the image in the image cache). You want the browser to use an image from the image cache because the browser can retrieve and display an image much faster from the local hard drive than from the Web server. The question is how to get the image file into the cache folder before the browser loads the Web page that calls for the image.

USE IT   One way to reduce image download times is to preload images that appear on other Web pages. Say, for example, that you have a multipage Web site on which visitors start at the index, or home page, and you want the graphics on the site's other pages to load quickly when the visitor moves on to those pages. To accomplish this, insert <img> tags for the graphics on the other pages at the bottom of the home page HTML, as follows:

```
<html>
<head>
  <title>Example of preloading images</title>
</head>
<body>

    Insert the Web document here. . .

  <img src="image1.jpg" width="1" height="1">
  <img src="image2.jpg" width="1" height="1">
</body>
</html>
```

In this example, the <img> tags instruct the Web browser to load the two images at the bottom of the Web page. However, the *width* and *height* attributes set to a value of "1" prevent the visitor from actually seeing the images onscreen. Although not visible onscreen, the Web browser still downloads the images from the Web server and stores a copy of the pictures in the image cache folder on the visitor's hard drive when the visitor retrieves the site's home page.

When the visitor leaves the home page for another page on the Web site, the browser will be able to retrieve the image(s) on that page from the image cache on the hard drive. As a result, the page will load quickly because the browser does not have to download image files from the Web server. When you create the <img> tags for the page on which you want the pictures displayed, use the image's actual height and width for the values of the *height* and *width* attributes in each of the image tags, as shown by the <img> tags in the following HTML:

```
<html>
<head>
  <title>Example of a normal Web document</title>
</head>
<body>

    Insert the Web document here. . .

  <img src="image1.jpg" width="200" height="75">
  <img src="image2.jpg" width="150" height="80">
</body>
</html>
```

Note that the <img> tags used to insert the pictures on the Web page on which the images are actually visible in this example are standard HTML <img> tags. The reason the Web page can load the images quicker is that the browser loads the images from the cache folder and does not have to download the pictures from the Web server. As such, the browser has almost instantaneous access to the images displayed on the page.

Bear in mind that even though the visitor cannot see the images you hide on a Web page (by setting the *width* and *height* attributes to one pixel each) the browser must still download the images along with the page. Therefore, a Web page that preloads (hidden) images takes longer to download than it takes to retrieve and display the visible content alone.

Using hidden images to preload graphics in the local cache works best on Web sites with a linear arrangement of content (that is, on sites where visitors normally visit pages in sequence). Say, for example, that the first page does not have any graphics and the next page in the series has four pictures. You could halve the time it takes to display the second page with the graphics by preloading two of the images and inserting <img> tags that display the images as 1-pixel dots on the first page without graphics.

Another way to reduce download times is to use the same graphics images on more than one Web page. Say, for example, that you create a graphics navigation bar, as shown here:

Instead of creating a different navigation bar for each page, use the same graphics image on all the pages. That way, the Web browser has to download the graphics navigation bar only one time, because the next time the browser needs to display the same graphics image (that is, the navigation bar), the browser can load the image from the image cache on the local hard drive. The same holds true for background graphics and all other images used on your Web site. When you plan a complex Web site, organize the site's pages so that you can use the same graphics images more than once. Moreover, when possible, preload images by hiding them as 1-pixel graphics at the bottom of pages with text only. Careful planning, and a little trickery, can turn an average Web site into an often-visited site with well-organized content and fast-loading Web pages.

Expanding the Web-Safe Color Palette with Dithering Techniques

When you create artwork for display on a Web page, color fidelity is a major concern. Ideally, you want the colors your visitors see in the image to be the same colors you used when you created the artwork. Unfortunately, with hundreds of different computer monitors and video cards on the market, it is doubtful that the colors you see on your monitor are exactly the same colors your visitors will see.

The Web-safe color palette reduces the amount of shifting that occurs when Web browsers display the same image on different monitors and video cards. Understand, however, that an *accurate* reproduction is often not an *exact* reproduction. Monitors and video cards not only display a multitude of colors, but they also let the user control how the colors look. Most monitors have brightness and contrast controls and many have options users can use to control the hue and saturation of those colors. As a result, a Web-safe shade of red will most likely be a slightly different shade of red on one monitor versus another.

Therefore, using Web-safe colors does not guarantee that the colors you use in your artwork will appear the same on all monitors; it just minimizes the chance that the colors you use will dither. Dithering is a process of mixing colors. When you use a color outside the displayable range of the visitor's video card, the video card attempts to approximate the color by mixing colors the video card can display.

USE IT   Although color mixing is used to create colors outside the displayable range of the monitor's video card, it can give a muddy look. If the GIF image contains words, reading the color-dithered text can be especially hard.

As long as text is not involved, you can use dithering to your advantage by creating colors outside the range of the browser-safe palette of 216 colors. Say, for example, that you want to create a Web page background in a color that lies outside the range of the 216-color browser-safe color palette. To create your custom background color, use an image-editing program such as Photoshop and create a 50-pixel-wide, by 50-pixel-tall RGB image.

For example, to create a background with a slightly lighter shade of blue than is available in the Web-safe color palette, paint alternating pixels in the 50 by 50 pixel matrix of the background image a darker shade of blue. Then, paint the remaining pixels a Web-safe, lighter shade of blue, as shown in Figure 6-31.

Finally, save the image as a GIF-formatted file with a meaningful name (such as blue.gif for this example).

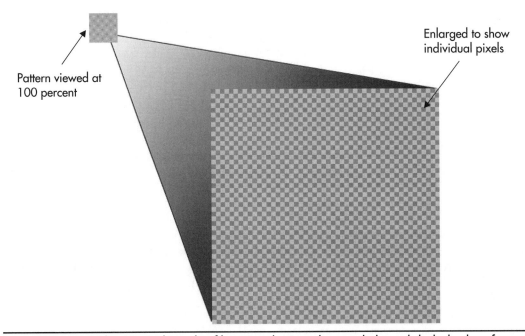

Pattern viewed at
100 percent

Enlarged to show
individual pixels

Figure 6-31   A 50 by 50 pixel graphic file painted using alternate light and dark shades of Web-safe blue

When you use the GIF in the Web page background (as shown by the <body> tag in the following HTML), the Web browser "paints" the background the light blue you want—between the lighter and darker shades of Web-safe blue:

```
<html>
<head>
  <title>Example of a Web page using a dithered color</title>
</head>
<body background="blue.gif">

   Web page body tags inserted here . . .

</body>
<html>
```

The trick to creating unique colors in a GIF image is to choose similar Web-safe colors. For example, select slightly different shades of the same color. Selecting colors that represent a harsh contrast (such as black and white) creates a visibly rough pattern within the image.

Using a controlled dither pattern to generate new colors, such as the light blue in this example, creates an image file with an extremely small file size, which guarantees that browsers can download the image quickly. Thus, you can use new colors created with small image files to make your Web site unique without making the page take longer to load.

Smoothing the Edges of Text Converted into a Graphic Through Anti-Aliasing

Web pages are a combination of many elements. Most likely, your pages will have text for visitors to read and graphics that, hopefully, enhance and support the text. Although using Web page graphics raises certain design issues (using only browser-safe colors, balancing image quality against file size, and so on), generally speaking, Web browsers can display the images you insert on the Web page.

Unfortunately, displaying text presents its own set of challenges—namely, displaying the text in the Web browser window using the typeface you want. For example, if you create text using the Arial typeface and Arial is not available on the visitor's computer, the browser will substitute the browser's default typeface for Arial—possibly Courier or Helvetica. (Visitors can use the browser's preference settings to select the default typeface to use when the Web page text calls for an unavailable typeface.) Moreover, site visitors can select the default color and size of the text. One way to solve the text appearance problem is to convert the text into a graphics image and then use an <img> tag to display the picture of the text onscreen.

Although converting an entire Web document into a graphics image would be impractical, sometimes using pictures of text makes sense. Suppose, for example, that you want to use your company logo on your Web page, and the logo is a combination of text and graphics. In addition, to further complicate matters, the text curves around the logo. Typeface issues aside, displaying standard Web page text along a curve (versus a square border) around an image is not possible.

USE IT   To solve the problem, edit the logo in an image-editing program such as Photoshop and make the text a part of the image. When you convert text to a "picture" of the text, you must decide whether to use the anti-aliased option.

Most graphic artists automatically specify anti-aliasing because using the option helps to make text you place in the image look smooth. The anti-aliased option tries to hide the fact that computer monitors display images using pixels, which have shapes like bricks in a wall. When you convert a vector image (text) into a graphics image, the image-editing program converts the mathematical form of the text (that is, the vector) into the raster form (that is, into pixels) in a graphics image.

If you turn on the anti-aliased option when converting text to an image, the image-editing program coats the edges of the text with colors. The added colors smooth the jagged appearance caused by the pointed edges of the pixels along the sides of the letter, as shown in Figure 6-32.

Although smoothing jagged edges may seem like a good thing to do all the time, anti-aliasing does not always work well on small text (under 14 points). By blurring the edges of each character in the text, anti-aliasing can make small letters too blurry to read. If you turn off anti-aliasing, the text appears in stark contrast to the background and may therefore appear slightly jagged to the viewer's eyes. However, the text will be easier to read, because the text is not blurry.

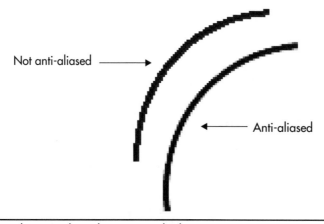

Not anti-aliased

Anti-aliased

Figure 6-32   The anti-aliased option applied to a vector image creates a visually smoother look to the edges

The following HTML code creates a Web page with two GIF images. The first image uses anti-aliasing when converting text into the GIF format, and the second image has anti-aliasing turned off, as shown in Figure 6-33:

```
<html>
<head>
  <title>Example of anti-aliasing applied to text</title>
</head>
<body>
  <center>
    <img src="antion.gif" width="500" height=200">
    <br>
    <img src="antioff.gif" width="500" height=200">
  </center>
</body>
<html>
```

As you can see in Figure 6-33, large text benefits from the anti-aliased option. Unfortunately, as the text becomes smaller, it becomes harder to read. Typically, text falling below 14 points is easier to read when converted to an image without the use of anti-aliasing. Using the anti-aliasing option creates one side effect that you should note: Because anti-aliasing coats the edges of the text with additional colors, the added colors will increase the final size of the saved file.

As with anything else on the Internet, always combine following the rules with visual confirmation. When converting text into a graphics image (that is, into a "picture" of the text), experiment and then choose the image that is the easiest to read.

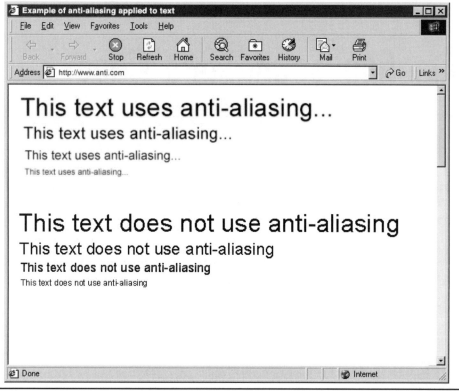

Figure 6-33   Large text appears readable using anti-aliasing; however, smaller text becomes harder to read

CHAPTER 7

Animation, Sound, and Video

TIPS IN THIS CHAPTER

▶ Creating a GIF Animation from Scratch   334

▶ Controlling GIF Animation Through Internal Settings   336

▶ Creating a Banner Ad Using GIF Animation   338

▶ Creating Smooth Transitions Between GIF Animation Frames Using Tweening   341

▶ Incorporating a Completed Flash Splash Screen into a Web Site   342

▶ Creating a Flash Movie from Scratch   345

▶ Building Text-Based Animations Using FlaX   348

▶ Broadcasting Streaming Audio and Video   348

▶ Creating Your Own Streaming Media   351

▶ Creating a Page that Features a Web Cam   352

▶ Integrating Video and Audio into a Web Site Using SMIL (Smile)   354

Browsing the Internet today without encountering Web pages that contain some form of animation, sound, video, or a combination of all three is almost impossible. From simple animated GIFs, to Flash movies, and even full-screen interactive images with sound and motion, adding animations to Web pages has the potential to enliven your designs. Unfortunately, the overuse of animation and sound can be annoying and a distraction to your visitors. Two opposing goals drive advances on the Internet:

- Web authors trying to please visitors want to transmit increasingly elaborate types of content (sound, animation, and video) over the Web.

- To reach Web site visitors, the file size for content must be small enough to load quickly, or the visitors grow impatient and move on to other sites.

Visitors demand more information. However, although they say, "Entertain and inform us," they are often unwilling to wait one moment longer for the additional content. Fortunately, the two opposing goals (design versus expectation) drive the development of new technologies that let you give visitors more information faster than ever before.

When you work with animation on the Web, you incorporate one or more technologies (Flash, Shockwave, GIF animation, or video and sound applications) with the ultimate goal of creating an eye-catching Web page. Creating animation on a Web page relies on the human eye's ability to retain an image (called *persistence of vision*). Persistence of vision refers to the fact that the shape of an image lingers on the eye after the image is removed from view or you look away. For example, go into a room, turn out the lights, and then flick the lights quickly on and off. Each time you switch the lights off, your eye retains a ghostly image of what you saw while the light was on. Persistence of vision causes you to see the ghostly images.

An animation is actually a series of still images displayed quickly one after another. The illusion of motion is created as your eye retains one image (persistence of vision) as the program "playing" the animation displays the next image onscreen. To create a smooth motion effect, the program must display each new image (or frame) within a fraction of a second of removing the last, so that the eye sees the new image just as the previous image fades.

The same thing happens in a movie theater. As you watch the movie, the projector displays a series of still images (typically 30 images [or frames] per second). Due to persistence of vision, your mind stitches the images together to create the illusion of motion. Of course, in both the movies and on a Web page, you are not limited to silent objects moving across the screen. Animation can also include speech and music.

For example, a lightning strike displayed onscreen has a far greater impact when accompanied by a clap of thunder. In addition, sound, in the form of a narration, background music, or special effects like the "clicking" of an interactive button, helps to set the mood of the page and keep your visitors entertained and focused.

Although adding animation and sound can bring life to what might otherwise be a dull or boring Web page, whether that life is necessary to the Web site you are designing is a question you must ask yourself before venturing into the world of animation.

Understanding Animation's Role in Web Design

The primary role of Web animation is to draw the attention of visitors to your Web site. However, Web animation can also entertain and inform. Young children (especially those that are just beginning to read) love movement and tend to focus on it. Therefore, you can use animation to grab and focus a young child's attention for an extended period on a concept you are trying to convey.

In addition, a Web page can use animation and sound to explain the steps in a complicated procedure or process. For example, an animated sequence (or perhaps a video) displaying the steps necessary to program a VCR to record a movie, accompanied by a narrator explaining the steps, is far more effective than a plain text document explaining the same procedure. The specific intent of the Web page you design will influence the type of animation and software required to create it. Animation is important to the design of a Web site, and as a Web designer, you can choose from several methods to achieve your specific goals.

Understanding Plug-In Software

Throughout this chapter, you will examine different types of multimedia content, such as Flash animations, streaming audio and video, QuickTime VR (virtual reality) tours, and more. Depending on an animation's file format, your Web browser may not provide built-in support you can use to display the animation. Instead, before you can view the animation, you must install special software (called a *plug-in*) that you normally download from the Web and install into your browser—sometimes as you are viewing the page that contains the object. For example, before you can display your first Flash animation, your browser must have a Flash plug-in. Years ago, users had to download the plug-in from the Macromedia Web site. Today, most newer browsers ship with the Flash plug-in already installed.

Normally, the HTML statements that place the animated object within a page will also include instructions the browser can use to locate and download the corresponding plug-in. Before it downloads and installs the plug-in, however, your browser displays a dialog box informing you that the page requires software not yet installed on your machine, and the location on the Web from which the browser will download the needed plug-in. If you agree to download the plug-in, your browser will retrieve the program and install it. If you do not let your browser perform the download, you will view the Web page contents minus the animated object. In the Windows environment, most plug-ins are ActiveX controls. Chapter 9 examines ActiveX objects in detail.

Understanding Dynamic HTML (DHTML)

In the beginning, Web content was static. After the browser finished loading a graphics image, the picture stayed in the same place within the browser window. Web designers found this too limiting on the creative process, and they looked for a way to add content that would change even after the visitor downloads a page.

In a simplistic way, Dynamic HTML (DHTML) makes this possible. Within a Web page, designers often produce DHTML content by using a scripting language, such as JavaScript, to access something called the *document object model* (DOM, an underlying software object) within the Internet browser. Basically, the DOM lets a script control the appearance of all the elements (that is, all objects) the browser displays on a Web page. What you must remember with respect to DHTML is that all processing occurs within the browser. DHTML uses client-side processing as opposed to a server-side operation.

Today, almost all visitors use Web browsers that let client-side scripts take control of the DOM. As such, designers can use scripts to alter and/or move the elements within a Web page. For example, you can use DHTML to change the text color as the visitor moves the mouse pointer over a word within a hypertext link. Although changing the color of text is not strictly animation, it does create a change onscreen that helps focus the visitor's attention. The following HTML file, DynamicDemo.html, uses JavaScript to change the color of text in a hyperlink (to a site that examines DHTML) as the user moves his or her mouse pointer onto or off of the link:

```
<!DOCTYPE html PUBLIC "-//W3C//DTD XHTML 1.0 Transitional//EN"
    "http://www.w3.org/TR/xhtml1/DTD/xhtml1-transitional.dtd">
<html xmlns="http://www.w3.org/1999/xhtml">

<head>
  <title>DHTML Demo of a Text Color Change Mouseover Effect</title>
</head>

<body bgcolor="#ADD8E6">
  <h1 align="center">HTML and Web Design Tips &amp; Techniques</h1>

  <hr />
  <p>Move your mouse pointer over the following links to see a
DHTML Text Mouseover event.<br />
    Click on any of the links to visit sites the examine DHTML.<br />
    <br />
  </p>

  <ul>
    <li><a href="http://www.dhtmlshock.com/"
        onmouseover="this.style.color='red'"
        onmouseout="this.style.color='blue'">DHTML Shock
        </a> - http://www.dhtmlshock.com/
    </li>

    <li style="list-style: none"><br /></li>

    <li><a href="http://www.w3schools.com/dhtml/dhtml_examples.asp"
        onmouseover="this.style.color='green'"
        onmouseout="this.style.color='blue'">DHTML Examples
        </a> - http://www.w3schools.com/dhtml/dhtml_examples.asp
    </li>

    <li style="list-style: none"><br /></li>
```

```
   <li><a href="http://www.dynamicdrive.com/"
        onmouseover="this.style.color='magenta'"
        onmouseout="this.style.color='blue'">Dynamic Drive
</a> - http://www.dynamicdrive.com/
   </li>

  </ul>

</body>
</html>
```

In this case, the HTML statements use the *onmouseover* and *onmouseout* events to specify the color the browser assigns to the link when the user moves his or her mouse pointer over and off of the link's text. The key point to understand about DHTML is that the processing occurs within the browser—meaning, DHTML requires client-side processing. Depending on the DHTML operations a Web page contains, the DHTML processing the browser must perform may cause a brief delay before the browser displays the page content.

DHTML was not created specifically with animation in mind, but it will let you alter HTML elements in a way that adds movement (action) to a Web page. For example, a DHTML script can simply tell the browser to keep changing the position of an image on the page, so that the picture travels around the screen. If you do this using several different images, you can move a series of graphic elements around each other. Most Web browsers support DHTML animation effects without requiring the visitor to download additional components. (Not forcing your visitors to stop and download plug-ins before displaying an animation effect on a Web page is a plus.) However, creating DHTML content that works the same way on all browsers is fairly difficult, so this sort of animation is not nearly as simple to make as a GIF animation, for example, which is discussed next. Actually coding the animation yourself is quite tedious and time-consuming. Fortunately, user-friendly software applications, such as Macromedia's Dreamweaver, help produce DHTML script code for you.

DHTML is fairly limited as to the type of animation effects it can produce, because all it can really do is move still images around the screen, and moving a still image around the screen is not really animation—it's simply movement. In order to add higher-quality, true animation to a Web page, use GIF animation, Flash, or Shockwave to achieve your goal. To see DHMTL in use, visit the following sites:

- http://www.hfe.org/resource/demo2/
- http://www.dhtmlcentral.com/
- http://www.webcoder.com/

Working with GIF Animation

Graphic Interchange Format (GIF) animation is the most popular form of animation on the Internet today. Several reasons account for its popularity:

- *GIFs are easy to create*   You can create GIF animation from a score of image- and Web design–applications, such as Macromedia Fireworks and Adobe ImageReady. In addition, you can go to shareware sites, such as http://www.shareware.com and http://www.tucows.com, to download shareware programs that create animated GIF files from existing images. Two popular shareware programs are GIF Builder (Macintosh) and GIF Construction Set (Windows).

- *GIFs require no special browser software*   Almost all Web browsers play GIF animations, which means that the browser requires no special software or plug-ins.

- *GIFs are a standard Web file format*   All browsers that support graphics images will display GIF files. In rare cases where the browser does not support GIF animation, the browser will still display a static version of the animation (typically the first frame in the animation sequence within the GIF file).

- *GIFs use streaming*   When a Web browser begins downloading the GIF animation, the browser displays the frames as it receives them. The visitor is not forced to wait until the browser finishes downloading the file before seeing the animation.

Animated GIF files work like traditional hand-painted, frame-by-frame animation created by companies such as Disney. Each GIF file contains a number of cells, with each cell representing one part of the animation. When you save the GIF file, the image-editing software stacks the images (that is, the cells) one on top of another and saves all them within a single file. When the Web browser opens the file, it displays the individual images one at a time, and creates a visual impression of movement, as shown here:

Frame 1   Frame 2   Frame 3   Frame 4

As we discuss in detail later in this chapter, in the Tip "Controlling GIF Animation Through Internal Settings," when you save a GIF animation, you select from a series of options that let you control the speed and duration of the animation. The program you use to create the GIF saves the options you select within the GIF file, and the Web browser interprets the choices when it opens the file to play the animation.

Because animation attracts attention, GIF animation is used extensively in marketing and advertising. Everyone has seen the ubiquitous banner ads that appear at the top of virtually every commercial Web page, advertising everything from Beanie Babies to magazine subscriptions.

Another reason for GIF animation's widespread use is the ease of inserting it into an HTML document. To place a GIF animation on a Web page, use the same <img> tag you use to insert graphics and artwork, as shown here:

```
<img src="neon.gif" width="50" height="50" />
```

The *src* attribute in this example instructs the Web browser to load a GIF file named neon.gif. The information that instructs the Web browser how to animate the GIF file (speed, number of loops) is embedded within the file itself and not written into the HTML code.

You can find numerous Web sites that offer free animated GIFs you can download and integrate into your Web site:

Animation Factory	http://www.animfactory.net/
All Free Original Clipart	http://www.free-graphics.com/
Animation City	http://www.animationcity.net/
imageif .net	http://www.imagif.net/

Within the Tip "Creating a GIF Animation from Scratch" later in this chapter, you will create your own GIF animations.

Working with Macromedia Flash

Flash is a multimedia development tool created by the Macromedia Corporation that lets you create full-screen animations, incorporating sound and interactivity using very small file sizes. Flash keeps the file sizes small through the use of vector images. Vector images are smaller than traditional bitmap images because they use math to describe the graphics instead of pixels. When you save a traditional bitmap image (GIF or JPEG), the file has to record and store information within the graphics file that describes each and every pixel, which creates large files. In contrast, when you save a vector graphic, the image uses mathematical formulas to save the image information. For example, assume that you use a graphics program to draw a picture of a line. If you store the image within a raster (bitmap) format, the file must store all the pixels that comprise the line, as well as those that make up the image background. In contrast, as shown in Figure 7-1, if you store the image in a vector format, the file will store an equation (such as the slope of the line) as well as the line's start and end points.

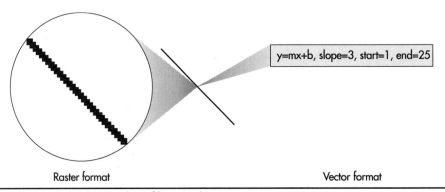

Raster format   Vector format

Figure 7-1   Vector graphics reduce file sizes by representing images using equations

Because files saved as vectors are small, the images download to the browser faster than traditional JPEG or GIF images. Vector images saved for use in Flash animation are defined as SVG image files, or Scalable Vector Graphics. SVG images can be resized (made larger or smaller) while the animation is playing, without loss of image quality. This means that you can create complicated Flash animation files, which load and play quickly on a visitor's computer.

Using Flash over traditional GIF animation offers several advantages:

- *Flash uses small image file sizes*   Smaller file sizes for vector images translates into fast-loading animations.

- *Flash enjoys cross-platform browser support*   Whether you use Microsoft Explorer or Netscape Navigator, or the Macintosh or Windows platform, does not matter. The plug-in that runs Flash animation is free and is available for most Web browsers.

- *Flash lets you resize images during animation*   Vector images resize with ease, creating images that look great at any size you decide to use.

- *Flash uses streaming technology*   When a visitor downloads a Flash animation, they do not have to wait for the entire file to download. The animation will start as soon as the visitor's Web browser receives enough of the Flash data to begin the animation.

- *Flash is interactive*   Flash lets you create interactive menus and navigation bars without prior experience in programming languages.

- *Flash incorporates JavaScript*   Flash is fully compatible with JavaScript. Because all browsers universally accept the JavaScript language, you can create even more complicated interaction between your page and its visitors.

- *Flash incorporates sound*   Flash works seamlessly with sound files, letting you create movement and audio in the same animation.

To design Flash animations, you use the Macromedia's Flash application, as shown in Figure 7-2. If you visit the Macromedia Web site, you can download a trial version of Flash, which you can use for 30 days to create your own Flash animations.

Although Flash is a popular way to create animation, it is not without competition. In 1999, Adobe released LiveMotion. Adobe LiveMotion creates full-screen animation with vector graphics similar to those used in Macromedia Flash.

Several Web sites offer free Flash animations you can download and use within your Web pages:

Extreme Flash	http://www.extremeflash.com/
Flash Kit	http://www.flashkit.com
freelayouts.com	http://www.freelayouts.com/
Macromedia	http://www.macromedia.com

In "Creating a Flash Movie from Scratch" later in the chapter, you will create your own Flash animation.

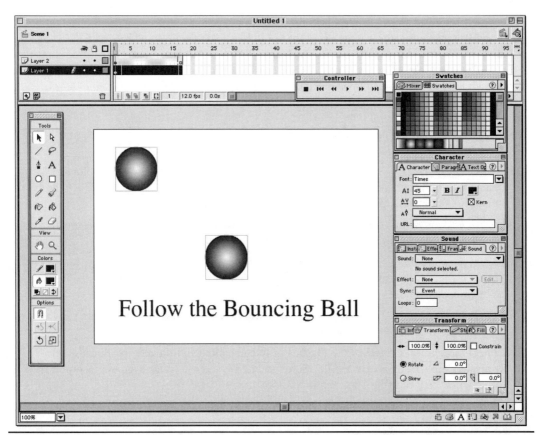

Figure 7-2   The Flash application lets you design and save animated Flash Web pages

Using Shockwave

Flash is not the only Web product produced by Macromedia. In the early '90s, Macromedia developed the Director application for use primarily in the creation of interactive media outside the Web environment. Director lets multimedia designers incorporate graphics, animation, sound, QuickTime movies, and interactive buttons into an application that users run on their computers. Director was, and still is, the major development program for media such as interactive computer games and instructional CDs.

In 1996, Macromedia expanded Director's capabilities by introducing Shockwave. Shockwave lets Web designers convert Director movies into interactive documents that are displayable on the Internet. Shockwave is a popular method for creating animation for the Internet (Shockwave files are called movies). However, Shockwave files lack the compact size of Flash animations, and creating shockwave movies requires extensive knowledge of a programming language called Lingo.

To create a Shockwave movie, you must first design the movie in Director, using the Lingo programming language, and then convert the Director movie into a Shockwave movie. With the cost of Director running approximately $1,000 and the steep learning curve of the Lingo language, Shockwave is a Web animation tool out of the reach of most Web designers, especially when Macromedia's Flash and Adobe's LiveMotion can give you much of the same flexibility and interactivity at a much lower cost, and without having to learn a programming language.

To place a Shockwave animation on a Web page, you can use either the <object> or <embed> tag. The following HTML statement, for example, illustrates how to use the <embed> tag to place a Shockwave movie within an HTML file:

```
<embed src="shock.dcr" height="400 width="400" name="shocking" />
```

In this example of an <embed> tag, the *src* attribute identifies the name of the shockwave movie (shock.dcr) the Web browser is to play, and the *width* and *height* attributes define the dimensions of the Shockwave movie "screen" within the Web browser application window. The *name* attribute specifies a way for forms and other HTML objects to communicate with the movie, as explained later in this chapter.

Several Web sites offer Shockwave applications you can download to take Shockwave for a test drive. Further, from the Macromedia Web site at http://www.macromedia.com/downloads, you can download a 30-day trial of Director Shockwave Studio. Several sites offer the source code for the Lingo programs the developers used to create the applications:

Shockwave.com	http://www.shockwave.com/sw/home/
Shockwave-sound.com	http://www.shockwave-sound.com/
Macromedia	http://www.macromedia.com

Understanding When and When Not to Use Animation

As previously discussed, animation attracts attention, it entertains, and it informs. However, as wonderful as animation is, there are concerns to using animation on a Web page:

- *Use animation to attract attention, but don't overdo it*   Animation is an attention grabber, but too much animation can be a problem. If you create animation to attract your visitor's attention, refrain from using more than one, or possibly two animations on each page.

- *Use animation to enhance the message of the Web page, but make sure that it adds value*   Attempt to use animation that relates to the other static information on the page. For example, is that rotating logo in the upper-left corner of the browser window contributing to the overall design and message of the page, or did you place it there simply to prove you could do it?

- *Do not use animation when it becomes distracting*   Avoid animation on Web pages that contain large bodies of text. Animation impacts the visitor's concentration and distracts from the reading of the text. Animation attracts attention; too much animation keeps the visitor from focusing.

- *Do not use animation for animation's sake*   Because animation files have larger file sizes, and consequently take longer for the Web browser to download and display, use animation only when it contributes to the page.

Remember, using animation is a two-edged sword. On the one hand, animation attracts attention and keeps visitors on your Web site. However, too much animation can detract from your primary message by distracting the site visitor. Create a balance between animation and the goal of the Web page. Ask yourself if the animation contributes to what you are trying to say, or is it animation for animation's sake?

Working with Sound on the Internet

If you don't believe that sound is part of a visual experience, watch a television show with the sound turned off. Although this might be an acceptable practice during commercials, television without sound creates only half the experience (many people would say the most important half). And it's not just the voices of the characters that keep the attention of a viewer riveted to the screen; the full experience also includes background music. How would you ever know, for example, that something bad was going to happen without the background music alerting you (the viewer) to the upcoming danger?

Just as the sound coming from a television helps set the mood for the audience, you can provide a more engaging experience for your site's visitors by adding sound to the text, graphics, and animations you use. A properly designed soundtrack helps your visitors gain a total experience by setting a mood that draws them into the content and thereby keeps them on the Web site. However, just as a well-designed soundtrack keeps visitors riveted to the page, a poorly designed soundtrack will drive them away. For example, constantly playing music in the background of a Web page is distracting, unless the music directly relates to the content—such as a Web site devoted to Brittany Spears playing her latest CD.

▶ **NOTE**

If you use music on your Web site, make sure you have permission from the artist, or from the production company that created it. This holds true for speeches as well as music. Make sure you have the right to use the material before you publish it on your Web site.

Although audio is now commonplace on the Internet, the World Wide Web used to be a silent medium. In 1996, when commercial browsers such as Netscape Navigator became more readily available to the public, a demand was generated for professional Web designers with high-quality media production skills.

Originally, the only sound formats available produced sound files so large it could take minutes or even hours to download a sixty-second music clip. Typically, visitors to a Web site expect results within seconds.

In late 1996, RealNetworks created the first version of RealAudio. RealAudio used "streaming" technology to allow Web browsers to download and play sound files directly on the visitor's computer. Streaming technology lets music or narration play while the Web browser is still downloading the sound file. In a normal situation, the Web browser downloads the start of the audio file and begins playing the portion of the file it has downloaded while, at the same time, continuing to retrieve the remainder of the file. Thus, visitors can listen to long audio clips without waiting a long time for a large audio file to download completely.

In competition with RealAudio is Apple's QuickTime, which functions in a similar way to RealAudio. Many Web sites exploit both the RealAudio and QuickTime formats and most users have previously downloaded the corresponding plug-ins. Here are some guidelines for using sound on the Internet:

- Use sound to communicate ideas through the use of dialog and narration.
- Use sound to improve a Web site's navigation. For example, use a clicking sound in conjunction with a rollover button.
- Use background music (where appropriate) to set the mood for the Web page. For example, to set the mood on a Web site dealing with life in the ocean, play the sound of surf gently rolling against the shoreline.
- Use sound to generate online revenue by the sale of audio and music clips. For example, let visitors play a portion of a new song, before purchasing.

The use of sound has changed the design and construction of Web sites. For example, some Web sites now play radio broadcasts (called Webcasts). Webcasts are used for everything from music to the live broadcast of important presidential speeches and major league baseball games. As time and technology advance, Web authors are realizing the importance of sound along with the other content of a Web page in generating a mood and keeping the attention of a Web visitor. Thousands of sites on the Web broadcast live. Examples include National Public Radio (http://www.npr.com) and MSNBC (http://www.msnbc.com).

▶ *NOTE*

If you decide to include music or sounds within your Web site, you should include a button on the site that allows the user to easily turn off the music or sounds. Many users will find it quite annoying when their coworker in the next cubicle cannot readily control the volume on his or her PC.

Just as graphic files are saved using specific formats such as JPEG and GIF, audio files have their own formats. Common sound file formats that work well on the Macintosh platform are AIF, AIFF, SND, AU, MP3, and MIDI (for music only). The Windows platform plays WAV, AU, SND, MP3, and MIDI (for music only) file formats. As you can see, several of the formats (AU, SND, MP3, and MIDI) can be used on both the Windows and Macintosh platforms. In addition to these formats, the MOV format used by QuickTime can be used to format music for both the Windows and Macintosh platforms. Also, using the Windows Media Player (which is available for the both the Mac and PC), users can play back Windows Media Format (WMF) files.

To capture audio using the Windows platform, you can use the built-in Sound Recorder or install and use an audio application such as Sound Forge. Both programs mentioned will capture audio using the WAV format (native to Windows), and let you save the file to several formats. To capture audio using the Macintosh platform, use the built-in recorder, or install and use an audio application such as Sound Edit Pro. Both capture audio using the AIFF format (native to Macintosh) and let you save the file to several formats.

▶ **NOTE**

To convert audio from one format to another, you can use a program such as Cool Edit, which you can download from http://www.syntrillium.com.

Several Web sites let you download audio clips for free, which you can then integrate into your Web site:

Midi-World	http://www.midi-world.net/
A1 Free Sound Effects	http://www.a1freesoundeffects.com/
TheFreeSite.com	http://www.thefreesite.com/Free_Sounds/Free_WAVs/

Adding Sound to a Web Page

To add a simple background sound to a Web page, you can place the <bgsound> tag within the page's header section, or you can use the <embed> tag within the Web page body section as shown here:

```
<head>
<bgsound src="music.au" />
</head>

<body>
<embed src="music.au" autostart="true"></embed>
</body>
```

These tags represent the minimal way of inserting a sound file into an HTML-based Web page. Because the <embed> tag will play in both Netscape Navigator and Internet Explorer, you may want to use it to place the sound file within your Web page. In the previous examples, the file named music.au would play once and not repeat. To instruct the sound to continually repeat, add the following attributes to the <bgsound> and <embed> tags (*hidden*, *loop*, *autostart*) as shown here:

```
<head>
 <bgsound src="music.au" hidden="true" loop="true" autostart="true"/>
</head>

<embed src="music.au" hidden="true" loop="true" autostart="true"></embed>
```

For anything more than a simple playback of a sound file, visitors to your site will need a plug-in–based solution such as Flash, QuickTime, or RealAudio, as previously discussed.

The HTML specification states that the preferred way to embed sound in a Web page is through the use of the <object> tag. However, until all major browsers support the <object> tag, you may simply want to continue to use the <embed> tag, as previously shown.

Incorporating Video into a Web Page

Creating video for display on a Web page is one of the fastest growing areas of Web design. Moreover, with the new technologies available, virtually anyone can create desktop video productions. If you are planning to create you own video, you'll want to consider several things before starting the project to ensure quality results:

- **Plan**   Always plan your video shots in advance. One way to do this is to sketch out the major sections of the video shoot using a storyboard. A storyboard contains small sketches of the frames: where the video shot takes place, who is in the video, what is needed (props, equipment) and what you expect that portion of the video to convey to the viewer.

- **Reduce camera movement**   When you shoot the video, keep movement down to a minimum. Not only does aggressive movement and zooming in and out look bad, they do not translate well when compressed into a format suitable for the Web. Many video compression programs save file size by repeating information in one frame to the next. If you constantly move the camera, the compression program has nothing to duplicate; therefore, not only is excessive movement distracting to the viewer, it creates a final production with a larger file size.

- **Watch the background**   Avoid high-contrast or excessively bright backgrounds. Excessively bright backgrounds cause the image to generate halos around the objects in the foreground, making them difficult to see. In addition, video cameras may compensate for the bright background, making objects in the foreground overly dark.

- **Keep the background simple**   Cluttered backgrounds cause images in the foreground to blend with the background. In addition, simple backgrounds (like solid-color backdrops) actually help the compression program to create a smaller file size for the finished production.

- **Use good lighting**   Although many video cameras let you record in low light, a low-light video looks dull and the finished production does not translate well to the Internet. Use good lighting to make the elements of the video stand out.

- **Stay focused**   Make sure the video stays well focused. When you compress the final production, some of the original quality of the movie is sacrificed to create a smaller file size. If the original image was slightly out of focus, the compressed Internet production will only be that much worse.

If you follow these simple steps when creating the video, you will be assured of the best quality for the finished Internet version.

Assembling a Video Production

After shooting the video, you will need a video-editing program to assemble the separate video clips into the finished production. VideoWave IV by MGI software is a reasonably priced application ($99) that lets you take video clips from several files and combine them. You can even include special effects such as subtitles, sound effects, and voice-over narration. Moving up the ladder, programs such as Adobe Premiere and iMovie give you more features, and even include an audio editing plug-in, as shown in Figure 7-3.

Although the use of video on the Internet is increasing, the ability of the Internet to download data, such as video files, quickly (bandwidth) has not caught up with the technology. For the present, unless your visitors are willing to suffer long download times, video clips must be short and use small

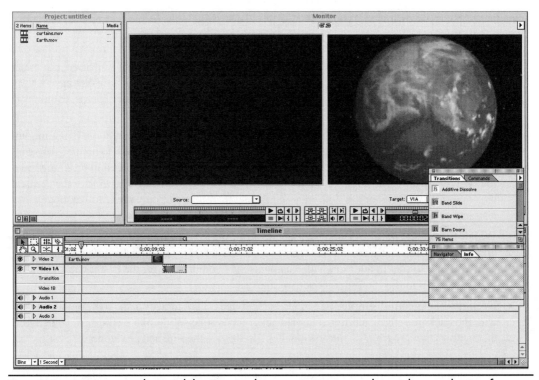

Figure 7-3   Programs such as Adobe Premier let you create a complete video production from one or more video clips, and even add special effects, titles, and audio

viewing areas, with low image and poor sound quality. With that said, video does have some excellent uses on the Internet:

- Use video to promote television shows and movies: industries that traditionally use trailers (short excerpts of the production).

- Use video to give visitors an impression of your personality. For example, a resume placed on the Internet would be enhanced by a short video. In this way, prospective employers get a chance to see what they might be buying.

- Product demos and walk-around video clips are better than a stationary photograph, and help prospective buyers actually *see* the product. Marketing sites such as http://www.toyota.com let car and truck shoppers actually walk around the vehicle with the use of virtual-reality programs such as Apple's VR modeling software (http://www.apple.com).

Of course, using any of these suggestions to create a video production assumes that visitors to your Web site will have the software plug-ins installed that they need to download and view the video. To get a look at Web sites that successfully integrate video, visit the following sites:

MTV	http://www.mtv.com/
EPSN	http://www.espn.com
AMC Theatres	http://www.amctheatres.com
Warner Brothers	http://www.warnerbros.com

Understanding Video Compatibility Issues and the World Wide Web

If you plan to add a video clip to your Web site, bear in mind that not everyone will be able to view your wonderful production. Viewing a video production requires that a Web browser has a plug-in that allows it to view the video. Both RealAudio and QuickTime have plug-ins that enable Web browsers to play video productions. However, downloading and installing a plug-in requires time and patience on the part of the visitor. Most surveys indicate that if visitors must stop and download a plug-in before viewing a video clip, most will simply leave the site.

Instead of forcing your visitors to download software, giving them a preview of the video might be better, possibly in a series of small still shots, and give them the option of downloading the software they need to view the movie. If the visitor knows what to expect, he or she might be willing to invest the time for the privilege of viewing your video, as shown in Figure 7-4.

Streaming vs. Downloading a Video Production

When you insert a video production into a Web page, you have the option of streaming the content or requiring the visitor to download the video completely prior to playback. Streaming video is played through a browser plug-in such as RealAudio or QuickTime and begins playing before the entire video file downloads. Typically, streaming video begins playing when it has downloaded enough of the file to continue playing the video while, at the same time, downloading the remainder of the file. One problem with streaming video is that the video file has to be compressed to a small size, so that it can load while it plays. Because some forms of video compression employ lossy techniques (compression by removing information), the video image suffers, and typically creates a poor quality playback. Further, as a browser (more specifically a video plug-in within the browser) downloads the streaming video, delays due to traffic on the Internet or a slow connection speed can delay the video's arrival, which disrupts the video playback, producing a choppy display or causing the images and audio to fall out of sync.

▶ **NOTE**

Streaming audio or video can place considerable processing demands on a server. If your site supports streaming operations, you should monitor your site's performance, as discussed in Chapter 12.

One alternative is to give the visitor the option of downloading a slightly larger (and better quality) version of the video file. While the video file is downloading, the visitor cannot view the video until the visitor's computer receives the entire file. For example, downloading a one-minute video might take five minutes. However, many visitors, after viewing the lower-quality streaming version, might be willing to wait the required time to download the better-quality version. In this case, as in many cases in Web design, putting in the extra work to give your visitors choices helps make a better, more user-friendly Web site.

Figure 7-4 Using still images to motivate users to download a video

One way to insert a video file into a Web page is to use an <a> tag that lets the visitor download the video file, as shown here:

```
<a href="company.avi">Click to view a video of our company</a>
```

In this example, the Web browser will download the video in the file company.avi after the visitor clicks on the anchor text "Click to view a video of our company." In the Tip "Broadcasting Streaming Audio and Video," you will learn how to broadcast streaming media from your Web site.

Taking Advantage of Virtual Tours

Many Web sites offer virtual tours that let users walk through homes that are for sale, to view the playing field from prospective seats for a sporting event (http://www.kcchiefs.com/fanfair/v_arrowhead.asp), view cities such as Vancouver (http://www.virtuallyvancouver.com/), tour famous landmarks such as the Pyramids (http://www.pbs.org/wgbh/nova/pyramid/explore/khufuall.html), and more. To take a virtual tour, you will normally need a QuickTime VR plug-in for your browser, which you can get from http://www.apple.com/quicktime. Figure 7-5, for example, shows a virtual tour of New York City that lets you compare different locations in the city as they appeared in 1907 to how they had changed by 1999 (http://www.pbs.org/wnet/newyork/hidden/contents.html).

To create a 360-degree virtual tour, developers use a tool such as Apple QuickTime VR Authoring Studio to "stitch" together images in the shape of a sphere. In general, to create the 360-degree panorama, you must have at least six photos (one facing forward, back, left, right, up, and down). The QuickTime VR Authoring Studio provides a tool called the Panorama Stitcher that sews the images in the shape of a sphere. Several Web sites present great virtual tours:

The Louvre Museum	http://www.louvre.or.jp/louvre/QTVR/anglais/index.htm
Submarines	http://www.pbs.org/wgbh/nova/subsecrets/
Virtual Earth	http://www.virtualearth.com
Apple's Cubic VR Gallery	http://www.apple.com/quicktime/products/gallery/

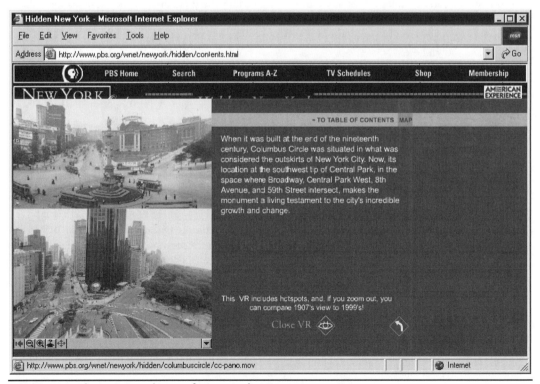

Figure 7-5 Taking a virtual tour of New York City

Depending on the product or topic your site presents, letting users view content via a virtual tour can be a very effective way to present information.

In conclusion, content has, and always will be, the focus of the Web visitor's attention, whether that content is text, still graphics, animation, audio, video, or a combination. Content is the reason a visitor goes online, and it will always be the first thing a visitor looks for in a Web page. Quality content is the most important aspect of Web page design. Without quality content, visitors will move to other sites to find what they need. Therefore, animation, video, and audio must support the content of the Web site, not be used simply to prove you can do it.

Remember that Web users are goal-oriented and very impatient. Always design your Web pages so that they quickly supply the answers visitors need. If you fail to do this one thing—supply quality content—all the video, animation, and audio in the world will not keep the visitors on your Web site.

Creating a GIF Animation from Scratch

GIF animation is the most widely used form of animation on the Internet. A GIF animation is composed of individual frames, or cells, each of which represents a single piece of the whole animation. Although GIF animations can be comprised of any type of images, they are typically clip art, cartoons, or text.

For example, creating an animated walking character generally involves 8 to 10 individual cells, (four to five cells per stride). Each one of the cells represents a part of the walking movement of the character, as shown here:

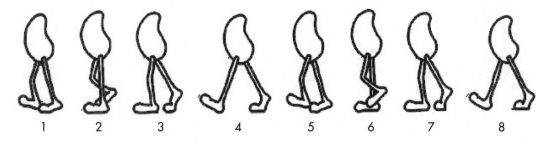

Because walking involves placing one foot in front of the other (as your parents so dutifully taught you when you were a child), to create a continuing animation of a person walking, you need to create only one walking cycle. When the animation reaches the last cell, it automatically returns to the first cell and repeats the animation all over again. Repeating a series of cells is called *cycling*.

USE IT   To create the individual cells, such as those shown previously, you can sketch them on paper and then scan them into your computer, or you can create the cells using any one of a number of image-editing programs such as Photoshop or ImageReady. In this example, the individual cells were created by sketching each one on paper and scanning them into individual layers in Adobe Photoshop.

After you complete the cells in the animation, you must assemble them in a GIF animation program. Check out http://www.shareware.com or http://www.tucows.com, for several Macintosh or Windows shareware programs (and don't forget, you are required to pay for shareware). GIF Construction Set, for example, sells for a modest price of $20. Other programs, such as Adobe's ImageReady, come with more features, but at a higher price. ImageReady comes bundled with Adobe Photoshop, which costs about $600. Figure 7-6 shows the individual walking cells opened in Adobe Photoshop.

After you have all the cells assembled in the animation program, you save the animation sequence to a file with a .gif extension. In this example, the file was saved as walking.gif. Finally, use an <img> tag to insert the completed GIF animation (that is, the file with the .gif extension) into a Web page's HTML statements as shown here:

```
<html>
<head>
  <title>This is a simple GIF animation</title>
</head>
<body>
  <center>
    <img src="walking.gif" alt="Animation" width="50" height="120" />
  </center>
</body>
</html>
```

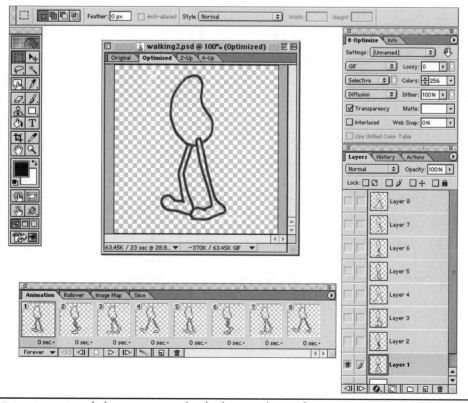

Figure 7-6   ImageReady lets you use individual image layers for use in an animation sequence

In this example, the *src* attribute in the image tag instructs the Web browser to load the GIF animation file named walking.gif.

Because GIF animations are supported by almost all Web browsers, creating a GIF animation file and inserting it into an HTML source document is almost certain to result in an animation that plays on the Web page. In a rare case where a visitor's browser does not support GIF animation, the visitor will see a still frame (typically the first cell in the animation).

Controlling GIF Animation Through Internal Settings

When you create and save GIF animation without modifying the animation settings, the application saves the file using the program's predefined settings. These settings typically instruct the Web browser to display a new cell, or frame, every tenth of a second, and continuously cycle (that is, repeat) the animation sequence. For example, if you create a GIF animation of a rotating logo, the logo will continue to rotate, displaying a new animation frame every tenth of a second, for as long as the Web page remains onscreen.

Although default settings may be fine for some animations, configuring the GIF animation's settings when you save the file is always best. Note that you save the settings that control the GIF animation playback within the GIF file, and not as a tag or attribute within the Web page HTML:

```
<img src="neon.gif" width="75 height="75" />
```

In this example, the <img> tag instructs the Web browser to load the GIF animation file neon.gif. The options that control the animation's playback are contained within the neon.gif file. After it loads the animation file, the Web browser extracts and executes the playback instructions it finds within the file.

USE IT   Suppose that you want to create a neon sign for your Web page. You would open a graphic in an image-editing application such as Photoshop, and use the program to create two GIF images. The first image represents the neon sign glowing, and the second shows the neon sign off. For example, the image in Figure 7-7 was created in Photoshop and opened in ImageReady.

All Web animation programs (such as ImageReady) give you the option to change the number of frames displayed per second (fps) and the number of times the image cycles (that is, the number of times the animation repeats).

- **Frames per second (fps)**   On the Internet, frame rates vary between 1 and 30 frames per second. To prevent the animation from appearing jittery, use a minimum of 10 fps to create the illusion of smooth movement in the animated GIF. However, in the case of a neon sign, to create a "buzzing" neon-like effect, you might reduce the number of frames per second.

- **Cycles**   The count that determines how many times the Web browser loops through the cells in the animation. Cycle counts can be forever (never stop cycling), or any number from 1 to 30,000.

The frames per second and number of times the animation cycles depend on the type of animation effect you are trying to create. For example, because a neon sign does not move like a typical

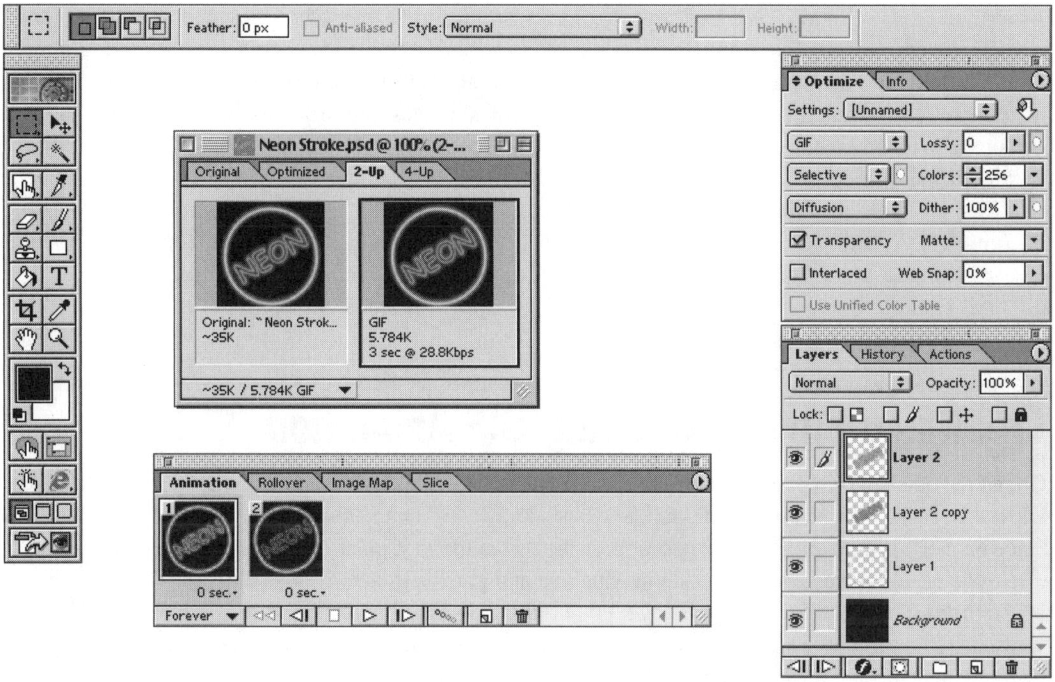

Figure 7-7   The two cells for the neon animation opened in ImageReady

animation (it just goes on and off), you set the frames per second to one second for the Neon sign "on" image, and one-half second for the sign "off" image. In addition, the sign's objective is to attract attention to the Web page, not continually annoy the visitor. Therefore, you might set the cycle count to 5 cycles, as shown here, so that the sign stops flashing after a while.

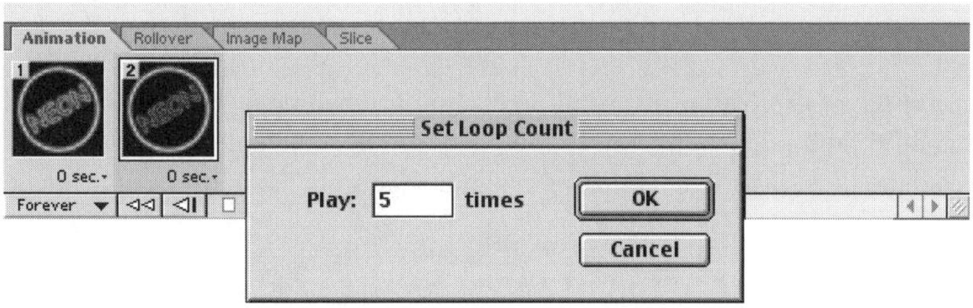

Some Web animation programs have an fps rate defined as No Delay or Zero Seconds. You should always select a specific period for the fps rate of the GIF animation as a number of seconds or fractions of a second. When you choose the No Delay or Zero Seconds option, you instruct the Web browser to flip through the animation frames as fast as possible. Therefore, you let the Web browser and the processor speed of the visitor's computer system determine your animation's appearance.

As a result, your animation will look great to some visitors and will look like an indistinguishable blur of motion to others.

When you save the animation to a disk file, the GIF animation program saves the cycle and frames per second settings within the file along with the graphics images that make up the animation sequence. When the Web browser opens the image, the browser adjusts the playback of the animation according to the settings you specified when you saved the file.

When the Web browser opens the neon.gif file, for example, the sign blinks on for one second and off for a half-second. After repeating this on/off sequence five times, the browser stops the animation on the last frame in the sequence. Notice that the last frame in the sequence shows the neon sign glowing, or "on." Therefore, when the animation stops, it will stop with the neon "on."

Creating a Banner Ad Using GIF Animation

One of the quickest ways to attract the attention of visitors to your Web site is with movement. Advertisers know this, so they create text and/or graphic images known as banner ads. Commercial Web sites typically place banner ads at the top of Web pages, because that is the first place your eyes go when the browser displays a page. Banner ads incorporate moving text and graphic images designed to attract your attention.

To insert a banner ad into a Web page, you could create the banner using Flash. However, doing so requires that the user's browser have plug-in software to run the animation. A simpler way would be to create and save the banner ad animation in the GIF format.

USE IT Begin by creating a new file in an image-editing program such as Photoshop. Base the width of the banner ad on the width of the Web page. Suppose, for example, that the width of the Web page is 800 pixels. You might then create the individual frames in the banner ad 750 pixels wide by 75 pixels tall.

▶ NOTE

The standard banner ad size on the Web is 468×60 pixels.

Because the width of the Web page is 800 pixels in this example, a 750-pixel banner ad will not crowd the left and right borders of the browser window. In this example, the individual frames of the animation create the illusion of lights blinking on and off around the border of the banner ad.

Note the different colors

To complete the animation, open the individual frames in a GIF animation program (such as ImageReady or GIF Construction Set) and set the frames per second and cycle count of the animation. In this example, you open the GIF image using GIF Construction Set, and set the frames per second (fps) rate to 0.5 seconds and the cycle to loop indefinitely, as shown in Figure 7-8.

To place the animated GIF onto a Web site, use HTML statements similar to the following:

```
<html>
<head>
  <title>Example of Banner Ad</title>
</head>
<body>
  <center>
    <img src="banner.gif" width="750" height="75" />
  </center>
<!--     **** Remainder of Web page ****      -->
</body>
</html>
```

In this example, the <img> tag's *src* attribute instructs the Web browser to load the GIF animation file (banner.gif), and the enclosing start and end center tags ( ) tell the Web browser to center the image at the top of the page. When the Web browser loads the page, the animation creates the illusion of blinking lights (every half-second) around the border of the banner ad graphic, and loops continuously.

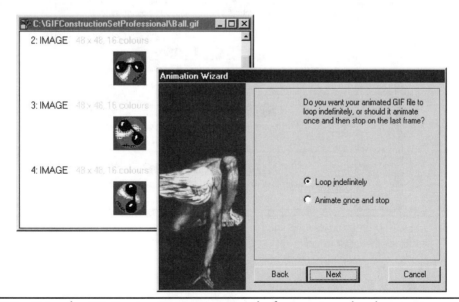

Figure 7-8 Using the GIF Construction Set to assign the frame rate and cycle count to a GIF graphic

You can add functionality to the banner ad by converting it into a hypertext, or clickable, link. For example, when visitors to your Web site click on the banner ad, it sends them to a Web site that has the product or service advertised for sale. To convert the banner ad in the previous example into a clickable link, enclose the <img> tag in the code within the start and end anchor tags (<a></a>) as shown here:

```
<a href="http://www.buyit.com/index.html">
  <img src="banner.gif" width="750" height="75" border="0">
</a>
```

In this example, when visitors to your Web site click on the banner ad, the <a> tag's *href* attribute instructs the Web browser to go to the Web site http://www.buyit.com and load the Web page index.html.

Because hyperlinks are identified by an underline (text), or a graphic surrounded by a border (designers refer to this as a *stroke*), the *border* attribute with a zero value is added to keep the Web browser from enclosing the banner ad with a stroke (by default, the stroke enclosing the graphic file is blue).

In addition to blinking lights, banner ads can include moving text, rotating logos, and even still images combined to create the illusion of a slide show. Figure 7-9 illustrates the use of moving text by making the words *Follow me to great bargains* move from left to right across the width of the banner ad. Because moving text is difficult to read onscreen, use a large font to make the words easier for the visitor to make out.

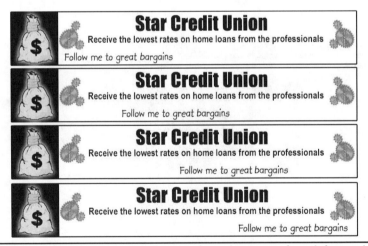

Figure 7-9   The GIF animation creates the illusion of words moving from left to right across the width of the banner ad

Creating Smooth Transitions Between GIF Animation Frames Using Tweening

In GIF animation, flipping through a series of still images creates the illusion of movement. Each image is a single part of the total animation sequence. For example, to create a GIF animation of a dog wagging its tail, you create several GIF images of a dog. In each image, the dog's tail is slightly up or down from its position in the image that precedes it in the sequence. When the browser plays the animation—that is, when the browser displays the images one after another in rapid succession—the visitor sees the illusion of movement (the tail wagging).

In most animation sequences, the abrupt change of one animation frame to the next is how you achieve the illusion of movement. However, at times you may want the transition of one animation frame to the next to be smooth, not abrupt.

Suppose, for example, that you create a neon sign using two GIF images. One image displays the neon sign glowing and the other displays the neon sign switched off. By displaying one image after the other rapidly, you can create the illusion of a neon sign flickering on and off.

USE IT   To make the neon sign pulse instead of flicker on and off, you use an animation technique called *tweening*. The *Tween* command lets you add or modify a series of new frames between two frames you created. Say, for example, that you have two graphic images of a neon sign. However, instead of the sign going on and off (flickering), you want to create the illusion of the neon sign pulsing (slowly going on and off). To accomplish this you need to create a series of intermediate frames where the neon sign slowly fades.

1. Open the two images in a Web-editing application such as Adobe ImageReady. In this example, assume that the frame with the neon sign turned on is frame 1, and frame 2 contains the layer with the neon turned off.

2. Click the Tween icon. ImageReady opens the Tween dialog box, shown in Figure 7-10.

   The following list briefly describes the settings you can use to control the tweening operation:

   • **All Layers**   Select All Layers to perform the Tweening option using all of the layers in the image.

   • **Selected Layer**   Select Selected Layer to use the layers selected for the animation. Because the neon animation contains two layers, and you want to use both in the animation, you will likely use the All Layers option instead.

   • **Position**   Select this option to vary the animation from the first to last cell. Because you want to create the illusion of pulsing on and off, select this option.

   • **Opacity**   When you select the Opacity option, the animation slowly fades to zero opacity.

   • **Effects**   Select this option to vary any layer effects applied to this image. Because you did not use any layer effects, you do not need to select this option.

   • **Tween With**   Click the Tween With option and select Next Frame to create the animation.

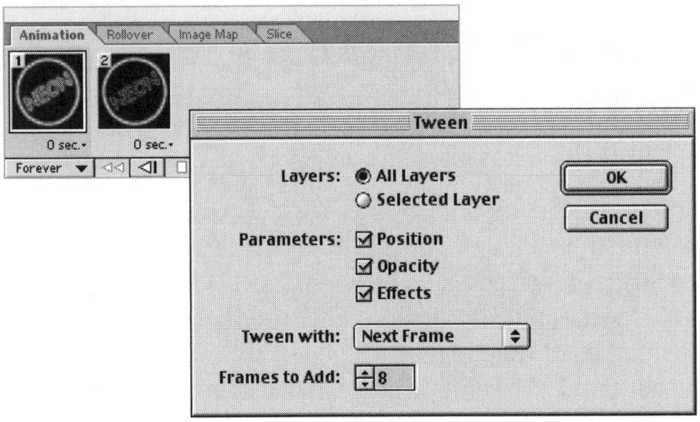

Figure 7-10 The Tween dialog box controls the characteristics of the Tween option

- **Frames To Add** Click in the Frames To Add input box and enter how many frames you want to create between the first and last frames. In this example, enter a value of 8.

3. Click OK to apply the Tween command to the image. ImageReady generates eight new frames, for a total of 10 animation frames, as shown here:

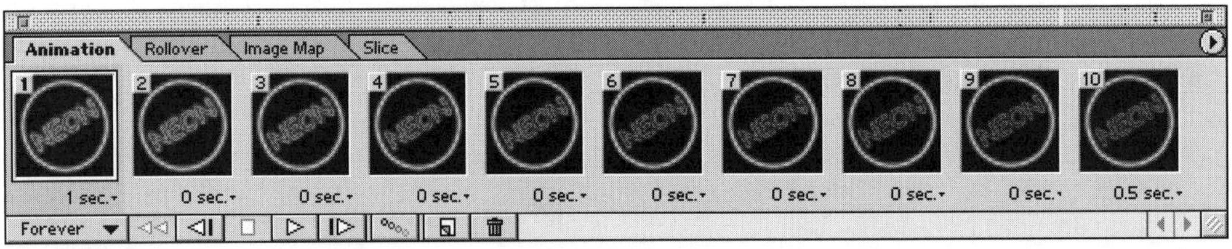

In essence, the *Tween* command creates a series of frames that slowly changed the image in frame 1 into the image in frame 2. When the browser plays the animation, the visitor will see the neon sign slowly pulsing rather than quickly flickering on and off. However, by adding the additional frames, you significantly increase the GIF's size, which will also increase the download time.

Incorporating a Completed Flash Splash Screen into a Web Site

Today, many Web designers use Flash to create animated *splash screens* that act as a short introduction to the site. Consider a splash screen as a ten- or fifteen-second commercial about who you are, what you have to offer, and why visitors should come into your site.

A splash screen is the first page the browser loads and is the first impression you make when visitors access your Web site. Flash is ideal for creating a splash screen because it creates small, fast-loading animation files and can incorporate eye-catching animation and sound.

When you use Flash to create a splash screen, your first consideration is how to display the finished Flash movie on the Web page. Remember, when you work with Flash, you are actually working with two elements: the HTML Web page and the Flash movie. You can choose to display the movie as a percentage of the available browser window size, or you can specify a size, such as 600×800 pixels. Flash movies, because they use vector graphics, are resolution-independent. As such, you can scale them to fit the current browser dimensions—without affecting the quality of the movie output.

A Flash document consists of several elements. There is a timeline, which holds text, images, clip art, and video; a stage, which displays your Flash movie; and a work area, that extends beyond the stage and holds elements that remain outside the visible frame of the final movie, as shown in Figure 7-11.

When you create the Flash document, the stage and timeline instruct the completed Flash movie exactly where and when things appear. Because Flash supports animation paths, not only will the movie elements appear on the Stage; in addition, the path animates the elements and lets you guide and scale them from one point to another. For example, you could place a logo in the upper-left corner of the stage, and use a path to move the logo to the middle of the stage and, at the same time, double the logo's size. Then, five seconds later return the logo to the upper-left corner of the stage

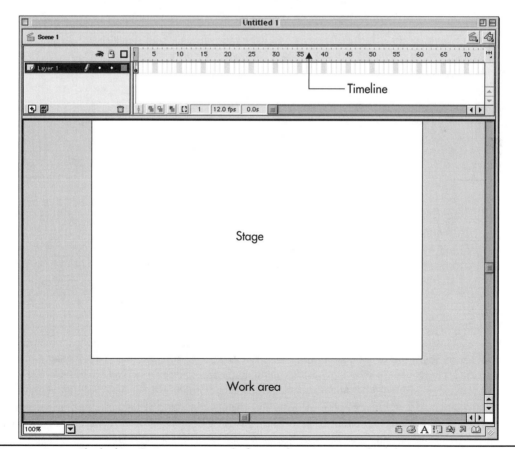

Figure 7-11   A Flash document is comprised of a timeline, stage, and work area

and shrink it back to its original size. Proper use of animation can attract visitors to what you want them to see, and help tell the story of your company in an entertaining and eye-catching way. However, don't forget that animation can also distract from your site's message. Use animation when it supports the message.

USE IT Technically, you don't need to use HTML to display a Flash movie—meaning, most browsers will simply open and display a Flash movie if you type the address of the movie file itself within your browser's address field. However, if you do not add HTML to control its size, the Flash movie will automatically scale to fit the width and height of the browser window. In most cases, it is better if you and not the visitor control the dimensions of the movie. To insert a Flash movie into an HTML document, you must consider the differences between Netscape Navigator and Internet Explorer. The main difference is that you use the <object> tag to insert a Flash movie you want Internet Explorer (and Netscape Navigator 6) to play and the <embed> tag to insert a Flash movie for Netscape Navigator version 4. When you open the following HTML statements within Internet Explorer, the browser will ignore the <embed> tag, which exists for Netscape Navigator. Likewise, if you open the following HTML within Netscape Navigator, the browser will ignore the <object> tag, which exists for Internet Explorer:

```
<object classid="clsid:D27CDB6E-AE6D-11cf-96B8-444553540000"
  codebase="http://download.macromedia.com/pub/shockwave/cabs/flash/
  swflash.cab#version=5,0,0,0"
  width="800"
  height="600"
    <param name="movie" value="splash.swf">
    <param name="quality" value="high">
    <param name="bgcolor" value="#ffffff>
  <embed src="splash.swf"
        quality="high"
        bgcolor="#ffffff"
        width="800"
        height="600"
        type="application/x-shockwave-flash"
        pluginspage="http://www.marcomedia.com/shockwave/download/
        index.cgi? P1_Prod_Version=ShockwaveFlash">
  </embed>
</object>
```

Before a browser can play a Flash movie, the browser must have special software called a Flash plug-in. Rather than simply not playing the Flash movie if a user's browser does not have the plug-in, the previous HTML specifies the location from which the browser can download the plug-in. If a user does not have the Flash plug-in, the browser will display a dialog box that gives the user the option of downloading and installing the plug-in. After the visitors install the plug-in, they can use it to view all other Flash animations in the future. In the previous HTML statements, the *codebase* attribute and the *pluginspage* attribute tell the browser the location from which the visitor can download the plug-in for Internet Explorer and Netscape Navigator, respectively. When you place a Flash animation on your Web site, you should structure your HTML as shown here to give the user the opportunity to install the plug-in.

Within the HTML file, the attributes serve the following purposes:

- *width* and **height**   The *width* and *height* of a Flash movie can be expressed in a percentage of the browser window or in pixels (the same for the <object> and <embed> tags).
- *movie*   The location of the Flash movie you are playing (<object> tag).
- *data*   The location of the Flash movie you are playing (<object> tag).
- *classid*   Identifies the ActiveX control that plays Flash movies (<object> tag).
- *codebase*   The location of the Flash ActiveX controls. This option allows the browser to download the player if it is not available (<object> tag).
- *src*   Identifies the location of the Flash movie (<embed> tag).
- *pluginspage*   The location of the Flash Player plug-in. This option allows the browser to download the player if it is not available (<embed> tag).
- *quality*   Sets the quality of the Flash movie; the options are High, Medium, Low (<object> and <embed> tags).
- *bgcolor*   Sets the background color of the Flash movie, not the HTML page (<object> and <embed> tags).
- *type*   This instructs the browser which plug-in to use to play the Flash movie.

You can use additional settings that will influence when the movie plays and how many times it plays. The preceding code instructs the Web browser to display and play the Flash movie splash.swf in a defined area of 800 by 600 pixels.

Creating a Flash Movie from Scratch

When you work with Flash, you are, in a sense, a movie director. Say, for example, that Hollywood decides to create a new movie. One of the first things they will do is hire a director. The director, in turn, works with actors, sound production crews, set designers, and camera operators to create the movie. In Flash, you are the director, and the actors are the elements within the Flash movie. Actors (or elements) can be text, clip art, photographic images, as well as sound and video.

If you do not have Flash, you can download a 30-day trial version of the software from the Macromedia Web site at http://www.macromedia.com/downloads. When you open Flash for the first time, you see a stage, surrounded by a work area. The stage and work area are where you place the separate pieces (elements) of the animation. In fact, think of the stage as the screen that projects your movie. When elements are on stage, they are visible within the movie; when they are in the work area, they are off-stage and therefore not visible, as shown previously in Figure 7-11.

Directly above the stage is the Flash timeline. Each element in a Flash movie has a timeline that tells the program when the element appears on the stage and when it disappears, or leaves the stage. You can add key frames to the timeline to move the element from one position on the stage to another.

For example, you might have a clip art image enter the Stage on the left, move across, and exit on the right, as shown here:

USE IT   To illustrate how Flash incorporates the stage and timeline to generate movement, you will create a simple, three-frame bouncing ball animation:

1. Start by opening up a new document in Flash (File | New), and name it **bounce**.

2. Select Frame 1 in the Timeline (refer to the previous illustration).

3. Select the Oval drawing tool from the toolbox and draw a circle in the upper-right corner of the stage. You can draw a perfect circle by holding down the SHIFT key while you draw the circle (the color of the circle is not important).

4. Select Frame 2 in the timeline, and add a keyframe (Insert | Keyframe). A small black dot will appear in Frame 2 indicating that it is a keyframe.

5. Select the Move tool (black arrow) from the toolbox and drag the circle to the bottom-center of the stage. Because you are moving the keyframe in Frame 2, you are actually moving a copy of the ball. You now have one ball in the upper-right corner, and one ball located at bottom-center.

6. Select Frame 3 in the Timeline, and add a keyframe (Insert | Keyframe). A small black dot will appear in Frame 3 indicating another keyframe.

7. Drag the bottom circle to the top-right of the stage. Because you are moving the keyframe in Frame 3, you are moving a copy of the ball. You now have three balls, top-left (Frame 1), bottom-center (Frame 2), and top-right (Frame 3).

To view the individual balls in each frame, click on the black dots associated with Frames 1, 2, and 3. As you select a specific frame, the balls appear (one at a time) on the stage, as shown in Figure 7-12.

To preview this simple animation, select Window | Toolbars | Controller (within Windows), or Window | Controller (on a Macintosh). The Controller window opens and displays some VCR type controls. Click the Play button in the Controller window (right-facing arrow) to preview the animation. If you want to see the movie displayed using the Flash Player, select Control | Test Movie. Flash will export the movie into a Flash (.swf) file and open it in the Flash Player.

To save the movie for use on the Internet, select File | Export Movie. Choose Flash Player as the movie format and name the file using the .swf extension. For example, you might name your bouncing ball movie bounce.swf.

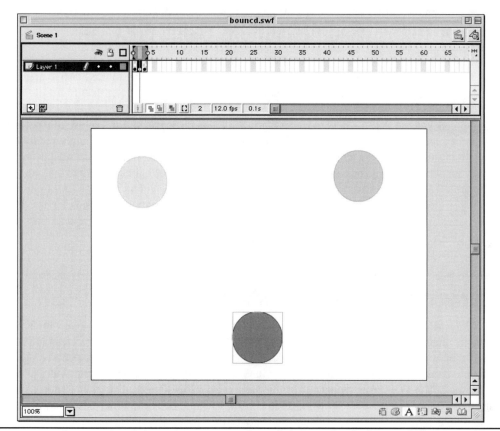

Figure 7-12   The completed document contains three frames with a ball in each frame

This example represents only the smallest fraction of the capabilities of the Flash application. Not only can you create simple keyframe shapes and move them across the Stage, you can also use tweening options to draw all the frames between the keyframes and generate a smoother animation. In addition, you can add more layers to the Timeline palette, and add other objects such as text and images, to enhance the presentation. Flash is truly a high-end, multimedia design tool for the Internet.

To help you get started with Flash, several sites on the Web offer Flash tutorials:

Flash Kit	http://www.flashkit.com
Flash Planet	http://www.flashplanet.com
Flaap.com	http://www.flaap.com/
Macromedia	http://macromedia-flash-5-infocenter.com/

Building Text-Based Animations Using FlaX

Macromedia Flash is one of the most powerful tools designers use for creating animations for use on the Web. Unfortunately, because Flash is such a powerful tool, learning to use Flash to create professional-quality animations can take developers a fair amount of time.

USE IT As you are learning how to create Flash animations, you can take advantage of a powerful shareware program named FlaX that lets you create a large number of high-quality Flash animations in a matter of minutes. To use FlaX, you simply type in the text message you want to animate, such as your company name or corporate slogan, and then choose the animation effect that you desire (see Figure 7-13 below).

After you create the effect that you desire, you can direct FlaX to export the animation to a Flash movie. Using Flax provides a fast and powerful way to create professional quality animations. To download FlaX, visit the GoldShell Web site at http://www.goldshell.com/flax.

Broadcasting Streaming Audio and Video

Across the AM, FM, and XM radio airways, radio stations broadcast signals to anyone who is willing to "tune in" their radios. Likewise, TV stations send their broadcasts across the airwaves (and across cables) at differing frequencies to their television audience. In a similar way, Internet-based radio and TV stations broadcast on the Internet—you can "tune in" by visiting the corresponding Web site using your browser. The Web hosts thousands of Internet-based radio stations that feature sports, news, music, and even talk shows. As shown in Figure 7-14, to "tune in" an Internet-based radio station, you simply visit the site's Web page using your browser.

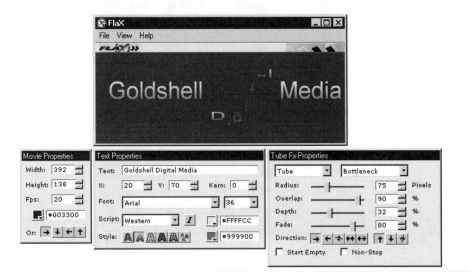

Figure 7-13   Using FlaX to create text-based animations

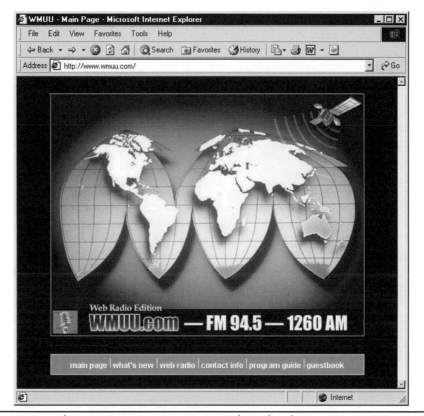

Figure 7-14   Using a browser to tune into an Internet-based radio station

For a larger listing of radio stations, visit the brs radio directory Web site at http://www.web-radio.fm/. Within the Web site, you can view listings of the stations by state, country, or by format (such as jazz, easy listening, oldies, sports, and talk).

Not to be outdone, several sites offer streaming video which you can view within a window on your screen, as shown in Figure 7-15. For a listing of sites that broadcast TV on the Web, visit http://www.tvradioworld.com, http://www.etown.edu/vl/radio.html, or http://dmoz.org/ Arts/Television/News/.

If you have a requirement to broadcast streaming video and audio from your Web site, you essentially have two options with respect to how you make your content available on the Web. First, you can use a third-party company to house and broadcast your data. Normally, such companies will charge you a monthly fee based on the amount of data they must house and a per MB fee for the data their site broadcasts on your behalf. Several companies on the Web offer streaming audio and video housing and broadcasting services:

| Bit Streaming Video | http://www.bitstreamingvideo.com/index.html |
| Host Express.com | http://www.hostexpress.com/real.html |

Prime Internet Network	http://www.primenetwork.net/hosting.html
Stream Audio	http://www.streamaudio.com

Your second option, and the more exciting option (although maybe not the more practical solution, if you must provide quality service 24/7) is to host your own streaming audio and video using your own broadcast server. For years, RealNetworks has been a leader in the field of streaming media. RealNetworks offers a trial server you can download and use on your system (the trial server will run for one year, but will only support 25 simultaneous connections). You can also purchase a full-featured streaming-media server from RealNetworks.

USE IT   To download and test drive the RealNetworks server, visit the RealNetworks Web site at http://www.real.com and follow the links to Products And Services and then search for free products. After the download completes, you will run the program to install the streaming-media server on your system. As soon as you have the server up and running, you will likely want to take it for a streaming-media test drive. To help you get started, the server installation provides some audio clips and video clips to which you (or other users) can connect from your site. To access the streaming media, you will normally include a port number, such as 8080, within the URL, as shown here:

```
http://www.yoursite.com:8080/ramgen/AudioClipName.rm
```

Behind the scenes, network applications refer to one another using numbers, which programmers refer to as *port numbers*. The HTTP browser and server, for example, refer to each other as "the application

Figure 7-15   Viewing streaming video on the Web

running at port 80." A port number is simply a value that corresponds to a specific application. The port number 8080 corresponds to the Real Media streaming server. When you include the port number 8080 in a URL, the remote server does not send the requests to the Web server (which is at port 80), but instead, sends the requests, in this case, to the streaming media server.

 ### *NOTE*

If your server sits behind a firewall, you may need to enable messages to pass through the firewall to port 8080, before your site can send streaming media (or receive requests for streaming media).

Creating Your Own Streaming Media

After you install a streaming-media server, you will likely want to create your own streaming video or audio files. To create a streaming audio file suitable for use by RealNetworks, you can use a program such as Cool Edit that you can download from http://www.syntrillium.com, as shown in Figure 7-16.

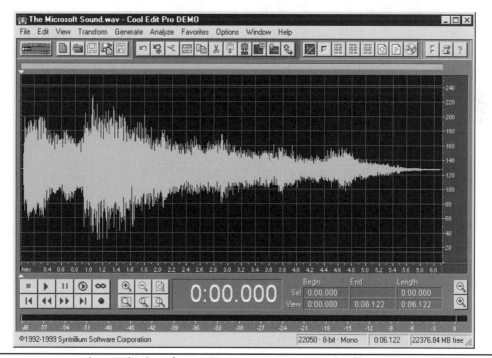

Figure 7-16   Using the Cool Edit software program to convert audio-file types

USE IT Using Cool Edit, you simply open an audio file, and then select File | Save A Copy As to store the file using the .rm (Real Media) format. Then, to place the file on your site for broadcasting, you can create a link to the audio clip within an HTML file, as shown here:

```
<a href="http://www.yoursite.com:8080/ramgen/AudioClipName.rm">
   Launch audio clip
</a>
```

On the Web, you can find several programs that will convert video files from one format to another, such as from AVI to QuickTime. The RealNetworks streaming media server supports MPEG and QuickTime video formats as well as Real video format (with the .rm extension). To place a streaming video within a Web page, you use a link similar to that shown here:

```
<a href="http://www.yoursite.com:8080/ramgen/VideoClipName.rm">
   Launch Streaming Video
</a>
```

Creating a Page that Features a Web Cam

The use of Web cams to provide real-time video has exploded. In the past, Web cams pointed at parks, national monuments, cityscapes, and so on. Today, news agencies point Web cams at city streets to provide users with up-to-the-minute traffic information, as shown in Figure 7-17.

Many companies have also found ways to integrate Web cams into their Web sites to provide valuable tools to customers. For example, many childcare facilities now offer a page that lets parents "look in" throughout the day. In another example, the Maricopa County Jail (in Arizona) uses a Web cam (at http://www.crime.com/info/jailcam.html) to let users view inmate life in the county jail. For a long list of Web cams, visit http://www.ispy.nl.

USE IT Creating a Web cam is actually quite straightforward. To begin, you can choose among many different video cameras to connect to your PC; you also have a variety of ways to connect the camera. Depending on the camera's type, you may connect the camera to a universal serial bus (USB), a TV adapter card, or even a serial port. To eliminate the need to run cabling from your PC to a camera, companies such as X10, whose site you can visit at http://www.x10.com, offer wireless cameras, similar to that shown in Figure 7-18, that can broadcast up to 100 feet to a receiver attached to your PC.

After you connect your camera to your PC, you must install software on your server (or a home PC) that can broadcast the video to users that connect to your site. Several Web sites offer software you can download for free that provides Web cam support:

Surveyor Corp.	http://www.webcamresource.com/
Dual View	http://www.dualview.com/
UK Software	http://www.msagentsoftware.com/easyfreewebcam/

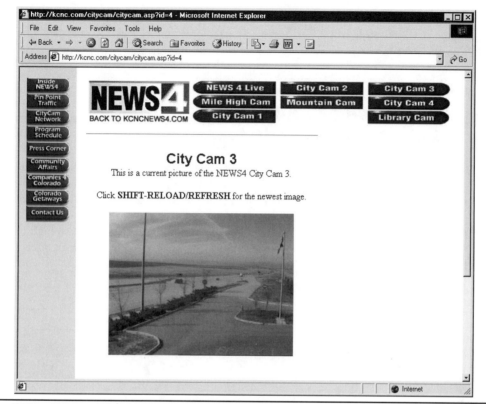

Figure 7-17   Using a Web cam to monitor street traffic

Figure 7-18   Using a wireless camera to create a Web cam page

Depending on the Web cam software you are using, the steps you must perform to integrate the Web cam into an HTML page will differ. Some software, for example, uses a Java applet, others an ActiveX object, and so on.

Integrating Video and Audio into a Web Site Using SMIL (Smile)

As they surf the Web, many users make extensive use of RealPlayer to play back streaming audio and video files. In the Tip "Broadcasting Streaming Audio and Video," you learned how to install a RealNetworks server to provide streaming media from your site. Many sites on the Web provide links to Real audio and Real video files. When the user clicks on a link that corresponds to a Real media object, the browser will normally launch the RealPlayer to play the object, as shown in Figure 7-19.

The following HTML statements, for example, illustrate how a site might integrate a streaming video clip into a Web page:

```
<html>
  <body>
    <h1>Test</h1>
    <hr>
    <a href="http://www.somesite.com:8080/ramgen/real8video.rm">
       Launch video
    </a>
  </body>
</html>
```

The RealPlayer and server exchange streaming media through port 8080. When you link directly to a real media object (either audio or video), you must specify the port number 8080 within the URL.

▶ **NOTE**

In addition to using HTTP to send requests to port 8080, which normally corresponds to a streaming media server, some URLs refer to the Real Time Streaming Protocol (RTSP) and port 554 to access a streaming media server (rstp://www.somesite.com:554/folder/filename). For more information on RSTP, you can view the specification at http://www.rstp.org.

Today, most designers consider a Web site's animation to be state-of-the-art if the Web site integrates Flash, animated GIFs, and streaming media—that's right, if the site uses the animation techniques this chapter presents. The state of animation on the Web, however, is changing. In the future, many sites will build complex animations using a special markup language called SMIL (pronounced "smile"). SMIL is an acronym for Synchronized Multimedia Integration Language. Like HTML (although SMIL more closely resembles XML), SMIL is based on start and end tags. Developers place the SMIL tags in a file with the .smi or .sml extension. Just as a browser uses a plug-in (player) to play a Real video

Figure 7-19   Using RealPlayer to play back a music video

or audio, the browser also uses a player to process the SMIL content you may embed within a Web page. Again, like HTML, SMIL sports myriad tags. To view the complete SMIL specification, visit the W3C Web site at http://www.w3.org/AudioVideo/.

SMIL exists to give you finer control over multimedia applications. This Tip gives you a brief overview of simple SMIL files. You can find a wide range of SMIL files on the Web, which you can examine to learn more about each SMIL tag and attribute.

Assume, for example, that you have a video file that does not have an audio track. Your video, which contains several different sports clips, resides in the file Sports.rm. Also assume that you want to play the audio file Music.rm as background music behind the video. The following SMIL file, Demo1.smi, uses the SMIL <par> tag to direct the player that supports SMIL operations to play the video and audio in parallel:

```
<smil>
  <body>
    <par>
      <video src="Sports.rm" />
      <audio src="Music.rm" />
    </par>
  </body>
</smil>
```

Just as an HTML file begins and ends with the <html> and </html> tags, a SMIL file begins and ends with <smil> and ends with </smil>. Assuming that you had media files named Sports.rm and Music.rm, you can test this SMIL file on your PC in one of several ways. (If you download a

RealAudio file and RealVideo file from the Web, you can rename the files to match the examples so you can test the SMIL application.)

To start, place the SMIL file and the two media files within the same folder. Then, using your browser, within the Windows environment, you can open the file by typing a URL in the form file://c:/foldername/Demo1.smi. Second, you can open the SMIL file directly within the RealPlayer. Third, if you are using a streaming media server, you can place the files on your server and then use your browser to open the file from the server.

In addition to the <par> tag that directs the player to play back objects in parallel, SMIL also provides a <seq> tag that directs the browser to play the items sequentially. The following SMIL statements, for example, would play the three audio files, beginning with One.rm, then Two.rm, and Finally.rm:

```
<smil>
  <body>
    <seq>
      <audio src="One.rm" />
      <audio src="Two.rm" />
      <audio src="Three.rm" />
    </seq>
  </body>
</smil>
```

SMIL, like HTML, provides attributes you can use within tags to fine-turn operations. For example, assume that you want to change the previous SMIL file, Demo1.smi, so that the music starts to play five seconds before the video. You can do so by using the *begin* attribute, as shown here, which directs the browser to wait five seconds after the file begins to start the video:

```
<smil>
  <body>
    <par>
      <video src="Sports.rm" begin="5s" />
      <audio src="Music.rm" />
    </par>
  </body>
</smil>
```

Just as your multimedia applications synchronize audio and video, you may also frequently want to synchronize the display of images and text. For example, assume that you are designing a high-end Karaoke Web site using SMIL. Within your Web site, you might place links to a variety of songs that you implement using SMIL. Within the SMIL files, you launch an audio file. As the audio file plays, your animation displays text on the screen in sync with the music.

To display text within a SMIL file, you must place the text in a specific format, called RealText (just as you store audio and video using Real audio and Real video). Second, to place images within a SMIL animation, you must store the images in the RealPix format. Using RealPix images and SMIL, you can fade images in and out as well as blur and merge images. The RealMedia Web site provides a toolkit for authors that you download for free and then use to create RealText and RealPix files.

When you download and install the RealNetworks server, the installation will place several SMIL files on your system whose contents you can examine using an editor such as Windows Notepad. Figure 7-20 shows the RealPlayer running the Africa.smi file, which at the time of this book's writing, was included with the RealNetworks streaming server.

Figure 7-20   Playing the Africa.smi file within the RealPlayer

CHAPTER 8

JavaScript

TIPS IN THIS CHAPTER

▶ Handling Older Browsers that Do Not Support Scripts   370

▶ Storing Multiple Values in One Variable by Using JavaScript Arrays   371

▶ Letting a Script Make Decisions and Process Accordingly   372

▶ Making Decisions Based on Two or More Conditions   374

▶ Executing Code When a Condition Is Not True   375

▶ Repeating Statements a Specific Number of Times   376

▶ Repeating Statements While a Condition Is True   377

▶ Responding to JavaScript Events   378

▶ Executing JavaScript Statements Within the Body of a Web Page   380

▶ Calling a User-Defined JavaScript Function   382

▶ Calling JavaScript Functions Within an Event Handler   384

▶ Looking Closer at JavaScript Event Handlers   385

▶ Creating an Interactive Navigation Bar with a Mouseover Effect   388

▶ Taking Advantage of the Scripting Object Model Arrays   390

▶ Referring to Web Page Objects by Name Instead of Position Number   392

▶ Leveraging the Contents of the Document Object   393

▶ Taking Advantage of the JavaScript Images Array 396

▶ Exploiting the JavaScript Links Array 398

▶ Changing Web Page Colors Using JavaScript 401

▶ Storing a Cookie on the Visitor's Hard Drive 402

▶ Formatting Cookie Data Using JavaScript 404

▶ Retrieving a Cookie Value from the Cookie File 406

▶ Removing a Cookie from the Cookie File 407

▶ Saving Time and Programming by Using Prewritten (External) Scripts 409

▶ Creating an Animation Using the onLoad Event 410

▶ Displaying Self-Changing Banners Using JavaScript 411

▶ Pointing Hyperlinks to New Files On-the-Fly 413

▶ Pre-caching Pictures to Reduce Image Display Time 415

▶ Creating a Scrolling Marquee Using JavaScript 416

JavaScript is a scripting language Web designers can use to automate tasks within a Web page. Before JavaScript, Web pages contained only graphics or audio files the Web browser was to display onscreen or play back through the computer's speaker(s). HTML tags can describe the way text should look; define things like hyperlinks, tables, and forms; and tell the Web browser to display the contents of files with pictures, movies, or sounds. However, HTML provides no way to tell the browser to carry out a sequence of instructions. As a result, without a scripting language like JavaScript, Web pages have no processing capabilities or any way to interact with the site visitor. For example, although visitors can enter information into forms, HTML only lets the browser send the data to the Web server, because HTML has no way of validating or doing anything else with the information the visitor types or the selections the visitor makes on a form.

Because Web designers need a way to tell Web browsers to do things in addition to displaying text and pictures and sending form data back to the Web server, Netscape (in collaboration with Sun Microsystems) developed JavaScript. Although JavaScript is a scripting language in that it lets you specify a set of commands you want the Web browser to execute, you cannot use JavaScript to create an external program that runs independent of the browser. As such, JavaScript is called a *scripting language*, because it lets you write a *script* (that is, a set of instructions) you want the Web browser to follow. Moreover, you embed the JavaScript statements that make up a script in the Web page HTML.

To write JavaScript, you do not need any special tools; you can use the same text editor you use to create a Web page. Moreover, most popular Web browsers (such as Netscape Navigator and Internet Explorer) have built-in JavaScript support. As such, site visitors don't need to install additional software on their computers; the browser can execute the JavaScript-based scripts you insert in the Web page HTML. All you have to do is enclose your JavaScript statements between a set of start and end script tags (<script></script>), which tell the Web browser to execute the statements instead of displaying them onscreen. For example, the JavaScript statements between the start and end script tags (<script></script>) in the following HTML write a line of text on the Web page and display a "Hello World!" message box, as shown in Figure 8-1:

```
<html>
<body>
   <h1>HTML and Web Design Tips & Techniques</h1>
   <p>This is text typed directly on the Web page.</p>

<script language="JavaScript">
<!--
   document.write("<p>This is a line of text inserted " +
                  "by a JavaScript statement.</p>");
   alert ("My first JavaScript script says: \"Hello World\"!");
// -->
</script>

   <p>Notice the Web browser displays the JavaScript popup<br>
      and waits before displaying the text that follows<br>
      the script embedded in the body of the page.</p>
</body>
</html>
```

Inserting JavaScript Statements in the Web Page HTML

To have the Web browser execute JavaScript statements as it initially displays the Web page, insert the statements between start and end script tags (<script></script>) placed where you want the browser to execute the script. When processing the HTML in the preceding example, the Web browser will display a heading and a single-line paragraph on the Web page. Next, the <script> tag tells the browser it is about to encounter the statements in a script. As a result, the browser does not display the text it finds onscreen. Instead, the browser treats the text on each line as an instruction to perform. In the preceding example, the browser reads *document.write* to mean that it is to execute the WRITE method (function) associated with the *document* object (that is, the current Web page). As such, the browser writes the quoted text within the parentheses on the current Web page ("This is a line of text inserted by a JavaScript statement.", in the preceding example).

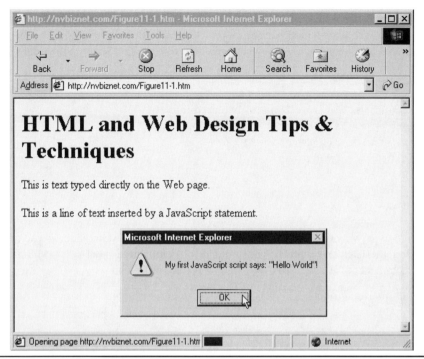

Figure 8-1   A message box displayed by a JavaScript alert statement

The text the JavaScript statement writes appears on the page between the first and second paragraphs of text, because the browser encounters the *document.write( )* function call at that point in the Web page HTML. When the Web browser continues on to the next JavaScript statement, the browser sees the *alert( )* function call and displays an (alert) message box with the text: "My first JavaScript script says: "Hello World"!" in response. Because the message box tells the browser to wait, the browser will not read and display the paragraph following the script until the visitor clicks OK at the bottom center of the message box.

The </script> tag after the last line of the script tells the Web browser it is no longer to interpret text it finds as JavaScript statements. Therefore, the Web browser will display the remaining three lines (in the last paragraph) onscreen. As is always the case, the Web browser works its way through the HTML for a Web page from top to bottom, left to right. Therefore, if you want the Web browser to execute another set of statements after it writes the last paragraph of text in the current example, you would enclose the additional statements you want the browser to execute in another set of start and end script tags (<script></script>) inserted just prior to the </body> tag.

Hiding Scripts from Browsers without JavaScript Support

Unfortunately, not all browsers support JavaScript. Moreover, browsers without JavaScript support do not recognize the start and end script tags (<script></script>) and will, therefore, ignore the tags.

As a result, such browsers will display the text *document.bgColor= "lightyellow"; document.fgColor= "magenta"* on the Web page rather than set the background color to light yellow and the foreground (that is, the default text color) to magenta when presented with the JavaScript in the following HTML:

```
<html>
<body>
  <h1>HTML and Web Design Tips & Techniques</h1>
<script language="JavaScript">
  document.bgColor="lightyellow";
  document.fgColor="magenta";
</script>
</body>
</html>
```

To keep browsers without JavaScript support from displaying the statements in a script onscreen, enclose the script's statements with HTML start and end comment tags (<!-- ... -->). For example, you would "comment out" the script in the example HTML as follows:

```
<script language="JavaScript">
<!--
  document.bgColor="lightyellow";
  document.fgColor="magenta";
// -->
</script>
```

Browsers that do not support JavaScript will ignore the start and end script tags (<script></script>) and everything between the HTML start and end comment tags. Conversely, JavaScript-aware browsers ignore the HTML comment tags when the tags occur within a set of start and end script tags. (The double slash [//] on the line above the </script> tag is a JavaScript comment indicator used to prevent JavaScript-aware browsers from mistaking the double dash [--] that begins the HTML end comment tag for a JavaScript code.)

Understanding JavaScript Functions

When programmers write programs, they normally group related instructions (statements) within a function. Each function has a unique name and should perform a single task. If you were to write a word-processing program, for example, you might create one function that you name *SpellCheck* that checks your document for spelling errors, a second function called *PrintDocument* that prints one or more copies of your document, and a third called *FileOperations* that opens or stores your file.

When you place JavaScript statements within a Web document, you will group your statements within functions. You might create one function that you name *validateForm*, which makes sure the visitor has entered the correct type of data (numeric or text) into all required fields on a form. You might create a second function that you name *calculateSalesTax*, which adds the total cost of items selected on a form and multiplies the sum by the local sales tax rate. The following statements, for example, create a function named *greetVisitor* that displays the message "Welcome to My Site" within a message box, as shown in Figure 8-2:

```
function greetVisitor()
{
 alert("Welcome to My Site");
 return;
}
```

Within a Web page, each JavaScript function must have a unique name. The function definition starts with the keyword *function*, followed by the function's name and then an optional list of parameters enclosed in parentheses. (You will learn how to use parameters to pass values into the function in "Passing Values to and from a JavaScript Function," later in this chapter.) After the function name and optional parameter list, you enclose the JavaScript statements that perform the function's task within left and right braces ({ }).

Most JavaScript statements you write should end with a semicolon (;). Because some Web browsers ignore carriage returns and line feed characters, omitting the optional semicolon at the end of your JavaScript statements can produce unpredictable results. To ensure proper execution, place a semicolon (;) at the end of each statement, whether you write statements one per line or write several statements on the same line within the script.

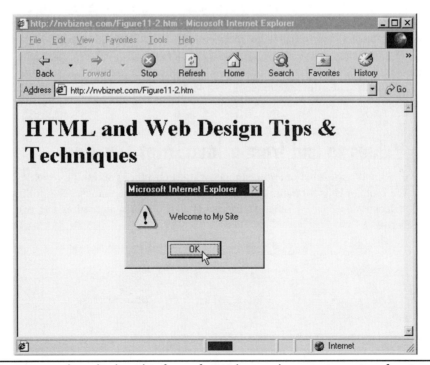

Figure 8-2   Message box displayed in front of a Web page by a statement in a function

At the end of each function (just before the closing right brace [}]), insert the keyword *return*. The return statement, as its name implies, returns control of the Web browser to the statement that called the function. To call a JavaScript function, write the function's name in an expression or as an independent statement within a function or script. For example, you might write the following HTML to have the Web browser call (that is, execute) the *greetVisitor()* function as the browser begins to load a Web page:

```
<body>
  <h1>HTML and Web Design Tips & Techniques</h1>
<script language="JavaScript">
<!--
  greetVisitor();
// -->
</script>
  <p>Notice the Web browser displays the JavaScript popup<br>
    and waits before displaying the text that follows<br>
    the script embedded in the body of the page.</p>
</body>
```

If you call a function from the body of a Web page (as shown by the *greetVisitor();* statement between the start and end script tags [<script></script>] in the preceding HTML), the browser stops reading the Web page HTML and executes the statements in the function. The browser does not return to the point in the page at which it called the function until the browser executes a *return* statement or reaches the closing brace (}) at the end of the function. As you will learn in "Responding to JavaScript Events" later in this chapter, you can also use event handlers to call JavaScript functions. If you use an event handler to call a function, the browser will continue to load and display the Web page while the event handler calls the function and then waits for the system to execute the statements in the function.

Passing Values to and from a JavaScript Function

When you call a JavaScript function, you can pass values into the function in variables called *parameters*. The function's list of parameters appears between the parentheses that follow the name in the function declaration. For example, the following code declares a function with two parameters: *Age* and *ShoeSize*:

```
function computeIQ(Age, ShoeSize)
{
 Age = Age * 2;
 alert("2 x Age = " + Age + "; Shoe Size = " + ShoeSize);
 return (Age * ShoeSize) / 2;
}
```

To pass values to the *computeIQ()* function, you include the parameters in the function call as follows:

```
IQ = computeIQ(YearsOld, 10);
```

When the browser calls *computeIQ()*, the browser will pass the value of the variable *YearsOld* to *computeIQ()* in the *Age* parameter and will pass the number 10 to the function through the *ShoeSize* parameter. In short, the browser assigns values to function parameters by position. That is, the browser assigns the first value in the function call to the first parameter in the declaration, the second value to the second parameter, and so on. Therefore, if you set *YearsOld* to 20 and then call *computeIQ()*, the function will display a message box that reads "2×Age = 40; Shoe Size = 10". Unlike the functions in previous examples, *computeIQ()* returns a value to the caller. To return a value from a function, insert the value you want to send back immediately after the keyword *return*, as shown on the last line before the closing brace (}) in this example.

Understanding JavaScript Reserved Words

When you name a function or create variables to store information as the Web browser executes statements in a function or script, you must choose function and variable names that do not conflict with the JavaScript *reserved words*, which are listed in Table 8-1. Reserved words are words that have special meaning within JavaScript. The word *function*, for example, identifies the start of a function declaration, just as the word *return* tells the browser to return to the point at which the browser called the function. If you try to use reserved words for function or variable names, the Web browser will abort execution of the script or function when it encounters the improper usage of the reserved word.

Using Comments to Explain Your Script's Processing

As you create scripts and functions, you can place notes among the JavaScript statements that explain the processing you want the browser to do. Programmers refer to such notes as *comments.* Placing comments throughout your code not only helps other developers understand your script, but may also help you to remember why your script uses specific statements—especially after you have not looked

abstract	continue	finally	instanceof	protected	throws
boolean	default	float	int	public	transient
break	delete	for	interface	return	true
byte	do	function	long	short	try
case	double	goto	native	static	typeof
catch	else	if	new	super switch	var
char	extends	implements	null	synchronized	void
class	false	import	package	this	while
const	final	in	private	throw	with

Table 8-1   JavaScript Reserved Words

at the script for several months. To place a comment within your JavaScript code, insert two forward slashes (//) and type your note, as shown here:

```
// This is a comment
```

When the Web browser encounters the double slashes, it ignores all text remaining on that line. In addition to single-line comments that start with a double slash (//), JavaScript also supports block comments that begin with a slash and an asterisk (/*) and which end with an asterisk and a slash (*/), as shown here:

```
/*
   The browser will ignore all the text it encounters
   after the slash-asterisk that starts the comment
   block until it reads the asterisk-slash that
   ends the multiline block comment.
*/
```

When the application encounters a block comment, the browser will ignore all the text that appears between the /* and */. Developers often "comment out" sections of code to determine the source of errors in script processing. Suppose, for example, that you had a Web page in which you defined the following JavaScript function:

```
function visitorSignIn(Form)
{
  if (Form.fname.value == "") return false;
  if (Form.lname.value == "") return false;
  if (Form.email.value == "") return false;

//load another Web page
   self.location = "htdocs/LoggedIn.htm"

  return;
}
```

If *visitorSignIn()* failed to display the new Web page (LoggedIn.htm) for some reason, you might comment out the first three statements in the function as follows:

```
function visitorSignIn(Form)
{
/*
  if (Form.fname.value == "") return false;
  if (Form.lname.value == "") return false;
  if (Form.email.value == "") return false;
*/
//load another Web page
   self.location = "htdocs/LoggedIn.htm"
```

```
 return;
}
```

Then, if the browser displays the page LoggedIn.htm after calling the function, you would know the "problem" must have something to do with the first three statements in the function, because without them, the function loads the new page. Similarly, if the browser still fails to load the new Web page, the error must involve the statement that is supposed to load the page (that is, *self.location*). After you correct the source of an error, be sure to remove the /* and */ or the // you used to turn one or more statements in a script or function into a comment during the test/debug process.

Declaring Variables Within a Script or Function

Within JavaScript statements, the script stores information by using variables. Unlike most programming languages, you do not specify the type of information you plan to store in a variable when you declare the variable. Instead, JavaScript assigns a data type to each variable based on the type of the data you store in the variable. Moreover, a variable's data type can change depending on the operation in which you use the variable. The following statements define several different variables:

```
var BookTitle, ChapterNumber;
var Publisher;
var StringValue = "10", var IntValue = 20;
var ConcatenatedValue = StringValue + IntValue;//Result: "1020"
var AdditionValue = IntValue + StringValue;    //Result: 30
```

Therefore, to declare variables within a script, you specify the variable name(s) after the keyword *var* (as shown in the first two lines). If you want to give a variable an initial value, you can follow the variable name with the assignment operator (=) and an initial value (as shown in the last three lines of the script). JavaScript imposes the following restrictions on variable declarations:

- A variable name cannot conflict with (that is, be the same as) a JavaScript keyword.
- Variable names must start with a letter or underscore character (_) and may contain numbers or letters after the first character.
- Variable names cannot contain any blanks or punctuation characters.

JavaScript names and keywords (like *var*) are case-sensitive, which means that *var* is a keyword, whereas *Var* is not. Similarly, *stringvalue* is a different variable name from *StringValue*.

Understanding JavaScript Operators

Operators let you combine variables and/or literal values into expressions that produce values, which you can then display, store in variables, or use as a part of other expressions. You can group JavaScript operators into several classes based on the operator's purpose. Table 8-2 shows JavaScript arithmetic operators that require two variables, values, or expressions (one on either side of the operator).

Operator	Purpose	Example
+	Addition	expression + expression
–	Subtraction	expression – expression
*	Multiplication	expression * expression
/	Division	expression / expression
%	Modulus (return the remainder of a division)	expression % expression

Table 8-2 JavaScript (Binary) Arithmetic Operators

Although you could classify the first three operators in Table 8-3 as arithmetic, they are called *unary* operators, because they require only one expression on which to operate.

When you place a double-plus (++) or double-minus (––) in front of a variable (that is, you *prefix* the operator), the operation takes place before the assignment of value. Conversely, if you place the increment or decrement operator after a variable (that is, you *postfix* the operator), the operation takes place after the assignment of value. For example:

```
i = 10;
j = i++;   //j=10, i=11
j = --i;   //i=9, j=9
```

The complement operator—that is, the exclamation point (!)—returns the reverse of the Boolean (true or false) value in a variable while leaving the value in the variable unchanged after. For example:

```
TestResult = true;
document.write(TestResult);   //true
document.write(!TestResult); //false
```

Comparison operators, as their group name implies, let you compare one expression, variable, or literal value to another. Typically, you use comparison operators (shown in Table 8-4) within conditional statements (such as *if* and *if-else*), and control loops (such as *while* and *for*).

Operator	Purpose	Example
++	Increment by 1	variable++ or ++variable
––	Decrement by 1	variable–– or ––variable
–	Negation	–expression
!	Complement (the *Not* operator)	!expression

Table 8-3 JavaScript Unary Operators

Operator	Purpose	Example
<	Less than	expression < expression
>	Greater than	expression > expression
<=	Less than or equal to	expression <= expression
>=	Greater than or equal to	expression >= expression
==	Equal to	expression == expression
!=	Not equal to	expression != expression
?:	Conditional (*if-else*)	(Boolean expression) ? TRUE expression : FALSE expression

Table 8-4 JavaScript Comparison Operators

The conditional operator (?:) is a special comparison operator used only in an assignment statement in which the operator functions as an *if-else* statement used to decide which of two values to assign. For example, in the following statement, if the expression in parentheses evaluates to True, the statement assigns the first value following the question mark (?) to the variable. Conversely, if the expression evaluates to False, the statement assigns the value that follows the colon (:), as shown here:

```
PassingThisClass = (GPA >= 2.0) ? "yes" : "no";
```

Logical operators let you compare two Boolean values. Typically, you will use the logical operators shown in Table 8-5 to compare the results of two comparison expressions in a conditional statement or control loop.

Conditional and Repetitive Processing

A script is a list of instructions the Web browser executes to accomplish a specific task. All the simple scripts you reviewed up to this point in the chapter have the Web browser start with the first statement and execute each statement, in order, to the end of the script or function. As your scripts become more complex, you will sometimes want the browser to execute one set of statements if one condition is true and, possibly, another set if the condition is false. In other words, you will want your browser to make decisions and respond accordingly. Scripts that make decisions perform *conditional*

Operator	Purpose	Example
&&	And	expression && expression
‖	Or	expression ‖ expression

Table 8-5 JavaScript Logical Operators

processing. In other words, based on the outcome of one or more conditions, the browser will execute specific statements.

To make decisions, your scripts must first perform some type of test. For example, one script might test if the password a visitor enters is correct and a second script might test if the phone number a visitor enters has the correct number of digits. To perform such tests, your scripts will use the JavaScript comparison operators listed previously in Table 8-4. *Comparison operators* let your scripts test how one value "compares" to another. In other words, using comparison operators, your scripts can test if one value is equal to, greater than, or less than a second value. When your scripts use relational operators to compare two values, the result of the comparison is either true or false—meaning, the two values either satisfy the comparison (true) or they do not (false). The Tip titled "Letting a Script Make Decisions and Process Accordingly" will show you how to use three different forms of *if-then-else* statements that let the Web browser decide which of the script's statements to execute based on the results of comparisons.

Closely related to decision making within your scripts is the ability to repeat one or more statements a specific number of times or until a known condition occurs. Two of the Tips that follow this introduction will show you how to use *for* statements and *while* loops to repeat operations in your scripts and functions. The *while* statement lets you create a loop in which the browser executes a set of JavaScript statements repeatedly as long as the specified condition remains true. Meanwhile, the *for* statement lets you create a loop in which the browser executes a set of statements a fixed number of times or until a predetermined event or condition occurs.

Inserting JavaScript Functions Within the Web Page HTML

Although you can define them elsewhere in the Web page HTML, embed your JavaScript functions at the end of the header section of the Web page (that is, just before the </head> tag at the beginning of the page). Placing your JavaScript functions in the Web page header guarantees that the Web browser will load the functions before the visitor can trigger an event that tells the browser to execute any one of them. Placing all the functions in a single location near the top of the Web page HTML also makes the functions easier for you to find when you need to modify them. (The Web browser will have no trouble in finding the functions it needs to execute, as long as you embed them somewhere in the HTML file.)

Handling Older Browsers that Do Not Support Scripts

As you learned at the beginning of this chapter, you embed JavaScript statements in your Web page HTML between start and end script tags (<script></script>). The browser executes the script when the browser loads the Web page or when you tell it to do so with a call to a user-defined function that contains the script's statements. Unfortunately, HTML's support for scripts is independent of the actual scripting language. When you include a script within an HTML document, you have no guarantee that the visitor's Web browser supports the execution of scripts. To alert a visitor when the browser does not support the execution of scripts, insert start and end no script support section tags (<noscript></noscript>) into the HTML document containing the script. The tags must appear somewhere within the Web page body (that is, somewhere between the page start and end body tags [<body></body>]). The best place to insert the <noscript> tag is immediately after a </script> tag.

USE IT Between the start and end no script support section tags (<noscript></noscript>), enter the text you want the browser to display when the Web browser does not support scripts. The following HTML code demonstrates the use of the start and end noscript support section tags(<noscript></noscript>):

```
<html>
<head>
  <title>A JavaScript example </title>
</head>
<body>
<script language="JavaScript">
<!--
  document.write("This is a JavaScript example!")
// -->
</script>
<noscript> No JavaScript support… SORRY!</noscript>
</body>
</html>
```

Although the script in this example simply tells the visitor that his or her browser does not have JavaScript support, you should provide additional content. For example, you might explain how to turn on JavaScript within the browser or provide a hyperlink a visitor can use to download a browser with JavaScript support (such as Netscape Navigator or Internet Explorer).

The interesting thing about the start and end no script support section tags (<noscript></noscript>) is that they are nonfunctional tags. If a browser supports scripts, it recognizes the tags and ignores the information between the tags. Browsers that do not recognize the <script> tag (that is, browsers without script support) also do not recognize the start and end no script support section tags (<noscript></noscript>). As a result, such browsers ignore the tags and simply display anything you place between the tags as ordinary Web page text.

Storing Multiple Values in One Variable by Using JavaScript Arrays

An array is a variable that contains a set of values of the same data type. Suppose, for example, that you have five items for sale and you need to track the count and price of each item you have on hand. You could create five variables to hold each of the five item counts and five other variables to hold the prices as follows:

```
var ItemCount1, ItemCount2, ItemCount3, ItemCount4, ItemCount5
var ItemPrice1, ItemPrice2, ItemPrice3, ItemPrice4, ItemPrice5
```

Now, imagine that you have an inventory of 100 different items. You will spend a lot of time declaring and typing variable names in function statements where you need to deal with the items all at once (such as to compute a total inventory value).

USE IT Fortunately JavaScript gives you a way to create a single variable that can hold any number of values you want—an *array*. For example, to create arrays that can hold the count and price for each item in an inventory of 100 items, you would use the following statements:

```
var ItemCount = new Array(100);
var ItemPrice = new Array(100);
```

Each of the two arrays, *ItemCount* and *ItemPrice*, has 100 storage areas called *elements*, and each element works like a variable, in that each element can hold one value. You reference each element in an array with an *index* by using the following syntax: *ArrayName[Index]*. Because JavaScript arrays are zero-based, the first item in an array has an index of zero (0). Therefore, to store the price and count of item 1, you would write something like this:

```
ItemCount[0] = 5;
ItemPrice[0] = 125.50;
```

Similarly, you would store the count and price of item 100 in array index 99 with statements like this:

```
ItemCount[99] = 10;
ItemPrice[99] = 89.95;
```

Letting a Script Make Decisions and Process Accordingly

The *if* statement lets your scripts perform a test and then execute statements based on the result of the test. The *if* statement normally performs a test using a JavaScript comparison operator. If the test result is true, the script executes the statement that follows the *if*. On the other hand, if the test result is false, the script ignores (skips) the statement that follows. The format of the *if* statement is as follows:

```
if (condition_is_true)
  statement;
```

USE IT Notice that you do not place a semicolon (;) after the *if (condition)* that starts the *if* statement because the *if* statement continues to the next line. The following script defines a *check18()* function that uses the *if* statement to compare the value stored in the variable *Age* to value 18. If the age is greater than or equal to 18, the script displays a message to the visitor. Otherwise, if the value is less than 18, the script simply returns control to the application that called the function:

```
function check18()
{
  var Age = 25;
```

```
if (Age >= 18)
  alert("Register to vote at www.VoterRegistration.com");
return;
}
```

When your scripts use the *if* statement for conditional processing, there will be times when your scripts must perform only one statement if the condition is true and other times when your script must perform several statements. When your script performs only one statement following an *if*, the statement is a *simple statement*:

```
if (Age >= 18)
  alert("Register to vote at www.VoterRegistration.com");
```

For your script to perform several statements when a condition evaluates as true, you must group the statements within left and right braces ({ }). The statements that appear within the braces make up a *compound statement*, as shown here:

```
if (Password != "Secret")
  {
  alert("Invalid Password");
  window.location = "htdocs/InvalidPassword.htm"
  }
```

▶ *NOTE*

It is not important that you remember the terms simple and compound statements, but rather that you know that you must group related statements within the left and right braces ({ }).

At the beginning of this Tip, you used an *if* statement to determine whether a visitor's age was greater than or equal to 18. If the condition was true, the script displayed a message to the visitor. If the condition was false, meaning the age was less than 18, the script did not display a message, it simply ended. In most cases, your scripts will want to specify one set of statements that executes when the condition is true and a second set that executes if the condition is false. To provide the statements that execute when the condition is false, your scripts must use the *else* statement. The format of the *else* statement is as follows:

```
if (condition_is_true)
  statement;
else
  statement;
```

The following script changes the *check18()* function to use an *if-else* statement to test whether the value of the *Age* variable is greater than or equal to 18. If the condition is true, the script will display a message reminding the visitor to vote. If the condition is false, the script will display a message telling the visitor to "Study hard and get good grades!":

```
function Check18()
{
 var Age = 15;

 if (Age >= 18)
   alert("Don't forget to vote!");
 else
   alert("Study hard and get good grades!");
 return;
}
```

Previously in this Tip, you used an *if-else* statement to execute one set of statements when a condition is true and another set of statements if the condition is false. There may be times, however, when your scripts must test several different related conditions. For example, assume that your script must determine a visitor's area code. To do so, your script must test for the many different cities. The following statement uses a series of *if-else* statements to illustrate a simplified example of the processing your script might perform:

```
if (City == "New York")
  AreaCode = 212;
else if (City == "Houston")
  AreaCode = 281;
else if (City == "Phoenix")
  AreaCode = 602;
else if (City == "Seattle")
  AreaCode = 206;
else
  AreaCode = 0;    // Program does not know city's area code
```

When the script performs the first *if* statement, it first tests whether the city is New York. If so, the script assigns the *AreaCode* variable the value 212. If the city is not New York, the script performs the *else if* to test if the city is Houston. The script will perform this processing for each city until it finds a matching city or it reaches the final *else* statement. If the script does not find a matching city, it assigns the variable *AreaCode* the value 0.

Making Decisions Based on Two or More Conditions

USE IT As your scripts become more complex, you sometimes must test more than one condition at a time. For example, your script might test if a visitor's age is greater than 20, and less than 50. Likewise, you might test whether a visitor owns a dog or a cat. To perform such operations, you will use the JavaScript logical AND operator (&&) and the logical OR operator (||). When your scripts use the logical AND or the logical OR operator to test more than one condition, you will place each condition within parentheses, as in the following *if* statement, which uses the logical OR operator to test whether the visitor owns a dog or a cat:

```
if ((VisitorOwnsaDog) || (VisitorOwnsaCat))
  // Statement
```

In a similar way, the following statement uses a logical AND operator to determine if a visitor's age is in the range 20 to 50:

```
if ((Age >= 20) && (Age <= 50))
  // Statement
```

When your scripts use the logical AND operator (&&), all the conditions within the statement must be true for the entire condition to evaluate as true. If any condition is false, the entire condition becomes false. For example, if the visitor's age is not greater than or equal to 20, the previous condition is false. Likewise, if the visitor's age is greater than 50, the condition is false. In order for the condition to be true, the visitor must be 20 or older and 50 or younger.

For a condition that uses the logical OR operator to evaluate as true, only one condition must be true. For example, if the visitor owns a dog, the previous condition is true. If the visitor owns a cat, the condition is true. Also, if the visitor owns both a dog and a cat, the condition is true. The only time the condition would be false is if the visitor owns neither a dog nor a cat, in which case both conditions are false and the overall condition evaluates as false.

Executing Code When a Condition Is Not True

USE IT   When your scripts test for specific conditions, you may sometimes want the scripts to perform specific statements when a condition is true. In a similar way, you may sometimes want your scripts to perform a set of statements when a condition is *not* true. The JavaScript *Not* operator—the exclamation point [!]—lets your scripts test whether a condition is not true. For example, the following statement tests whether the visitor does not own a car:

```
if (!Owns_a_Car)
  // Statement
```

The *Not* operator converts a false condition to true and a true condition to false. For example, assume that the visitor does not own a car. The variable *Owns_a_Car* would contain the value false. When the JavaScript performs the condition using the *Not* operator, JavaScript uses the variable's current value (false), and applies the *Not* operator. The *Not* operator makes the false value true. The entire condition then evaluates as true, and the script performs the corresponding statement. The following statement uses the *Not* operator to test if a visitor's password is not equal to "Secret":

```
if (Password != "Secret")
  // Statement
```

Repeating Statements a Specific Number of Times

One of the most common operations your scripts will perform is to repeat one or more statements a specific number of times, in which case you will use the *for* statement. When your script uses a *for* statement, the script must specify a variable, called a *control variable*, that keeps track of the number of times the loop executes. For example, the following *for* loop uses the variable *Count* to keep track of the number of times the script has executed the loop, so processing will stop with the fifth iteration:

```
for (Count = 1; Count <= 5; Count++)
  // Statement;
```

USE IT   The *for* statement consists of four parts: an initialization, a test condition, the statements that are to repeat, and an increment. To begin, the statement *Count = 1;* assigns the control variable's starting value. The *for* loop performs this initialization one time, when the loop first starts. Next, the loop tests the condition *Count <= 5;*. If the condition is true, the *for* loop will execute the statement that follows. If the condition is false, the loop will end, and the script will continue its execution with the first statement that follows the loop. If the condition is true and the *for* loop executes the statement, the loop will then increment the variable *Count* using the statement *Count++*. Finally, the script tests the condition *Count <= 5;*. If the condition is still true, the script will execute the statements, and the process of incrementing and then testing the variable *Count* will repeat. The following script creates the *oneToFive()* function that uses the *for* loop to display the values 1 through 5:

```
function oneToFive()
{
 var Count;
 for (Count = 1; Count <= 5; Count++)
   alert("Count = " + Count);
}
```

Within a *for* loop, you are not restricted to incrementing the value by 1. The following *for* loop, for example, displays every fifth number from 0 through 25:

```
for (Count = 0; Count <= 25; Count += 5)
   alert("Count = " + Count);
```

Note the statement the *for* loop uses to increment the variable *Count*:

```
Count += 5;
```

When you want to add a value to a variable's current value and then assign the result to the same variable, JavaScript lets your scripts do so in one of two ways. First, assuming that your script must add the value 5 to the variable *Count*, your script can do as shown here:

```
Count = Count + 5;
```

Second, JavaScript lets you use the shorthand notation shown here to add the value 5 to the variable *Count*:

```
Count += 5;
```

Because it is easier to write, programmers commonly use this shorthand notation within loops. When you use a *for* loop, JavaScript does not limit your loops to counting up. The following *for* loop, for example, counts down from 10 to 1:

```
for (Count = 10; Count >= 1; Count--)
  // Statement
```

Finally, JavaScript also does not restrict a *for* loop to using integer values for the control variable. The following statement, for example, uses a floating-point value, which the loop initializes to 0.0 and then increments by 0.10:

```
for (Value = 0.0; Value <= 1.0; Value += 0.10)
  // Statement
```

Repeating Statements While a Condition Is True

In the preceding Tip, you learned that the JavaScript *for* loop lets your scripts repeat one or more statements a specific number of times. For situations in which your scripts must loop as long as a specific condition is true, but not necessarily a specific number of times, your scripts can use the JavaScript *while* loop. The general format of the *while* loop is as follows:

```
while (Condition_Is_True)
  statement;
```

USE IT   When your script encounters a *while* loop, your script first tests the specified condition. If the condition is true, the script will execute the *while* loop's statements. After the last statement in the loop executes, the *while* loop again tests the condition. If the condition is still true, the loop's statements will repeat, and this process will continue. When the condition finally becomes false, the loop will end, and your script will continue its execution at the first statement that follows the loop. The following script uses a *while* loop to prompt the visitor to enter a password repeatedly, until the visitor enters the password "Secret":

```
function getPassword()
{
```

```
var Password = "";  // Assign an initial value != "Secret"

while (Password != "Secret")
  Password = prompt("Password", "");
alt("You're in!");
}
```

Responding to JavaScript Events

Near the beginning of this chapter, you learned how to call (that is, how to execute) a JavaScript function by typing the function's name as a statement in a script or as part of an expression. Sometimes, however, you want the browser to call a function in response to an event that occurs some time after the browser loads the Web page. For example, you might have an "exit" function you want the browser to execute when the visitor clicks a hyperlink to move on to another Web page. Similarly, you might want the browser to call a form validation function when the visitor clicks a form's Submit button.

Fortunately, JavaScript provides a number of *event handlers* you can insert in your HTML tags to watch for specific events. When an event occurs, the event handler monitoring it will tell the Web browser to execute the statement or function you associated with the event. Table 8-6 summarizes JavaScript events and what triggers them to occur.

Event	Applies to	Occurs When	Event Handler
abort	Images	Visitor aborts the loading of an image (for example, by clicking a link or clicking the Web browser's Stop button)	*onAbort*
blur	Frames, windows, and all form elements	Visitor removes input focus from a frame, form element, frame, or window	*onBlur*
click	Checkboxes, hyperlinks, image map hotspots, pushbuttons, radio buttons, Submit buttons, Reset buttons	Visitor clicks a form element or hyperlink	*onClick*
change	Select lists, text fields, textarea fields	Visitor changes the value in a form element	*onChange*
error	Images, windows	Web browser encounters an error in loading a document or an image	*onError*
focus	Frames, windows, and all form elements	Visitor gives input focus to a frame, form element, or window	*onFocus*
load	Document body	Web browser loads the Web page	*onLoad*

Table 8-6   JavaScript Events that Trigger the Execution of a Statement or Function

Event	Applies to	Occurs When	Event Handler
mouseout	Areas, hyperlinks	Visitor moves mouse pointer out of an image map hotspot or off of a hyperlink	*onMouseout*
mouseover	Areas, hyperlinks	User moves mouse pointer over a hyperlink or into an area with an image map hotspot	*onMouseover*
reset	Forms	Visitor clicks a form's Reset button	*onReset*
select	Text fields, textarea fields	Visitor selects an input field on a form	*onSelect*
submit	Forms	Visitor clicks a form's Submit button	*onSubmit*
unload	Document body	Visitor exits the Web page	*onUnload*

Table 8-6   JavaScript Events that Trigger the Execution of a Statement or Function *(continued)*

If you want a JavaScript event handler to tell the Web browser to execute a function you declared on the page, you must associate the function with a specific event handler that watches for the event to occur. For example, if you want to greet the user with a message in a dialog box as the browser loads the page, you would assign a JavaScript function to the *onLoad* event handler. Likewise, if you want to highlight a hyperlink (text or graphics image) as the visitor moves the mouse pointer across it, you would assign JavaScript functions to the *onMouseover* and *onMouseout* event handlers.

USE IT   To assign a JavaScript function to an event, select the event's event handler and then decide which of the Web page objects you want the event handler to monitor. Next, add the event handler to the HTML tag used to insert the object on the Web page. Suppose, for example, that you use the following code to place a button labeled "Click Me!" on the Web page:

```
<form>
  <input type="button" value="Click Me!"
    onClick="youClickedIt()">
</form>
```

By inserting the *onClick* event handler in the button's <input> tag you tell the *onClick* event handler to monitor the button for a mouse click. When the visitor clicks the button, the event handler tells the Web browser to execute the *youClickedIt()* function. Similarly, if you want the browser to call a function when the visitor moves the mouse pointer over a hyperlink, insert the *onMouseover* event handler in the hyperlink's <a> tag as follows:

```
<a href="http://www.NVBizNet.com" onMouseover="youAreOnIt()">
  NVBizNet.com</a>
```

Placing the *onMouseover* event handler in the hyperlink's <a> tag instructs the *onMouseover* event handler to tell the Web browser to execute the *youAreOnIt()* function whenever the visitor moves the mouse pointer across or onto the hyperlink's anchor text. In short, you associate an event with a particular object on a Web page by placing the event handler in the object's tag as: *eventHandler="functionCall()"*. Or, if you want to execute one or more statements instead of calling a function, insert in the object's HTML tag an event handler reference in the form of *eventHandler="statements"*.

Executing JavaScript Statements Within the Body of a Web Page

As you have learned, a JavaScript function is a set of statements that perform a specific task. There are two types of functions: those that you create, and those JavaScript provides. Whereas functions you create are called *user-defined functions,* those that come standard with JavaScript are called *built-in functions.* As you read about JavaScript, you will find that programmers (especially those who work with object-oriented programming languages) also refer to functions as *methods.*

Within an object-oriented language (such as JavaScript), functions (methods) often correspond to a specific object (such as a document, that is, a Web page, or something on the Web page such as a form, a pushbutton, or a hyperlink). As you will learn, JavaScript defines several objects that you can use in the scripts you create. For example, JavaScript associates a *document* object with your Web page. Using the *document* object, you can use JavaScript to manipulate the text and other elements (objects) the Web page contains.

USE IT   Each JavaScript object will have one or more functions you can call to perform a specific task. To call an object's function (that is, to call one of the methods associated with an object), you specify the object's name, followed by a dot (.) and then the method (function) name. For example, to use the document object's *write* method to place text on the current Web page, you would write a JavaScript statement similar to the following in your script:

```
document.write("Message");
```

To JavaScript, the current Web page is the *document* object, and its *write* method (as the function's name implies) writes the text you pass to it on the Web page. Therefore, to have the Web browser execute a function (that is, a method) associated with an object, you write the function call as *objectName.method()* in your JavaScript. The following HTML code, for example, calls the *document.write()* method (that is, the *document* object's *write* method) twice to display the text "Welcome to the Web page with my first JavaScript script.", as shown in Figure 8-3.

```
<html>
<body>
   <h1>HTML & Web Design Tips & Techniques</h1>
   <p>The following Script will insert text on a Web page.</p>

<script>
<!--
```

```
//write a line of text on the Web page
  document.write("<p><b>Welcome to the Web page ");
  document.write("with my first JavaScript script.</b></p>");
// -->
</script>

  <p>If your Web browser supports JavaScript you will see
     a "Welcome" message just before this text.
</body>
</html>
```

Note the script in this example calls the *document.write( )* method twice due to the publisher's restriction that lines of code in this book must wrap at column 64. When you call the same method to write text onto a Web page, you can pass a string of whatever length you like. As such, you could (and would) display the second paragraph in this example using a single *document.write( )* method call.

When you use the *document.write( )* method to insert text on a Web page, be sure to include any HTML formatting tags along with the text you want displayed. Notice that the text in the second *document.write( )* function call in the current example did not start with the <p> tag. As a result, when the Web browser read the HTML generated by the function, it displayed the second text string (on the same line) right after the text from the first function call.

You can also use JavaScript string manipulation operators (you learned about earlier in this chapter) to create the text string you pass to the *document.write( )* method. For example, the preceding code used two *document.write( )* function calls to write a single line of text. If you wanted to break up a long text string in your code for formatting purposes, while still having the browser display it as a single line of text, you could use multiple *document.write( )* function calls (as shown in the example). Or, you could use the plus (+) string concatenation operator and a single function call as follows:

```
document.write("<p><b>Welcome to the Web page " +
               "with my first JavaScript script.</b></p>");
```

HTML & Web Design Tips & Techniques

The following Script will insert text on a Web page.

Welcome to the Web page with my first JavaScript script.

If your Web browser supports JavaScript you will see a "Welcome" message just before this text.

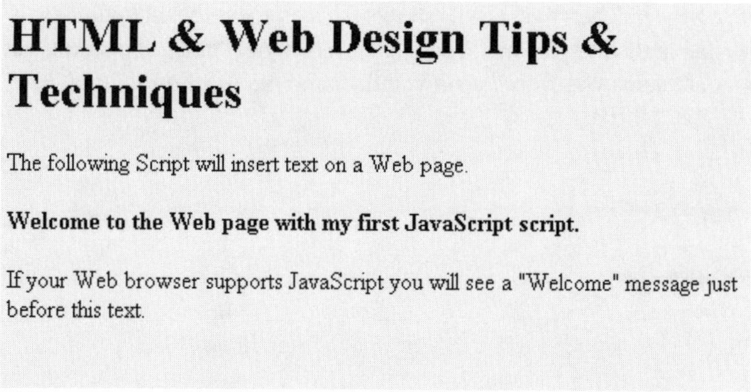

Figure 8-3   A Web page with a JavaScript-generated "Welcome" message

Calling a User-Defined JavaScript Function

In the preceding Tip, you learned that functions you write are called *user-defined* functions while those that come standard with JavaScript itself are called *built-in* functions (or methods). You also learned how to call built-in functions (such as the *document.write()* method) by writing the function call as: *objectName.method()* in a JavaScript statement. Writing *document.write("message")* in a JavaScript statement, for example, tells the Web browser to call the *document* object's *write* method (function) and pass to it the text string "message."

USE IT   The JavaScript built-in functions are associated with an object (such as the *document* object, or Web page); the user-defined functions you write are not. As such, instead of calling a user-defined function by referring to an object and a function as *objectName.functionName()* in a JavaScript statement, you call a function you create by simply including its name in a statement or expression. For example, the following HTML tells the Web browser to call a user-defined function named *helloWorld* after it calls the *document.write()* method to insert a line of text on the Web current Web page:

```
<script>
<!--
//write a line of text on the Web page
  document.write("<p>Click the mouse on the OK button to continue.</p>")
//call the user-defined JavaScript function "helloWorld"
  helloWorld();
// -->
</script>
```

As you may have guessed, before you can call a user-defined function, you have to "define" or declare the function. Programmers refer to statements that define the function's name and list its statements as the function's *declaration*. The following HTML statements first show the *helloWorld()* function declaration, which occurs between the first set of start and end script tags (<script></script>) within the Web page header. Then the HTML shows the statement that actually "calls" the function just before the </script> tag in the body of the Web page. (When you "call" a function, you tell the Web browser to execute statements you listed when you declared the function.)

```
<html>
<head>
<script language="JavaScript">
<!--
  function helloWorld()
  {
  alert("Hello from my first JavaScript function!")
  return;
  }
// -->
</script>
```

```
</head>
<body>
  <h1>Web Page with a JavaScript Function</h1>
  <p>The following Script will display the message box.</p>

<script>
<!--
//write a line of text on the Web page
  document.write("<p>Click OK to continue.</p>")
//call the JavaScript function "helloWorld()"
  helloWorld();
// -->
</script>

  <p>Now that you have cleared the message box,
    how do you get it to display again?</p>
  <p>After all, there is no HTML "looping" tag to tell the
    browser to read through the Web page HTML and execute
    the function again. </p>
</body>
</html>
```

As is always the case, the <script> tag in the Web page header tells the Web browser it is to treat everything until the subsequent </script> tag as JavaScript statements. However, when the Web browser reads the JavaScript in the header section of the HTML in the current example, it loads the user-defined JavaScript function *helloWorld()* into memory, but does not execute the function's statements. This behavior (of not executing statements when reading a function declaration) has nothing to do with the fact that you declared the function in the Web page header. Whenever the Web browser encounters the keyword *function* in a script, the browser knows that it is about to read a function declaration and not a statement it is supposed to execute immediately. As a result, the browser simply reads into memory the function name, its parameters (between parentheses following the name), and the function's statements (everything between the left and right brackets [{}] that follow the function's parameter list).

By convention, the browser does not execute the statements in a JavaScript function (such as the *helloWorld()* function in the current example) until you tell it to do so. As mentioned previously, you can *call* a function (that is, tell the Web browser to execute the statements in a function) by writing the function's name in a statement of a script you insert between start and end script tags (<script></script>) in the body section of a Web page. Moreover, as you will learn in the next Tip, you can use an event handler to tell the Web browser to call a function based on an event (such as clicking a hyperlink on the Web page) or an element (such as an input field or push button) on a form. As a general rule, you should put all of your JavaScript function declarations between a single set of start and end script tags (<script></script>) in the header section of the Web page HTML (as shown in the current example).

Because the browser loads the contents of the header section first, putting all of your function declarations in the header ensures that the browser has read them into memory by the time it reaches the point in the Web page HTML where you make your first function call. Loading user-defined functions before displaying any portion of the Web page also ensures the functions you have associated with event handlers will be available (and not undefined) when the visitor starts interacting with the objects on the Web page and thereby triggering events that cause event handlers to call your functions.

Calling JavaScript Functions Within an Event Handler

In the preceding Tip you learned how to call (that is, how to execute the statements in) a JavaScript function by writing a statement that includes the function's name. You can also have the Web browser execute a JavaScript function automatically in response to an event. The events to which you can have the Web browser react include when the browser loads or unloads a Web page and when a user clicks or moves the mouse pointer over a pushbutton, hyperlink, or field on a form. An event handler is an item you add to an HTML tag that tells the Web browser to execute a JavaScript statement or to call a function in response to something the browser or user has done.

USE IT   For example, if you want the Web browser to "do something" before it unloads a Web page, add the *onUnload* event handler to the Web page <body> tag. The *onUnload* event handler in the <body> tag of the Web page defined by the following HTML statements will display a message box similar to that shown in Figure 8-4, whenever the Web browser leaves the current Web page.

```
<html>
<body onUnload="alert('Thanks for stopping by!')">
   <h1>HTML & Web Design Tips & Techniques</h1>
   <p>Go to <a href="http://www.NVBizNet.com">NVBizNet.com</a>.
   </p>
</body>
</html>
```

The Web browser performs the same action whether it is replacing the Web page in response to a click on a hyperlink or a click on the browser's Back, Forward, or Refresh button. Whenever the visitor tells the browser to unload the current Web page and replace it with another page (or even the same Web page), the *onUnload* event handler in this example tells the Web browser to display a message box. The visitor must then click OK at the bottom of the message box before the Web browser will unload the Web page in favor of another. In addition to executing one or more JavaScript statements, you can also have an event handler call a user-defined or built-in function.

Figure 8-4   Message box displayed each time the Web browser unloads the Web page

For example, the *onClick* event handler in the <a> tag of the following HTML statements tells the Web browser to call the user- defined function *youWannaLeave( )* when the visitor clicks the <a> tag's hyperlinked text:

```
<html>
<head>
<script>
<!--
  function youWannaLeave()
  {
   alert("Leaving so soon?");
  }
// -->
</script>
</head>
<body>
  <h1>HTML & Web Design Tips & Techniques</h1>
  <p>Go to <a href="http://www.NVBizNet.com"
           onClick="youWannaLeave()">NVBizNet.com</a>.</p>
</body>
</html>
```

Thus, using an event handler to execute a statement or to call a function is a two-step process. First, identify the Web page object with which you wish to associate the event. Second, insert the event handler you want to use into the object's HTML tag as *eventHandler="statement"' or eventHandler="functionName()"*. In the first example of the current Tip, in which the event relates to unloading the body (that is, the content) of the Web page itself, you inserted the onUnload event handler in the <body> tag. Similarly, in the second example, in which the event relates to the visitor's click of a hyperlink, you inserted the *onClick* event handler in the hyperlink's <a> tag. The following Tip contains a table that shows you a list of all of the JavaScript event handlers and the action of the visitor or Web browser for which the event handler is waiting. For now, the important things to understand are that you place event handlers in the HTML tags, and you can use event handlers to execute one or more statements or to call a function.

Looking Closer at JavaScript Event Handlers

Event handlers are special items you use within HTML tags to have the Web browser execute a JavaScript statement or call a function when the visitor clicks or moves the mouse over items on the Web page. In fact, JavaScript provides an event handler for just about anything a user can do to interact with a Web page. In addition, JavaScript even provides event handlers such as *onLoad* and *onUnload* that deal with actions the browser takes on the Web page itself. Moreover, you can use *onResize* and *onMove* to watch for the visitor moving or changing the size of the Web browser application window.

The first column in Table 8-7 lists the names of the available event handlers. The table's second column (on the right) explains the visitor or Web browser action that triggers each event along with the HTML tags in which you can insert the event handler. To use an event handler to execute a JavaScript function or statement(s), select the object on the Web page you want the Web browser to monitor. Then, insert the name of the event handler along with the statement(s) the Web browser is to execute or function it is to call in the tag you used to put the object on the page as *eventHandler="Statement(s)"* or *eventHandler="functionName()"*.

Event Handler	Occurs When
onAbort	Visitor aborts the loading of an image (for example, by clicking a hyperlink or the browser's Stop button). Tag: <img>
onBlur	Visitor removes the input focus from a window, frame, or form element. Tags: <body>, <frame>, <frameset>, <ilayer>, <input>, <layer>, <select>
onChange	Visitor changes the value in a form element such as a text area or text field, or makes a new selection on a selection list. Tags: <input>, <select>
onClick	Visitor clicks a hyperlink or a form element such as a checkbox, pushbutton, radio button, Reset button, or Submit button. Tags: <a>, <area>, <body>, <input>
onDoubleClick	Visitor double-clicks a hyperlink or a form element such as a checkbox, pushbutton, radio button, Reset button, or Submit button. Tags: <a>, <area>, <body>, <input>
onDragDrop	Visitor drags and drops an object onto the Web browser window. Tags: <body>, <frame>, <frameset>
onError	Browser encounters an error when loading an image or Web page. Tags: <body>, <frame>, <frameset>, <img>
onFocus	Visitor moves the input focus to a window or form element. Tags: <body>, <frame>, <frameset>, <ilayer>, <input>, <layer>, <select>
onKeyDown	Visitor depresses a key on the keyboard. Tags: <a>, <body>, <frame>, <frameset>, <img>, <input>
onKeyPress	Visitor presses or holds down a key in a text area form element. Tags: <a>, <body>, <frame>, <frameset>, <img>, <input>
onKeyUp	Visitor releases a key in a text area form element. Tags: <a>, <body>, <frame>, <frameset>, <img>, <input>

Table 8-7 JavaScript Event Handlers, Descriptions of Events They Handle, and the Tags in Which You Can Insert Them

Event Handler	Occurs When
onLoad	After the browser loads a Web page or image. Tags: <body>, <frame>, <frameset>, <img>, <layer>
onMouseDown	Visitor depresses a mouse button. Tags: <a>, <body>, <input>
onMouseOut	Visitor moves the mouse pointer out of an image map area or off of a hyperlink. Tags: <a>, <ilayer>, <layer>
onMouseOver	Visitor moves the mouse pointer into an image map area or onto a hyperlink. Tags: <a>, <ilayer>, <layer>
onMouseUp	Visitor releases a mouse button. Tags: <a>, <body>, <input>
onMove	Visitor or script moves the application window. Tags: <body>, <frame>, <frameset>
onReset	Visitor clicks the Reset button on a form. Tag: <form>
onResize	Visitor or script changes the size of the application window. Tags: <body>, <frame>, <frameset>
onSelect	Visitor selects text in a form text area or text field. Tag: <input>
onSubmit	Visitor clicks the Submit button on a form. Tag: <form>
onUnload	Before the browser replaces the Web page with another Web page. Tags: <body>, <frame>, <frameset>

Table 8-7   JavaScript Event Handlers, Descriptions of Events They Handle, and the Tags in Which You Can Insert Them *(continued)*

USE IT   Suppose, for example, that you want the Web browser to call a user-defined function named *calculateTotals( )* when the visitor clicks a particular pushbutton on a form. Insert the *onClick* event handler in the pushbutton's definition as shown by the last item in the following <input> tag:

```
<form>
  <input type="button" name="CalcTotals" value="Calc"
       onClick="calculateTotals()">
</form>
```

Then, as a result of the *onClick* event handler in the <input> tag in the current example, the Web browser will execute the statements in the *calculateTotals( )* function whenever the visitor clicks the button named CalcTotals.

Creating an Interactive Navigation Bar with a Mouseover Effect

During your travels among sites on the Web, you have no doubt come across navigation bars (or menus) whose buttons change appearance as you move the mouse pointer over them. JavaScript lets you create navigation bars that exhibit similar mouseover effects. All you need are two different graphics images for each button on the navigation bar and *onMouseOver()* and *onMouseOut()* event handlers in the <a> tag that defines the hyperlink anchored to each button on the menu bar. For example, you can use HTML statements similar to the following to display a navigation menu such as the one shown in Figure 8-5.

```
<html>
<body>
<table>
  <tr>
    <td width="87" height="34">
      <a href="Figure8-5.htm">
      <img border="0" src="images/YellowChoice1.jpg"
           width="87" height="34"></a></td>
    <td width="87" height="34">
      <a href="Figure8-5.htm">
      <img border="0" src="images/YellowChoice2.jpg"
           width="87" height="34"></a></td>
    <td width="87" height="34">
      <a href="Figure8-5.htm">
      <img border="0" src="images/YellowChoice3.jpg"
           width="87" height="34"></a></td>
  </tr>
</table>
</body>
</html>
```

By inserting a picture between a set of start and end hyperlink anchor tags(<a></a>), you can use the graphics image as you would hyperlinked text. When the visitor clicks anywhere on a graphics image (button) in the navigation bar, the browser retrieves the Web page named by the *href* attribute in the <a> tag that precedes each picture.

USE IT To add a mouseover (also called a rollover) effect to the navigation bar, you need the Web browser to change the graphics image displayed when the site visitor moves the mouse pointer over any one of the buttons on the menu. Therefore, you need two graphics images, one for when the mouse pointer is over the menu button and one for when it is not. (For best results, make sure the two images are approximately the same size.) Next, you need to declare a JavaScript function similar to the following that will swap images by changing the image *src* property in the document's *images* array. (When you replace one image with another in the *images* array, the Web

Figure 8-5   Graphics "buttons" on a static navigation bar

browser automatically displays the new image onscreen in place of the original image in the browser's application window.)

```
<script language="JavaScript">
<!--
  function newImage(ImageIndex, NewButton)
  {
//generate the pathname to the new image file
   NewButton = "images/"+NewButton+".jpg"
//substitute the new image for the existing image
   document.images[ImageIndex].src = NewButton
   return;
  }
// -->
</script>
```

The first statement in the *newImage()* function uses the string passed in the *NewButton* parameter to generate the pathname of the image the Web browser is to display onscreen. The function's second executable statement then replaces the pathname of the current image in the *src* property of the document's *images* array with the pathname of the new image the browser is to display. (The value of the *ImageIndex* parameter tells the function which *src* property in the array to replace.) After you declare—preferably in the header section of the Web page—a function (such as *newImage()*) that swaps image pathnames, you need only to add the *onMouseOver* and *onMouseOut* events to each <a> tag as follows:

```
<table>
  <tr>
    <td width="87" height="34">
      <a href="Figure8-3.htm"
         onMouseOver="newImage(0,'CyanChoice1')"
         onMouseOut="newImage(0,'YellowChoice1')">
      <img border="0" src="images/YellowChoice1.jpg"
           width="87" height="34"></a></td>
    <td width="87" height="34">
      <a href="Figure8-3.htm"
         onMouseOver="newImage(1,'CyanChoice2')"
         onMouseOut="newImage(1,'YellowChoice2')">
      <img border="0" src="images/YellowChoice2.jpg"
```

```
        width="87" height="34"></a></td>
  <td width="87" height="34">
    <a href="Figure8-3.htm"
       onMouseOver="newImage(2,'CyanChoice3')"
       onMouseOut="newImage(2,'YellowChoice3')">
    <img border="0" src="images/YellowChoice3.jpg"
       width="87" height="34"></a></td>
  </tr>
</table>
```

The *onMouseOver* event handler tells the Web browser to call the *newImage()* function each time the visitor places the mouse pointer over the hyperlink, that is, over the graphics image "button" on the navigation bar. Similarly, the *onMouseOut* event tells the Web browser to call the *newImage()* function when the visitor moves the mouse pointer off the hyperlink (that is, of the graphics image) on the navigation bar. When you review the code, you will see that the *onMouseOver* event handler passes a new (cyan versus yellow) image to the *newImage()* function while the *onMouseOut* event handler passes the original (yellow) image specified by the *src* attribute within the <img> tag to the *newImage()* function. As a result, the navigation bars "buttons" appear as shown in Figure 8-5, except for the one button over which the site visitor has placed the mouse pointer, which appears as shown in Figure 8-6.

Taking Advantage of the Scripting Object Model Arrays

JavaScript "sees" a Web page as a set of properties and objects stored in an array named *document*. The properties that the Web browser stores in the *document* array include the Web page foreground (that is, text), background, and hypertext colors, cookies, form elements, images, and so on. By modifying the values stored in the document array, you can change not only the appearance of a Web page but also the objects on the page. For example, you might read the contents of the *document.cookies* property to determine settings the visitor previously selected for Web page background and text colors. You could then set the values of *document.bgColor* and *document.fgColor* to change the colors of the background and Web page text (respectively) to the selections the visitor made. After changing the Web page colors, you would likely also set the values of *document.linkColor* and *document.vlinkColor* to change the colors of unvisited and visited hyperlink text so that neither is the same color as the Web page background or its nonhyperlinked text. In short, the elements in the document array let you change the Web page content and appearance based on cookie values or visitor input at the Web browser.

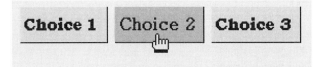

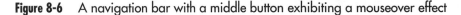

Figure 8-6   A navigation bar with a middle button exhibiting a mouseover effect

USE IT To set or view a Web page property, start with the word *document*, add a dot(.), and then the name of the property. For example, the following JavaScript—when inserted after the start <body> tag in the Web page HTML—will display the Web page title, URL, and date last modified as part of the Web page:

```
<script>
<!--
   document.write ("<b>Web Page Title: </b>" +
                    document.title + "<br>");
   document.write ("<b>URL/Web Address: </b>" +
                    document.URL + "<br>");
   document.write ("<b>Last modified on: </b>" +
                    document.lastModified  + "<br>");
//-->
</script>
```

In addition to the properties that describe the Web page and the way it looks, the document array also includes arrays that in turn hold the properties of the objects inserted on the page. Web page objects described by their own arrays within the document array include anchors, applets, embeds, forms, frames, images, links, and plug-ins. The Web browser puts information about each of the objects on a Web page into the array that bears the object's name. For example, the browser puts the properties of plug-ins into the *document.plugins* array, the properties of hyperlinks into the *document.links* array, the properties of images into the *document.images* array, and so on.

You can reference the properties of objects on the Web page through the document array in the same manner that you referenced the properties of the Web page itself as: *document.objectType [ObjectTypeIndex].property*. For example, you access the value of the *src* attribute (or URL) of the third image on the Web page as *document.images[2].src*. (Remember, the first element in a JavaScript arrays has an index of zero (0), so the third element has an index of two (2) and not three (3).)

The form element in the document array is a special case. Not only is the form element an array (like the *images*, *links*, and *plugins* objects) to let you address each of perhaps several forms on a Web page, but the *document.forms* element is itself an array. Therefore, whereas you can address the properties of a form (such as its name, method, action, and so on) as *document.forms[FormIndex]. property*, you address the properties of each of the elements on a form as *documents.forms[FormIndex]. elements[ElementIndex].property*. The Web page shown in Figure 8-7 has five objects: three graphics images, one form, and three hyperlinks. Note that the two graphics buttons (Submit and Clear) near the bottom of the page in this example are actually hyperlinked images, thus count as both image and hyperlink objects.

As the Web browser displays the objects on the Web page shown in Figure 8-7, the browser puts the properties of the graphics image inserted with the first <img> tag in the Web page HTML into the first element of the document *images* array: *document.images[0]*. Similarly, the browser stores the properties of the second graphic it finds in the Web page HTML (the Submit button graphic) into the second element of the document *images* array: *document.images[1]*. Moreover, the browser stores the properties of the third image on the page (the Reset button graphic) into the third element of the document *images* array: *document.images[2]*. (As is the case with all other objects on the Web page,

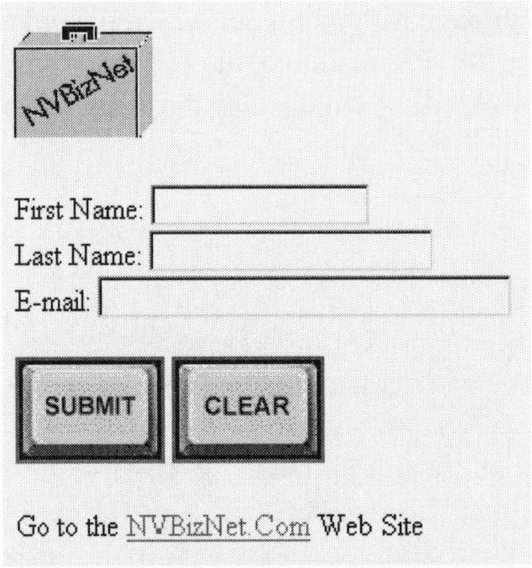

Figure 8-7 A Web page with five JavaScript addressable objects

the browser stores the properties of each image in its object type (in this case, *images*) array in the order in which it finds the <img> tags in the Web page HTML.)

The browser stores the properties (name, length, action method, and so on) of the first (and only) form on the current Web page into the first element of the document *forms* array: *document.forms[0]*. Like a Web page itself, a form normally has more than one element. (The form in the current example has three elements: the three text input fields.) To store the properties of a form's elements, the Web browser must create the document *forms* array as an array of *elements* arrays. After doing so, the Web browser can store the properties of the elements of the form in the current example in *document.forms[0]. elements[0]*, *document.forms[0].elements[1]*, and *document.forms[0].elements[2]*. (The browser stores the form element properties in the *document.forms elements* array in the order in which they are defined on the form.) Finally, the browser stores the properties of the three hyperlinks on the page in the current example in the document *links* array elements: *document.links[0]*, *document.links[1]*, and *document.links[2]* in the order in which it finds the hyperlink <a> in the Web page HTML. (The Web has three hyperlinks—one anchored to each of the buttons at the bottom of the form and the third anchored to the text "NVBizNet.Com" at bottom of the page.)

Referring to Web Page Objects by Name Instead of Position Number

In the preceding Tip, you learned how to use the document array to access the properties of the objects on a Web page. However, to work with an object's properties you must first determine the object's position (or index) in the document array. To determine the index, count the HTML tags used to insert objects of the same type, until you reach the tag for the object you want. After you know the object's index, you can reference any of the object's properties as *document.objectType*

[ObjectTypeIndex].property. For example, to set the *src* attribute (or property) of the third image on a Web page, you might tell the Web browser to execute the JavaScript statement:

```
document.images[2].src = "images/NVBizNet.JPG";
```

JavaScript arrays use zero-based indexing, which means that the third array element resides at *document.images[2]*. Therefore, the preceding statement will change the source (or pathname) of the image inserted on the Web page by the third <img> tag. (After you change the *src* property of an image in the document *images* array, the Web browser will change the image displayed on the Web page.)

Referring to Web page objects by number becomes tedious if there are many of the same type on the page. Suppose, for example, that you want to replace an image near the end of a Web page with another picture. You must first determine the image's index in the document array by counting the <img> tags that precede the <img> tag whose *src* property you want to change. If you have twenty or thirty thumbnail images on the page, you will be doing a lot of counting, which will increase your likelihood of making an error.

USE IT   Conversely, if you name a Web page object, you can then work with the object's properties by name as *document.ObjectName.property*. For example, if the Web page HTML includes the following <img> tag:

```
<img name="logo" width="78" height="61"
  src="images/picture.GIF">.
```

Without counting the number of <img> tags that precede the <img> tag whose *src* attribute you want to change, you can replace the image on the Web page with another picture by telling the Web browser to execute a JavaScript statement such as this:

```
document.logo.src = "images/NVBizNet.JPG";
```

Although the current example only shows you how to use an object's name in place of an array name and index value, the same holds true for the other types of objects as well. In other words, if an object on a Web page includes the *name* attribute in the tag that inserts the object on the page, you can replace *objectType[ObjectTypeIndex]* with the name of the object and write the JavaScript reference to one of the object's properties as *document.ObjectName.property*.

Leveraging the Contents of the Document Object

Before the Web browser draws a Web page onscreen, the browser creates a *document* object. As it reads the Web page HTML, the browser stores Web page attribute values (such as background color, foreground color, title, and so on) in the document object. The browser also adds to the document object arrays in which the browser stores the properties of forms, hyperlinks, images, and Java applets inserted on the page.

One way in which to take advantage of the document object is to fill in form elements for your visitor. Suppose, for example, that you have a Web page with an order form. Rather than have a customer fill in the name, shipping address, and billing information each time he or she places an order, store these values in a cookie on the visitor's hard drive. You can than retrieve the cookie values previously stored from the document object's *document.cookie* property and use them to fill in the form elements within the document object's *document.forms* array.

USE IT   Another way to use the document object is to prevent visitors from linking directly to a Web page within the members-only section of a Web site. The *document.referrer* property gives the URL of the Web page with the hyperlink used to get to the current page. If the character string stored in *document.referrer* is blank or does not include your site's domain name, your script can have the browser load the login screen by executing a statement similar to this:

```
self.location = "http://www.NVBizNet.com/login.htm"
```

(*Document.referrer* is blank when the visitor types the URL into the browser Address field or clicks a bookmark or favorite.) In this example, the Web browser displays the login page (login.htm) rather than the Web page the visitor requested.

The following sections discuss Web page properties and object arrays you can access in the browser-created *document* object. At the end of each description, you will find the format for or an example of a JavaScript statement you can include in a script to view and (in some cases) change the value of a Web page property. (Properties of the *document* object's *images* and *links* object arrays are discussed in the next two Tips.)

alinkColor   *alinkColor* is the color of the "active" hyperlink on the Web page. A hyperlink is "active" during the brief moment after the visitor clicks it and before the Web browser follows the hyperlink to another Web page. To set the color you want the Web browser to use when displaying an "active" hyperlink, execute a JavaScript statement in the form *document.alinkColor = ActiveLinkColor* (where *ActiveLinkColor* is a hexadecimal triplet that gives the RGB color values in the form "#RRGGBB").

anchors   This is a read-only array of "named" hyperlinks (that is, anchor objects) whose <a> tags include a *name* attribute. You can only use the anchors property to retrieve the number of "named" hyperlinks on the Web page with a JavaScript statement such as *AnchorCount = document.anchors.length.*

applets   This is an array of methods and properties from all Java applets defined between start and end applet tags (<applet></applet>) on the Web page. You can access any public properties and execute any public methods defined in a Java applet on a Web page by referring to a public applet property as *document.applets[AppletIndex].property* and a public applet method with: *document.applets[AppletIndex].method( ).* If the <applet> tag has a *name* attribute, you can use *document. AppletName.property* and *document.AppletName.method(). To retrieve the number of Java applets* on a Web page, execute a JavaScript statement such as *AppletCount = document.applets.length.* (You will learn more about Java applets in the Java chapter later in this book.)

bgColor   This is the current color of the Web page background. You can change the color of the Web page background with a statement such as *document.bgColor = BackgroundColor* (where *BackgroundColor* is a hexadecimal triplet that gives the RGB color values in the form "#RRGGBB").

cookie A cookie is a string of up to 4,096 (4K) characters that you can store on the site visitor's hard drive. (You will learn how to create and save a cookie in a Tip later in this chapter.) To retrieve a cookie's name and value pairs into a string you can parse, tell the Web browser to execute a statement such as *CookieValue = document.cookie*.

domain This is the domain name of the Web server that sent the Web page to the browser. You can retrieve the Web server's domain name with a statement such as *DomainName = document.domain*. (The Web browser uses the information in the *domain* property as the filename of the document's cookie file.)

embeds An array of fields and methods from all objects inserted on the Web page using the start and end embedded object tags (<embed></embed>). (Typically, you embed files, for which the Web browser must use a plug-in to display—such as QuickTime (.mov) files.) If the embedded object is Java-enabled, you can access one of its fields as *document.embeds[EmbeddedObjectIndex].field* (or by name as *document.EmbeddedObjectName.field*, if the <embed> tag has a *name* attribute). You can execute a method in a Java-enabled embedded object as *document.embeds[EmbeddedObjectIndex]. method()* (or by name as *document.EmbeddedObjectName.method()*, if the <embed> tag includes a *name* attribute). To retrieve the number of embedded objects on a Web page, execute a JavaScript statement such as *EmbeddedObjectCount = document.embeds.length*.

fgColor This is the color of the Web page text content not modified by a *color* attribute in a <font> tag. To change the color of the text, execute a statement such as *document.fgColor = TextColor* (where *TextColor* is a hexadecimal triplet that gives the RGB color values in the form "#RRGGBB").

forms This is an array of properties and methods for all form objects on the Web page. The chapter on HTML forms (earlier in this book) discusses the methods and properties available for each form object and for each of the elements within the form objects. In general, you can access a form property with *document.forms[FormIndex].property* (or *document.FormName.property*) and a form method with a JavaScript statement in the form *document.forms[FormIndex].method()* (or *document. FormName.method()*). To work the property of an element on the form, in turn, use a JavaScript statement in the form *document.forms[FormIndex].elements[ElementIndex].property* (or *document. FormName.ElementName.property*). Similarly, to execute a form element's method, refer to the method you want to use in a JavaScript statement as *document.forms[FormIndex].elements [ElementIndex].method()* (or *document.FormName.ElementName.method()*).

images This is an array of properties for images inserted on the Web page with <img> tags. The read-only image properties you can retrieve are *name*, *border*, *complete*, *height*, *width*, *vspace*, and *hspace*. You can also use JavaScript to retrieve and modify an image's *lowsrc* and *src* properties. To access an image property use *document.images[ImageIndex].property* or *document.ImageName. property*.

lastModified This is a read-only character string that contains the local date and time at which the Web page was last modified. To retrieve the *lastModified* property, use a JavaScript statement such as *LastModified = document.lastModified*.

linkColor   The color of unvisited hyperlinks on the Web page. To set the color you want the Web browser to use when displaying unvisited hyperlinks, execute a JavaScript statement such as *document. linkColor = LinkColor* (where *LinkColor* is a hexadecimal triplet that gives the RGB color values in the form "#RRGGBB").

links   This is an array with the properties of the hyperlinks on the Web page. The hyperlink properties you can access and modify through the links array are hash, hostname, host, href, pathname, port, protocol, search, and frame. To work with a property of a particular hyperlink, use *document.links[LinkIndex]. property* or *document.LinkName.property*.

referrer   This is a read-only string with the Web address of the Web page that contains the hyperlink the visitor used to get to the current page. For example, if the site visitor clicked a hyperlink on the Web page index.htm at NVBizNet.com to get to the current Web page, you can retrieve the full URL of the index.htm Web page on the NVBizNet.com Web site with a statement such as *CameFromURL = document.referrer*. (The value of *document.referrer* will be blank if the visitor retrieved the current Web page by entering a URL into the browser's Address field or if the visitor selected the current page from the browser's list of favorites.)

title   This is a read-only string with the title of the current Web page as defined by the text between start and end title tags (<title></title>). You can retrieve the value of the Web page title with a statement such as *PageTitle = document.title*.

url   This is a read-only string with the full URL (that is, the Web address) of the current Web page. You can retrieve the value of the URL with a statement such as *CurrentURL = document.url*.

vlinkColor   This is a the color of previously visited hyperlinks on the Web page. To set the color you want the Web browser to use when displaying previously visited hyperlinks, execute a JavaScript statement such as *document.vlinkColor = LinkColor* (where *LinkColor* is a hexadecimal triplet that gives the RGB color values in the form "#RRGGBB").

Taking Advantage of the JavaScript Images Array

The Web browser stores the properties of each image inserted on the Web page in the *images* array. As you learned in the preceding Tip, the *images* array is a part of the document object in which the Web browser stores all the objects on and properties of the current Web page. Each time the browser finds an <img> tag in the Web page HTML, it adds another element to the *images* array in the document object.

Using the *document.images* array, you can change the graphics images displayed on a Web page. In a previous Tip ("Creating an Interactive Navigation Bar with a Mouseover Effect"), you learned how to create a mouseover effect by using the *document.images* array to swap one graphic for another whenever a visitor moved the mouse pointer over an image on the page. You might also use the *document.images* array to enhance the experience of visitors with dial-up Internet connections by letting the visitor decide whether to display high resolution (slower-loading) images or lower resolution alternates.

Say for example that you have a page with a large number of images. High resolution color images tend to have large file sizes, which means that the the Web browser may take an unacceptably long time to load such images over a low-bandwidth (dial-up) Internet connection. Therefore, prior to displaying a Web page with a gallery of images, use a form element on a prior page to ask the visitor which version of the images he or she wants to see. (Visitors with high speed connections will most likely choose the higher resolution images.) Then, when you display the Web page with the images, set the *src* property of each image (*document.images[ImageIndex].src*) to the URL of the high resolution (larger file size) image or to the lower resolution version of the picture based on the visitor's form input.

Using a script at the Web browser to change the images displayed on a Web page is faster than the traditional method that would require a server-side script to retrieve and process the visitor's form input and then use a processor such as ASP or PHP to generate a new Web page. Swapping images in a script at the Web browser eliminates the transfer overhead of sending additional requests to the Web server and the time it would take the Web server to rebuild the Web page. The browser-based script works with the page the browser already received from the Web server—simply changing the URLs of the images and leaving the remainder of the Web page HTML intact.

The following sections discuss properties the browser stores in each of the *images* array's elements. At the end of each description, you will find the format for a JavaScript statement you can use in a script to view (and in the case of the *lowsrc* and *src* properties, change) the value of an image property. Although the majority of the properties are read-only, you can use the (updateable) "src" property to change images on the Web page on-the-fly. For example, by creating two versions of a graphic, one plain and one highlighted, you can create a mouseover effect by having the Web browser swap the highlighted graphic for the plain one when the visitor moves the mouse pointer over the image.

border   This is a read-only value that specifies the width in pixels of the border around an image. You can retrieve the value of the *border* attribute specified in the picture's <img> tag with a JavaScript statement in the form *BorderWidth = document.images[ImageIndex].border* or *BorderWidth = document.ImageName.border*.

complete   This is a read-only Boolean value that remains false until the Web browser has finished retrieving the image file from the Web server. For example, you can use the following *while* loop to wait for an image to download from the Web server before swapping it for another image on the Web page:

```
while (!document.ImageName.complete)
{
}
```

height   This is a read-only value that gives the height of the image in pixels. You can retrieve the picture's height with a JavaScript statement of the form *ImageHeight = document.images [ImageIndex].height* or *ImageHeight = document.ImageName.height*.

hspace   This is a read-only value that gives the number of pixels of blank space the Web browser is to leave between the picture and adjacent content (or the Web page margin) to the left and right of the graphics image. You can retrieve the value of *hspace* with a JavaScript statement of the form *HorizontalSpace = document.images[ImageIndex].hspace* or *HorizontalSpace = document.ImageName.hspace*.

lowsrc   This is the pathname of the low-resolution image the Web browser is to load to give the visitor something at which to look while the browser downloads the normal, high-resolution picture specified by the <img> tag's *src* attribute. You can set the value of *lowsrc* with a JavaScript statement in the form *document.images[ImageIndex].lowsrc = LowResImagePathname* or *document.ImageName. lowsrc = LowResImagePathname*.

name   This is a read-only string with the name assigned to the graphics image by the *name* attribute in the <img> tag. You can retrieve the value of the image name with a JavaScript statement of the form *ImageName = document.images[ImageIndex].name*.

src   This is the pathname of the graphics image you want the Web browser to display on the Web page. You can change the graphics image displayed by setting the value of the *src* property with a JavaScript statement of the form *document.images[ImageIndex].src = NewImagePathname* or *document.ImageName.src = NewImagePathname*.

vspace   This is a read-only value that gives the number of pixels of blank space the Web browser is to insert above and below the picture and content adjacent to the graphics image on the Web page. You can retrieve the value of *vspace* with a JavaScript statement of the form *VerticalSpace = document.images[ImageIndex].vspace* or *VerticalSpace = document.ImageName.vspace*.

width   This is a read-only value that gives the width of the image in pixels. You can retrieve the picture's width with a JavaScript statement of the form *ImageWidth = document.images [ImageIndex].width* or *ImageWidth = document.ImageName.width*.

Exploiting the JavaScript Links Array

The document object's *links* array lets you work with the properties of hyperlinks inserted on the Web page with <a> tags and hotspots on images as defined by <area> tags. Both Netscape Navigator and Internet Explorer (version 4 and above) let you modify (as well as display) the properties of links array elements. Therefore, you can change, on-the-fly, the Web page (or other file) the Web browser loads when the visitor clicks a hyperlink. As such, you can create a banner ad by writing a script that changes the image displayed on a page as well as the URL of the Web page the browser will retrieve when the visitor clicks on the banner image. Similarly, you can have hyperlinks move to different portions of a Web page (or to different Web pages altogether) based on the time of day or day of the week—all without having to change the Web page at the Web server either manually or through a server-side script.

As it reads the Web page HTML, the browser fills the document object's *links* array with the properties of all <a> tags (that is, hyperlinks) and image map hotspot <area> tags the browser finds, in the order in which it encounters the tags. The following sections discuss properties the browser stores about each hyperlink in the links array's elements. At the end of each description, you will find the format for a JavaScript statement you can use in a script to view or change the value of the property described.

hash   This is the portion of the *href* attribute in a hyperlink anchor that includes the hash mark (#) and the name of the fragment identifier that follows the hash mark (#). If the visitor clicks a hyperlink that has a fragment identifier, the Web browser will display the portion of the Web page that starts with an <a> tag whose *name* attribute is set to the value of the fragment identifier. You can retrieve the name of the fragment identifier from the hyperlink's *href* attribute with a statement of the form *FragmentIdentifier = document.links [LinkIndex].hash.* Conversely, you can change the fragment identifier (thereby pointing the hyperlink to a new location within a Web page) with a statement of the form *document.links[LinkIndex].hash = NewFragmentIdentifier.*

host   This is the IP address or domain name portion of a hyperlink's *href* attribute value. For a given hyperlink, the value of the *host* property differs from the value of the *hostname* property (discussed next) only in that the *host* property includes the port number (80, by default) that the Web browser is to use when communicating with the Web server. To retrieve the domain name (or IP address), including port number, from a hyperlink, execute a statement such as *HostNameWithPort = document.links[LinkIndex].host* or *HostNameWithPort = document.links[LinkIndex].host.*

hostname   This is the IP address or domain name portion of a hyperlink's *href* attribute value. You can retrieve the value of the hostname in a hyperlink with a JavaScript statement of the form *HostName = document.links[LinkIndex].hostname.* You can also change the domain name (or IP address) in a hyperlink with *document.links[LinkIndex].hostname = NewHostName.*

href   This is the value of the hyperlink's target address (including the bookmark, if any) assigned to the *href* attribute in the hyperlink's <a> tag or <area> tag. You can retrieve the hyperlink's target address with a JavaScript statement of the form *HyperlinkTarget = document.links[LinkIndex].href.* You can also change a hyperlink's target by assigning a new value to the *href* property with a JavaScript statement of the form *document.links.[LinkIndex].href = NewTargetAddress.*

pathname   This is the pathname portion of a URL. For example, given the hyperlink *<a href="http://www.NVBizNet.com/htdocs/clients.htm>Client List</a>*, the *pathname* property will contain the string "/htdocs/clients.htm" on Netscape Navigator and "htdocs/clients.htm" on Internet Explorer. You can retrieve a hyperlink's pathname with a statement of the form *Pathname = document.links[LinkIndex].pathname.* You can also change the pathname of the Web page retrieved by clicking the hyperlink, by assigning a new value to the pathname property with a statement of the form *document.links[LinkIndex].pathname = NewPathname.* (When assigning a new pathname, be sure to include the leading slash [/] in the new pathname for both Internet Explorer and Netscape Navigator.)

port   This is the port number on which to communicate with the Web server. The port number, if present, follows the domain name or IP address. For example, in a hyperlink with a *href* attribute value of "http://www.NVBizNet.com**:80**/clients.htm", the port number is 80. You can retrieve the port number with a statement of the form *PortNumber = document.links[LinkIndex].port*. A hyperlink need not include a port number, because the Web browser will set the port number to 80, by default. Internet explorer will return "80" unless the hyperlink specifies a different port number; Netscape Navigator will return no port number unless the hyperlink includes one.

protocol   This is the delivery protocol portion of the hyperlink's target. You will find the delivery protocol at the beginning of the hyperlink's *href* attribute before the two forward slashes (*//*). The protocol, which indicates the way in which the Web browser is to retrieve its target Web page or other file, may be one of the following:

- **file**   The browser is to retrieve the document from a local computer or from a disk on a local computer or network workstation
- **ftp**   The browser is to retrieve the document using an FTP program
- **gopher**   The browser is to retrieve the document using the Gopher protocol
- **http**   The browser is to retrieve a Web page
- **mailto**   The browser is to launch the system's default e-mail program and create a message to the address specified in the hyperlink
- **JavaScript**   The hyperlink points to a file with JavaScript statements

You can retrieve the value of a hyperlink's protocol property with a JavaScript statement of the form *DeliveryProtocol = document.links[LinkIndex].protocol*.

search   This is the query string portion of the hyperlink's *href* attribute, including the leading question mark (?). If present in the hyperlink, the query string follows a question mark (?). When the visitor clicks the hyperlink's anchor text or graphics image, the browser passes the query string to a CGI program on the Web server for processing. You can retrieve the value of a hyperlink's *search* property with a JavaScript statement of the form *SearchString = document.links[LinkIndex].search*. You can also change the search string with a statement in the form *documents.links[LinkIndex].search = SearchString* (where *SearchString* is a string such as "?fname=konrad&lname=king").

target   This is the name of the window or frame in which the Web browser is to display the document it retrieves when the visitor clicks the hyperlink's anchor text or graphics image. By default, the browser will replace the Web page in the current window with the new Web page. However, if the hyperlink's <a> tag includes a *target* attribute setting other than "_self", the Web browser will leave the original Web page onscreen and display the Web page it retrieves in a different window or frame. You can retrieve the name of a hyperlink's target frame or window with a JavaScript statement of the form *FrameName = document.lists[ListIndex].target*. You can also change the hyperlink's target window or frame with a statement in the form *document.lists[ListIndex].target = NewFrameName*.

Changing Web Page Colors Using JavaScript

When you design a Web page, you may want to specify a color scheme so that the page will look the same to all visitors and not change foreground, background, and hyperlink colors based on the browser's settings. Unfortunately, no matter how good the color scheme looks on your own system, some visitors may have problems viewing your content if you use colors other than the default black text on a white or gray background. For example, colorblind visitors may not be able to see one or more of the colors you used, or you may have specified colors beyond the capabilities of the visitor's display. Whatever the reason for the problem, you can use a JavaScript function to get around the "color issue" by letting visitors select a color scheme they find more appealing.

Table 8-8 lists the Web page properties you can use to change the colors the Web browser is using to display the page text, background, and hyperlinks. Remember, the browser stores all the Web page properties in a *document* object as it reads the Web page HTML. To change the Web page color scheme, you need only to change the values of the *document* object's color properties.

The following JavaScript function will set the Web page color scheme based on the value of the *ColorScheme* parameter passed to the function by the Web browser. Although the *selectScheme()* function has only two color schemes, you can add additional selections by adding more *else if {...}* statement blocks that set the five document color properties to other values:

```
<script>
<!--
function selectScheme(ColorScheme)
{
 if (ColorScheme == "1")
   {
    document.alinkColor = "#008080";   //Teal
    document.bgColor = "#FFFFE0";       //Light Yellow
    document.fgColor = "#A52A2A";       //Brown
    document.linkColor = "#008000";    //Green
    document.vlinkColor = "#FF00FF";   //Magenta
   }
 else if (ColorScheme == "2")
   {
    document.alinkColor = "Ivory";
    document.bgColor = "Lightblue";
    document.fgColor = "Magenta";
    document.linkColor = "Darkred";
    document.vlinkColor = "SlateGray";
   }
 return;
}
//-->
</script>
```

Property	Description
alinkColor	The color of the hyperlink as the visitor clicks it
bgColor	The Web page background color
fgColor	The color of the Web page nonhyperlink text
linkColor	The color of unvisited hyperlinks
vlinkColor	The color of visited hyperlinks

Table 8-8   Document Object Color Properties

After you declare the preceding function in the Web page header, you need only make it accessible to the site visitor by inserting a button or a hyperlink with an *onClick* event handler that calls the function. For example, the following code will place two buttons on the Web page:

```
<form>
   <input type="button" value="Color Scheme 1"
          onClick="selectScheme(1)">
   <input type="button" value="Color Scheme 2"
          onClick="selectScheme(2)">
</form>
```

If the visitor clicks either button, the Web browser will call the *selectScheme()* function, which in turn, will change the colors of the background, foreground, and hyperlinks on the page.

Storing a Cookie on the Visitor's Hard Drive

A "cookie" is a string with up to 4,096 (4K) characters that you can tell the Web browser to store on a visitor's hard drive. Cookies give you a way to store information about the site visitor that you can retrieve each time the visitor returns to the site—so long as the visitor uses the same Web browser and computer system. Each Web browser type stores all cookie data in a single file unique to the browser. As such, if you use Internet Explorer on one visit to a site and Netscape Navigator on the next, Netscape Navigator will not retrieve the cookies previously saved by Internet Explorer.

Without cookies, you have no way of determining what happened the last time the visitor came to the site—or even if the visitor has ever been to your site before. If you store a cookie on the visitor's hard drive, the Web browser can retrieve information saved to the cookie file during subsequent visits. For security reasons, the Web browser can only write data to and read data from a cookie file as opposed to writing and reading files with private information on your hard drive. Moreover, the script on a Web page can only read cookies written by scripts on Web pages from the same domain (that is, Web pages sent from the same Web server).

USE IT   To set a cookie, that is to add a cookie to the cookie file on the visitor's hard drive, execute a JavaScript statement in the following form:

```
document.cookie = "CookieName=Cookievalue [;expires=ExpDate]
[;domain=DomainName][;path=Pathname][;secure]
```

The only required values when saving a cookie are the cookie's name and text data you want to save. The following sections discuss the optional values you can store with a cookie.

expires   This is the date (in GMT format) when the cookie expires. After a cookie expires, the Web browser will no longer provide its value to any script and will remove the cookie from the cookie file. If you do not supply an expiration date, the cookie will be available only until the visitor exits the Web browser. If you set the cookie to expire prior to the local date and time, the Web browser will remove the cookie from the cookie file.

domain   By default, scripts on Web pages from the same domain as the Web page that wrote the cookie can retrieve the cookie's value. By adding a domain value to the cookie, you can further restrict access to specific Web servers within the domain. For example, if a script on a Web page from NVBizNet.com wrote the cookie, scripts on Web pages from NVBizNet.com and SQLServer. NVBizNet.com can retrieve the cookie's data. If you set *domain="SQLServer.NVBizNet.com"* when you save the cookie, only scripts on Web pages sent from the SQLServer.NVBizNet.com Web site will be able to read the cookie.

path   By default, any Web page from the same path as the Web page that created the cookie can retrieve the cookie from the cookie file. By adding a pathname to the cookie, you can specify the path from which a Web page must come in order to have access to the cookie. For example, if a script on a Web page from "/htdocs" stored the cookie, Web pages stored in "/htdocs", "/htdocsabc", "htdocs/xyz", and so on can retrieve the cookie. If you include *path="/htdocs/cookieddocs/"* when you save the cookie, only Web pages stored on a path that starts with *"/htdocs/cookiedocs"* can read the cookie. Similarly, if you include *path="/"*, the script on any Web page from the Web site can retrieve the cookie, because the path for every Web page on the site starts with "/" (the site's root).

secure   If you add the *secure* keyword when storing the cookie, only Web pages sent over a secure (HTTPS) connection can read the cookie's value.

The following JavaScript statements add two cookies to the cookie file. The first cookie (named *Email*) expires July 14, 2002. Meanwhile, the second cookie (named *pwd*) has the same expiration date; however, only browsers with a secure (HTTPS) connection to the Web server can read the cookie:

```
<script>
<!--
  document.cookie =
"Email=kki@NVBizNet.com;expires=Sun, 14 Jul 2002 00:00:00 GMT";
  document.cookie =
"pwd=king;expires=Sun, 14 Jul 2002 00:00:00 GMT;secure";
```

```
// -->
</script>
```

Formatting Cookie Data Using JavaScript

USE IT   In the preceding Tip, you learned how to save cookie data to a file on the visitor's
computer. Unfortunately, the format of the cookie data is easy to forget, and calculating
GMT-formatted expiration dates is tedious at best. As such, you may want to include the following
setCookie( ) function between start and end script tags (<script></script>) in the header section of
Web pages that need to store cookies:

```
function setCookie(CookieName,CookieValue,ExpDate,Domain,Path,
                    Security)
{
 var CookieData = CookieName;

//store letters and numbers as themselves, but store any
//symbols or spaces in the cookie value as an ASCII code
 CookieData = CookieData + "=" + escape(CookieValue);

//check for optional parameters values
 if (ExpDate.value != "")
   CookieData = CookieData + "; expires=" +
                    ExpDate.toGMTString();
 if (Domain != "")
   CookieData = CookieData + "; domain=" + Domain;
 if (Path != "") CookieData = CookieData + "; path=" + Path;
 if (Security == "secure") CookieData = CookieData + "; secure"
//insert the cookie in the cookie file
 document.cookie = CookieData;
 return ;
}
```

The *setCookie( )* function in this example accepts the cookie name, value, expiration date, domain,
path, and security restrictions and puts them into the required format before inserting the cookie within
the cookie file.

After you include the *setCookie( )* function in your Web page header, you can tell the browser to call the
function with cookie data you want to save. Suppose, for example, that your Web page has the following
form definition, which asks the visitor to enter a first name, last name, and e-mail address:

```
<form name="RegistrationForm">
  <table>
```

```
    <tr><td>First Name:</td>
        <td><input type="text" name="fname" size="20"></td></tr>
    <tr><td>Last Name:</td>
        <td><input type="text" name="lname" size="20"></td></tr>
    <tr><td>E-mail:</td>
        <td><input type="text" name="email" size="20"></td></tr>
    <tr><td><input type = "button" value = "Register"
            onClick="visitorSignIn(RegistrationForm)"></td></tr>
    </table>
</form>
```

When the visitor clicks the Register button at the bottom of the form, the browser calls the *visitorSignIn()* function, which in turn, validates the form data and then calls the *setCookie()* function. To use the form, declare the *visitorSignIn()* function between the start and end script tags (<script></script>) in the Web page header:

```
function visitorSignIn(Form)
{
 if (Form.fname.value == "") return false;
 if (Form.lname.value == "") return false;
 if (Form.email.value == "") return false;

//Generate an expiration date one year from today
 var ExpDate = new Date ();
 ExpDate.setTime (ExpDate.getTime() +
                  (365 * 24 * 60 * 60 * 1000));

//Write the cookies that store the first name, last name,
//and e-mail address
  setCookie("FirstName",Form.fname.value,ExpDate,"","/","");
  setCookie("LastName",Form.lname.value,ExpDate,"","/","");
  setCookie("eMailAddr",Form.email.value,ExpDate,"","/","");

//load another Web page
  self.location = "htdocs/LoggedIn.htm"
}
```

The first three statements of the *visitorSignIn()* function tell the browser to return to the registration form if any of the form's fields are blank. The three calls to the *setCookie()* function near the end of the *visitorSignIn()* function store data in the form's fields as three cookie values in the cookie file.

Retrieving a Cookie Value from the Cookie File

As you learned from a previous Tip in this chapter, the Web browser creates an object named *document* when it receives a Web page from the Web server. The browser stores Web page properties and the properties of the objects inserted on the page in the *document* object. In addition, the browser reads the cookie file and stores in the *document.cookie* property the name/value pairs from cookies that scripts on the Web page can use. Before you can use a specific cookie's value, you must extract the value from the string of all available cookie names and values in the *document.cookie* property.

 The following JavaScript function will return a single cookie's value from the document object's cookie property:

```
function cookieValue(FirstChar)
{
//Semicolons separate the cookie name/value pairs in
//document.cookie property. Find the index of first
//semicolon that follows the start of the cookie value
 var LastChar = document.cookie.indexOf (";", FirstChar);
 if (LastChar == -1)
   LastChar = document.cookie.length;

 return unescape(document.cookie.substring(FirstChar, LastChar));
}
```

The *unescape()* function in the last statement of the *cookieValue()* function converts escape sequences in the cookie's value to the ASCII symbol they represent. Remember, in the preceding Tip, you used the *escape()* function when you stored the cookie value. As a result, the browser stored "kki@NVBizNet.com" in the cookie file as "kki%40NVBizNet.com". The *unescape()* function converts the escape sequence "%40" back into an at sign (@) symbol.

Before you can call the *cookieValue()* function, however, you must know where the value of the cookie you want starts among the string of all cookie name/value pairs in *document.cookie*. The following function will find the first character in the value of the cookie whose name you pass to the function in the *CookieName* parameter. After it calls the *cookieValue()* function, the *getCookieValue()* function will return the cookie value associated with the name you passed to the function in the *CookieName* parameter:

```
function getCookieValue(CookieName)
{
 CookieName = CookieName + "=";
 var NameLength = CookieName.length;
 var CookieLength = document.cookie.length;
 var FirstChar = 0;
 var LastChar = 0;

 while (FirstChar < CookieLength)
```

```
{
  LastChar = FirstChar + NameLength;
  if (document.cookie.substring(FirstChar, LastChar) ==
      CookieName)
    return cookieValue (LastChar);
//go 1 character past the space between cookie name/value pairs
  FirstChar = document.cookie.indexOf(" ", FirstChar) + 1;
  if (FirstChar == 0) break;
 }
 return null;
}
```

Therefore, to retrieve cookie values from the *document.cookie* property by name, first declare the *cookieValue()* and *getCookieValue()* functions between start and end script tags (<script></script>) in the Web page header. You can then insert a script such as the following in the body of the Web page to retrieve and display the names and e-mail address from cookies stored in the preceding Tip, as shown in Figure 8-8:

```
<script>
<!--
  document.RegForm.fname.value = getCookieValue("FirstName");
  document.RegForm.lname.value = getCookieValue("LastName");
  document.RegForm.email.value = getCookieValue("eMailAddr");
// -->
```

Removing a Cookie from the Cookie File

As the browser scans the cookie file, looking for cookies to add to the document object's *cookie* property for the current Web page, it removes any cookies that have expired. Remember, when you save a cookie, you save the expiration date along with the cookie's name and value. Because each cookie increases the cookie file's size and the cookie file can hold at most 200 cookies for any single

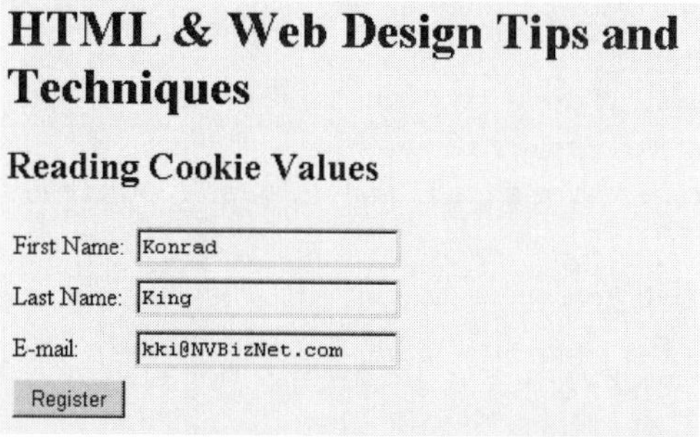

HTML & Web Design Tips and Techniques

Reading Cookie Values

First Name: Konrad

Last Name: King

E-mail: kki@NVBizNet.com

Register

Figure 8-8   A form with data retrieved from cookie values stored in *document.cookie*

domain, you want to delete cookies you no longer need. Because the Web browser automatically removes expired cookies from the cookie file, simply set the expiration date of the cookie you want to delete to a date and time in the past.

USE IT If you declare the following function between a set of start and end script tags (<script></script>) in your Web page html (preferably in the header section), you can call the *deleteCookie()* function anytime you want to delete a cookie:

```
function deleteCookie (CookieName)
{
 document.cookie = CookieName +
   "= ; expires=Thu, 01 Jan 1970 00:00:01 GMT";
 return
}
```

The *deleteCookie()* function "expires" the cookie by setting the cookie's expiration date to the earliest usable date (one second past midnight on 01 January 1970). Because the *correct* local time on any computer is long after the 01 January 1970 at present, calling *deleteCookie()* will cause a Web browser to delete from the cookie file the cookie whose name you pass to the function in the *CookieName* parameter. Suppose, for example, that you previously stored a cookie named *toDelete*. If you execute the statement *deleteCookie("toDelete");* (as shown near the end of the following code sample), the Web browser will remove the cookie, as shown in Figure 8-9:

```
<html>
<head>
<script language="JavaScript">
<!--
  function deleteCookie (CookieName)
  {
   document.cookie = CookieName +
     "= ; expires=Thu, 01 Jan 1970 00:00:01 GMT";
   return
  }
// -->
</script>
<body>
  <h1>HTML & Web Design Tips and Techniques</h1>
  <h2>Deleting Cookie Values </h2>
  <h3>Cookies available before calling "deleteCookie()"</h3>

<script language="JavaScript">
<!--
  document.write('<p>cookie = ' + document.cookie+'</p>');
  deleteCookie ("toDelete");
  document.write('<h3>Cookies available AFTER calling ' +
```

```
                        '"deleteCookie()"'</h3>');
  document.write("<p>cookie = " + document.cookie+'</p>');
// -->
</script>
</body>
</html>
```

Saving Time and Programming by Using Prewritten (External) Scripts

As you add to your JavaScript library, you will no doubt write some functions and scripts you can use on several Web pages. The cookie maintenance and display functions you saw in the previous three Tips are a good example. You could simply cut and paste the functions to set, retrieve, and delete cookies between start and end script tags (<script></script>) on each Web page that needs them. However, by using the *src* attribute in a <script> tag to include an external script file, you can save the time you would otherwise spend searching for and copying JavaScript code into your Web pages. Moreover, telling the Web browser to read code stored in other files reduces the amount of "clutter" in your HTML document, which lets you zero in on the tags you need to change to keep the site's content up to date.

 USE IT To tell the Web browser to include functions and scripts stored in external files, add the *src* attribute to the start <script> tag as <script src="*RelativePath/ScriptFilename*">. Suppose, for example, that you store script files in a folder named scripts and Web pages in the hotdocs folder—both at your Web site's root. To include functions (or scripts) stored in the scripts folder on a Web page stored in the htdocs folder, the HTML would look something like this:

```
<head>
  <script src="../scripts/GetCookieValue.js"></script>
</head>
```

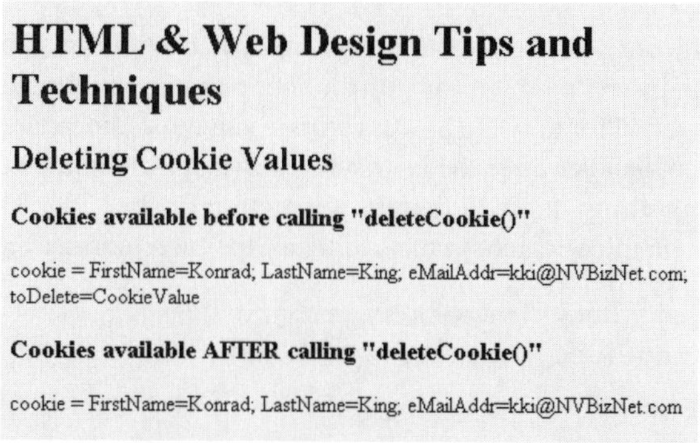

HTML & Web Design Tips and Techniques

Deleting Cookie Values

Cookies available before calling "deleteCookie()"

cookie = FirstName=Konrad; LastName=King; eMailAddr=kki@NVBizNet.com; toDelete=CookieValue

Cookies available AFTER calling "deleteCookie()"

cookie = FirstName=Konrad; LastName=King; eMailAddr=kki@NVBizNet.com

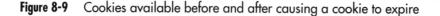

Figure 8-9 Cookies available before and after causing a cookie to expire

The *../scripts* in the code sample is the relative path to the script file you want the browser to include. In this case, the HTML tells the browser it can find the script file *relative* to the current Web page (stored in the htdocs folder) by moving up one level in the folder hierarchy (to the Web site's root folder), and then down one level to the scripts folder. If you were to include the same script file in a Web page (such as index.htm) stored at the root of the Web site, your <script> tag would read as follows:

```
<head>
  <script src="scripts/getCookieValue.js"></script>
</head>
```

In this case, the path relative to the current Web page tells the browser to start from the current folder (the Web site's root) and move down one level into the scripts folder. You can include as many sets of start and end script tags (<script></script>) as necessary to include the files with the scripts and functions you need on the Web page. For example, if you stored the cookie management functions you learned about in the previous three Tips in three files, the HTML you would use to include the files would look like this:

```
<head>
  <script src="../scripts/SetCookie.js"></script>
  <script src="../scripts/GetCookieValue.js"></script>
  <script src="../scripts/DeleteCookie.js"></script>
</head>
```

Note that scripts you save in external files have no start and end script tags (<script></script>).

Creating an Animation Using the *onLoad* Event

You create an animation on a Web page by displaying one image after another in rapid succession. Each picture in an animation, like each frame in a movie, is slightly different from the one that precedes it. Your mind perceives motion (that is animation) as objects in one location in a picture seem to "move" to a new location when the Web browser replaces the current image with the next.

USE IT By adding the *onLoad* event to an <img> tag, you can tell the Web browser to replace the image the tag inserts on the page with another picture each time the browser is finished loading an image. To get a feel for how the process works, you must understand that the Web browser activates the *onLoad* event handler *after* the browser loads (that is, displays) the image on the Web page. Thus, the following <img> tag will display the picture Frame1.jpg. Then the browser will trigger the *onLoad* event handler, which, in turn, will call the (user-defined) *nextImage()* function:

```
<img name="animation" src="images/Frame1.jpg"
     onLoad="nextImage(document.animation.src)">
```

The *nextImage()* function creates the animation effect. As shown by the following code, each time the Web browser calls *nextImage()*, the function changes the *src* property of the image named animation in the document object's images array. Changing the *src* property causes the Web browser to load (that is, display) another image, which, in turn, triggers the *onLoad* event, and the process repeats:

```
<script>
<!--
  function nextImage(ImageSource)
  {
  var i = ImageSource.indexOf (".jpg",0);
  var NextFrame = ImageSource.substring(i-1, i);
  if (NextFrame == "1")
    document.animation.src = "images/Frame2.jpg";
  else if (NextFrame == "2")
    document.animation.src = "images/Frame3.jpg";
  else if (NextFrame == "3")
    document.animation.src = "images/Frame4.jpg";
  else
    document.animation.src = "images/Frame1.jpg";
  return;
  }
// -->
</script>
```

The animation displayed by the preceding code has four frames (that is, four different pictures) and repeats indefinitely. To stop the animation sequence after it plays once, remove the two statements just before the function's *return;* statement. If you do not load the first image again after you load the last, the browser will call *nextImage()* once more after loading Frame4.jpg. However, during the final pass, *nextImage()* makes no change to the document object's *src* property, because none of the function's *if* statements evaluate to true. As a result, the animation stops, because the Web browser does not trigger the *onLoad* event again, because the function did not tell the browser to load another picture.

Displaying Self-Changing Banners Using JavaScript

Banner ads—almost every business-oriented Web site has them. The concept is simple, display a small graphic image that advertises a company or product. Rather than fill the entire screen with advertisements (and drive your visitors away permanently), you can display an (unlimited) series of advertisements in a small area onscreen by replacing one picture with another at timed intervals. In fact, displaying banner ads is a lot like creating an animation (which you learned about in the preceding Tip). Both animations and self-changing banner ads require the Web browser to display a series of pictures, one after another. With a banner ad, however, you want the browser to leave each picture onscreen for 5–10 seconds, so that the visitor has enough time to view the ad.

USE IT To create a self-changing (rotating) banner, include an *onLoad* event handler such as the following in the Web page HTML's <body> tag:

```
<body onLoad="rotateBanner('images/Banner1.jpg')">
```

In this case, the *onLoad* event handler tells the Web browser to call the user-defined function *rotateBanner( )* after the browser loads (displays) the Web page in the application window. Although a JavaScript function can change the image displayed on a Web page, a function cannot add a new image to the page. As such, you must display the initial banner graphic by inserting an <img> tag similar to that shown near the middle of the following HTML, somewhere in the Web page body:

```
<h1>HTML & Web Design Tips and Techniques</h1>
<h2>Rotating Banner Ad</h2>
<table>
  <tr><td><img name="banner" src="images/Banner1.jpg"></td>
  </tr>
</table>
```

Finally, declare a *rotateBanner( )* function similar to the following between start and end script tags (<script></script>) in the header section of your Web page HTML:

```
function rotateBanner(BannerSrc)
{
 var TimerID
//swap the picture
 document.banner.src = BannerSrc;

//wait for timeout and call myself to swap next picture
 if (BannerSrc == "images/Banner1.jpg")
   TimerID = setTimeout("rotateBanner('images/Banner2.jpg')",5000);
 else if (BannerSrc == "images/Banner2.jpg")
   TimerID = setTimeout("rotateBanner('images/Banner3.jpg')",5000);
 else if (BannerSrc == "images/Banner3.jpg")
   TimerID = setTimeout("rotateBanner('images/Banner4.jpg')",5000);
 else
   TimerID = setTimeout("rotateBanner('images/Banner1.jpg')",5000);
 return;
}
```

Each time *rotateBanner( )* changes the *src* property of the image named animation in the document object's images array, the Web browser will display the new image onscreen. The built-in *setTimeout( )* function creates the "rotating" banner effect by calling the *rotateBanner( )* function recursively every five seconds to change the banner on the Web page. The syntax of the *setTimeout( )* function call may appear a bit confusing at first. However, the idea is the function evaluates the expression supplied as the first parameter after the number of milliseconds specified in the second parameter. Thus, given the syntax *TimerID* = setTimeout("*expression*", *DelayInMilliseconds*), the first call to *setTimeout()* in the example script tells the browser to call the *rotateBanner()* function after 5,000 milliseconds (that is, after 5 seconds), and pass the pathname of the "next" banner to display (*images/Banner2.jpg*). To display your own banner ads, simply replace the pathnames in the example with the pathnames of your banner ad graphics and adjust the millisecond delay in each *setTimeout()* function call to the amount of time you want each ad to stay onscreen. You can increase or decrease the number of ads by inserting or removing *else if* statements.

Note that almost all (and perhaps all) banner ads let visitors click the banner ad graphic to follow a hyperlink to the Web page with the advertised product or service for sale. In the next tip, you will learn how to change not only the graphics image, but also the hyperlink associated with the banner ad.

Pointing Hyperlinks to New Files On-the-Fly

When a visitor clicks hyperlinked text or on an image map hotspot, the Web browser retrieves the Web page (or other file) specified by the *href* attribute in the hyperlink's <a> tag. Normally, you want the Web browser to retrieve the same file every time the visitor clicks a particular hyperlink. Sometimes, however, you may find it convenient to point the hyperlink to a new file based on the date or the graphics image onscreen when the visitor clicks the mouse. Fortunately, the *links* array in the documents object has three properties you can change to point a hyperlink to a new file: *hash*, *pathname*, and *href*.

USE IT   The *hash* property lets you change everything to the right of a hash mark (#) in the hyperlink. As such, the *hash* property lets you change the name of the target bookmark without changing the file the browser will retrieve. Suppose, for example, that you have a hyperlink such as the following, which points to a bookmark named monday on the events.htm Web page:

```
<a href="http://www.NVBizNet.com/htdocs/events.htm#monday">
   Today's Events</a>
```

Assuming this is the first hyperlink on the page, you can execute the statement: *document.links[0].hash = "tuesday"* to change the hyperlink's target to "http://www.NVBizNet.com/htdocs/events.htm#tuesday". Therefore, if *events.htm* has a bookmarked section for each day of the week, you can use a single hyperlink to move to the current day's section whenever the visitor clicks the anchor text Today's Events. You need only write a script that uses the date object's *getDay()* method to determine the day of the week and then assigns the current day to the *hash* property each time the browser loads the Web page.

The *pathname* property lets you change everything between the domain name and the hash mark (#) in the hyperlink. As such, the *pathname* property lets you change the pathname of the file you want the browser to retrieve without changing the domain name or bookmark (if any). Suppose, for example, that you have a hyperlink such as the following, which points to a file named Jan.htm in the /news/2001 folder:

```
<a href="http://www.NVBizNet.com/news/2001/Jan.htm#birthday">
   This Month's Birthdays</a>
```

Assuming that this is the second hyperlink on the page, executing the statement *document.links[1].pathname = "/news/2001/Feb.htm"* will change the hyperlink's target to "http://www.NVBizNet.com/news/2001/Feb.htm#birthday". (Notice the reference to the "birthday" bookmark was not lost during the assignment.) Therefore, if you store the company's monthly newsletters in the /news/2001 folder on the Web site, you can use a single hyperlink to move to the "birthday" section of the current month's newsletter whenever the visitor clicks the anchor text This Month's Birthdays. You need only write a script that uses the date object's *getYear()* and *getMonth()* methods to build a pathname based on the year and month and then assigns the new path and filename to the *pathname* property each time the browser loads the page.

The *href* property lets you change the hyperlink's entire URL. As such, setting the *href* property in the *links* array has the same effect as specifying a new value for the *href* attribute in the hyperlink's <a> tag. Suppose, for example, that you have a rotating banner and want to let visitors move to a company's Web site by clicking the company's banner ad. First, anchor a hyperlink to the banner graphic with HTML similar to this:

```
<a href="http://www.NVBiznet.com">
  <img border="0" name="banner" src="images/Banner1.jpg"></a>
```

Next, update the function that rotates the banner ads by adding statements that assign the company's Web address to the *href* property (such as those in the first group of *if..else* statements in the following function):

```
function rotateBanner(BannerSrc)
{
 var TimerID
//swap the picture
 document.banner.src = BannerSrc;

//update the banner's hyperlink to the company's Web site
 if (BannerSrc == "images/Banner1.jpg")
   document.links[0].href = "http://www.NVBizNet.com"
 else if (BannerSrc == "images/Banner2.jpg")
   document.links[0].href = "http://www.NVBizNet2.com"
 else if (BannerSrc == "images/Banner3.jpg")
   document.links[0].href = "http://www.osborne.com"
 else
   document.links[0].href = "http://www.mcgrawhill.com"

//wait for timeout and call myself to swap next picture
 if (BannerSrc == "images/Banner1.jpg")
   TimerID = setTimeout("rotateBanner('images/Banner2.jpg')",5000);
 else if (BannerSrc == "images/Banner2.jpg")
   TimerID = setTimeout("rotateBanner('images/Banner3.jpg')",5000);
 else if (BannerSrc == "images/Banner3.jpg")
   TimerID = setTimeout("rotateBanner('images/Banner4.jpg')",5000);
```

```
else
   TimerID = setTimeout("rotateBanner('images/Banner1.jpg')",5000);
return;
}
```

Pre-caching Pictures to Reduce Image Display Time

Pre-caching graphics images is a technique by which you tell the Web browser to retrieve pictures from the Web server now, in anticipation that you may need to display the images later. By telling the browser to retrieve the pictures in the background (that is, while the visitor is doing other things on the Web page), you can eliminate the download delay the visitor would experience when clicking a thumbnail to display a larger picture. Similarly, if your Web page makes extensive use of scripts that display graphics images for mouseover effects or animations, you will want to pre-cache images not yet displayed. A pre-cached image will appear onscreen immediately when the browser calls for it instead of after a (perhaps lengthy) delay while waiting for the Web server to send the image to the browser. Suppose, for example, that your Web page has the eight thumbnails shown in Figure 8-10.

USE IT   You can pre-cache the images the browser will display when the visitor clicks the thumbnails by adding an *onLoad* event handler to either the Web page <body> tag or to one of the thumbnail <img> tags. For example, if you add the following *onLoad* event handler to the <img> tag for the last thumbnail displayed in Figure 8-10, the Web browser will call the user-defined function *preCache()*:

```
<td><a href="images/Pix8.jpg">
      <img onLoad="preCache()" border="0"
            src="images/Pix8_small.jpg"></a></td>
```

Your *preCache()* function, in turn, will be something like this:

```
function preCache()
{
 var Pictures = new Array();
 for (i=1; i<=8; i++)
 {
  Pictures[i] = new Image();
  Pictures[i].src = "images/Pix"+i+".jpg";
 }
 return;
}
```

After creating a new array named *Pictures*, the function uses the *new Image()* constructor to create new image objects into which it then loads images from the Web server. The Web browser does not display the images as the function downloads them from the Web site. However, the browser does store the image files in the system cache. When the visitor clicks one of the thumbnails for a larger

HTML & Web Design Tips and Techniques

Image Pre-cache

Figure 8-10   A Web page with eight thumbnails displayed while the browser loads the larger images

picture the *preCache()* function retrieved, the browser can fetch the larger picture from the local cache (that is, from the local system's memory or hard drive). Thus, downloading each thumbnail's larger image to the system's cache lets the browser avoid the download delay normally incurred when the browser has to retrieve the image from the Web server. As a result, the corresponding larger picture appears onscreen immediately after the visitor clicks a thumbnail. If you decide to pre-cache graphics images, make sure that the browser loads pictures inserted on the Web page before you call the *preCache()* function. After all, your intent is to load images into the system cache so the browser can display the pictures more quickly *if* the visitor asks to see them. The last thing you want to do is to make the visitor wait to see other images while you load a bunch of pictures into the system cache—especially if the visitor decides not to look at the pictures in the end.

When deciding where to place the *onLoad* event handler that calls the *preCache()* function, you must understand the way the browser retrieves and displays the Web page content. The browser first writes the text and renders the forms and tables as it finds them in the HTML. Next, the browser opens several simultaneous connections to the Web server to download graphics images inserted on the page. If you place the *onLoad* event handler on the last <img> tag in the Web page HTML, you can make sure the browser has at least *started* to download all thumbnails before calling the pre-cache function. Moreover, if the thumbnails are not all the same size, and you have a choice as to their arrangement, assign the pathname of the thumbnail with the largest file size to the *src* attribute of the last <img> tag. That way, by the time the browser is finished loading the last, largest thumbnail, and the *onLoad* event handler calls the *preCache()* function, the Web browser will have loaded all the thumbnails.

Creating a Scrolling Marquee Using JavaScript

The <marquee> tag has been around for quite some time. Unfortunately, only Internet Explorer supports the tag at present. As a result, when you use the <marquee> tag to display a line of scrolling text on your Web site, visitors using Netscape Navigator see a line of regular, nonmoving text.

Fortunately, JavaScript has timer and string manipulation functions you can use to turn a single-line text field on a form into the display area for a scrolling text marquee.

USE IT To create a scrolling marquee, first define a form with two text fields—a hidden field to hold the marquee's text and a visible field in which to display the moving text. For example, the following HTML will create a form that lets you display a marquee with up to 50 characters visible at any one time:

```
<form name="marquee">
  <input type="hidden" name="marquee_text"
         value=
"Welcome to JavaScript in HTML & Web Design Tips & Techniques!">
  <input type="text" name="display_area" size="50">
</form>
```

If you want to display a different length marquee, change the value of the *size* attribute to the maximum number of characters you want displayed onscreen. (Also, be sure to set the *value* attribute to the text string you want the marquee to scroll across the screen.) Next, to create the scrolling text effect, insert the following function between a set of start and end script tags (<script></script>) in your Web page header:

```
var StartPos = 0;
function scrollingMarquee()
{
 var i
 var Padding = 20 ; //number of spaces between repeats
 var ScrollingText = document.marquee.marquee_text.value;
 var StringLength = document.marquee.marquee_text.value.length;
 var TimerID;
//Padding is the number of blanks between the end of the
//scrolling text and the start of the next copy of the text.
 for(i=1; i<=Padding; i++) ScrollingText += " ";
 ScrollingText += ScrollingText
 document.marquee.display_area.value =
   ScrollingText.substring(StartPos, StartPos + StringLength +
                           Padding);
 if(StartPos++ == (StringLength + (Padding - 1))) StartPos=0;

//Wait 200 milliseconds before moving right 1 character
 TimerID = setTimeout("scrollingMarquee()",200);
}
```

Remember, you can have as many forms as you want on a Web page, so placing a marquee on a page does not prevent you from accepting visitor input on another form. Moreover, you can place your form(s) in a table. As such, you can use a table with hidden borders to place the scrolling marquee (that is, the form field with the "scrolling" text) exactly where you want it to appear on the Web page.

CHAPTER 9

Java Applets and ActiveX Objects

TIPS IN THIS CHAPTER

▶ Using an Applet to Create a Pop-Up Navigation Menu   437

▶ Using an Applet to Animate a Text String   440

▶ Using an Applet to Display and Print a Calendar for Any Year   442

▶ Using an Applet to Display a Passage at Random from a Text File   443

▶ Using an Applet to Create a Navigation Menu that Runs in Its Own Window   444

▶ Using an Applet to Scroll the Contents of a File Vertically Within a Rectangular Box Onscreen   448

▶ Using an Applet to Animate an Image Along a Sine Wave   450

▶ Editing Java Source Code to Build a Custom Applet   452

▶ Using the Microsoft Chat ActiveX Control to Add Internet Chat to a Web Page   457

▶ Using Only ActiveX Objects with Internet Explorer   460

In Chapter 8, you learned how to create scripts using JavaScript that you place within your HTML files. When a Web browser encounters JavaScript, the browser executes the corresponding statements. Although JavaScript provides many capabilities you can use to create simple scripts, JavaScript does not provide the tools programmers need to create multimedia applications that manipulate sounds and graphics or enable programmers to interact with remote data, such as a corporate database. To develop high-end applications for the Web, many programmers use the Java programming language.

Specifically, using Java, programmers create Web-based applications, called *applets*. Using the HTML <applet> tag, Web developers integrate the Java applet into a Web page, in much the same way that you would place a graphic within a Web page using the <img> tag. When the browser encounters an <applet> tag within an HTML page, the browser will download and run the specified applet from the server. Java applets are well suited for use on the Web because:

- Java applets are generic, meaning that the same applet will run under Windows, Linux, MacOS, and more (Java's generic nature makes applets more *portable*, meaning that programmers can easily move the applet among different computer types that run different operating systems).

- Java applets cannot access a user's disk or files, which means that an applet cannot place a virus on the user's system, and the applet cannot access information stored on the user's disk.

This chapter examines the steps you must perform to integrate Java applets into your Web pages. This chapter also presents several ready-to-run applets you may want to put to immediate use. Java applets are programs, and Java is a powerful programming language. This chapter will not teach you how to program in Java. However, this chapter will show you how to download the Java programming tools and use them to make simple changes to Java programs. From the Web, you can retrieve the program statements for many Java applets. Often, you can customize the applets by making a few simple changes to the program code, such as changing the names of files the program manipulates or text the program displays. This chapter shows you how to make such changes to a Java program and then how to rebuild the applet to put your changes into effect.

In addition to using Java to implement Web applications, many sites rely on ActiveX objects (similar to programs) to perform specific tasks. Using an ActiveX object, for example, a Web site might display a stock ticker or a status bar that indicates the percentage of a task (such as a file download) that the Web browser has completed. ActiveX objects differ from Java applets as follows:

- ActiveX objects are not generic. Unlike a Java applet that supports Windows, Linux, the Mac, and more, ActiveX objects exist only for the Windows platform.

- ActiveX objects are not safe. Unlike a Java applet that runs within the browser and that cannot access a user's files and disk, an ActiveX object resides on the user's disk and has access to all the system's resources. A malicious ActiveX object, for example, could introduce a virus and could steal, corrupt, or destroy information on a user's disk.

Given that ActiveX objects support only Windows and that ActiveX objects are not safe, you may be wondering why you would want to use ActiveX objects—a fair question. Because ActiveX objects reside on a user's system, the objects can interact with Windows. As a result, programmers can create very powerful solutions using ActiveX. Across the Internet, the fact is that most users surf the Web using Windows. Because ActiveX objects are not safe, you should use only ActiveX objects that you create yourself, those created by programmers whom you know and trust, and those that you download from a trusted Web site (such as Microsoft). This chapter will show you the steps you must perform to integrate ActiveX objects into your Web pages.

Understanding How a Browser Executes a Java Applet

A Java applet resides within a file. For years, Java programmers used the <applet> tag to place a Java applet within a Web page. As shown here, you use an <applet> tag to reference the applet's filename:

```
<applet code="Demo.class">
</applet>
```

Although browsers still support the <applet> tag, you should use, according to the W3C, the <object> tag as shown here to insert Java applets within a Web page:

```
<object code="Demo.class">
</object>
```

As you examine HTML files that use Java applets, you will find widespread use of the <applet> tag. The W3C, however, has deprecated the <applet> tag in favor of the <object> tag. In the future, in theory, browsers may stop supporting the <applet> tag. However, because of the tag's current widespread use, browsers will likely continue to support the tag for some time to come. Further, until all browsers fully support the <object> tag, you may find fewer compatibility problems by using the <applet> tag as shown throughout this chapter.

When the browser encounters the <applet> tag, the browser must download the applet from the server, much like the browser must download a graphic when it encounters an <img> tag. Java applet files use the .class file extension. In this case, the <applet> tag directs the browser to download an applet file named Demo.class. After the browser downloads the applet file, the browser will execute the applet's statements. Figure 9-1 illustrates the process the browser performs to identify, download, and execute a Java applet.

Normally, when programmers create applications, the program code the programmer writes is specific to a hardware and operating system platform. For example, a programmer might create an application that can run on a Intel-based processor (or compatible CPU) running Windows, or the programmer might create code for a Motorola processor running MacOS. If the programmer must support both environments (the Mac and Windows), the programmer must create two separate programs. The Windows-based program will not run on the Mac and vice versa.

In contrast to applications programmers create using other programming languages, Java applets are not constrained by platform. Rather than program code that is specific to the Intel processor or the Motorola processor, Java applets contain a generic set of instructions, which programmers refer to as *bytecode*. After a browser downloads a Java applet, the browser converts the generic bytecode into machine-specific code that the user's CPU can execute. In other words, if the browser is running on a Windows-based system, the browser converts the bytecode into Intel-specific instructions. Likewise,

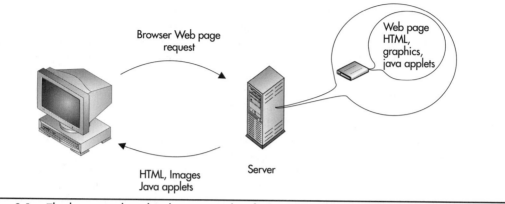

Figure 9-1   The browser downloads Java applets from a Web server

if the browser is running on a Mac, the browser converts the bytecode into Motorola-specific instructions. By using generic bytecode, the same Java applet can run on a variety of platforms, as shown in Figure 9-2.

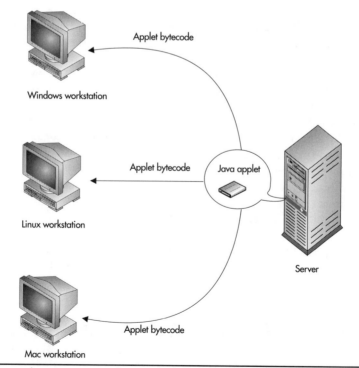

Figure 9-2   Java applets use generic bytecode, which the browser translates into machine-specific code, which lets the same applet run on various machine types

You may be wondering why all programmers do not simply use Java to create applications that can run on all system types. The problem with Java's generic bytecode is that the browser must translate the program code into a processor-specific program each time the application runs. This translation process adds overhead, which causes a delay before the program runs. Further, the processor-specific code the browser generates is often less efficient than the instructions a programming language can create for a specific processor. Thus, if you run equivalent Java and C++ programs side by side, the C++ program will normally execute faster. Also, each time the user runs the applet, the browser must download the applet. In contrast—as you will learn later in this chapter—when a Web site uses an ActiveX object, the site must download the object only one time. After that, the object will reside on the user's disk, and applications that use the object will always use the local copy.

Performance issues aside, however, the generic nature of Java applets is well suited for Web-based applications that may be run by users using a variety of system types and operating systems. Further, the Java security model protects users from viruses and other threats present in programs that users download from the Web.

Understanding Why Java Applets Are Safe to Run

Any time a user downloads an executable program from the Web, the user puts his or her system at risk of infection from a computer virus or other malicious programs that may try to steal information that resides on the user's disks.

Java applets are not stand-alone executable programs. You cannot, for example, download a Java applet and simply run the applet from within Windows or Unix. Instead, applets can run only within a browser.

When Sun Microsystems developed the Java programming language, the developers focused on security and the threats to user systems from running programs that users download from the Web. To eliminate threats such as viruses and information theft, Java applets cannot access resources (specifically files) that reside on the user's disk. As shown in Figure 9-3, Java simply does not provide programmers with the tools they need to perform operations on the user's PC. Further, Java applets cannot read system properties, load library files, or open network connections to sites other than the host from which they were downloaded.

As you have learned, the user's Web browser executes the Java applet. Programmers refer to the specific software within the browser that executes applets as the *Java Virtual Machine (JVM)*. When a browser encounters an <applet> tag within an HTML file, the browser essentially hands off the applet to the Java Virtual Machine, which, in turn, downloads, translates (the bytecode into processor-specific code), and executes the applet.

Programmers often refer to the security model that the Java Virtual Machine uses to run applets as the sandbox. You can think of the sandbox as a security fence that surrounds the applet and keeps the Java program away from the private areas in memory and your hard drive.

Understanding How a Browser Executes an ActiveX Object

ActiveX objects are like Java applets in that they let you add programs to a Web page. On the Web, you can find thousands of ActiveX objects (which programmers also call *ActiveX controls*) that perform a wide range of tasks, from displaying a message marquee to generating voice output from

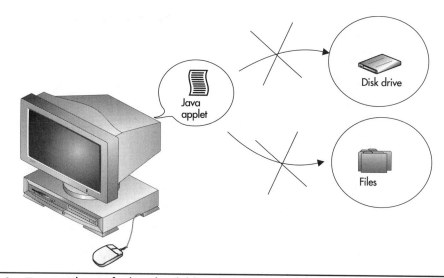

Figure 9-3 To provide a safe downloadable solution, Java applets prevent disk and file operations

text, or that let you implement voice recognition within your programs and Web pages! To locate ActiveX objects, begin your search at the following Web sites:

- http://activex.microsoft.com/activex/activex/
- http://visualbasic.about.com/cs/activexfree/
- http://webreference.com/programming/activex.html
- http://activex.microsoft.com
- http://zdnet.com/devhead/

ActiveX, unlike Java, is not a programming language. Rather, ActiveX is a means of integrating objects written in different languages within the Windows environment. Unfortunately, years after its initial release, ActiveX is still Windows specific (so there are no ActiveX objects for Unix systems or the Macintosh), and ActiveX support does not come standard in Netscape Navigator. (Microsoft, Macromedia, and other major software companies provide plug-ins that allow Netscape Navigator to run ActiveX objects, but these plug-ins do not come standard with the Web browser.)

As with a Java applet, to use an ActiveX object, you place a tag within an HTML file at the location where you want the object to appear on the Web page. To place an ActiveX object on a page, you use an <object> tag.

Unlike Java applets, which run within the browser, ActiveX objects must reside on the user's disk. If the user visits a Web page that uses an ActiveX object and the user does not have the object installed on his or her disk, the Web server will try to download the object to the user's computer. Normally, depending on the user's security settings, the Web browser will display a dialog box, similar to that shown in Figure 9-4, that warns the user that he or she is about to download an ActiveX object.

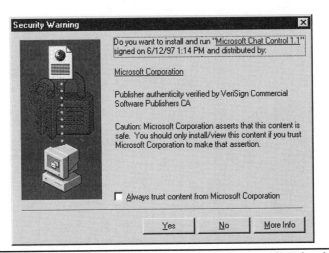

Figure 9-4   A dialog box warning the user that he or she is about to download an ActiveX object

The browser warns the user about ActiveX objects because, unlike Java applets, which have a security model that prevents them from accessing the user's files and disk, ActiveX objects are not safe. An ActiveX object must actually reside on the user's disk (or more specifically, on the Web pages that the user visits) before the user can use the object. Furthermore, unlike Java applets, which execute within a sandbox that prevents the applets from accessing system resources, ActiveX objects can access all of the files and resources on a computer. After the user downloads an ActiveX object, a Web page can interact with the object using a scripting language, such as VBScript or JavaScript.

If the visitor is too trusting and accepts an ActiveX object from an unknown Web site, the visitor might just wind up installing a program that contains a virus or that sends the user's personal data (or perhaps the entire contents of the hard drive) to an unauthorized party. As a designer, your job is to put ActiveX objects only from trusted sources (such as Microsoft, Macromedia, or programmers you trust) on your Web pages.

Programmers create ActiveX objects using myriad programming languages, such as Visual Basic and Visual C++. This chapter will not teach you how to write ActiveX objects. Instead, this chapter shows you how you can integrate existing ActiveX objects into your Web pages.

Placing a Java Applet Within a Web Page

As you have learned, a Java applet is a program that a Web browser runs as part of your Web page content. To embed an applet in a Web page, you use the start and end applet tags (<applet> </applet>). Within the <applet> tag, you use the *code* attribute to specify the filename of the Java applet (which will have a .class file extension, or a .jar file extension if the applet requires multiple files). You may also use other attributes that specify the size of the window within which the applet will run as well as values you want to pass to the applet, such as a text message you want the applet to display.

The following tags, for example, will embed an applet that resides in the file appletClassName.class on a Web page:

```
<applet code="appletClassName.class" height=150 width=150>
</applet>
```

When the browser encounters the <applet> tag, the browser must download the applet from the server, much like the browser must download a graphic when it encounters an <img> tag. In this example, the Web browser will expect to find the applet file appletClassName.class in the same folder as the Web page in which you embedded the applet. The *height* and *width* attributes tell the Web browser to give the applet a 150-pixel by 150-pixel viewable area (that is, to make the Java program's input-output screen 150 pixels high by 150 pixels wide).

As the original developer of the Java programming language, Sun Microsystems offers many sample Java applets on its Web site (http://java.sun.com). Figure 9-5, for example, shows a Java applet that you can use to display a simple analog clock on a Web page.

To get started with Java, you will first use Sun's analog clock applet, which you can download from either Sun's Web site or this book's Web site at http://www.Osborne.com. When you download the application, you will actually download a Zip file, named demo.zip, that contains applet's .class files (in this case, AnalogClock.class, CustomParser.class, JavaClock.class, and ParamParser.class) to a folder on your Web site. After you download the Zip file, you must then unzip the file's contents. When you unzip the file, place the applet's .class files in a folder in which you can create an HTML document that will contain the applet.

Next, create an HTML file, named FirstApplet.html, that contains the following <applet> tag, which embeds the Java analog clock applet onto a Web page:

```
<applet code="JavaClock.class" width="150" height="150">
</applet>
```

Using your browser, open the file FirstApplet.html. When the browser encounters the <applet> tag, the browser will load the applet file. After the browser translates the applet's generic bytecode, the browser runs the applet, displaying the analog clock shown in Figure 9-5.

Although the analog clock applet uses the four .class files previously listed, you specify only one, JavaClock.class, in the <applet> tag. When you embed an applet that has multiple .class files, the applet's documentation will tell you the name of the class to assign to the *code* attribute.

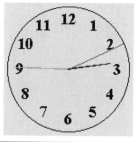

Figure 9-5 The original analog clock applet developed by Sun Microsystems

Specifying the Applet's Location on a Web Page

An applet, like a picture, takes up space on your Web page, and you locate the applet's viewable area (as you do a graphics image) by placing the start and end applet tags (<applet> </applet>) in the Web page HTML where you want the applet to appear on the page. The Web browser takes care of executing the Java code in the applet and displaying the results in the applet's viewable area. Within a Web page, you treat applets as you do other objects, such as images, text, animations, and video clips—meaning, in general, that you only have to determine the size of the applet's output area and where you want the area to appear on your Web page. For example, the following HTML statements insert the analog clock applet on a Web page, below the text at the top of the page and between the two images, as shown in Figure 9-6:

```
<html>
<body bgcolor="#ADD8E6">
  <h1><center>HTML and Web Design Tips & Techniques</center></h1>
  <p>The clock appears on the page below this text and between
     the two pictures. In this example, the applet's location
     is controlled by the location within the Web page HTML of
     the tags used to insert the applet on the page. The
     applet appears after content inserted before the applet's
     tags in the HTML, before content inserted after the
     applet's start and end applet tags.</p>
  <img src="images/pix1_small.jpg">
  <applet code="JavaClock.class" width="150" height="150">
  </applet>
  <img src="images/pix2_small.jpg">
</body>
</html>
```

Similarly, if you want text to flow around an applet, as shown in Figure 9-7, you would use code similar to the following:

```
<html>
<body bgcolor="#ADD8E6">
  <h1><center>HTML and Web Design Tips & Techniques</center></h1>
  <hr><img align="left" src="images/pix2_small.jpg">
  This text appears to the right of the first image on the
  page. The text flows along the right-hand side of the image
  because the align attribute tells the browser to place the
  image flush with the left-hand margin.<hr>
```

```
<p><applet align="right" code="JavaClock.class"
        width="150" height="150"></applet>

This text is to the left of the second "image"; that is, the
applet on the Web page. Although the text follows the
applet's tags in the Web page HTML, it appears before
(that is, to the left of) the applet because the align tag
tells the browser to put the applet along the right-hand
margin and flow text in the same paragraph with the applet
along the applet's left-hand side. </p>
</body>
</html>
```

Within the Web page, you can use the *align* attribute to tell the Web browser where to place text in relation to both an image and an applet. In this example, align="left" in the <img> tag tells the browser to place the image along the left side of the page and to flow text along the picture's right side. Similarly, align="right" in the <applet> tag tells the browser to place the applet flush with the right margin and float text along the left side of the applet's viewable area.

When you want an applet—that is, the applet's viewable area—to appear at a specific location on the Web page, you can use an HTML table (as you learned from Tips in Chapter 2) or a rule on a Cascading Style Sheet (as you learned from Tips in Chapter 4). For example, to center an applet on

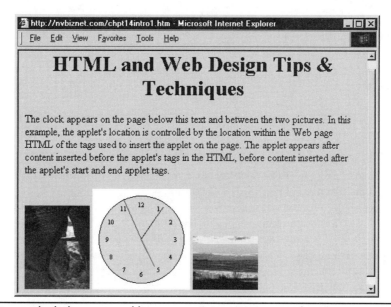

Figure 9-6   An applet below text and between two images on a Web page

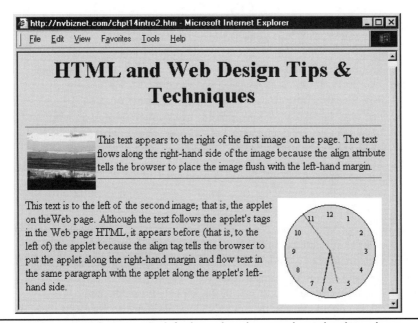

Figure 9-7 A Web page with an image left aligned and an applet right aligned

a Web page between two columns of text, as shown in Figure 9-8, you might use a table with zero-width (hidden) borders, as follows:

```
<html>
<body>
  <h1><center>HTML and Web Design Tips & Techniques</center></h1>
  <hr>
  <center>
    <table border="0">
      <tr><td width="150">
          Text in the first column of the table appears to
          the left of the applet</td>
        <td width="150">
          <applet code="JavaClock.class"
                width="150" height="150"></applet></td>
        <td width="150">
          Text in the third column (from the left) in the
          table appears to the right of the applet, because
          the applet itself is in the second column, which
          happens to be the center column of a three-column
```

```
            table.</td>
        </tr>
      </table>
    </center>
  </body>
</html>
```

In short, you treat your Java applet as you would an image you insert on a Web page. As with an image, decide where you want the applet's rectangular viewable area to appear and then insert the start and end applet tags (<applet></applet>) in the Web page HTML next to other objects or within a table cell to position the applet at a specific location on the page.

Passing Parameter Values to an Applet

On the Web, you can find dozens of sites with hundreds of applets you can use on your Web pages. Some applets come complete with source code you can modify and then compile to customize the applets to suit your needs. However, most applets let you specify initial values, called *parameters*, which you can use to change the applet's appearance and output without having to do any programming whatsoever.

When you download an applet from the Web, the documentation the programmer provides with the applet will tell you the name and purpose of each parameter the applet will accept. To pass values

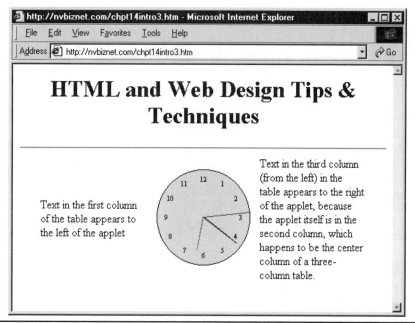

Figure 9-8   A Web page with an applet positioned between columns of text using a table

to an applet, you simply insert a <param> tag with the name and value of each parameter you want to pass between the applet's start and end applet tags (<applet></applet>), as shown here:

```
<applet code="AppletName.class"
        width="PixelWidth" height="PixelHeight">
  <param name="ParameterName1" value="ParameterValue1">
  <param name="ParameterName2" value="ParameterValue2">
  <param name="ParameterNameN" value="ParameterValueN">
</applet>
```

To better understand how passing parameter values to a Java applet lets you customize the applet's processing, consider Sun Microsystems' NervousText.class applet that animates the letters in a text string by bouncing the letters in a nervous fashion, as shown next. You can download the NervousText applet from the Sun Microsystem Java Web site or from this book's Web site at http://www.Osborne.com.

After you download and unzip the NervousText applet, you can embed the applet within an HTML page using the following <applet> tag:

```
<applet code="NervousText.class"
        width="468" height="50"></applet>
```

Although the text displayed by NervousText provides an interesting animation effect, you will want to change that text that the applet displays before you use the applet to display bouncing text on your Web pages. Without parameters, you would have to download the applet's Java source file (NervousText.java), edit the text string that the applet animates (Hot Java), and then compile the program into a new Java .class file that you embed on the Web page. Fortunately, the NervousText applet lets you use a parameter to pass the string to animate, which means that you do not have to do any programming to change the text that the applet displays.

To have the applet NervousText.class animate the string "I'm nervous until I have my java." you would use the <param> tag when you embed the applet in your Web page, as follows:

```
<applet codebase="/java" code="NervousText.class"
        width="510" height="50">
  <param name="text" value="I'm nervous until I have my java." >
</applet>
```

After you load the HTML file that contains the <param> tag to specify a parameter within your browser, the applet will use the parameter text, as shown here:

If the parameter value you pass changes the amount of space that the applet needs to display its output, you must increase the values of the *width* and *height* attributes in the <applet> tag accordingly. In this example, the increase in the animated text's length requires you to increase the width of the area allocated to the applet on the Web page. If size of the area you specify (with the *width* and *height* attributes in the <applet> tag) is too small, the browser will simply cut off that portion of the applet's output that does not fit. (If the applet's documentation does not specify the dimensions of the applet's output area, or if you pass a parameter value to change the applet's output, you may need to experiment with different *height* and *width* attribute values until you get the sizing just right.)

Understanding Java Archive (.jar) Files

One criticism of Java applets is the amount of time the Web browser takes to download the applet files. Each time the browser retrieves a Web page with an embedded applet, the browser must retrieve the applet, as it does graphics images, sound files, and all other embedded objects. Applets that are larger and more complex often require multiple class files, each of which the browser must download before the applet can run.

To reduce download times, Java programmers often store an applet's files (class files, graphics files, sound files, and so on) within a Java Archive (or *.jar*) file. You can think of a .jar file as similar to a compressed Zip file. By storing an applet's files in a single .jar file, the programmer reduces the amount of time the Web browser takes to download the applet from the Web server.

To use a .jar file when you embed an applet, you must add the *archive* attribute to the <applet> tag, as follows:

```
<applet code="JavaClock.class" width="150" height="150"
        archive="Clock.jar">
</applet>
```

In this case, when the browser encounters the <applet> tag, the browser will establish an HTTP connection with the server and request the Clock.jar Java Archive file. If the archive file does not exist, most browsers will try to retrieve the applet's individual .class files instead. Note that the name of the archive file need not be the same as the name of the applet's main .class file.

Understanding the codebase Attribute

If you keep your Java .class files in a folder other than the one in which you store your HTML documents, you must use the *codebase* attribute within the <applet> tag to tell the Web browser where to find the .class file you specify in the *code* attribute. Suppose, for example, that you keep your Web page files in the Web site's HTDocs folder and your Java applet .class files in a folder named Classes. If both folders are in the Web site's root folder, you would use the *codebase* attribute within the <applet> tag as follows to embed the JavaClock.class applet:

```
<applet codebase="/Classes" code="JavaClock.class"
        width="150" height="150">
</applet>
```

You can also use the *codebase* attribute to tell the browser to embed a Java applet that resides at a different Web site into a Web page. To embed a remote applet, you simply specify the full URL of the folder that contains the applet's .class files in the *codebase* attribute. For example, to embed the analog clock applet in the Classes folder on www.NVBizNet2.com on your Web page, you would use the following *codebase* attribute:

```
<applet codebase="http://www.nvbiznet2.com/classes"
        code="JavaClock.class" width="150" height="150">
</applet>
```

▶ **NOTE**

Be careful when you embed applets stored at other Web sites. Remember that the Web browser must download all of the applet's .class files after the browser retrieves the Web page on which you inserted the applet. If someone deletes the .class files or moves them to a different folder, the Web browser will be unable to retrieve them and therefore unable to display the applet on your Web page. Unless you control the content on the remote site, to ensure that the applet is available when you need it, download the applet's .class files to a folder on your Web site.

Embedding an ActiveX Object in a Web Page

Like a Java applet, an ActiveX object provides program code that you want a Web browser to run as part of your Web page content. To embed an ActiveX object in a Web page, insert the object as you would an applet, except instead of using the <applet> tag (which you would use to insert an applet), use a set of start and end object tags (<object></object>) to place the ActiveX object on the page.

Suppose, for example, that you want to display the stock ticker from the Microsoft Network (MSN) financial Web site (at http://moneycentral.msn.com) on your page. You would insert the following code in the Web page HTML where you want the stock ticker (shown here) to appear on the Web page:

```
<object id="StockTicker" width="100%" height="34"
  type="application/x-oleobject"
  classid="clsid:52ADE293-85E8-11D2-BB22-00104B0EA281"
  codebase="http://fdl.msn.com/public/investor/v7
/ticker.cab#version=7,1999,1104,1">

  <param name="ServerRoot" value="http://moneycentral.msn.com" />
  <param name="NewsTarget" value="_newstop" />
  <param name="BackgroundColor" value="0x00ADD8E6" />

<!-- The following <embed> tag lets Netscape Navigator v 6.1
```

```
   (and later) run the ActiveX Control -->

 <embed type="application/x-eskeractivex" id="StockTicker"
   clsid="52ADE293-85E8-11D2-BB22-00104B0EA281"
   codebase="http://fdl.msn.com/public/investor/v7
/ticker.cab#version=7,1999,1104,1"
   width="100%" height="34"
   serverroot="http://moneycentral.msn.com"
   BackgroundColor="0x00ADD8E6"
   newstarget="_newstop" value="0x00ADD8E6" />
</object>
```

After reviewing the <object> tag's contents, you will notice several similarities between it and the <applet> tag. The attributes within an <object> tag have the following meanings:

- **id** A unique name you assign to the object so that other objects on the same Web page can communicate with the object and so you can work with the object (by name) in any scripts inserted on the page.

- **width**, **height** The object's initial dimensions in pixels. Bear in mind that an ActiveX object can change the size (and location) of its display area. While the stock ticker in this example and the Macromedia Shockwave animation (you will embed in the next example) stay within the dimensions defined, an ActiveX pop-up menu, for example, will start at the size of a standard pushbutton and expand to whatever dimensions it needs to display all of the items on the menu.

- **type** Optional attribute that identifies the type of content you are embedding.

- **classid** Attribute that identifies the object's implementation: that is, the name of the runtime program you want to execute. The long string of digits and letters assigned to the *classid* attribute is a 128-bit value known as a globally unique identifier (GUID). The programmer that writes the ActiveX application that runs a special software tool (GUIDGEN.EXE) to create a unique GUID—meaning no two programs ever have the same GUID.

- **codebase** Attribute that specifies the location where the browser can find and download the program specified by the *classid* attribute, if necessary. (If the browser previously downloaded and installed the ActiveX object, the browser will use the local copy instead of downloading the program again.) If you omit the *codebase* attribute, the browser will expect to find the implementation (that is, the ActiveX program) in the same folder as the document in which you embedded the object. In this example, the *codebase* attribute instructs the browser that the implementation is within a .cab file. (Programmers put a program that requires more than one file for installation in a .cab file, much like Java developers use .jar files.)

- **param** Values you wanted passed to the ActiveX program at run time. Normally parameters contain setup information and initial values for program variables.

Although the *classid* and *codebase* attributes seem to have undecipherable values, do not worry about how the values are generated. The programmer who writes your ActiveX program or the documentation of the program you download from the Internet will give you both of these values.

Your main job as a designer is to decide what you need the ActiveX object to do and where you want the object to appear on your Web page. The programmers will write and compile the program, use an application named genuid.exe to generate a unique 128-bit identifier for the program, and store the code (that is, the implementation) in a folder on the Web server. After you read the documentation (or question the programmer), you simply plug in the values provided to you for the *classid* and *codebase* attributes.

Making ActiveX Objects Work with Netscape Navigator and Internet Explorer

Unfortunately, the two companies whose browsers are likely to be used by 95 percent of your site's visitors have not been able to agree on the "best" way to embed external programs in Web pages. While Internet Explorer uses <object> tags and ActiveX objects to add functionality to the browser, Netscape Navigator uses <embed> tags and plug-ins (which are external helper programs).

The result, and the part that concerns you as a designer, is that Netscape Navigator will not run an ActiveX object until you install a program-specific plug-in. Moreover, Netscape Navigator requires you to use an <embed> tag instead of an <object> tag to embed the program you want the browser to execute. Fortunately, you can insert start and end embed tags (<embed></embed>) within start and end object tags (<object></object>), and each browser will ignore the HTML intended for the other. The plug-in you must download and install differs depending on your version of Netscape Navigator.

You can find plug-ins that provide Netscape Navigator with ActiveX support at several Web sites. You might first visit http://www.esker.com, which offers a plug-in you can download that supports a wide range of ActiveX controls. In addition, you can find links to other plug-ins and explanation of the steps you should follow for your specific version of Netscape at http://www.mozilla.org.

For example, if you want to play a Shockwave animation (ants.swf) stored in the same folder as your Web page, you might insert the following statements on the page where you want the animation to appear:

```
<object
    classid="clsid:D27CDB6E-AE6D-11cf-96B8-444553540000"
    codebase="http://download.macromedia.com/pub/shockwave/cabs/flash
/swflash.cab#version=5,0,30,0"
    width="300" height="120">
    <param name="movie"    value="ants.swf">
    <param name="quality" value=high>
    <param name="salign"   value="TL">

  <embed
    src="ants.swf"
    quality="high"
    pluginspage="http://www.macromedia.com/shockwave/download
/index.cgi?P1_Prod_Version=ShockwaveFlash"
    type="application/x-shockwave-flash"
    width="200" height="200" salign="TL">
  </embed>
</object>
```

When Internet Explorer encounters the preceding code, the browser uses the attributes and parameters found prior to the <embed> tag to start the Shockwave animation (and to download Shockwave Player, if necessary). Netscape Navigator, on the other hand, will ignore the HTML up to the <embed> tag and use the code between the start and end embed tags (<embed></embed>) to play the animation (and download the plug-in, if necessary).

Understanding Signed Objects

Because ActiveX objects can be unsafe, you should download and install ActiveX objects only from programmers or companies that you trust. Often, programmers who develop trusted ActiveX objects will attach a digital signature to the object that users who download the object can examine to confirm that the individuals or company claiming to have developed the object is authentic (meaning that they are who they claim to be). In addition, if an ActiveX control contains a valid certificate, users can be confident that a hacker did not intercept and change the object as it made its way across the Internet. Within Windows, for example, many users will direct their browsers to automatically install and use signed objects, as opposed to prompting the user for permission before installing the objects. If a system's security level directs the browser to prompt the user before it downloads and installs an ActiveX object, the browser will display a Security Warning dialog box similar to that shown previously in Figure 9-4 when an <embed> tag calls for an ActiveX object not already installed on the user's system.

Within the Security Warning dialog box, you can view certificate information by clicking the publisher's name. Your browser, in turn, will display a Certificate dialog box, within which you can view the specifics of the setting, as shown in Figure 9-9.

To give users greater security control, Windows assigns two levels of security for ActiveX controls: safe for initialization and safe for scripting. When a programmer specifies that an ActiveX control is safe for initialization, the programmer is stating the control will not misbehave (meaning that the object will work correctly, and a script cannot cause the object's code to fail or to perform a malicious operation), regardless of the initial values the user may assign to the control using <param> tags. If Internet Explorer encounters an ActiveX control within an HTML page that is not safe for initialization and the <object> tag contains one or more <param> tags that initialize the object, Internet Explorer may, depending on your security settings, display a dialog box that alerts you to a potential security violation.

When a programmer marks an ActiveX control as safe for scripting, the programmer is stating that the control will behave properly, regardless of how a script manipulates the control. Again, if Internet Explorer encounters an ActiveX control within an HTML page that is not marked as safe for scripting, the browser may, depending on your security settings, display a dialog box that warns of a potential security violation.

Fine-Tuning Java and ActiveX Security Settings

To prevent your browser from downloading Java applets or ActiveX objects without your knowledge or permission, Windows lets you assign settings that dictate how the browser handles the applets and objects. Using the security settings, for example, you might direct the browser to download and

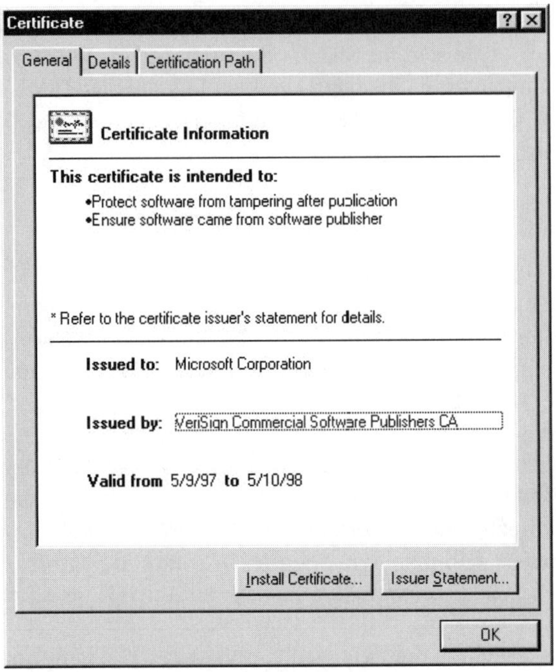

Figure 9-9   Viewing the specifics of an object's certificate

install signed objects automatically, but to prompt you before downloading unsigned objects. To use the Windows security settings to control Java and ActiveX objects, perform these steps:

1. Select the Start menu Settings option and choose Control Panel. Windows will open the Control Panel window.

2. Within the Control Panel, double-click the Internet Options icon. Windows will display the Internet Properties dialog box.

3. Within the Internet Properties dialog box, select the Security tab. Windows will display the Security sheet.

4. Within the Security sheet, click the Custom Level button. Windows will display the Security Settings dialog box, shown in Figure 9-10.

5. Within the Security Settings dialog box, use the radio buttons to select the setting levels you desire and then click OK to return to the Internet Options dialog box. Then click OK within the Internet Options dialog box to exit the dialog box.

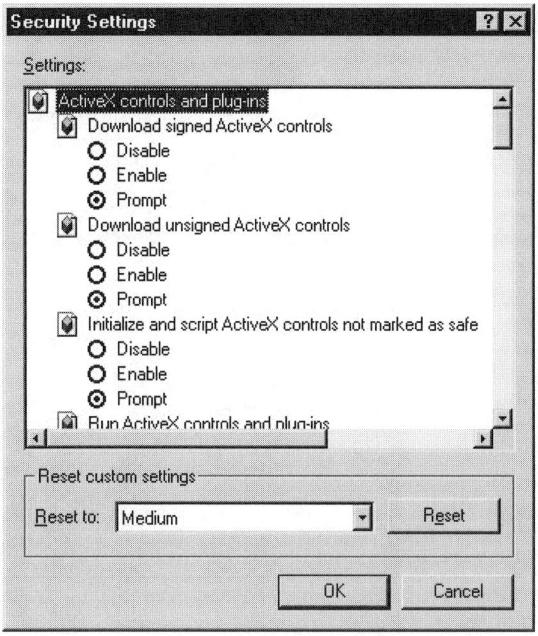

Figure 9-10   Setting Java and ActiveX security within the Security Settings dialog box

▶ *NOTE*

Within Internet Explorer, you can access the Internet Options dialog box by selecting Tools |
Internet Options.

Using an Applet to Create a Pop-Up Navigation Menu

As you increase the number of Web pages available on your Web site, you must increase the number
of entries on your navigation menu. After all, you want to let your visitors jump to specific pages
without forcing them to go through several other pages first. Unfortunately, increasing the number of
hypertext links on your navigation menu also means increasing the menu's size, which often forces
you to split content into two pages. PopupNavigator.class, an applet written by Branko Dimitrijevic,
provides a solution that lets you present a navigation bar in the form of a hierarchical menu. To save
space, the applet appears on the screen as a pushbutton that, when clicked, displays a pop-up menu
over the Web page content, as shown in Figure 9-11.

When a user clicks the pushbutton, the browser will launch the applet, which displays the pop-up
menu. Within the menu, the user simply clicks the menu choice he or she desires. The applet then
retrieves and displays an HTML document linked to the visitor's choice. The Web page that
corresponds to the menu option can reside at the current Web site or at another site. If the visitor

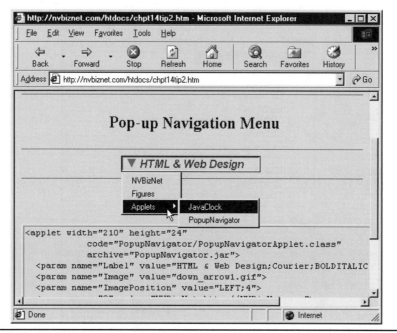

Figure 9-11   The PopupNavigator applet after a mouse click

moves the mouse pointer over a menu choice that has a right arrow (such as Applets in Figure 9-11), the applet will display a submenu of additional choices.

USE IT   You can view and download the PopupNavigator.class applet and its source code at http://www.osborne.com. After copying PopupNavigator.zip to a folder on your computer, extract the .class (Java applet), .gif (picture), and .jar (Java Archive) files from the compressed (Zip) file. To use the pop-up navigation menu on a Web page, copy all .gif files and either the .jar file or all of the .class files into the same folder as the Web page. Then insert HTML statements similar to the following on the page where you want the pop-up menu button to appear:

```
<applet align="center" width="210" height="24"
        code="PopupNavigator/PopupNavigatorApplet.class"
        archive="PopupNavigator.jar">
  <param name="Label"
   value="HTML & Web Design;Arial;BOLDITALIC;16;RED;200 255 0">
  <param name="Image" value="down_arrow1.gif">
  <param name="ImagePosition" value="LEFT;4">

  <param name="0" value="NVBizNet;http://www.NVBizNet.com">
  <param name="1" value="Figures;ListOfFigures.htm">
  <param name="2" value="Applets;">
```

```
    <param name="2;0" value="JavaClock;Chpt09Tip1.htm">
    <param name="2;1" value="PopupNavigator;Chpt09Tip2.htm">
</applet>
```

▶ **NOTE**

PopupNavigator.jar is a Java Archive file that contains the applet's .class files in a compressed format. To reduce download times, you should use a .jar file when one is available. The applet will function the same way whether you use the .class files or the .jar file. To use the .jar file, you must use the archive *attribute in the* <applet> *tag to specify the name of the Java Archive file. Without an* archive *attribute, the start applet tag* <applet> *tells the browser to load the applet's .class files.*

The parameters you use to set up the pop-up menu are described next.

label   A semicolon (;) delimited string with the label you want on the pushbutton and a description of how you want the label and the pushbutton itself to look. The syntax of the label's value string is "<label>;<typeface>;<font style>;<font size>;<label text color><button color>". If you omit the label parameter altogether, the applet will display "Navigate" as the pushbutton's label text. You can also use browser default values for <typeface>, <font style>, and <size> by omitting these values from the value string. When specifying the label text or button color, either use the Netscape Navigator color name or express the color as a triplet of decimal numbers (with a space between each number) that indicates the RGB values that make up the color. If you omit <label text color> or <button color>, the applet will display black text on a gray (control) button.

image   The pathname (URL) of an image you want displayed on the pushbutton. If you want only a text label, omit the *image* parameter. For example, the preceding code labels the button "HTML & Web Design" by setting the *label* parameter's value to "HTML & Web Design;Arial;BOLDITALIC;16; RED;200 255 0".

imageposition   The location of the image (specified by the image parameter) in relation to the sides of the pushbutton. Here are the possible values:

- **CENTER**   Center the image on the button.
- **LEFT, RIGHT, TOP,** and **BOTTOM**   Position the image relative to the middle of the left, right, top, or bottom of the pushbutton. For example, value="LEFT;4" tells the applet to position the image 4 pixels away (toward the center of the button) from the left side of the button.
- **ABSOLUTE**   Position the image at specific (x,y) coordinates within the pushbutton. For example, value="ABSOLUTE;24;16" tells the applet to position the image at coordinates $24(x)$, $16(y)$ relative to the top left corner of the pushbutton.

<menu item>   the parameter tag <param> for each menu item has a *name* attribute that consists of a semicolon (;) delimited set of integer coordinates. The parameter tag's *value* attribute consists of the item text followed by a semicolon and then the URL of the Web page that the applet is to display when the visitor selects the menu choice.

 USE IT   Although the menu in the example at the start of this Tip has only two levels, you can create a hierarchical menu with as many submenus as you want—meaning that submenus can have submenus that, in turn, can have submenus, and so on. For example, to add two levels of submenus to the Figures option in the preceding example, you would change the parameter declarations as follows:

```
<param name="0" value="NVBizNet;http://www.NVBizNet.com">
<param name="1" value="Figures;">
<param name="2" value="Applets;">

<param name="1;0" value="Chapter 1; ">
<param name="1;1" value="Chapter 2; ">
<param name="1;0;0" value="Chapter 1, Figure 1;Fig1-1.htm">
<param name="1;0;1" value="Chapter 1, Figure 2;Fig1-2.htm">
<param name="1;1;0" value="Chapter 2; Figure 1;Fig2-1.htm">
<param name="1;1;1" value="Chapter 2; Figure 2;Fig2-2.htm">

<param name="2;0" value="JavaClock;Chpt09Tip1.htm">
<param name="2;1" value="PopupNavigator;Chpt09Tip2.htm">
```

Notice that menu items that lead to submenus when selected (such as Figures, Applets, and Chapter 1) have only the item text and no URL. Conversely, menu items that have no submenus (such as NVBizNet, Chapter 1, Figure 1, Chapter 2, and Figure 2) have both the item text that the browser is to display as the (sub)menu choice and the URL of the Web page that the applet is to tell the browser to retrieve.

Using an Applet to Animate a Text String

When you want to draw a visitor's attention to a banner or text passage, animate it. Because characters on a page normally remain unchanged, animated text (that is, text that changes) attracts attention. One way to animate text is to create a marquee that moves text across the screen. Another way is to use an applet, such as AnimText.class, that continuously changes the size of each of the characters in a stationary string.

USE IT   You can view and download the AnimText.class applet and its source code at http://www.osborne.com. After copying AnimText.zip to a folder on your computer, extract AnimText.class from the compressed file. Next, to use the applet on a Web page, copy the applet's .class file (AnimText.class) into the same folder as the Web page. Then insert HTML similar to the following on the page where you want the animated text to appear:

```
<applet code="AnimText.class" width="575" height="65">
    <param name="text"    value="HTML and Web Design">
    <param name="font"    value="TimesNewRoman">
    <param name="style"   value="PLAIN">
    <param name="fgcolor" value="blue">
    <param name="bgcolor" value="255:255:255">
    <param name="type"    value="wave">
    <param name="min"     value="14">
    <param name="max"     value="48">
    <param name="align"   value="center">
</applet>
```

To specify the text, the text's appearance, and the animation effect, you can pass the following parameters to the applet:

- **text**   The text string you want to animate. Default: "Welcome to Java!".
- **font**   The typeface you want the applet to use. Default: "TimesRoman".
- **style**   The font style: plain, bold, or italic. Default: "plain".
- **fgcolor**   The text color expressed as a word or as a string of three colon (:) delimited RGB values (as shown by the *bgcolor* setting in the preceding code). The possible word color values are red, blue, green, yellow, white, orange, cyan, and magenta. Default: "black".
- **bgcolor**   The applet's background color expressed either as a word (as shown by the *fgcolor* setting in the preceding code) or as a string of three colon (:) delimited RGB values. The possible word color values are the same as those listed for *fgcolor*. Default: "lightgray".
- **type**   Controls whether the applet increases and decreases the size of all characters in the text string together (blink) or independently (wave). In addition to blink and wave, you can set the *type* attribute to random and let the visitor's computer select which of the two effects to use when animating the text. Default: "wave".
- **max**   The maximum character size, in points. Default: "28".
- **min**   The minimum character size, in points. Default: "8".
- **align**   You can align text flush left, flush right, or centered between the sides of the applet. Default: "center".

If you want to use the animated text as a hyperlink, simply insert the applet as you would a hyperlinked image between a set of start and end anchor tags (<a></a>). Set the *href* attribute in the start anchor tag to the URL of the Web page you want the browser to display when the visitor clicks the animated text.

Using an Applet to Display and Print a Calendar for Any Year

When you ask users to enter a specific date (such as when reserving a hotel room) or to enter a date range (for example, when asking for time off from work), users often will need to refer to a calendar. Thus, your visitors will find the calendar.class applet helpful when they need to look up a date but do not have a printed calendar at hand. The calendar.class applet, written by Kerry Newman, lets visitors not only view but also print a hard copy of the calendar for an entire year of the visitor's choice.

USE IT   You can view and download the calendar.class applet (shown in Figure 9-12) and its source code at http://www.osborne.com.

After copying KNCalendar.zip to a folder on your computer, extract calendar.class from the Zip file. To use the applet to display a calendar on a Web page, copy the .class file into the same folder as the Web page. Then insert HTML similar to the following on the page where you want the calendar to appear:

```
<applet code="calendar.class" width="780" height="680">
</applet>
```

You cannot use parameters to customize the calendar's appearance or change its size. However, your site visitors can use the FontColor and BackColor buttons on the calendar to change the text and

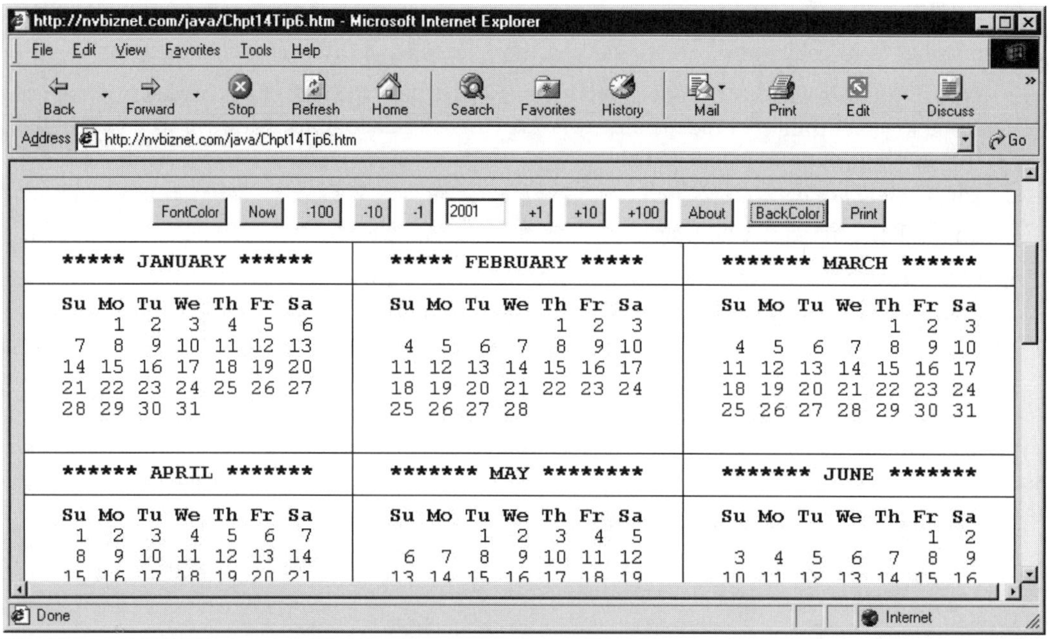

Figure 9-12   A calendar displayed by the calendar.class applet

background colors. Of course, the KNCalendar.zip file does include the Java source code (in calendar.java). Therefore, if you have installed a Java compiler on your computer, such as the one in the free Java software development kit at the Sun Microsystems Web site, you can always modify the applet to accept parameters such as the initial date, colors, and size.

Using an Applet to Display a Passage at Random from a Text File

One of the challenges in designing a Web site is to keep your content fresh, so visitors continue to come back. The PetQuotes.class applet lets you display passages, one at a time, from a text file. By using random selection to choose the passage to be displayed, the applet will likely display a different passage each time the visitor's browser retrieves the Web page, as shown in Figure 9-13.

Although the applet (as written) will retrieve the text to be displayed only from a file named PetQuotes.txt, you can place any lines of text you want in the file. Thus, you can use the PetQuotes.class applet to display jokes, quotations, or any other type of text you choose to place in the file.

USE IT You can view and download the PetQuotes.class applet and its source code at http://www.osborne.com. After copying PetQuotes.zip to a folder on your computer, extract PetQuotes.class and PetQuotes.txt from the compressed file. Next, to use the applet on a

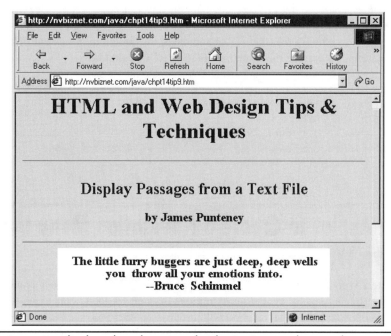

Figure 9-13   Quotation displayed on the screen by the PetQuotes.class applet

Web page, copy the two files (PetQuotes.class and PetQuotes.txt) into the same folder as the Web page. Then insert HTML similar to the following on the page where you want the text passage to appear:

```
<applet code="PetQuotes.class" width="410" height="72">
  <param name="font"      value="Arial">
  <param name="font_size" value="18">
  <param name="color"     value="black">
  <param name="bgcolor"   value="white">
</applet>
```

To change the appearance of the text and the applet's background color, you can pass the following parameters:

- **font**   The typeface you want the applet to use. Default: "TimeRoman".
- **font_size**   The character size, in points. Default: "18".
- **color**   The text color. Possible values are black, white, lightgray, gray, darkgray, red, pink, orange, yellow, green, magenta, cyan, and blue. Default: "black".
- **bgcolor**   The text color. Possible values are black, white, lightgray, gray, darkgray, red, pink, orange, yellow, green, magenta, cyan, and blue. Default: "white".

To supply your own quotes, jokes, or other text passages for the applet to display, edit the file PetQuotes.txt. On the first line in the file, enter the number of lines of text in the file. Then, on the second and subsequent lines, enter the lines of text you want displayed. Enter each passage and source on a separate line as <text passage>||<source>. Note the double-pipe symbol (‖) between the text of each quotation or passage and the source (that is, the author) of the quotation or passage. The following file illustrates sample content you might include in the PetQuotes.txt file:

```
3
Some men dream of doing great things. Others stay up late and
 get them done.||Anonymous
Sometimes a scream is better than a thesis.||Ralph Waldo Emerson
I've been on a diet for two weeks and all I've lost is two
 weeks.||Totie Fields
```

Using an Applet to Create a Navigation Menu that Runs in Its Own Window

When you create a Web site, you want to make it easy for the site visitor to move from page to page or to jump to a particular page. If visitors have to move through 15 documents to get to the page they want, some might bookmark the page, but most will just go to another Web site that is easier to navigate. To make site navigation easy, you can insert a menu of hyperlinks on each of the site's Web pages.

The only problem with navigation menus is that they can take up a lot of room on large sites due to the number of hypertext links you must include in the menu.

Fortunately, you can use the MenuApplet.class applet to display a navigation menu with as many as 400 hyperlinks—without sacrificing room on the screen for your Web site's content. Because the applet displays the menu in a new window, you have to allow room for only a single pushbutton on each of your site's Web pages to let your visitors call for the navigation menu when they want to use it, as shown in Figure 9-14.

Moreover, the applet helps you organize the pages on your site by letting you split the site's pages into 20 categories, with 20 menu items per category.

USE IT   You can view and download the MenuApplet.class applet and its source code at http://www.osborne.com. After copying MenuApplet.zip to a folder on your computer, extract the two .class files (MenuApplet.class and LabelButton.class), the .ini file (MenuApplet.ini), and the menu Web page (menu.html) from the compressed file. After you edit the contents of the .ini file and the .html file (as discussed in the following paragraphs), copy the .class files, MenuApplet.ini, and menu.html to the same folder as the Web pages on which you want to insert the Site Menu buttons that call the MenuApplet.class applet.

The MenuApplet.ini file contains the categories and menu items that the applet presents to the visitor on the navigation menu. There are two types of lines in the .ini file: those that start and end

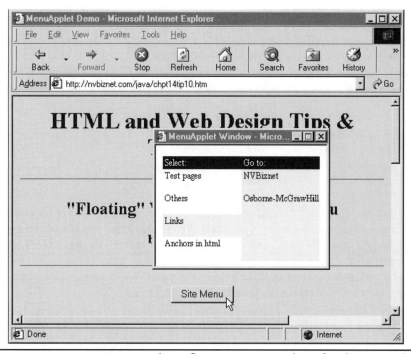

Figure 9-14   A navigation menu opened in a floating (new) window after the visitor clicks a pushbutton on a Web page

with a plus sign (+), and those that start with a backslash (\). Lines that start (and end) with a plus sign (+) are menu categories, which the applet displays in its left column, under the heading "Select." Lines that start with a backslash (\) are menu items, which the applet displays in its right column, labeled "Go To." When the visitor clicks a category in the applet's Select column, the applet displays the menu items in the category selected in the Go To column. Similarly, when the visitor clicks a menu item in the Go To column, the applet tells the Web browser to retrieve and display a Web page in the window whose name you pass to the applet through the *targetWindow* parameter (discussed later in this Tip).

Use a text editor to open MenuApplet.ini and replace the file's contents with your own categories and menu items. When you open the file the first time, you will see entries similar to the following:

```
+Test pages+
\test1\ "test_html/test1.html"
\test2\ "test_html/test2.html"


+Links+
\Osborne-McGrawHill\ "http://www.Osborne.com/"
\NVBizNet\            "http://www.NBVizNet.com"
```

To add a category to the menu, type the category text between plus signs (+) such as the category entries +Test pages+ and +Links+ shown in this example. To add menu items to a category, type the menu item text between backslash characters (\) followed by the relative address or URL that the browser is to retrieve, in quotation marks. In this example, \test1\ is a menu item in the Test pages category, and "test_html/test1.html" is the relative address of the Web page that the browser is to retrieve when the visitor clicks the test 1 menu choice. Note that you must define each menu choice within a category, and each category can have at most 20 menu choices.

If you look at the contents of the menu Web page (menu.html), you will see that it contains code similar to the following that embeds the MenuApplet.class applet in the Web page:

```
<applet code="MenuApplet.class" width="222" height="144">
  <param name="targetWindow" value="LoadHere">
  <param name="fontType"      value="TimesRoman">
  <param name="fontStyle"     value="0">
</applet>
```

Bear in mind that the MenuApplet.class applet lets you display a navigation menu in a window other than the one in which you are displaying your site's Web pages. Thus, you embed the menu applet in its own menu Web page (menu.html, in this example) and not in the Web page HTML of any of your site's content pages.

To customize the applet, use a text editor to open the menu Web page menu.html and set the following three parameters to the values you want the applet to use:

- **targetWindow**   The window in which you want the applet to display the Web page retrieved when the visitor clicks a menu choice. Default: "_self".

- **fontType**   The typeface you want the applet to use when displaying the menu's categories and items. Default: "Helvetica".

- **fontStyle**   A number from 0 to 3, inclusive, that specifies the font style of the menu text. 0 = plain, 1 = bold, 2 = italic, and 3 = bold + italic. Default: "0" (that is, plain).

To give visitors access to the menu, insert the following form definition on your Web pages where you want visitors to see the pushbutton they can click to display the navigation menu:

```
<form>
  <input type="button" name="NavButton" value="Site Menu"
         OnClick="window.open('menu.html', 'SiteNavMenu',
         'menubar=no, height=166, width=244')">
</form>
```

The form definition in this example will insert a standard pushbutton labeled Site Menu. When the visitor clicks the pushbutton, the Web browser executes the pushbutton's JavaScript, which opens the menu Web page (menu.html) in a new window named SiteNavMenu. The MenuApplet.class applet (embedded in the menu.html Web page) then displays the navigation menu in the SiteNavMenu window.

One last consideration you must take into account is the size of the window in which you want the MenuApplet.class applet to display the navigation menu. To calculate the height of the window, review the menu definition you created in MenuApplet.ini and determine whether your menu has more categories or more menu items in a single category. Then use the formula

```
height = (n + 1) * 18
```

where n is the maximum number of categories or maximum number of links in a single category, whichever is greater. To calculate the width, use the formula

```
width >= 12 + (p * 7) + (q * 7)
```

where p is the number of characters in the longest category name, and q is the number of characters in the longest menu item entry.

After you calculate the height and width, assign these values to the *height* and *width* attributes in the start applet tag <applet> in the menu Web page HTML (that is, in the file menu.html). Then, whatever values you compute for the applet's height and width, make them add 20 pixels to each dimension and assign those values to the *height* and *width* parameters the JavaScript passes to the *window.open()* function in the input tag <input> you use to put the Site Menu button on the Web page.

An added benefit of using the applet is that you will be able to make changes to the navigation menu at any time (by modifying the MenuApplet.ini file) and have those changes reflected immediately on all pages where you inserted the Site Menu pushbutton. (Using a traditional navigation bar inserted on each page, you would have to make the same menu change repeatedly on each of the site's pages.)

Using an Applet to Scroll the Contents of a File Vertically Within a Rectangular Box Onscreen

If you must scroll a single line of text horizontally across the screen, Internet Explorer lets you specify the text you want to scroll between a set of start and end marquee tags (<marquee></marquee>). For a more flexible solution, you might write JavaScript to perform the same function, since Netscape Navigator does not support the marquee tags, but both Netscape and Internet Explorer support JavaScript. When you want to display more than one line of text on the screen at the same time and scroll the text horizontally, you need something more than a simple marquee; you need the NewsScroller applet.

The NewsScroller applet, written by E. A. Graham, Jr., lets you scroll the text from an ASCII file vertically within a rectangular area on a Web page, as shown in Figure 9-15.

Within the input file to be displayed, the applet lets you designate single and multiline headings, messages, and clickable (that is, hyperlink-like) text, each in its own color.

USE IT You can view and download the NewsScroller applet and source code at http://www. osborne.com. After copying NewsScroller.zip to a folder on your computer, extract Scroller.jar and News.txt from the compressed file. Next, to use the applet on a Web page, copy the Java Archive file Scroller.jar and the news message file News.txt into the same folder as the Web page. Then insert HTML similar to the following in the Web page HTML where you want the scrolling text to appear:

```
<applet code="crackers.Scroller.NewsScroller.class"
        archive="scroller.jar" width="400" height="150">
  <param name="DataFile"   value="News.txt">
  <param name="ClickColor" value="#0000FF">
  <param name="HeadColor"  value="#FF0000">
  <param name="Font"       value="Serif">
  <param name="FontSize"   value="18">
  <param name="MousePause" value="">
  <param name="TopPause"   value="0">
  <param name="Refresh"    value="0">
  <param name="Foreground" value="#000000">
  <param name="Background" value="#FFFFFF">
  <param name="Border"     value="8">
  <param name="Picture"    value="bg_gif.gif">
  <param name="Target"     value="_top">
  <param name="SleepTime"  value="30">
  <param name="Scrollby"   value="1">
</applet>
```

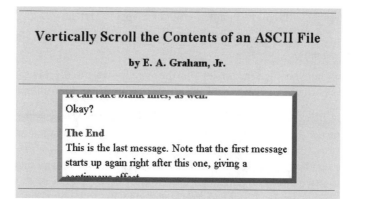

Figure 9-15   The NewsScroller applet scrolling text vertically on an area of a Web page

To customize the applet, you can pass the following parameters:

- **DataFile**   The relative address or URL of the file with the headlines, hypertext links, and messages you want to display. Default: "News.txt".

- **ClickColor**   The color (expressed as a hexadecimal triplet) that the applet will use to display clickable (that is, hyperlink) text in the data file. Default: "#0000FF" (blue).

- **HeadColor**   The color (expressed as a hexadecimal triplet) that the applet will use to display heading text in the data file. Default: "#FF0000" (red).

- **Font**   The typeface in which to display the text in the data file. Default: "Serif".

- **FontSize**   The point-size of the scrolling text. Default: "12".

- **MousePause**   If you pass this parameter, even with a value of "", NewsScroller will stop scrolling the text when the visitor moves the mouse pointer over the applet, and start scrolling text again when the visitor moves the mouse off the applet. For text scrolling uninterrupted by mouse movements, omit the *MousePause* parameter.

- **TopPause**   The number of milliseconds you want each heading to pause when the applet scrolls the heading to the top of the viewable area. Default: "0".

- **Refresh**   The number of minutes to wait before re-reading the news file. Default: "0" (meaning no refresh).

- **Foreground**   The color (expressed as a hexadecimal triplet) that the applet will use to display message text in the data file. Default: "#000000" (black).

- **Background**   The color (expressed as a hexadecimal triplet) of the applet background. Default: "#FFFFFF" (white).

- **Border** The pixel width of the boarder around the applet. Default: "0".

- **Picture** The relative filename or URL of the graphics image file you want to use as the applet's background.

- **Target** The frame in which the applet tells the Web browser to display the Web page that the browser retrieves when the visitor clicks the hypertext link in the scrolling text.

- **SleepTime** The number of milliseconds that the applet waits between updates. Default: "30".

- **ScrollBy** The number of pixels that the applet scrolls during each update cycle. Default: "1".

To customize the text that the applet displays, use a text editor to open and modify the contents of the file you specified in the *DataFile* parameter, News.txt by default. Your news file consists of heading, hyperlink, frame, message, and end data, denoted by the following tags:

- **@HEAD** Indicates that heading data follows. Each news item starts with a @HEAD (heading) line. Heading data may flow across multiple lines. The next @URL, @MSG, or @END tag terminates the heading tag.

- **@URL** Indicates that hyperlink data follows. The applet will treat any text up to the next @END tag as part of the hyperlink that the visitor can click to load another Web page.

- **@FRAME** Indicates that the name of a target frame or target window follows. The @FRAME tag must follow a @URL tag in the preceding line.

- **@MSG** Indicates that message data follows. You terminate a message by placing an @END tag on the line following the last line in a message.

- **@END** Indicates that the line in the news file is an end message line.

Review the contents of News.txt, which you extracted from NewsScroller.zip, for an example that shows how to define headings, hyperlinks, and messages for the applet to display.

Using an Applet to Animate an Image Along a Sine Wave

The preceding Tip shows how to animate text by executing an applet that moves the text left to right (or right to left) across the screen along a sine wave. Instead of scrolling text along a sine wave to create an animated banner, you can use the SinLogo.class applet to animate an otherwise static image such as a logo, as shown in Figure 9-16.

Note that the letters in the logo at the top in Figure 9-16 appear level. Conversely, the characters in the logo at the bottom of the figure are at different heights, showing the way the applet aligns the bottom of the logo along the curves of a sine wave.

USE IT You can view and download the Sinlogo.class applet and its source code from http://www.osborne.com. After copying Sinlogo.zip to a folder on your computer, extract

Figure 9-16   Two views of the same logo: static logo at the top, animated logo at the bottom

Sinlogo.class from the compressed file. Next, to use the applet on a Web page, copy the Sinlogo.class and an image you want to animate into the same folder as the Web page. Then insert HTML similar to the following in the Web page HTML where you want the shimmering image to appear:

```
<applet code="Sinlogo.class" width="363" height="97">
   <param name="image_logo" value="Web4.gif">
   <param name="angle_add"  value="1.9">
   <param name="bg_red"     value="0">
   <param name="bg_green"   value="0">
   <param name="bg_blue"    value="0">
</applet>
```

To adjust the animation effect in the applet, you can pass the following parameters:

- **image_logo**   The pathname of the GIF or JPG file you want to use the applet to animate.
- **angle_add**   The factor (that is, the amount) by which the applet shifts the bits in the image away from the base sine curve. The higher the value, the more the different parts of your image will move up and down. Default: "0.5".
- **bg_red**   The "red" value of the RGB background color (expressed as a decimal value).
- **bg_green**   The "green" value of the RGB background color (expressed as a decimal value).
- **bg_blue**   The "blue" value of the RGB background color (expressed as a decimal value).

The applet works by turning the color of the pixels in a portion of your image to the background color while at the same time turning the color of the pixels in the background of another portion of the picture to the image color. Thus, the most important parameters to set are *bg_red*, *bg_green*, and *bg_blue*, which tell the applet the color of the background, so the applet can make portions of the image seem to disappear and reappear along the curved shape of a sine wave.

Editing Java Source Code to Build a Custom Applet

Throughout this chapter, you used the <param> tag to customize Java applets to meet your specific needs. On the Web, you can find hundreds of ready-to-run applets that you can download and incorporate into your Web pages. Normally, you can use the <param> tag to customize the applets, just as you have done in the previous tips. Some applets, however, do not accept setup parameters. To customize those applets that do not let you pass setup values through <param> tags, you must edit the Java program statements that the programmer defined to create the applet. Therefore, you can customize such applets only if the programmer lets you download the *source code* file that contains the statements. Before you begin to update Java applets by editing the program statements, you must understand the steps the programmer performs to create an applet.

When a programmer creates a program, he or she uses a programming language, such as Java, Visual Basic, or C++, to specify the instructions the computer is to perform. The programmer places the instructions (that is, the program statements) in a file that programmers refer to as the program's (or in this case, the applet's) *source file*. Just as you can use a range of text editors to create an HTML document, programmers can use various editors to create an applet's source file. Likewise, just as your HTML pages use the .htm or .html file extension, Java source files use the extension .java.

Earlier in this chapter, you examined the NervousText applet, which bounces around onscreen the letters within a text message to make the letters appear jittery. The following statements comprise the source code for a simplified version of the applet, which you will name Nervous.java. (The Java programming language is case sensitive, which means that it considers the uppercase and lowercase versions of a single letter to be two different letters. Therefore, when you create the source file Nervous.java, make sure that you create the file using an uppercase "N" within the filename.)

```java
import java.awt.event.*;
import java.awt.Graphics;
import java.awt.Font;
import java.applet.Applet;

public class Nervous extends Applet implements Runnable
  {
    String banner;
    char bannerChars[];
    Thread runner = null;

    public void init()
      {
        banner = "I'm nervous!";
        int bannerLength = banner.length();

        bannerChars =  new char[bannerLength];
        banner.getChars(0, banner.length(), bannerChars, 0);

        resize(15*(bannerLength + 1), 50);
```

```
      setFont(new Font("TimesRoman", Font.BOLD, 36));
   }

public void start()
  {
    runner = new Thread(this);
    runner.start();
  }

public synchronized void stop()
  {
    runner = null;
  }

public void run()
   {
     Thread me = Thread.currentThread();

     while (runner == me)
       {
           try {
             Thread.sleep(100);
           } catch (InterruptedException e){ }

           repaint();
       }
   }

public void paint(Graphics g)
   {
     for(int i=0, length = banner.length(); i < length; i++)
       {
           int x = (int) (10*Math.random() + 15*i);
           int y = (int) (10*Math.random() + 36);
           g.drawChars(bannerChars, i, 1, x, y);
       }
   }
}
```

It is not important that you understand the specific purpose of the statements within the Java source file. Instead, this tip's goal is for you to download and use the Java Software Development Kit (SDK) from Sun Microsystem's Java Web site so you can build your first Java applet.

As you have learned, a Java applet consists of a generic bytecode (that is, a file full of ones and zeros) that the browser executes. To convert the statements that appear within the Java source file into the ones and zeros that comprise the bytecode that your Web browser executes, programmers use a special program called a *compiler*. As shown in Figure 9-17, the compiler converts the statements (referred to as *code*) within the Java source file into bytecode. A Java source file normally has a .java extension, and the compiler stores the bytecode it produces in a file that has a .class extension. (As you saw in previous tips, to embed an applet into your Web page, you set the *code* attribute within an <applet> tag to the name of the file with the applet's bytecode.)

For most programming languages, such as Visual Basic or C++, programmers must purchase a compiler, which may cost several hundred dollars. Sun Microsystems, however, offers the Java Software Development Kit, which contains the Java compiler (along with other programming tools and sample programs), for free! You can download the Java SDK from http://www.java.sun.com.

The Java SDK is large (over 30MB). To download the SDK, you will need ample disk space and patience as you wait for the download to complete. When you download the SDK, you will receive an executable file that you will run to install Java on your system. (To create Java applets, you must have the Java compiler installed on your system; to run Java applets, you need only a browser.) After the download completes, you must run the program to install the Java SDK on your system. The installation lets you select the folder within which you want to place the Software Development Kit's files. For simplicity, install the Java folder in your disk's root directory (the installation will create a folder within the root directory within which it places the files). After the Java SDK installation completes, you must perform a few simple housekeeping tasks before you can use the compiler to build your first applet.

The Java compiler is a command-line program, meaning that you do not run the compiler within a window per se, but rather, from a system prompt. To help you get the compiler up and running under various operating systems (or versions of operating systems), Sun's Java Web site provides step-by-step instructions. For instructions on installing the compiler within the Windows environment (Windows 9x, 2000, and XP), visit http://java.sun.com/j2se/1.3/install-windows.html#Environment.

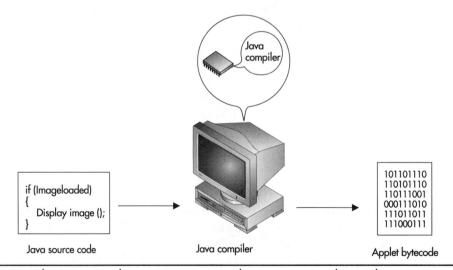

Figure 9-17   The Java compiler converts source code statements into bytecode

To give you a better understanding of the compiler's installation process, the remainder of this Tip discusses the steps you must perform to install the compiler within the Windows 9*x* environment.

First, within the Windows environment, you run the Java compiler from a command-line prompt within an MS-DOS window. To open an MS-DOS window, select Start | Run. Windows will display the Run dialog box. Within the Run dialog box, type **command** and press ENTER.

The name of the directory that contains the Java programming tools depends on the version of the Java SDK you installed. Before you can use the compiler to create Java applets, however, you must add the name of the directory that contains the tools to your command path, defined by the PATH entry within your system's AUTOEXEC.BAT file. To select the root directory (which contains the AUTOEXEC.BAT file), at the command prompt type **CHDIR ** and then press ENTER:

```
C:\Windows> CHDIR  \   <Enter>
C:\>
```

The name of the folder that contains the Java programming tools will normally begin with the letter *J*. To locate the folder, type the following DIR command and then press ENTER. Windows will then display a directory list similar to the one shown here.

```
C:\> DIR \J* /A:D <Enter>
 Volume in drive C has no label
 Volume Serial Number is 07CF-0713
 Directory of C:\

JAMSAM~1          <DIR>        11-04-99   7:10a Jamsa Media Group
JBUILD~1          <DIR>        05-01-00   3:36p JBuilder3
JREXPR~1          <DIR>        05-01-00   3:44p JableREXpress
JOBS              <DIR>        01-15-01  10:16a Jobs
J2SDK1~1 0-B      <DIR>        12-01-01   2:20p j2sdk1.4.0-beta3
           0 file(s)               0 bytes
           5 dir(s)         920.94 MB free
```

In this case, the Java programming tools reside in the directory J2DSK~1.0-B. Write down the name of the directory within which the Java files are stored on your system (if the name appears to contain a space, replace the space with a period). Using Windows Notepad, edit the root directory file AUTOEXEC.BAT:

```
C:\> notepad \autoexec.bat   <Enter>
```

Within the AUTOEXEC.BAT file, locate the PATH entry. At the end of the entry, add a semicolon, the current drive letter, a colon, a slash, and the name of Java directory followed by \BIN, as shown here:

```
PATH C:\WINDOWS\SYSTEM;C:\J2SDK~1.0-B\BIN
```

Save the file's contents and exit the editor. Use the EXIT command to close the MS-DOS window; then shut down and restart your system.

After your system restarts, you are ready to compile Java applets. In this case, you will download (or type) the program statements for the Nervous.java source file. You can download the file from this book's Web site at http://www.Osborne.com. If you type the statements, pay very close attention to your use of uppercase and lowercase letters. Place the file in a folder on your disk, which in this case you might simply name MyJava. Next, again open an MS-DOS window. Use the CHDIR command to select the directory within which you stored the Nervous.java file. For example, if you placed the file in the MyJava directory, use the following CHDIR command:

```
C:\Windows> CHDIR  \MyJava  <Enter>
C:\MyJava>
```

To compile the Nervous.java source file, issue the following javac command from within the folder in which you stored your Java source file:

```
C:\MyJava>  javac  Nervous.java  <Enter>
```

If the Java compiler successfully compiles the program, it will create the file Nervous.class within the same folder as the applet's source file. If you typed the file and the compiler displays error messages, edit the file and compare its statements closely to the text that appears in this book. The letters and symbols you type must match, exactly, those the book presents. If, when you run the javac command, your system displays the message "Bad command or file name," the PATH entry in your AUTOEXEC.BAT file is not pointing correctly to the file that contains the Java programming tools.

After you successfully compile the applet, create the following HTML file, Nerves.html, which embeds your newly created applet on a Web page for your browser to execute:

```
<html>
<head><title>Nervous</title></head>
<body>
  <hr>
  <applet code="Nervous.class" width=375 height=50>
    <param name=text value="Java Development Kit 1.2">
  </applet>
  <hr>
</body>
</html>
```

Open the file Nerves.html within your browser (if you stored the HTML document in the directory C:\MyJava, for example, you would type **file://C:/MyJava/Nerves.html** in your Web browser's Address field and press ENTER). Your Web browser will then load the Web page with your embedded applet, which displays the bouncing text, "I'm nervous."

Next, exit your Web browser and use your editor to open the file Nervous.java. Look for the following line:

```
banner = "I'm nervous!";
```

Change the line to your name, as shown here:

```
banner = "Konrad King";
```

Save the file's contents and exit the editor. Then issue the following javac command at the MSDOS command prompt to rebuild your applet:

```
C:\MyJava> javac Nervous.txt <Enter>
```

Each time you change the code within the Java source file, you must compile the code using the Java compiler (javac) to put your change into effect. In this case, the Java compiler will overwrite the contents of Nervous.class with the bytecode for the modified Java source file (Nervous.java) so that the next time you load the Web page, Nerves.html, within your Web browser, the embedded applet (Nervous.class) will display your name. That's all there is to building or changing and rebuilding Java applets.

► *NOTE*

Depending on the number of characters in the text you want the applet to display, you may need to increase the width of the applet by changing the width *attribute within the <applet> tag that embeds the applet on your Web page.*

Using the Microsoft Chat ActiveX Control to Add Internet Chat to a Web Page

In the previous tips within this chapter, you used Java applets to add various capabilities to your Web sites. The tips that follow show you how to use ActiveX objects on your Web pages. As discussed earlier in this chapter, an ActiveX object differs from a Java applet in that you must download and install the object (that is, the ActiveX control) on your system, as opposed to downloading and running an applet tucked safely within a browser. Moreover, if you are using Netscape Navigator, you must download and install a plug-in that provides the browser with support for the specific ActiveX control that you want to execute.

Before Instant Messaging from AOL (and now Microsoft) and before Internet phone service from companies like Net2Phone, people talked to each other on the Internet using Internet Relay Chat (IRC). Even today, with e-mail, text-messaging pagers, cellular phones, and lower long-distance rates, IRC is still immensely popular. Microsoft Chat lets you put a basic chat control such as that shown in Figure 9-18 on your Web pages.

After connecting to an IRC server and either joining an existing chat room or starting a new one, the visitor can type messages in the lower left pane. The control then displays messages the visitor types, along with messages typed by other people in the same chat room, in real time within the control's upper left pane. (The control uses the right pane to list the names of the people in the room.)

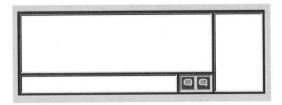

Figure 9-18   The Microsoft Chat IRC ActiveX control

USE IT   Many companies have found chat sessions a convenient way to let customers speak directly to customer support. Chat rooms are especially convenient for new product releases, when several customers have the same questions about installation and (new) features. Companies can save time and money by answering the questions once in a chat forum, so that many customers can read the answers instead of the company's having to answer the same questions repeatedly by phone over the company's toll-free support number. To use the Microsoft Chat control on a Web page, insert code similar to the following in the Web page HTML where you want the chat control's input and output panes to appear:

```
<object id="Chat"
   classid="clsid:D6526FE0-E651-11CF-99CB-00C04FD64497"
   align="baseline" border="0" width="600" height="200"
   standby="Downloading the Microsoft Chat Control"
   type="application/x-oleobject">
   <param name="MaxMessageLength" value="2000">
   <param name="MaxHistoryLength" value="32767">
   <param name="UIOption" value="4095">
   <param name="BackColor" value="255">
<!-- the following uses the esker.com activeX plug-in to insert
     the chat ActiveX control on a Web page displayed within
     Netscape Navigator Version 6.1 and later. -->
   <embed type="application/x-eskeractivex"
     id="Chat"
     clsid="D6526FE0-E651-11CF-99CB-00C04FD64497"
     width="600" height="200"
     MaxMessageLength="2000"
     MaxHistoryLength="32767"
     UIOption="4095"
     BackColor="255"
   </embed>
</object>
```

Note that the code in this example has an <embed> tag that loads the Microsoft Chat ActiveX control onto the Web page when it is displayed by Netscape Navigator. Remember that you must install the plug-in that lets Netscape Navigator execute the ActiveX control before the browser will load and display the ActiveX object on the Web page. The <embed> tag in this example requires you to install the ActiveX plug-in np6esk32.dll, available at http://www.esker.com, before the Microsoft Chat control will appear on the Web page. The value you assign to the <embed> tag's *type* attribute will vary depending on the ActiveX plug-in you use for your version of Netscape Navigator.

You can customize the chat control by passing the following parameters:

- **Standby**   Text the Web browser displays while downloading the Microsoft Chat control.

- **MaxMessageLength**   The maximum number of characters the visitor can type in the outgoing message area (that is, into the lower left pane) before clicking one of the two Send buttons to the right of the pane.

- **MaxHistoryLength**   The number of characters the control will allow to accumulate in the message (history) list area (that is, in the upper left pane) before deleting the oldest text.

- **BackColor**   A number from 0 to 255, inclusive, that sets the color of the border between control's panes.

In addition to the Microsoft Chat control itself, you need to provide the visitor a form for entering the name of the IRC server, chat room, and chat topic and a nickname to use while in the room. Moreover, the visitor will need the pushbuttons shown at the bottom of the form in Figure 9-19 to join or start a chat room, control the interaction with other members, and clear the messages from the message list area as desired.

Download MSChatPage.htm from http://www.osborne.com for an example of a fully functional Web page with an embedded Microsoft Chat ActiveX control. Feel free to rearrange the form's fields and text labels. The VBScript functions called when the visitor clicks the form's pushbuttons are

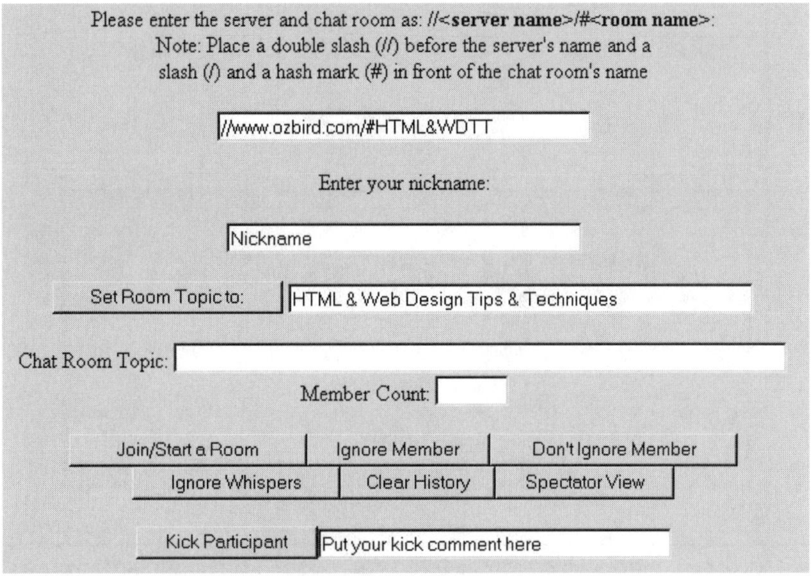

Figure 9-19   Form that lets the visitor enter login information and send control commands to the Microsoft Chat client by clicking pushbuttons

located at the bottom of the Web page HTML. (Each VBScript function calls a method—that is, a function—within the Microsoft Chat control to perform the action indicated by the label on the form pushbutton used to call the function.)

Using Only ActiveX Objects with Internet Explorer

One of the challenges of using ActiveX objects on your Web pages is supporting users running Netscape. As you have learned, before Netscape can use an ActiveX object, you must have a plug-in that supports the object. Unfortunately, not all plug-ins support all ActiveX objects. For example, the Microsoft marquee control lets you display the contents of a Web page vertically, horizontally, or diagonally within a rectangular area on a Web page, as shown in Figure 9-20. The Microsoft marquee control displays the text, background, and graphics images as the visitor would see them by visiting the Web page itself. Thus, the marquee control gives you a way of scrolling text as well as graphics images as a rotating banner. Unfortunately, many of the Netscape plug-ins do not support the marquee control.

USE IT To use the Microsoft marquee control on a Web page, you would normally first create an HTML file that contains the contents you want the marquee to scroll. Then, within the HTML file for the page within which you want to place the marquee, you insert HTML statements

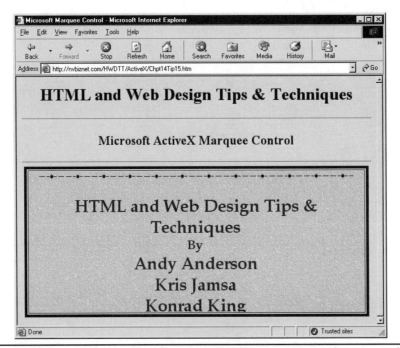

Figure 9-20 Marquee control, which scrolls one Web page in a rectangular area within another page

similar to the following at the page location where you want the scrolling page content to appear (replace the URL that appears in the *szURL* parameter with the URL for the HTML page whose content you want to display):

```
<object id=marquee width="640" height="260"
  classid="clsid:1a4da620-6217-11cf-be62-0080c72edd2d">
  <param NAME="szURL"
      value="http://www.NVBizNet.com/HWDTT/BookInformation.htm">
  <param NAME="ScrollDelay" value=300>
  <param NAME="LoopsX" value=-1>
  <param NAME="LoopsY" value=-1>
  <param NAME="ScrollPixelsX" value=0>
  <param NAME="ScrollPixelsY" value=-10>
  <param NAME="Whitespace" value=0>
  <param NAME="Zoom" value=100>
</object>
```

You can customize the marquee by passing the following parameters:

- **szURL**   The URL of the source Web page you want the marquee to display.
- **ScrollDelay**   The number of milliseconds between updates.
- **LoopsX**   The number of times the program is to scroll the content horizontally. A value of −1 means forever.
- **LoopsY**   The number of times the program is to scroll the content vertically. A value of −1 means forever.
- **ScrollPixelsX**   The number of pixels the program is to shift the marquee's contents horizontally each update cycle. A negative value scrolls the content right to left, and a positive value scrolls the content left to right.
- **ScrollPixelsY**   The number of pixels the program is to shift the marquee's contents vertically each update cycle. A negative value scrolls the contents upward, and a positive value scrolls the content downward.
- **Whitespace**   The amount of blank space (in pixels) that the program is to leave between successive copies of the source Web page.
- **Zoom**   The percentage by which to increase (or decrease) the size of the source Web page within the marquee.

USE IT   One solution to using ActiveX objects is to embed the objects only for users who are running Microsoft Internet Explorer. The previous <object> tag, for example, prevents the page from using the object for Netscape browsers by not including an <embed> tag, which Netscape requires. Rather than simply ignoring the Netscape users, however, you may want your Web page to perform one operation (such as embedding the ActiveX object) for Internet Explorer users and a different operation (such as loading a similar Java applet) for Netscape users.

The following Active Server Page, for example, uses the HTTP_USER_AGENT value to determine information about the user's browser. If the string the function returns contains the letters MSIE, the script knows that the user is running Microsoft Internet Explorer and so the script places statements in the HTML file that embed the ActiveX object. If the user is running a browser other than Internet Explorer, the script does not embed the object:

```
<%
  if instr(1,Request.ServerVariables("HTTP_USER_AGENT"),"MSIE") > 0 then
      Response.Write "<object id=marquee width=""640"" height=""260"""
      Response.Write "classid=""clsid:1a4da620-6217-11cf-be62-0080c72edd2d"">"
      Response.Write "<param NAME=""szURL""
value=""http://www.NVBizNet.com/HWDTT/BookInformation.htm"">"
      Response.Write "<param NAME=""ScrollDelay"" value=300>"
      Response.Write "<param NAME=""LoopsX"" value=-1>"
      Response.Write "<param NAME=""LoopsY"" value=-1>"
      Response.Write "<param NAME=""ScrollPixelsX"" value=0>"
      Response.Write "<param NAME=""ScrollPixelsY"" value=-10>"
      Response.Write "<param NAME=""Whitespace"" value=0>"
      Response.Write "<param NAME=""Zoom"" value=100>"
      Response.Write "</object>"
  else
      Response.Write "<applet
          code=""crackers.Scroller.NewsScroller.class""
          archive=""scroller.jar"" width=""400"" height=""150"">"
      Response.Write "<param name=""DataFile""    value=""News.txt"">"
      Response.Write "<param name=""ClickColor"" value=""#0000FF"">"
      Response.Write "<param name=""HeadColor""   value=""#FF0000"">"
      Response.Write "<param name=""Font""        value=""Serif"">"
      Response.Write "<param name=""FontSize""    value=""18"">"
      Response.Write "<param name=""MousePause""  value="""">"
      Response.Write "<param name=""TopPause""    value=""0"">"
      Response.Write "<param name=""Refresh""     value=""0"">"
      Response.Write "<param name=""Foreground""  value=""#000000"">"
      Response.Write "<param name=""Background""  value=""#FFFFFF"">"
      Response.Write "<param name=""Border""      value=""8"">"
      Response.Write "<param name=""Picture""     value=""bg_gif.gif"">"
      Response.Write "<param name=""Target""      value=""_top"">"
      Response.Write "<param name=""SleepTime""   value=""30"">"
      Response.Write "<param name=""Scrollby""    value=""1"">"
      Response.Write "</applet>"
  end if
%>
```

CHAPTER 10

PHP4

TIPS IN THIS CHAPTER

▶ Sending Data from an HTML Form to a PHP Script — 484

▶ Using PHP to Parse and Extract Form Results — 488

▶ Using PHP to Send an E-Mail Message — 491

▶ Determining Whether a Visitor's Web Browser Accepts Cookies — 493

▶ Using PHP and a Disk File to Set Up Username/Password Access to a Web Site — 496

▶ Preventing Visitors from Linking Directly to Pages on Your Site — 498

▶ Using a PHP Session to Establish a Persistent Connection Between a Site Visitor and the Web Server — 499

▶ Creating a MySQL Database and Tables — 502

▶ Displaying SQL Query Results in an HTML Table on a Web Page — 504

▶ Using PHP to Generate a Random Password — 507

▶ Using PHP and MySQL to Set Up Username/Password Access to a Web Site — 509

▶ Preventing Visitors from Changing Variable Values with URL Arguments — 511

▶ Using PHP and MySQL to Track Where Visitors Go on Your Web Site — 512

▶ Determining the Visitor's IP Address for Web Page Requests Sent Through a Proxy Server — 514

▶ Preventing One Visitor from Assuming Another Visitor's PHP
   Session Identity   516

▶ Using PHP Functions to Create Web Page Templates   517

▶ Using PHP to Add File Upload Functionality to a Web Page   520

PHP is a tool that lets you create Web pages on-the-fly. In the past, Web sites consisted of static Web pages with text, graphics, and perhaps flashy (but unchanging) multimedia effects and animations. Today, visitors expect sites that let them store and query database data and to create new Web content based on requests made while using the site's resources. PHP (which originally stood for Personal Home Page tools) is a hypertext preprocessor that lets you generate Web page content on-the-fly. You can place statements for the PHP processor to execute in a separate file or embed the statements within other Web page HTML.

Figure 10-1 shows the steps involved in retrieving and displaying a PHP Web page. When a Web browser requests a PHP Web page (that is, a file with an extension, usually .php, associated to the PHP processor), the Web server sends the request to the PHP processor. The processor, in turn, reads the document that the browser wants to retrieve. As it goes through the file, line by line, the PHP

1) The Web browser sends an HTTP request for a PHP Web Page to the Web Server.
2) The Web server passes the request for the Web page to the PHP parser.
3) The PHP parser finds and retrieves the PHP Web page (that is, a file with a .php extension).
4) The PHP parser executes the PHP statements in the PHP document and creates a Web page from statement output and the HTML the parser finds in the file.
5) The PHP parser passes the new Web page to the Web server.
6) The Web server sends the page generated by the PHP parser to the Web browser.

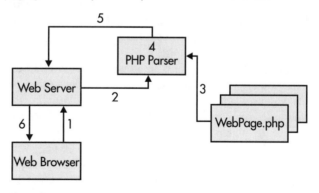

Figure 10-1   PHP Web page processing

processor executes PHP statements enclosed within start PHP (<?php or <?) and end PHP script tags (?>). The processor writes the output generated by the PHP statements it executes as well as all the text outside start and end PHP tags to a (virtual, in Web- server memory) Web page that the Web server eventually sends to the Web browser.

By having the PHP processor generate the Web page HTML after the Web browser sends a request for a PHP Web page to the Web server, you can do things like generate pages with browser-specific HTML and pages that display different content depending on who the visitor is or based on the time of day. In short, PHP lets you convert your Web site from a collection of static Web pages visitors can view into an application running on the Web server with a Web page user interface.

Suppose, for example, that you want to display the current time on your Web page. If you code the page statically (using only standard HTML), you will spend your whole day updating the Web page (once per minute) to make sure the time is correct when a visitor retrieves the page. Conversely, by inserting a PHP statement that dynamically writes the current time on the Web page after a Web browser requests the page, you can have the PHP processor update the time on the page automatically. After receiving a request for a PHP Web page, the processor creates a page that contains the non-PHP statement (that is, static) content from the Web page file on disk and inserts the current time returned by the PHP built-in *date( )* function.

Whereas client-side scripting languages (such as JavaScript) run within the Web browser, PHP is a server-side language, which means a program on the Web server (and not the Web browser) executes PHP scripts embedded in the Web page HTML. In technical terms, PHP is a cross-platform, markup language–embedded, server-side scripting language, which means:

- You can run most PHP code without alteration on Web servers running a variety of operating systems such as Linux, Mac OS, RISC OS, Unix, and Windows.

- You embed PHP statements within your Web page document either alone or alongside the HTML, XHTML, or XML tags you use to define the page for the Web browser.

- When the Web browser requests a Web page with embedded PHP statements, the Web server sends the request to the PHP processor. The PHP processor, in turn, locates the requested file and executes the embedded PHP code in the file, replaces the PHP statements with output (if any), and passes the results to the Web server. The Web server then passes the page returned by the PHP processor to the Web browser.

The elegance of using PHP is that the Web browser never works with the PHP embedded in the Web page. Unlike JavaScript, VBScript, Jscript, or other client-side scripting languages, when you write PHP scripts, you need not worry whether the visitor's Web browser supports PHP. To create a PHP-enabled Web page, you simply embed the PHP commands you want executed within the Web page HTML and give the Web page document an extension (such as .php) associated with execution by the PHP processor. When the Web browser requests a Web page with the .php extension, the Web server knows to send the document request to the PHP processor and send the Web page returned from the processor to the Web browser for display. The PHP processor executes the PHP statements and ensures that the Web page sent to the Web server (and then on to the Web browser) is properly formatted with tags the browser understands.

Understanding the History of PHP

By reviewing a (very) brief history of PHP, you can see how the origins of the language have influenced its current usage. Some time in 1994, Rasmus Lerdorf wrote several Perl scripts to determine who was visiting his personal Web page. Over time, more and more Web developers became interested in his scripts, and he released them as a package called the Personal Home Page Tools in the spring of 1995—hence the first meaning of PHP. The initial PHP toolset, which Lerdorf referred to as "a CGI wrapper written in Perl," contained a few server-side macros and simple utilities, such as a hit counter and a guest book.

Due to the growing interest in his Perl scripts, Lerdorf rewrote his parsing engine and incorporated a tool to parse input from HTML forms, called the Form Interpreter (FI), and added mSQL database support. The combined package, released in mid-1995, was called PHP/FI or PHP2. Soon thereafter, Web developers began using the tools to perform ever more complicated tasks. PHP's "open source" policy allowed a group of developers led by Zeev Suraski and Andi Gutmans to rewrite the PHP processor again in 1997. The code they released became the foundation of PHP3 (that is, PHP version 3), which was quickly adopted by more than 1,000,000 Web sites over other server-side scripting languages such as Microsoft's Active Server Pages (ASP) and Allaire's ColdFusion.

The most recent version of PHP (PHP4, that is, PHP version 4) is available free of charge (from various Web sites, including http://www.PHP.net) and open source, which means you can download the PHP processor's source code and "look under the hood," if you so desire. However, being free and open source does not account for the fact that PHP is in use on over 6,000,000 domains to date. PHP has become the server-side scripting language of choice for many Web servers because of the following reasons:

- PHP can run on either Windows NT or Unix, which makes it easy to build complex Web sites for either platform.

- PHP has a simple yet elegant object-oriented syntax and excellent documentation (available both in books from various authors and [for free] online). Moreover, PHP's constructs are familiar to developers who have used procedural or object-oriented programming languages. Thus, if you know C, C++, Java, Pascal, or Visual Basic, learning to write PHP scripts and functions will be a easy—you will not feel as if you are learning a completely new programming language.

- PHP is tailored to the Web developer by allowing the developer to perform tasks with a few function calls (inserted within the Web page HTML), what can only be done with expert knowledge and cumbersome code in other scripting languages.

- PHP is very fast. Unlike ASP, which tends to bog down an Internet Information Server (IIS) when parsing many complex ASP pages at once, you can compile, optimize, and cache PHP scripts in memory—thereby allowing the Web server to serve a large number of PHP Web pages without a noticeable degradation in performance.

Downloading and Installing PHP

The purpose of this chapter is to teach you how to use PHP to create dynamic Web content. However, before you can use PHP, you need a working Web server, PHP itself, and (arguably) an SQL database management system (DBMS) such as MySQL. Showing you how to download and install a Web server, PHP, and MySQL on several platforms is beyond the scope of this book. In fact, as a designer, you will normally rely on your Internet Service Provider (ISP) to perform these installation tasks for you. However, because you must sometimes make your case for providing PHP and MySQL support, showing how inexpensive (free) and easy it is to install the applications may go a long way toward getting your ISP to install them for you to use.

If you are working with a Linux or a Unix platform, your Web server of choice is most likely the Apache Web server, which your ISP can download free of charge from the Apache Software Foundation site at http://www.apache.org. If you are working with a Windows platform (NT/2000/XP), you will most likely be using Microsoft's Internet Information Server (IIS). If your ISP did not install IIS with the Windows operating system, he or she can download version 4.0 of the software as part of the NT Option Pack from the Microsoft site at http://www.microsoft.com/ntserver/nts/downloads/ recommended/ NT4OptPk/. (Note that the CD-ROM for most new Window products such as 2000 Professional, 2000 Server, and XP Professional includes the latest version of IIS.)

After installing the Web server software, your ISP can download and install PHP. If you are working with a Linux or Unix machine, the ISP must not only retrieve the PHP source code but also compile it using an ANSI C compiler such as gcc or g++, which he or she can download from the GNU Web site at http://www.gnu.org/gnulist/production/. You can retrieve the latest version of PHP from http://www.php.net. Download both the PHP source to compile and the documentation, which will guide you through the installation and help you select the necessary configuration options.

Configuring PHP on Windows NT running IIS is much simpler than compiling and configuring PHP for the Apache Web server on a Linux or Unix machine. Proceed to the PHP Web site at http:// www.php.net and click the Downloads hyperlink. In the Win32 Binaries section of the downloads Web page, click the hyperlink to download the PHP compressed file and then on the hyperlink to download the PHP installation program (as of this writing, PHP 4.0.6 Zip Package and PHP 4.0.6 Installer, respectively). When prompted, store both files in the same folder (such as C:\PHP) on the Web server. Remember, PHP is a server-side scripting language. As such, you install and run the language processor on the Web server.

Next, unzip the PHP compressed file (currently, php-4.0.6-Win32.zip) and then execute the PHP InstallShield installation program (currently, php406-installer.exe). The installation program will prompt you to enter the pathname of the folder in which you unzipped the PHP processor's files and the folder and version of IIS (or Personal Web Server) to which you want to add PHP support. After completing its work, the installation program will ask you to let it reboot your NT/2000/XP server to finish the installation process. If you have any problems during the installation, or want to perform a manual installation, print and review the contents of the install.txt file in the PHP folder.

▶ *NOTE*

The Windows PHP installer installs the CGI version of PHP and will configure the Web server to send Web pages with .php (versus .htm or .html) extensions to the PHP processor. PHP4 for Windows comes in two flavors—a CGI executable (php.exe) and several Web server application program interface (SAPI) modules (such as php4isapi.dll for IIS). Although the SAPI form of PHP4 provides significant improvements in performance over the CGI version, SAPI modules are new and (as of this writing) not yet considered "production quality." As such, before performing a manual PHP installation to make use of an SAPI module, be sure to read the install.txt file in the PHP folder for the types of errors you might encounter. If you need a reliable, production Web server, use the CGI version of the PHP executable until the SAPI version is fully tested and certified as the production version on the PHP Web site (http://www.php.net).

After you install PHP, test your installation with a small Web page such as the following:

```
<html>
<body>
  <?php phpinfo();?>
</body>
</html>
```

For example, save the preceding HTML on the Web server in a file named test.php (assuming you opted to use the .php extension for PHP-parsed Web pages during the installation process). Then, use your browser to retrieve the Web page (test.php) and display results similar to those shown in Figure 10-2.

If everything is working properly, PHP will return information on the processor's current version followed by PHP configuration, environment, and variable information. If your browser's application window remains blank, or if the browser displays an error message, a problem exists with the PHP installation, or the PHP processor could not find the Web page (with the .php extension) you tried to retrieve from the Web server. Refer to the last two pages of the install.txt file (in the PHP folder) for help in resolving these and other issue(s) if your PHP installation attempt is unsuccessful. If install.txt does not give you all the information you need, check the support page on the http://www.php.net Web site.

Understanding PHP Start and End Tags

When the PHP processor retrieves a file to parse, you must set statements intended for the processor apart from those intended for the Web browser. PHP provides three start and end tags you can use to enclose the code you want the PHP processor to execute:

```
<?php  <php statements>  ?>
<?  <php statements>  ?>
<script language="php">  <php statements>  </script>
```

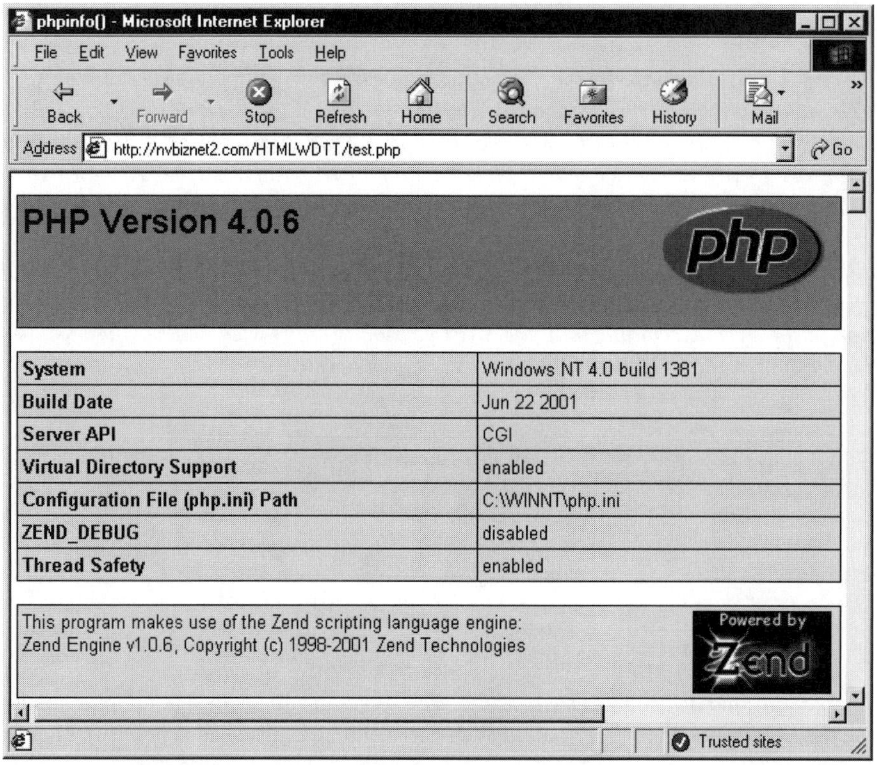

Figure 10-2 Web page returned by PHP when sent a Web page that calls the *phpinfo()* function

You are probably already familiar with the third set of PHP code delimiters, because the PHP start and end script tags (<script></script>) are the same HTML tags you use to delineate client-side scripts embedded in the Web page HTML. By setting the scripting language to "php" (versus "JavaScript" or "VBScript", for example), you tell the PHP processor to execute the embedded script's statements instead of passing them on to the browser. Thus, any one of the start script tags "<?php", "<?", or <script language="php"> tells the PHP processor that it has encountered statements to execute in the Web page HTML. The PHP processor will execute all statements it reads until the processor encounters the matching end script tag ("?>" or </script>).

The following code uses each of the PHP start and end tags to produce the Web page HTML shown in Figure 10-3. Note that neither of the PHP start script tags ("<?php", "<?") has a "closing" greater-than sign (>) you see at the end of normal HTML tags. (That is, the PHP start script tag is "<?php" or "<?" and not "<?php>" or "<?>".) Similarly, the PHP end script tag "?>" has no "opening" less-than sign (<):

```
<html>
<head><title>PHP Start and End Tags</title></head>
<body bgcolor="#ADD8E6">
  <h1><center>HTML and Web Design Tips & Techniques</center></h1>

  <?php echo "<p><hr>";
       echo "The current date is: "; ?>

  <?echo gmDate("l, F d, Y.");
    echo "<br><br>The current time is: ";
  ?>

  <script language="php">
   echo gmDate("h:i:s A");
   echo "</p>";
  </script>

  <hr>
  The PHP processor ignores the heading at the top of the page,
  this text, and the horizontal rule (line) above this text.
  The PHP processor simply passes them on to the Web browser for
  display.
</body>
</html>
```

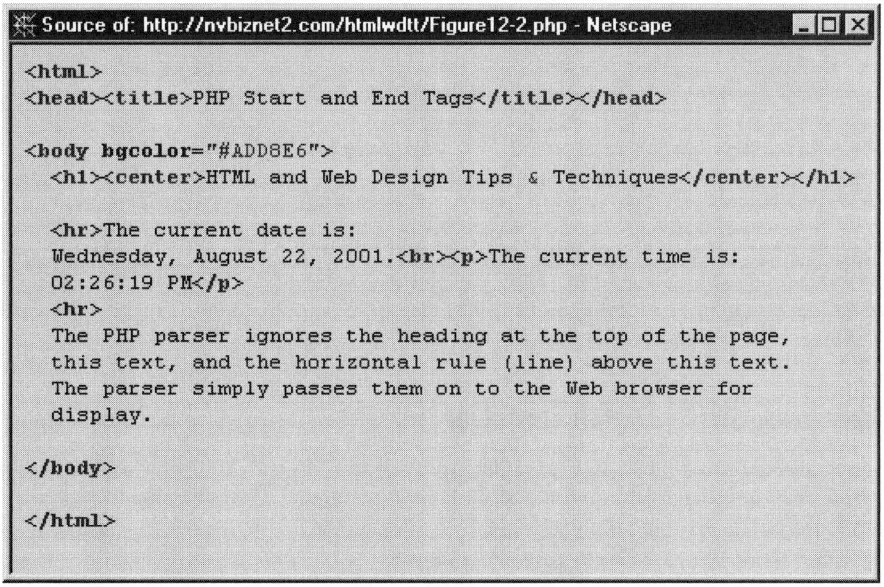

```
Source of: http://nvbiznet2.com/htmlwdtt/Figure12-2.php - Netscape    _ □ ✕

<html>
<head><title>PHP Start and End Tags</title></head>

<body bgcolor="#ADD8E6">
  <h1><center>HTML and Web Design Tips & Techniques</center></h1>

  <hr>The current date is:
  Wednesday, August 22, 2001.<br><p>The current time is:
  02:26:19 PM</p>
  <hr>
  The PHP parser ignores the heading at the top of the page,
  this text, and the horizontal rule (line) above this text.
  The parser simply passes them on to the Web browser for
  display.

</body>

</html>
```

Figure 10-3   Web page HTML generated by the PHP processor

Notice that the Web page the PHP processor passes back to the Web server to send to the Web browser contains HTML tags and text in place of the PHP statements the processor executed. (You can view the Web page source the browser received from the Web server by selecting View | Source in Internet Explorer and View | Page Source in Netscape Navigator.)

Understanding PHP Statement Syntax

The PHP scripts in the Web page HTML at the end of the preceding section show you two important things. First, you can embed PHP scripts within your Web page HTML by simply delimiting those scripts with the PHP start and end script tags (<? …?> or <?php … ?>) or HTML start and end script tags (<script language="php"> … </script>). Second, you can embed HTML tags within PHP scripts, as long as you enclose those tags within quotes and tell the PHP processor to *echo* (that is, print) them in the Web page HTML the processor sends back to the Web server. For example, the following statement will insert a horizontal rule tag (<hr>) within the Web page HTML the PHP processor sends back to the Web server:

```
<?php echo "<hr>"; ?>
```

Using the Semicolon (;) Statement Terminator

Whether embedding a script within a Web page with HTML (XHTML or XML) statements or in a file by itself, you must terminate each statement in a PHP script (including the last) with a semicolon (;). Thus, the syntax of a single-statement PHP script is as follows:

```
<start script tag> <php statement>; <end script tag>
```

and the syntax for a multistatement script is as follows:

```
<start script tag> <php statement>; <php statement>;
  <php statement>; <last php statement>; <end script tag>
```

As shown by the syntax in this example, you can place multiple PHP statements on the same line within the PHP document. PHP requires only that you terminate each statement with a semicolon (;). However, to make your code more readable, place each PHP statement on its own line (as shown by the example code in the preceding section).

Using the Backslash (\) Escape Character

As mentioned in the preceding section, you can embed HTML tags in your PHP scripts by enclosing those tags between quotes (" ") following the PHP *echo* command. You can also use the PHP *echo* statement to insert plain text onto the Web page by enclosing the text in quotes. However, the following script will cause the PHP processor to generate an error:

```
<?php echo "<p>PHP is the "bomb"!</p>"; ?>
```

PHP thinks that the quote (") before the *b* in *bomb* signals the end of the text the *echo* statement is to insert in the Web page, and *bomb* is undefined.

To include a quotation mark (or other symbol you want the passer to insert and not interpret) within quoted text, place a backslash (\) in front of the quotation mark (or symbol) you want PHP to include on the Web page. For example, to show the text "PHP is the "bomb"!" on the Web page, write the preceding script as follows:

```
<?php echo "<p>PHP is the \"bomb\"!</p>"; ?>
```

Inserting Comments in a PHP Script

PHP gives you three symbols you can use to insert comments in your code: "#", "//", and "/* .. */". Inserting comments in your PHP scripts is an excellent habit. Though ignored by the PHP processor, comments remind you (and tell others) why you wrote certain portions of the script in a particular way or what you are trying to accomplish with the script in general. You might also use comments during the development process to figure out exactly where a processor-reported error occurs. By commenting out a section of code (that is, by telling the processor to ignore lines of code as "comments"), you can make an error "go away." Then, by "uncommenting" one line of code at a time until the processor reports the error again, you can figure out which line of code produced the error—the last line of code you changed from a comment back into an executable statement within the script.

The following code shows how you can use each of the three comment delimiters to add comments to your PHP scripts:

```
<html>
<body bgcolor="#ADD8E6">
  <h1><center>HTML and Web Design Tips & Techniques</center></h1>
<!--
  the script will display the current system date onscreen
-->
  <?echo gmDate("l, F d, Y.");

# The pound sign (or hash mark)(#) lets you insert a single
# line of comments

// The same is true for the double slash (//). If you use a
// single-line comment delimiter (// or #), you must place that
// delimiter as the first character in each line of comments.

/* If you want to use multiline comments, without placing a #
   or // in on each line, use the C-style comment delimiter /*,
```

```
  and PHP will ignore anything you type until the PHP processor
  reads the end comment delimiter */
   echo "<br>";
 ?>
</body>
</html>
```

By the way, the statement *echo gmDate("l, F d, Y.");* in the preceding code tells the processor to call the built-in *gmDate()* function, which in turn, retrieves the current GMT (Greenwich Mean Time) date and time. The letters passed to the function form a *formatting string* in which certain special letters (such as *l*, *F*, *d*, and *Y* in this example) tell the parser which portions of the date and time to print. The function prints all other nonspecial characters (such as the commas [(,)] and period [(.)] used for punctuation in this example) in the formatting string as is. Figure 10-4 shows the HTML that the PHP processor will produce when it executes the preceding code.

Notice that only the HTML comments show up in the Web page HTML—along with the HTML tags and content the browser is to display, of course. PHP comments—although saved in the Web page file—are ignored by the PHP processor and not passed on to the Web server in the Web page the PHP processor returns.

Understanding Variables

A variable is a memory location set aside to hold a value. To make it easy to store and retrieve the data in memory, PHP lets you use a meaningful name to refer to each memory location. For example, to store the name the visitor used to log in to your Web site, you might name the memory location you use to hold the name *$username*. Similarly, you might use *$item_number* to store the item number a visitor selected for purchase, and use *$amount_purchased* to store the total value of the visitor's purchases.

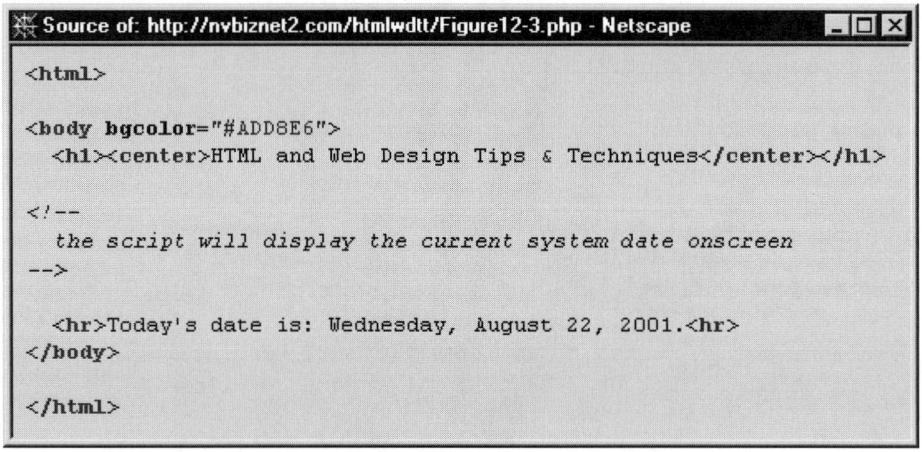

```
<html>

<body bgcolor="#ADD8E6">
   <h1><center>HTML and Web Design Tips & Techniques</center></h1>

<!--
   the script will display the current system date onscreen
-->

   <hr>Today's date is: Wednesday, August 22, 2001.<hr>
</body>

</html>
```

Figure 10-4   Web page HTML produced by a PHP script with comments

PHP places few limits on the names you can use for variables. You can use an unlimited number of characters in a PHP variable name. However, each variable must start with a dollar sign ($) followed by a letter or an underscore (_). The remainder of the characters in the name can be any combination of letters, numbers, and underscores (_). Other special symbols, such as +, -, /, *, &, ", @, and so on, are not allowed. Bear in mind that PHP variable names are case-sensitive, which means that the following code will produce two different variables:

```
$username = "Konrad King";
$userName = "Andy Anderson";
```

You will use four main types of variables in your PHP scripts—integer, float (also called real or double), string, and array. When using variables in your scripts, you need not declare the variables first. (In fact, because PHP has no variable declaration statements, the only way to "declare" [that is, to create] a variable in PHP is to assign a value to a new variable name or to call the *array()* constructor function to create an empty array.) When you assign a value to a variable, PHP not only associates a memory location with the variable's name, but also determines the variable's data type based on the value you place in the variable. For example, the following script creates a variable of each of the four data types, assigns a value to each variable, and then displays the values of the variables on a Web page, as shown in Figure 10-5:

```
<html>
<body bgcolor="#ADD8E6">
  <h1><center>HTML and Web Design Tips & Techniques</center></h1>
  <hr>
  <?
//create a string variable
  $authorName = "Konrad King";
//create an integer variable
  $familyMemberCount = 3;
//create an array
  $petsNames[0] = "Samantha";
  $petsNames[1] = "Caesar";
  $petsNames[2] = "Floppy";
//create a floating point (that is a real or double) variable
  $yearsInNevada = 7.5;
//display all variables on a Web page.
  echo "$authorName, the author of several computer-related ";
  echo "books, has lived in Nevada for $yearsInNevada years.";
  echo "<br> There are $familyMemberCount people in the ";
  echo "author's family, plus three pets named: ";
  echo "$petsNames[0], $petsNames[1], and $petsNames[2]"
  ?>
</body>
</html>
```

> ## HTML and Web Design Tips & Techniques
>
> Konrad King, the author of several computer-related books, has lived in Nevada for 7.5 years.
> There are 3 people in the author's family, plus three pets named: Samantha, Caesar, and Floppy

Figure 10-5   The values of PHP variables displayed on a Web page

Understanding Operators

The basic function of a PHP *operator* is to change the value of a variable or to work with the value of a variable or literal in some way. In the preceding example, the PHP script used the assignment operator—that is, the equal sign (=)—to assign an initial value (string, integer, and floating point) to each variable created within the script. PHP has four main types of operators:

- **Assignment operators**   These are used to assign a value to a variable or to change a variable's current value by performing an arithmetic operation or string concatenation. The assignment operators are described in the following table:

Assignment Operator	Purpose	Example
=	Assign a value	$variable = expression $a = 5; $b = $a + 7; $c = 6 * $d;
+=	Add the value that follows the equal sign (=) to the current value of the $variable	$variable += expression $a = $a + 5; (same as) $a += 5;
−=	Subtract the value that follows the equal sign (=) from the $variable's current value	$variable −= expression $a = $a − 10; (same as) $a −= 10;
/=	Divide the $variable's value by the (nonzero) value that follows the equal sign (=)	$variable /= nonzero expression $a = $a / 10; (same as) $a /= 10;
*=	Multiply the $variable's value by the value that follows the equal sign (=)	$variable *= expression a = a * 25; (same as) a *= 25;
%=	(Modulus)—Divide the $variable's current value by the value that follows the equal sign (=) and place the remainder from the division in the $variable	$variable %= expression $a = $a % 15; (same as) $a %= 15;
.=	(Concatenation)—Concatenate the string or numeric value that follows the equal sign (=) onto the string $variable's current value	$variable .= " string value" $variable .= numeric value $a = $a . "bcd"; (same as) $a .= "bcd";

- **Arithmetic operators**   These are used to perform (as you might expect) arithmetic operations (such as addition, subtraction, multiplication, and/or division) on the values of two or more variables or literal numbers in an expression. The arithmetic operators are described in the following table:

Arithmetic Operator	Purpose	Example
+	Addition	expression + expression
–	Subtraction	expression – expression
*	Multiplication	expression * expression
/	Division	expression / expression
%	Modulus (return the remainder of a division)	expression % expression

- **Comparison operators**   These are used to compare one expression, variable, or literal value to another. Typically, you use comparison operators within conditional statements (such as *if* and *if-else*), and control loops (such as *while* and *for*). The comparison operators are listed in the following table:

Comparison Operator	Purpose	Example
<	Less than	expression < expression
>	Greater than	expression > expression
<=	Less than or equal to	expression <= expression
>=	Greater than or equal to	expression >= expression
==	Double equal sign (=)—Equal to	expression == expression
===	Triple equal sign (=)—Identical to	$variable === literal value
!=	Not equal to	Expression != expression

- **Logical operators**   These are used to compare two Boolean (that is, true or false) values. Typically, you will use logical operators to compare the results of two comparison expressions in a conditional statement or control loop. The logical operators are described in the following table:

Logical Operator	Purpose	Example
&&, and	And	expression && expression
||, or	Or	expression || expression
!	Not (exclamation point [!])—negates the value of an expression	!expression

Understanding Conditional and Repetitive Processing

A PHP script is a list of instructions you want the PHP processor (running on the Web server) to execute to accomplish a specific task. All the simple scripts you reviewed up to this point in the chapter have the processor start with the first statement and execute each statement, in order, to the end of the script. As your scripts become more complex, you will sometimes want the PHP processor to execute one set of statements if one condition is true, and, possibly, another set if the condition is false. In other words, you will want the processor to make decisions and respond accordingly. When you write scripts that instruct the processor to make decisions, you are performing *conditional processing*. In other words, based on the outcome of one or more conditions, the processor will execute specific statements.

To make decisions, your scripts must first perform some type of test. For example, one script might test if the password a visitor entered is correct, and a second script might test if the phone number a visitor entered has the correct number of digits. To perform such tests, your scripts will use the PHP comparison operators listed previously. Comparison operators let your scripts test how one value "compares" to another. In other words, by using comparison operators, the PHP processor can test if one value is equal to, greater than, or less than a second value. When the processor uses comparison operators to compare two values, the result of the comparison is either true or false— meaning, the two values either satisfy the comparison (true) or they do not (false).

Closely related to decision making within your scripts is the ability to repeat one or more statements a specific number of times or until a known condition occurs. The *while* statement lets you create a loop in which the processor executes a set of statements repeatedly as long as the specified condition remains true. The *for* statement lets you create a loop in which the PHP processor executes a set of statements a fixed number of times.

Using the *if* Statement to Test a Condition

The *if* statement lets you use a PHP comparison operator to instruct the PHP processor to perform a test and then execute statements based on the result of the test. If the test result is true, the processor executes the statement that follows the *if*. On the other hand, if the test result is false, the processor ignores (skips) the statement that follows. The format of the *if* statement is as follows:

```
if (condition_is_true)
    statement;
```

Notice that you do not place a semicolon (;) after the *if (condition_is_true)* that starts the *if* statement because the *if* statement continues to the next line.

When you use the *if* statement for conditional processing, you will sometimes want the processor to perform only one statement if the condition is true, and other times when you want the processor to execute several statements. When your script tells the processor to perform only one statement following an *if*, you are using a *simple statement*:

```
if ($state == "ca")
    echo "The state entered was California.";
```

To instruct the PHP processor to perform several statements when a condition evaluates as true, you must group the statements within left and right braces ({ }). The statements that appear within the braces make up a *compound statement*, as shown here:

```
if ($username != "Konrad")
  {
   header("Location: http://NVBizNet2.com/htmlwdtt/InvalidUser.htm");
   exit;
  }
```

▶ **NOTE**

Remembering the terms simple statement *and* compound statement *is not important, but rather, that you know that you must group related statements (that is, statements within a statement block) within the left and right braces ({}).*

In the two previous examples, the processor uses an *if* statement to determine whether it is to execute one or several statements. In the first example, the processor inserted text on the Web page if the condition was true. Similarly, in the second example, the processor redirected the Web browser to a new Web page if the condition was true—that is, if the value of the *$username* variable was not "Konrad". In both examples, if the condition was false, the processor skipped executing the statement(s) in the *if* statement block. In most cases, however, you will want the processor to execute one set of statements when the condition is true and a second set of statements if the condition is false. To provide the statements that execute when the condition is false, your scripts must use the *else* statement. The format of the *else* statement is as follows:

```
if (condition_is_true)
    statement;
else
    statement;
```

The following script uses an *if-else* statement to check whether the value in *$username* is "Konrad", and if so, takes the visitor to the Welcome.htm Web page. Otherwise, the processor will redirect the visitor to the InvalidUser.htm page:

```
if ($username == "Konrad")
  {
   header("Location: Welcome.htm");
   exit;
  }
else
  {
   header("Location: http://NVBizNet2.com/htmlwdtt/InvalidUser.htm");
   exit;
  }
```

In addition to using an *if-else* statement to execute one set of statements when a condition is true and another set of statements if the condition is false, you may sometimes want the processor to test several different related conditions or the same condition repeatedly. For example, assume that your script must determine a visitor's area code by testing the value in *$city* for a match with various city names whose area codes are known to the script. The following statement uses a series of *if-elseif* statements to illustrate a simplified example of the processing the processor might perform:

```
if ($city == "New York")
   $areaCode = 212;
elseif ($city == "Houston")
   $areaCode = 281;
elseif ($city == "Phoenix")
   $areaCode = 602;
elseif ($city == "Seattle")
   $areaCode = 206;
else
   $areaCode = "**UNKNOWN**";
```

When the PHP processor executes the *if* statement, it first tests whether the city is New York. If so, the processor assigns the *$areaCode* variable the value 212. If the city is not New York, the processor performs the following *else if* to test if the city is Houston. The PHP processor will perform this processing for each city until it either finds a matching city or reaches the final *else* statement. If the processor does not find a matching city, it assigns to the variable *$areaCode* the string value "**UNKNOWN**".

Use the *if-elseif* structure shown in the preceding example to execute a statement (or set of statements) when you are testing for inequality (the value of a variable being less than, greater than, or not equal to another value) or when you want to test the values of multiple, related variables. When you want to base statement execution on a single variable being equal to a number or string, PHP provides a *switch* statement more suitable (than an *if-elseif* structure) for this purpose. For example, the following *switch* statement is more intuitively obvious and elegant than the *if* and *elseif* statements in the previous example:

```
switch ($city)
{
 case "New York":
   $areaCode = 212;
   break;
 case "Houston":
   $areaCode = 281;
   break;
 case "Phoenix":
   $areaCode = 602;
   break;
 case "Seattle":
   $areaCode = 206;
```

```
    break;
 default:
    $areaCode = "**UNKNOWN**";
}
```

When it encounters a *switch* statement, the processor compares the value of the expression that follows the keyword *switch* to each of the values in the *case* clauses. If the values match, the PHP processor executes the statement(s) that follows the matching *case* clause until the processor encounters the end of the *switch* statement or a *break* statement. If none of the *case* clause values matches the value in the *switch* clause, the processor will execute the statement(s) associated with the *default* clause.

The *break* statements in the preceding example are important because they instruct the PHP processor to stop executing *case* clause statements and continue execution at the first statement following the *switch* statement. For example, if you were to omit the break in the "Houston" *case* clause, the processor would first assign 281 and then 602 to the *$areaCode* variable.

You may sometimes omit the *break* statement on purpose. Suppose, for example, that you want to execute the same statement(s) for multiple *case* clause values, such as in the first three *case* clauses in the following switch statement:

```
switch ($city)
{
 case "Henderson":
 case "Las Vegas":
 case "Pahrump":
    $areaCode = 702;
    break;
 case "New York":
    $areaCode = 212;
    break;
 case "Houston":
    $areaCode = 281;
    break;
 case "Phoenix":
    $areaCode = 602;
    break;
 case "Seattle":
    $areaCode = 206;
    break;
 default:
    $areaCode = "**UNKNOWN**";
}
```

Because Henderson, Las Vegas, and Pahrump have the same area code (702), you want the PHP processor to execute the *$areaCode = 702;* assignment statement whenever the *$city* has any one of the three names.

Using Logical Operators to Test Two or More Conditions

As your scripts become more complex, you will sometimes want the processor to test more than one condition at a time. For example, your script might test if a visitor's annual income is greater than $25,000 and less than $75,000. Likewise, you might test whether a visitor has a good credit history or if the visitor is a first-time homebuyer. To perform such operations, you will use the PHP logical *AND* operator (&& or "and") and the logical OR operator (|| or "or"). When your scripts use the logical *AND* or the logical *OR* operator to test more than one condition, you will place each condition within parentheses, as shown by the following *if* statement, which uses the logical *OR* operator to test whether the visitor has good credit or is a first-time homebuyer:

```
if (($hasGoodCredit) || ($firstTimeHomeBuyer))
   statement;
```

In a similar way, the following statement uses a logical *AND* operator to determine if a visitor's income is in the range $25,000 to $75,000:

```
if (($income >= 25000) && ($income <= 75000))
   statement;
```

When your scripts use the logical *AND* operator, all the conditions within the statement must be true for the entire condition to evaluate as true. If any condition is false, the entire condition becomes false. For example, if the visitor's income is not greater than or equal to $25,000, the previous condition is false. Likewise, if the visitor's income is greater than $75,000, the condition is false. In order for the condition to be true, the visitor's income must be greater than or equal to $25,000 and less than or equal to $75,000.

For a statement that uses the logical *OR* operator to evaluate as true, only one condition must be true. For example, if the visitor has good established credit, the previous condition is true. If the visitor is buying his or her first home, the condition is true. Moreover, if the visitor has good credit and is buying his or her first home, the condition is true. The only time the condition would be false is if the visitor does not have good credit and is not buying a first home, in which case both conditions are false, and the overall condition evaluates false.

Using the *for* Statement to Repeat Statements a Specific Number of Times

One of the most common operations your scripts will perform is to instruct the PHP processor to repeat one or more statements a specific number of times, in which case you will use the *for* statement. A PHP *for* statement has three expressions and a simple or compound statement with the following syntax:

```
for (expression1, expression2, expression3) statement;
```

The PHP processor evaluates the first expression (*expression1*) once at the beginning of the loop. At the start of each iteration, the processor evaluates the second expression (*expression2*). If the second expression evaluates as true, the PHP processor executes the statement or group of statements within a begin-end block ({ }) as in:

```
for (expression1, expression2, expression3)
  {
    statement;
    statement;
       ...
    statement;
  }
```

Conversely, if the second expression evaluates as false, the PHP processor stops executing the *for* loop. At the end of each iteration, the PHP processor evaluates *expression3*.

You can use any legal PHP expressions you want within a *for* loop and any or all three of the expressions may be empty. However, an empty second expression (*expression2* in the preceding syntax) means that the PHP processor will execute the *for* loop indefinitely. Thus, the following *for* loop with empty second and third expressions will terminate only when the conditional *break* statement within the loop (*if $count == 10 break;*) causes the PHP processor to continue execution with the first statement that follows the *for* loop:

```
for ($count = 1;;)
  {
    echo "Count = $count<br>";
    if ($count == 10) break;
    $count = ++$count;
  }
```

As another example, the following *for* statement (with three non-empty expressions) displays the first ten values in the *$stateNames* array:

```
for ($stateIndex = 0; $stateIndex <= 9; ++$stateIndex)
  echo "\$stateNames[$stateIndex] = $stateNames[$stateIndex]<br>";
```

The third expression increments the variable *$stateIndex* after each iteration of the *for* loop. While the second expression (*$stateIndex <= 9*) is true, the PHP processor will execute the *for* loop's statement block—a single *echo* statement in this example.

Using a *while* Loop to Repeat Statements While a Condition Is True

In the preceding section, you learned to use PHP *for* loops to instruct the PHP processor to repeat one or more statements a specific number of times. For situations in which you want the PHP processor to loop as long as a specific condition remains true, but not necessarily a specific number of times, you can use the PHP *while* loop. The general format of the *while* loop is as follows:

```
while ($conditionIsTrue)
{
 statement;
 statement;
}
```

When the PHP processor encounters a *while* loop, the processor first tests the specified condition (within the parentheses after the keyword *while*). If the condition is true, the processor will execute the *while* loop's statement block (that is, the statements within the braces [{}] that follow the *while* clause). After executing the last statement in the loop, the processor again tests the condition. If the condition is still true, the processor executes the *while* loop's statements again, then checks the condition again, and so on. When the condition finally becomes false, the processor continues execution at the first statement that follows the last statement in the *while* loop.

The PHP *do-while* loop is similar to the *while* loop in that the *do-while* loop also instructs the browser to repeat a set of statements while a condition is true. However, instead of checking the condition before executing the statements in the loop (as is the case with the *while* loop), the *do-while* loop checks the condition after executing the loop's statements. The general format of the *do-while* loop is as follows:

```
do
{
  statement;
  statement;
}
while ($conditionIsTrue)
```

Because the processor tests the condition after executing the *do-while* loop's statements, the processor will execute the statements in the loop at least once—even if the condition the processor tests is false before the processor executes the loop's statements the first time.

Sending Data from an HTML Form to a PHP Script

If PHP were not able to retrieve information from a site visitor, the scripting language would offer little more than is already available with standard HTML. After all, displaying things such as the date, time, and visitor count does not give a Web page dynamic content of interest to site visitors. True, the values of these items will change. However, the overall content of the Web site—that is, the information a visitor would visit the site to view—remains static unless you give the visitor a means of telling the Web server what he or she wants to see. You can use HTML forms to let the visitor send information to the Web server, and PHP scripts to act on the information sent (by the visitor) to create new Web page content.

As you learned in Chapter 3, after a visitor fills in a form's text elements, makes radio button and check box selections, and then clicks on the form's Submit button, the Web browser sends the form results to the Web server. However, the Web server does not "understand" the data sent by the browser. As a result, the Web server must pass the data (that is, the form results) to another program for processing. Traditionally, Web browsers passed the form results to Perl scripts for processing. Nowadays, you have the Web server send form results not only to Perl scripts, but also to Java Servlets, Active Server Pages (ASP), and (as you will learn in this Tip) PHP scripts.

When you read about forms (in Chapter 3), you learned about the various attributes you can use in a <form> tag. The two attributes important to PHP's interaction with the form results are the *action* and *method* attributes. By setting the *action* attribute in a <form> tag to the URL of a PHP Web page, you can tell the Web server to pass the form results (sent to the Web server by the Web browser when the visitor clicks the form's Submit button) to a PHP script. The *method* attribute tells the Web browser the way in which the browser is to send the form results to the Web server.

Suppose for example, that you create a Web page with the following form definition:

```
<form action="http://www.NVBizNet2.com/HWDTT/Chpt10Tip01.php"
      method="GET">
  First Name: <input type="text" name="firstName" size="20"><br>
  Last Name: <input type="text" name="lastName" size="20"><br>
  E-Mail: <input type="text" name="emailAddr" size="30"><br>
  <input type="submit" value="submit">
  <input type="reset" value="reset">
</form>
```

After the visitor clicks the form's Submit button, the Web browser will send the form results to the Web server using the GET method. The GET method tells the Web browser to append the form's name/value pairs (that is, the form results) onto the URL to which the Web server passes the form data (http://www.NVBizNet2.com/HWDTT/Chpt10Tip01.php in this example), as shown by the Address field of the Web browser application window in Figure 10-6.

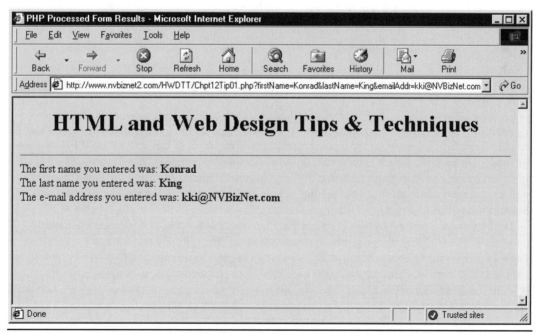

Figure 10-6   Web browser Address field with form results sent using the GET method

In this example, the Web browser passes the name/value pairs "firstName=Konrad", "lastName=King", and "emailAddr=kki@NVBizNet.com".

The "name" portion of the name/value pair in the form results comes from the *name* attribute of the form element's definition and the "value" portion of the pair is the information the visitor entered into the form element itself. Thus, in this example, the visitor entered "Konrad" into the *firstName* element, "King" into the *lastName* element, and "kki@NVBizNet.com" into the *emailAddr* element to produce the form results shown in Figure 10-6. By reviewing the Web browser Address field in Figure 10-6, you can see that the GET method caused the browser to format the form results as the URL:

```
http://www.nvbiznet2.com/HWDTT/Chpt10Tip01.php?firstName=Konrad
&lastName=King&emailAddr=kki@NVBizNet.com
```

from the *action* attribute in the <form> tag, followed by a question mark (?) and the three name/value pairs from the form as:

```
firstName=Konrad
lastName=King
emailAddr=kki@NVBizNet.com
```

An ampersand (&) separates each of the name/value pairs in the form results appended onto the URL.

One disadvantage of using the GET method is the very public nature of the form results transmission—the visitor can view all form results in the Address field of the browser application window. Moreover, form results transmitted as part of a URL are logged in the browser's history list, the Web server's log files, and (if used) a proxy server's cache. If you do not want the browser to display the form results sent to the Web server or leave a copy of the results in easily accessible locations, use the POST method as shown in the following <form> tag:

```
<form action="http://www.NVBizNet2.com/HWDTT/Chpt10Tip01.php"
      method="POST">
```

After the visitor clicks the Submit button on a form using the POST method, the browser sends the name/value pairs that make up the form results to the Web server in the body of an HTTP request (instead of as part of a URL). As a result, the Web browser's address field will show only the URL specified by the *action* attribute and none of the form results. Moreover, using the POST method lets you transmit more information, because there is a physical limit as to the number of characters the browser can transmit as part of a URL.

Deciding which method to use (POST or GET) to transmit form results is largely a matter of preference. The HTML 4.01 specification states you *should* use the GET method if the application that will process the form results retrieves information but makes no changes. Conversely, you should use the POST method whenever the application that processes the form results updates existing data or stores the form results in a file or database. However, these are just guidelines—they are not hard and fast rules. Therefore, you might use other criteria to make your selection.

For example, if the visitor might want to bookmark the URL resulting from submitting a search form or if the URL contains information you want to analyze later (by using a Web server log file analyzer to determine the most common search terms), use the GET method. Conversely, if the form results contain sensitive or personal/private information or if the form results are part of a transaction that should be performed only once (such as a stock purchase or a balance transfer between bank accounts), use POST.

USE IT   Whether you use the POST or GET method to send form results to the Web server, the PHP processor automatically creates variables named after the form elements and stores the visitor's input into those variables. Thus, within your PHP script, you can refer to the data submitted through a form element by using the form element name preceded by a dollar sign ($).

Suppose, for example, that your Web page has the form definition given at the beginning of this Tip:

```
<form action="http://www.NVBizNet2.com/HWDTT/Chpt10Tip01.php"
      method="GET">
  First Name: <input type="text" name="firstName" size="20"><br>
  Last Name: <input type="text" name="lastName" size="20"><br>
  E-Mail: <input type="text" name="emailAddr" size="30"><br>
  <input type="submit" value="submit">
  <input type="reset" value="reset">
</form>
```

You can use the form results in a PHP script such as the one in the body of the following PHP Web page by saving the page to the URL given by the *action* attribute in the <form> tag:

```
<html>
<head>
  <title>PHP Processed Form Results</title>
</head>
<body bgcolor="#ADD8E6">
  <h1><center>HTML and Web Design Tips & Techniques</center></h1>
  <hr>
  <?echo "The first name you entered was: ";
    echo "<b>$firstName</b><br>";
    echo "The last name you entered was: ";
    echo "<b>$lastName</b><br>";
    echo "The e-mail address you entered was: ";
    echo "<b>$emailAddr</b><br>";
  ?>
</body>
</html>
```

Given the value of the *action* attribute in the form definition for this example, you would save the preceding PHP Web page to a file named Chpt10Tip01.php in the HWDTT folder on the NVBizNet2.com Web site.

Note that the variable names in the PHP script are case-sensitive. Thus, the Web server will pass the form element named *firstName* and the element's value to the PHP variable *$firstName*.

However, as you learned earlier in this chapter, *$firstName* is not the same as *$FirstName*. As such, to use the value entered in the *firstName* element, you must use the PHP *$firstName* variable (spelled and capitalized exactly the same as the form element name).

Using PHP to Parse and Extract Form Results

The preceding Tip shows you how to retrieve forms data values into your PHP scripts. In short, you can refer to the value in a form element using a PHP variable whose name matches the value of the form element's *name* attribute. Thus, your PHP script would use *$firstName* to refer to the value entered in a form element defined as follows:

```
<input type="text" name="firstName" size="20">
```

Before using PHP to process form results, you need to check if the visitor entered valid data in all the form's required elements. Often, you will also need to make sure that each item entered is of the proper data type and within an acceptable range of values. For the sake of efficiency, you normally instruct the Web browser to validate data entered into a form's elements before sending the form results to the Web server.

To perform all form validation at the Web server would increase Web server overhead and use Internet bandwidth unnecessarily. A visitor may forget to fill in several required form elements and/or enter values that are out of bounds. Verifying form results at the Web server would require that the visitor wait while the Web browser sends invalid data to the Web server only to receive a message detailing what needs to be fixed. In the process of submitting form results, the visitor may send bad form results across the Internet several times (taking up bandwidth) and the Web server may have to check the same form data results repeatedly (using up server resources).

By using a JavaScript or VBScript function embedded in the Web page to validate form results at the Web browser, you can prompt the visitor to fix data entered into the form before the browser sends the form results to the Web server. Therefore, letting the Web browser validate data entered into a form before sending the form results to the Web server keeps the Web browser from sending form results multiple times. Instead, the JavaScript or VBScript used to validate the form alerts the visitor to errors in the data entered (or omitted) and forces the visitor to correct the data before sending the form results (once) to the Web server.

Even after validating form results within the Web browser, you should perform a second, final check of the form's data at the Web server as well. Theoretically, the JavaScript or VBScript functions embedded in the Web page HTML will prevent the visitor from submitting invalid data. Unfortunately, some Web browsers do not support scripting languages, and for safety, some site visitors will instruct a browser with script support not to execute scripts embedded on a Web page. Therefore, to make sure you only process valid data, check the form results at the Web server one last time.

USE IT To check whether the visitor entered something into a (single-line) text element or a (multiline) text area, you can simply use the equality comparison operator (==) and compare the form element's value to a zero-length string, as in this example:

```
if (trim($firstName) == "")
  {
   echo "<b>** Invalid - Enter Name **</b><br>";
   $formResultsValid = false;
  }
```

PHP also provides several built-in functions you can use to determine if the data entered in a text element is numeric [*is_numeric()*, *is_real()*, and *is_integer()*]. After you determine whether the visitor entered data (and perhaps, specifically numeric data) in a text field, you can perform further comparison tests to ensure that the text or numeric data entered is within a valid range of values.

Unlike radio buttons, each check box on a form is an individual entity and is not part of a named group. To ensure that the visitor has made a selection from at least one of what you want to treat as a set of check boxes, give each check box a unique name, as shown in the following code:

```
<input type="checkbox" name="windows" value="Windows">Windows
<input type="checkbox" name="mac"     value="Macintosh">Mac
<input type="checkbox" name="unix"    value="UNIX">Unix
```

Because the Web browser sends only the name/value pairs of the check boxes into which the visitor clicked a check mark (or an *X*), you can then use logical *AND* operators (&&) in code such as the following to ensure the visitor made at least one selection:

```
if ((!isset($windows)) && (!isset($mac)) &&
    (!isset($unix)))
  {
   echo "You must select Windows, Mac, or Unix<br>";
   $formResultsValid = false;
  }
```

The PHP built-in *isset()* function returns true if the value of the variable you pass to the function has been set. Because the browser passes only the value of check marked (that is, selected) check boxes, the values of check boxes not check marked will have no value in the PHP script.

The Web browser handles radio buttons in groups based on a group name you assign to the *name* attribute in each radio button's <input> tag. Whereas you give each check box in a form a different (unique) name, you give the radio buttons in the same group a single name. For example, the following code creates a group of two radio buttons under the radio button group name of *giveOutEmailAddr*:

```
<input type="radio" value="Yes" name="giveOutEmailAddr">Yes
<input type="radio" value="No"  name="giveOutEmailAddr">No
```

The Web browser lets the visitor select only a single entry within any one radio button group. However, the browser does not force the visitor to make at least one selection. Therefore, to ensure that the visitor made one selection from a group of radio buttons, use the PHP built-in function *isset()* in code similar to the following:

```
if (!isset($giveOutEmailAddr))
  {
   echo "<b>Please tell us if we can give out your".
         " e-mail address.</b><br>";
   $formResultsValid = false;
  }
```

The Web browser passes only a name/value pair for the (one) selected radio button in a button group through the button group's name. As such, if the user makes no selection, the browser does not pass a value to the button group's PHP variable.

Finally, suppose your form has a list box defined by code similar to the following:

```
<select size="6" name="currentOS[]" multiple>
  <option value="Windows98">Windows 98</option>
  <option value="WindowsME">Windows ME</option>
  <option value="WindowsXP">Windows XP</option>
  <option value="MacOs">Macintosh</option>
  <option value="Unix">Unix</option>
  <option value="Linux">Linux</option>
</select>
```

Note the brackets ([]) that follow the list box element's name. If you simply name the list box *currentOS*, PHP will only have access to the value of a single option (the last one toward the bottom of the option list) that the visitor selects. This is fine if you omit the *multiple* attribute from the <select> tag, which means the Web browser will let the visitor make only a single selection from the list. By appending the brackets ([]) to the list box name, you instruct the Web browser to return the values of all selections the visitor makes as an array.

To determine if the visitor made at least one selection within the list box, you would again use the PHP *isset()* built-in function as follows:

```
if (!isset($currentOS))
  {
   echo "<b>** You must select the operating system(s) " .
        "you use. **</b><br>";
   $formResultsValid = false;
  }
```

Putting together what you have learned in this Tip then, your overall form results validation script will consist of the following:

```
<?
  $formResultsValid = true;
/*
  Statements that display element names and values for valid
  form element data set; and that display element names,
```

```
   "error message" and set the $formResultsValid (Boolean)
   variable to false for each element with invalid data.
*/
  if ($formResultsValid)
    {
/*
    PHP code that processes the form results with user-defined
    and/or built-in PHP functions or a script typed either here
    or in an included external PHP Web page.
*/
     echo "<hr>";
     echo "<b>The information you entered has been submitted ".
          "for processing.<br>Thank you!</b>";
    }
//** If the form is invalid, give the visitor a "Back" Button **
  else
    {
     echo "<form method=POST>";
     echo "<input type=\"button\" value=\"Correct Form\"".
          " onClick=\"self.history.back()\">";
    }
?>
```

For a complete listing of the form definition and validation script used in this example, download the Chpt10Tip02 from http://www.osborne.com.

Using PHP to Send an E-Mail Message

Many Web sites have hyperlinks that let site visitors send e-mail messages to people associated with the site (such as the Webmaster, company employees, or departments such as customer service, marketing, human resources, and so on). To create a hyperlink that instructs a Web browser to send an e-mail message, set the *href* attribute in the hyperlink's <a> tag to "mailto:" followed by the e-mail address to which the browser is to send the message.

For example, to send an e-mail message to kki@NVBizNet.com, you might insert the following hyperlink on a Web page:

```
<a href="mailto:kki@NVBizNet.com">Konrad King</a>
```

Unfortunately, using "mailto:" to instruct the Web browser to send an e-mail message works only in a limited number of situations. If the visitor has not configured the Web browser to start the e-mail application or if the visitor has not properly configured the e-mail application itself, the browser will be unable to send the message as desired. Fortunately, PHP has a built-in *mail()* function you can use to instruct the Web server to send the e-mail message through a local—or on a Windows platform, through a remote—Simple Mail Transport Protocol (SMTP; that is, e-mail) server. By taking the Web browser out of the loop, you no longer have to depend on the visitor's having the proper software configuration to send an e-mail message successfully.

USE IT Before you can use the PHP *mail()* function, your ISP must specify the SMTP server (or, for a Unix platform, the path to the Sendmail program) in the PHP.ini file. For example, if your ISP's Web server runs under Windows NT, have the ISP open the PHP.ini file in the winnt folder. Then, set the SMTP and sendmail_from settings in the mail function section of the INI file, similar to the following:

```
[mail function]
SMTP =  smtp.lvcablemodem.com ; for Win32 only
sendmail_from =  kki@NVBizNet.com ; for Win32 only
;For Unix only. You may supply arguments as well (default: 'sendmail -t -i').
;sendmail_path =
```

To send an e-mail message, create a form such as the one shown in Figure 10-7, and set the *action* attribute in the form's <form> tag to the URL of the PHP Web page with the script that sends the form results as an e-mail message.

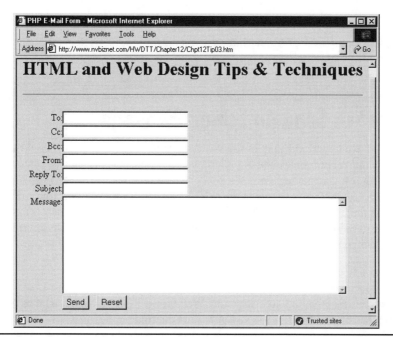

Figure 10-7   A form that lets a site visitor send an e-mail message through a PHP script

In general terms, the PHP script will pass the values entered in the form shown in Figure 10-7 as parameters to the built-in PHP *mail()* function. The *mail()* function, in turn, will pass the parameter values to either the Sendmail program (Unix) or to an SMTP server.

The syntax of the PHP *mail()* function call is as follows:

```
mail($recipientList, $subject, $message [, $headerList
    [, $parameterList]]);
```

Here is a description of the syntax:

- *$recipientList*   String that contains a list of e-mail addresses separated by commas (,)
- *$subject*   String with the "Subject:" line of the e-mail message
- *$message*   String which contains the body of the e-mail message
- *$headerList*   (Optional parameter) string with text the *mail()* function is to place in the e-mail header. Separate each header item with a carriage return/new line combination (\r\n).
- *$parameterList*   Command line parameter string the *mail()* function is to pass to the Sendmail program or SMTP server

Thus, a PHP *mail()* function call might look something like this:

```
mail("kki@NVBizNet.com,konrad@NVBizNet.com",
    "Test message to say hello",
    "This is the body of the message"
    "From: me\r\nReply-To: secret@xyz.com\r\n".
      "X-Sender: PHP\r\nCc: userID@domain.com");
```

Of course, the script in the PHP Web page to which the Web browser sends the form results (*Chpt10Tip03*, in this example) passes string variables and not literals as parameters to the *mail()* function. You can download the Web page HTML for the form shown in Figure 10-7 and the source for the PHP script used to process the form results from http://www.osborne.com.

Determining Whether a Visitor's Web Browser Accepts Cookies

Cookies are small text data items the Web server can store and retrieve from a cookie file on the visitor's hard drive. Normally, the HTTP protocol is *stateless*, which means that when a Web server responds to a browser's HTTP request, the server has no idea if there was a previous request from the same visitor. The Web server simply sends files (Web pages, graphics images, and so on) to the Web browser in response to the browser's HTTP requests. Previous pages viewed and interactions with Web page objects (such as form element selections or entries) have no effect on the content of each new page retrieved.

However, if you have a subscription site to which the visitor must log in for access to nonpublic or custom content, the server must have some way to keep track of the visitor's state as "logged-in" while the visitor moves from page to page on the site. Otherwise, the visitor must log in repeatedly as he or she moves from one restricted-access page to another. Cookies let the Web server maintain the visitor's state information by storing the following information:

- A visitor's preferences for a site and the Web pages he or she visited previously
- A key that links the visitor with the personal data you stored about the visitor in the site's database
- A "session" key that allows the visitor to log in once and remain logged in until the visitor leaves the site or exits the Web browser
- A visitor's product selections on an e-commerce site so you can present items selected on a order form when the visitor is ready to check out and pay for his or her selections

Unfortunately, because some developers use cookies to gather information on consumers without their knowledge, and worse yet, sell the information to others, you can expect some of your site visitors will set their Web browsers not to accept cookies. If processing performed by scripts on your site's Web pages depends on storing and retrieving cookie data, use PHP scripts to test whether the visitor's Web browser accepts cookies before you let the visitor onto the site.

USE IT To test if the browser will accept cookies, insert the following PHP script to write a "test" cookie before the Web page HTML in your site's login page or index page:

```
<?
//create a date string to use as the "test" cookie value
 $today = getDate();
 $dateString =  $today['month']." ".$today['mday'].", ".
   $today['year'];

//attempt to set the cookie
 setcookie("TestCookie", $dateString);
?>
//display the remainder of the index page or login page content
```

If you pass only Web pages with a .php extension to the PHP processor, and your site's index page (that is, the site's home page) has an .htm extension, insert the home page content after the preceding script in a Web page with a .php extension, such as LoginPage.php. Then, insert an *onload* attribute such as the following that loads the PHP Web page in the start <body> tag of the site's home page (usually index.htm or default.htm):

```
<body onload="document.location='LoginPage.php'">
```

Next, in the PHP Web page the browser loads when the visitor exits the site's login or index page, insert the following script:

```
<?
//create a date string against which to test the cookie value
 $today = getDate();
 $dateString =  $today['month']." ".$today['mday'].", ".
   $today['year'];

if (!empty($testCookie))
 {
  if ($testCookie == $dateString)
   {
//validate username and password here & if valid move
//to the "logged in" screen
    header("Location: LoggedIn.htm");
    exit;
   }
 }
//If no cookie was set, display a page asking the visitor to
//set the browser to accept cookies.
 header("Location: NeedCookies.htm");
 exit;
?>
```

You must spread the cookie test across two Web retrievals, because the Web browser passes and accepts cookie information only as part of a Web page header. Thus, the *setcookie()* function call in the first PHP script creates a cookie the Web server sends to the Web browser in the login or index page header. The Web browser, in turn, stores the cookie data (the current date, in this example) in the site's cookie file on the visitor's hard drive. When the visitor moves on to another of the site's pages, the Web browser sends all the site's cookies (TestCookie, in this example) to the Web server as part of the HTTP request for the new page.

When the Web server receives the request for a PHP Web page, the server passes the HTTP (Web page) request and the cookie data to the PHP processor for processing. The PHP processor, in turn, can access each cookie value in a variable with the same name as the cookie preceded by a dollar sign ($). Thus, in this example in which the *setcookie()* function created a cookie named *testCookie*, the PHP processor can check the value of *$testCookie* to see if the cookie's value is the current date. If *$testCookie* is undefined or has a date other than the current date, the Web browser failed to store the cookie created by *setcookie()*, which means that the Web browser does not accept cookies. As a result, the PHP processor directs the Web server to load the Web page NeedCookies.htm, which prompts the visitor to change the processor's cookie preferences to accept cookies. Conversely, if *$testCookie* contains the current system date, the Web browser stores the cookie *setcookie()* created, and the PHP processor loads the Web page that lets the visitor access the site's content.

Using PHP and a Disk File to Set Up Username/Password Access to a Web Site

When you set up a Web site with members-only content, you need a way to let authorized users log in to the site while preventing those not authorized from retrieving the site's Web pages. You can use an HTML form such as the one shown in Figure 10-8 to prompt the site visitor for the username and password that will give him or her access to the site's restricted content.

To keep things simple, set the *name* attribute of the form's first element to "username" and the second element to "password". To pass the username and password the visitor enters into the form to a PHP script, set the *action* attribute in the form's <form> tag to the name of the PHP Web page with the login script as follows:

```
<form method="post" action="Chpt10Tip05.php" name="loginForm">
```

In this example, the filename of the PHP Web page with the username/password authentication script is Chpt10Tip05.php. (You can download the login form Chpt10Tip05.htm and the login script Chpt10Tip05.php from http://www.osborne.com.)

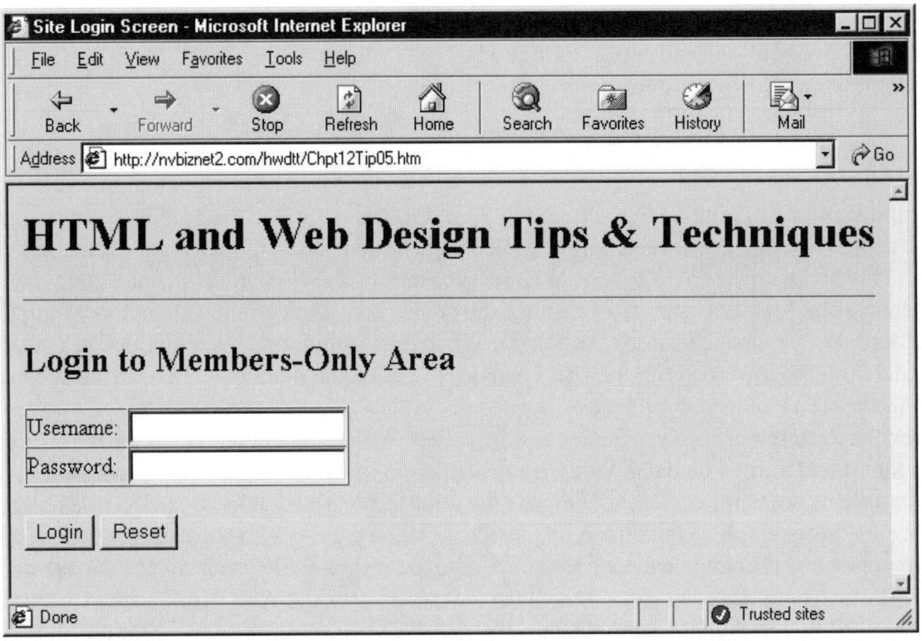

Figure 10-8   Username/Password Login Form

USE IT   After making sure that the visitor entered both a username and a password into the login
form's elements, the PHP script (in Chpt10Tip05.php) uses the built-in *fopen()* function
to open a text file named password.txt, which contains the valid username/password pairs. When you
review the script, you will see the following code used to read the contents of the password.txt until
the script finds a username/password pair in the file that matches the username and password the
visitor entered on the login screen:

```
if ($fp = fopen("c:\\password.txt", "r"))
  {
   while (feof($fp) == 0)
     {
//read 1 line of up to 1,000 characters from the password file
      $line = trim(fgets($fp,1000));
//each line in the password file is formatted as:
//"username,password".
      $userPass = split(",", $line);
//check for a matching of both username and password
      if (($userPass[0] == $username) and ($userPass[1] == $password))
        {
         header ("Location: Chpt10LoginSuccessful.htm");
         exit;
        }
     }
//invalid username / password entered.
   header ("Location: Chpt10AccessDenied.htm");
   exit;
  }
```

If the script finds a match, the PHP processor calls the *header()* function to pass to the Web browser
a Web page in the members-only area of the site (Chpt10LoginSuccessful.htm, in this example).
Conversely, if the script is unable to find a match before reaching the end of the password.txt file, the
PHP processor passes the "invalid login" page (Chpt10AccessDenied.htm) to the Web browser and
denies the visitor access to the site.

To prevent the visitor from using the Web browser to display the contents of the username/
password file, store the file outside the Web site's folders. (Otherwise, the visitor could display the
contents of the text file by entering the filename into the browser's Address field.) As long as the
PHP processor has sufficient access rights, you can place the file with the authorized username/
password pairs in any folder on the server's hard drive. Moreover, to increase security by making
it more difficult for visitors to guess the name of the authentication file, use a filename with letters
and numbers and avoid using *password* or *username* in the name.

QUICK TIP

When you set a form input element's type *attribute to "password", the Web browser obscures what the visitor enters into the element from view by displaying an asterisk (*) in place of each character the visitor types. However, when the Web browser submits all form data (including data in password elements), it sends it as (unencrypted) ASCII text. As such, a hacker could tap into the Internet, steal and read (as plain text) the body of the HTTP message in which the Web browser sends the form data results to the Web server.*

To safeguard sensitive information, use the Secure Socket Layer (SSL) protocol to encrypt the data transmissions between the Web server and the Web browser. SSL encryption occurs outside the scope of PHP—meaning that SSL encryption is transparent to your PHP scripts. When using a secure connection, the Web browser encrypts the HTTP requests (including those for PHP Web pages) that the browser sends to the Web server. After receiving an encrypted HTTP request, the Web server decrypts the message and passes the (decrypted) request to the PHP engine. The engine, in turn, retrieves the PHP Web page, executes the scripts and functions in the page, and sends the Web page generated to the Web server. The Web server, in turn, places the page into the body of an HTTP response, which the server then encrypts and sends to the Web browser. Upon receipt of the HTTP response (that is, the Web page requested from the Web server), the Web browser decrypts the message and displays the Web page.

To set up secure processing (in which the Web server and Web browser send encrypted messages), speak with the ISP hosting your Web site. After your ISP obtains and installs the required keys and certificates, your scripts will run, for the most part, unchanged. The only difference you will notice is that your secure URLs will start as "https://" instead of the standard (unsecure) "http://". Thus, to use a secure connection when moving from one PHP Web page to another, use the following, for example:

    header ("Location: https://www.NVBizNet2.com/LoginScript.php"

in place of:

    header ("Location: http://www.NVBizNet2.com/LoginScript.php"

Preventing Visitors from Linking Directly to Pages on Your Site

In the preceding Tip, you learned how to use a login form and a text file to restrict access to a Web site by requiring visitors to enter a valid username/password pair. Unfortunately, if you use only a login page, visitors can access members-only content without providing a valid username/password by bypassing the login screen altogether.

Suppose, for example, that the login script you wrote to check the username/password pair sends the LoginSuccess.htm Web page to the Web browser if the visitor enters a valid username/password pair. If you use only a login screen to secure the site's pages, a visitor could skip the login process and access the site's content by bookmarking a restricted page (such as LoginSuccess.htm, in this example) or by entering the URL of any members-only page into the browser's Address field.

USE IT To prevent visitors from retrieving restricted pages directly (without first logging into the site), place all the site's members-only content on PHP Web pages, that is, on Web pages with a .php extension. Then, insert a PHP script similar to the following before the first line of HTML in each restricted-access page:

```
<?
//retrieve the URL of the Web page with the hyperlink used to
//retrieve the current page
 $fromPage = getEnv("HTTP_REFERER");

//make sure that the "referrer" contains the URL of a Web page that
//is allowed to link to a page in the members-only section of
//the Web site
  if ((substr($fromPage,0,31) !=
        "http://www.nvbiznet2.com/hwdtt/") and
      (substr($fromPage,0,27) !=
        "http://nvbiznet2.com/hwdtt/"))
   {
//if not from a valid page, display a page with a custom error
//message or simply send the login screen to the visitor's Web
//browser instead of the page requested
     header ("Location: http://NVBizNet2.com/hwdtt/LoginScreen.htm");
     exit;
   }
?>
```

The Web browser sends the URL of the Web page with the hyperlink used to retrieve a Web page as "HTTP_referer" in the header of the HTTP request the Web browser sends to the Web server. If the visitor retrieves a Web page from the login screen or by clicking a hyperlink on any page within the "/hwdtt" folder on the NVBizNet2.com Web site, the *getenv( )* function will return a string that starts http://www.NVBizNet2.com/hwdtt/ or http://NVBizNet2.com/hwdtt/.

To use the preceding script on your Web pages, use your site's .com address and the pathname of the folder in which you store the site's members-only content in the *if* statement. In addition, replace the URL in the *header( )* function call with the URL of your login page in the next-to-last line of the script.

Using a PHP Session to Establish a Persistent Connection Between a Site Visitor and the Web Server

In a discussion about the World Wide Web, a *session* is a series of related interactions between a site visitor and the Web server, which take place over an extended period. A session might consist of a series of transactions a visitor makes while transferring money between bank accounts, while paying bills through a Web-based bill payment service, or while updating a stock portfolio. During a session, the visitor might make multiple requests to execute the same script or the visitor may execute a variety of scripts on several of the site's Web pages. In short, a session starts when the visitor retrieves one of a site's Web pages and ends when the visitor exits the Web browser or moves on to another Web site.

One way to make data persistent—that is, to have variables retain their values from one HTTP request to the next—is to instruct the Web server to send the variables (names and values) to the visitor's Web browser as cookies. The Web browser, in turn, stores in a (cookie) file the Web browser creates on the visitor's hard drive all the cookies sent from a particular site.

Another way to create persistent variables is to have the PHP processor store the values of the variables in a session file at the Web server. When you install PHP, the installation program prompts you for the name of the session save path, which is the pathname of the folder in which you want PHP to create the session files. Typically, you will have PHP store session files in the \PHP\sessiondata folder on the same drive on which you install the PHP itself. Therefore, if you install PHP on the D drive, you will have PHP create session files in the D:\PHP\sessiondata folder.

By using session variables instead of cookies, you avoid having to pass the variable data values between the Web server and Web browser with each HTTP request. Instead of several data values, the Web server sends only one "key" value—the session ID—to the Web browser as a cookie named PHPSESSID. The browser then passes the session ID to the Web server with each HTTP request, and the PHP processor uses the session ID to identify the file (on the Web server's hard drive) that contains the persistent data values available to scripts the visitor might run during the session.

USE IT   To establish a session, call the *session_start()* function in a PHP script to create a cookie (PHPSESSID) with a randomly generated session ID. The Web server must pass all cookies (including PHPSESSID) to the Web browser within the Web page header. As such, the PHP processor must execute a *session_start()* function call that creates and inserts the cookie with the session ID into the Web page header before the script outputs any other content to the page.

Thus, if you plan to use persistent (session) variables, insert the following code at the start of your site's login script or at the start of the first PHP Web page the visitor retrieves when accessing the site:

```php
<?php session_start(); ?>
```

If the visitor previously started a session on the Web site and did not subsequently exit the Web browser, calling the *session_start()* function will continue or re-establish the session with the same session ID generated earlier. Otherwise, the *session_start()* function call will generate a new session ID at random and insert the ID as a cookie (named PHPSESSID) into the Web page header. If the visitor has his or her browser preferences set to Prompt Before Accepting Cookies, the Web browser will display a message box similar to that shown in Figure 10-9 when the browser receives the Web page with the session ID cookie (PHPSESSID) in the page header.

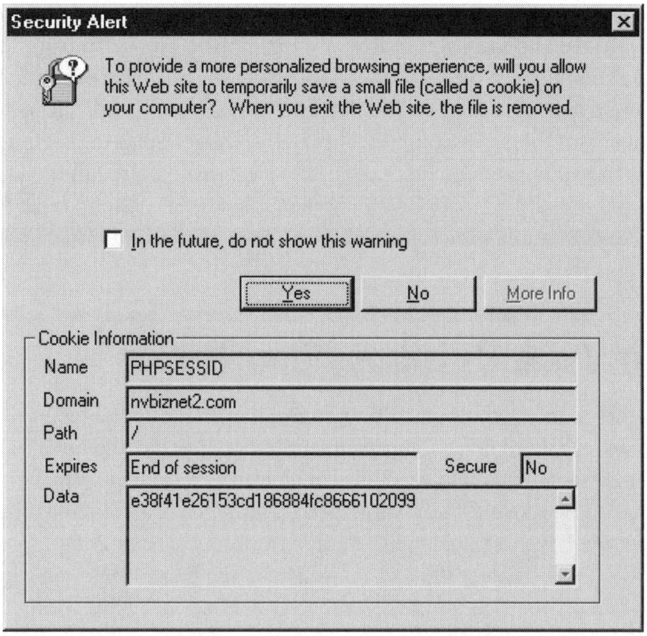

Figure 10-9   The Web browser "Accept Cookie" message box displayed when establishing a new session

After you call the *session_start( )* function to establish the session ID and alert the PHP processor that you plan to use persistent (session) variables, you can register the variables whose values you want the processor to maintain in the session file. To register a variable, pass the quoted variable name without the leading dollar sign ($) to the *session_register( )* function as shown in the following code that registers four persistent-valued, global variables (*$s_firstName*, *$s_lastName*, *$s_address*, and *$s_phoneNumber*):

```
<?
 session_register("s_firstName", "s_lastName", "s_address",
                 "s_phoneNumber");
?>
```

You can assign the value you want the processor to maintain in a persistent variable anytime after you register the variable. However, you can only call the *session_register( )* function before the processor outputs *any* content (even so much as a single space) to the current Web page. (Calling the *session_register( )* function to register a session variable does not change (or set) the variable's current value.)

For an example showing scripts that establish a session and then use session variable values on various Web pages, retrieve and view the source code in Chpt10Tip07.zip from http://www .osborne .com. The script at the beginning of the PHP Web page Chpt10Tip07.php executes the *session_start()* function call to generate a unique session ID and start the session. Next, the *session_register()* function call near the end of the login script in Chpt10Tip07Login.php registers several session variables and assigns to two of them the username and password entered in the login form (on the Chpt10Tip07.php page). Finally, Chpt10GetPI.php and Chpt10GetPI2.php have forms that let the visitor enter personal information, which the script in Chpt10ShowInfo.php displays onscreen.

Creating a MySQL Database and Tables

In a previous Tip in this chapter you learned how to use the PHP built-in *fopen()* function to open a text file on the Web server's hard drive. You then learned how to use the built-in *fgets()* function to retrieve the text file's contents, one line at a time, in an effort to find a username/password pair that matched the username and password the visitor entered into the elements of a "login" form.

Now, suppose that you have a text file with the list of products your company sells. Using what you already know, you could create a PHP script that calls the *fgets()* function repeatedly to retrieve the product data one line (or item) at a time. Then, by executing an "echo" statement or calling the built-in *print()* function after each read, you could write a script that displays the product list on a Web page. Thus, you can use PHP and text files on the Web server to create content on-the-fly. In the current example, the Web page with your company's product list does not exist until the site visitor retrieves the PHP Web page with the script that generates the list.

An SQL database, like a text file, is simply a collection of data. However, unlike text files in which applications store data in unstructured chunks, a DBMS controls all interactions with the data in an SQL database and organizes the data for fast, easy access and manipulation. As a result, it would take an unacceptably long time to search through a text file of several thousand username /password pairs for a match required to grant the user access to a Web site. Meanwhile, a DBMS can perform the same search (on tens of thousands of records) in a fraction of a second. Similarly, a DBMS could display a list of specific products or a single product (versus a list of all products) more quickly than a script reading the text file with the product list from beginning to end.

PHP comes with built-in functions that let you not only retrieve but also update the data stored in several of the most popular DBMS products such as DB2, FrontBase, Informix, InterBase, mSQL, MS SQL Server, MySQL, Oracle, ODBC, PostgreSQL, and Sybase. Check with your ISP or database administrator (dba) to see which of these products is available for you to use to supply data to your PHP scripts. If none is installed, you may find MySQL of particular interest. MySQL is a multiuser DBMS you can download free of charge from http://www.MySQL.com and is available for both the Windows and Unix platforms.

 Regardless of the DBMS product to which you have access, you will need to create a database to hold the tables your PHP scripts can use to store and retrieve information.

To create a database, use the SQL CREATE DATABASE statement. Suppose for example that you want to create a database in which to create tables that hold data for use when working with the examples in this book's Tips. You might use the first letter in each word of the book's title as the database name (**H**TML & **W**eb **D**esign **T**ips & **T**echniques yields *HWDTT*). Therefore, to create a database for this book's example tables execute the SQL CREATE DATABASE statement as follows:

```
CREATE DATABASE hwdtt;
```

The syntax of the SQL CREATE DATABASE statement is this:

```
CREATE DATABASE <database name>
```

After you create a database, you will need to create tables in which to store your data. A complete discussion of data normalization (that is, using relational database concepts to determine what data to include in which tables) is beyond the scope of this book. What is important to understand now is that an SQL table consists of rows of related information arranged in columns. Each row (sometimes—albeit loosely—called a *record*) consists of related data items. For example, if you wanted to create a table of usernames and passwords, each row in the table would contain a valid username/password pair—with the username in one column and the associated password in another. To create such a table, first tell the DBMS which database you want to use and then execute an SQL CREATE TABLE statement as follows:

```
USE hwdtt;
CREATE TABLE webSiteUsers
   (username VARCHAR(20) NOT NULL,
    password VARCHAR(20) NOT NULL);
```

The syntax of an SQL CREATE TABLE statement is as follows:

```
CREATE TABLE <table name>
 (<column name> <column type> [<column attribute list>],
 ...
   <last column name><last column type> [<last attribute list>])
```

To be useful, your SQL table needs data, which you can add using SQL INSERT statements. For example, to insert usernames and passwords into the *webSiteUsers* table, you can execute an INSERT statements such as:

```
INSERT INTO webSiteUsers (username, password)
   VALUES ("Konrad", "abc2125");
INSERT INTO webSiteUsers (username, password)
   VALUES ("Gracie", "157WXY3");
```

The syntax of an SQL INSERT statement is this:

```
INSERT INTO <table name> (<column1, column2, ..., columnN)
  VALUES (value1, value2 ..., valueN)
```

Next, to use the table in this example, you can submit a query in the form of an SQL SELECT statement to the DBMS. For example, to display the usernames and passwords in the table, you can execute the SQL SELECT statement:

```
SELECT username, password FROM webSiteUsers;
```

To test whether a visitor entered a valid username, you can add a WHERE clause that tells the DBMS to return only those rows in which the username and password matched the values the visitor entered into the elements of the login form. For example, if the visitor entered *Konrad* into the username element and *wrongPass* into the password element of the login form, your query would be this:

```
SELECT COUNT(*) FROM webSiteUsers
WHERE username="Konrad" AND password="wrongPass";
```

If the query returns "1", the username/password pair submitted is valid, because it is an entry in the table. Conversely, if the visitor submitted a username/password pair not in the table (as is the case in this example), the query returns "0" to indicate that no user in the table has the username and password combination submitted in the query.

The next Tip shows you how to insert data into an SQL table and how to submit queries that retrieve the SQL table data using PHP scripts.

Displaying SQL Query Results in an HTML Table on a Web Page

To retrieve and display data from a database onto a Web page, your PHP script must do three things. First, the script must establish a connection with the DBMS by calling a built-in PHP "database connect" function (such as *mysql_connect()*, which lets PHP connect to a MySQL DBMS). Second, the script needs to send a query to the DBMS through the database connection using a built-in "SQL query" function (such as *mysql_query()*, which lets PHP send SQL statements to the MySQL DBMS for execution). Third, after the DBMS places query results in an output buffer at the Web server, the script must retrieve the data stored in the buffer and display the information on a Web page. For example, if you are working with MySQL, your script might use the built-in *mysql_fetch_array()* function to retrieve the data in one row of SQL query results (from the DBMS output buffer) and place the row's column values into the elements of an array. Next, the script might execute an *echo* statement or make a *print()* function call to display the database field values (from the array) onto the Web page.

USE IT   Suppose, for example, that you are using the MySQL DBMS and want to display in an
HTML table on your Web page the data in an SQL table named *products* within the
HWDTT database (that is, within the HTML and Web Design Tips and Techniques database). First,
execute a *mysql_connect()* function call such as the following:

```
$link = mysql_connect($db_host, $db_user, $db_pass);
```

$db_host contains the string "localhost" (if the MySQL server is running on the same system as
the Web server) or a string with the IP address of the computer running the MySQL Server with
which you want to connect. (Speak with the ISP hosting your Web site to get the IP address of the
computer with the SQL server you will be using.) The remaining two parameters, *$db_user* and
$db_pass, are the username and password the function needs to log in to the MySQL DBMS. (If
you are working with a default installation of MySQL, you can log in with *$db_user* = "root" and
$db_pass = "".)

Within the *mysql_connect()* function, the PHP processor assigns the DBMS connection handle
to the *$link* variable or returns the Boolean false if the connection attempt fails. Because things do
sometimes go wrong, use an *if* statement to check if the *$link* is false and display an error message
on the Web page if necessary. If the connection attempt succeeds, use a function call such as the
following to select the database with the table(s) whose data you want to query:

```
if (!mysql_select_db($db_name, $link))
  {
//Statements to handle a failed "USE database" statement.
  }
else
  {
//Processing after a successful database connect and select.
  }
```

A MySQL server normally manages several databases, so you need to choose the database with
the table(s) whose data you want to use. In this example, *$db_name* contains the string "HWDTT"
and *$link* contains the database connection handle generated by the successful *mysql_connect()*
function call. As before, check the value returned by the PHP function call [*mysql_select_db()*, in this
case] to make sure your database selection was successful; the function returns true for success or
false to indicate failure.

After successfully connecting to the MySQL DBMS and selecting a database, call the *mysql_
query()* function with a statement similar to the following to send the query (or other SQL command)
you want the DBMS to execute:

```
$result = mysql_query($query, $link);
```

In this example, in which you want to display the contents of the *products* table, *$query* contains
the SQL statement SELECT * FROM products ORDER BY description. As before, *$link* contains

the database connection handle returned by the successful *mysql_connect()* function call made near
the start of the script. *mysql_query()* returns false (if the DBMS was unable to execute the SQL
statement submitted for some reason) or a pointer to the location where the DBMS placed the query's
output (that is, a pointer to where the DBMS placed the query's results set).

To retrieve the query results (that is, the rows of data the query selected from the *products* table),
call the *mysql_fetch_array()* repeatedly to retrieve each row of query results and store the row's
column values in an array. Then display the values in the array on the Web page. For example, the
following script retrieves the number of fields (returned in the query results), the names and types
of those fields, and then displays the column values within each row of query results (returned by
each *mysql_ fetch_array()* function call) in an HTML table the script constructs on the Web page:

```
//determine the number of fields returned in the results set
  $fields = mysql_num_fields($result);
//start the HTML table definition
  echo "<center><table border='1' cellpadding='5'>";
//display column names as HTML table headings
  echo "<tr>";
    for ($i=0; $i < $fields; $i++)
      {
        echo "<th>" . mysql_field_name($result, $i) . "</th>";
        $fieldType[$i] = mysql_field_type($result, $i);
      }
  echo "</tr>";


//display query results in the HTML table's rows and columns
  while ($array = mysql_fetch_array($result))
    {
    echo "<tr>";
    for ($i=0; $i < $fields; $i++)
      {
      if ($fieldType[$i] <> "string")
        echo '<td align="right">';
      else
        echo '<td align="left">';
      echo "$array[$i]</td>";
      }
    echo "</tr>";
    }
  echo "</table></center>";
```

You can retrieve the complete PHP script described in this Tip by downloading Chpt10Tip09.php
from the Osborne Web site at http://www.osborne.com. By changing the connection information and
the SQL query, you can use the script to retrieve and show the results set from any SQL query within
the elements of an HTML table on a Web page. The script displays the names of the columns returned
by the query in a "heading" row across the top of the HTML table and displays the query results
themselves in rows below the headings.

Using PHP to Generate a Random Password

When you create a members-only Web site, you want to make sure your subscribers use passwords that unauthorized users cannot guess. Because people try to think of passwords that are easy to remember, they often use the names of family members or friends, the numbers in memorable dates, or some nickname or phrase they are fond of saying. Unfortunately, such "memorable" words, numbers, or combinations of words and numbers are also easy for someone acquainted with the member to figure out.

By using the built-in PHP *mt_rand( )* function to generate a password that consists of random letters and numbers, you can prevent new members from choosing easily compromised passwords. Unfortunately, if a password is hard to remember, the member is likely to forget it. As such, to keep your members happy and to avoid a flurry of phone calls for forgotten passwords, you will need to provide an on-line mechanism members can use to retrieve passwords previously assigned. One often used method is to have a program on the site send the initial and forgotten passwords to the member's e-mail address.

USE IT To use a PHP script to assign a random password, you need a Web page with a form such as the one shown in Figure 10-10, which lets the visitor enter a username and an e-mail address.

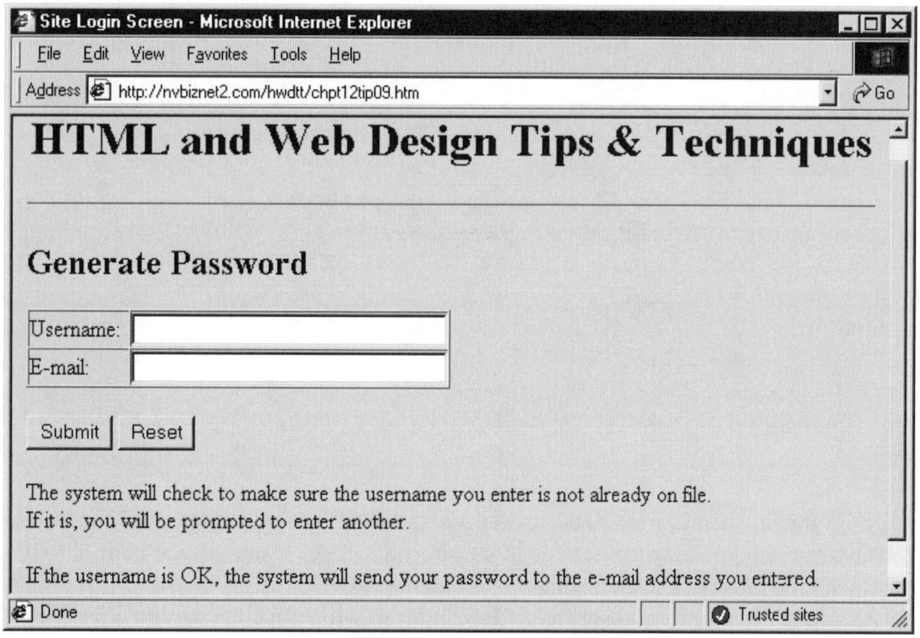

Figure 10-10   Web page prospective members can use to request a PHP generated password

As indicated by the text at the bottom of the page shown in Figure 10-10, the PHP script will generate a password of five to eight characters after the visitor enters a username not already in-use by another member. The script randomizes not only the characters in the password but also the length of the password itself for added security. (A password is more difficult to crack when the person trying to guess what the password is also does not know its length.)

You can use a PHP script similar to the following to generate a random password:

```
function generatePassword()
 {
//"seed" the random function and determine the password length
  mt_srand ((double)microtime() * 1000000);
  $passwordLength = mt_rand (5, 8);


//set ASCII range for random character generation
//ascii 48-57 inclusive are characters 0 to 9
//ascii 65-90 inclusive are characters A to Z
//ascii 97-122 inclusive are characters a to z
  $lowerBound = 48;
  $upperBound = 122;
//Exclude symbols
  $excludeSymbols = array(':',';','<','=','>','?','@','[',
                      chr(92),']','^','_','`');
//create the random password
  $i = 0;
  $password = "";
  while ($i < $passwordLength)
    {
      mt_srand ((double)microtime() * 1000000);
      $letter = chr(mt_rand ($lowerBound, $upperBound));
      if (!in_array ($letter, $excludeSymbols))
        {
          $password .= $letter;
          $i++;
        }
    }
  return $password;
 }
```

Next, insert the username, e-mail address, current IP address, system date, and the (randomly generated) password in the *usernames* table in the site's database. Then, call the built-in PHP *mail()* function to send the password to the member's e-mail address.

When a new member logs in, a user-defined login script will search the *usernames* table for a matching username/password pair. If the script can match the username and password stored in the database table with the username and password the visitor entered in the login form, the login script "activates" the account. In the current example (not shown here but performed by the PHP script in

Chpt10Tip10Login.php), the login script writes the system date into the last_login column of the visitor's record in the usernames table to activate the account.

You can retrieve the Web pages with the forms and PHP scripts described in this Tip by downloading the file Chpt10Tip10.zip from the Osborne Web site at http://www.osborne.com.

Using PHP and MySQL to Set Up Username/Password Access to a Web Site

In "Using PHP and a Disk File to Set Up Username/Password Access to a Web Site" earlier in this chapter, you learned how to set up a restricted access (that is, members-only) Web site using PHP and a text file with the site's username/password pairs stored on the Web server's hard drive. Unfortunately, placing the site's authorized user list in a text file has several inherent problems. For example:

- Each time you add username/password pairs to the file, you increase the time it takes a user to log in. It takes longer and longer for the login script to scan the access file (from beginning to end) for matching username/password pairs as the file gets larger.

- Deleting or changing username/password pairs in the access file is a manual, tedious, and error-prone process. As a result, someone may inadvertently render the access file unusable to the authentication script by changing the required <username>,<password> format of each line.

- Network users (such as the system administrator and others with privileged accounts) might not recognize the access file's name and delete the file while "cleaning up" folders to free up disk space (thereby denying everyone access to the Web site). Or, these users may simply view the file's contents and thus get a complete (albeit, unauthorized) list of your site's usernames and passwords.

By storing username/password pairs in an SQL database, you can avoid all these problems. Everyone authorized to work with the access table must do so through the DBMS. Therefore, no one can corrupt the format of the lines in the access file by adding, removing, or changing username/password pairs. Moreover, you can control who does what in the file by granting some users "insert only" and others "insert", "delete", "view", and/or "update" access. Moreover, whether the site has 10 or 10,000 members, it will take the PHP login script the same (short) amount of time to search for a matching username/password pair when a member logs onto the site.

USE IT   To use a table in a MySQL database as the site's access control list, first create the table in which to store the site's usernames and passwords with an SQL CREATE statement:

```
CREATE TABLE siteAccessList
(username VARCHAR(30) PRIMARY KEY,
 password VARCHAR(15) NOT NULL);
```

The SQL CREATE statement in this example creates a two-column database table for usernames and passwords. The first column, username, can store hold up to 30 characters, and the PRIMARY

KEY attribute specifies that every row in the table must have a unique, nonblank (and NOT NULL) value in the username column. The second column (password) can hold up to 15 characters and each row must have a non-NULL password.

Next, execute INSERT statements such as the following to add to the table username/password pairs subscribers can use to log in to the Web site:

```
INSERT INTO siteAccessList VALUES ("Konrad","King");
INSERT INTO siteAccessList VALUES ("Sally","Fields");
INSERT INTO siteAccessList VALUES ("Craig","Berry");
```

(To prevent nonsubscribers from "guessing" passwords and thereby gaining unauthorized access to the Web site, you should not use last names for passwords as shown in this example.) Each of the three INSERT statements creates a new row in the table, placing the first item in the VALUES list in the first table column and the second item into the second column.

After a visitor enters his or her username and password into a login form and clicks the form's "Login" button, a PHP script such as the following connects with the MySQL database and determines if the username/password pair entered is in the site access list:

```
<?
 $db_host = "localhost";
 $db_user = "root";
 $db_pass = "";
 $db_name = "hwdtt";

//Connect to MySQL DBMS
 $link = mysql_connect($db_host, $db_user, $db_pass);

//Select the database with the siteAccessList table
 mysql_select_db($db_name, $link);

//formulate the query and then send it to DBMS for execution
 $query = "SELECT username FROM siteAccessList ".
          "WHERE username = \"$username\" ".
          "AND    password = \"$password\"";
 $result = mysql_query($query, $link);

//Check the number of rows in the query results set. If the
//username/password is on file, the query will produce exactly
//1 row of results. If not, mysql_num_rows() will find that the
//query returned zero (0) rows.
 if (mysql_num_rows($result) == 0)
   header ("Location: Chpt10AccessDenied.php");
 else
   header ("Location: Chpt10Tip10LoginSuccessful.php");
?>
```

After calling the *mysql_connect()* function to log in to the MySQL server, the script calls the *mysql_select_db()* function to select the database that contains the site access list (*siteAccessList*, in this example). Next, the script builds the query (that is, the SQL SELECT statement) that instructs the DBMS to return the table rows with a username/password pair that matches the username and password the visitor entered in the login form. After the script calls the *mysql_query()* function to send the query to the DBMS, the DBMS executes the query and places the list of rows with matching username/password pairs it finds in an output buffer.

The *mysql_num_rows()* function call returns the number of rows the DBMS returned by executing the SQL SELECT statement submitted by the *mysql_query()* function call. If the *mysql_num_rows()* function in the *if-else* statement at the end of the scrip returns "1", the visitor is authorized to enter the site. Conversely, if the *mysql_num_rows()* function returns "0", the script prevents the visitor from accessing the site's members-only content, because the username/password pair the visitor entered is not one of those in the site access list.

You can retrieve the Web page with the login form and the PHP Web page with the login script described in this Tip by downloading the file Chpt10Tip11.zip from the Osborne Web site at http://www.osborne.com.

Preventing Visitors from Changing Variable Values with URL Arguments

To pass form results to a PHP script, you can use either the GET method or the POST method. As you learned in Chapter 3, the POST method causes the Web browser to send form results to the Web server in the body of an HTTP request. The GET method, meanwhile, appends the form results onto the URL to which the Web server is to pass the form results. Unfortunately, being able to pass variable values to a PHP script by appending variable name/value pairs onto the URL of a PHP Web page (as the GET method does) poses a potential security problem. Visitors might append values for variables you do not want changed.

Suppose, for example, that your site has a login screen that requires the visitor to enter a valid username/password pair. After a valid login, your login script establishes a PHP session and sets a persistent variable such as *$s_username* to the name the visitor used to log in to the Web site. Prior to a valid login, *$s_username* is unset (that is, undefined), so you might place an *if* statement such as the following at the beginning of each of the PHP Web pages in the members-only area to prevent unauthorized access:

```php
<?php
 session_start();
 if (!isset($s_username))
   {
     header("Location: http://www.NVBizNet2.com/LoginScreen.htm");
     exit;
   }
?>
```

Unfortunately, if the site visitor enters into the Address field of the Web browser the URL of a page in the members-only area as follows, the PHP engine will set the value of *$s_username* to "Konrad":

```
http://www.NVBizNet2.com/LoggedIn.php?s_username=Konrad
```

Because the *$s_username* variable has a value when checked by the *if* statement at the start of the PHP Web page, the visitor is allowed to retrieve the page, although he or she never logged in.

USE IT To prevent visitors from setting session variables (and thereby circumventing your login process), pass all your form results using the POST method. In so doing, you can check to make sure the site visitor has not entered any URL arguments with code such as the following:

```php
<?php
 if ($HTTP_SERVER_VARS["argc"] != 0)
   {
    header("Location: $PHP_SELF");
    exit;
   }
?>
```

By passing any form results in the bodies of HTTP requests, you make sure that none of the PHP Web pages expects URL arguments. Therefore, if the PHP processor detects any arguments appended to a URL, the processor should (and does) reload the PHP Web page again—without arguments.

Using PHP and MySQL to Track Where Visitors Go on Your Web Site

After you create a Web site, you often want to track who visits the site, what pages they view, and (perhaps) the URL of the Web page with the hyperlink on which the visitor clicked to get to the page on your site. To create a comprehensive access log of every visit for all your site's pages, talk to the ISP hosting your Web site. Most commercial Web servers (including IIS) come with a built-in capability to generate W3C-compliant site usage logs. After the Web server generates a standard usage log, you can use an off-the-shelf usage log analyzer (or write an application of your own) to read the ASCII log file and display information on the site's page views using both text graphics charts.

If your ISP will not turn on the Web server's logging functions (due to the space required for the log files and the server overhead involved in maintaining them), or if you want only to track access to certain pages, you can use a MySQL table and a few PHP scripts to create your own usage reports. Suppose, for example, that you execute the following SQL CREATE statement to create a table named *UsageLog* in a MySQL database:

```
CREATE TABLE UsageLog
(visitor_IP    TEXT,
```

```
page_URL        TEXT,
DT_retrieved    TIMESTAMP,
referer_URL     TEXT,
session_ID      TEXT,
session_views INTEGER);
```

You can then insert code that calls the following user-defined function at the start of each PHP Web page for which you want to track the usage by adding a row into the *UsageLog* table in the MySQL database:

```
<?
 function recordPageHit($db_host, $db_user, $db_pass, $db_name, $sessionID)
 {
  global $REMOTE_ADDR, $PHP_SELF, $link, $result;

//to save space, use str_replace() to strip off the //"http://"
//from the URL. Also, use explode() to remove the query,
//if any, that follows the "?" in a URL
  $referer = explode("?",
    str_replace("http://", "", getenv("HTTP_REFERER")));

//call a user-defined function to connect with the MySQL DBMS
  if (connectToDB($db_host, $db_user, $db_pass, $db_name))
    {
//Only insert one row per page per session. If the visitor
//views a page multiple times, keep track of the number of
//visits to the page during the session in the "session_views"
//column of
    $query = "UPDATE UsageLog ".
             "SET session_views = session_views + 1 ".
             "WHERE session_ID = '$sessionID' ".
             " AND page_URL   = '$PHP_SELF'";
    $result = executeQuery($query);

//Check if the UPDATE statement found a row for the page.
//If not, insert a row for the page into the table. A page will
//have only one row of stats per session
    if (!mysql_affected_rows($link))
      {
        $query = "INSERT INTO UsageLog ".
                 "(visitor_IP, page_URL, referer_URL, ".
                 "session_ID, session_views) ".
               "VALUES ('$REMOTE_ADDR', '$PHP_SELF', ".
                     "'$referer[0]', '$sessionID', 1)";
        $result = executeQuery($query);
```

```
        }
     }
  }
?>
```

Copy the PHP source code for the preceding function, as well as the user-defined function *connectToDB()* (used to connect to a MySQL DBMS near the beginning of *recordPageHit()*), onto your computer by downloading the file Chpt10Tip13.zip from the Osborne Web site at http://www.osborne.com. Chpt10Tip13.php (also included in the Zip file) shows you the statements you need to insert at the top of your PHP Web page files to start a session and then call the *recordPageHit()* function.

Note that the *recordPageHit()* function calls the same user-defined function (*executeQuery()*, which is also included in Chpt10Tip13.zip) to both update an existing row in the *UsageLog* table and to insert a new one. When working with MySQL, you use the same PHP built-in function (*mysql_query()*) to send to MySQL any statements (such as SELECT, INSERT, UPDATE, CREATE, DROP, and so on) you want the DBMS to execute. (Bear in mind that logging each Web page request can bog down your Web server if you get an appreciable amount of traffic and thereby reduce your site's scalability.)

Determining the Visitor's IP Address for Web Page Requests Sent Through a Proxy Server

In the preceding Tip, you learned how to create a MySQL table and use PHP scripts (some saved as user-defined functions) to log page views by inserting rows of data into the SQL table. In addition to generating reports on the number of pages and which specific pages a visitor retrieves during a session, you might want to identify each visitor to your site by IP address. Given the table *UsageLog* (created in the preceding Tip), you could submit an SQL query such as the following to get a list of IP addresses used during sessions the Web server started during the previous 14-day period:

```
SELECT visitor_IP 'Visitor IP', session_ID 'Session ID',
       DATE_FORMAT(DT_retrieved, '%m/%d/%y %T') 'Date & Time'
FROM   usageLog
WHERE  (TO_DAYS(NOW()) - TO_DAYS(DT_retrieved)) <= 14
GROUP BY visitor_IP, session_ID;
```

Each computer on the Internet has a unique Internet Protocol (IP) address. Typically, the Internet Service Provider (ISP) used to connect the computer to the Internet assigns the IP address to the computer from the "bank" of IP addresses the ISP controls. When you use your browser to send an HTTP request for a Web page to a Web server, the Web server uses the IP address the Web browser sends in the HTTP request header to route the Web page you requested back to your computer. As mentioned previously, each computer connected to the Internet (either directly or through an ISP's equipment) has its own IP address. However, multiple workstations that access the Net through a single proxy server appear to have the same IP address (that is, the proxy server's IP address) to those on the "Internet side" of the proxy server. (Companies usually place a proxy server between computers on the company's internal network and the Internet for security reasons.)

When a visitor accesses your site through a proxy server, the visitor's computer sends the HTTP request for a Web page at your site to a proxy server. The proxy server (a computer on the internal company network that is also connected to the Internet) analyzes the message that the network user wants to send out onto the Internet. If the message passes the proxy server's "rules" tests, the proxy server notes the IP address of the computer sending the request, replaces the IP address in the REMOTE_ADDR field of the request header with its own, and then sends the HTTP request on to the Web server.

At the Web server, processing occurs as normal. The Web server (or PHP engine if the visitor requested a PHP Web page) finds the Web page requested. Then, the Web server sends the page back to the IP address in the REMOTE_ADDR field of the HTTP request. Thus, when a proxy server stands between the network user and the Internet, the Web server sends the Web page to the proxy server as the computer requesting the Web page. After the proxy server receives the Web page, the server checks the message for viruses and other "illegal" content. If all is okay, the proxy server sends the HTTP response on to the IP address of the workstation that sent the HTTP request manually.

As far as your site visitor is concerned, everything worked as it normally does, because the proxy server, acting as a middleman, is transparent to the visitor. (The Web visitor sent a request for a Web page to the Web server, and the Web server sent the requested page back to the browser.) However, at the Web server, your PHP script can no longer retrieve the visitor's (true) IP address from the REMOTE_ADDR field in the HTTP message header. Remember, the proxy server replaced the visitor's IP address in the REMOTE_ADDR field with its own.

Fortunately, the proxy server sends the visitor's IP address in the HTTP_X_ FORWARDED _FOR field instead. Therefore, to keep from missing the IP address information from visitors that come to your site through a proxy server, use the following code to determine the visitor's true IP address (which you can then store as *visitor_IP* in the UsageLog table):

```
<?
//the proxy server inserts HTTP_X_FORWARDED_FOR data into the
//message header if there is no proxy server, getenv() returns
//either blank or NULL

 $visitorIP = getenv("HTTP_X_FORWARDED_FOR");

//if there is no proxy server then retrieve the IP address from
//the REMOTE_ADDR field in the header

 if (($visitorIP == null) or ($visitorIP == ""))
   $visitorIP = getenv("REMOTE_ADDR");
 else
   {
//parse the IP address sent as:  proxy_IP [,] visitor_IP

   list ($proxyIP, $visitorIP) = split('[,]', $visitorIP);
```

```
        $visitorIP = ltrim($visitorIP);
    }
?>
```

You can retrieve the PHP source code in the preceding script and the user-defined function (*Chpt10Tip14Insert()*) used to store visitor data (including the visitor's true IP address) by downloading the file Chpt10Tip14.zip from the Osborne Web site at http://www.osborne.com.

Preventing One Visitor from Assuming Another Visitor's PHP Session Identity

When you want to use variables with persistent values (that is, variables that maintain their values as the visitor moves from page to page on the Web site) you can either use cookies or call the built-in *session_start()* function to start (or continue) a PHP session. If you use cookies, the Web browser stores the cookie values in the site's cookie file on the visitor's computer. Conversely, if you start a PHP session, the PHP processor stores the names and values of session variables in a session file on the Web server.

The PHP processor creates session files in the folder you specified when you installed the engine. By default, the PHP installation program sets the session save path to \PHP\SessionData on the same drive on which you installed PHP. Thus, if you installed PHP on the D drive, the installation program will, by default, set the session save path to D:\PHP\SessionData. (You can call the PHP built-in function *session_save_path()* to display the pathname of the folder in which PHP will create the session file.)

The name of the session file is sess_<$PHPSESSID>. If a PHP script calls the *session_start()* function when the *$PHPSESSID* variable is undefined, the *session_start()* function will place a 32-character text string into *$PHPSESSID*, append the 32-character string onto *sess_* to form the session filename, and use the session filename to create the session file in the save path folder. Suppose, for example, that the *session_start()* function call in a script sets *$PHPSESSID* to "d06205502d1bb3a0f2553bac4de763ad". The PHP processor will create the session file *D:\PHP\SessionData\sess_ d06205502d1bb3a0f2553bac4de763ad* in which to store the session variables. (You create session variables by passing the names of the session variables you want as parameters in a *session_register()* function call.)

If a PHP script calls the *session_start()* function when *$PHPSESSID* already has a 32-character value, the PHP processor will use the session ID (that is, the value in *$PHPSESSID*) to locate and open the existing session file. After opening the session file, the PHP processor will retrieve the session variable names and values previously stored in the file.

Unfortunately, the PHP processor does nothing to prevent a site visitor from initially setting or changing the value of the current session ID. Suppose, for example, that I know that the PHP processor assigned the session ID "d06205502d1bb3a0f2553bac4de763ad" when you retrieved www.NVBizNet.com/secret.php. I can steal your session by retrieving the same Web page as http://www.NVBizNet.com/secret.php?PHPSESSID =d06205502d1bb3a0f2553bac4de763ad on another computer. Moreover, because session files remain on the Web server long after a site visitor moves on to another Web site or closes the Web browser altogether, I can take over your session after you have left the site—so you would have no idea that I had done so.

To prevent one visitor from assuming another's "session identity," remove any session ID arguments passed as part of the URL by inserting the following script at the start of your PHP Web pages that use sessions:

```
<?
  if (isset($queryString))
    {
//Build a string starting with the first occurrence
//of PHPSESSID passed in the URL arguments.
    $sessionIDArgument = strstr($queryString,"PHPSESSID");
    if ($sessionIDArgument <> "")
      {
//If "PHPSESSID" is indeed one of the URL arguments, build a
//string consisting of the remaining URL arguments. Then, use
//that string to replace the "remaining URL arguments" with ""
//in the sessionIDArgument string
      $remainingArguments = strchr($sessionIDArgument,"&");
      $sessionIDArgument = str_replace($remainingArguments,"",
                            $sessionIDArgument);
//replace the session ID argument (PHPSESSID=xxx) with ""
      $queryString =
        str_replace($sessionIDArgument,"",$queryString);
      $newURL = $PHP_SELF . "?" . $queryString;
      $newURL = str_replace("?&","?",$newURL);
//Retrieve the current PHP Web page without the PHPSESSID
//argument in the URL
      header ("Location: $newURL");
      }
    }
```

You can retrieve the PHP source code used in the preceding script by extracting the file StripSessionIDFromURL.php from the Chpt10Tip15.zip archive file on the Osborne Web site at http://www.osborne.com.

Using PHP Functions to Create Web Page Templates

When creating a Web site with many Web pages, you will probably have content that you want to include on (just about) every Web page. For example, on a company Web site, you will often place the same heading (with the company name and logo) at the top of each page and perhaps some sort of copyright information at the bottom. Moreover, if you create a site navigation menu, you will want to include the same set of hyperlinks on any Web page on which you display the menu. By writing PHP

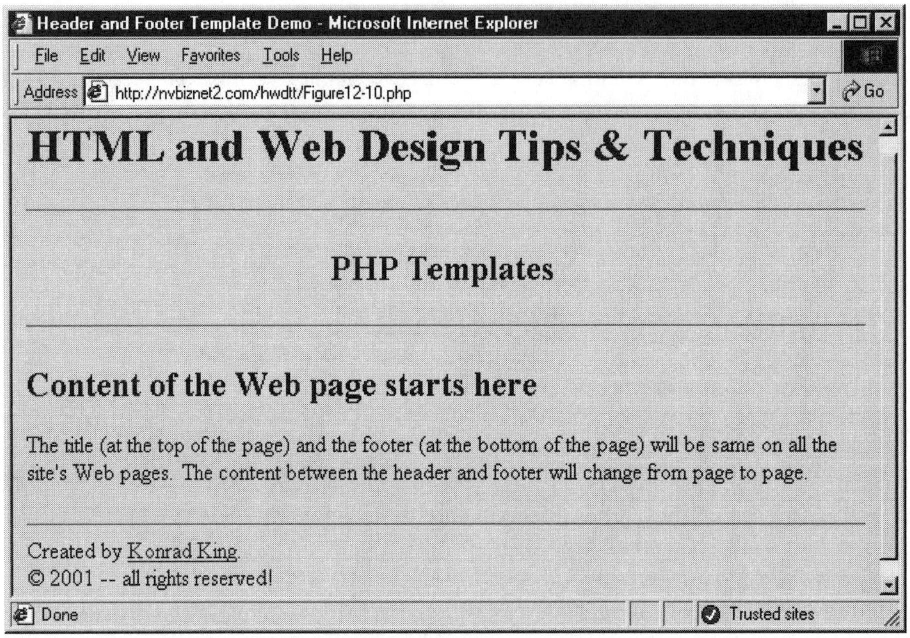

Figure 10-11 Web page on which PHP inserted a common header and footer

functions that produce templates (with the common page header, footer, navigation menu, and so on) that you can use on multiple PHP Web pages, you can save yourself a lot of time (and typing).

Suppose, for example, that you want all your site's pages to have the title, background color, and footer information shown in Figure 10-11.

You could create two PHP functions to generate the templates with the content you want to display on each page. For example, the following function will display the page heading shown previously in Figure 10-11:

```php
<?
function startHTML($title, $heading = "")
{
 echo '<html>
      <head>';
 echo "<title>$title</title>";
 echo '</head>
      <body  bgcolor="#ADD8E6">
      <h1><center>HTML and Web Design Tips & Techniques</center></h1>
      <hr>';
```

```
  if ($heading <> "")
    echo "<h2><center>$heading</center></h2>";
  return;
}
?>
```

Similarly, the following function will display a page footer:

```
<?
function endHTML()
{
 echo '<hr>
        Created by <a href="mailto:kki@NVBizNet.com">Konrad King
                   </a>.<br>
        &copy; 2001 -- all rights reserved!';
 echo "</BODY>
 </HTML>";
 return;
}
?>
```

After saving the functions in this example to files named StartHTML.php and EndHTML.php, include the following code in your Web page HTML to use the templates when creating the site's Web pages:

```
<?
 include ('StartHtml.php');
 include ('EndHTML.php');
 startHTML("Header and Footer Template Demo","PHP Templates");
?>
 **** The content that changes from page to page goes here! ****
<?
 endHTML();
?>
```

Of course, the more complex the template the PHP function generates (and the greater the number of pages on which you use the template), the more time and effort you save by not having to type the HTML that the PHP functions generate into multiple Web page documents. Moreover, when you need to make a site-wide update, such as changing the company phone number in the heading at the top of the page or the contact information in the page footer, you need only make the change once. After you change the PHP function that creates the header or footer template you want to update, all the site's pages will reflect the change the next time a visitor retrieves any Web page from the site.

Using PHP to Add File Upload Functionality to a Web Page

When you want to transfer files from one computer to another across the Internet, you typically use an FTP client application to logon to an FTP server. (FTP is short for *file transfer protocol*, and an *FTP client* is a program that implements the client-side functions defined in the FTP specification.) When you need a simple way to let your site visitors upload (that is, place) files in a folder on your Web server's hard drive, FTP servers provide capabilities you may not want your visitor to have. For example, FTP servers typically let the user upload and download files, list the contents of folders, and delete, rename, and create both files and folders. If you are developing a Web site for an accounting office or payroll processing company, for example, you may only want to give your client's clients the ability to send files with accounting or payroll data to the Web site.

USE IT   To let your site visitor upload files (without using an external FTP client program), set the *type* attribute in a start <input> tag to "file" as shown in the following form definition:

```
<form action="Chpt10Tip17Upload.php" method="POST"
      ENCTYPE="multipart/form-data">
  Select File:<input type="file" name="uploadFile" size="50">
  <br>
  <input type="submit" value="Upload">
</form>
```

The *file* form element lets the visitor enter into a single-line textbox on the form the pathname of a file on a local or network drive that the Web browser is to send to the Web server. Instead of typing the full pathname of the file the browser is to upload, the visitor can click a browser-supplied Browse button to the right of the form element and then use the window's Choose File dialog box to search for and select the file to send. Both Netscape Navigator (v3.0 and above) and Internet Explorer (v4.0 and above) support the "file" option for the *type* attribute in a start input tag <input>.

After the visitor clicks the form's Submit button (labeled "Upload", in this example), the browser sends the file specified in the "file" form element to the Web server along with any other form results. The PHP script specified by the *action* attribute in the <form> tag (Chpt10tip17Upload.php, in this example) stores the file in a folder at the Web server. You can retrieve the Web page with the "file upload" form and the PHP script used to store a file on the Web server by downloading the file Chpt10Tip17.zip from the Osborne Web site at http://www.osborne.com.

Before a site visitor uses the file upload form, have your PHP script call the *opendir()* function to select an existing folder into which to store the file the browser sends to the Web server. (If you do not explicitly select a target folder, the PHP processor will place the uploaded file(s) in the same folder as the Web page with the form used to upload the file(s).) Suppose, for example, that you want to store files the browser sends in a subfolder named upload within the same folder as the Web page on which you placed the file upload form. The following PHP statements first try to open the upload folder, and if the folder does not exist, will call the *mkdir()* function to create the folder before calling the *opendir()* function again:

```
if (!$handle = @opendir("upload"))
  {
  mkdir ("upload", 0666);
  $handle = opendir("upload");
  }
```

(The at sign [@] in front of the first *opendir()* function call tells the PHP processor to suppress any warning messages such as "Warning: Folder does not exist".)

You can use either relative or absolute addressing for the pathnames you supply to the *opendir()* and *mkdir()* functions. In this example, the script uses relative addressing to open (and create, if necessary) a subfolder named "upload" within the same folder used to store the PHP Web page with the script being executed by the PHP processor.

A PHP script refers to the *contents* of a file sent through a form element in the same way the script refers to text and numbers in the form data results set. Whether working with file contents or scalar (that is string or numeric) values, the script refers to the data received from a form element as the variable formed by inserting a dollar sign ($) in front of the form element's name. In this example, the *name* attribute of the form element used to upload files is *uploadFile*. Therefore, the PHP script will use the variable *$uploadFile* to refer to the contents of the file whose pathname the visitor entered into the *uploadFile* element on the form.

When submitting a form with an input element of type "file", the Web browser sends not only the contents of the file but also the file's name, type, and size in the form results. The PHP processor, in turn, automatically stores the uploaded file to a temporary location on the Web server and creates four variables the PHP script can use when working with the uploaded file. The names of the four variables all stem from the name of the form element used to upload the file. In the current example, the name of the form element into which the visitor enters the filename to upload is *uploadFile*. Thus, the PHP processor creates the following variables:

- *$uploadFile*   The full pathname to the uploaded file contents on the Web server (for example /tmp/php098XM0). Use *$uploadFile* in the script to refer to the uploaded file's contents.
- *$uploadFile_name*   The original name of the file on the visitor's computer.
- *$uploadFile_type*   The MIME type of the file, if known.
- *$uploadFile_size*   The size of the file, in bytes.

The PHP built-in *move_uploaded_file()* function lets a PHP script move a file from one location to another. Thus, for the current example, you would write the following *move_uploaded_file()* function call to move the file the Web browser sent from the Web server's form results buffer to a file in the folder whose pathname the script stored in the *$dir* variable:

```
move_uploaded_file($uploadFile, $dir/$uploadFile_name);
```

To inform the visitor of the success or failure of the attempt to move the uploaded file from the Web server's temporary form results buffer to the file's new, permanent location within the folder given by *$dir*, call the *move_uploaded_file()* function within an *if* statement as follows:

```
if (move_uploaded_file ($uploadFile, "$dir/$uploadFile_name"))
  echo "OK: File \"$uploadFile_name\" uploaded successfully.";
else
  echo "ERROR: File \"$uploadFile_name\" upload unsuccessful!";
```

▶ *NOTE*

When writing a script that lets visitors upload files to a folder on your Web site, make sure that the script prevents the visitor from uploading files with extensions used to denote files the Web server will pass on to the PHP, ASP, Perl, or other server-side script processors running at the server. If you do not, a visitor could do something malicious, such as upload a PHP Web page named deleteFiles.php to the site, and then retrieve the file with his Web browser. The Web server, having received an HTTP request for a file with a .php extension, will pass the PHP Web page (with the script that deletes files on the Web server) to the PHP processor for execution.

CHAPTER 11

Active Server Pages (ASP)

TIPS IN THIS CHAPTER

▶ Controlling the Flow of Content from Web Server to Web Browser Through the
  HTML Output Stream   539

▶ Preventing the Web Browser from Displaying Stale Active Server Pages   543

▶ Redirecting the Web Browser to Another Web Page   545

▶ Maintaining Variable Values Between HTTP Requests with the
  Cookies Collection   547

▶ Retrieving Form Results from the ASP Form Collection   550

▶ Retrieving Form Results from the ASP QueryString Collection   553

▶ Retrieving Information from the Server Variables Collection   556

▶ Connecting to a MySQL DBMS Through the MyODBC Driver   559

▶ Setting Up Username/Password Access to a Web Site   562

▶ Starting a Session and Working with Session Variables   565

▶ Executing SQL Queries and Displaying Query Results Sets Within an
  HTML Table   568

▶ Displaying Banner Ads with the Microsoft Banner Ad Rotator   573

▶ Tracking Microsoft Banner Ad Rotator Impressions and Click-Throughs   576

▶ Handling "Status: 404 Not Found" Errors   580

When you create a Web page using HTML alone, the page is static (that is, unchanging). Although you might spruce up the page with pictures, animations, and other multimedia effects, every visitor that requests the page will see the same content—until your next manual update. To display dynamic (that is, constantly changing) content on a Web page, you need more than just HTML. For example, to display something as basic as the current date and time using only HTML requires that you constantly edit the Web page throughout the day—everyday! Even if you display only the current date on a site's home page, each time you create a new site, you have yet one more Web page you must edit at 12:01 A.M. each day.

Active Server Pages let you create dynamic Web pages by combining HTML tags and text content with instructions written in a scripting language such as VBScript, JScript (the Microsoft version of JavaScript), PerlScript, Python, or Rexx (to name a few). The HTML tags and text provide the static (unchanging) portion of the page. Meanwhile, the script generates the dynamic (that is, changing) content you want the Web server to insert. For example, rather than type (and then have to update) the current date and time on a Web page manually, you could insert between "<%" and "%>" delimiters in an Active Server Page the VBScript statements shown in the seventh and eight lines of the following code:

```
<!DOCTYPE HTML PUBLIC "-//W3C//DTD HTML 4.0//EN">
<html>
<body bgcolor="#ADD8E6">
   <h1><center>HTML and Web Design Tips & Techniques</center></h1>
   <hr>
   Welcome Web Surfer!<br>
   In Las Vegas, the current time and date is: <% = time %> on
   <% = date %>.<br>
   Each time you refresh (or reload) the Web page the time (and
   once a day) the date will change.
</body>
</html>
```

When a Web browser requests an Active Server Page (typically a file with an .asp extension), the Web server finds the Web page and passes the document to the ASP script host, which within the Windows environment, resides in the file asp.dll on the Web server. The ASP script host parses the document and sends script statements it finds enclosed within start script (<%) and end script (%>) tags to the appropriate script engine for processing. Thus, under Windows, asp.dll passes VBScript embedded in an Active Server Page file to the VBScript engine, JScript statements to the JScript engine, and so on.

The script engine, in turn, interprets the script's statement(s) and returns the output (if any) as a string of HTML (tags and text) to the asp.dll script host. Then, the script host inserts the script output in place of the script within the Active Server Page document and passes the updated page to the Web server. The Web server, in turn, sends the Web page to the browser that requested it, as shown in Figure 11-1.

If Active Server Pages let you display only a changing date and time on a Web page, they would hardly be worth the effort involved in creating the technology. Fortunately, using a server-side script

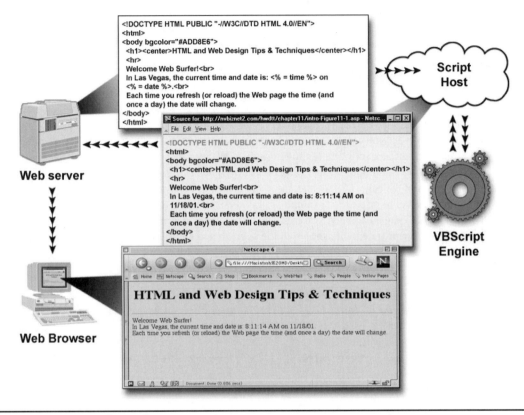

Figure 11-1 Active Server Page processing

to display a date and time on a Web page is only the simplest example of what you can do with Active Server Pages. As you will learn in this chapter, with the proper scripts, you can customize Web page content based on who is visiting your Web page, the Web browser he or she is using, and actions the visitor takes during the visit (or session). Suppose, for example, that you use your bank's Active Server Pages to manage your checking, saving, or credit card account(s). Scripts embedded within the bank's Web pages generate the HTML and text to display your account information. When someone else logs onto your bank's site, that visitor sees his or her account data (and not yours) at the same Web address.

In addition to displaying dynamic and custom Web page content, designers also use scripts embedded within Active Server Pages to process form results. Suppose, for example, that you log on onto your bank's Web site and fill out an HTML form to transfer money from one account to another. After you click the form's Submit button, your Web browser sends the information you entered into the form (that is, the form results) to the URL given by the *action* attribute within the form's <form> tag. If the URL names an Active Server Page, the Web server passes the Web document (specified by the URL) along with form results to the ASP script host. The script host passes the amount you specified and the account selections you made (or entered) on the HTML form to a script engine, which in turn, executes script statements that update your account information stored in database tables.

Understanding What You Must Have to Create and View Active Server Pages

To create an Active Server Page, you need only a text editor, such as Notepad, which comes standard with all versions of Windows. Or, you can use any one of a number of Web page development tools such as Microsoft's Visual InterDev or FrontPage, Allaire's HomeSite, Adobe's GoLive, or Macromedia's Dreamweaver to create Active Server Pages. An Active Server Page is simply an ASCII text file, typically with an .asp extension. As such, when you use a Web site development tool to create an Active Server Page, you can edit the page either with the same tool or with any of the other tools or with a text editor (such as Notepad). Just remember, to be treated as an Active Server Page, your Web document's filename must have an extension that associates the file with the asp.dll scripting engine. (Typically, Active Server Pages have an .asp file extension, because site administrators associate (designate) files with an .asp extension for processing by the asp.dll application.)

To publish Active Server Pages (that is, to make Active Server Pages available on the Internet or your company's Intranet), you need a Web server that supports Active Server Pages. Microsoft developed the Active Server Page technology. Therefore, it comes as no great surprise that Microsoft's Web server, the Internet Information Server (IIS), supports Active Server Pages. If the ISP hosting your Web site is running Windows NT Server 4.0, he or she may have installed IIS 2.0 (which has Active Server Pages version 1.0 support). The IIS Web server version 3.0 is part of Windows NT 4.0 Service Pack 3, and IIS 4.0 is available free as part of the Window NT 4.0 Option Pack. (As of this writing, you can download Option Pack 4 from the Microsoft Web site at http://www.microsoft.com/ NTServer/downloads/ recommended/NT4OptPk/default.asp.) Both IIS 3 and IIS 4 come with the asp.dll that provides Active Server Pages version 2.0 support. Windows 2000 includes IIS version 5.0, which supports Active Server Pages version 3.0.

In addition to IIS (version 2 and later), Microsoft's Personal Web Server (PWS), which is available within the Windows NT 4.0 Option Pack mentioned previously, also provides Active Server Pages support. (By the way, you can run the Personal Web Server on Windows NT Workstation or Windows 95 and above.) If you publish your Web site on a non-IIS (or PWS) Web server, you may still be able to use Active Server Pages. Find out if your ISP installed Active Server Page extensions from a company like Chili!Soft or Halcyon Software. Once installed, Chili!Soft ASP, for example, lets you run Active Server Pages on Web servers from Apache, Lotus, Netscape, and Microsoft running on Microsoft, Sun, and IBM platforms.

To view Active Server Pages, you need a Web browser. Because the Web server (and not the Web browser) executes scripts embedded in Active Server Pages, any Web browser will do. One of the strengths of server-side script execution (that is, having the Web server rather than the Web browser execute scripts) is that only the Web server need support the scripting language used to write the embedded scripts. The script host running on the Web server is responsible for sending the script to the proper scripting engine and for inserting script output (if any) within the Web page as standard HTML tags and text the Web browser can understand and display.

Understanding Active Server Page Start and End Tags

As mentioned previously, when the Web browser requests an Active Server Page, the Web server retrieves the document and passes the Web page to the asp.dll script host. To set server-side script statements (which the script host sends to the script engine for processing) apart from HTML statements (which the script host returns verbatim to the Web server), enclose the server-side script statements between start and end script tags as follows:

```
<%  <VBScript statements>  %>
```

VBScript is the default server-side scripting language for the IIS Web server. As such, when you use <%" and "%> delimiters to embed VBScript statements you want executed on an IIS Web server, you need not specify a scripting language. Conversely, if you embed a server-side script written in another scripting language, you must identify the language by name using the *language=* @ command. For example, to embed a script written in JScript within an Active Server Page, you must include the following *language=* @ command before the first line of server-side scripting you want the script host to process:

```
<% @language = JScript %>
<%  <JScript statements>  %>
```

Creating a Simple Active Server Page

To create an Active Server Page with a few statements for the VBScript engine to process, start your favorite text editor (such as Windows Notepad) and enter the following code:

```
<!DOCTYPE HTML PUBLIC "-//W3C//DTD HTML 4.0//EN">
<html>
<head>
  <title>ASP Server-Side Script Start and End Tags</title>
</head>
<body bgcolor="#ADD8E6">
  <h1>
    <center>HTML and Web Design Tips & Techniques</center>
  </h1>
  <hr>
  <% @language = VBScript %>
  <%
    Response.Write "<p>The <b>Web server</b> date and time are: "
    Response.Write(now())
  %>
</body>
</html>
```

In this example, the ASP script host adds the first ten HTML statements (starting with the DOCTYPE declaration and ending with the <hr> tag) to the Web page the script host is building. Thus, the server-side script in this example starts with the following statement on line 1:

```
<% @language = VBScript %>
```

The *@language* command in this statement tells the host that the script(s) embedded on the Web page has VBScript statements. As such, the script host will pass the statements between start and end script tags (<% ... %>) (in lines 13 and 14) to the VBScript engine for processing. As the VBScript engine returns the output from each of the two *Response.Write* method calls to the script host, the host adds the text returned to the Web page HTML.

For now, do not worry about the various objects and methods available to your Active Server Page scripts—you will learn about them later in this chapter. Understand that *Response.Write* is a method (that is, a function call) that lets you add text to your Web page HTML. The first call to *Response.Write* adds the quoted string you typed in this example, whereas the second call returns the current date and time for the script host to add to the Web page.

Now, save your Web page to an .asp file (such as *ASP_Test1.asp*) on the Web server.

Next, open the HTML document in your Web browser to display a page similar to that shown in Figure 11-2.

Note that you must retrieve the Active Server Page you created through a Web server with Active Server Page Support (such as Microsoft's IIS). (If the Web server does not support Active Server

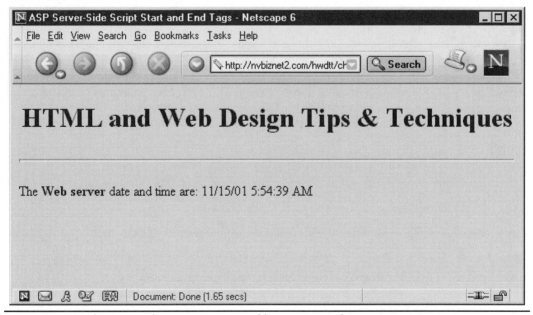

Figure 11-2   Web page with content generated by a script within an Active Server Page

Page files, the server will simply send the requested document to the Web browser as is, and the Web browser will display the VBScript within the page as text content.) Conversely, a Web server with Active Server Page support passes the Active Server Page you request (such as *ASP_Test1.asp*) to the script host (also running at the Web server). The script host, in turn, calls on a script engine to execute the statements in the embedded script(s) to create the Web page that Web server eventually sends to your Web browser for display. For example, to retrieve an Active Server Page such as the one you created in the preceding example through the NVBizNet2.com Web server, enter **http://www .NVBizNet2.com/HWDTT/ASP_Test1.asp** into your Web browser's Address field.

The Web page the ASP script host passes back to the Web server contains HTML tags and text in place of the VBScript statements the script host sent to the VBScript engine for processing. You can view the Web page source the browser received from the Web server by selecting View | Source in Internet Explorer and View | Page Source in Netscape Navigator.

Adding Comments to an Active Server Page Script

Inserting comments in your Active Server Page scripts is an excellent habit. Though ignored by the script engine, comments remind you (and tell others) why you wrote certain portions of the script in a particular way or what you are trying to accomplish with the script in general. In addition, you might use comments during the development process to figure out exactly where a processor-reported error occurs. By commenting out a section of code (that is, by telling the script engine to ignore lines of code as "comments"), you can make an error "go away." Then, by "uncommenting" one line of code at a time until the processor reports the error again, you can figure out which line of code produced the error—usually the last line of code you change from a "comment" back into an executable statement in the script.

The specific character or sequence of characters you use to denote a comment depends on the scripting language in which you write the embedded script. In VBScript, for example, you use the single quote (') or "tick mark" to start a comment. You can use a tick mark to place a comment at the end of a line of code or to make an entire line a comment. However, once you start a comment, the script engine will treat the remaining text on the line as part of the comment.

For example, the three lines after the start script tag (<%) in the following HTML are comments:

```
<html>
<head>
   <title>Comments within an Active Server Page Script</title>
</head>
<body bgcolor="#ADD8E6">
   <h1><center>HTML and Web Design Tips & Techniques</center></h1>
   <% @language = VBScript %>
   <%
' the following will display text on the Web page and could
' just as easily be written using plain HTML (vs. using the
' Response.Write method)
```

```
    Response.Write "<hr>" 'draw a horizontal line
    Response.Write "<p>The <b>Web server</b> date and time are: "

    Response.Write(now()) ' call the now() function to get the
                          ' current date and time
    %>
</body>
</html>
```

When processing the embedded script in this example, the VBScript engine ignores the three lines of comments. Similarly, the script engine processes the following *Response.Write* method calls to add an <hr> tag and the current date and time to the Web page HTML, while ignoring the comment text that follows the tick mark within each statement:

```
Response.Write "<hr>" 'draw a horizontal line
Response.Write(now()) ' call the now() function to get the
                      ' current date and time
```

Hiding ASP Source Code from the Web Site Visitor

While surfing the net, you have undoubtedly noticed that you can view the HTML used to define a Web page in your Web browser (for example, by selecting View | Source if using Internet Explorer or by selecting View | Page Source if using Netscape Navigator). Bear in mind, when you view a Web document's source code in this manner, you see only the *client-side* HTML—that is, the HTML previously sent from the Web server to the Web browser.

Viewing the page source in the Web browser does not let a Web surfer view the server-side script statements embedded within the Active Server Page that generated the HTML. Remember, the Web server passes a browser requested Active Server Page to the script host (asp.dll). The script host executes the script (by sending the script to the appropriate scripting engine) and replaces the script's statements with HTML and text output from the script. The entire process occurs before the Web server sends the Active Server Page to the Web browser. As such, server-side scripting hides scripts from view by the Web surfer. Therefore, to view script statements, you must view the Active Server Page on the Web server itself and not as presented within the Web browser.

The fact that a site visitor cannot view Active Server Page script statements in the Web browser has several important and valuable consequences. For example, if you are writing an Active Server Page that queries a database for information, you need to code connection details within the Web document. These connection details as well as the query itself may contain sensitive information you do not want disclosed to the site visitor. Fortunately, executing the connection script and query at the Web server means that the server sends only the HTML-formatted query results (and not the username, password, and SQL query used to retrieve the information) to the Web browser. Similarly, if your Active Server Page executes a script with a proprietary formula used to perform a calculation or determine a price, running the script at the Web server and sending only the result to the Web browser lets algorithms remain secret by keeping them away from prying eyes.

Understanding the Active Server Page Objects

When someone says the word *object* in everyday conversation, you think of things like a desk, chair, book, television, car, and so on. In the "real" world, objects are things you can see, touch, and/or smell. In programming terms, an *object* is a conceptual "thing" like a spreadsheet, a Web document, customer information, a shopping cart used in making online purchases, and so on. Each object has a set of properties and methods. An object's *properties* are attributes that describe the object or its state. *Methods*, meanwhile, are actions you can take on the object.

All Active Server Pages have seven built-in objects. As such, any script embedded in an Active Server Page can use the properties and methods available in the *Application*, *ASPError*, *ObjectContext*, *Request*, *Response*, *Server*, and *Session* objects. You need not memorize the object names. You need to understand only that each object has a set of properties that provide related information and a group of methods that give your scripts a certain type of functionality. The *Session* object, for example, lets you track and manipulate information about a visitor and his or her interactions with the site's pages during the course of a single visit. Meanwhile, the *Request* object lets you access and work with information (such as form results, the query string, and cookies) that the Web browser sends to the Web server as part of an HTTP request. Conversely, the *Response* object lets you create a Web page in response to a Web browser's request.

As you learn to use them in the Tips you read later in this chapter, you will become familiar with the properties and methods found within each of the built-in objects. For now, let's focus on the *Response* object to get a general idea of how a script might use an Active Server Page object and its methods.

Using the *Response.Write* Method to Send Information to a Web Browser

When the Web server receives an HTTP request from a Web browser, the server responds with the requested data (that is, by sending a Web page or other file), with a redirect message, or with an error message. The response message body contains the HTML the Web browser is to display and the message header contains directives and/or information about the content in the body.

For example, if the Web server receives an HTTP request for an HTML document to which the server has access, the Web server responds by reading and sending the contents of the Web page to the Web browser. When responding to an HTTP request for an Active Server Page, however, the Web server calls on the asp.dll script host to create a Web page using the methods available within the *Response* object. After the script host has finished its job, the Web server reads the *Response* object data and sends it as an HTML output stream to the Web browser for display.

You can use the *Response* object's *Write* method to insert text (both content and HTML tags) anywhere within the Web document, or to create the Web page entirely. To insert text on a page, simply pass the text you want to add within a variable or as a string literal (that is, as text within quotes) to the *Response.Write* method as shown here:

```
<%
Response.Write "<html><body>"
Response.Write _
```

```
   "<p>Both text and HTML tags are fair game as parameters " & _
   "for the Response object Write method.</p>"
Response.Write _
   "<p>The ampersand(&) is the VBScript string " & _
   "concatenation character and the underscore (_) lets " & _
   "you continue a single statement across multiple lines.</p>"
Response.Write "</body></html>"
%>
```

Note that the ampersand (&) is the VBScript string concatenation character and the underscore (_) is for line continuation. Thus, in this example, the underscore (_) allows the second *Response.Write* method call to extend across three lines for formatting purposes. (Text in this manuscript must wrap at column 64.) The ampersand (&) at the end of the second line tells VBScript to pass the quoted text on lines two and three as a single (concatenated) text string to the *Response.Write* method.

As noted by the text in this example, you can pass to the *Response.Write* method both HMTL tags to format the Web page content as well as the content itself. Therefore, if you typed the preceding code into an Active Server Page file such as ASP_Test2.asp, the script host creates the following Web page HTML when the visitor requests the document from the Web server:

```
<html>
<body>
   <p>Both text and HTML tags are fair game as parameters
      for the Response object Write method.</p>
   <p>The ampersand(&) is the VBScript string concatenation
      character and the underscore (_) lets you continue a
      single statement across multiple lines.</p>
</body>
</html>
```

Writing the Double Quote (") Character on a Web Page

Sometimes you want to enclose words on a Web page within quotes. Suppose, for example, you want to enclose "Response.Write" in quotes as shown in this sentence. Because the *Response.Write* method requires that you enclose string literals (that is, quoted text) within quotes, you cannot simply type a double quote (") character around the text you want to display in quotes on the Web page. For example, the following code will generate an error:

```
<%
Response.Write _
   "The "Response.Write" method lets you add text content and " & _
   "HTML tags to the Web page HTML."
%>
```

When the VBScript engine reads the quotation mark (") that follows "the", the script engine expects to see a carriage return and linefeed character combination to end the statement. Instead, the script engine finds more text and reports the following error:

```
Microsoft VBScript compilation error '800a0401'
Expected end of statement
```

VBScript gives you three ways to have the *Response.Write* method display a double quote (") on a Web page: use two sets of double quotes (""), call the *chr()* function, or pass the HTML escape syntax ("). For example, the following three lines of code each display "Response.Write" in quotes on a Web page:

```
<html>
<body>
<%
 Response.Write _
    "You can use double, double quotes to display quotation" & _
    " marks around ""Response.Write"" on a Web page.<br>"
 Response.Write _
    "You can use the Chr() function to display quotation " & _
    "marks around " & Chr(34) & "Response.Write" & Chr(34) & _
    ".<br>"
 Response.Write _
    "Or, you can use HTML escape syntax to place quotation " & _
    "marks around &quot; Response.Write &quot;."
%>
</body>
</html>
```

When the *Response.Write* method detects a set of two double quotes (""), it knows the first quotation mark is part of the text and not meant to terminate the string literal. Thus, to fix the code in the first example within this section, you could rewrite the script as follows:

```
<%
Response.Write _
    "The ""Response.Write"" method lets you add text content and " & _
    "HTML tags to the Web page HTML."
%>
```

A second way to display a double quote (") on a Web page is to have the *Response.Write* method insert the output from a *chr()* function call into the Web page. You used the *Response.Write* method to insert function call results earlier in this chapter. At that time you wrote the following code to display the current date and time (returned by the VBScript *now()* function) on the Web page:

```
<%
Response.Write(now())
%>
```

Similar to the VBScript engine passing the value returned by the *now()* function call to the *Response.Write* method, you can have the script engine pass the value returned by the *chr()* function to insert a double quote character. Thus, once you know that the double quote (") has an ASCII character value of 34, you can display double quotes around "Response.Write" with the following code:

```
<%
Response.Write _
  "The " & chr(34) "Response.Write" & chr(34) & "method lets" & _
  " you add text content and HTML tags to the Web page HTML."
%>
```

Each *chr(34)* function call within the script returns a double quote character. The ampersand (&) character tells the VBScript engine to append the character returned by the *chr()* function call onto the portion of the string the script engine already built. As a result, the VBScript engine simply passes the double quote (") that the *chr()* function returns to the *Response.Write* method as part of a long string literal.

The third way to display a double quote (") on a Web page is to insert the HTML escape syntax that instructs the Web browser to create it. As mentioned previously, you can use *Response.Write* to insert not only text but also HTML tags and other codes into the Web page HTML. Although it tells the Web browser to display a double quote, """ is simply a six-character string to the *Response.Write* method. Therefore, you can display double quotes (") around "Response.Write" as follows:

```
<%
Response.Write _
  "The &quot;Response.Write&quot; method lets " & _
  "you add text content and HTML tags to the Web page HTML."
%>
```

Using the *With* Keyword Shortcut

When working with an Active Server Page object, you often use several properties or call the object's methods multiple times. Rather than repeat the object's name in your code, you can save yourself some typing by using the *With* keyword. For example, to create a Web page with an HTML table, you might create an Active Server Page with the following script:

```
<%
  Response.Write "<html>"
  Response.Write "<body bgcolor='#ADD8E6'>"
  Response.Write "<h1><center>" & _
```

```
    "HTML and Web Design Tips & Techniques</center></h1><hr>"
  Response.Write & _
    "<table align='center' width='200' border='1'>"
  Response.Write "<tr><td>First Name</td><td>Konrad</td></tr>"
  Response.Write "<tr><td>Last Name</td><td>King</td></tr>"
  Response.Write "<tr><td>Total Due/td><td>234.25</td></tr>"
  Response.Write "</table>"
  Response.Write "</body>"
  Response.Write "</html>"
%>
```

Rather than repeatedly type the response object's name, use the keyword *With*, as shown here:

```
<%
  With response
    .write "<html>"
    .write "<body bgcolor='#ADD8E6'>"
    .write "<h1><center>" & _
      "HTML and Web Design Tips & Techniques</center></h1><hr>"
    .write "<table align='center' width='200' border='1'>"
    .write "<tr><td>First Name</td><td>Konrad</td></tr>"
    .write "<tr><td>Last Name</td><td>King</td></tr>"
    .write "<tr><td>Total Due/td><td>234.25</td></tr>"
    .write "</table>"
    .write "</body>"
    .write "</html>"
  End With
%>
```

Although the VBScript in this example uses the *With* keyword only as a shortcut for the *Response* object, you can use the *With* shorthand with any VBScript object.

Using *Response.Write* to Display Variables

Variables are items you create to store information in your code. Each variable names a memory location set aside to hold a value. To make it easy to store and retrieve the data in memory, script languages let you use a meaningful name to refer to each memory location. VBScript, for example, requires that each variable start with a letter, but lets you use any combination of up to 255 letters, underscores (_), and numbers to define a variable name. Therefore, you might store the name the visitor used to log in to your Web site in a memory location named *username*. Similarly, to store the product code of an item the visitor wants to purchase you might use *productCode* and the variable *totalPurchaseAmount* to store the total value of the visitor's purchases.

To declare a variable in VBScript, use the keyword *Dim* (which stands for Dimension) followed by one or more variable names. VBScript has but one data type (called *variant*), so you do not specify the type of data a variable will hold when you declare its name. Each time you place a value in a variable, VBScript decides how the value is stored based on the value's data type. Therefore, you might make the following variable declarations at the start of your script:

```
DIM tableStart, tableEnd, tdLeft, tdRight, tdEnd
DIM trStart, trEnd
DIM custName (1)       'creates a 2 item array
DIM totalDue
```

With the exception of the third statement, which creates an array (*custName*) that can hold two values, each variable declared in this example can hold a single string or numeric item. Thus, if you write the following statement in your script, *totalDue* will be numeric:

```
totalDue = 235.45
```

If you write the following statement in another part of the script, VBScript will make *totalDue* a character string instead:

```
totalDue = "None"
```

You can use variable names in statements either alone or in combination with numeric or string literals. Thus, all the *Response.Write* method calls in the following code are legal:

```
<%
  DIM authors$(1), authorList

  authors(0) = "Andy Anderson"
  authors(1) = "Konrad King"
  authorList = authors(0) + " & " + authors(1)

  With response
    .write "<html><body>"
    .write "<p>The authors are Konrad King & Andy Anderson</p>"
    .write "<p>The authors are Konrad King & " & authors(0) & _
           "</p>"
    .write "<p>The authors are " & authorList & "</p>"
    .write "</html></body>"
  End With
%>
```

(Note that the first element in a VBScript array has an index of 0 and not 1.)

As an example of how you might use variables, consider rewriting the code in the previous section using variables instead of string literals, as in the following example:

```
<html>
<body bgcolor="#ADD8E6">
  <h1><center>HTML and Web Design Tips & Techniques</center></h1>
```

```
  <hr>
<%
 DIM tableStart, tableEnd, tdLeft, tdRight, tdEnd
 DIM trStart, trEnd    'will hold string values
 DIM custName (1)      'create a two item array
 DIM totalDue          'will hold a numeric value

 tableStart = "<table align='center' width='200' border='1'>"
 tableEnd = "</table>"
 tdLeft = "<td width='70' align='left'>"
 tdRight = "<td width='130' align='left'>"
 tdEnd = "</td>"
 trStart = "<tr>"
 trEnd = "<trEnd>"
 custName(0) = "Konrad"
 custName(1) = "King"
 totalDue = 234.25

 With Response
   .Write tableStart
   .Write trStart
   .Write tdLeft & "First Name" & tdEnd
   .Write tdRight & custName(0) & tdEnd & trEnd
   .Write trStart
   .Write tdLeft & "Last Name" & tdEnd
   .Write tdRight & custName(1) & tdEnd & trEnd
   .Write trStart
   .Write tdLeft & "Total Due" & tdEnd
   .Write tdRight & totalDue & tdEnd & trEnd
   .Write tableEnd
 End With
%>
</body>
</html>
```

By substituting variable names for table tags, you make it easy to apply styles to rows and/or columns in a table—without a lot of typing. Suppose, for example, you want to change the alignment and background color of all the cells in the table's right-hand column. Rather than change multiple <td> tags, using a variable (such as *tdRight*, in this example), you can change the formatting of all the cells in the column at once by changing a single assignment statement:

```
tdRight = "<td width='130' align='center' color='white'>"
```

Of course, the more rows and columns in a table, the more time and effort you save by making a single change that affects the format of a column or row throughout the table.)

Controlling the Flow of Content from Web Server to Web Browser Through the HTML Output Stream

Although Active Server Page scripts may perform many functions, the primary reason for using Active Server Pages is to create HTML pages for the Web server to send to a site visitor. As you learned earlier in this chapter, the ASP script host uses the *Response.Write* method to insert text and tags into the HTML document the Web server sends to the browser. The HTML output stream is a queue (or buffer) of information, which the Web server receives from the ASP script host and sends to the Web browser.

For the most part, the ASP script engine builds each Web page in the same way. The script engine first clears the temporary storage space (the HTML output stream) in which it will build the Web page. Next, the script engine starts adding information in the order in which the Web browser expects to receive it—HTTP header data first, followed by the HTML tags and text that make up the content the visitor sees onscreen. Thus, the HTML output stream (that is, the buffer in which the script host builds the Web page), starts out empty. Then, the script host adds static HTML stored in the Active Server Page document and the output from embedded scripts. After the script host copies the static HTML and has the script engine execute all the scripts embedded within the Active Server Page, the script host notifies the Web server that processing is complete. The Web server, in turn, sends the contents of the HTML output stream to the Web browser.

Normally, waiting until all processing is complete before sending the buffer contents to the Web browser is fine. However, if the Active Server Page has a script that takes a long time to complete, you may want to send partial results or at least a status message to let the visitor know the script is working on his or her request. Otherwise, the visitor might give up, thinking the Web page (or perhaps the Web server) is "unavailable," because the server has not sent the page requested. Unless you instruct it to do otherwise, the Web server sends the output buffer's contents only after the script host has finished all processing. The *Response* object has one property (*Response.Buffer*) and three methods (*Response.Flush*, *Response.Clear*, and *Response.End*) you can use to control the way the script host buffers the HTML output stream.

USE IT   Use the *Response.Buffer* property to specify whether the Web server is to buffer the output created by an Active Server Page. Setting the *Response.Buffer* property to true tells the Web server to hold output created until the script host has processed all scripts or until the script host calls either the *Response.Flush* or *Response.End* method (discussed later in this Tip). Conversely, setting the *Response.Buffer* property to false lets the Web server control the flow of output to the Web browser. Rather than waiting for the script host to finish processing, the Web server checks the output buffer periodically and sends any data the script host has placed in the HTML output stream.

Suppose for example, that your Active Server page has the following script:

```
<%
CONST oConnection = _
"DRIVER={MySQL};SERVER=NVBizNet2;UID=root;PWD=;DATABASE=hwdtt"
 DIM connObj, totalSales
 Response.Buffer = true
 Response.Write _
    "<!DOCTYPE HTML PUBLIC ""-//W3C//DTD HTML 4.0//EN"">"
 Response.Write "<html><body>"
 Response.Write _
    "<p>One moment please. Processing query...</p>"
 Set connObj = server.createobject ("adodb.connection")
 connObj.ConnectionString = oConnection
 connObj.Open
 Set totalSales = connObj.execute _
    ("SELECT SUM(InvoiceTotal) AS TotalSold FROM invoices")
 Response.Write "Total sales: " & totalSales("TotalSold")
%>
</body>
</html>
```

The script host places into the output buffer the <html> and <body> tags followed by the text "One moment please. Processing query…." However, the Web server sends nothing to the Web browser until the script host finishes processing the query in the second half of the script. As a result, the visitor sees the "One moment please" message at the same time he or she receives the query results. If the query takes 30 seconds to execute, the visitor may give up, because "nothing happened" after clicking the hyperlink to retrieve the Active Server Page with the total sales figure.

To have the Web browser send the "One moment please…" message immediately, set the *Response.Buffer* property to false as shown here:

```
<%
 CONST oConnection = _
    "DRIVER={MySQL};SERVER=NVBizNet2;UID=root;PWD=;DATABASE=hwdtt"
 DIM connObj, totalSales
 Response.Buffer = false
 Response.Write _
    "<!DOCTYPE HTML PUBLIC ""-//W3C//DTD HTML 4.0//EN"">"
 Response.Write "<html><body>"
 Response.Write _
    "<p>One moment please. Processing query...</p>"
        '<connection & query statements ...>
 Response.Write "Total sales: " & totalSales
```

```
%>
</body>
</html>
```

Note that you can only change the *Response.Buffer* property's value while the output buffer is empty. As such, the statement that sets *Response.Buffer* to false (or true) must appear within the Active Server Page before any static HTML (including <html> and <body> tags) and statements that place data into the output buffer.

In the preceding example, the script host again places the "One moment please" message into the output buffer. However, this time, the Web server sends the HTML tags and the message to the Web browser as soon as the server detects them within the HTML output stream. After the script host executes the query and outputs the total sales figure and the </body> and </html> tags (30 seconds later, in this example), the Web server sends the data to the Web browser for display, as shown in Figure 11-3.

The *Response.Flush* method tells the Web server to send the current contents of the output buffer to the Web browser immediately, while the script host continues processing the script. You would flush the output buffer to the client (that is, send its contents to the Web browser) when you want to display partial results or status messages while the script host finishes script processing. Displaying interim results may prevent the visitor from growing impatient and moving on rather than waiting for the results of a complex or multipart query. To use the *Response.Flush* method, simply insert the following line in your Active Server Page script:

```
<% Response.Flush %>
```

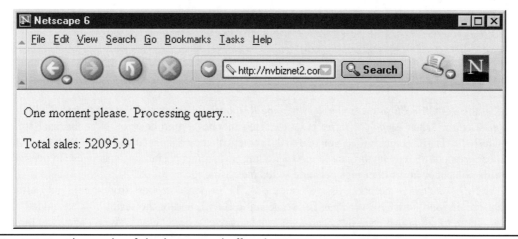

Figure 11-3   The results of displaying nonbuffered HTML output stream contents

Suppose, for example, that your script must execute three queries—each of which takes 20 seconds to complete. To keep the visitor from thinking the system is down during the minute it takes to generate the final result, you can use code such as the following to display interim totals:

```
<%
CONST oConnection = _
"DRIVER={MySQL};SERVER=NVBizNet2;UID=root;PWD=;DATABASE=hwdtt"
DIM connObj
DIM office1Sales, office2Sales, office3Sales
Response.Buffer = true
Response.Write _
    "<!DOCTYPE HTML PUBLIC ""-//W3C//DTD HTML 4.0//EN"">"
Response.Write "<html><body>"
Response.Write _
  "<p>One moment please. Processing query...</p>"
        '<connection & query 1 statements ...>
Response.write "Finished 1 of 3. Office 1 sales = " & _
  office1Sales & "<br>"
Response.Flush
        '<connection & query 2 statements ...>
Response.write "Finished 2 of 3. Office 2 sales = " & _
  office2Sales & "<br>"
Response.Flush
        '<connection & query 3 statements ...>
Response.Write "Finished 3 of 3. Office 3 sales = " & _
  office2Sales & "<br>"
Response.Write "Grand Total sales: " & _
  (office1Sales + office2Sales + office3Sales)
%>
</body>
</html>
```

Call the *Response.Flush* method only when the *Response.Buffer* property is set to true. Calling *Response.Flush* when *Response.Buffer* is set to false generates a runtime error. Note that each time you flush the HTML output buffer, you add to the content already displayed within the Web browser's application window. As such, be sure to use Cascading Style Sheet positioning statements to overwrite existing content or insert <br> tags between status messages.

The *Response.Clear* method erases all but the HTTP response headers from the output buffer. Therefore, if your Active Server Page has some static HTML and/or the script host has added some output to the HTML output stream, you can start over with a "blank" Web page by calling *Response.Clear*. As was the case with the *Response.Flush* method, the *Response.Buffer* property must be set to true, or calling *Response.Clear* will generate a runtime error.

You might use *Response.Clear* after displaying interim results, so that the site visitor sees the final result on a Web page without status messages or interim totals. For example, you might replace the final two *Response.Write* calls in the previous example with the following:

```
Response.Clear
Response.Write _
  "<!DOCTYPE HTML PUBLIC ""-//W3C//DTD HTML 4.0//EN"">"
Response.Write "<html><body>"
Response.Write "Per Office and Grand Total Sales</title><body>"
Response.Write "Office1 Sales: " & office1Sales & "<br>"
Response.Write "Office2 Sales: " & office2Sales & "<br>"
Response.Write "Office3 Sales: " & office3Sales & "<br>"
Response.Write "Grand Total sales: " & _
    (office1Sales + office2Sales + office3Sales)
```

If you want to stop all script processing and send the buffered output to the Web browser, use the *Response.End* method. When you call *Response.End*, the script host will neither process more script statements nor send any remaining static HTML it finds within the Active Server Page. You might use the *Response.End* method to abort processing if you discover you cannot complete a multipart procedure partway through. Suppose for example, that the office 2 sales database is not available, so you cannot compute the grand total sales. By checking the error return from the database connect statement, you could abort on error by inserting the following code in your script:

```
If errorOnConnect
  Response.Write "Query Aborted! Office 2 Data not available."
  Response.Write "<\body><\html>"
  Response.End
End If
```

Notice the script places <\body> and <\html> tags into the HTML output stream before calling the *Response.End* method. Remember, calling *Response.End* halts further script processing. Moreover, the script host does not copy any remaining static HTML (such as the </body></html> tags that follow the script) from the Active Server Page to the output buffer.

Preventing the Web Browser from Displaying Stale Active Server Pages

You may have noticed that the first time you visit a Web page it often takes longer for the Web browser to retrieve and display the page completely than on subsequent visits. The reason for the apparent difference in download speed is often due to Web page caching. The first time you visit a Web page, your browser must retrieve the page from the Web server. However, after the first visit, the browser can display the same page from the browser's Internet content cache on your (local) hard drive. On a Windows machine, Internet Explorer, for example, caches Web pages you visit along with graphics, sound, and other multimedia files used on those pages within the C:\Windows \ Temporary Internet Files folder on your hard drive.

Caching and serving Web pages from a local hard drive (or from a proxy server's hard drive when accessing the Internet through a proxy server) is not a problem when dealing with static Web pages. However, Active Server Pages are, by nature, dynamic. Unfortunately, as far as the Web browser is concerned, the Web page generated by the script host is simply an ordinary, static Web document with an .asp extension. Because the .asp at the end of the filename means nothing special to the Web browser, the browser caches and subsequently displays from cache, Active Server Pages. As a result, the Web page the browser displays when you return to a page may not have the same content you might see if the browser retrieved the page from the Web server rather than the browser's cache.

The *Response.Expires* and *Response.ExpiresAbsolute* properties let you stop Web browsers from displaying out-of-date content by setting an expiration date and/or time for cached files. Until the cached page expires, a Web browser displays the cached copy of a Web page rather than requesting the page from the Web server. After the cached page expires, however, the Web browser must download a "fresh" copy of the page from the Web server when the visitor returns to the page.

USE IT   Suppose, for example, that you have an Active Server Page whose content you update once per month. When making changes on 1/1/2002, you insert the following statement within the script that generates the Active Server Page content:

```
<% response.ExpiresAbsolute = #01/31/2002# %>
```

By setting the cached page expiration to the date (and time) scripts on the page will change the Web page content, you prevent the visitor from seeing stale, cached information.

The syntax you use to set the *Response.ExpiresAbsolute* property is as follows:

```
Response.ExpiresAbsolute = #<expireDate[ <expireTime>]>#
```

Thus, in the preceding example, all cached copies of the Active Server Page you edit on 01/01/2002 will expire at midnight on 01/31/2002. (Omitting the time when setting the *Response.ExpiresAbsolute* property causes the cached page to expire at midnight on the expiration date.) If you want the cached page to expire at 3:15pm in the afternoon on 2/1/2002 instead, you would use:

```
<% Response.ExpiresAbsolute = #02/01/2002 3:15:00pm# %>
```

Setting the expiration date to a specific date and/or time requires that you manually edit the script (to change the expiration date) at the start of each new period. As such, you will find it more convenient to set a cached page valid for a set number of minutes rather than until a specific date (and time). Suppose, for example, that you have an Active Server Page that displays stock quotes and your Web server receives new quote data every 15 minutes. To keep cached content up to date, you would use the *Response.Expires* method to specify the number of minutes until a cached page expires by using the following syntax:

```
Response.Expires = <minutes>
```

Thus, to force the Web browser to reretrieve the Active Server Page from the Web server whenever cached data is more than 15 minutes old, add the following statement to the script that generates the Active Server Page content:

```
<% Response.Expires = 15 %>
```

On a final note, to prevent Web browsers from displaying stale Active Server Page content, you must also make allowances for those proxy servers that do not honor page expiration dates (and times). When a Web visitor accesses the Internet through a proxy server, the proxy server (like the Web browser) stores a copy of Web pages retrieved within a cache folder on the proxy server's local hard drive. When the Web browser requests a Web page already in the proxy server's cache, the proxy server sends to the Web browser the page from the cache rather than retrieving the page from the Web server again. Thus, the Web browser will request a new page from the Web server after the page in the browser's cache folder expires. However, if the proxy server ignores cached page expirations, the proxy server may send the Web browser a page with stale content from the proxy server cache.

To prevent proxy servers from sending stale Active Server Pages, set the *Response.CacheControl* property to "Private". When you leave the *Response.CacheControl* property set to the default, "Public", the proxy server will cache the page in a folder on the proxy server's hard drive. Conversely, when you set the *Response.CacheControl* to "Private", the proxy server will not. Therefore, to ensure that the proxy server will retrieve a Web page from the Web server each time, include the following statement either just before or after you set the page expiration date or time:

```
<% Response.CacheControl = "Private" %>
```

Redirecting the Web Browser to Another Web Page

As visitors surf the Web they often bookmark (that is, add to their lists of favorites) Web pages to which they want to return. Although repeat traffic is normally a good thing, you must sometimes prevent visitors from jumping directly to specific pages within your site. Suppose, for example, that you want your visitors to log in or register before viewing the site's content. If a visitor bypasses the login process by using a bookmark to jump directly to a content page, you need a way to redirect that visitor to the Web page with the login/registration form automatically. The *Response.Redirect* method lets you move a site visitor onto a Web page other than the one he or she requested.

 USE IT In addition to redirecting a visitor to a different page as part of a login security scheme, you might also do so in order to balance the load among servers in a Web server farm, or if you move a Web site from one .com address to another. Suppose, for example that you run two Web servers, NVBizNet.com and NVBizNet2.com, and want to balance their workloads to speed things up. As a result, you move some Web sites hosted on NVBizNet.com to NVBizNet2.com. Unfortunately, previous visitors may have bookmarked site home pages on the original server (NVBizNet.com). To move visitors that reach NVBizNet.com looking for sites that are now on NVBizNet2.com, insert the following code at the start of Active Server Pages on NVBizNet.com:

```
<% Response.Redirect "http://www.NVBizNet2.com/default.asp" %>
```

When the script engine executes the *Response.Redirect* method, the command takes effect immediately. The script host processes no more statements within the current Active Server Page.

Instead, the Web server sends a message to the Web browser, which tells the browser to request another Web page. Thus, in this example, the Web browser first sent a message to NVBizNet.com requesting an Active Server Page. Rather than send the page (now served by another Web server) to browser, the NVBizNet.com Web server sends a redirect message, which tells the browser to request default.asp from NVBizNet2.com. The Web browser, in turn, requests and displays the default.asp home page from NVBizNet2.com.

In addition to sending a visitor to a site on another Web server or to a different Web site on the same Web server, you can use the *Response.Redirect* method to move the visitor from one page to another within a single Web site. When the new page you want the Web browser to retrieve is within the current Web site, drop the "http://" and the .com address from the URL you provide to the *Response.Redirect* method. Supply the relative address of the new page to the method instead. Suppose, for example, you want to prevent visitors from linking directly to Active Server Pages within a members-only area— bypassing your site's login form. Insert code similar to the following at the start of each Active Server Page you want to secure:

```
<%
  DIM referer, wwwReferer
  wwwReferer = Left(Request.ServerVariables("HTTP_REFERER"),31)
  referer = Left(Request.ServerVariables("HTTP_REFERER"),27)
  If ucase(wwwReferer) <> "HTTP://WWW.NVBIZNET2.COM/HWDTT/" And _
     ucase(referer) <> "HTTP://NVBIZNET2.COM/HWDTT/"
    Response.Redirect "/loginScreen.asp" Then
  End If
%>
```

If a visitor enters the URL of a Web page into the browser's Address field or selects a page from a list of favorites (or bookmarks), the "HTTP_REFERER" value within the HTTP request the Web browser sends is blank. Conversely, when a visitor clicks a hyperlink, the Web browser sends the URL of the Web page with the hyperlink as the "HTTP_REFERER" value HTTP request the browser sends to the Web server. Thus, in the preceding example, when a visitor retrieves a Web page after logging on (through the login screen) or by clicking a hyperlink on any other page within the /hwdtt folder on NVBizNet2.com, calling the *Request.ServerVariables* method, as follows, returns a string that starts http://www.NVBizNet2.com/hwdtt/ or http://NVBizNet2.com/hwdtt/:

```
Request.ServerVariables("HTTP_REFERER")
```

The statement in this example retrieves the value of "HTTP_REFERER" which the Web browser placed in the HTTP request sent to the Web server.

To use the preceding script on your Web pages, test for your site's .com address and the pathname of the folder in which you store the site's members-only content within the *if* statement. In addition, replace the URL passed to the *Response.Redirect* method with the URL of your site's login page in the next-to-last line of the script.

Because the *Response.Redirect* method uses the HTTP message header to tell the Web browser to retrieve another Web page, a script can only call the *Response.Redirect* method when the HTML output buffer is empty (or contains only HTTP header data). If you want to redirect the Web browser to a new page after the script has already generated some Web page HTML, use the *Response.Clear* method to clear the output buffer first. Then, call the *Response.Redirect* method to tell the Web browser to move onto another page.

Maintaining Variable Values Between HTTP Requests with the Cookies Collection

As mentioned previously in this book, the client-server relationship between Web browser and Web server is "stateless." The Web server maintains no information about the client from one request to the next. In general, the server waits for a Web browser (any Web browser) to send an HTTP request. After receiving a request, the Web server responds with no memory of previous connections (if any) between itself and the Web browser that sent the request. Unfortunately, if you have a members-only Web site or an e-commerce site, you need some way to keep track of the visitor as he or she moves from page to page. Otherwise, the visitor must log in repeatedly, because a Web page request provides no way to let the Web server know that the visitor has already logged in.

A cookie is a small amount of text the Web server tells the Web browser to write within the Web site's "cookie file" on the visitor's computer. Many visitors see cookies as an intrusion on their privacy and turn off the browser's ability to store cookies, or at least force the browser to ask permission before saving cookie data. However, a cookie can only store data the visitor voluntarily provides or general information about the visitor's connection (found within the HTTP header of a Web page request). Moreover, a browser sends to the Web server only those cookies the Web server previously sent to the Web browser for storage. Thus, if you visit www.NVBizNet.com and www.yahoo.com, your browser will not send to the Yahoo.com Web server any cookie information the browser stored when you visited the NVBizNet.com Web site, and vice versa.

USE IT   Use the *Response.Cookies* collection to set cookie values and the *Request.Cookies* collection to retrieve them. For example, to create a single-session cookie—that is, a cookie that remains on the visitor's system only until he or she exits the Web browser—your script need only provide the cookie's name and value using the following syntax:

```
Response.Cookies("<cookieName>") = "<cookieValue>"
```

Thus, to set single-session cookies named *firstName* and *lastName* to "Konrad" and "King", respectively, insert the following code within an Active Server Page Script:

```
<%
  Response.Cookies("firstName") = "Konrad"
  Response.Cookies("lastName") = "King"
%>
```

If you want to make a cookie's value persistent (that is, remain valid past the end of the current session), set the cookie's *Expires* property either to a specific date or to a length of time. After the cookie expires, the Web browser will no longer send the cookie name/value pair to the Web server when making an HTTP request. For example, to set a cookie named *userName* to expire on January 5, 2003, use the following:

```
<% Response.Cookies("userName").Expires = "January 5, 2003" %>
```

Similarly, to set the *userName* to expire in 30 days from today, use the built-in VBScript *Date()* function as follows:

```
<% Response.Cookies("userName").Expires = Date + 30 %>
```

Suppose, for example, that your site had a visitor registration form similar to that shown in Figure 11-4 in which the text element names are *firstName*, *lastName*, *streetAddress1*, *streetAddress2*, *city*, *state*, *zipCode*, and *eMailAddress*.

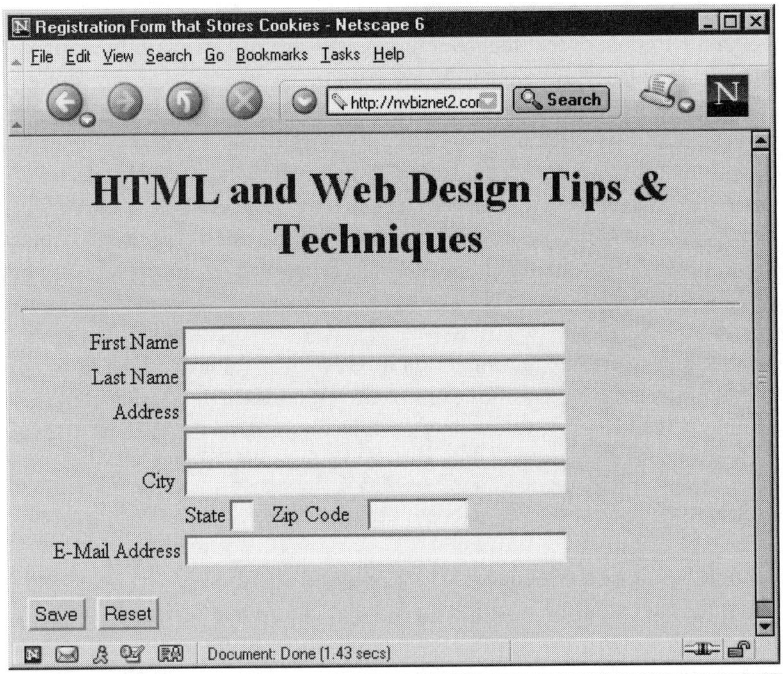

Figure 11-4   Registration form that stores name, street address, and e-mail address in a cookies file

By calling the following subroutine within your site's login script, you could store the visitor's name, address, and e-mail address in the site's cookie file until the date specified by *expDate*:

```
<%
'Subroutine "StoreCookie" stores a cookie value
 Sub StoreCookie(cookieName, cookieValue, expDate)
   Response.Cookies(cookieName) = cookieValue
   Response.Cookies(cookieName).Expires = expDate
 end sub

'store the name, street address, and e-mail address in
'cookies for later use
 StoreCookie "firstName",Request.Form("firstName"), Date + 30
 StoreCookie "lastName",Request.Form("lastName"), Date + 30
 StoreCookie "streetAddress1",Request.Form("streetAddress1"), _
   Date + 30
 StoreCookie "streetAddress2",Request.Form("streetAddress2"), _
   Date + 30
 StoreCookie "city",Request.Form("city"), Date + 30
 StoreCookie "state",Request.Form("state"), Date + 30
 StoreCookie "zipCode",Request.Form("zipCode"), Date + 30
 StoreCookie "eMailAddress",Request.Form("eMailAddress"), _
   Date + 30
%>
```

If the visitor returns to the site before a cookie's expiration date, you can use the *Request.Cookies* method to load the cookie value into its element within the registration form as shown here:

```
<form name="RegistrationForm" action="RegisterVisitor.asp"
  method="POST">
<%
With Response
  .Write "First Name: <input type='text' name='firstName'" & _
    "size='40' value='" & request.Cookies("firstName") & _
    "'><br>"
  .Write "Last Name: <input type='text' name='lastName'" & _
    "size='40' value='" & request.Cookies("lastName") & _
    "'><br>"
  .Write "Address 1: <input type='text' " & _
    "name='streetAddress1' size='40' value='" & _
    request.Cookies("streetAddress1") &"'><br>"
  .Write "Address 2: <input type='text' " & _
```

```
        "name='streetAddress2' size='40' value='" & _
     request.Cookies("streetAddress2") &"'><br>"
  .Write "City: <input type='text' name='city'" & _
     "size='40' value='" & request.Cookies("city") &"'><br>"
  .Write "State: <input type='text' name='state'" & _
     "size='4' value='" & request.Cookies("state") & _
     "'>  "
  .Write "Zip Code: <input type='text' name='zipCode'" & _
     "size='10' value='" & request.Cookies("zipCode") &"'><br>"
  .Write "E-Mail Address: <input type='text' " & _
     "name='eMailAddress' size='40' value='" & _
     request.Cookies("eMailAddress") & "'><br><br>"
 End With
%>
  <input type="submit" value="Save">   
  <input type="reset">
</form>
```

To delete a cookie, set its value to an empty string, or set the cookie's *Expires* property to a date (or time) in the past. For example, either of the following statements will delete the cookie named *userName* from the Web site's cookie file:

```
<% Response.Cookies("userName") = "" %>
<% Response.Cookies("userName").Expires = Date - 1000 %>
```

Retrieving Form Results from the ASP Form Collection

Retrieving input from HTML form elements lets your Active Server Page scripts customize page content to the needs and desires of your site visitors. True, even without visitor input, server-side scripts can insert dynamic information such as the current date and time, stock quotes, weather information, and so on. However, the current time and temperature in Las Vegas is likely of little interest to a resident of Juneau, Alaska. Similarly, a current price quotation for stocks with the symbols MSFT, INTU, BAC, and GM would be of limited use to someone who owns other stocks and may be of no interest to a bond investor. To be useful, server-side scripts that generate content must first find out what a visitor wants to see and then supply the information requested. Fortunately, the Web server makes HTML form data available to your scripts as a collection of name/value pairs within the Active Server Page Request object.

After a visitor fills in a form's text elements, makes radio button and checkbox selections, and then clicks on the form's Submit button, the Web browser sends the form results to the Web server. The *action* and *method* attributes within the <form> tag tell the Web server where to send the data and how the browser "packaged" it. When the *action* attribute in a <form> tag is set to the URL of an Active Server Page, the Web server passes the page named by the attribute to the ASP script host. Depending on the *method* attribute's value (either GET or POST), the Web server places the form results in either the *QueryString* or the *Form* collection within the *Request* object.

When the <form> tag's *method* is GET, the Web browser appends the form results onto the URL, and the Web server places the form data in the *Request.QueryString* collection. Similarly, when the *method* attribute's value is POST, the Web browser sends the form results within the HTTP message body, and the Web server passes the form data to the script as the *Request.Form* collection.

Suppose, for example, that your Web page has the following HTML form definition:

```
<form action="http://www.NVBizNet2.com/HWDTT/FormResults.asp"
      method="POST">
 First Name: <input type="text" name="firstName" size="20"><br>
 Last Name: <input type="text" name="lastName" size="20"><br>
 E-Mail: <input type="text" name="eMailAddr" size="30"><br>
 <input type="submit" value="Submit">
 <input type="reset" value="Reset">
</form>
```

After the visitor clicks the form's Submit button, the Web browser will send the form results to the Web server using the POST method. As such, the Web server will retrieve the form name/value pairs the Web browser sends from the HTTP message body and place them in the Active Server Page *Request.Form* collection.

USE IT An Active Server Page collection is an array of values a script can retrieve by numeric index or keyword. Conveniently, a script can use a form element's name as the keyword to retrieve the element's value from the *Request.Form* collection. Thus, for the form defined in the previous example, you can use the following script to retrieve the form results:

```
<!DOCTYPE HTML PUBLIC "-//W3C//DTD HTML 4.0//EN">
<html>
<body>
<%
  DIM firstName, lastName, eMailAddr
'retrieve the form results
  firstName = Request.Form("firstName")
  lastName = Request.Form("lastName")
  eMailAddress = Request.Form("eMailAddr")

'display the form results
  With Response
    .write "<b>First Name: </b>" & firstName & "<br>"
    .write "<b>Last Name: </b>" & lastName & "<br>"
    .write "<b>E-mail Address: </b>" & eMailAddress & "<br>"
  End With
%>
</body>
</html>
```

Although the script in this example simply retrieves and then displays the form data values in the *Request.Form* collection, your script can do anything you need with values submitted through an HTML form. The important thing to understand is that you can retrieve a form element value from the *Request.Form* collection.

If you retrieve form results by index rather than keyword, you can create a reusable confirmation that displays form element names and the values entered or selected. To retrieve form results by name, you must know the form element names when you write the script. The advantage in creating a reusable confirmation page is that you can write a single script that will display form results from forms with different element counts and names. For example, you can embed the following script in an Active Server Page to display form element names and values from any form that "posts" its results set:

```
<!DOCTYPE HTML PUBLIC "-//W3C//DTD HTML 4.0//EN">
<html>
<body>
<%
  DIM i
'display element names and form results
  With Response
    For i = 1 To Request.Form.Count
      .Write "<b>" & Request.Form.Key(i) & " : </b>" & _
        Request.Form(i) & "<br>"
Next
  End With
%>
</body>
</html>
```

The *Request.Form* collection has one property (*Count*) and two methods (*Item* and *Key*). When adding items (values) and keys (names) to a collection, the Web server stores the number of items it adds within the collection's *Count* property. Thus, in this example, the *Request.Form.Count* property holds the number of name/value pairs the Web browser passed to the Web server as form results. To work with the "names" (that is, with the "keys") in a collection, use the *Request.Form.Key* method, which lets you retrieve the "name" portion of the name/value pairs within the collection. Similarly, to work with the values stored in the collection, use the *Request.Form.Item* method, which retrieves the "value" portion of a form results name/value pair.

Note that you can avoid unnecessary typing by omitting the *Item* when retrieving form element values from a collection, as shown here:

```
Response.Write "<b>" & Request.Form.Key(1) & " : </b>" & _
  Request.Form.Item(1) & "<br>"
Response.Write "<b>" & Request.Form.Key(1) & " : </b>" & _
  Request.Form(1) & "<br>"
```

Both statements in this example produce the same result.

Retrieving Form Results from the ASP QueryString Collection

HTML forms let you retrieve information from site visitors. On an e-commerce site, visitors select products, enter payment details, and provide delivery instructions through forms. Prior to making a purchase, the visitors may use forms to log in to their accounts on the Web site or to search for product data or installation and use instructions about items for sale. Noncommerce sites also use forms that let members log in to execute transactions (such as transferring money between accounts or making stock purchases), or to retrieve information (such as stock quotes, weather reports, or perhaps a list of movies playing at local theatres). In short, forms let a site visitor specify content that an Active Server Page script running at the Web server is to provide or work the script it is to perform.

To keep form results private, you set the *method* attribute in the <form> tag to POST, so that the Web browser sends the form results within an HTTP message body. You might use the POST method to submit order details or a visitor's name, address, and phone number. Moreover, if the form includes highly sensitive information, such as a credit card number, username/password, or account numbers, you would also establish a secure connection between Web browser and Web server. When using the POST method to send form results across a secure connection, the form results travel across the Internet encrypted within the HTTP message body.

Conversely, when you want to record the form results in the Web server's log file for later analysis or want to let visitors create bookmarks (or favorites) they can use to resubmit the same form results without filling out the form again, set the <form> tag's *method* attribute to "GET". When using the GET method to submit form results, the Web browser still sends the name and value from each form element to the URL specified by the <form> tag's *action* attribute. However, instead of "hiding" the form results within the HTTP message body (as it does when using the POST method), when using the GET method, the Web browser appends the string of name/value pairs as part of the URL to which the browser submits the form results.

Suppose for example, that you create a Web page with the following form definition:

```
<form action="http://www.NVBizNet2.com/HWDTT/StockQuotes.asp"
     method="GET">
  <table>
    <tr><th colspan="3">Stocks to Watch</th></tr>
    <tr><td><input type="text" name="s1" size="6"></td>
        <td><input type="text" name="s2" size="6"></td>
        <td><input type="text" name="s3" size="6"></td></tr>
    <tr><td><input type="text" name="s4" size="6"></td>
        <td><input type="text" name="s5" size="6"></td>
        <td><input type="text" name="s6" size="6"></td></tr>
  </table>
  <p><input type="submit" value="Submit">
     <input type="reset"  value="Reset"></p>
</form>
```

After the visitor clicks the form's Submit button, the Web browser sends the form results to the Web server using the GET method. The GET method tells the Web browser to append the form results onto the URL specified by the <form> tag's *action* attribute. Thus, in this example, the browser appends the form results onto the URL http://www.NVBizNet2.com/HWDTT/Quotes.asp, as shown in the Address field of the Web browser application window in Figure 11-5.

USE IT When the HTTP message with the form results reaches the Web server, the server copies the name/value pairs from the URL into the Active Server Page *Request.QueryString* collection. An Active Server Page collection is an array of values a script can retrieve by either numeric index or by name. Conveniently, form element names are the "keywords" a script must use to retrieve form element values from the *Request.QueryString* collection by name. Thus, for the form defined in the previous example, you might use the statements in the first half of the following script to retrieve form results:

```
<!DOCTYPE HTML PUBLIC "-//W3C//DTD HTML 4.0//EN">
<html>
<body>
<%
  DIM symbol(6), i
'retrieve the form results
  symbol(1) = Request.QueryString("s1")
  symbol(2) = Request.QueryString("s2")
  symbol(3) = Request.QueryString("s3")
  symbol(4) = Request.QueryString("s4")
  symbol(5) = Request.QueryString("s5")
  symbol(6) = Request.QueryString("s6")
'display the form results
  With Response
    For i = 1 To Request.QueryString.Count
      .Write "<b>Symbol " & i & "</b>: " & symbol(i) & "<br>"
    Next
  End With
%>
</body>
</html>
```

The script in this example first retrieves form element values by name from the *Request.QueryString* collection and assigns the values to elements within an array named *symbol*. Then, the script calls on the *Response.Write* method to display each value submitted on the Web page. Your script will, of course, do something more with values submitted. However, the important thing to understand is that you retrieve the values entered on forms submitted using the GET method from the *Request.QueryString* collection. Moreover, you can retrieve each element's value from the collection by name.

In fact, you normally retrieve form element values by name—so long as the form element's names are meaningful. In the preceding example, however, the form element's names do nothing to describe

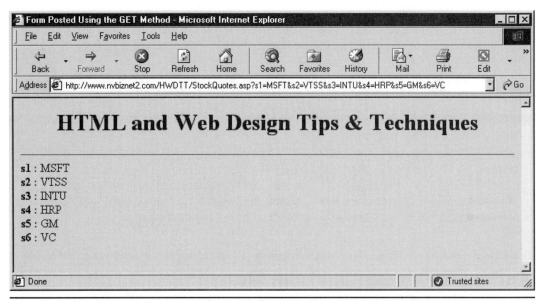

Figure 11-5   Web browser Address field with form results sent using the GET method

the element values. Therefore, in this instance, it is more convenient to retrieve form element values from the *Request.QueryString* collection by numeric index rather than by name as shown here:

```
<!DOCTYPE HTML PUBLIC "-//W3C//DTD HTML 4.0//EN">
<html>
<body>
<%
  DIM i
'retrieve & display the form results both values and names
  With Response
    For i = 1 To Request.QueryString.Count
      .Write "<b>" & Request.QueryString.Key(i) & " : </b>" & _
        Request.QueryString(i) & "<br>"
Next
  End With
%>
</body>
</html>
```

As is true for all Active Server Page collections, the *Request.QueryString* collection has one property (*Count*) and two methods (*Item* and *Key*). When adding items (values) and keys names) to a collection, the Web server stores the number of items it added to the collection within the collection's *Count* property. Therefore, in this case, the Web server sets the *Request.QueryString.Count* property to the number of name/value pairs it found within the form results. The *Request.QueryString.Key* method lets you retrieve the "name" portion of the form result's name/value pairs, and the *Request.QueryString.Item* method lets you retrieve the "value." Note that when you refer to a collection item by index or key value, the *Item* method call is implied. Therefore, in this example where "s1" is the key (that is, the name) of the first item in the *Request.QueryString* collection, the following statements are equivalent:

```
Response.Write Request.QueryString.Item(1)
Response.Write Request.QueryString(1)
Response.Write Request.QueryString.Item("s1")
Response.Write Request.QueryString.("s1")
```

To avoid unnecessary typing, you normally omit *Item* when retrieving form element values from a collection, as shown by the second and fourth statements in this example.

Retrieving Information from the Server Variables Collection

With each Web page request, a browser sends some information about itself and its Internet connection. An Active Server Page script can use the information a browser sends to limit site access based on IP address, customize page content to take advantage of features supported only by certain browsers, track who referred a visitor to the site, warn the visitor before sending sensitive data over nonsecure connections, and so on.

The Web server stores the HTTP header data and other information the Web browser sends within the *Request.ServerVariables* collection. Like other Active Server Page collections, the *Request.ServerVariables* collection consists of a list of names, called "keys", and their associated values. To get data from the collection, you simply specify the key whose value you want to retrieve. For example, to retrieve and display the visitor's IP address, your script might use the REMOTE_ ADDR key as shown in the following code:

```
<% DIM visitorIPAddress
   visitorIPAddress = Request.ServerVariables("REMOTE_ADDR")
   Response.Write _
     "<p>Thank you for visiting from IP Address: " & _
     visitorIPAddress & "<br>To combat unauthorized " & _
     "credit card use, we store your IP address with each " & _
     " transaction processed.</p>"
'<... other script statements ... >
%>
```

USE IT   As mentioned previously, the *Request.ServerVariables* collection contains information
the Web browser sends with each HTTP request that it sends to the Web server. The
Request.ServerVariables collection contains such things as HTTP headers, cookies, the visitor's
IP address, the query string, and the URLs of the current and referring Web pages. To get a list of all
the names and values available within the *Request.ServerVariables* collection (similar to that shown
in Figure 11-6), you can use the following code:

```
<!DOCTYPE HTML PUBLIC "-//W3C//DTD HTML 4.0//EN">
<html>
<head>
  <title>Request.ServerVariables Items & Associated Values
  </title>
</head>
<body>
<% DIM itemName
   For Each itemName In Request.ServerVariables
     Response.Write "<b>" & itemName & " = </b>" & _
       Request.ServerVariables(itemName) & "<br>"
   Next
 %>
</body>
</html>
```

As the VBScript *For-Each* loop iterates through the *Request.ServerVariables* collection, the script
engine places into the variable *itemName* the key (that is, the name) associated with each value within
the collection. The *Response.Write* method then displays the collection item's name and value on the
Web page.

You can use an item in the *Request.ServerVariables* collection item to make some Active Server
Pages available only to visitors from workstations on your company's intranet. Given that your ISP
allocated to your company the 256 IP addresses within the range 24.234.31.000–24.234.31.255, you
can limit access to company computers only, by placing the following script at the start of the Active
Server Page file:

```
<% DIM visitorIPAddress
   visitorIPAddress = Request.ServerVariables("REMOTE_ADDR")
   If Left(visitorIPAddress,10) <> "24.234.31." Then
     Response.Redirect("/")
   End If
 %>
```

```
Request.ServerVariables Items & Associated Values - Microsoft Internet Explorer        _ □ ✕

File   Edit   View   Favorites   Tools   Help                                          ▓

ALL_HTTP = HTTP_ACCEPT:image/gif, image/x-xbitmap, image/jpeg, image/pjpeg, application/vnd.ms-excel,
application/vnd.ms-powerpoint, application/msword, */* HTTP_ACCEPT_LANGUAGE:en-us
HTTP_CONNECTION:Keep-Alive HTTP_HOST:nvbiznet2.com HTTP_USER_AGENT:Mozilla/4.0 (compatible;
MSIE 5.5; Windows 98) HTTP_ACCEPT_ENCODING:gzip, deflate
ALL_RAW = Accept: image/gif, image/x-xbitmap, image/jpeg, image/pjpeg, application/vnd.ms-excel,
application/vnd.ms-powerpoint, application/msword, */* Accept-Language: en-us Connection: Keep-Alive Host:
nvbiznet2.com User-Agent: Mozilla/4.0 (compatible; MSIE 5.5; Windows 98) Accept-Encoding: gzip, deflate
APPL_MD_PATH = /LM/W3SVC/1/ROOT
APPL_PHYSICAL_PATH = d:\Inetpub\wwwroot\
AUTH_PASSWORD =
AUTH_TYPE =
AUTH_USER =
CERT_COOKIE =
CERT_FLAGS =
CERT_ISSUER =
CERT_KEYSIZE =
CERT_SECRETKEYSIZE =
CERT_SERIALNUMBER =
CERT_SERVER_ISSUER =
CERT_SERVER_SUBJECT =
CERT_SUBJECT =
CONTENT_LENGTH = 0
CONTENT_TYPE =
GATEWAY_INTERFACE = CGI/1.1
HTTPS = off
HTTPS_KEYSIZE =
HTTPS_SECRETKEYSIZE =
HTTPS_SERVER_ISSUER =
HTTPS_SERVER_SUBJECT =
INSTANCE_ID = 1
INSTANCE_META_PATH = /LM/W3SVC/1
LOCAL_ADDR = 24.234.49.5
LOGON_USER =
PATH_INFO = /hwdtt/chapter11/Figure11-6.asp
PATH_TRANSLATED = d:\Inetpub\wwwroot\hwdtt\chapter11\Figure11-6.asp
```

Figure 11-6   List of *Request.ServerVariables* collection item names and values

The VBScript *If-Then* statement in this example checks to ensure that the visitor's IP address is within the acceptable range of IP addresses. If the IP address is not one of the 256 allowed to view the page, the *Response.Redirect* method call instructs the Web browser to load the Web site's default index page.

Connecting to a MySQL DBMS Through the MyODBC Driver

One of the most powerful (and often used) features of Active Server Page scripts is their ability to retrieve and display data from an SQL database. Much of the content visitors want when they visit a Web site is stored within database tables. Banks keep account balances, transaction data, and other financial information on customers within tables. Brokerage houses use tables to store such things as securities transactions, deposits, withdrawals, transfers of money, and information about publicly traded companies. Stores take orders, monitor inventory, and manage charge card accounts—all by executing SQL statements that act on database table data. In fact, when you (like your site visitors) go online to access account information, make a purchase, or check the status of an order chances are great that you are working with an SQL database. Behind the scenes, server-side scripts retrieve data from database tables to generate the Web page content you see. In addition, scripts update the data within the database when directed to do so by instructions you enter and send to the Web server through HTML forms.

Before it can submit queries and other SQL statements for processing, an Active Server Page script must establish a connection with the database management system (DBMS). To connect with the MySQL DBMS, for example, an Active Server Page script must have an open database connectivity (ODBC) driver to act as a go-between. The script passes a string (with connection/login instructions or an SQL statement) to the ODBC driver. The ODBC driver, in turn, puts the string into a format the DBMS (such as MySQL) understands and sends the connection/command string to the DBMS for processing. The ODBC driver then formats output (such as a query results set) produced by the DBMS and passes the statement's results to the Active Server Page script.

USE IT   As of this writing, the MyODBC driver an Active Server Page script must have to communicate with the MySQL DBMS does not come bundled with the MySQL application. You can download the MyODBC driver from http://www.MySQL.com/Downloads/. (Click on the MyODBC hyperlink within the APIs section of the Web page, and follow the download instructions for your operating system.) Retrieve the MyODBC.zip (archive) file from the Web site and store it within a folder (such as C:\My Download Files) on the computer with the MySQL DBMS. Next, extract the files in the archive to a folder such as C:\My Download Files\MyODBC. Finally, perform the following steps to complete the installation process:

1. Find Setup.exe within the folder in which you extracted the files within the MyODBC archive file.

2. Double-click Setup.exe to start the installation program. Setup.exe, in turn, will display the Microsoft ODBC Setup message box.

3. Click Continue. The installation program, in turn, will display the Install Drivers dialog box.

4. Click MySQL in the Available ODBC Drivers list box and then click OK. The installation program, in turn, will display the Data Sources dialog box.

5. Click Close and then click OK at the bottom of the Microsoft ODBC Setup message box to exit the installation program.

When you click Close in Step 5, the installation program installs the MyODBC driver on your system and displays the Microsoft ODBC Setup Complete message box. Click OK in the message box to exit the installation program and return to the Windows desktop.

After you install the ODBC driver for the MySQL DBMS (MyODBC), your ASP scripts can connect to the DBMS using a connection string with the following syntax:

```
DRIVER={MySQL};SERVER=<Web server computer name>;
  UID=<username>;PWD=<password>;DATABASE=<database name>
```

Suppose, for example, that your Web server is on a computer named NVBizNet2 and you want to connect with a database named hwdtt. (The database name comes from the first letter in each word of this book's title—**H**TML & **W**eb **D**esign **T**ips & **T**echniques.) You would use a connection string such as the following:

```
DRIVER={MySQL};SERVER=NVBizNet2;UID=root;PWD=;DATABASE=hwdtt
```

In this example, the Active Server Page script logs in as username root with no password. Thus, to display the results of a query within an HTML table on a Web page, your active Server Page script might call a subroutine similar to the following:

```
<%
  Sub SubmitQuery (queryString)
    Const cMySQLConStr = _
 "DRIVER={MySQL};SERVER=NVBizNet2;UID=root;PWD=;DATABASE=hwdtt"

    Dim objMySQLCon, objResultsSet
    Dim field

'Create DBMS connection object
    Set objMySQLCon = Server.CreateObject("ADODB.Connection")

    With objMySQLCon
'open the connection to the MySQL DBMS, submit the query
'and store the query results set in a VBScript object
      .ConnectionString = cMySQLConStr
      .Open
      Set objResultsSet = .Execute (queryString)

'display the query on the Web page
      Response.Write "<center><p><b>Results Set for: </b>" & _
        queryString & "</p></center><hr>"
```

```
'display column names and query results within an HTML table
     Response.Write _
        "<center><table border='1' cellpadding='5'>"

'display SQL Table column names in the HTML table header row
     Response.Write "<tr>"
        For Each field In objResultsSet.Fields
           Response.Write "<th>" & field.Name & "</th>"
        Next
     Response.Write "</tr>"

'display SQL Table column names in the HTML table header row
     Do While Not objResultsSet.EOF
        Response.Write "<tr>"
          For Each field In objResultsSet.Fields
             Response.Write "<td>" & field & "</td>"
          Next
        Response.Write "</tr>"

'move the rowpointer to the next row in the results set
        objResultsSet.MoveNext
     Loop

     Response.Write "</table></center>"
   End With
  End Sub
%>
```

As shown in this example, the following script statements use the connection object (*objMySQLCon*) *Open* method to open a connection to with a MySQL database:

```
objMySQLCon.ConnectionString = cMySQLConStr
objMySQLCon.Open
```

The script then uses the *Set* statement shown here to submit the query in *queryString* to the DBMS and transfer the query results to the object *objResultSet*:

```
Set objResultsSet = objMySQLCon.Execute (queryString)
```

VBScript stores the query results as the *Fields* collection within the results set (or record set) object *objResultsSet*, in this example. As such, query results are stored as key/item (that is, name/value) pairs within the *objResultsSet* object. You can work with both the item name (or key) and its value. In this example, the script first inserts the keys (the column names from the SQL table), as a heading row across the top of an HTML table. Then, the script works its way through the results set one row at a time, displaying the item value in each results set row beneath its corresponding heading in the HTML table.

Setting Up Username/Password Access to a Web Site

To set up a Web site that has members-only content, you must provide a way to ensure that only authorized visitors (that is, "members") can retrieve the site's restricted pages. Typically, sites with restricted content will have both public and private (restricted) areas. The site's public area consists of Web pages with content available to all who visit. Meanwhile, the Web server lets only those visitors with established accounts retrieve pages within the restricted, members-only area.

USE IT   Each member account has a username and password the visitor must supply for access to restricted content. To let authorized visitors log in to the site, create an HTML form that prompts the visitor for an account username and password. For example, you might save the following form definition in a Web page document named Login.htm:

```
<form action="http://www.NVBizNet2.com/HWDTT/authenticate.asp"
      method="POST">
  Username: <input type="text" name="username" size="20"><br>
  Password: <input type="password" name="password" size="20">
  <br><br><input type="submit" value="Login">
          <input type="reset" value="Reset">
</form>
```

Set the *action* attribute within the <form> tag to the URL of the Active Server Page with the site's authentication/login script. In this example, the *action* attribute specifies the Active Server Page authenticate.asp. Thus, after the visitor enters his or her username and password into the form and clicks on the form's Submit button, the Web browser will send the form results to the script embedded within the Web page authenticate.asp. If the username and password entered match a username/ password pair on file, the script lets the visitor proceed to a page within the members-only area.

You can store site member username/password pairs in a disk file or within an SQL database table. The Active Server Page script that authenticates the visitor login searches the list of username/ password pairs for a set that matches the pair entered into the HTML form on the site's login page. If the script finds a matching username/password pair, the script moves the visitor from the login page to a Web page within the members-only area. Conversely, if the username/password typed into the form has no match in the site's username/password (access) list, the script denies access to the site and returns the visitor on the login page to try again.

When you store usernames and passwords within an SQL table, each row in the table contains a valid username/password pair—with the username in one column and the associated password in another. To create such a table, first tell the SQL database management system (DBMS) which database you want to use and then execute an SQL CREATE TABLE statement as follows:

```
USE hwdtt;
CREATE TABLE siteAccessList
   (username VARCHAR(20) NOT NULL,
    password VARCHAR(20) NOT NULL);
```

The first statement in this example tells the DBMS to use the hwdtt database. (The database name comes from the first letter in each word of this book's title—**H**TML & **W**eb **D**esign **T**ips & **T**echniques.) The syntax of an SQL CREATE TABLE statement is as follows:

```
CREATE TABLE <table name>
 (<column name> <column type> [<column attribute list>],
...
   <last column name><last column type> [<last attribute list>]);
```

To be useful, your SQL table needs a list of usernames and passwords, which you can add by using SQL INSERT statements. For example, to insert data into the *siteAccessList* table, you would execute an INSERT statement such as the following:

```
INSERT INTO siteAccessList VALUES ("Kris", "mfe2275");
INSERT INTO siteAccessList VALUES ("Andy", "687fc");
```

The syntax of an SQL INSERT statement is as follows:

```
INSERT INTO <table name> (<column1, column2, ..., columnN)
   VALUES (value1, value2 ..., valueN);
```

(As shown in this example, if the INSERT statement provides the values of all columns in a row, you can omit the columns list that follows the <table name> in the statement.)

Next, to use the table in this example during the login process, the Active Server Page script must connect with the DBMS and submit a query in the form of an SQL SELECT statement. For example, to display the usernames and passwords in the table you would execute the SQL SELECT statement:

```
SELECT username, password FROM siteAccessList;
```

To test if a visitor entered a valid username/password pair, add a WHERE clause that tells the DBMS to return only those rows in which the username and password matched the values the visitor typed into the form on the login page. For example, if the visitor entered "Andy" into the username element and "pass1454" into the password element of the login form, your query would be as follows:

```
SELECT COUNT(*) FROM siteAccessList
WHERE username="Andy" AND password="pass1454"
```

If the query returns "1", the visitor entered a valid username/password, because the username and password entered is an entry within the site's members list. Conversely, if the visitor submitted a username/password pair not in the table (as is the case in this example) the query returns "0" to indicate no account has the username and password combination submitted.

Before submitting its query, the Active Server Page script must establish a connection with the database that has the table of account usernames and passwords. The *Server.CreateObject* method in the following code creates a database connection object.

```
<% Set objMySQLCon = Server.CreateObject("ADODB.Connection")
   objMySQLCon.ConnectionString = _
 "DRIVER={MySQL};SERVER=NVBizNet2;UID=root;PWD=;DATABASE=hwdtt"
   objMySQLCon.Open
%>
```

The connection object's *ConnectionString* property contains the values necessary for the script to log in to the DBMS. In this example, the *objMySQLCon.Open* method uses the MySQL ODBC driver to connect with the MySQL DBMS on the NT server named NVBizNet2. The connection logs in under the username (UID) root, which has no password, and elects to use the hwdtt database.

After establishing a connection with the DBMS, use the connection object's *Execute* method to submit a query as shown here:

```
<%
  queryString = _
    "SELECT COUNT(*) Count FROM siteAccessList" & _
  " WHERE username = '" & Request.Form("username") & "'" & _
  " AND   password = '" & Request.Form("password") & "'"
  Set objResultsSet = objMySQLCon.Execute (queryString)
  If objResultsSet.Fields("Count") = 1 Then
    Response.Redirect "/hwdtt/MemberWelcome.asp"
  End If
%>
```

In this example, the script uses the connection object (*objMySQLCon*) *Execute* method (*objMySQLCon.Execute*) to submit a query string (*queryString*) to the MySQL DBMS. The DBMS, in turn, executes the query and returns the rows of columns that match the search criteria (that is, the query's results set) within the *objResultsSet* object.

The query in this example will always return a single row of results in a column named *Count*. [*Count(*)* in the query submitted is an SQL aggregate function that returns the count of table rows that satisfy the search condition(s) in the query's WHERE clause.] If the DBMS finds a matching username/password pair in the *siteAccessList* table, the DBMS sets the *Count* field to "1", and the script redirects the Web browser to the Welcome page within the site's members-only area. Conversely, if either the username or the password typed into the login form is invalid, the DBMS returns zero (0) in the *Count* field. The script then moves on to HTML tags and text (not shown here), which prompts the visitor to log in again.

You can retrieve the Web page with the login form and the Active Server Page with the login authentication script described in this Tip by downloading the file Chpt11Tip09.zip from the Osborne Web site at http://www.osborne.com.

Note that setting a form element's *type* attribute to "password" obscures text the visitor enters into the element from view. (The Web browser displays an asterisk [*] in place of each character the visitor types into the element.) However, after the visitor clicks the Submit button, the Web browser sends all form data (including text typed into a password element) as unencrypted ASCII text. As such, a hacker could tap into the Internet and read (as plain text) the body of the HTTP message in which the Web browser placed the username and password it sent to the Web server.

To safeguard sensitive information (such as usernames and passwords), ask the ISP hosting your site to set up the Secure Socket Layer (SSL) protocol. The ISP must first obtain a *security certificate* for your Web site from a certificate authority such as VeriSign Corporation (http://www.versign.com), Thawte Consulting (http://www.thawte.com), or Entrust (http://www.entrust.com). After the ISP installs the security certificate for your site on the Web server, the Web server and Web browser will encrypt the HTTP messages before sending them across the Internet. Having the Web browser and server encrypt their transmissions protects your form results (and other message content) from unauthorized access, because a hacker viewing an encrypted HTTP message body sees only an unintelligible jumble of characters, numbers, and special symbols.

SSL encryption and decryption occur outside the scope of your Active Server Page scripts—meaning you can use the same login (or other) script whether communicating across a secure or nonsecure connection. The only difference you will notice is that your secure URLs will start with https:// instead of the standard (nonsecure) http://. Thus, to use a secure connection when sending form results to an Active Server Page script, you would use a URL like https://www.NVBizNet2 .com/hwdtt/authenticate.asp in place of a URL like http://www.NVBizNet2.com/hwdtt /authenticate.asp.

After receiving an encrypted HTTP request for an Active Server Page, the Web server decrypts the message and passes decrypted data (such as form results) along with the Web page requested to the ASP script host. The script host, in turn, calls on a script engine to execute the Active Server Page script(s) embedded within the Web page and sends the script output back to the Web server. The Web server, in turn, places the script-generated page into the body of an HTTP response, which the server then encrypts and sends to the Web browser. Upon receipt of the HTTP response (that is, the Web page requested from the Web server) the Web browser decrypts the message and renders the page.

Starting a Session and Working with Session Variables

An Active Server Page session is a continuous period during which a visitor interacts with a Web site. A session might consist of a single or a series of transactions and the visitor might retrieve one or several Web pages during the course of a single session. For example, during a session, a visitor might check the weather on a local news site. Or, the visitor might log in to a bank's Web site to check account balances, pay bills online, and transfer money between accounts. In short, an Active Server Page session begins when a visitor requests the first Active Server Page from a site and ends when the visitor leaves the site, when a script abandons the session, at the expiration of a timeout interval, or (immediately) if the visitor's browser refuses the session cookie.

Sessions are an important Web site design tool because they let Active Server Pages scripts use variables that maintain their state (that is, variables that keep their values) throughout the visitor's stay on the Web site. As a visitor moves from page to page on a site, you can use session variables to keep track of the visitor's personal data (such as name, address, and phone number), items the visitor puts into an online shopping cart, selections he or she makes on multipage forms, and so on. Although you could create persistent variables with cookies and hidden form elements, by using session variables, you reduce the amount of data that must pass between the Web server and browser with each HTTP request.

The Web server sends only one "key" value, the session ID, to the Web browser at the start of the session. The session ID is a cookie named ASPSESSIONID (or ASPSESSIONID*XXXXXXXX* on

Internet Information Server [IIS] version 4 and later). Then, instead of several cookie values or hidden form elements, the Web browser passes only the session ID cookie to the Web server with each Web page request. The Web server, in turn, uses the cookie to identify the file (on the Web server's hard drive) that contains the persistent data values (that is, the session variables) the server makes available to scripts through the Active Server Page Session object. A typical session ID cookie looks something like one of the following (depending on the version of IIS):

```
ASPSESSIONID=908JIJFAOI83UKNOINGUHDNE
ASPSESSIONIDPPFFFEER=908JIJFAOI83UKNOINGUHDNE
```

On a Web server, each session ID cookie is a unique, pseudo-random series of letters and numbers used to identify the visitor to the Web server. Thus, session ID cookies are like ID cards the Web server hands out to each site visitor. When a Web browser asks for an Active Server Page, the Web server checks if the browser passed a session ID cookie (that is, if the browser presented the visitor's ID card). If the browser failed to present an ID, the Web server sends a session ID cookie to the Web browser along with the Active Server Page the visitor requested. Conversely, if the Web browser sent a session ID cookie along with the Active Server Page request, the Web server uses the ID to retrieve information the server previously stored during the course of the visitor's session. The Web server makes the information available through session variables within the Active Server Page *Session* object.

USE IT   Thus, your Active Server Page scripts need take no special action to start a session—the Web server does so for you automatically. When the browser requests an Active Server Page without sending a session ID cookie, the Web servers starts a new session and sends the session ID cookie to the Web browser. If the Web browser accepts the cookie, the browser will return the cookie with all subsequent Web page requests the visitor makes during the session. When the Web browser sends the ASPSESSIONID (or ASPSESSIONID*XXXXXXXX*) cookie, the Web server matches the cookie value with a server-side list. After it finds a match, the Web server opens the browser's session file on the server's hard drive and makes session variables available through the *Session* object.

The Web server stores session variables as a collection within the Active Server Page *Session* object. Thus, each session variable, like items in other Active Server Page collections, consists of a key (that is, a name) and an associated value. To create a new session variable, you simply assign a value to a new key as shown here:

```
Session("firstName") = "Konrad"
Session("lastName") = "King"
```

To change the value of a session variable, assign the new value to an existing key. For example, given the two session variables created in the preceding example, the following code will display "Konrad King is now Konrad Kingsly" on a Web page:

```
Response.write(Session("firstName") & " " & _
  Session("lastName") & " is now "
Session("lastName") = "Kingsly"
Response.write(Session("firstName") & " " & _
  Session("lastName")
```

Notice that you can use session variables in expressions and as function or method parameters. Simply insert the object name (such as the name of the collection) and the key (that is, the name of the session variable) you want to use within the expression or in the function or method call parameter list.

Remember, session variables use memory resources on the Web server during the session. When the visitor requests a Web page, the server retrieves session variables (and their values) from disk and stores them in memory within an in-memory *Session* object. Therefore, be sure to delete session variables you no longer need during the course of a session. To remove a session variable from the collection, set the variable's value to "Empty" as shown here:

```
Session("orderTotal") = Empty
```

Bear in mind that setting a session variable's value to a null string ("") or setting the value to "Nothing" as follows is not the same as setting the value to "Empty":

```
Session("productCode1") = ""
Session("procuctQty1") = Nothing
```

Null-valued items are still items (with a null value) within the *Session* variable collection. Paradoxically, in VBScript, *Nothing* is an object, which is not empty. As such, both null and *Nothing* session variables take up Web server memory during the session. To free memory resources, you must set the session variable's value to "Empty" so the Web server will remove it from the collection.

In addition to persistent values, a Web server also creates a timer for each session. When it starts the session, the Web server sets the timer's *Session.Timeout* property at twenty minutes in IIS version 4 (ten minutes in IIS version 5). The timer starts at its initial default value and counts down to zero (0). When the timer reaches zero (0), the Web server ends the Active Server Page session and abandons all information associated with the session. You can set the *Session.Timeout* property at any point during a session with a script statement such as this:

```
Session.Timeout = 1
```

The statement in this example sets the session timeout to one (1) minute. (You cannot set the *Session.Timeout* property to fractions of minutes.)

Each time it receives a request from the browser associated with a session, the ASP script host resets a session's timer to the initial default. Therefore, as long as the visitor continues to request pages, the session remains active. When the visitor stops interacting with the Web site, the ASP script host stops resetting the *Session.Timeout* property, which then reaches zero (0) and causes the Web server to end the session.

The primary purpose of the session timer is to prevent the Web server from storing session data indefinitely—thereby using up memory resources and disk space unnecessarily. Ideally, the Web browser would send a "logoff" message to the Web server when the visitor moves on to another Web site or exits the browser altogether. Unfortunately, due to the stateless nature of HTTP, that does not happen. Instead, the browser just stops sending requests to the Web server. Of course, "timing-out" a visitors session leads to a conflict when the visitor lets the browser "sit" on a Web page without making a request during the timeout period, and then interacts with the page again.

When a Web browser presents a session ID cookie for a session the Web browser has already abandoned, the Web server no longer has the session's data in memory (or on disk). As such, the Web server treats the session ID cookie as invalid. To avoid expending resources involved in generating a new cookie, the Web server lets the browser keep the same cookie value but creates a new *Session* object it associates with the session ID cookie. Therefore, your Active Server Page scripts should use the *isEmpty()* function to make sure that session variables they use still exist when scripts use variables they do not create themselves. For example, the following script checks for session variables it needs (*username* and *password*) and redirects the visitor to the site's login page if either is no longer present within the session variables collection:

```
If isEmpty(Session("username")) Then
  Response.Redirect "/hwdtt/Chapter11/Tip10-Login.htm"
End If
If isEmpty(Session("password")) Then
  Response.Redirect "/hwdtt/Chapter11/Tip10-Login.htm"
End If
```

Note that if you set a timeout value after which a page is no longer accessible, be sure to let the visitor know the timeout period somewhere on the Web page. It can be very frustrating to be in the middle of filling out a long form, get interrupted by a phone call, and then return to form data entry only to find the timeout expired and you have to start over.

Executing SQL Queries and Displaying Query Results Sets Within an HTML Table

A typical static Web page consists of text and graphics images. Even if you add an animation or two, every visitor still sees the same content, albeit in an enjoyable and perhaps more memorable form. To be truly dynamic, a Web page must vary its content based on the data a visitor requests. The challenge for you as a Web page author is that you cannot anticipate every possible data query your visitors might make. Fortunately, you can use Active Server Page scripts to let visitors submit queries directly to a database and the *Response.Write* method to display the query results.

USE IT To retrieve and display data from an SQL database on a Web page, a script needs three objects—a *Connection* object, an object to hold the query's results set, and the Active Server Page *Response* object. The *Server.CreateObject* method lets you create a database connection object as shown in the following code:

```
Dim objMySQLCon
Set objMySQLCon = Server.CreateObject("ADODB.Connection")
objMySQLCon.ConnectionString = _
  "DRIVER={MySQL};SERVER=NVBizNet2;UID=root;PWD=;DATABASE=hwdtt"
objMySQLCon.Open
%>
```

Set the connection object (*objMySQLCon*, in this example) *ConnectionString* property to the values necessary to log in to the DBMS. Then, use the connection object *Open* method to open a connection to the DBMS. In this example, *objMySQLCon* uses the MySQL ODBC driver to open a connection with the MySQL DBMS on a computer named NVBizNet2. The script logs on as the username (UID) root, which has no password, and elects to use the hwdtt database. After executing the connection object's *Open* method, the script can submit statements to the DBMS.

Although you could let visitors type queries into an HTML form element, most sites have the visitor execute predefined queries or stored procedures. Suppose, for example, that you have an Active Server Page named *GetOrderNumber.asp* with the following script:

```
<%
  If Not IsEmpty (Request.Form("Status")) Then
    Dim objMySQLCon, rsOrderDetail
    Set objMySQLCon = Server.CreateObject("ADODB.Connection")
    objMySQLCon.ConnectionString = _
 "DRIVER={MySQL};SERVER=NVBizNet2;UID=root;PWD=;DATABASE=hwdtt"
    objMySQLCon.Open
    SET rsOrderDetail = objMySQLCon.Execute( _
         "SELECT orderNum FROM orders WHERE orderNum = '" & _
            Request.Form("orderNum") & "'")
    If Not rsOrderDetail.EOF Then
      Response.Redirect("ShowOrderStatus.asp?OrderNum=" & _
        Request.Form("orderNum"))
    End If
  End If
%>
<!DOCTYPE HTML PUBLIC "-//W3C//DTD HTML 4.0//EN">
<html>
<body bgcolor="#ADD8E6">
    <!-- Web Page Text and Form Definition -->
</body>
</html>
```

Note that the script in this example resides above the Web page HTML within the Active Server Page *GetOrderNumber.asp* shown in Figure 11-7.

The script first checks the Form collection's *Status* item to see if the visitor clicked on the form's Status button to retrieve the Active Server Page. If the visitor has not yet clicked the Status button, the ASP script engine displays the order number entry form as defined here:

```
<form method="post" action="GetOrderNumber.asp"
     name=OrderNumEntry>
<%
  If Not IsEmpty (Request.Form("Status")) Then
    Response.Write _
      "<b>The order number you entered was not found. " & _
```

```
      "Please try again.</b><br>"
  Else
    Response.Write _
      "Please enter your order number and then click " & _
      "on the ""Status"" button.<br>"
  End If
%>
  <input type="text" name="orderNum" size=20"><br><br>
  <input type="submit" name="Status" value="Status">
  <input type="reset" value="Reset">
</form>
```

(Note that the *action* attribute in the <form> tag instructs the Web browser to retrieve *GetOrderNumber.asp*—the same Active Server Page into which visitors enter the order number.)

If the Web browser retrieved the Active Server Page *GetOrderNumber.asp* after the visitor clicked the form's Status button, the *Status* item in the *Request.Form* collection will not be "empty," and the ASP script host will execute the script. To determine if the order number entered is valid, the script

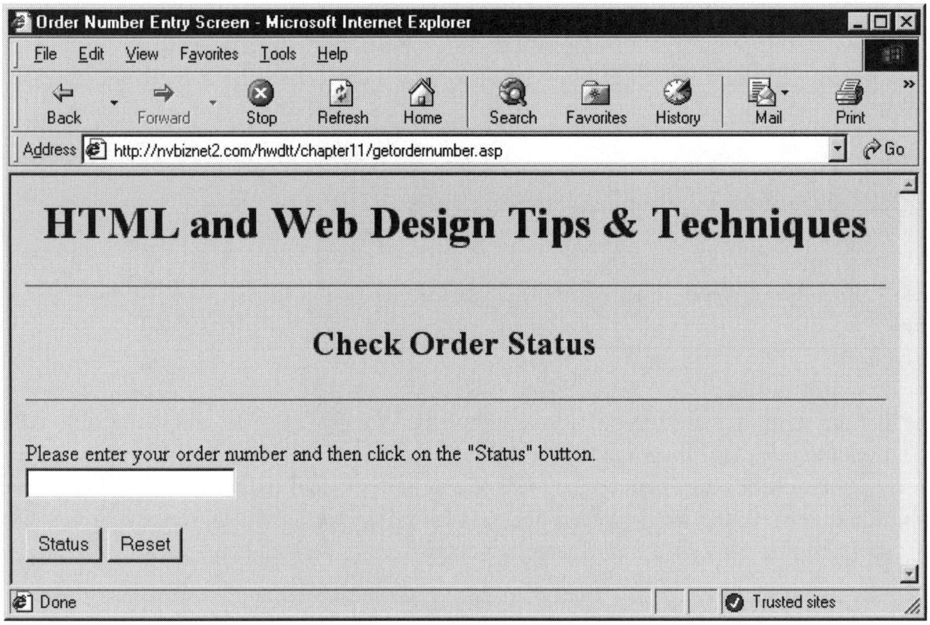

Figure 11-7   Active Server Page with an order number entry form

calls the *Connection* object's *Execute* method to submit a query to the SQL *orders* table as shown here:

```
SET rsOrderDetail = objMySQLCon.Execute( _
    "SELECT orderNum FROM orders WHERE orderNum = '" & _
        Request.Form("orderNum") & "'")
If Not rsOrderDetail.EOF Then
  Response.Redirect("ShowOrderStatus.asp?OrderNum=" & _
    Request.Form("orderNum"))
End If
```

The results set object's "end of file" property (*rsOrderDetail.EOF*, in this example) is true immediately after the script executes a query only if the query returns no rows. In this example, if *rsOrderDetail.EOF* is true immediately after executing the query, the order number is not on file within the SQL *orders* table. Conversely, if the order number is on file, the *rsOrderDetail.EOF* will be false, and the script will direct the browser to retrieve the Active Server Page *ShowOrderStatus.asp*. (*ShowOrderStatus.asp* has a script that displays the header, item detail, and status of the order.)

Each time you call the *Connection* object's *Execute* method to submit a query, the DBMS returns zero, one, or several rows of query results. In this example, the script embedded within the Active Server Page *ShowOrderStatus .asp* creates three variables as follows to hold the results sets of the three queries the script performs:

```
DIM rsOrderDetail, rsOrderItems, rsOrderStatus
```

Objects in which scripts store DBMS query results start as ordinary VBScript variant data type variables. When you assign the results set returned by *Connection.Execute* method calls, as shown here, the variables become objects:

```
With objMySQLCon
  Set rsOrderDetail = .Execute( _
      "SELECT orderDate FROM orders " & _
      "WHERE orderNum = '" & orderNum & "'")
  Set rsOrderItems = .Execute( _
      "SELECT orderItems.itemNum 'Item Number', " & _
          "description Product, units Quantity " & _
      "FROM orderItems, itemMast " & _
      "WHERE orderNum = '" & orderNum & "' " & _
      "AND   itemMast.itemNum = orderItems.itemNum " & _
      "ORDER BY itemMast.itemNum")
  Set rsOrderStatus = .Execute( _
      "SELECT Description Stage, dateStarted Started, " & _
          "dateCompleted Completed " & _
      "FROM orderStatus " & _
      "WHERE orderNum = '" & orderNum & "' " & _
      "ORDER BY stepNumber")
End With
```

The conversion from VBScript variant variable to results set object is important. As objects, each of the three results sets (*rsOrderDetail*, *rsOrderItems*, and *rsOrderStatus*) has methods and properties you can use to display the rows and columns (fields) within the results set.

For example, the *rsOrderInfo* object has only one row, because the query by order number returns the header information for a single order. As such, you can display order header information using the *Response.Write* method to place values within the row's columns on the Web page as follows:

```
Response.Write "<b>Order Number: </b>" & orderNum & "<br>" & _
    "<b>Order Date: </b>" & rsOrderDetail.Fields("orderDate")
```

Unlike *rsOrderInfo*, both *rsOrderItems* and *rsOrderStatus* might have more than one row of query results. As such, you will use the VBScript *Do-Until* loop to display each row of query results in these objects as shown here:

```
With Response
    .Write "<table border='1' cellpadding='5'>"

'display SQL Table column names in the HTML table header row
    .Write "<tr>"
      For Each field In rsOrderItems.Fields
        .Write "<th>" & field.Name & "</th>"
      Next
    .Write "</tr>"

'display SQL Table column names in the HTML table header row
    Do While Not rsOrderItems.EOF
      .Write "<tr>"
        For Each field In rsOrderItems.Fields
          If field <> "" Then
            .Write "<td>" & field & "</td>"
          Else
            .Write "<td> </td>"
          End If
        Next
      .Write "</tr>"
'move the row pointer to the next row in the results set
      rsOrderItems.MoveNext
    Loop
    .Write "</table>"
End With
```

In this example, the script calls the *Response.Write* method repeatedly (until the property *rsOrderItems.EOF* is set to true) to add rows from the results set (in *rsOrderItems*) to an HTML table on the Web page. The *EOF* property stands for "End of File" and is set to true when the *rsOrderItems.MoveNext* method moves the row pointer past the last row of query results.

You can retrieve the Active Server Pages with the scripts described in this Tip by downloading the file Chpt11Tip11.zip from the Osborne Web site at http://www.osborne.com.

Displaying Banner Ads with the Microsoft Banner Ad Rotator

Since the Internet's inception, Web site developers have followed the commercial television model—free programming/content paid for by commercials/banner ads. As you create Web sites, you will no doubt be asked to include a banner ad campaign of some sort in your designs. On an online store, banner ads will likely advertise the store's products and special sale items. Nonstore sites that present information or provide software, graphics, or other multimedia content for download sell banner ad space to third parties. These companies, in turn, advertise products site visitors may want to purchase.

Typically, a site will have more than one sponsor or advertise several products. As such, you will normally display multiple banner ads within the same "billboard" area on the Web page. To do so, you need a banner ad rotation system that randomly (or sequentially) selects and displays banner ads one at a time from a list of ads. Microsoft provides a free software application called the Ad Rotator you can use. When you install the Personal Web Server (PWS), Internet Information Server (IIS) version 4, or IIS version 5, the installation program installs the Ad Rotator as part of the default installation process.

USE IT   To use the Ad Rotator, you must create a rotator schedule file and a redirection file. Within the *rotator schedule file* you list the banner ad graphics images you want the Ad Rotator to display. The *redirection file*, meanwhile, is an Active Server Page with an embedded script that generates a "click-through" by sending the Web browser on to a target page when the visitor clicks on the banner ad. We discuss the rotator schedule file first and then the redirection file near the end of the Tip.

The rotator schedule file has the following format:

```
REDIRECT  redirectionFileURL
WIDTH     bannerWidthInPixels
HEIGHT    bannerHeightInPixels
BORDER    imageBorderWidthInPixels
*
bannerImageURL1
bannerRedirectionURL1
bannerImageAltAttribute1
bannerWeight1
bannerImageURL2
bannerRedirectionURL2
bannerImageAltAttribute2
bannerWeight2
< ... additional banner descriptions ... >
```

Though not required, name your Ad Rotator schedule file something like AdRotatorSchedule.asp and store it within a folder such as BannerAds on the Web site. Although neither the filename nor the folder name suggested here is mandatory, using meaningful names for files and folders will make things easier to find as you maintain the site over time.

The first four lines of the rotator schedule file contain information that applies to all banner ads displayed during the banner ad rotation. Each line starts with a keyword: REDIRECT, WIDTH, HEIGHT, or BORDER. The following list describes the information you place after the keyword on each of the first four lines in the file:

- **REDIRECT**   Followed by the URL of the redirection file. When a visitor clicks on a banner ad, the ad's hyperlink directs the Web browser to retrieve the redirection file. The redirection file, in turn, is an Active Server Page with a script that sends the visitor to the banner ad's target Web page. If you save the redirection file as AdRedirect.asp within the BannerAds folder on the NVBizNet2.com Web site, for example, the first line in the schedule file would read:
  REDIRECT http://www.NVBizNet2.com/hwdtt/BannerAds/AdRedirect.asp
  Or, you might use the redirection file's full virtual path, which is
  /hwdtt/BannerAds/AdRedirect.asp in this example.

- **WIDTH**   Followed by the width of the banner ads in pixels.

- **HEIGHT**   Followed by the height of the banner ads in pixels.

- **BORDER**   Followed by the width of the border the Web browser is to display around each ad in pixels.

Following the first four lines in the schedule file is a line with only an asterisk (*). This line separates the global information applicable to all banners from the groups of four-line descriptions that apply to individual banner ads. The format of each four-line banner description is as follows:

- *bannerImageURL*   The URL or full virtual path of the image to be displayed as a banner ad. For example, to display a banner ad graphic named SomeBanner.gif stored within the BannerAds folder on the NVBizNet2.com Web site, replace *bannerImageURL* with http://www.NVBizNet2.com/BannderAds/SomeBanner.gif or /hwdtt/BannerAds/SomeBanner.gif.

- *bannerRedirectionURL*   The URL of the banner ad's target Web page, that is, the Web page to which the visitor is sent if he or she clicks on the banner ad.

- *bannerImageAltAttribute*   The *alt* attribute within the banner ad graphic's <img> tag. The Web browser displays the *alt* attribute text while loading the banner ad graphics image or if the visitor disabled images or is using a text-only Web browser.

- *bannerWeight*   How often the Ad Rotator is to display a banner ad relative to other banner ads listed within the rotator schedule file. Suppose, for example, the rotation schedule has two banner ads—one with a *bannerWeight* of 10 and the other with a *bannerWeight* of 5. The Ad Rotator will display the banner ad with the *bannerWeight* of 10 twice as often as the banner ad with the *bannerWeight* of 5.

To display a banner ad, use the *Server.CreateObject* method to create an Ad Rotator object and then call the object's *GetAdvertisement* method. For example, to display a banner ad at the top of a site's home page (that is, its index page) save the following VBScript within the file Index.asp in the site's root folder:

```
<% Option Explicit
   DIM adRotatorObj
   SET adRotatorObj = Server.CreateObject("MSWC.AdRotator")
%>
<!DOCTYPE HTML PUBLIC "-//W3C//DTD HTML 4.0//EN">
<html>
<body>
<!-- Display the Banner Ad -->
  <center>
<%
  Response.Write _
    adRotatorObj.GetAdvertisement( _
      "/hwdtt/BannerAds/AdRotatorSchedule.asp")
%>
  </center>
  <h1>HTML & Web Design Tips and Techniques</h1>
  <p>*** Homepage Content ***</p>
</body>
</html>
<!-- Destroy/delete the Ad Rotator object -->
<% Set adRotatorObject = Nothing %>
```

In this example, the third line of the script calls the *Server.CreateObject* method to create the Ad Rotator object (*adRotatorobj*). The *Response.Write* method near the center of the Active Server Page inserts output similar to the following returned by the *GetAdvertisement* method call:

```
<a href="http://www.NVBizNet2.com/hwdtt/BannerAds/AdRedirect.asp?
    URL=http://www.NVBizNet.com/default.htm&
    image=/BannerAds/NVBizNet.GIF">
  <img src="/BannerAds/NVBizNet.GIF"
    alt="Visit NVBizNet for Web Page Design Tips"
    width="400" height="60" border="1"></a>
```

Therefore, after clicking on the banner ad displayed at the top of the Web page, the Web browser retrieves the Ad Rotator redirection file (http://www.NVBizNet2.com/hwdtt/BannerAds/ AdRedirect.asp, in this example). As mentioned earlier in this Tip, it is up to the script within the redirection file to move the Web browser on to the banner ad's target page. (Remember, a banner ad's purpose is to get the visitor to go to a Web page on the advertiser's site by clicking on the ad graphic.) By moving the Web browser to a redirection file first, you can execute code within the redirection file to track click-throughs (as you will learn to do in the next Tip).

Note that the hyperlink generated by the Ad Rotator passes the target URL and banner image pathname to the script within the redirection file through a query string. (In the preceding example, the query string was: "*URL=http://www.NVBizNet.com/default.htm&image=/hwdtt/BannerAds/ NVBizNet.GIF*".) Thus, the redirection file (*AdRedirect.asp*, in the preceding example) must have at least the following code:

```
<% Response.Redirect Request.QueryString("URL") %>
```

After the visitor clicks the banner ad in the previous example, the Web browser retrieves the Active Server Page AdRedirect.asp. The script embedded within AdRedirect.asp, in turn, retrieves the Web address of the banner ad's target page from the *URL* query string argument and redirects the browser to http://www.NVBizNet.com/default.htm, in this example.

You can retrieve the Ad Rotator Schedule file, the Ad Rotator Redirection file, and the Active Server Page with the script that uses the Ad Rotator to select a banner ad to display by downloading the file Chpt11Tip12.zip from the Osborne Web site at http://www.osborne.com.

Tracking Microsoft Banner Ad Rotator Impressions and Click-Throughs

To defray development costs and provide site content free of charge, many Web sites sell banner ad space to companies with products or services for sale. In addition to enticing visitors to go to other Web sites, banner ads are often used to advertise products or specials available on the current site. Amazon.com, for example, might display banners that advertise books on their best-sellers list or new releases from popular authors. Whether a banner ad is geared to sell the site's products or to attract visitors to make purchases at other sites, advertisers are concerned with two things— impressions and click-throughs.

Impressions are the number of times visitors see a particular banner ad. The more impressions, the more likely the ad will present itself to a visitor that wants to buy the product advertised. Impressions are a function of both the number of times a banner ad rotator displays the banner graphic on a Web page and how often visitors retrieve the page. A banner ad on a page retrieved 100 times per hour, for example, generates fewer impressions than a banner ad on a page that averages 1,000 visitors during the same period. The more visitors that see an ad and the more often the ad rotator displays the banner, the higher the likelihood that visitors will click the banner ad and purchase the product advertised.

Click-throughs are even more important than impressions. A *click-through* occurs whenever a visitor clicks the banner ad to retrieve the Web page for the product or service advertised. Think of television commercials. Getting a viewer to watch an advertisement is one thing; getting the viewer to go out and make a purchase is another (more important thing, from the advertiser's standpoint).

Whereas television advertisers must rely on marketing studies to determine how many times a television commercial led to a purchase, you can track a visitor's reaction to a banner ad much more closely. With Active Server Page scripts, you can count and store in a database the number of times the ad rotator displays a Web page (that is, the number of impressions) and how often visitors click the banner to get more information (that is, the number of click-throughs). Advertisers use impression and click-through statistics to determine the effectiveness of a banner ad campaign. Web site owners, meanwhile, use the same statistics to set advertising rates—the higher the average impression and click-through counts, the more advertisers are willing to pay to place a banner ad on a Web page.

USE IT   To accumulate impression and click-through data for later analysis, execute SQL statements such as the following to create an SQL table within a database:

```
USE hwdtt;
CREATE TABLE bannerAdStats
  (targetURL          VARCHAR(60) NOT NULL,
   imageURL           VARCHAR(60) NOT NULL,
   impressionCount    INTEGER,
   clickThroughCount INTEGER);
```

The first statement in this example tells the DBMS to use the hwdtt database. (The database name comes from the first letter in each word of this book's title—HTML & Web Design Tips & Techniques.) The second statement creates the SQL table (*bannerAdStats*) in which Active Server Page scripts will store impression and click-through counts.

The Microsoft Banner Ad Rotator (which comes standard with Personal Web Server (PWS), Internet Information Server (IIS) version 4 and IIS version 5) selects a banner ad from a list of ads within a "rotator schedule" file and displays the ad on a Web page. To use the Ad Rotator to display a banner ad, you insert lines of VBScript similar to the following within an Active Server Page:

```
<%
  SET adRotatorObj = Server.CreateObject("MSWC.AdRotator")
  Response.Write _
    adRotatorObject.GetAdvertisement( _
      "/hwdtt/BannerAds/AdRotatorSchedule.asp")
%>
```

While the first line of the script creates an Ad Rotator object (*adRotatorObj*), the *Response.Write* method call (which starts on the script's second line) displays the banner ad returned by the *adRotatorObject.GetAdvertisement* method call.

To track the number of impressions, that is, the number of times the *GetAdvertisement* method selects a particular banner ad, insert the following function at the start of the Active Server Page on which you display the banner ad:

```
<%
  Function DisplayRotatorAd(adRotatorObj,rotatorScheduleFile)
    Dim objMySQLCon
```

```
    DIM strAdRotatorHTML, intImageStart, strImageURL

'have the Ad Rotator generate HTML to display banner ad
  strAdRotatorHTML = adRotatorObj.GetAdvertisement( _
                         rotatorScheduleFile)
'find the graphics image URL in the HTML the Rotator Ad returns
  intImageStart = InStr(1, strAdRotatorHTML, "image=") + 6
  strImageURL = Mid(strAdRotatorHTML, intImageStart, _
    InStr(intImageStart, strAdRotatorHTML, """") - intImageStart)

'Connect to the DBMS and update the impression count
  Set objMySQLCon = Server.CreateObject("ADODB.Connection")
  With objMySQLCon
    .ConnectionString = _
 "DRIVER={MySQL};SERVER=NVBizNet2;UID=root;PWD=;DATABASE=hwdtt"
    .Open
    .Execute "UPDATE bannerAdStats " & _
            "SET impressionCount = impressionCount + 1 " & _
            "WHERE imageURL = '" & strImageURL & "'"
    .Close
  End With
  DisplayRotatorAd = strAdRotatorHTML
End Function
%>
```

Statements in the first half of the script call the Ad Rotator object *GetAdvertisement* method to generate the HTML that will display the banner ad as a hyperlink on the Web page. The script parses the HTML returned by the Ad Rotator and extracts the URL of the image used in the banner ad. Next, the statements in the script's second half connect with a MySQL DBMS and update the graphic's impression count in the SQL *bannerAdStats* table.

Note the *DisplayRotatorAd()* function returns the output of the *adRotatorObject.GetAdvertisment* method call. Therefore, you must replace the *GetAdvertisement* method call in this Tip's first example script with the *DisplayRotatorAd()* function call as shown here:

```
<%
  SET adRotatorObj = Server.CreateObject("MSWC.AdRotator")
  Response.Write _
    DisplayRotatorAd(adRotatorObj, _
                     "/hwdtt/BannerAds/AdRotatorSchedule.asp")
%>
```

If you read the Tip that precedes this one, you already know the *GetAdvertisement* method call generates HTML similar to the following:

```
<a href="http://www.NVBizNet2.com/hwdtt/BannerAds/AdRedirect.asp?
    URL=http://www.NVBizNet.com/default.htm&
    image=/hwdtt/BannerAds/NVBizNet.GIF">
  <img src="/hwdtt/BannerAds/NVBizNet.GIF"
    alt="Visit NVBizNet for Web Page Design Tips"
    width="400" height="60" border="1"></a>
```

The specific HTML returned by the *GetAdvertisement* method call in your script will depend on the banner descriptions in your rotator schedule file. However, the *href* attribute within the <a> tag created will always point to the Ad Rotator redirection file. (You specify the URL of the Ad Rotator redirection file after the keyword *REDIRECT* in the first line within the Ad Rotator Schedule file.)

When the visitor clicks on the banner ad, the Web browser passes to the script within the redirection file a query string that names the banner ad's target page and the ad's image file pathname. In this example, the banner ad's target Web page is http://www.NVBizNet2.com/hwdtt/BannerAds/AdRedirect.asp, and the query string passed to the Active Server Page redirection file is *URL=http://www.NVBizNet.com/default.htm&image=/hwdtt/BannerAds/NVBizNet.GIF*.

A script within the rotator redirection file (AdRedirect.asp, in this example) is responsible for redirecting the Web browser to the banner ad's target page. Therefore, the redirection file is also a good place in which to update a banner ad's click-through statistic. To increment the click-through count for the banner ad that the visitor clicked, use code similar to the following within the Ad Rotator redirection file:

```
<%
  Dim objMySQLCon, strImageURL, strTargetURL

'parse the query string into two variables
  strImageURL = Request.QueryString("image")
  strTargetURL = Request.QueryString("URL")

'open a connection to the DBMS and increment the click-through
'count
  Set objMySQLCon = Server.CreateObject("ADODB.Connection")
  With objMySQLCon
    .ConnectionString = _
  "DRIVER={MySQL};SERVER=NVBizNet2;UID=root;PWD=;DATABASE=hwdtt"
    .Open
    .Execute "UPDATE bannerAdStats " & _
          "SET clickThroughCount = clickThroughCount + 1 " & _
          "WHERE imageURL = '" & strImageURL & "' " & _
          "AND   targetURL = '" & strTargetURL & "' "
    .Close
  End With
  Response.Redirect Request.QueryString("URL")
%>
```

The script in this example retrieves the banner ad target and graphics image URLs from the query string passed to the Active Server Page (AdRedirect.asp) in which the script resides. After updating the *bannerAdStats* table, the script closes the database connection and then calls the *Response.Redirect* method to redirect the Web browser to the banner ad's target.

▶ *NOTE*

In order for the SQL UPDATE statements in the scripts shown within this Tip to work, you must insert both the banner ad image URL and the ad's target URL into the SQL table in which you track the banner ad impressions and click-throughs (bannerAdStats, *in this example). Therefore, each time you add a banner description to the Ad Rotator schedule file, execute INSERT statements such as the following within the DBMS:*

```
INSERT INTO bannerAdStats VALUES
    (bannerRedirectionURL, bannerImageURL, 0, 0);
```

Substitute the name of your banner statistics table for *bannerAdStats* and replace *bannerRedirectionURL* with the URL of the banner ad's target Web page and *bannerImageURL* with the URL of the graphics image used for the banner ad.

For a description of the Ad Rotator schedule and redirection files, please read the Tip that precedes this one. You can retrieve the Active Server Page that displays the banner ad, the rotator schedule file, and the rotator redirection file used in the examples described within this Tip by downloading the file Chpt11Tip13.zip from the Osborne Web site at http://www.osborne.com.

Handling "Status: 404 Not Found" Errors

The Web server includes a status code within the header of each HTTP response it sends to a Web browser. The status code indicates the success or failure of the Web browser's request. Status codes in the range 200–299 indicate success; status codes in the range 400–499 indicate failure due to some error in the Web browser's request. For example, the Web server sends the status code "200" in the HTTP header when the browser's GET request (that is, the browser's Web page retrieval request) was successful. On the other hand, the Web server sends a status "404" in the HTTP message header to indicate the Web browser's GET request failed, because the Web server was unable to find the Web page the browser requested.

In addition to the status code 404, a Web server normally sends a generic and largely unhelpful Web page titled "HTTP 404 Not Found" when a site visitor mistypes a Web address or clicks on a hyperlink that targets a page or resource no longer available on the Web server. The default status 404 error page is not helpful because it is a dead-end. Text on the page tells the visitor the desired Web page was not found. However, the generic error page does not provide a search form or hyperlinks that help the visitor find and navigate to other resources on the Web site. Fortunately, developers are starting to customize Web server "Status: 404 Not Found" Web pages to make them more visitor-friendly.

A good error page (if there is such a thing as a "good" error) has the following characteristics:

- The page acknowledges that an error has occurred and explains the problem in terms the visitor can understand.

- The page includes an apology that the error occurred—even when the error is due to a visitor mistyping a Web address.

- The page includes links to the site's search page and links to the site's most popular resources.

For examples of custom error pages currently available on the Web, visit the following Web addresses to display status 404 error pages with the following features:

- **http://www.microsoft.com/InvalidURL**   A site map, drop-down selection lists of hyperlinks to product, support, and general information areas on the Web site, and a search form

- **http://www.yahoo.com/InvalidURL**   Links to the site's roster of products, buttons on which a visitor can click to move to popular areas (such as auctions, messenger, e-mail, and so on), and a search form

- **http://www.4guysfromrolla.com/InvalidURL**   A site index, links to the site's resources (organized by section, columnist, and type of information), links to the site's most viewed pages, a search form, and even a link to a Web page that tells you how to create your own custom status 404 error page

USE IT   To replace the generic status 404 "The page cannot be found" error page, you must do two things: create a custom error page and instruct the Web server to send your page rather than the Web server's default error page. For example, you might use an Active Server Page such as the following to display a custom status 404 error page like the one shown in Figure 11-8:

```
<% Option Explicit
  Function BadUrl()
    Dim objEMail, strBadURL
    strBadURL = _
      Right(Request.QueryString, Len(Request.QueryString) - 4)
    Set objEMail = Server.CreateObject("CDONTS.NewMail")
    objEmail.To = "kki@NVBizNet.com"
    objEmail.From = "Error404.asp@NVBizNet2.com"
    objEmail.Subject = "Error 404 Occurred on NVBizNet2.com"
    objEmail.Body = _
      "An Error 404 (File Not Found) Error Occurred at " & _
      Now() & ". The missing page is: " & strBadURL & ". " & _
      "The visitor used a hyperlink on -->" & _
      Request.ServerVariables("HTTP_REFERRER") & _
      "<-- to retrieve the page."
    objEMail.Send
    BadURL = strBadURL
```

```
   End Function
%>
<!DOCTYPE HTML PUBLIC "-//W3C//DTD HTML 4.0//EN">
<html>
<head><title>NVBizNet2 - Web Page Not Found</title></head>
<body bgcolor="#ADD8E6">
  <h1><center>HTML and Web Design Tips & Techniques</center>
  </h1><hr><center><h2>Web Page Not Found</h2></center><br>
<%
  Response.write "<p><b>Sorry, the document you requested " & _
    "(" & BadURL & ") was not found on NVBizNet2.com.</b><br>"
%>
  Perhaps you typed the address incorrectly, or the page you
  want was moved to a new location.</p>
  <p>When you reached this page, the Webmaster
  <a title="Send an E-Mail Message to the Webmaster"
    href="mailto:kki@NVBizNet.com?
      subject=Status 404 - Page Not Found on NVBizNet2.com">
    (Konrad King - kki@NVBizNet.com)</a> was sent an automated
  e-mail to let him know the site has a missing document. He
  will correct the situation shortly.</p>
  <p>Perhaps one of the following links can assist you in
  finding the document you want or take you to another page you
  will find useful:
  <ul>
    <li><a href="http://www.NVBizNet.com">NVBizNet.com</a></li>
    <li><a href="/">NVBizNet2.com (Homepage)</a></li>
    <li><a href="http://nvbiznet.com/HWDTT/HTML&WDTT_TOC.htm">
      Site Map</a></li>
    <!-- links to other pages of interest -->
  </ul></p>
  <p>Or... enter one or more keywords to search the site for
  the page you want:<br>
  <form method="POST" action="\Search\SearchPage.asp">
    <input type="submit" value="Search" name="Search">
    <input type="text" name="keywords" size="30">
  </form></p>
</body>
</html>
```

In addition to providing content for the site visitor, the *BadURL()* function at the beginning of the Active Server Page in this example sends an e-mail message to the site's Web master. The *BadURL()* function uses the CDONTS e-mail component (which comes with the Internet Information Server [IIS]) to send a message that indicates when the error occurred, the URL the visitor was trying to

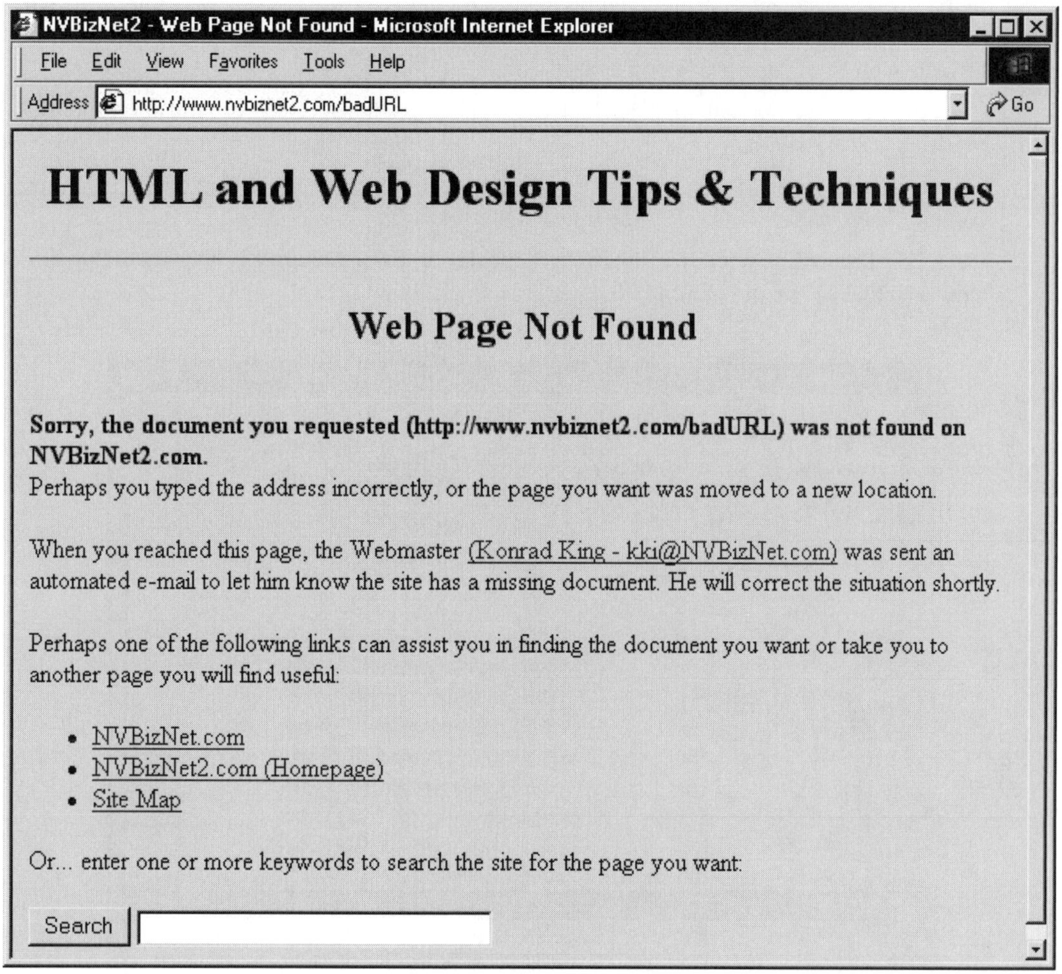

Figure 11-8   Custom status 404 error page

retrieve, and the URL of the Web page with the hyperlink that referred the visitor to the "missing" page. After creating the Active Server Page with the code in the previous example, save the new error page to a filename such as Error404.asp either within the Web site's root folder or within a subfolder.

Next, modify the Web server's setup to have the Web server send your Active Server Page to the Web browser when the server detects a status 404 error. For example, to have IIS version 4 or version 5 send a custom status 404 error page, perform the following steps:

1. Choose Start | Programs | Microsoft Internet Information Server | Internet Service Manager. Windows NT, in turn, will display the IIS Management Console.

2. In the IIS Management Console's right-hand pane, right-click the Default Web Site icon, and select Properties from the pop-up menu. The Management Console, in turn, will display the Default Web Site Properties dialog box.

3. Click the Custom Errors tab to display a list of Web pages the Web server sends in response to various error statuses.

4. Use the vertical scroll bar to scroll the list of error pages until you see 404 in the HTTP Error column. Then, click 404 to select the status 404 error page.

5. Click Edit Properties. Windows, in turn, will display an Error Mapping Properties dialog box similar to that shown in Figure 11-9.

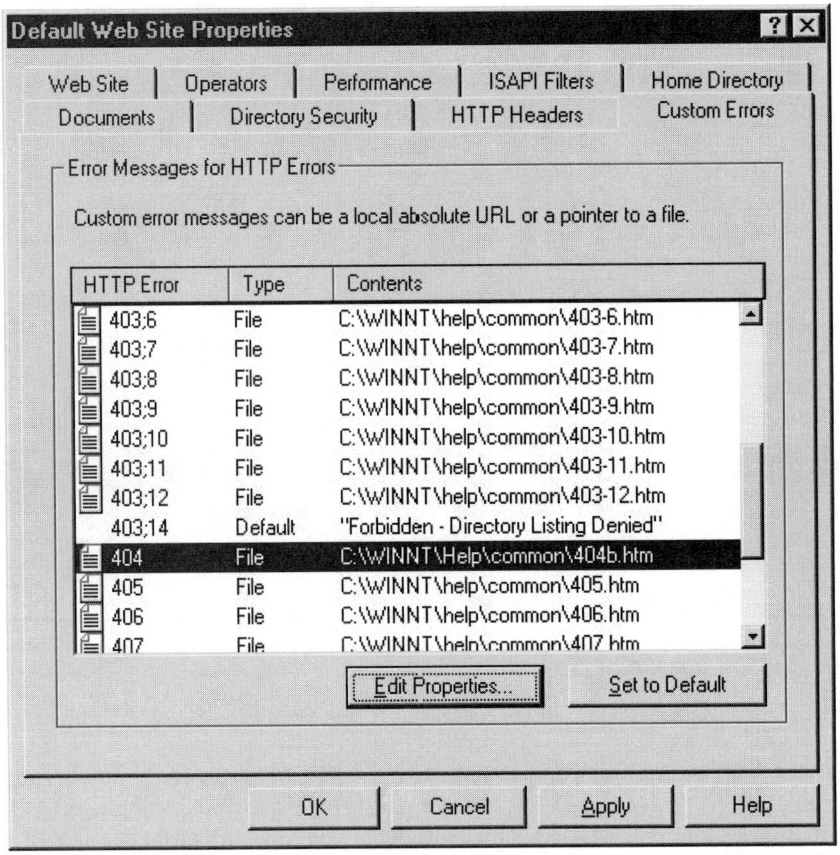

Figure 11-9 The Internet Information Server (IIS) Error Mapping Properties dialog box

6. Click the drop-down list button to the right of the Message Type field and select URL. Windows, in turn, will change the label of the field below Message Type from File to URL.

7. Into the URL field, type the full relative address of the custom status 404 error page you want the Web server to use. For example, if you saved the error page you created earlier in this Tip to the file Error404.asp in the Web site's root directory, type **/Error404.asp** into the URL field.

8. Click OK at the bottom of the Error Mapping Properties dialog box. Windows, in turn, will save your changes, close the dialog box, and return to the Default Web Site Properties dialog box.

9. Click OK at the bottom of the Default Web Site Properties dialog box. Windows, in turn, will return to the IIS Management Console application window.

After you complete Step 9, click the Close button in the upper right-hand corner of the IIS Management Console application window to exit (close) the application and return to the Windows desktop.

CHAPTER 12

Security and Performance

TIPS IN THIS CHAPTER

▶ Downloading and Installing a Public Key, Digital Signature, and Server ID   600

▶ Creating a Secure Web Page Under IIS   601

▶ Installing a Software-Based Firewall   603

▶ Fine-Tuning a Firewall's Port Assignments   605

▶ Reducing Your Site's Exposure to Viruses   607

▶ Improving Performance and Security by Disabling Printer and File Sharing   610

▶ Using Client Certificates to Restrict User Access   612

▶ Auditing System Events to Detect Intruders   614

▶ Exploiting the NTFS File System   617

▶ Disabling Remote Services   620

▶ Analyzing Your System's Vulnerability   623

▶ Processing Credit Card Data   625

▶ Taking a Close Look at Web Site's Performance Chain   625

▶ Creating a Web Farm   631

▶ Monitoring Server Performance   631

Throughout this book, you have examined a wide variety of tools you can use to create powerful Web sites. In this chapter, you will first focus on protecting your Web site. Specifically, you will learn steps you can perform to defend your site against the most common hacker attacks and how to protect user transactions using secure pages. You will learn, for example, how to create secure pages, which direct a browser and server to exchange encrypted messages using the secure sockets layer. You will also learn how to install and configure a firewall that filters the network messages that can enter your site. Further, you will learn how to use audit trails and intrusion detection to discover potential hacker attacks.

Then you will look at ways you can improve your Web site's performance by eliminating bottlenecks that slow down the operations your site performs. You will examine a Web server's performance chain, which begins with the server's connection to the Web and continues through the server's use of random access memory (RAM), fast disk drives, caching, and more. In short, this chapter shows you how to put the finishing touches on a professional-quality Web site.

Understanding Hacker Threats

After your site is up and running, hackers may attack it in numerous ways:

- By intercepting, viewing, and possibly modifying the HTTP-based messages your server exchanges with client browsers.

- By accessing files that reside on your server that may contain sensitive information such as customer credit card data.

- By launching thousands of requests at your server that consume your site's resources and prevent your site from responding to other visitors.

- By infecting your files, disks, or e-mail messages that enter your site with a computer virus.

- By breaking CGI-based scripts to gain access to your server.

This chapter examines specific ways you can reduce your site's risks to each of these types of attack.

Understanding How Hackers Intercept and Possibly Change Network Messages

When programs send information across the Internet to a remote computer, the messages do not simply travel directly from the sending computer to the message recipient. Instead, as shown in Figure 12-1, to reach a remote computer, a message passes through numerous sites on the Net.

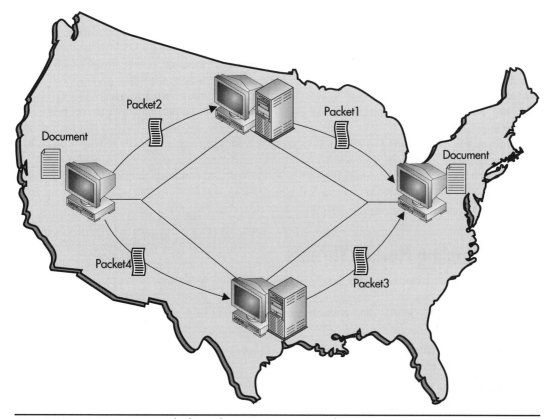

Figure 12-1   A message travels through many sites as it makes its way across the Net

To better understand how messages hop from one system to another as they travel across the Net, issue the *tracert* command (the command's name is an abbreviation for trace route), which displays a list of the sites through which a message travels as it makes its way to a remote site. The following output, for example, illustrates the path a message traveled from the author's PC to reach yahoo.com:

```
C:\> tracert  yahoo.com  <Enter>

Tracing route to yahoo.com [216.115.108.243]
over a maximum of 30 hops:

1   179ms 200ms 200ms   arc-4a.hou.mindspring.net [207.69.219.84]
2   170ms 190ms 200ms   cisco-f0-1-0.hou.mindspring.net [207.69.219.65]
3   190ms 200ms 200ms   206.181.103.185
4   199ms 180ms 180ms   iah2-core1-s3-1.atlas.icix.net [165.117.64.250]
5   169ms 200ms 190ms   dfw3-core3-pos4-3.atlas.icix.net [165.117.50.85]
6   179ms 178ms 197ms   165.117.52.198
7   295ms 189ms 199ms   so-4-1-0.mp2.Dallas1.Level3.net [209.247.10.109]
```

```
8   205ms 210ms 239ms   so-2-0-0.mp1.SanJose1.Level3.net [209.247.9.114]
9   239ms 210ms 240ms   gige9-2.ipcolo4.SanJose1.Level3.net [64.159.2.138]
10  232ms 210ms 240ms   ge-3-3-0.msr1.pao.yahoo.com [216.115.101.42]
11  229ms 239ms 220ms   vlan29.bas2-m.snv.yahoo.com [216.115.100.126]
12  210ms 250ms 250ms   yahoo.com [216.115.108.243]
```

Trace complete.

In this case, to reach yahoo.com, a message had to pass through 11 intermediate sites. Each time a message arrives at a site, that system's network software examines the message to determine whether the message is destined for that site. If so, the network software sends the message to the appropriate program, such as an e-mail application or Web server. If the message is not destined for that site, the network software forwards the message to another host that puts the message closer to its destination.

At any point during a message's travels, a hacker whose system the message travels past can read and change the message contents. Assume, for example, that the message contains credit card information. As the message flows through the hacker's system, the hacker can read and store (steal) the credit card data, as shown in Figure 12-2.

In Chapter 3, when you examined HTML-based forms, you learned that when a user submits a form's contents, behind the scenes the browser sends the form's data to the server using the HTTP protocol. Unfortunately, HTTP passes messages using plain text, which means that it is very easy for a hacker to view a message's contents. To better understand how a hacker can intercept and view message packets, download and install the CommView program from http://www.webattack.com/get/commview.shtml. Using CommView, you can view the contents of a wide range of message types that enter your system. Figure 12-3, for example, illustrates the contents of an HTTP message within the CommView utility.

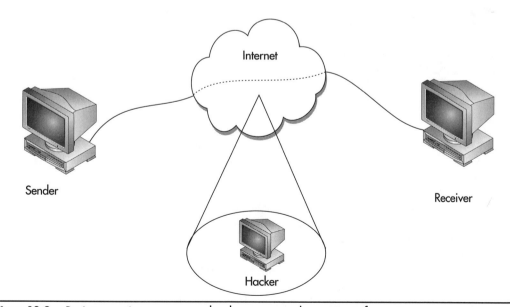

Figure 12-2   By intercepting messages, hackers can steal sensitive information

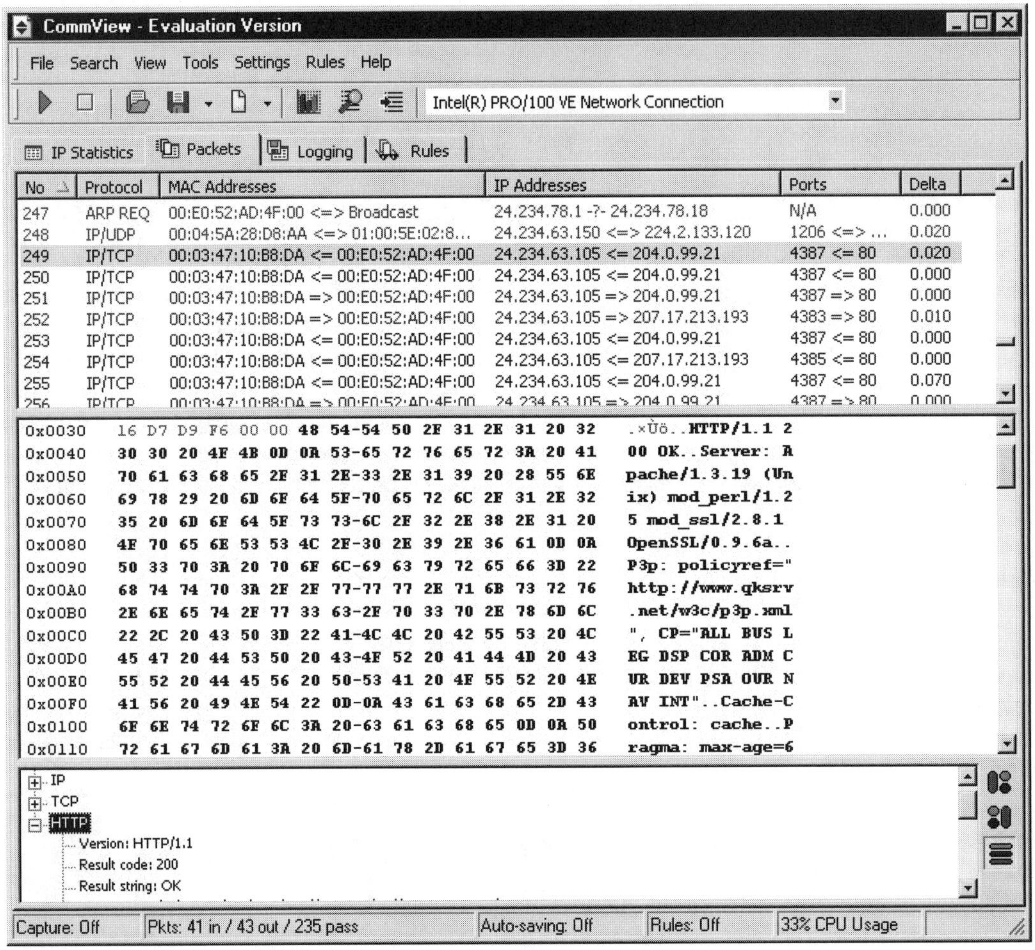

Figure 12-3 Using the CommView program to view HTTP messages

A hacker can use a program similar to CommView to monitor the messages that arrive at his or her computer. Because the number of messages passing through the hacker's system can be quite large, a sophisticated hacker might use a program that scans the messages for data that takes the form of a credit card number, expiration date, and so on.

In addition to viewing the information a message contains, a hacker can change the contents of the messages he or she intercepts. For example, assume that a hacker intercepts a message that contains a purchase order. The hacker might, as shown in Figure 12-4, change the order quantity and ship-to address, so that he or she also receives goods as a part of your order.

To protect your site's messages from interception and modification by a hacker in this way, you can use encryption and secure Web pages, as discussed later in the section "Understanding How Encryption Protects Messages You Send Across the Net."

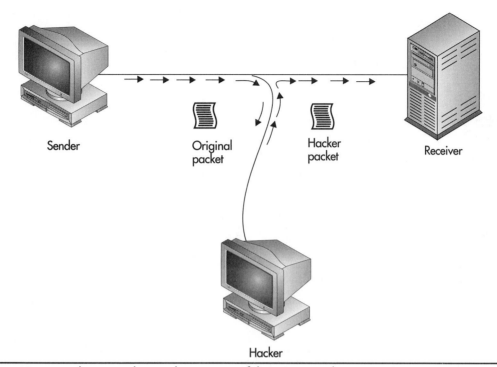

Sender   Original   Hacker   Receiver
          packet   packet

Hacker

Figure 12-4   Hackers can change the contents of the messages they intercept

Understanding How Hackers Break into a System

Across the Internet, many systems let users log into the network from remote locations. A company might, for example, let its salespeople log onto the company's network when they travel, so they can view, create, or update order information or simply access their e-mail. Likewise, a system might let programmers, Web developers, and other users connect from remote locations to upload or download files. Depending on the system's configuration, users may, as shown in Figure 12-5, gain remote access to the system using a dial-up modem or the Internet. When a system is available for remote access, hackers may exploit the remote access programs and services to break into the network.

To break into a network using remote access, a hacker normally must specify a valid username and password. Unfortunately, a hacker may gain access to valid usernames and passwords using a number of techniques:

- Using a password cracking program that attacks the system's password file.
- Targeting common default accounts for which the network administrators have not changed the password.
- Simply asking a user who has a valid account for his or her username and password.

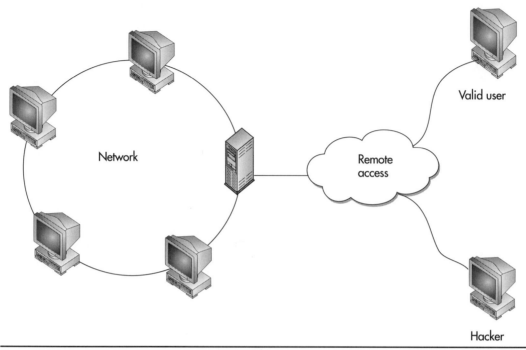

Figure 12-5 Remote access provides users (and hackers) who are not physically connected to the network a way to access network resources

If your site does not require remote access, you should disable the remote services as discussed in this chapter's Tip, "Disabling Remote Services."

Understanding Password Cracking Software

Password cracking is a technique hackers use to gain access to systems that are protected by usernames and passwords. Television shows and movies often portray hackers as magnificent guessers who can quickly break into a system simply by guessing a username and password. Fortunately, the process is not quite that easy. Today, many operating systems have the ability to lock out an account after a user fails to give a correct username/password pair a specific number of tries. For example, assume that a hacker learns your username and tries to log into the system by guessing your password. If the hacker guesses five incorrect passwords, the operating system would likely lock your account, so that neither you nor the hacker can use your account until your system administrator unlocks it. Although being locked out of your own account in this way can be inconvenient, it will make you aware of the fact that someone is trying to gain access to your account.

Years ago, before operating systems disabled accounts after a number of failed logins, hackers would run special programs called password crackers that repeatedly entered username and password combinations. Using the password cracker, the hacker could try thousands of different username/password combinations in a matter of minutes.

Most operating systems store user account information (which includes usernames and passwords) within a file. To prevent users from viewing the password information, the operating system normally encrypts the file. Unfortunately, on the Web you can download a variety of programs that decrypt and display passwords within a Unix/Linux system, a Windows NT system, and even Windows 2000. The best way to protect these files is to protect the administrator accounts on your system.

Normally, a hacker will first try to access a site's administrator accounts. To make it more difficult for hackers to attack the administrator accounts, many sites assign less meaningful names to the accounts, rather than using usernames such as NetworkAdmin and RemoteAdmin. This means that the hacker will need to search harder to obtain access to the key accounts, which may, in and of itself, be enough to convince the hacker to move on to an easier site.

Protecting Default Accounts

When you first install an operating system or large application program (such as a database management system), the software normally provides several default accounts that you can use to perform the installation, test system settings, and so on. Unfortunately, many users fail to disable these default accounts after installing the application. Many hackers break into systems across the Internet simply by using default accounts that have not been disabled.

If you are a system administrator, take time now to examine your site's list of accounts. Make sure to change the password for all default accounts and, better yet, disable the default accounts you do not need. As you examine the list of accounts, make sure you can readily identify each account's purpose. Further, you can often improve your site's security by restricting many user accounts to access during working hours only.

Understanding Social-Engineering Attacks

One of the easiest ways for hackers to gain access to a system is simply for the hacker to ask a user for his or her username and password. Network administrators refer to such hacker attacks as social-engineering attacks. Often, the hacker may call an unsuspecting user and use a dialog similar to the following to gain access to a site:

Hacker: *Good morning. This is Konrad in the data processing department. Later today, you will receive an e-mail message that states that as a part of our network security initiative, we want all users to change their passwords tomorrow morning at 8:30.*

User: *Okay.*

Hacker: *To monitor the process, I need to record your current username and password.*

User: *Okay.*

Hacker: *Let me have your username first.*

User: *Smith.*

Hacker: *Can you spell out your password for me?*

User: *Yes. It is t-o-o-b-u-s-y.*
Hacker: *Great. Make a note to change your password tomorrow morning.*

After the hacker gains access to a username and password, the hacker can access the system. To protect your site from such attacks, you must train your users never to divulge their account information. Let them know that your data processing department will never ask them for such information, and that they should never tell another individual, even an employee, their username and password.

Understanding How Hackers Deny Access to Your System

When a hacker is unable to break into your site, the hacker may try to prevent others from accessing your system by performing a denial-of-service attack, which consumes your system's resources, either in part (which slows down your site) or in total (which prevents visitor access). A few years ago, for example, hackers shut down the Whitehouse e-mail services by bombarding the e-mail address with tens of thousands of large e-mail messages. Although the hackers themselves were not able to break into the Whitehouse site, their actions denied the site's service to others.

The following simple HTML file, ReloadForever.html, uses a <meta> tag to direct the browser to download a large graphics file from the site www.SomeVictim.com every 30 seconds. By disabling caching, the HTML file forces the Web server to send the requested Web page content every 30 seconds. While the server is responding to this request, it cannot service others. A hacker might, for example, open 10 or more browser windows within which he or she loads the ReloadForever.html page. The greater the number of windows in which the hacker opens this simple file, the more the hacker reduces the server's ability to serve others.

```
<html>
<meta http-equiv="Refresh" content="30" />
<img src="http://www.SomeVictim.com/LargeImageFile.jpg" />
</html>
```

To protect your site from such denial-of-service attacks, you can use a firewall, which watches for repetitive HTTP requests or similar repeated requests. Additionally, you can examine your site's log files. In this chapter's Tips, you will learn how to install and configure a firewall and how to enable and monitor your system's log files.

Understanding How Hackers Attack CGI Scripts

In Chapter 3, you learned how to create HTML-based forms that visitors can complete and submit to an application that runs on the Web server. Normally, programmers create the applications the server runs to process the forms using a programming language such as Perl or PHP. For years, hackers have targeted CGI scripts to break into Web sites. That's because often the script programs that run on the Web server have the ability to access data stored on the server's hard drive. Depending on the processing a script performs, a hacker may be able to (mis)use the script by running it with values that the hacker assigns from outside the form submission process. Further, if the hacker can access the Web server's hard drive, the hacker may be able to replace the script file with one of his or her own. Depending on the processing the hacker's new script performs, it could take considerable time for the site's administrators to detect the change. The hacker's script, for example, might simply add a line that e-mails a copy of all credit card information to the hacker's e-mail account.

As you read about hacker threats, you will encounter discussions of buffer overflow attacks, which let the hacker break out of the script to gain access to the server in such a way that the hacker can then run any program installed on the server! In Chapter 3, when you created HTML-based forms, you created text fields, for example, that let the user type a specific number of characters. A buffer overflow occurs when a user (not necessarily a hacker) submits more data than the script expects to store. For example, assume that an HTML form lets a user submit a street address that contains up to 128 characters. However, due to a programming error, the script provides space for only 64 characters for the street address. Because most street addresses visitors enter require less than 64 characters, the script may run for a long time, with no problems. However, when a visitor eventually enters more than 64 characters, the script will cause a buffer overflow error.

The problem with buffer overflow errors is that some scripting languages (normally a compiled program) cause the script processor (that is, the program that executes the script's statements on the server) to fail. Depending on the operating system the server is running, such errors can provide the hacker with access to the server and the files it contains. To exploit buffer overflow errors, a hacker first causes the script processor to fail. Then, after the hacker gains access to the server, the hacker can copy or delete files or run other programs that reside on the server.

As you have learned, as messages travel across the Internet, a hacker can intercept and possibly change the message contents. If the hacker is aware that a server is running an operating system and script processor that is susceptible to buffer overflow errors, the hacker might intercept a valid message destined for the site and then change the message contents so that the data causes a buffer overflow error.

Over the years, operating system developers, script processor developers, and programmers who create Web scripts have become aware of the risks of buffer overflow errors. Most newer applications, therefore, do not fail after a buffer overflow error in such a way that a hacker can gain control of the server. To better understand the dangers of buffer overflow errors, visit the CERT Web site at http://www.cert.org and search for known buffer overflow vulnerabilities (see Figure 12-6). Using the CERT Web site, you can also search for known vulnerabilities on other software you use, such as PHP, ActiveX, Active Server Pages, IIS, and more.

Understanding How Firewalls Protect Your Site

To protect a network from hacker attacks, many network administrators place a firewall between the Internet and the network. The firewall filters the network messages that pass from the Internet into the network. Do not confuse network messages with e-mail messages. Network messages correspond to the data that programs such as Web browsers and chat programs send from one computer to another.

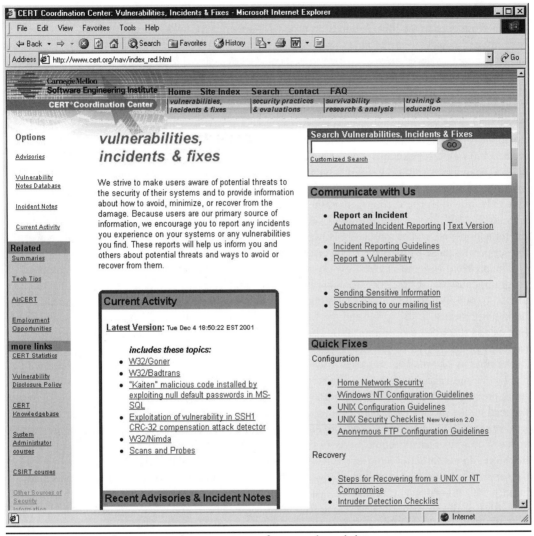

Figure 12-6 Using the CERT Web site to view software vulnerabilities

A firewall can be a special hardware box or a PC running firewall software. Figure 12-7 shows how a firewall filters the messages that arrive at a network.

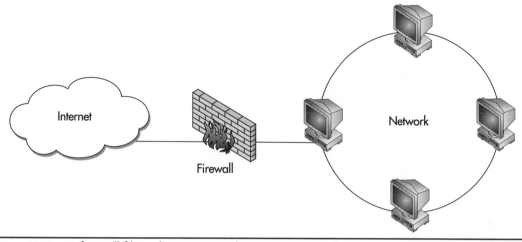

Figure 12-7   A firewall filters the messages that enter a network

In this case, the firewall allows only HTTP-based messages sent from a remote browser to enter the network. The firewall prevents messages from applications such as chat programs or file transfer programs (like FTP) from entering the network. In the Tip "Installing a Software-Based Firewall," you will learn how to install and configure a firewall to secure your Web site.

Understanding How Encryption Protects Messages You Send Across the Net

As you have learned, when messages travel across the Net, a hacker can intercept, view, and possibly change their contents. Unfortunately, it is impossible to prevent hackers from intercepting messages that travel past the hacker's computer. However, by encrypting the messages that you send, you prevent the hacker from viewing information within the messages and from being able to change the messages in a meaningful way.

To exchange encrypted messages, two programs, such as the browser and the server programs, must first agree on the encryption algorithm they will use to encrypt the messages. Assume, for example, that the browser and server encrypt data by increasing or decreasing letters by one letter. For example, the programs might encrypt the letters ABC as BCD by increasing each letter by one, or the letters ZYX would become YXW by decreasing each letter by one. After the browser and server determine which method they will use (in this case, increasing or decreasing letters), they must agree on the count by which they will increase or decrease the characters. You can think of the count they agree on as the encryption key. For example, the browser and server might decide to use the method that increases letters and then decide to increase each letter by 2, so that the letters ABC become CDE.

Obviously, encryption algorithms on the Web involve much more than simply shifting letters up or down. However, the process the programs use to determine the algorithm and choose a key is similar to that just discussed. When a Web browser initiates a secure transaction on the Web, the browser first sends the server a list of the encryption algorithms that the browser supports. The server, in turn, examines the list and selects an algorithm that both it and the browser support and then sends a message to the browser that specifies the selected algorithm. However, before the two programs can use the algorithm to encrypt messages, the programs must agree on an encryption key.

Assume, for example, that the server, when it sends the message that contains the encryption algorithm the programs will use, also includes the key that the two will use to encrypt and decrypt messages. Because the server cannot encrypt the message until the browser knows the encryption key, the server would need to send the message in the clear—that is, unencrypted. If a hacker intercepts the message, the hacker will know not only the encryption algorithm, but also the encryption key, which means that the hacker could later intercept and decrypt the encrypted messages that the browser and server exchange. To prevent the hacker from intercepting the encryption key and algorithm, the server uses a special encryption key—the server's public encryption key—to encrypt the key value that browser and server will later use when encrypting messages they exchange during the secure session. This means that before a client and server can start a secure session, the Web server must have a public key (as discussed in the next session) that it can send to the Web browser.

Understanding Public Key Encryption

Today, to send encrypted e-mail messages or to establish secure Web site connections, users make extensive use of public key encryption. To receive encrypted messages, a user gets two special keys: a private key that the user protects and a public key that the user can freely distribute to everyone in the world.

Assume, for example, that you want to send an encrypted e-mail message to George Bush. To do so, you must know his public key, which he may have sent to you in a previous message, or which he may have placed on a public key server (which is accessible to any user). Using George Bush's public key, you would encrypt your message. Later, when he receives your message, he would decrypt it using his private key. In other words, to send you an encrypted message, a user encrypts the message using your public key. When you receive the message, you decrypt it using your private key.

The public key encryption scheme is unique in that anyone can have your public key. The only thing a user can do with your public key is encrypt messages that you can later decrypt using your private key. Your public key is different from your private key. A user, for example, cannot use your public key to decrypt messages that other users send to you.

Finding a User's Public Key

In the Tip "Downloading and Installing a Public Key, Digital Signature, and Server ID" you will learn how to download and install your own encryption keys and digital signature. A digital signature is a unique value that you can attach, for example, to your e-mail messages to authenticate you to the recipient (so that the recipient knows that you actually sent the message) and validate that a hacker has not intercepted the message and changed its contents as it made its way across the Net.

Normally, after you receive your own public key, you send it to your associates, friends, and family via an e-mail message, so they can use the key to encrypt the messages they send to you. In addition, you can post your public key on a public key ring that resides on the Web. When a user to whom you have not sent your public key needs to encrypt a message to send to you, the user can search the public key servers for your key. Figure 12-8 shows a public key server at MIT that you can use to search for a user's public key.

After the user locates your key, the user can use it to the encrypt messages he or she sends to you.

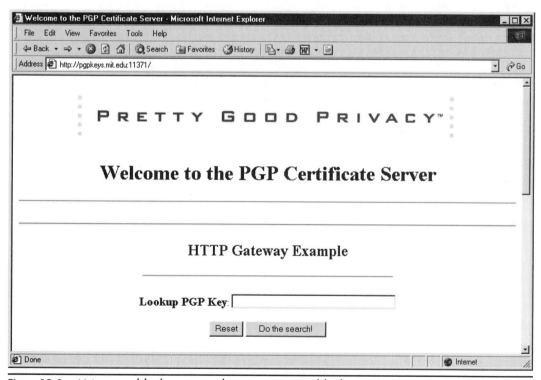

Figure 12-8   Using a public key ring to locate a user's public key

Downloading and Installing a Public Key, Digital Signature, and Server ID

Before a user can send you encrypted e-mail, you must get your own public and private encryption keys. There are several ways for you to get your own public and private encryption keys. The VeriSign Web site, http://www.verisign.com, lets you download a trial set (valid for 60 days) of public and private keys, or you can simply purchase the encryption keys from the site. The download instructions you receive from VeriSign list the steps you must follow to begin using your keys. In addition, from the M.I.T. Web site at http://web.mit.edu/network/pgp.html, you can download software for free if you plan to use PGP (Pretty Good Privacy) encryption. Using either key type, users can use your public key to send you encrypted messages that you can later decrypt using your private key. Both Web sites provide instructions that walk you through the steps for sending and receiving encrypted e-mail messages.

Similarly, before your Web server can perform secure operations, you must install a digital certificate (also called a secure server ID) for use by your Web server software. After you enable the certificate and your site's secure communications, users can request secure pages from your site by preceding your site's Web address with the https:// prefix (note the *s* in the prefix, which indicates a secure connection).

Several companies, which users refer to as Certification Authorities, offer Web server IDs over the Internet. In general, after investigating your company, the Certification Authority issues a server ID that vouches for your right to use your company name and Web address. Normally, before a Certification Authority issues a server ID, it reviews your company's credentials, such as your Dun & Bradstreet number and articles of incorporation. After the Certification Authority authenticates your company, it issues you a server ID that you can use to enable secure transactions on your Web site. Depending on the level of investigation that the Certification Authority performs, it can take several weeks (or more) for you to receive a server ID for your organization.

Normally, when you connect to a secure Web page, you can view the site's server ID (certificate) from within your browser, as shown in Figure 12-9.

Across the Web, you can download a digital certificate from several different Certification Authorities. Before you purchase a server ID, make sure that the certificate type is compatible with your server software. Most server ID certificates support the secure socket layer (SSL), which is the protocol most Web servers use to implement secure operations.

USE IT To get you started, VeriSign offers a trial server ID that you can download, install, and use for a 14-day period. You can use the trial server ID to prepare your software as you wait for the Certification Authority to issue your company's permanent server ID, or if you are simply interested in learning how to create secure Web sites, you can download and install the trial server ID and use it for 14 days. Further, VeriSign will tell you how to set up the server ID for use with your particular server software. To download the trial server ID, visit VeriSign at http://www.verisign.com.

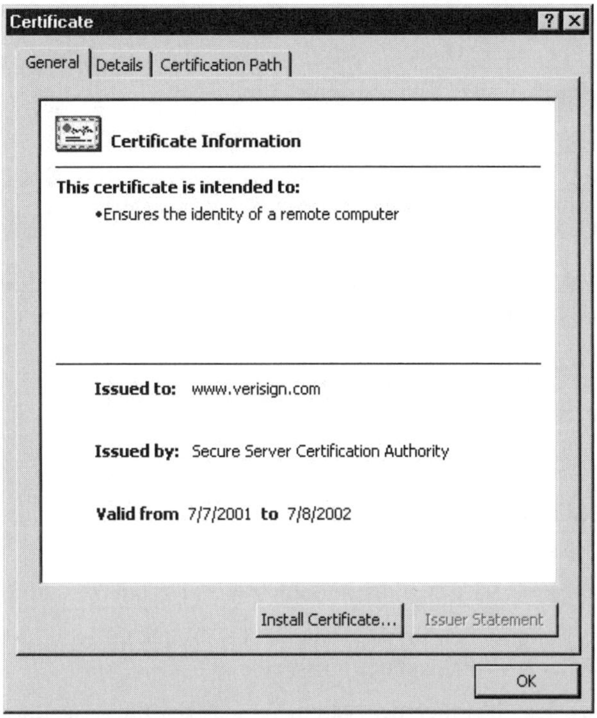

Figure 12-9   Viewing a site's digital certificate within a Web browser

Creating a Secure Web Page Under IIS

When you download and install a server ID, as discussed in the preceding Tips, you normally will receive step-by-step instructions you must follow to use the ID with your particular server type. To help you better understand the process, this Tip examines the steps you must perform to use a server ID with IIS.

USE IT   After you download a server ID from a Certification Authority, you must install the ID on your server and then enable the secure communication capabilities built into IIS. To start, you will use the Web Server Certificate Wizard to install the server certificate file for use on your Web site. To run the Web Server Certificate Wizard, perform these steps:

1. Choose Start | Settings | Control Panel. Windows will display the Control Panel.

2. Within the Control Panel, double-click the Administrative Tools icon. Windows will open the Administrative Tools window.

3. Within the Administrative Tools window, double-click the Internet Services Manager.

4. Within the Internet Services Manager, right-click the Web site you want to secure. Internet Services Manager will display a pop-up menu.

5. Within the menu, select the Properties option. Internet Services Manager will display the site's Properties dialog box.

6. Within the Properties dialog box, select the Directory Security tab. Windows will display the Directory Security sheet.

7. Within the Server Communications section of the Directory Security sheet, click the Server Certificate button. Internet Services Manager will start the Web Server Certificate Wizard.

After you install the certificate, you must enable your server's secure communication capabilities by performing these steps:

1. Choose Start | Settings | Control Panel. Windows will display the Control Panel.

2. Within the Control Panel, double-click the Administrative Tools icon. Windows will open the Administrative Tools window.

3. Within the Administrative Tools window, double-click the Internet Services Manager.

4. Within the Internet Information Services snap-in, right-click the icon for the Web site you want to secure. Windows will display a pop-up menu.

5. Within the menu, select the Properties option. Windows will display the site's Properties dialog box.

6. Within the Properties dialog box, click the Advanced button. Windows will display the Advanced Multiple Web Site Configuration dialog box.

7. Within the Advanced Multiple Web Site Configuration dialog box, make sure that the Multiple SSL Identities of This Web Site pane contains the port value 443.

8. Click the Directory Security tab. Windows will display the Directory Security Sheet.

9. Within the Directory Security sheet, click the Secure Communications Edit button. Windows will display the Secure Communications dialog box, shown in Figure 12-10.

10. Within the Secure Communications dialog box, configure your Web server to require a secure channel by selecting the Require Secure Channel (SSL) check box. Optionally, select the Require 128-Bit Encryption check box to force the secure connection to use 128-bit encryption. (Not all browsers support 128-bit encryption. If you do not select 128-bit encryption, your server will use 40-bit.)

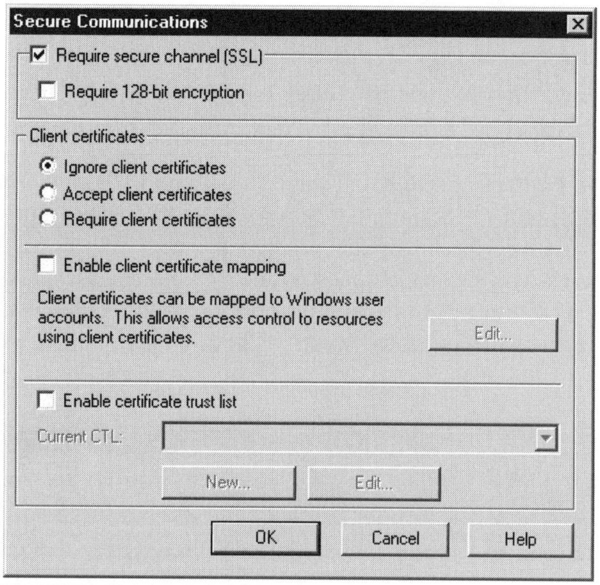

Figure 12-10   The Secure Communications dialog box

Installing a Software-Based Firewall

A firewall protects a site by sitting between the site and the rest of the Internet. All network messages destined for the site must first pass through the firewall. By configuring the firewall's message filters, you can control which messages can and cannot enter the site. A firewall can be hardware or software based. On the Web, several companies offer trial firewall software that you can download and try for free; normally, the trial software lets you use the firewall for a 30-day period:

McAfee	http://www.mcafee.com
Network Ice	http://www.networkice.com
Symantec	http://www.symantec.com
Tiny Software	http://www.tinysoftware.com
Zone Labs	http://www.zonelabs.com

If you are the administrator for a professional site that does not yet use a firewall, you should immediately download and install several different trial versions to better understand the features you need and how to use them. Take time to experiment with the firewall. For example, you might want to use the firewall to disable incoming FTP packets that a remote user generates by running an FTP program to upload or download files to or from your site. However, if you disable FTP packets and then try using FTP to connect to your site, the FTP command will fail.

USE IT Many network administrators install and configure firewalls on the Web sites they manage and leave their home PC exposed to hackers. Recently many software companies have begun to offer personal firewalls for home users. Using a personal firewall, you can close up potential holes a hacker can exploit as you visit remote sites on the Web. Several sites that sell personal firewalls on the Web will let you run software that examines your PC for vulnerabilities. For example, Figure 12-11 shows the output generated by the Symantec Security Check program, which you can run from the Symantec Web site.

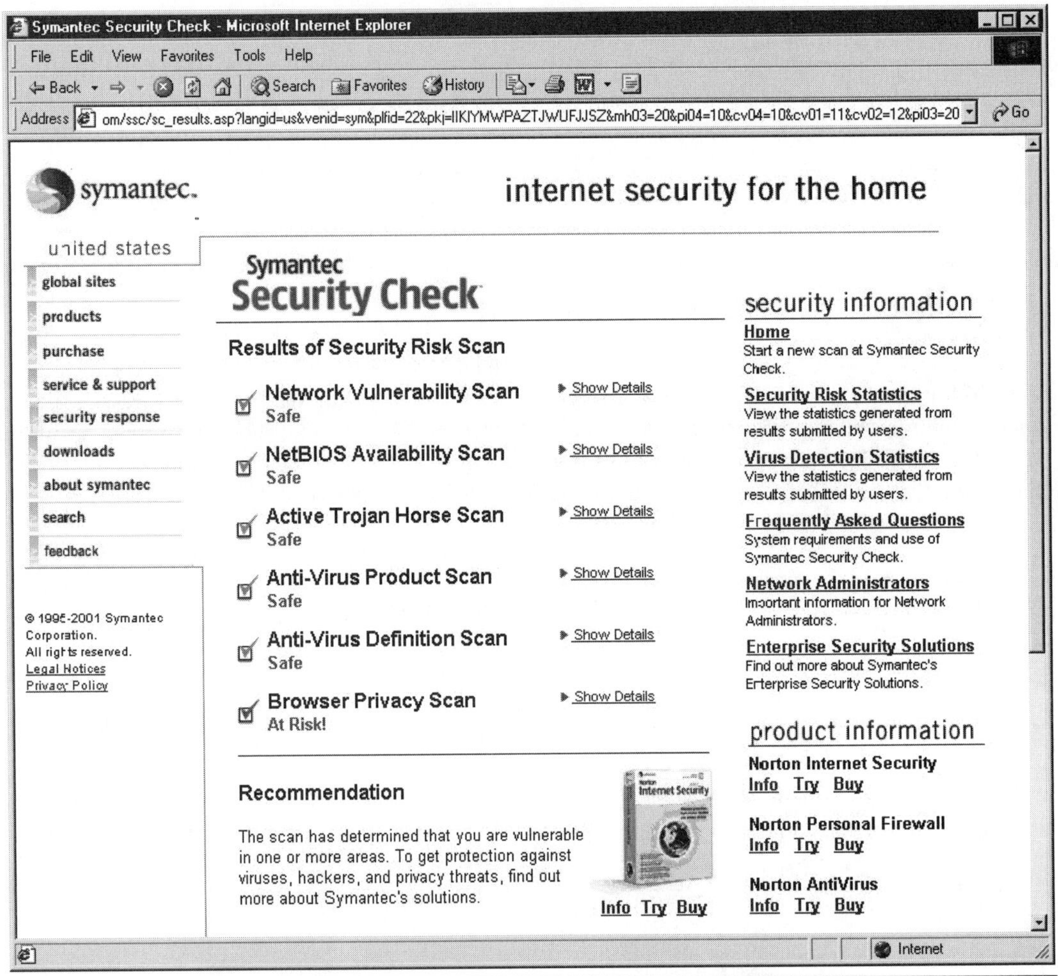

Figure 12-11 Testing your system vulnerabilities from the Symantec Web site

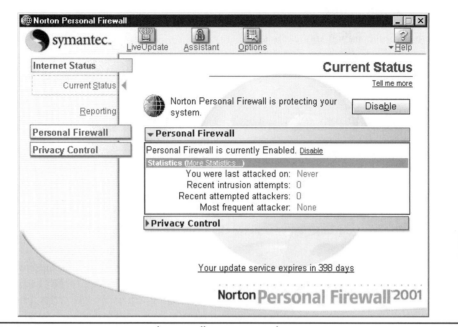

Figure 12-12   Using Norton Personal Firewall to protect a home PC

Using a personal firewall, such as Norton Personal Firewall, you can protect your system against Java applets, ActiveX controls, and attempts by programs to access unused application ports. Figure 12-12 (above) shows a screen from Norton Personal Firewall.

As you experiment with the trial versions of the firewall software, you should download and install a personal firewall from one company and then run the vulnerability test from another company's Web site to determine the effectiveness of each trial firewall program.

Fine-Tuning a Firewall's Port Assignments

To communicate over a network, the sending program must specify the address of the remote computer. In addition, the sending program must identify the application on the remote computer to which it is sending the message. For example, when a browser sends a Web page (HTTP) request to a Web server, the sending program (that is, the Web browser) must specify the Internet protocol address of the remote site and the fact that the message is for the Web server application that is running at the site.

Network programs specify remote applications using a number that programmers refer to as the application's *port number*. For example, to send a message to a Web server, a browser sends a message to port 80 (which corresponds to the HTTP protocol). Periodically, as you surf the Web, you may encounter a URL that includes port number 80, such as www.SomeSite.com:80/Filename.html. Across the Internet, various protocols correspond to specific port numbers. Programmers refer to the first 1,024 port numbers as well-known ports. The following list shows the port numbers that correspond to several common applications:

Port Number	Application
21	File transfer protocol (FTP)
23	Telnet
25	Simple mail transport protocol (SMTP)
80	Hypertext transport protocol (HTTP)
139	NetBIOS session service

Most firewalls let you control the flow of messages into your network by preventing messages bound for specific ports from entering your network, as shown in Figure 12-13.

USE IT   As you configure your firewall, you may find it easier to first disable messages to all ports and then turn on access to only those specific ports you require. Depending on the firewall you are using, the steps you must perform to restrict or allow port use will differ. Figure 12-14, for example, shows how to filter specific ports within Norton Personal Firewall.

Internet programs can use up to 65,536 different port numbers. As you configure ports within a firewall, you should refer to the list of port assignments at http://www.iana.org/assignments/port-numbers.

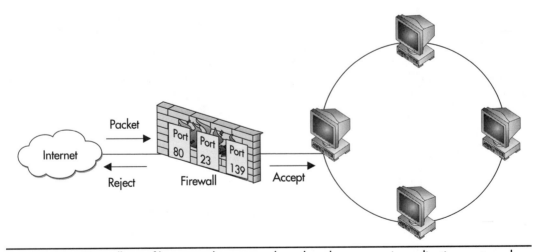

Figure 12-13   Firewalls can filter network messages based on the message's application port number

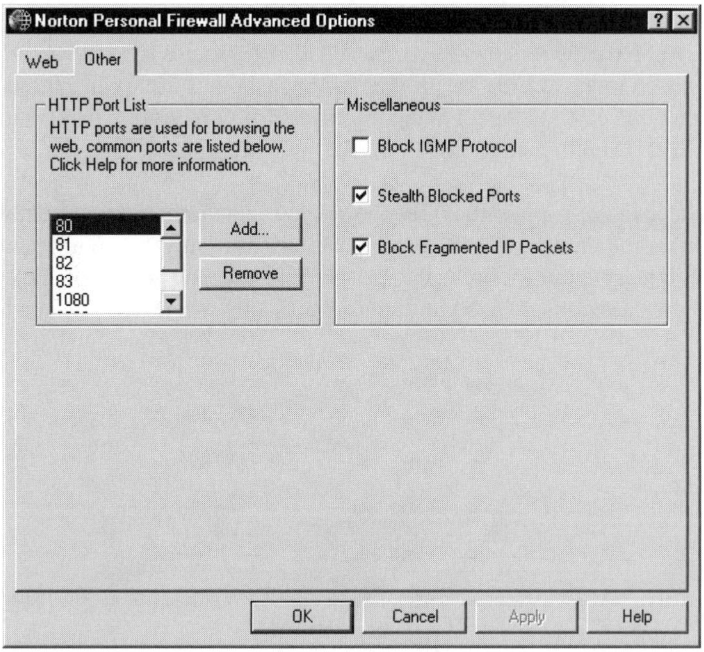

Figure 12-14   Using Norton Personal Firewall to filter messages based on port numbers

Reducing Your Site's Exposure to Viruses

In 2001, computer viruses cost businesses over $11 billion in lost time, damaged files, and more. Leading the way was the Code Red virus, which cost businesses over $3 billion dollars—which, by the way, fell far short of the nearly $10 billion cost of the Love Bug virus in 2000. Computer viruses are a threat to any PC that connects to the Net.

Simply put, if you have computers and users connected to a network (particularly the Internet), your network and each of its PCs are exposed to computer viruses.

Years ago, to infect a PC with a virus, a user had to run an infected program. Prior to the Internet, users typically received an infected program via a floppy disk given to them by another user. With the advent of computer bulletin board systems, with users downloading programs to their computers, the virus threat increased; however, the user still had to run a program to infect his or her system.

Today, many application programs, such as Microsoft Word, Excel, and even PowerPoint, possess macro capabilities that let users automate specific tasks. Using an Excel macro for example, a user might automatically calculate the interest rates and monthly payments for a mortgage. Likewise, within

Microsoft Word, a user might use a macro to spell check a document and to add a header and footer automatically before printing the document's contents. Although macros let users extend an application's capabilities in powerful ways, macros are programs, and malicious users can exploit them to spread viruses. As a result, users can now infect their systems with a virus simply by opening a Word or Excel document that contains a macro-based virus.

USE IT To reduce the risk of a virus infection on your network, every system within your network—the servers as well as the workstations—must be running current virus-detection software. If you are using a firewall to protect your site (and you should be), your firewall may also support virus detection, which you should use as a front-line defense (see Figure 12-15).

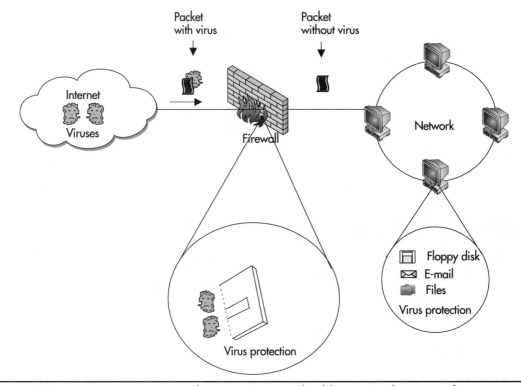

Figure 12-15 To protect your network, every computer should run virus-detection software

If you are not currently running virus-detection software, several sites on the Web offer free trial software you can download and use for a 30-day period:

AVG 6.0 Anti-Virus System	http://www.grisoft.com
Norton AntiVirus	http://www.symantec.com
PC-cillin	http://www.trendmicro.com
VirusScan	http://www.mcafee.com

One of the keys to reducing the threat of viruses is to train users never to run programs they download from the Web (many companies include directives within their employee manuals that state that employees must not install or download any programs without prior written approval). You must instill in your users the understanding that they should never open a document, program, or e-mail attachment that they receive from a user they do not know, and that they should never open any file without first using virus-detection software to scan the file for viruses.

After you install virus-detection software, it is very important that you keep the software current. Each day, hackers and other malicious programmers work on new virus programs. Thus, for your virus-detection software to be effective, you must update the software's list of known viruses on a regular basis (at least once a month). Normally, after you purchase virus-detection software, you can update the virus list for a year or more for free. After that, you can subscribe to the company's virus data file update service for a nominal fee.

In Chapter 9, you examined ActiveX objects, which users can download as they browse the Web. To protect your network, you must instruct your users to treat ActiveX objects as programs, which means that users should not download and install objects without permission. Moreover, users should download and install only signed objects that have a digital certificate that authenticates the developer and verifies that a hacker did not intercept the object and attach a virus to it as it made its way across the Net. Further, users should not download and install an ActiveX object until they have examined the object using their virus-detection software.

Finally, to better defend your system against virus infections, you should study and be aware of the current threats. Several Web sites maintain listings of the current virus threats. One of the best sites for both hacker and virus information is CERT, at http://www.cert.org, shown in Figure 12-16.

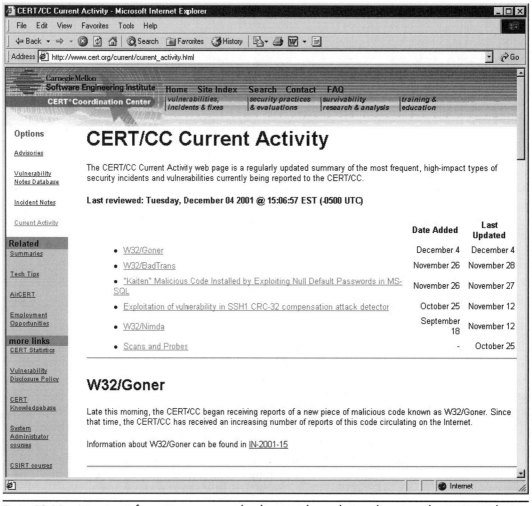

Figure 12-16   Viewing information on recent hacker attacks and virus threats at the CERT Web site

Improving Performance and Security by Disabling Printer and File Sharing

If you are running Windows software within your network, the Client for Microsoft Networks software lets you share files and printers with other users. If, for example, you double-click the Network Neighborhood icon (which resides on the Windows desktop), the Client for Microsoft Networks software lists the PCs, workgroups, and printers that exist in your network. The Client for Microsoft Networks software runs on top of your network software, meaning, within most networks, that it sits on top of the TCP/IP protocol.

USE IT   If the workstations on your network do not share files and printers (printers that connect
to a users' PCs as opposed to a printer that attaches directly to the network), you should
remove support for the Client for Microsoft Networks from each user's system by performing these steps:

1. Select Start | Settings | Control Panel. Windows will open the Control Panel window.

2. Within the Control Panel, double-click the Network icon. Windows will display the
   Network dialog box, shown in Figure 12-17.

3. On the Configuration tab of the Network dialog box is a list of installed components.
   Select the Client for Microsoft Networks entry and then click Remove.

USE IT   If you are using a cable-modem connection, you essentially are working on a network
that consists of your PC and the cable company. If, for some reason, your system must
support Client for Microsoft Networks, turn off printer and file sharing. Otherwise, you may leave
your system exposed to a hacker who gains access to your cable company's computer system. To
turn off file and printer sharing within Windows, perform these steps:

1. Select Start | Settings | Control Panel. Windows will open the Control Panel window.

2. Within the Control Panel, double-click the Network icon. Windows will display the
   Network dialog box, shown in Figure 12-17.

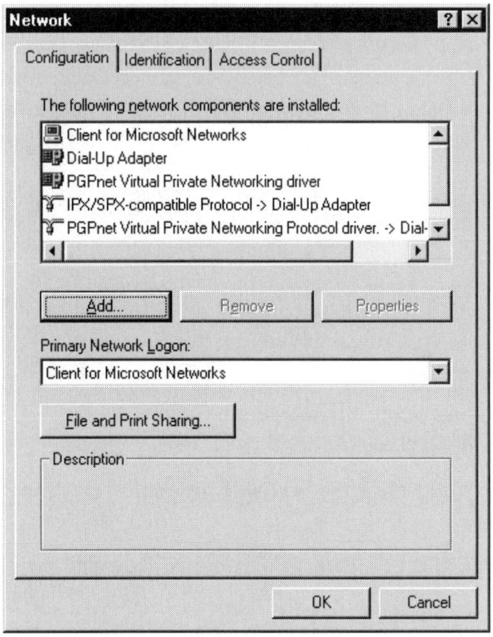

Figure 12-17   The Network dialog box

3. Within the Network dialog box, click the File and Print Sharing button. Windows will display the File and Print Sharing dialog box.

4. Within the File and Print Sharing dialog box, click each check box to remove the check marks and then click OK.

Using Client Certificates to Restrict User Access

To access a secure Web site, a browser and server use the secure sockets layer (SSL) to encrypt the HTTP-based messages they exchange. To use SSL, a client does not have to have a public key. Instead, the server must have a digital certificate (which contains the server's public key). That explains why, for example, you can connect to secure Web sites across the Web despite the fact that you may not have a public key. Behind the scenes, when your browser connects to a secure site, your browser and site's Web server exchange messages that contain information about the encryption techniques each supports. Then the server sends your browser a message that contains the server's public key. The Web server does not encrypt the message in which it sends its public key. Your browser, in turn, will use the server's public key to encrypt a message that contains numbers that each can use to generate a session key that both the server and browser can then use to encrypt and decrypt the messages they exchange.

If your Web site contains applications that access sensitive data (such as corporate human resources information or sales data), you may want to restrict the users who can run the applications to those who can authenticate themselves using a digital certificate (a client certificate). In some cases, you may require only that a user accessing a resource have a certificate, meaning that any certificate will do. In other cases, you may require a specific certificate, which means that you will likely map the certificate to an account you create on your system for the user. Before you can use client certificates within Internet Information Server (IIS), you must first assign a certificate to the server.

USE IT   To enable client certificates within IIS, perform these steps:

1. Select Start | Settings | Control Panel. Windows will display the Control Panel window.

2. Within the Control Panel window, double-click the Administrative Tools icon. Windows will open the Administrative Tools window.

3. Within the Administrative Tools window, double-click the Internet Services Manager icon. Windows will display the IIS snap-in.

4. Within the IIS snap-in, right-click the Web site (or page) you desire. Windows will display a pop-up menu.

5. Within the pop-up menu, select Properties. Windows will display the item's Properties dialog box.

6. Within the Properties dialog box, click the Directory Security tab. Windows will display the Directory Security sheet, shown in Figure 12-18.

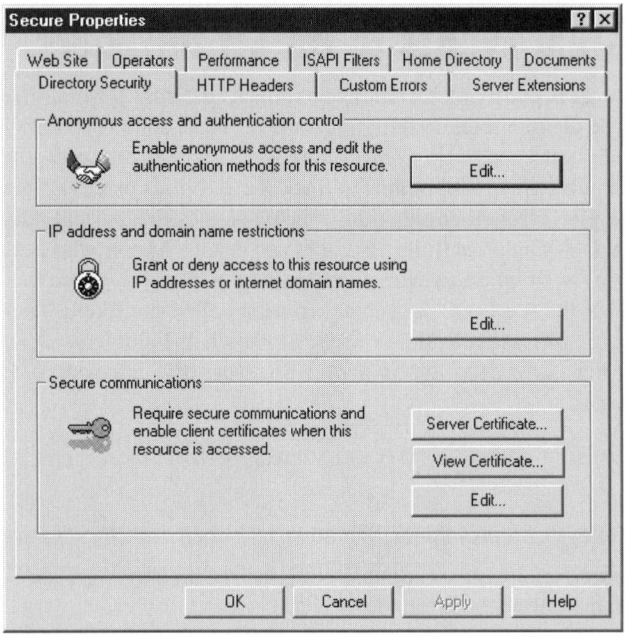

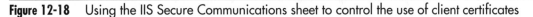

Figure 12-18   Using the IIS Secure Communications sheet to control the use of client certificates

7. Within the Secure Communications section, click Edit. Windows will display the Secure Communications dialog box. Next, select the Require secure channel (SSL) check box, placing a check mark in the box. To connect to the page in the future, the user must use a secure connection.

8. Within the Client Certificates field, select the setting you desire and then click OK. Table 12-1 briefly describes the settings you can use.

Setting	Purpose
Accept Client Certificates	The server will accept, but will not require, a client certificate.
Require Client Certificates	The server will require a client certificate before the user can connect to the resource.
Ignore Client Certificates	The server will ignore client certificates.

Table 12-1   Settings that Control the Use of Client Certificates in IIS

Auditing System Events to Detect Intruders

Across the Internet, hackers use many techniques to attack systems. Normally, as hackers perform their attacks, they cause the operating system to generate events so that you may be able to detect an ongoing attack or track down the hacker after the fact. In general, an *audit trail* consists of one or more log files the operating system maintains to track the activities users perform. Within the Unix environment, for example, different applications create log files that system administrators can view to monitor system events. Using audit trails may help you catch a hacker who has successfully broken into your system. More important, however, audit trails may alert you to the fact that a hacker attack is in progress. Within Windows 2000, a special program called the Event Viewer lets system administrators view a log of various system events, as shown in Figure 12-19.

The Event Viewer logs three event types: application, security, and system. In this Tip, your focus will be on security events.

USE IT   To display the Windows 2000 Event Viewer, perform these steps:

1. Select Start | Settings | Control Panel. Windows will open the Control Panel.
2. Within the Control Panel window, double-click the Administrative Tools icon. Windows will display the Administrative Tools window.
3. Within the Administrative Tools window, double-click the Event Viewer icon. Windows will display the Event Viewer.

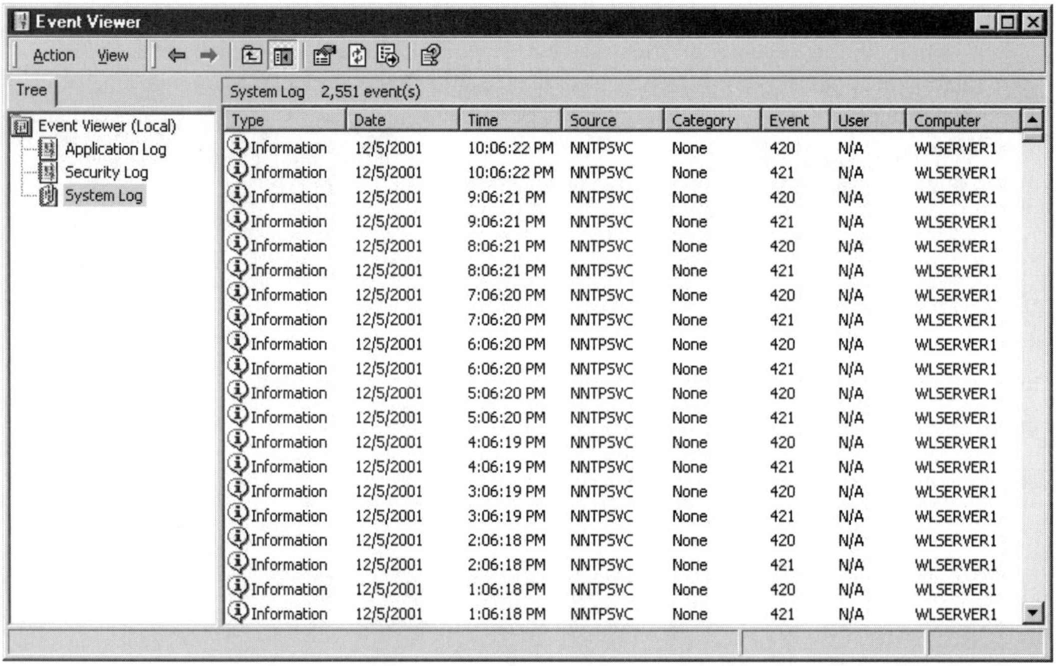

Figure 12-19   Within Windows 2000, administrators use the Event Viewer to monitor system logs

4. Within the Event Viewer, click the Security entry. The Event Viewer will display the security log, as shown in Figure 12-20.

Within the Event Viewer, you can view details about a specific event by double-clicking the event's entry within the log file. The Event Viewer will display an Event Properties dialog box that describes the event, as shown in Figure 12-21.

To monitor security events within Windows 2000, you must first enable security logging. Depending on whether your system uses domain-level or local-level policies, the steps you must perform to enable security logging will differ.

USE IT To enable security settings within a system that uses local-level policies, for example, you would perform these steps:

1. Select Start | Settings | Control Panel. Windows will open the Control Panel.

2. Within the Control Panel window, double-click the Administrative Tools icon. Windows will display the Administrative Tools window.

3. Within the Administrative Tools window, double-click the Local Security Policy icon. Windows will display the Local Security Settings window.

4. Within the Local Security Settings window, double-click the policy you want to audit. Windows will display the Local Security Policy Setting dialog box.

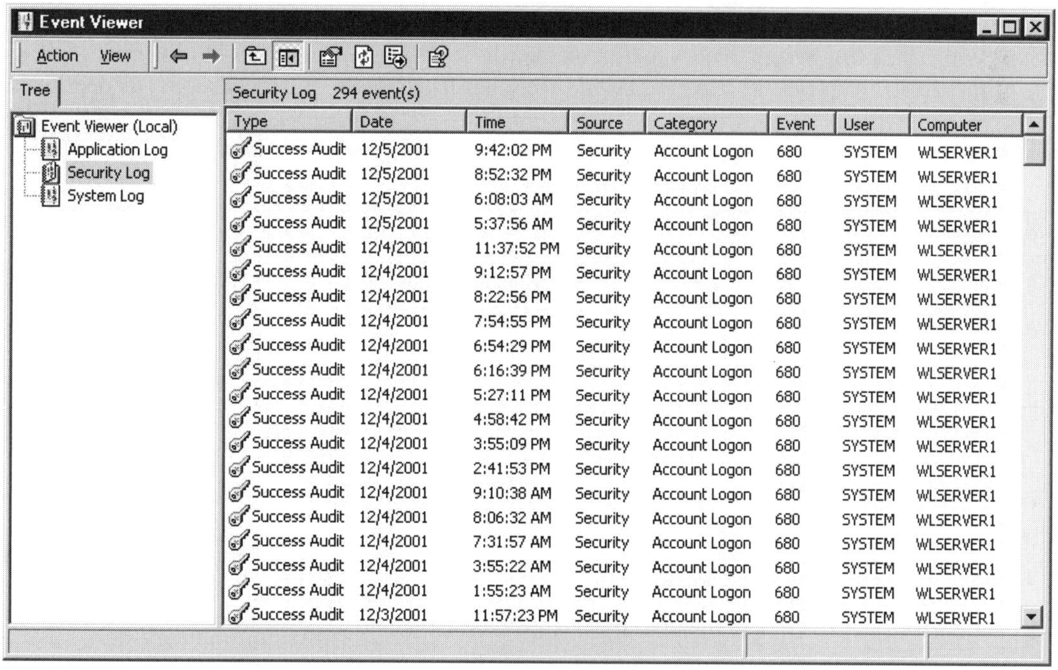

Figure 12-20   Viewing the security log within the Event Viewer

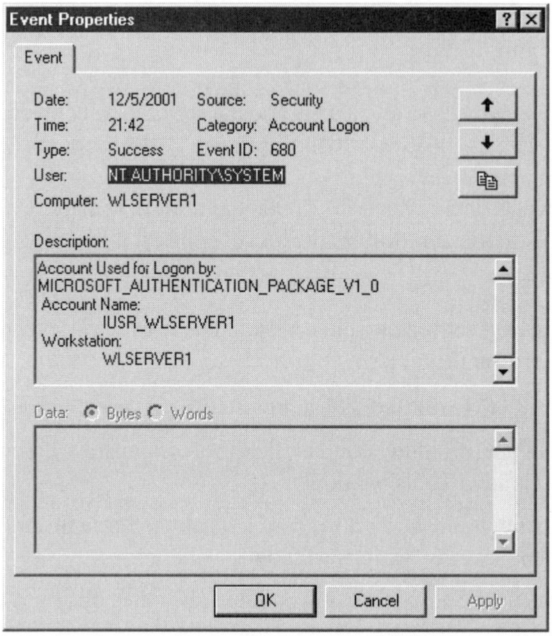

Figure 12-21 Viewing specifics about an Event

5. Within the Local Security Policy Setting dialog box, select the Success check box to enable logging for successful operations; select the Failure check box to enable logging for unsuccessful operations.

Using the Local Security Policy settings, you can set the policies briefly described in Table 12-2.

Policy	Purpose
Account Logon	Tracks logon and logoff operations for which this computer authenticated the account.
Account Management	Tracks all changes to user and system accounts.
Directory Service Access	Tracks the use of the active directory.
Logon Events	Tracks all users logging onto or off of this computer.
Object Access	Tracks each access to a directory, file, registry, or printer object.
Policy Change	Tracks changes to accounts rights, audit policies, and trust policies.
Privilege Use	Tracks each user's exercise of a privilege.
Process Tracking	Tracks when programs run, end, and duplicate handles.
System Events	Tracks system operations that change log files.

Table 12-2 Security Settings that Windows 2000 Should Log

Exploiting the NTFS File System

Within an operating system, special software called the *file system* manages the files and folders that reside on your disk. Each time you create, change, delete, or rename a file or folder, you interact with the file system. If you are using a Windows NT or Windows 2000 server, you can improve your site's security by using the NT file system (NTFS).

Using NTFS, you can assign specific permissions to each file and folder. These permissions control which users can access a resource and what each user can do with it. Should a hacker gain access to your server, for example, the file permissions that you assign to files and folders may limit the information the hacker can access.

USE IT To determine your current file system, perform these steps:

1. On the Windows desktop, double-click the My Computer icon. Windows will display the My Computer window, which displays icons for each of your disk drives.

2. Within the My Computer window, right-click the icon that corresponds to your hard drive. Windows will display a pop-up menu.

3. Within the pop-up menu, select the Properties icon. Windows will display the disk's Properties dialog box, which displays the file system type, as shown in Figure 12-22.

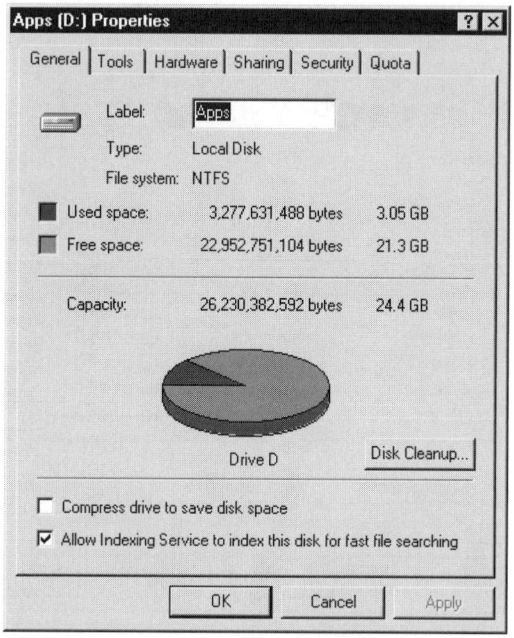

Figure 12-22   Using a disk's Properties dialog box to view the file system type

As discussed, using NTFS you can assign to files specific permissions that control which users can access each of them and how.

USE IT   To assign permissions to a file or folder within NTFS, perform these steps:

1. Within Windows Explorer, right-click the file or folder you want to protect. Windows will display a pop-up menu.

2. Within the pop-up menu, select Properties. Windows will display the Properties dialog box.

3. Within the Properties dialog box, click the Security tab. Windows will display the Security sheet, as shown in Figure 12-23.

4. Within the Security sheet, click the Add button to add users or groups to the permission list. Windows will display the Select Users or Groups dialog box.

5. Within the Select Users or Groups dialog box, click the user or group you want to add. To add multiple users or groups, hold down the CTRL key on your keyboard as you click the mouse on the entries. After you select the users and groups you want, click OK.

6. Within the Security sheet, choose the security settings you want to allow or deny for the new users or groups and then click OK.

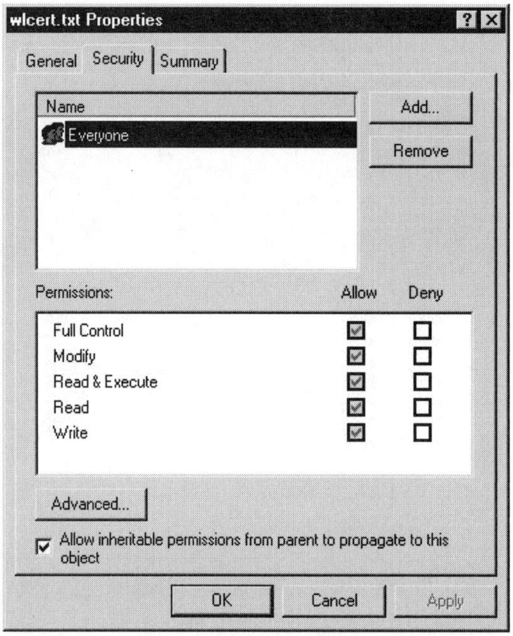

Figure 12-23   Viewing a file's Security sheet within the Properties dialog box

Another advantage of NTFS is that it lets you encrypt files and folders on your disk. Again, should a hacker gain access to your server, the hacker will not be able to view the encrypted file's contents. After you encrypt a file within NTFS, you can continue to use the file just as you always have. NTFS will decrypt the file's contents automatically for you each time you open the file (or a file within an encrypted folder). NTFS encrypts files based on your username, so should another user later access the system, that user cannot decrypt your files.

USE IT To encrypt a file or folder using NTFS, perform these steps:

1. Within Windows Explorer, right-click the file or folder you want to encrypt. Windows will display a pop-up menu.
2. Within the pop-up menu, click the Properties option. Windows displays the Properties dialog box.
3. Within the Properties dialog box, click the Advanced button. Windows will display the Advanced Attributes dialog box, as shown in Figure 12-24.
4. Within the Advanced Attributes dialog box, select the Encrypt Contents to Secure Data check box, placing a check mark in the box. Click OK.

The only disadvantage of encrypting files is that each time you open or save the file, NTFS must either decrypt or encrypt the file's contents. The process of encrypting and decrypting files adds overhead, which, on a busy server, could degrade performance. Because most users, however, do not normally open and save files in quick succession, most will not notice the slight overhead introduced by encryption and decryption. Likewise, within a Web environment, there are many files whose contents you would not encrypt, such as the HTML files that users download when they visit your site.

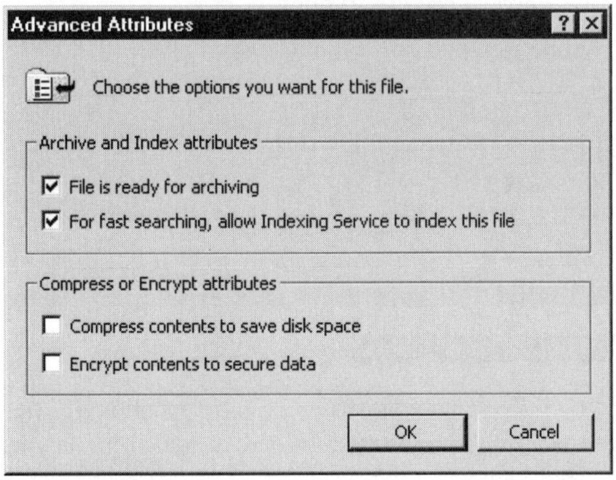

Figure 12-24   Using the Advanced Attributes dialog box to encrypt a file

Finally, to improve your site's security, you may want to know which users access what files or folders and when.

USE IT   Using NTFS, you can enable auditing for specific files and folders by performing these steps:

1. Within Windows Explorer, right-click the file or folder you want to audit. Windows will display a pop-up menu.
2. Within the pop-up menu, choose Properties. Windows will display the Properties dialog box.
3. Within the Properties dialog box, click the Security tab. Windows will display the Security sheet.
4. Within the Security sheet, click the Advanced button. Windows will display a dialog box that contains the file's current permissions.
5. Within the dialog box, click the Audit tab. Windows will display the Audit dialog box.
6. Within the Audit dialog box, click the Add button. Windows will display the Select User or Group dialog box.
7. Within the Select User or Group dialog box, choose the users or groups whose actions you want to audit.

After you enable auditing, the NTFS will place entries in the Event Viewer as discussed in the Tip "Auditing System Events to Detect Intruders."

USE IT   If you are not currently using the NTFS file system, you can convert your disk to NTFS by performing these steps:

1. Using backup software, perform a complete backup of the files that reside on the disk.
2. Close the applications you are currently running.
3. Select Start | Run. Windows will display the Run dialog box.
4. Within the Run dialog box, type **CMD** and press ENTER. Windows will open a console window.
5. Within the console window, issue the following *convert* command, replacing *drive:* with the drive letter of the disk drive you want to convert to NTFS:

```
C:\> convert  drive:  /fs:ntfs  <Enter>
```

Disabling Remote Services

Many Web sites let users log into the network from a remote location. If your site does not need to allow users to access the system from remote locations, you should disable your site's remote services to reduce the risk of a hacker's exploiting the services to gain access to your system. Depending on the operating system your system is running, the steps you must perform to prevent remote access will differ. For example, within the Unix/Linux environment, you should remove support for Telnet as well as remote capabilities, including remote logins (*rlogin*) and remote shell (*rsh*) operations. Further, at a minimum, you should disable anonymous FTP operations, and if your site does not require users to be able to upload and download files using FTP, you should disable FTP completely.

USE IT   Within Windows 2000, you can disable remote services by performing these steps:

1. Select Start | Settings | Control Panel. Windows will display the Control Panel window.

2. Within the Control Panel, double-click the Administrative Tools icon. Windows will display the Administrative Tools window.

3. Within the Administrative Tools window, double-click the Services icon. Windows will display the Services window, as shown in Figure 12-25.

4. Within the Services window, double-click one of the Remote services, such as Remote Access Connection Manager. Windows will display a dialog box, within which you can configure the service.

5. Within the dialog box, select Disabled from the Startup Type pull-down list and then click OK.

6. Repeat steps 4 and 5 for each of the Remote entries.

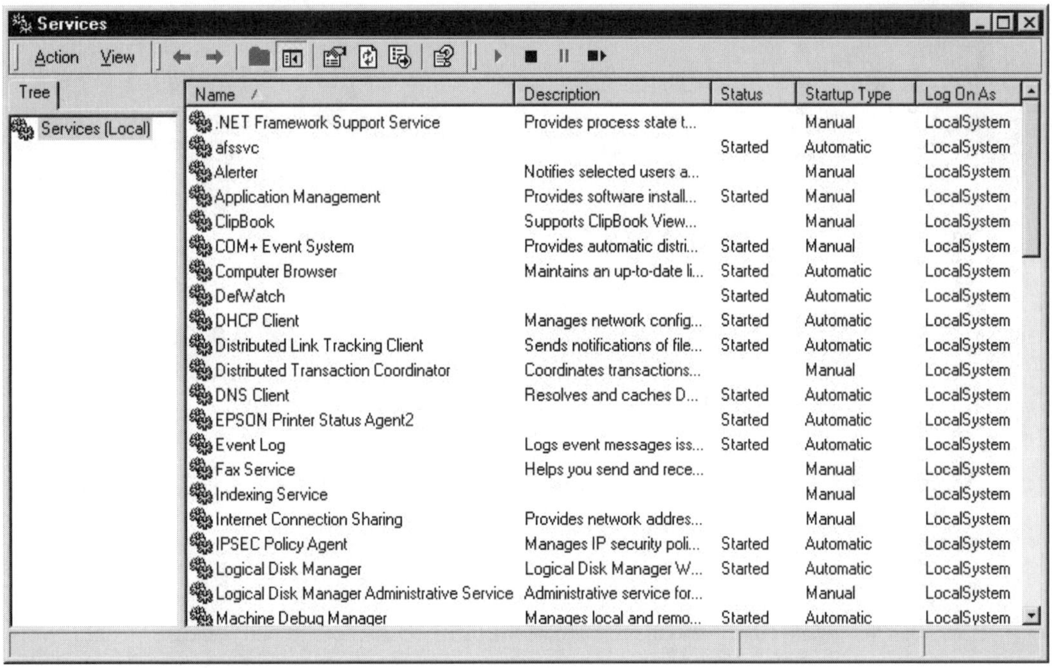

Name	Description	Status	Startup Type	Log On As
.NET Framework Support Service	Provides process state t...		Manual	LocalSystem
afssvc		Started	Automatic	LocalSystem
Alerter	Notifies selected users a...		Manual	LocalSystem
Application Management	Provides software install...	Started	Manual	LocalSystem
ClipBook	Supports ClipBook View...		Manual	LocalSystem
COM+ Event System	Provides automatic distri...	Started	Manual	LocalSystem
Computer Browser	Maintains an up-to-date li...	Started	Automatic	LocalSystem
DefWatch		Started	Automatic	LocalSystem
DHCP Client	Manages network config...	Started	Automatic	LocalSystem
Distributed Link Tracking Client	Sends notifications of file...	Started	Automatic	LocalSystem
Distributed Transaction Coordinator	Coordinates transactions...		Manual	LocalSystem
DNS Client	Resolves and caches D...	Started	Automatic	LocalSystem
EPSON Printer Status Agent2		Started	Automatic	LocalSystem
Event Log	Logs event messages iss...	Started	Automatic	LocalSystem
Fax Service	Helps you send and rece...		Manual	LocalSystem
Indexing Service			Manual	LocalSystem
Internet Connection Sharing	Provides network addres...		Manual	LocalSystem
IPSEC Policy Agent	Manages IP security poli...	Started	Automatic	LocalSystem
Logical Disk Manager	Logical Disk Manager W...	Started	Automatic	LocalSystem
Logical Disk Manager Administrative Service	Administrative service for...		Manual	LocalSystem
Machine Debug Manager	Manages local and remo...	Started	Automatic	LocalSystem

Figure 12-25   The Windows 2000 Services window

There are times when users have a legitimate need to access a network remotely. If you have one or more users who access the network via dial-up operations, you can increase your system security by using a call-back system, similar to that shown in Figure 12-26.

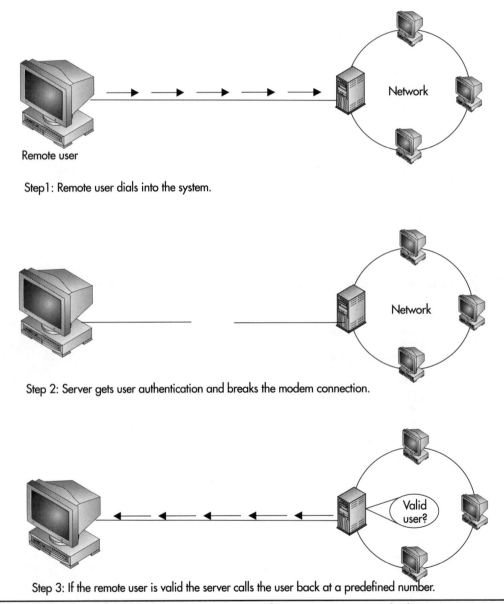

Remote user

Step1: Remote user dials into the system.

Network

Step 2: Server gets user authentication and breaks the modem connection.

Network

Valid user?

Step 3: If the remote user is valid the server calls the user back at a predefined number.

Figure 12-26   A call-back system increases security for remote operations by limiting access to known phone numbers

Using a call-back system, the remote user dials into the system using his or her modem. Depending on the call-back software, the user may simply need to dial into a specific number, or the user may also be required to provide a username and password or digital certificate after dial-up. The call-back system will then disconnect the call and call the user back at a predetermined number, such as the phone number of a modem at the user's remote office or home. In this way, a hacker at any other location cannot access the system remotely, because the call-back system will not place a call back to the hacker's modem.

If you are running a Unix-based site that requires remote access, you should disable the Unix *r* commands previously discussed and replace them with applications such as *ssh* (secure shell) that use the secure sockets layer to encrypt the messages users exchange with the site. On the Web, you can find implementations of *ssh* for a wide range of workstations, including Linux and Windows systems.

USE IT   If your server is Unix or Linux based, you should also consider disabling the *finger* and *whois* commands, which hackers can use to gain more information about system users. Using the *finger* command, for example, a hacker can determine which users are currently logged on. Then, using *whois* to view specifics about a user, the hacker may be able to guess the user's username and password or to contact the user and simply ask the user his or her username and password (a social-engineering attack).

▶ **NOTE**

If you have specific remote services you must support, you can improve your site's security by restricting remote service operations to specific times of the day. For example, by disabling a remote service during nonworking hours, you reduce the opportunity for a hacker to break into a system.

Analyzing Your System's Vulnerability

Several Web sites exist that you can use to test your site for common vulnerabilities. Most of the tests these sites perform examine network-specific issues, as opposed to operating system vulnerabilities. Fortunately, there are several utilities you can download and run that perform such specific tests. For example, within the Unix/Linux environments, administrators often run a program named SATAN (which stands for Security Administrator Tool for Analyzing Networks). Using SATAN, Unix administrators can identify such vulnerabilities as holes in the network file system (NFS) or file transport protocol (FTP) application, as well as possible exposure through remote shell configurations and other services.

► *NOTE*

Many Unix/Linux administrators are concerned about hackers running SATAN against the administrator's site to determine vulnerabilities that the hackers can later exploit. To prevent a hacker from running SATAN against a Unix/Linux site, some sites install the Courtney or Gabriel application, both of which detect when SATAN is running against a system. You can download these applications from the Computer Incident Advisory Capability Web site, at http://ciac.llnl.gov/ciac/ ToolsUnixNetMon.html.

If you are using a Windows NT or Windows 2000 server, you can use a program such as LANguard Network Scanner, which you can download to test your system, as shown in Figure 12-27.

To learn more about key security programs, visit http://www.insecure.org/tools.html, which features a list of the Top 50 Security Tools.

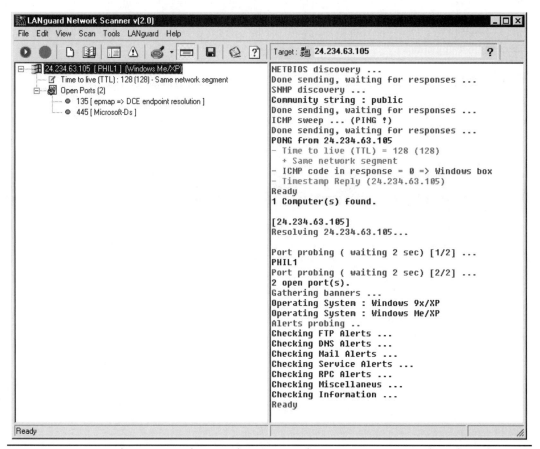

Figure 12-27   Using the LANguard Network Scanner utility to examine a Windows-based system's vulnerabilities

Processing Credit Card Data

Earlier in this chapter, you learned how to create a secure Web site, which is the first step you must perform if you want to accept credit cards. Next, you must establish a merchant account with a bank that lets you accept credit card payments. On the Web, several companies, such as PSiGate, at http://www.psigate.com, offer software that you can use to easily integrate credit card processing into Active Server Pages and other scripting technologies. Using the credit card processing software, the scripts you create can easily authorize and process credit card payments.

To accept a credit card purchase, a Web site normally creates an HTML-based form that prompts the user for credit card information. By placing the form on to a page that users access securely (using https:// to launch an SSL-based connection), you prevent a hacker from intercepting a user's credit card information as the information makes its way across the Net.

Your primary challenge as a Web designer, however, is storing the credit card information on your site after the secure transaction is completed. To maintain a record of your credit card transactions, you must store the credit card data within one or more files. Unfortunately, if you leave the credit card information on your server's hard drive, you expose the credit cards to the risk of theft by a hacker. In the past, hackers have successfully broken into Web sites and stolen files that contain credit card information that the site stored in a plain-text file (meaning that the file was not encrypted). When you store credit card information, you must determine how you will protect the information from hackers as well as your own employees (such as programmers and database administrators who likely have access to the data).

Ideally, you should move credit card information off of your server as quickly as possible. The longer the data remains on your server, the greater the risk of theft. Regardless of where you store the credit card data, you should store the information in an encrypted file.

Because storing credit card information can be a challenging process, you may find it easier initially to outsource your company's credit card operations to a larger company that performs such e-commerce operations on a regular basis.

Taking a Close Look at a Web Site's Performance Chain

Depending on whom you ask, the definition of Web site performance will differ. To a user visiting a site, performance is a measure of the site's responsiveness—the length of time the user must wait to see the results desired. To a Web site administrator, performance often is a measure of the site's user or hit capacity, meaning the number of simultaneous or near simultaneous hits the site can process in a given period of time. By focusing on the site's capacity, Web administrators take slow network connections (such as dial-up connections) out of the equation. Although it may be fair from a server-performance perspective to eliminate the user's connection speed from the equation, Web page designers must fully consider the ramifications of slow download times on the pages they create.

As shown in Figure 12-28, to truly measure a Web site's performance, you must take into account several factors, the combination of which creates a performance chain that influences the site's responsiveness as perceived by the visitor.

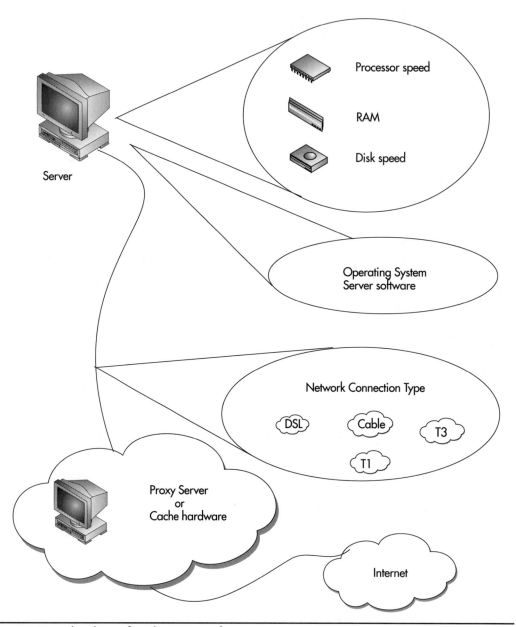

Figure 12-28   The chain of Web server performance

In the Tip "Monitoring Server Performance," you will learn how to monitor your server's CPU use and available free memory to determine whether your server has sufficient processing resources to handle its current workload. Further, you will learn how to use log files to determine the number of hits you are receiving and the frequency of hits.

In addition to monitoring your server's performance, you can gain significant insight into your server's basic capabilities, as compared to other servers on Web, by running special benchmark programs. Several Web sites offer benchmark programs you can download and run on your server. The benchmarks simulate a range of user operations, so you can measure such server capabilities as these:

- Ability to support simultaneous connections.

- Support for connections at a limited line speed.

- Processing of dynamic GET operations as well as static GET and POST operations.

- Support for persistent connections (HTTP 1.1).

- Ability to process dynamic ad rotations using cookies and table lookups.

- File access speed.

- Support for socket-based communication.

- Secure operations such as SSL-based transactions.

Most of the benchmark programs are available for major server platforms, such as Windows 2000, Unix/Linux (Apache), and so on. Further, to help you understand the processing the benchmarks perform, you can normally download the source code programmers wrote to create the benchmark. With the source code in hand, you can compile the code into an executable program for use on your server platform.

USE IT   For specifics on Web server benchmark programs, visit the following sites:

SpecWeb	http://www.specbench.org
Webstone	http://www.mindcraft.com/webstone
Webbench	http://www.zdnet.com/zdbop

After you run the benchmark programs, you may want to take a closer look at your server's hardware capabilities. The following sections briefly examine aspects of your server that you may want to consider as you evaluate your server's performance.

Network Connection Type

Across the Web, sites connect to the Internet in a variety of ways: using high-speed T1 connections, or digital subscriber line (DSL) connections, or cable modems. Depending on the site's connection type, the speed at which the visitor can download data will differ. Table 12-3 briefly describes the speeds of common connection types.

Connection Type	Description	Download Speed	Upload Speed
ISDL	ISDN DSL	144 Kbps	144 Kbps
HDSL	High bit-rate DSL	1.5 Mbps	1.5 Mbps
SDSL	Symmetric DSL	1.5 Mbps	1.5 Mbps
ADSL	Asymmetric DSL	Based on distance, up to 9 Mbps	Based on distance, down to 384 Kbps
RADSL	Rate Adaptive DSL	Varies	Varies
VDSL	Very high bit-rate DSL	Up to 50 Mbps	Up to 16 Mbps
Satellite	TV satellite	Up to 500 Kbps	Up to 60 Kbps
Cable	TV cable	Up to 1.5 Mbps	Up to 1.5 Mbps
T1	Leased line	Up to 1.5 Mbps	Up to 1.5 Mbps
T3	Leased line	Up to 45 Mbps	Up to 45 Mbps

Table 12-3   Common Server Connection Speeds

USE IT   Depending on your connection type, you can find different sites on the Web that will measure your connection's true bandwidth. For example, if you connect your site to the Web using a cable modem, you should visit http://www.bandwidthplace.com/speedtest and run the bandwidth evaluation shown in Figure 12-29. Similarly, if you are using a DSL connection, you should visit http://www.dslreports.com/stest to measure your connection's bandwidth.

PC Processing Speed

Within the PC, the CPU is the workhorse that executes the instructions within the operating system and server programs. In general, the faster your server's CPU speed, the faster your site's performance. CPU speed is measured in cycles per second, or Hertz. The CPU contains a clock that ticks a specific number of times per second; each time the clock ticks, the CPU executes an instruction. Within a 500 MHz (500 megahertz) CPU, for example, the clock ticks 500 million times per second. Likewise, within a 2 GHz (2 gigahertz) CPU, the clock ticks 2 billion times per second. Most users normally assume that using a 2 GHz CPU, which is four times faster than a 500 MHz CPU, would make the server four times faster. Unfortunately, that is not the case. In the Tip "Monitoring Server Performance," you will learn how to measure your CPU's use. Assume that your server normally maintains a 20 percent CPU utilization rate (which is actually quite high). If you were to upgrade a 500 MHz processor to a 2 GHz processor, you would see gains from the CPU's faster speed only when the CPU is in use (which means 20 percent of the time). Thus, rather than making your server four times faster (which would

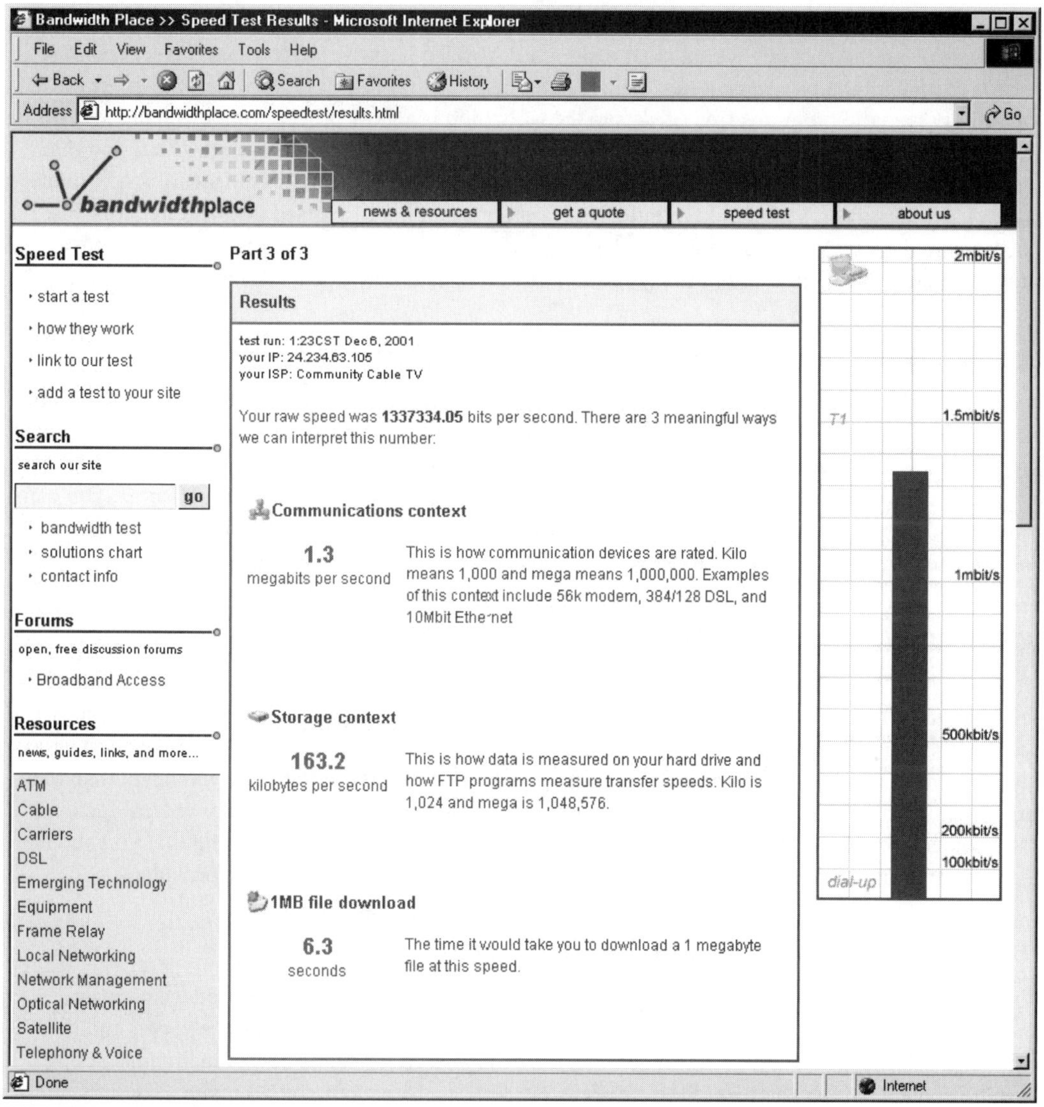

Figure 12-29 Measuring the true bandwidth of a cable-modem connection

be the case if your CPU were in use 100 percent of the time), the 2 GHz CPU would increase the server's performance by only 80 percent:

```
Performance improvement = (Percentage of use) * (Speed gained)
                        = (20%) * (4)
                        = 80%
```

The amount of RAM the server contains is also key to performance. Before a CPU can run a program, the program and the program's data must reside in RAM. To improve performance, a server must be able to hold all the programs it runs on a regular basis within RAM. Otherwise, the server must continually load the programs from disk into RAM, which is a slow process (the mechanical disk drive is much slower than the computer's electronic RAM). Most administrators will tell you that the more RAM your server contains, the better. However, rather than simply throwing RAM (and money) at your server, you should monitor your server's amount of unused physical memory (as discussed in the Tip "Monitoring Server Performance"). If your server is not running short on physical memory, adding more RAM will not improve your server's performance.

Disk Access Time

Because a disk drive is a mechanical device (has moving parts), the disk drive is much slower than the computer's electronic components. Server administrators improve performance by adding more RAM, to reduce slow disk operations. That said, many server applications must eventually read or write information to or from disk. By monitoring the disk operations your server performs, you can gain an understanding of how much a faster disk drive would improve your server's performance. For most servers, spending more money to purchase a faster disk drive is a good initial investment.

Operating System and Server Application

The operating system and applications that a server runs have a very significant impact on the server's performance. On the Web, you can find numerous benchmark reports that compare and contrast operating system performance under various server loads. In general, however, for most Web sites, any of the major operating systems will offer more than adequate performance. If you have a site that receives millions of hits a day, the operating system's performance will be a more critical factor. If you manage a smaller site, your priorities should be ease of management (meaning that you should use an operating system with which you are familiar), security, and, finally, performance.

Proxy Servers and Web Caching Devices

Within a Web site, the contents of many HTML-based pages never change. To reduce overhead on the server, many sites place a proxy server or Web-caching device between the server and the Internet, as shown in Figure 12-30. In general, the proxy server or cache device maintains a copy of static content, which can be used to satisfy user requests. Depending on your site's use of static pages, the overhead on your server that you eliminate using such a front end can be quite significant. Further, many sites allow the proxy server to perform simple Active Server Pages (ASP) or PHP operations that generate output that does not depend on data stored on the server. For the specifics on integrating a proxy server or Web cache into your site, visit http://wwwcache.ja.net/servers.

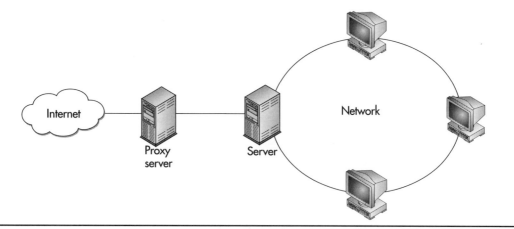

Figure 12-30   Using a proxy server or Web-caching device to reduce server overhead

Creating a Web Farm

As your Web traffic increases, managing your site can become much more difficult. Because users expect your system to be up and running 7 days a week, 24 hours a day, performing even simple operations, such as installing new software and restarting the system, can become challenging. To simplify such operations, some sites use a Web farm that consists of two or more identical sites (which administrators often call *mirrored sites*). As shown in Figure 12-31, a Web farm uses one server that receives the incoming messages. That server then forwards messages (requests) to one of the mirrored sites. If you must restart one of the mirrored servers, or if one of the mirrored servers fails, the front-end server can simply route messages to one of the other servers.

Using a Web farm, a busy site can perform load balancing by spreading the site's requests across multiple servers. If the site becomes very busy, administrators can simply add another server to the Web farm.

Although Figure 12-31 implies that the servers within the Web farm reside in close proximity to one another, the servers could reside at geographically dispersed locations. In fact, by placing servers in different regions, you better protect your site from disasters, such as fires or floods. In addition, you reduce the risk that a single network failure will prevent users from accessing your site.

Monitoring Server Performance

Most network administrators will argue that to provide optimal performance, you should always use your fastest computer as your Web server. Further, many administrators have strong opinions regarding a Web server's minimum hardware configuration, such as the minimum amount of RAM the server should use. The reality, however, is that your server's performance must support your server's workload. If your server runs only Web software and your site experiences only a few

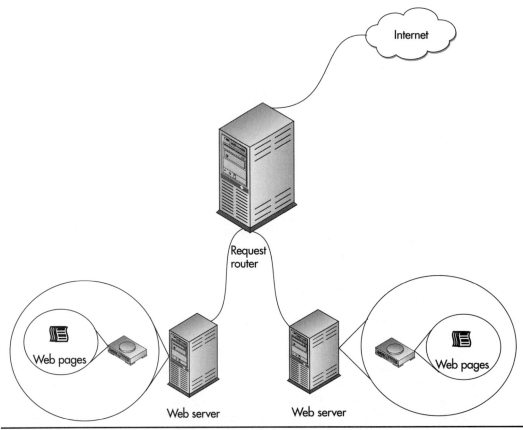

Figure 12-31 A Web farm consists of multiple identical (mirrored) servers

hundred (or even a few thousand) hits per hour, a low-end PC will more than likely meet your needs. Rather than guess whether your server hardware is sufficient, you should monitor your server's performance.

USE IT Normally, the first two indicators that your server's hardware may not be sufficient are the percentage of CPU use and the amount of available physical memory. Within Windows 2000, you can quickly monitor these two settings by performing these steps:

1. Press the CTRL-ALT-DEL keyboard combination. Windows 2000 will display the Windows Security dialog box.

2. Within the Windows Security dialog box, select Task Manager. Windows will open the Windows Task Manager dialog box.

3. Within the Windows Task Manager dialog box, select the Performance tab. Windows will display your system's current CPU use and physical memory use, as shown in Figure 12-32.

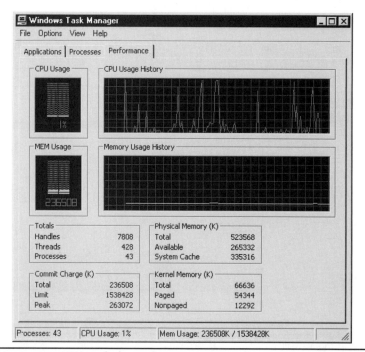

Figure 12-32　Monitoring CPU and physical memory use within Windows 2000

In addition, Windows 2000 lets you monitor a wide range of performance settings using the Performance window, shown in Figure 12-33.

To use the Performance window to monitor your server, perform these steps:

1. Select Start | Settings | Control Panel. Windows will open the Control Panel window.

2. Within the Control Panel, double-click the Administrative Tools icon. Windows will open the Administrative Tools window.

3. Within the Administrative Tools window, double-click the Performance icon. Windows will open the Performance window, shown in Figure 12-33.

4. To monitor a specific item within the Performance window, click the plus sign (+) that appears in the window's toolbar. Windows will display the Add Counters dialog box, as shown in Figure 12-34.

5. Within the Add Counters dialog box, select the object you want to monitor and then the specific characteristic of the object, which Windows 2000 refers to as a *counter*, and then click OK.

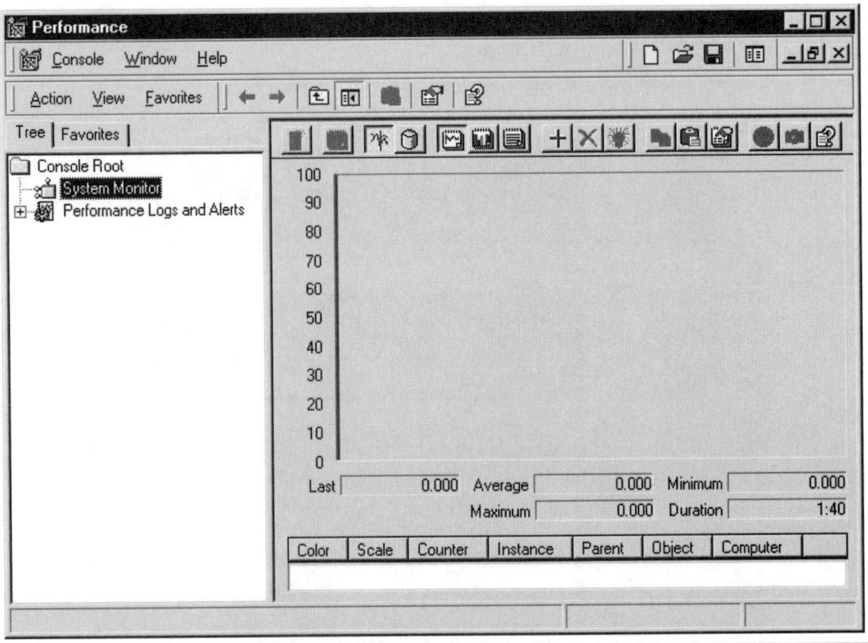

Figure 12-33 Using the Windows 2000 Performance window to monitor a server's performance

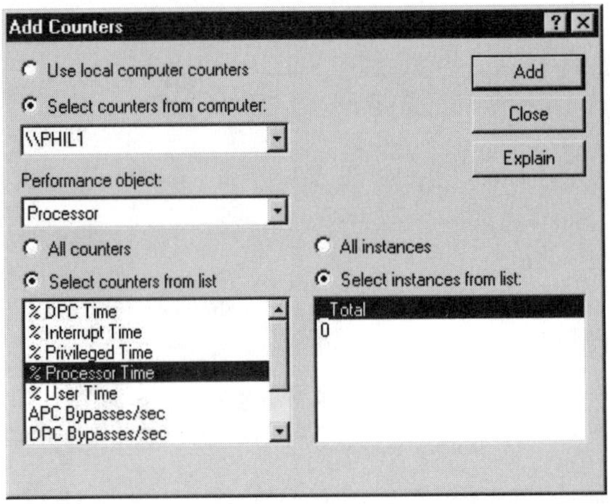

Figure 12-34 Using the Add Counters dialog box to select an item for performance monitoring

Most servers also let you enable logging so you can see the actual operations that browsers are asking the server to perform (such as the specific HTML pages that browsers are requesting). Using the log file, you can monitor your site's use, get accurate hit statistics, and more. The following output is an example of the type of contents that the IIS log file produces:

```
152.163.188.195 [04/Dec/2001:22:11:34 -0500]
    "GET /bands-up1.gif HTTP/1.0" 200 437
152.163.188.193 [04/Dec/2001:22:11:34 -0500]
    "GET /bands-over1.gif HTTP/1.0" 200 437
152.163.188.227 [04/Dec/2001:22:11:34 -0500]
    "GET /links-over1.gif HTTP/1.0" 200 360
152.163.188.161 [04/Dec/2001:22:11:34 -0500]
    "GET /home-over2.gif HTTP/1.0" 200 386
152.163.188.194 [04/Dec/2001:22:11:42 -0500]
    "GET /CommercialButtonOver.jpg HTTP/1.0" 200 5889
152.163.188.197 [04/Dec/2001:22:11:44 -0500]
    "GET /emailButtonOver1.jpg HTTP/1.0" 200 945
152.163.188.228 [04/Dec/2001:22:12:02 -0500]
    "GET /gallery2.html HTTP/1.0" 200 16808
152.163.188.164 [04/Dec/2001:22:12:16 -0500]
    "GET /a12.jpg HTTP/1.0" 200 10273
152.163.188.195 [04/Dec/2001:22:12:16 -0500]
    "GET /aaron1.jpg HTTP/1.0" 200 16805
152.163.188.228 [04/Dec/2001:22:13:59 -0500]
    "GET /phone-_.jpg HTTP/1.0" 200 3870
```

If the number of hits to your Web site is large, so too will be the size of the server's log file. The larger the log file, the more difficult it will be for you to gain meaningful information from the log file simply by viewing its contents.

USE IT On the Web, several companies offer software tools you can use to manipulate a large log file to extract the information you need:

SurfStats Log Analyzer	http://www.surfstats.com/
AWStats	http://awstats.sourceforge.net/
WebTrends Log Analyzer	http://www.webtrends.com/products/log/default.htm

Index

Note: Page numbers in *italics* refer to illustrations or charts.

NUMBERS and SYMBOLS
404 errors. *See* "Status: 404 not found" errors
@font-face declarations, CSS rules for embedding fonts
    within XHTML Web pages, 250–251
@import command, XHTML media attributes, 260
@import statements, CSS (Cascading Style Sheets), 168–169
@language command, ASP (Active Server Pages), 528, 529
@media rule. *See* CSS @media rule
; (semicolon) statement terminator, PHP4, 472
\ (backslash) escape character, PHP4, 472–473
" (double quote character), writing on Web pages, 533–535
<!-- --> (comment) tags, 24–25
    See also comments
    JavaScript and, 362

A
a:active pseudoclass, hyperlinks appearance, *191*
<a> (anchor) tags
    graphical hyperlink anchors, 300–301
    href attribute, 58–59, 93–95
    hyperlinks and, 40
    image map simulation, 100–101
    links arrays (JavaScript) and, 398–399
    multiple <iframe> tags, 256–257
    target attribute, 58, 59
    thumbnail images within tables, 93–95
    video and, 332
abort event, JavaScript events, *378*
absolute pathnames, relative pathnames comparison, 14–16
absolute positioning, overlapping text, 178
absolute and relative values for dimensioning
    cells, 85–86
    <table> tags, 84–85
"Accept Cookie" message box, sessions via PHP4, *501*
accessing Web sites via ASP, 562–565
    See also ASP (Active Server Pages)
    action attribute, 562
    ConnectionString property, 564

Count field, 564
Execute method, 564
HTTP (HyperText Transport Protocol), 565
security certificates, 565
Server.CreateObject method, 563–564
SQL CREATE TABLE statements, 563
SQL INSERT statements, 563
SQL SELECT statements, 563
SSL (Secure Socket Layer) protocol, 565
type attribute, 564
username/password pairs, 562–563
accessing Web sites via PHP4, 496–498, 509–511
    See also MySQL databases and tables; PHP4
    action attribute, 496
    fopen( ) function, 497
    header( ) function, 497
    HTTP (HyperText Transport Protocol), 498
    mysql_connect( ) function, 511
    mysql_num_rows( ) function, 511
    mysql_query( ) function, 511
    mysql_select_db( ) function, 511
    name attribute, 496
    SQL CREATE statements, 509–510
    SQL INSERT statements, 510
    SSL (Secure Socket Layer) protocol, 498
    username/password pairs, 509
accesskey attribute
    <input> tags, 120
    <label> tags and form shortcut keys, 149
action attribute
    accessing Web sites via ASP, 562
    accessing Web sites via PHP4, 496
    <form> tags, 117
    replacing Submit and Reset buttons with images,
       141–142
    retrieving form results from ASP Form collection, 550
    retrieving form results from ASP QueryString
       collection, 553–554
    sending data from HTML forms to PHP scripts,
       484–485, 486, 487

sending form results via e-mail, 143, 144
SQL queries and results via ASP, 570
Active Server Pages. *See* ASP
ActiveX objects, 419–420, 422–424, 460–462
   See also Java applets
   embedding in Web pages, 432–435
   marquee control, 460–462
   Microsoft Chat IRC, 457–460
   security, 424
   Security Settings dialog box, 435–437
   virus-detection software and, 609
Ad Rotator, 573–580
   See also ASP (Active Server Pages); banner ads
   bannerImageAltAttribute description, 574
   bannerImageURL description, 574
   bannerRedirectionURL description, 574
   bannerWeight description, 574
   BORDER keyword, 574
   GetAdvertisement method, 575, 577–579
   HEIGHT keyword, 574
   REDIRECT keyword, 574
   redirector file, 573
   Response.Redirect method, 576
   Response.Write method, 575, 577
   rotator schedule file, 573–574
   Server.CreateObject method, 575
   tracking impressions and click-throughs, 576–580
   WIDTH keyword, 574
Add Counters dialog box, monitoring Web server
   performance, 633, *634*
addToList( ) function, selection list items availability,
   134–135, 136
Adobe Photoshop. *See* Photoshop
advertisements. *See* banner ads
a:hover pseudoclass, hyperlinks appearance, *191*, 192
align attribute
   aligning cell content horizontally and vertically,
     86–87, *88*
   aligning tables on Web pages, 89
   <hr> (horizontal rule) tags, 46
   inserting Java applets into Web pages, 427
   multiple <iframe> tags, 255
aligning cell content horizontally and vertically, 86–88
   See also tables
   align attribute, 86–87, *88*
   valign attribute, 87, *88*
aligning labels, form elements and CSS, 206–209
aligning tables on Web pages, 89
   See also tables
aligning text and graphics, 37–39
   <center> tags, 39
   <img> (image) tags, 38
   <p> (paragraph) tags, 38–39
aligning Web page content via borders, 108–110
   See also tables
   border attribute, 109–110
aligning Web page text. *See* text-align property

a:link pseudoclass, hyperlinks appearance, *191*
alinkColor property
   JavaScript document object color properties, *402*
   JavaScript document objects, 394
alpha property, filter properties, *205*
alt attribute and <img> (image) tags, 37, 278–281
alt attribute and text-only viewers, 278–281
   See also graphics; <img> (image) tags
   height attribute, 279
   longdesc attribute, 281
   width attribute, 279
analyzing system vulnerabilities, 623–624
   See also security
   LANguard Network Scanner, *624*
   SATAN (Security Administrator Tool for Analyzing
     Networks), 623–624
anchor tags. *See* <a> tags
anchors arrays, JavaScript document objects, 394
animation, 316–357
   banner ads, 338–340
   broadcasting streaming audio and video, 348–351
   determining use of, 325–326
   DHTML (Dynamic HTML), 318–320
   Flash, 322–323, *324*, 342–348
   GIF (Graphics Interchange Format), 320–322, 334–342
   onLoad events and, 410–411
   overview, 317–318
   persistence of vision, 317
   plug-in software, 318
   Shockwave, 324–325
   sine wave and SinLogo.class (Java applets), 450–451
   SMIL (Synchronized Multimedia Integration
     Language) and, 354–357
   sound and, 326–328
   streaming audio and video, 351–352
   video and, 328–332
   virtual tours, 332–334
   Web cams and, 352–354
   Web design and, 318
animation and onLoad events, 410–411
   See also JavaScript
   <img> (image) tags, 410
   nextImage( ) function, 411
   onLoad event handler, 410
   src attribute, 411
animation programs, GIF animation, 334–335
AnimText.class, Java applets, 440–441
anti-aliasing, 313–315
   See also graphics; images
<applet> tags, 420
   See also Java applets
   code attribute, 424–425
   codebase attribute, 431–432
   inserting Java applets into Web pages, 424–425
applets arrays, JavaScript document objects, 394
arrays
   document, 390–392

images. *See* images arrays (JavaScript)
JavaScript, 371–372
links. *See* links arrays (JavaScript)
ASP (Active Server Pages), 524–585
    accessing Web sites via, 562–565
    Ad Rotator, 573–580
    comments, 530–531
    connecting to MySQL DBMS via MyODBC driver, 559–561
    cookies collection, 547–550
    creating, 527, 528–530
    hiding ASP source code from Web site visitors, 531
    HTML output stream, 539–543
    @language command, 528, 529
    marquee control (ActiveX), 462
    objects, 532–539
    overview, 525–527
    preventing Web browsers from displaying "stale," 543–545
    publishing, 527
    PWS (Personal Web Server) and, 527
    redirecting Web browsers, 545–547
    Response object, 532
    Response.Buffer property, 539–541
    Response.Clear method, 542–543
    Response.End method, 543
    Response.Flush method, 541–542
    Response.Write method, 529, 532–539
    retrieving form results from ASP Form collection, 550–552
    retrieving form results from ASP QueryString collection, 553–556
    retrieving information from Server Variables collection, 556–558
    scripts and, 525–527
    sessions, 565–568
    SQL queries and results via, 568–573
    start and end tags, 525, 528–531
    "Status: 404 not found" errors, 580–585
    VBScript engine and, 525, *526*, 529, 530
    Web browsers and, 527
    Web servers and, 527
attributes, 9
    assigning sets of to multiple page elements, 11
    <font> tags and, 10
    minimization of, 227
    XHTML values enclosed in quotes, 227
audio. *See* sound
auditing NTFS (NT file system), 620
auditing system events to detect intruders, 614–616
    See also security
    enabling security settings, 615–616
    Event Viewer log, 614–615
    Local Security Policy Setting dialog box, 616
auto value, cursor types, *214*
a:visited pseudoclass, hyperlinks appearance, *191*

B

<b> (bold) tags
    character formatting tags, 41–42
    formatting text, 8
background attribute
    <table> tags, 80–81
    <td> (table data) tags, 80–81
    tiled backgrounds, 301–302
background images, positioning watermarks and, 196–199
background images and colors, 78–81
    See also tables
    cells, 79
    style attribute, 81
    <table> tags and background attribute, 80–81
    <table> tags and bgcolor attribute, 80–81
    <td> (table data) tags, 78–81
    <td> (table data) tags and background attribute, 80–81
    <td> (table data) tags and bgcolor attribute, 80
    <td> (table data) tags and bordercolor attribute, 78
background-color property, style attribute, 81
background-image property
    CSS (Cascading Style Sheets), 196
    CSS (Cascading Style Sheets) and border graphics, 194–196
    positioning background images and watermarks, 196–197
    style attribute, 81
background-position property, positioning background images and watermarks, 198–199
background-repeat setting, positioning background images and watermarks, 197–198
backgrounds
    cell color, 107–108
    tiled, 301–304
backslash (\) escape character, PHP4, 472–473
BadURL( ) function, "Status: 404 not found" errors, 582–583
banner ads, 338–340
    See also GIF animation; JavaScript
    Ad Rotator, 573–576
    <img> (image) tags, 339–340
    self-changing (JavaScript), 411–413
bannerImageAltAttribute description, Ad Rotator, 574
bannerImageURL description, Ad Rotator, 574
bannerRedirectionURL description, Ad Rotator, 574
banners, drop-shadow effect and text, 193–194
bannerWeight description, Ad Rotator, 574
benchmark programs, Web sites, *627*
bgcolor attribute
    cell background colors, 108
    Flash animation, 345
    hexadecimal color values, 81–82
    <table> tags, 80–81
    <td> (table data) tags, 80
bgColor property
    JavaScript document object color properties, *402*
    JavaScript document objects, 394

<bgsound> tag, background sound, 328
<blockquote> tags, 47, *48*
blur event, JavaScript events, *378*
blur property, filter properties, *205*
<body> tags
    HTML section tags, 4
    <img> (image) tags and, 269
    XHTML, 224
bold tags. *See* <b> tags
border attribute
    aligning Web page content via borders, 109–110
    <img> (image) tags, 37
    JavaScript images arrays, 397
    <table> tags, 70, 72, 75–76
    tables, 69–70, 75–78
    tables and form layout, 147
border graphics, 194–196
    See also CSS (Cascading Style Sheets)
    background-image property, 194–196
    tiles, 194–196
BORDER keyword, Ad Rotator, 574
border properties, CSS (Cascading Style Sheets), 186–187
border-color properties, style attribute, 77–78
bordercolor attribute
    hexadecimal color values, 81–82
    <table> tags, 76–77
    <td> (table data) tags, 78
bordercolordark attribute, <table> tags, 76–77
bordercolorlight attribute, <table> tags, 76–77
borders
    aligning Web page content via, 108–110
    inserting Java applets into Web pages, 428–429
    nesting tables to control, 99, *100*
bounding boxes, transparent GIFs and, 304

 (line break) tags, <p> (paragraph) tags and, 27–31
breaking into systems, 591–594
    See also hacker threats; security
    default accounts protection, 593
    password-cracking software, 592–593
    social-engineering attacks, 593–594
    username/password pairs, 591–592
broadcasting streaming audio and video, 348–351
    See also animation; streaming audio and video;
      streaming vs. downloading video
    port numbers, 350–351
    radio, 327, 348–349
    RealNetworks server, 350
    Web sites, *349–350*
browsers. *See* Web browsers
buffer overflow errors, CGI script attacks, 595
bullets. *See* lists and bullets
button objects, 153–154
    See also forms
    <input> tags, 153–154
    type attribute, 154
    value attribute, 154

bytecode
    editing Java source code, 453–454
    Java applets, 420–422

C

caching images. *See* pre-caching images; preloading and
    caching images
calendars, KNCalendar.zip (Java applets), 442–443
call-back systems, disabling remote services, 622–623
calling JavaScript functions within event handlers, 384–385
    onClick event handler, 385
    onUnload event handler, 384
calling user-defined JavaScript functions, 382–384
    <script> tags, 383
cameras, Web, 352–354
<caption> tags, tables and, 70
captions, thumbnails with, 209–212
case sensitivity of XHTML, 225
CDATA section (XHTML)
    See also XHTML
    hiding scripts and CSS (Cascading Style Sheets),
      231–232
cellpadding attribute, <table> tags, 83–84
cells
    See also tables
    aligning content horizontally and vertically, 86–88
    background colors, 107–108
    background images and colors, 79
    images and links in, 98
    relative and absolute values for dimensioning, 85–86
    spanning multiple columns or rows, 72–74
cellspacing attribute, <table> tags, 83–84
<center> tags, aligning text and graphics, 39
CERT Web site, virus-detection software, *610*
Certificate dialog box, embedding ActiveX objects in Web
    pages, 435, *436*
certificates
    See also digital signatures; security
    accessing Web sites via ASP, 565
    client, 612–613
    embedding ActiveX objects in Web pages, 435, *436*
CGI script attacks, 594–595
    See also hacker threats; security
    buffer overflow errors, 595
change event, JavaScript events, *378*
character formatting tags, 41–42
    See also symbols and special characters
    <b> (bold) tags, 41–42
    <cite> tags, 42
    <code> tags, 42
    <del> tags, 42
    <em> (emphasis) tags, 42
    <i> (italic) tags, 42
    <q> (quotation) tags, 42
    <strong> tags, 42
    <sub> (subscript) tags, 42

\<sup\> (superscript) tags, 42
\<u\> (underline) tags, 42
chat, Microsoft Chat IRC ActiveX control, 457–460
checkboxes, 124–126
    See also forms
    \<input\> tags and type attribute, 124–126
    parsing and extracting form results via PHP4, 489
checked attribute, \<input\> tags, 125, 127
checked property, validating radio button group selections, 129
children and parents, CSS (Cascading Style Sheets) and inheritance, 165–166
chr( ) function, Response.Write method, 534, 535
chroma property, filter properties, *205, 206*
\<cite\> tags, character formatting tags, 42
class attribute
    aligning labels via form elements and CSS, 209
    overlapping text, 179
    text-align property and, 180
class names, multiple CSS rules and single selectors, 172
classes, multiple CSS rules and single selectors, 170–171
classid attribute
    Flash animation, 345
    \<object\> tags, 433, 434
click event, JavaScript events, *378*
click-throughs, tracking. *See* tracking impressions and click-throughs
client certificates, 612–613
    See also certificates; security
    Directory Security tab, 612, *613*
    SSL (Secure Socket Layer) protocol, 612
clip art, saving. *See* GIF (Graphics Interchange Format) files
clock example, inserting Java applets into Web pages, 425–432
CLUTs (color lookup tables), cross-platform issues for graphics, 275
\<code\> tags, character formatting tags, 42
code attribute
    \<applet\> tags, 424–425
    editing Java source code, 454
codebase attribute
    \<applet\> tags, 431–432
    Flash animation, 344, 345
    inserting Java applets into Web pages, 431–432
    \<object\> tags, 433, 434
color
    cell background, 107–108
    CSS rules for adding to XHTML tables, 247–249
    hexadecimal values, 81–83
    JavaScript document object color properties, 401–402
    Web-safe color palette, 298–300, 311–313
color attribute, \<font\> tags, 33–35
color lookup tables (CLUTs), cross-platform issues for graphics, 275
colorful horizontal rules, 294–296
    See also graphics
    \<hr\> (horizontal rule) tags, 294–295
    \<p\> (paragraph) tags, 296
Colors dialog box, hexadecimal color values, 82–83

cols attribute
    \<frameset\> tags, 58
    \<textarea\> tags, 121, 122
colspan attribute
    CSS rules for adding color to XHTML tables, 248
    \<td\> (table data) tags, 72, 74
    \<tr\> (table row) tags, 72, 74
columns, 183–185
    See also CSS (Cascading Style Sheets)
    \<div\> tags, 183–184
    padding properties, 185
    width property, 183–184
comments
    \<!-- --\> tags, 24–25, 362
    ASP (Active Server Pages), 530–531
    JavaScript, 365–367
    PHP4, 473–474
CommView program, intercepting and changing network messages, 589–590
complete attribute, JavaScript images arrays, 397
compound statements, PHP4, 479
compressing photographs. *See* JPEG (Joint Photographic Experts Group) format
conditional and repetitive processing
    JavaScript, 369–370
    PHP4, 478–484
connecting to MySQL DBMS via MyODBC driver, 559–561
    See also ASP (Active Server Pages); MySQL databases and tables
    objResultsSet object, 561
    Open method, 561
    Set statements, 561
Connection objects, SQL queries and results via ASP, 568, 571
connection speeds, 627–628
    See also performance
ConnectionString property
    accessing Web sites via ASP, 564
    SQL queries and results via ASP, 569
"container" elements, XHTML, 226–227
container tags, HTML, 4
converting HTML to XHTML. *See* HTML Tidy
cookie property
    JavaScript document objects, 395
    retrieving values from cookie files, 406
CookieName parameter
    removing cookies from cookie files, 408
    retrieving values from cookie files, 406
cookies, 402–409
    See also JavaScript
    formatting cookie data, 404–405
    JavaScript document objects and, 394
    preventing session masquerading, 516
    removing from cookie files, 407–409
    retrieving values from cookie files, 406–407
    sessions via ASP, 565–566, 568
    sessions via PHP4, 500
    storing on visitors' hard drives, 402–404

cookies acceptance (determining via PHP4), 493–495
    See also PHP4
    onload attribute, 494
    setCookie( ) function, 495
cookies collection, 3, 547–550
    See also ASP (Active Server Pages)
    Expires property, 548
    maintaining variable values between HTTP requests,
        547–550
    Request.Cookies collection, 547–549
    Request.Cookies method, 549–550
cookieValue( ) function, retrieving values from cookie files,
    406–407
Cool Edit, streaming audio and video, 351–352
copyright issues for Web graphics, 270–272
    See also graphics
    release forms, 271–272
copyright symbol, symbols and special characters, 43, *44*
Count field, accessing Web sites via ASP, 564
Count property
    Request.Form collection, 552
    Request.QueryString collection, 555–556
countSelections( ) function, validating radio button group
    selections, 129
Courtney program, detecting SATAN (Security Administrator
    Tool for Analyzing Networks), 624
CPU processing speed, 628–630
    See also performance
    monitoring Web server performance, 632–633
    RAM and, 630
CREATE DATABASE statements, MySQL databases and
    tables, 503
CREATE statements, accessing Web sites via PHP4, 509–510
CREATE TABLE statements
    accessing Web sites via ASP, 563
    MySQL databases and tables, 503
    tracking visitors via PHP4 and MySQL, 512–513
creating Web pages, 5–6, 11–13, *14*
    See also Web pages
    overview, 11
    text editors, 11–12
    Web layout applications, 13, *14*
    word processors, 12–13
credit card processing, security, 625
cross-platform issues for graphics, 274–276
    See also graphics
    CLUTs (color lookup tables), 275
    Photoshop, 276
crosshair value, cursor types, *214*
CSS (Cascading Style Sheets), 158–218
    adding to Web pages, 166–170
    background-image property, 194–196
    border graphics, 194–196
    border properties, 186–187
    children and parents, 165–166
    columns, 183–185
    columns and padding properties, 185, 211

    creating, 162–166
    cursor types, 212–213, *214*
    drop-shadow effect, 192–194
    embedding, 166–167
    filter properties, 203–206
    float attribute, 200
    float property, 199–200
    floating images and text, 199–200
    font-family property, 172–174
    font-size property, 174–176
    form elements and, 206–209
    <h*n*> (heading level) tags, 163, 169–170
    hiding via CDATA section (XHTML), 231–232
    hyperlinks appearance, 191–192
    icap class (initial caps), 189–190
    @import statements, 168–169
    indenting paragraphs, 188
    inheritance, 164–166
    layering Web page elements, 214–215, *216*
    letter-spacing property, 188
    line-height property, 183, 188–189
    <link> tags, 167–168
    list-style-image property, 202
    list-style-position property, 202
    list-style-type property, 201–202, *203*
    margin properties, 181–183
    multiple declarations, 163
    multiple rules and single selectors, 170–172
    overlapping text, 177–179
    overview, 159–162
    <p> (paragraph) tags, 163
    padding properties, 185, 211
    parents and children, 165–166
    position property, 159, 178–179
    positioning background images and watermarks,
        196–199
    rules, 159, 160, 162, 163–164
    rules for adding color to XHTML tables, 247–249
    selector {rule} statements, 163
    separating content from appearance, 161–162
    <style> tags, 159–160, 162, 164
    style attribute, 169–170
    table selector, 164
    terminology, 163–164
    text size keywords for XHTML, 242–245
    text-align property, 179–181
    thumbnails with captions, 209–212
    <ul> (unordered list) tags, 164
    validator, 216–218
    word spacing, 188
CSS @media rule
    printing XHTML Web pages, 263
    XHTML media attributes, 259–260
CSS page-break-before and page-break-after properties,
    printing XHTML Web pages, 261–263
CSS rules for adding color to XHTML tables, 247–249
    See also tables; XHTML

colspan attribute, 248
<tbody> tags, 247–248
<td> (table data) tags, 248
<tfoot> tags, 247–248
<th> (table heading) tags, 249
<thead> tags, 247–248
<tr> (table row) tags, 247
CSS rules for embedding fonts within XHTML Web pages, 249–251
    EOT (Embedded Object Type) files, 250–251
    <font> tags, 249–250
    @font-face declarations, 250–251
    font-family property, 249–250
    PFR (Portable Font Resource) files, 250–251
CSS validator, 216–218
    "Errors" section, 216
    Validator screen, 217, *218*
cursor property, cursor types, 212, 213
cursor types, 212–213, *214*
    See also CSS (Cascading Style Sheets)
    auto value, *214*
    crosshair value, *214*
    cursor property, 212, 213
    default value, *214*
    hand value, *214*
    help value, *214*
    move value, *214*
    resize values, *214*
    text value, *214*
    title attribute, 212
    tool tips, 212, 213
    wait value, *214*
cycle counts, GIF animation, 336–338
cycling cells, GIF animation, 334

D

data attribute, Flash animation, 345
<dd> tags, definition lists, 52–53
default accounts protection, breaking into systems, 593
default value, cursor types, *214*
definition lists, 52–53
    <dd> tags, 52–53
    <dl> tags, 52–53
    <dt> tags, 52–53
<del> tags, character formatting tags, 42
deleteCookie( ) function, removing cookies from cookie files, 408–409
denying access to systems, 594
    See also hacker threats; security
    ReloadForever.html, 594
DHTML (Dynamic HTML), 318–320
    See also animation; HTML (HyperText Markup Language)
    DOM (document object model) and, 318–319
    DynamicDemo.html, 319–320
    onmouseover and onmouseout events, 320

digital signatures
    See also certificates; security
    downloading and installing, 600, *601*
    embedding ActiveX objects in Web pages, 435
Dim keyword, Response.Write method and variables display, 536–537
Director. *See* Shockwave animation
Directory Security tab, client certificates, 612, *613*
disabled attribute
    enabling/disabling form elements "on-the-fly," 154–156
    <input> tags, 120
disk access time, performance and, 630
DisplayRotatorAd( ) function, tracking impressions and click-throughs, 578
dither patterns, JPEG files, 283
dithering techniques, Web-safe color palette, 311–313
<div> tags
    columns, 183–184
    form elements and CSS, 207–209
    margin properties, 182
    thumbnails with captions, 210–212
<dl> tags, definition lists, 52–53
<!DOCTYPE> element, 228–229, 237–238
    See also XHTML
    DTD (Document Type Definition), 237–238
    FPI (formal public identifier), 237
    Transitional XHTML DTD, 238
    validating XHTML, 239, 241
<!doctype> tags, HTML, 23–24
document arrays, 390–392
    See also JavaScript
    images and, 391–392
    properties and, 390–392
document object color properties (JavaScript), 401–402
    alinkColor property, *402*
    bgColor property, *402*
    fgColor property, *402*
    linkColor property, *402*
    selectScheme( ) function, 401
    vlinkColor property, *402*
document objects (JavaScript), 393–396
    See also JavaScript
    alinkColor property, 394
    anchors arrays, 394
    applets arrays, 394
    bgColor property, 394
    color properties, 401–402
    cookie property, 395
    cookies and, 394
    domain property, 395
    embeds arrays, 395
    fgColor property, 395
    forms arrays, 395
    images arrays, 395
    lastModified property, 395
    linkColor property, 396

links arrays, 396
referrer property, 396
title property, 396
url property, 396
vlinkColor property, 396
Document Type Definition. *See* DTD
DOM (document object model), DHTML (Dynamic HTML)
   and, 318–319
domain property
   JavaScript document objects, 395
   storing cookies on visitors' hard drives, 403
downloading
   HTML Tidy (converting HTML to XHTML), 233–234
   PHP4, 468
   preloading and caching images, 309–311
   public keys, digital signatures, and server IDs, 600, *601*
   PWS (Personal Web Server), 16–17
downloading vs. streaming video, 331–332
   See also broadcasting streaming audio and video
drop-down lists, 129–132
   See also forms
   <option> tags, 130, 132
   <select> tags, 129–131, 132
drop-shadow effect, 192–194
   See also CSS (Cascading Style Sheets)
   banners, 193–194
<dt> tags, definition lists, 52–53
DTD (Document Type Definition)
   HTML <!doctype> tags, 23–24
   Transitional XHTML, 238
   validating XHTML, 239, 241
   XHTML, 225, 228–229, 237–238
Dynamic HTML. *See* DHTML
DynamicDemo.html, DHTML (Dynamic HTML), 319–320

E

e-mail
   sending form results via, 143–144
   sending messages via PHP4, 491–493
editing Java source code, 452–457
   See also Java applets
   bytecode, 453–454
   code attribute, 454
   Java compiler, 454–455, 456
   Java programming tools, 455
   Java SDK, 454, 455
   javac command, 457
   Nervous.java, 452–453, 456–457
   source files, 452
<em> (emphasis) tags, character formatting tags, 42
<embed> tags
   ActiveX objects, 434–435
   Shockwave animation, 325
   sound, 328
Embedded Object Type (EOT) files, CSS rules for embedding
   fonts within XHTML Web pages, 250–251

embedding ActiveX objects in Web pages, 432–435
   See also inserting Java applets into Web pages;
      Java applets
   Certificate dialog box, 435, *436*
   digital signatures, 435
   <embed> tags, 434–435
   Internet Explorer, 434
   Netscape Navigator, 434–435
   <object> tags, 432–433, 434
   signed objects, 435
embedding CSS (Cascading Style Sheets), 166–167
embedding fonts, CSS rules and XHTML Web pages, 249–251
embeds arrays, JavaScript document objects, 395
empty tags
   HTML, 5
   XHTML, 226–227
encryption, 597–599
   See also security
   NTFS (NT file system), 619
   overview, 597–598
   public key, 598–599
enctype attribute
   <form> tags, 117
   sending form results via e-mail, 144
EOT (Embedded Object Type) files, CSS rules for
   embedding fonts within XHTML Web pages, 250–251
error event, JavaScript events, *378*
"Errors" section, CSS validator, 216
event handlers (JavaScript), 384–387
   See also JavaScript
   calling functions within, 384–385
   onAbort event handler, *386*
   onBlur event handler, *386*
   onChange event handler, *386*
   onClick event handler, *386*
   onDoubleClick event handler, *386*
   onDragDrop event handler, *386*
   onError event handler, *386*
   onFocus event handler, *386*
   onKeyDown event handler, *386*
   onKeyPress event handler, *386*
   onKeyUp event handler, *386*
   onLoad event handler, *387*
   onMouseDown event handler, *387*
   onMouseOut event handler, *387*
   onMouseOver event handler, *387*
   onMouseUp event handler, *387*
   onMove event handler, *387*
   onReset event handler, *387*
   onResize event handler, *387*
   onSelect event handler, *387*
   onSubmit event handler, *387*
   onUnload event handler, *387*
   overview, 385–386
Event Viewer log, auditing system events to detect intruders,
   614–615

events (JavaScript), 378–380
    See also JavaScript
    abort event, *378*
    blur event, *378*
    change event, *378*
    click event, *378*
    error event, *378*
    focus event, *378*
    load event, *378*
    mouseout event, *379*
    mouseover event, *379*
    onClick event handler, 379
    reset event, *379*
    select event, *379*
    submit event, *379*
    unload event, *379*
Execute method
    accessing Web sites via ASP, 564
    SQL queries and results via ASP, 571
expiration dates, removing cookies from cookie files, 407–408
expires keyword, storing cookies on visitors' hard drives, 403
Expires property, cookies collection, 548
external scripts, 409–410
    See also JavaScript
    <script> tags, 409–410

F

face attribute, typefaces, 26–27
farms, Web, 631, *632*
fgColor property
    JavaScript document object color properties, *402*
    JavaScript document objects, 395
filter properties, 203–206
    See also CSS (Cascading Style Sheets)
    alpha property, *205*
    blur property, *205*
    chroma property, *205, 206*
    fliph property, *205, 206*
    glow property, *205, 206*
    gray property, *205, 206*
    invert property, *205, 206*
    mask property, *205, 206*
    shadow property, *205, 206*
    wave property, *205, 206*
    width property and, 204
    xray property, *205, 206*
finding public keys, public key encryption, 599
finger command, disabling remote services, 623
firewalls, 595–597, 603–607
    See also security
    port assignments, 605–606, *607*
    software-based, 603–605
    virus-detection software and, 608
Fireworks image-editing program, 292
Flash animation, 322–323, *324*, 342–348
    See also animation
    adding splash screens to Web sites, 342–345

    advantages of, 323
    bgcolor attribute, 345
    classid attribute, 345
    codebase attribute, 344, 345
    creating, 345–347
    data attribute, 345
    FlaX shareware, 348
    height attribute, 345
    movie attribute, 345
    <object> tags, 344
    pluginspage attribute, 344, 345
    quality attribute, 345
    src attribute, 345
    type attribute, 345
    vector graphics, 322–323
    Web sites, *323, 347*
    width attribute, 345
FlaX shareware, Flash animation, 348
fLeft class, thumbnails with captions, 210–211
fliph property, filter properties, *205, 206*
float attribute, CSS (Cascading Style Sheets), 200
float property
    CSS (Cascading Style Sheets), 199–200
    form elements and CSS, 207
floating images and text, 199–200
    See also CSS (Cascading Style Sheets)
    float property, 199–200
focus event, JavaScript events, *378*
<font> tags, 10
    attributes and, 10
    color attribute, 33–35
    CSS rules for embedding fonts within XHTML Web
        pages, 249–250
    size attribute, 32–33
    typefaces, 26–27
@font-face declarations, CSS rules for embedding fonts
    within XHTML Web pages, 250–251
font-family property, 172–174
    See also CSS (Cascading Style Sheets)
    CSS rules for embedding fonts within XHTML Web
        pages, 249–250
    <p> (paragraph) tags, 173–174
    selecting typefaces, 172–174
font-size property
    CSS (Cascading Style Sheets), 174–176
    text size keywords for XHTML, 243
fontStyle parameter, navigation menus (Java applets), 447
fontType parameter, navigation menus (Java applets), 447
fopen( ) function, accessing Web sites via PHP4, 497
for attribute, <label> tags and form shortcut keys, 149
for statements
    JavaScript, 376–377
    PHP4, 482–483
<form> tags, 117–119
    See also forms
    action attribute, 117
    enctype attribute, 117

id attribute, 118
method attribute, 118, 134
name attribute, 118
onReset attribute, 118
onSubmit attribute, 118, 134
retrieving form results from ASP Form collection,
   550–551
retrieving form results from ASP QueryString
   collection, 553–554
sending data from HTML forms to PHP scripts,
   484–485, 486, 487
target attribute, 118
title attribute, 119
form elements and CSS, 206–209
See also CSS (Cascading Style Sheets)
aligning labels, 206–209
class attribute, 209
<div> tags, 207–209
float property, 207
<span> tags, 207–209
formal public identifier (FPI), XHTML <!DOCTYPE>
   element, 237
formatting
character tags, 41–42
<hr> (horizontal rule) tags, 44–46
<pre> (preformatted text) tags, 54–55
formatting cookie data, 404–405
See also cookies; JavaScript
setCookie( ) function, 404, 405
visitorSignIn( ) function, 405
formatting text, 6–8
<b> (bold) tags, 8
<i> (italic) tags, 8
<p> (paragraph) tags, 7
<u> (underline) tags, 8
forms, 112–156
button objects, 153–154
checkboxes, 124–126
disabled attribute, 154–156
drop-down lists, 129–132
<form> tags, 117–119
hiding input in password fields, 152–153
hotmail example, 113, *114*
<label> tags and form shortcut keys, 148–149
multiline input fields, 120–122
<optgroup> tags (grouping XHTML selection list
   items), 245–247
overview, 113–119
parsing and extracting results via PHP4, 488–491
passing values via hidden fields, 151–152
processing of, 115–117
radio buttons, 126–129
replacing Submit and Reset buttons with images,
   141–143
Reset buttons, 138–140
results of. *See* parsing and extracting form results
   via PHP4

retrieving results from ASP Form collection, 550–552
retrieving results from ASP QueryString collection,
   553–556
selection list items availability, 134–136
selection list values and hidden fields, 136–137
sending data to PHP scripts, 484–488
sending results via e-mail, 143–144
single-line input fields, 119–120
Submit buttons, 140–143
tables and form layout, 145–147
ValidateForm( ) function, 123–124
validating data, 122–124
validating radio button group selections, 128–129
validating selection list choices, 132–134
validating via onClick attribute, 149–150
forms arrays, JavaScript document objects, 395
FPI (formal public identifier), XHTML <!DOCTYPE>
   element, 237
fps (frames per second), GIF animation, 336–338
<frame> tags, src attribute, 58
frames, 57–60
<frame> tags, 58
<frameset> tags, 58
inline (XHTML), 251–257
<noframes> tags, 60
frames simulation, 104–107
See also tables
framesets, 104
<frameset> tags, 58
cols attribute, 58
navigation menus, 56
FTP (file transfer protocol), upload file functionality via
   PHP4, 520
functions (JavaScript), 362–365, 380–385
See also JavaScript
built-in, 380
calling user-defined, 382–384
calling within event handlers, 384–385
executing statements within Web pages, 380–381
inserting within HTML, 370
overview, 362–364
passing values between, 364–365
write method, 380–381

G

Gabriel program, detecting SATAN (Security Administrator
   Tool for Analyzing Networks), 624
Get Info dialog box, graphics size, 270, *271*
GET method
preventing visitors from changing variable values via
   URL arguments, 511
retrieving form results from ASP Form collection, 551
retrieving form results from ASP QueryString
   collection, 553–554
sending data from HTML forms to PHP scripts, 485–487

GetAdvertisement method
    Ad Rotator, 575, 577–579
    tracking impressions and click-throughs, 577–579
getCookieValue( ) function, retrieving values from cookie files, 406–407
GetOrderNumber.asp, SQL queries and results via ASP, 569–570
GIF (Graphics Interchange Format) files, 268
    See also graphics; graphics file formats
    animation, 320–322, 334–342
    interlaced mode, 286, *287*
    noninterlaced mode, 286
    RLE (Run Length Encoding) compression, 286
    tips, 288
    transparent. *See* transparent GIFs
GIF animation, 320–322, 334–342
    See also animation
    animation programs, 334–335
    banner ads, 338–340
    creating, 334–336
    cycle counts, 336–338
    cycling cells, 334
    fps (frames per second), 336–338
    <img> (image) tags, 321, 335–336
    internal settings, 336–338
    src attribute, 322, 336
    tweening, 341–342
    Web sites, *322*
glow property, filter properties, *205*, *206*
graphical hyperlink anchors, 300–301
    See also graphics; hyperlinks
    <a> (anchor) tags, 300–301
    <img> (image) tags, 301
graphics, 264–315
    See also images; <img> (image) tags
    aligning, 37–39
    anti-aliasing, 313–315
    balancing text and graphics on Web pages, 272–274
    colorful horizontal rules, 294–296
    copyright issues for Web, 270–272
    creating, 267
    cross-platform issues, 274–276
    file formats, 268–269
    Get Info dialog box and size of, 270, *271*
    GIF (Graphics Interchange Format) files, 268, 286–288
    graphical hyperlink anchors, 300–301
    image-editing programs, 291–292
    <img> tags. *See* <img> (image) tags
    inserting into Web pages, 269–270
    interlaced option, 288–289
    Internet access speeds and, 270
    JPEG (Joint Photographic Experts Group) format, 102, 268, 283–286
    lowsrc attribute, 296–298
    making images appear to load faster, 288–289
    overview, 265

PNG (Portable Network Graphic) format, 268–269, 290, *291*
    preloading and caching images, 309–311
    progression option, 288–289
    scanners and, 292–294
    smoothing edges. *See* anti-aliasing
    thumbnails and retrieving full size images, 307–309
    tiled backgrounds, 301–304
    transparent GIFs, 304–307
    Web design and, 265–267
    Web-safe color palette, 298–300, 311–313
graphics file formats, 268–269
    GIF (Graphics Interchange Format) files, 268, 286–288
    JPEG (Joint Photographic Experts Group) format, 102, 268, 283–286
    PNG (Portable Network Graphic) format, 268–269, 290, *291*
gray property, filter properties, *205*, *206*
grouping XHTML selection list items. *See* <optgroup> tags
gutter size, Web page, 110–111

H

<h*n*> (heading level) tags, 32
    CSS (Cascading Style Sheets), 163, 169–170
hacker threats, 587–595
    See also security
    breaking into systems, 591–594
    CGI script attacks, 594–595
    denying access to systems, 594
    intercepting and changing network messages, 587–590, *591*
    overview, 587
hand value, cursor types, *214*
hash attribute, JavaScript links arrays, 399
hash property, pointing hyperlinks to new files "on-the-fly," 413
<head> tags
    HTML, 4
    XHTML, 224
header( ) function, accessing Web sites via PHP4, 497
heading level tags. *See* <h*n*> tags
headings, table. *See* <th> tags
height attribute
    alt attribute and text-only viewers, 279
    <embed> tags, 325
    Flash animation, 345
    <iframe> tags, 253
    <img> (image) tags, 37, 277–278
    JavaScript images arrays, 397
    <object> tags, 433
    preloading and caching images, 309–310
    <table> tags, 84–85
    tables and form layout, 145–146
    <td> (table data) tags, 85
    <th> (table heading) tags, 86
HEIGHT keyword, Ad Rotator, 574

help value, cursor types, *214*
hexadecimal color values, 81–83
    See also <table> tags; tables
    bgcolor attribute, 81–82
    bordercolor attribute, 81–82
    Colors dialog box, 82–83
hidden fields
    passing values via, 151–152
    selection list values and, 136–137
hiding ASP source code from Web site visitors, 531
    See also ASP (Active Server Pages)
hiding input in password fields, 152–153
    See also forms
    type attribute, 153
hiding scripts and CSS (Cascading Style Sheets), CDATA
    section (XHTML), 231–232
hiding scripts from Web browsers without JavaScript support,
    361–362
    See also JavaScript
horizontal rule tags. *See* <hr> (horizontal rule) tags
host attribute, JavaScript links arrays, 399
hostname attribute, JavaScript links arrays, 399
hotspots, image map simulation, 100
<hr> (horizontal rule) tags, 44–46
    align attribute, 46
    colorful horizontal rules, 294–295
    noshade attribute, 46
    size attribute, 46
    width attribute, 46
href attribute
    <a> (anchor) tags, 58–59, 93–95
    hyperlinks, 40–41
    image map simulation, 101
    JavaScript links arrays, 399
    <link> tags, 167
    multiple <iframe> tags, 257
    pointing hyperlinks to new files "on-the-fly," 413,
        414–415
    replacing Submit and Reset buttons with images, 142
    thumbnail images within tables, 93–95
    thumbnails and retrieving full size images, 307, 308–309
hspace attribute, JavaScript images arrays, 398
<html> tags
    HTML section tags, 4
    XHTML section tags, 223–224
HTML (HyperText Markup Language)
    aligning text and graphics, 37–39
    animation, 316–357
    ASP (Active Server Pages), 524–585
    attribute minimization, 227
    attributes, 9
    character formatting tags, 41–42
    comments, 24–25
    container tags, 4
    converting to XHTML. *See* HTML Tidy
    creating Web pages, 5–6
    CSS (Cascading Style Sheets), 158–218

definition lists, 52–53
DHTML (Dynamic HTML) and, 318–320
displaying multiple Web pages. *See* frames
DTD (Document Type Definition), 23–24
empty tags, 5
formatting text, 6–8
forms, 112–156
frames, 57–60
graphics, 264–315
HTTP (HyperText Transport Protocol) and, 1–2
hyperlinks, 40–41
inserting JavaScript functions within, 370
Java applets and, 418–462
JavaScript and, 358–417
navigation menus, 56–57
nested lists, 51–52
overview, 1–2
pathnames, 14–16
performance, 625–635
PHP4 and, 464–522
PWS (Personal Web Server) and, 16–21
section tags, 4–5
security, 586–625
symbols and special characters, 42–44
tables, 62–111
typefaces, 26–27
Web browsers and, 1, 2–3
XHTML and, 220–263
HTML Tidy (converting HTML to XHTML), 233–237
    configuration options, 236–237
    conversion steps, 235–236
    downloading, 233–234
    Tidy Configuration dialog box, *235*
    Tidy Output dialog box, *236*
    TidyGUI.exe, 234–235
HTML Validation service, validating XHTML, 239–242
HTTP (HyperText Transport Protocol), 1–2
    accessing Web sites via ASP, 565
    accessing Web sites via PHP4, 498
    "Status: 404 not found" errors, 580–585
HTTP_X_FORWARDED_FOR field, IP address
    determination, 515
hyperlinks, 40–41
    See also graphical hyperlink anchors
    <a> (anchor) tags, 40
    defined, 40
    href attribute, 40–41
    pointing to new files "on-the-fly," 413–415
    preventing linking to Web pages via PHP4, 498–499
    sending e-mail messages via PHP4, 491
    <u> (underline) tags caveat, 41
hyperlinks appearance, 191–192
    See also CSS (Cascading Style Sheets)
    a:active pseudoclass, *191*
    a:hover pseudoclass, *191*, 192
    a:link pseudoclass, *191*
    a:visited pseudoclass, *191*

I

<i> (italic) tags
    character formatting tags, 42
    formatting text, 8
icap class (initial caps), CSS (Cascading Style Sheets), 189–190
id attribute
    <form> tags, 118
    <input> tags, 119, 125, 127
    <object> tags, 433
    <select> tags, 131
    <textarea> tags, 121
ID cookies, sessions via ASP, 565–566, 568
if statements, 372–376
    See also JavaScript
    multiple conditions, 374–375
    Not operator, 375–376
    overview, 372–374
    PHP4, 478–481
    SQL queries and results via PHP4, 505
if-else statements, PHP4, 479–480
if-elseif structures, PHP4, 480–481
<iframe> tags, 252–257
    See also inline frames (XHTML)
    height attribute, 253
    multiple, 255–257
    name attribute, 253–254
    scrolling attribute, 253
    src attribute, 253
    target attribute, 254
    width attribute, 253
IIS (Internet Information Server)
    client certificates, 612–613
    server IDs, 601–602, *603*
    "Status: 404 not found" errors, 583–585
IIS log file, monitoring Web server performance, 635
image map simulation, 100–101
    See also tables
    <a> (anchor) tags, 100–101
    hotspots, 100
    href attribute, 101
image maps, 65–66
image parameter, pop-up navigation menus, 439
Image Size dialog box, Photoshop, 294
image tags. *See* <img> tags
image-editing programs, 291–292
    See also graphics
    Macromedia Fireworks, 292
    Photoshop, 292
    src attribute, 291
imageposition parameter, pop-up navigation menus, 439
images
    See also graphics; <img> (image) tags
    anti-aliasing, 313–315
    border graphics, 194–196

    caching. *See* pre-caching images; preloading and caching images
    document arrays and, 391–392
    file formats, 268–269
    floating text and, 199–200
    making appear to load faster, 288–289
    pre-caching, 415–416
    preloading and caching, 309–311
    replacing Submit and Reset buttons with, 141–143
    slicing for quick loading, 102, *103*
    smoothing edges. *See* anti-aliasing
    thumbnail within tables, 93–95
    thumbnails with captions, 209–212
    tiled backgrounds, 301–304
    wrapping text around, 91–93
images arrays, JavaScript document objects, 395
images arrays (JavaScript), 396–398
    See also arrays; JavaScript
    border attribute, 397
    complete attribute, 397
    height attribute, 397
    hspace attribute, 398
    lowsrc attribute, 398
    name attribute, 398
    overview, 396–397
    src attribute, 398
    vspace attribute, 398
    width attribute, 398
images and links in cells, 98
    See also tables
    src attribute, 98
    <table> tags, 98
    <td> (table data) tags, 98
<img> (image) tags, 35–37, 269–270, 277–282, *283*
    See also graphics; images
    aligning text and graphics, 38
    alt attribute, 37
    alt attribute and text-only viewers, 278–281
    animation and onLoad events, 410
    banner ads, 339–340
    <body> tags and, 269
    border attribute, 37
    dimensioning, 277–278
    GIF animation, 321, 335–336
    graphical hyperlink anchors, 301
    graphics, 269–270
    height attribute, 37, 277–278
    lowsrc attribute, 296–298
    pre-caching images, 415
    preloading and caching images, 309–310
    src attribute, 36, 269
    title attribute and tool tips, 281–282, *283*
    width attribute, 37, 277–278
    XHTML, 269
@import command, XHTML media attributes, 260
@import statements, CSS (Cascading Style Sheets), 168–169

impressions, tracking. *See* tracking impressions and click-throughs
indenting paragraphs, CSS (Cascading Style Sheets), 188
Indexed Color dialog box, Photoshop, 299, *300*
inheritance, CSS (Cascading Style Sheets), 164–166
initial caps (icap class), CSS (Cascading Style Sheets), 189–190
inline frames (XHTML), 251–257
    See also frames; XHTML
    <iframe> tags, 252–257
<input> tags
    accesskey attribute, 120
    button objects, 153–154
    checkboxes, 124–126
    checked attribute, 125, 127
    disabled attribute, 120
    id attribute, 119, 125, 127
    maxlength attribute, 120
    name attribute, 120, 125, 127
    radio buttons, 126–127
    readonly attribute, 120
    single-line input fields, 119–120
    size attribute, 120
    tabindex attribute, 120
    type attribute, 119, 124–127, 138
    value attribute, 120, 125, 127
<input> tags and type attribute
    checkboxes, 124–126
    radio buttons, 126–127
    Reset buttons, 138
INSERT statements
    accessing Web sites via ASP, 563
    accessing Web sites via PHP4, 510
    MySQL databases and tables, 503–504
inserting graphics into Web pages, 269–270
inserting Java applets into Web pages, 424–432
    See also embedding ActiveX objects in Web pages;
      Java applets
    align attribute, 427
    <applet> tags, 424–425
    borders, 428–429
    clock example, 425–432
    codebase attribute, 431–432
    .jar (Java Archive) files, 431
    overview, 424–425
    <param> tags, 430
    passing parameter values, 429–431
    positioning Java applets, 426–429
installing
    PHP4, 468–469
    public keys, digital signatures, and server IDs, 600, *601*
    PWS (Personal Web Server), 17–18
intercepting and changing network messages, 587–590, *591*
    See also hacker threats; security
    CommView program, 589–590
    tracert command, 588–589
interlaced mode, GIF files, 286, *287*

interlaced option, graphics, 288–289
Internet access speeds, graphics and, 270
Internet Explorer
    embedding ActiveX objects in Web pages, 434
    using only ActiveX objects, 460–462
Internet Information Server. *See* IIS
invert property, filter properties, *205, 206*
IP address determination, 514–516
    See also PHP4
    HTTP_X_FORWARDED_FOR field, 515
IP addresses, PWS (Personal Web Server) and, 19–21
isEmpty( ) function, sessions via ASP, 568
isset( ) function, parsing and extracting form results via PHP4, 489–490
italic tags. *See* <i> tags
Item method
    Request.Form collection, 552
    Request.QueryString collection, 556

J

.jar (Java Archive) files, inserting Java applets into Web pages, 431
Java applets, 418–462
    ActiveX objects and, 419–420, 422–424, 460–462
    AnimText.class, 440–441
    <applet> tags, 420
    bytecode, 420–422
    codebase attribute, 431–432
    editing Java source code, 452–457
    embedding ActiveX objects in Web pages, 432–435
    inserting into Web pages, 424–432
    .jar (Java Archive) files, 431
    JVM (Java Virtual Machine), 422
    KNCalendar.zip, 442–443
    Microsoft Chat IRC ActiveX control and, 457–460
    navigation menus, 444–447
    NewsScroller applet, 448–450
    <object> tags, 420
    overview, 419–420
    passing parameter values to, 429–431
    PetQuotes.class, 443–444
    pop-up navigation menus, 437–440
    positioning, 426–429
    security, 422
    Security Settings dialog box, 435–437
    SinLogo.class, 450–451
    Web browser and, 420–422
Java compiler, editing Java source code, 454–455, 456
Java programming tools, editing Java source code, 455
Java SDK, editing Java source code, 454, 455
javac command, editing Java source code, 457
JavaScript, 358–417
    See also scripts
    <!-- --> (comment) tags and, 362
    animation and onLoad events, 410–411
    arrays, 371–372

banner ads, 411–413
built-in functions, 380
comments, 362, 365–367
conditional and repetitive processing, 369–370
cookies, 402–409
declaring variables, 367
document arrays, 390–392
document object color properties, 401–402
document objects, 393–396
event handlers, 384–387
events, 378–380
external scripts, 409–410
for statements, 376–377
functions, 362–365, 370, 380–385
hiding scripts from Web browsers without JavaScript
    support, 361–362
if statements, 372–376
images arrays, 396–398
inserting functions within HTML, 370
inserting statements into HTML, 360–361
links arrays, 398–400
<marquee> tags, 416–417
naming Web page objects, 392–393
navigation bars, 388–390
<noscript> tags, 370–371
operators, 367–369
overview, 359–360
passing values between functions, 364–365
pointing hyperlinks to new files "on-the-fly," 413–415
pre-caching images, 415–416
repetitive and conditional processing, 369–370
reserved words, 365
<script> tags, 360–361
self-changing banner ads, 411–413
user-defined functions, 382–384
while loops, 377–378
write method, 380–381
JPEG (Joint Photographic Experts Group) format, 283–286
See also graphics; graphics file formats
dither patterns, 283
graphics file formats, 268
lossy compression, 284
nonprogressive mode, 284
progressive mode, 284, *285*
slicing images for quick loading, 102
tips, 285–286
"justify" option, text-align property, 180
JVM (Java Virtual Machine), 422
See also Java applets

K

Key method
    Request.Form collection, 552
    Request.QueryString collection, 556
KNCalendar.zip, Java applets, 442–443

L

<label> tags and form shortcut keys, 148–149
    See also forms
    accesskey attribute, 149
    for attribute, 149
label attribute, <optgroup> tags (grouping XHTML selection
    list items), 246
label parameter, pop-up navigation menus, 439
LabelButton.class, navigation menus (Java applets), 445
labels, aligning via form elements and CSS, 206–209
@language command, ASP (Active Server Pages), 528, 529
LANguard Network Scanner, analyzing system
    vulnerabilities, *624*
large keyword, text size keywords for XHTML, *243*
larger keyword, text size keywords for XHTML, 244
lastModified property, JavaScript document objects, 395
layering Web page elements, 214–215, *216*
    See also CSS (Cascading Style Sheets)
    z-index property, 215, *216*
length property, validating radio button group selections, 129
letter-spacing property, CSS (Cascading Style Sheets), 188
<li> tags, nested lists, 52
line break tags. *See*
 tags
line-height property, CSS (Cascading Style Sheets), 183,
    188–189
<link> tags, 167–168
    See also CSS (Cascading Style Sheets)
    href attribute, 167
    media attribute, 167–168
    type attribute, 167
linkColor property
    JavaScript document object color properties, *402*
    JavaScript document objects, 396
links. *See* hyperlinks
links arrays, JavaScript document objects, 396
links arrays (JavaScript), 398–400
    <a> (anchor) tags and, 398–399
    hash attribute, 399
    host attribute, 399
    hostname attribute, 399
    href attribute, 399
    overview, 398–399
    pathname attribute, 399
    port attribute, 400
    protocol attribute, 400
    search attribute, 400
    target attribute, 400
list boxes, parsing and extracting form results via PHP4, 490
list-style-image property, CSS (Cascading Style Sheets), 202
list-style-position property, CSS (Cascading Style Sheets), 202
list-style-type property, 201–202, *203*
    See also CSS (Cascading Style Sheets)
    style attribute, 202
    <ul> (unordered list) tags, 202, *203*
    values, *201*

lists
  definition, 52–53
  form drop-down, 129–132
  nested, 51–52
  ordered (<ol> tags), 48–50
  selection. *See* selection lists
  unordered (<ul> tags), 50–51
lists and bullets, 96–97
  See also tables
  <ul> (unordered list) tags, 96
load event, JavaScript events, *378*
Local Security Policy Setting dialog box, auditing system
  events to detect intruders, 616
log files, tracking visitors via PHP4 and MySQL, 512–513
longdesc attribute, alt attribute and text-only viewers, 281
lossless compression, PNG files, 290
lossy compression, JPEG files, 284
lowsrc attribute, 296–298
  See also graphics; <img> (image) tags
  JavaScript images arrays, 398

M

Macintosh, cross-platform issues for graphics, 274–276
macro-based viruses, virus-detection software, 607–608
Macromedia Director. *See* Shockwave animation
Macromedia Fireworks image-editing program, 292
Macromedia Flash. *See* Flash animation
mail( ) function, sending e-mail messages via PHP4, 491–493
mailto:, sending form results via e-mail, 144
maps, image. *See* image map simulation; image maps
margin properties, 181–183
  See also CSS (Cascading Style Sheets)
  <div> tags, 182
margin width, Web page, 110–111
<marquee> tags, 416–417
  See also JavaScript
marquee control (ActiveX), 460–462
  See also ActiveX objects
  ASP (Active Server Pages), 462
mask property, filter properties, *205, 206*
maxlength attribute, <input> tags, 120
media attributes, <link> tags, 167–168
media attributes (XHTML), 257–260
  See also XHTML
  CSS @, 259–260
  @import command, 260
@media rule. *See* CSS @media rule
medium keyword, text size keywords for XHTML, *242*
memory
  CPU processing speed and, 630
  monitoring Web server performance, 632–633
<menu item> parameter, pop-up navigation menus, 439–440
MenuApplet.class, navigation menus (Java applets), 445–447
menus, navigation. *See* navigation menus; pop-up
  navigation menus
messages, intercepting and changing network, 587–590, *591*

method attribute
  <form> tags, 118, 134
  retrieving form results from ASP Form collection,
    550–551
  retrieving form results from ASP QueryString
    collection, 553
  sending data from HTML forms to PHP scripts, 485
Microsoft Chat IRC ActiveX control, 457–460
  See also ActiveX objects
mkdir( ) function, upload file functionality via PHP4, 520–521
monitoring Web server performance, 631–635
  See also performance
  Add Counters dialog box, 633, *634*
  CPU processing speed, 632–633
  IIS log file, 635
  RAM, 632–633
  Web sites, *635*
  Windows Task Manager dialog box, 632–633, *634*
mouseout and mouseover events, JavaScript events, *379*
move value, cursor types, *214*
move_uploaded_file( ) function, upload file functionality via
  PHP4, 521–522
movie attribute, Flash animation, 345
mt_rand( ) function, random passwords via PHP4, 507
multiline input fields, 120–122
  See also forms
  <textarea> tags, 120–122
multiple attribute, <select> tags, 131, 132–133, 134
multiple conditions, JavaScript if statements, 374–375
multiple CSS rules and single selectors, 170–172
  See also CSS (Cascading Style Sheets)
  class names, 172
  classes, 170–171
  p.critical text style, 171
  p.regular text style, 171
multiple declarations, CSS (Cascading Style Sheets), 163
multiple <iframe> tags, 255–257
  See also <iframe> tags; inline frames (XHTML)
  <a> (anchor) tags, 256–257
  align attribute, 255
  href attribute, 257
  onClick events, 256–257
  target attribute, 256, 257
multiple Web pages, displaying. *See* frames
MyODBC driver, connecting to MySQL DBMS via, 559–561
MySQL databases and tables, 502–504
  See also PHP4
  accessing Web sites via PHP4, 509–511
  connecting to via MyODBC driver, 559–561
  SQL CREATE DATABASE statements, 503
  SQL CREATE TABLE statements, 503
  SQL INSERT statements, 503–504
  SQL SELECT statements, 504
  tracking visitors via PHP4 and MySQL, 512–514
mysql_connect( ) function
  accessing Web sites via PHP4, 511
  SQL queries and results via PHP4, 504, 505

mysql_fetch_array( ) function, SQL queries and results via PHP4, 504, 506

mysql_num_rows( ) function, accessing Web sites via PHP4, 511

mysql_query( ) function
    accessing Web sites via PHP4, 511
    SQL queries and results via PHP4, 504, 505–506

mysql_select_db( ) function, accessing Web sites via PHP4, 511

N

name attribute
    accessing Web sites via PHP4, 496
    <embed> tags, 325
    <form> tags, 118
    <iframe> tags, 253–254
    <input> tags, 120, 125, 127
    JavaScript images arrays, 398
    parsing and extracting form results via PHP4, 489
    replacing Submit and Reset buttons with images, 142
    <select> tags, 131
    sending data from HTML forms to PHP scripts, 486
    sending form results via e-mail, 143
    Submit buttons, 141
    <textarea> tags, 121
    validating radio button group selections, 128

naming Web page objects, JavaScript, 392–393

navigation bars, 388–390
    See also JavaScript
    newImage( ) function, 389
    onMouseOut event handler, 388–390
    onMouseOver event handler, 388–390

navigation menus, 56–57
    <frameset> tags, 56

navigation menus (Java applets), 444–447
    fontStyle parameter, 447
    fontType parameter, 447
    LabelButton.class, 445
    MenuApplet.class, 445–447
    pop-up, 437–440
    targetWindow parameter, 446

navigation sidebars, 97–98
    See also tables

Nervous.java, editing Java source code, 452–453, 456–457

nested lists, 51–52
    <li> tags, 52

nesting
    tables to control borders, 99, *100*
    XHTML elements, 224–225

Netscape Navigator, embedding ActiveX objects in Web pages, 434–435

Network dialog box, disabling printer and file sharing, *611*

network messages, intercepting and changing, 587–590, *591*

newImage( ) function
    navigation bars, 389
    pre-caching images, 415

newOption( ) function, selection list items availability, 136

NewsScroller applet, 448–450
    See also Java applets

nextImage( ) function, animation and onLoad events, 411

<noframes> tags, frames and, 60

noninterlaced mode, GIF files, 286

nonprogressive mode, JPEG files, 284

Norton Personal Firewall, software-based firewalls, *605*

<noscript> tags, JavaScript, 370–371

noshade attribute, <hr> (horizontal rule) tags, 46

Not operator, JavaScript if statements, 375–376

Nothing session variables, sessions via ASP, 567

now( ) function, Response.Write method, 535

NTFS (NT file system), 617–620
    See also security
    auditing, 620
    determining current file system, 617
    encryption, 619
    permissions, 618

O

<object> tags
    classid attribute, 433, 434
    codebase attribute, 433, 434
    embedding ActiveX objects in Web pages, 432–433, 434
    Flash animation, 344
    height attribute, 433
    id attribute, 433
    Java applets, 420
    param attribute, 433
    sound, 328
    type attribute, 433
    width attribute, 433

objects, ASP (Active Server Pages), 532–539

objResultsSet object, connecting to MySQL DBMS via MyODBC driver, 561

ODBC (open database connectivity), connecting to MySQL DBMS via MyODBC driver, 559–561

<ol> (ordered list) tags, 48–50
    start attribute, 50
    type attribute, 50

onAbort event handler, JavaScript event handlers, *386*

onBlur event handler, JavaScript event handlers, *386*

onChange event handler, JavaScript event handlers, *386*

onClick attribute, validating forms via, 149–150

onClick event handler
    calling JavaScript functions within event handlers, 385
    JavaScript event handlers, *386*
    JavaScript events, 379

onClick events, multiple <iframe> tags, 256–257

onDoubleClick event handler, JavaScript event handlers, *386*

onDragDrop event handler, JavaScript event handlers, *386*

onError event handler, JavaScript event handlers, *386*

onFocus event handler, JavaScript event handlers, *386*

onKeyDown event handler, JavaScript event handlers, *386*

onKeyPress event handler, JavaScript event handlers, *386*

onKeyUp event handler, JavaScript event handlers, *386*

onload attribute, cookies acceptance (determining via PHP4), 494

onLoad event handler
    animation and onLoad events, 410
    JavaScript event handlers, *387*
    pre-caching images, 415, 416
    self-changing banner ads (JavaScript), 412

onLoad events, animation and, 410–411

onMouseDown event handler, JavaScript event handlers, *387*

onMouseOut event handler
    JavaScript event handlers, *387*
    navigation bars, 388–390

onMouseOver event handler
    JavaScript event handlers, *387*
    navigation bars, 388–390

onmouseover and onmouseout events, DHTML (Dynamic HTML), 320

onMouseUp event handler, JavaScript event handlers, *387*

onMove event handler, JavaScript event handlers, *387*

onReset attribute
    <form> tags, 118
    Reset buttons, 139

onReset event handler, JavaScript event handlers, *387*

onResize event handler, JavaScript event handlers, *387*

onSelect event handler, JavaScript event handlers, *387*

onSubmit attribute
    <form> tags, 118, 134
    Submit buttons, 141
    validating radio button group selections, 129

onSubmit event handler, JavaScript event handlers, *387*

onUnload event handler
    calling JavaScript functions within event handlers, 384
    JavaScript event handlers, *387*

Open method
    connecting to MySQL DBMS via MyODBC driver, 561
    SQL queries and results via ASP, 569

opendir( ) function, upload file functionality via PHP4, 520–521

operating systems and server applications, performance and, 630

operators
    JavaScript, 367–369
    PHP4, 476–477, 482

<optgroup> tags (grouping XHTML selection list items), 245–247
    See also forms; XHTML
    label attribute, 246

<option> tags
    drop-down lists, 130, 132
    selected attribute, 132
    value attribute, 132

ordered lists, <ol> tags, 48–50

overflow errors, CGI script attacks, 595

overlapping tags caveat, XHTML, 224–225

overlapping text, 177–179
    See also CSS (Cascading Style Sheets)
    absolute positioning, 178
    class attribute, 179

    <p> (paragraph) tags, 179
    position property, 178–179
    relative positioning, 178

P

<p> (paragraph) tags
    See also paragraphs
    aligning text and graphics, 38–39

 (line break) tags and, 27–31
    colorful horizontal rules, 296
    CSS (Cascading Style Sheets), 163
    font-family property, 173–174
    formatting text, 7
    overlapping text, 179

padding properties
    CSS (Cascading Style Sheets) and columns, 185, 211
    thumbnails with captions, 211

page layout, tables and, 72

page-break-before and page-break-after properties, printing XHTML Web pages, 261–263

<par> tags, SMIL (Synchronized Multimedia Integration Language), 355–356

paragraphs
    See also <p> tags
    indenting via CSS (Cascading Style Sheets), 188

<param> tags
    inserting Java applets into Web pages, 430
    pop-up navigation menus, 439–440

param attribute, <object> tags, 433

parameter values, passing to Java applets, 429–431

parents and children, CSS (Cascading Style Sheets) and inheritance, 165–166

parsing and extracting form results via PHP4, 488–491
    See also forms; PHP4; retrieving form results from ASP...
    checkboxes, 489
    form results validation script, 490–491
    isset( ) function, 489–490
    list boxes, 490
    name attribute, 489
    radio buttons, 489–490

passing parameter values to Java applets, 429–431

passing values between JavaScript functions, 364–365

passing values via hidden fields, 151–152
    See also forms
    type attribute, 151
    validateAndSubmit( ) function, 152
    value attribute, 151

password fields, hiding input in, 152–153

password-cracking software, breaking into systems, 592–593

passwords
    See also username/password pairs
    accessing Web sites via ASP, 562–565
    accessing Web sites via PHP4, 496–498, 509–511
    preventing linking to Web pages via PHP4, 498–499
    random via PHP4, 507–509

path keyword, storing cookies on visitors' hard drives, 403
pathname attribute, JavaScript links arrays, 399
pathname property, pointing hyperlinks to new files "on-the-fly," 413–414
pathnames, relative vs. absolute, 14–16
p.critical text style, multiple CSS rules and single selectors, 171
performance, 625–635
    chain of Web server, 625, *626*
    connection speeds, 627–628
    CPU processing speed, 628–630
    disk access time, 630
    monitoring Web server, 631–635
    operating systems and server applications, 630
    overview, 625–627
    proxy servers and Web-caching devices, 630, *631*
    Web farms, 631, *632*
    Web sites, *627*
permissions, NTFS (NT file system), 618
persistence of vision, animation, 317
Personal Web Manager, 18, *19*
    See also PWS (Personal Web Server)
Personal Web Server. *See* PWS
PetQuotes.class, Java applets, 443–444
PFR (Portable Font Resource) files, CSS rules for embedding fonts within XHTML Web pages, 250–251
photographs, compressing. *See* JPEG (Joint Photographic Experts Group) format
photos. *See* graphics; images
Photoshop
    cross-platform issues for graphics, 276
    Image Size dialog box, 294
    image-editing programs, 292
    Indexed Color dialog box, 299, *300*
    Save For Web dialog box, 289, 305, *306*
    transparent GIFs, 305–306
    Web-safe color palette, 299, *300*
PHP4, 464–522
    accessing Web sites via, 496–498, 509–511
    backslash (\) escape character, 472–473
    comments, 473–474
    compound statements, 479
    conditional and repetitive processing, 478–484
    cookies acceptance (determining via), 493–495
    downloading and installing, 468–469
    for statements, 482–483
    history of, 467
    if statements, 478–481
    if-else statements, 479–480
    if-elseif structures, 480–481
    IP address determination, 514–516
    logical operators, 482
    MySQL databases and tables, 502–504
    operators, 476–477, 482
    overview, 465–466
    parsing and extracting form results, 488–491
    preventing linking to Web pages via, 498–499

preventing session masquerading, 516–517
preventing visitors from changing variable values via URL arguments, 511–512
random passwords via, 507–509
repetitive and conditional processing, 478–484
<script> tags, 470
semicolon (;) statement terminator, 472
sending data from HTML forms to PHP scripts, 484–488
sending e-mail messages via, 491–493
sessions via, 499–502
SQL queries and results via PHP4, 504–506
start and end tags, 469–472
statement syntax, 472–474
switch statements, 481
tracking visitors via PHP4 and MySQL, 512–514
upload file functionality, 520–522
variables, 474–476
Web page templates, 517–519
while loops, 483–484
PHP processor, preventing session masquerading, 516
pictures. *See* graphics; images
plug-in software, animation and, 318
pluginspage attribute, Flash animation, 344, 345
PNG (Portable Network Graphic) format, 268–269, 290, *291*
    See also graphics; graphics file formats
    lossless compression, 290
pointing hyperlinks to new files "on-the-fly," 413–415
    See also JavaScript
    hash property, 413
    href attribute, 413, 414–415
    pathname property, 413–414
pop-up navigation menus, 437–440
    See also Java applets
    image parameter, 439
    imageposition parameter, 439
    label parameter, 439
    <menu item> parameter, 439–440
    <param> tags, 439–440
    PopupNavigator.class, 437–439
port assignments, firewall, 605–606, *607*
port attribute, JavaScript links arrays, 400
port numbers, broadcasting streaming audio and video, 350–351
Portable Font Resource (PFR) files, CSS rules for embedding fonts within XHTML Web pages, 250–251
position property
    CSS (Cascading Style Sheets), 159, 178–179
    overlapping text, 178–179
positioning background images and watermarks, 196–199
    See also CSS (Cascading Style Sheets)
    background-image property, 196–197
    background-position property, 198–199
    background-repeat setting, 197–198
    tiles, 196
    watermarks, 197–198
positioning Java applets, 426–429

POST method
 preventing visitors from changing variable values via
  URL arguments, 511
 retrieving form results from ASP QueryString
  collection, 553
 sending data from HTML forms to PHP scripts, 486–487
<pre> (preformatted text) tags, 54–55
pre-caching images, 415–416
 See also JavaScript
 <img> (image) tags, 415
 new Image( ) constructor, 415
 onLoad event handler, 415, 416
 preCache( ) function, 416
p.regular text style, multiple CSS rules and single selectors, 171
preloading and caching images, 309–311
 See also downloading; graphics
 height attribute, 309–310
 <img> (image) tags, 309–310
 width attribute, 309–310
prepFormResults( ) function, selection list values and hidden
 fields, 137
PreResetProc( ) function, Reset buttons, 140
preventing linking to Web pages, 498–499
 See also PHP4
preventing session masquerading, 516–517
 See also PHP4
 cookies, 516
 PHP processor, 516
 session_start( ) function, 516
preventing visitors from changing variable values via URL
 arguments, 511–512
 See also PHP4
 GET method, 511
 POST method, 511
preventing Web browsers from displaying "stale" ASP, 543–545
 See also ASP (Active Server Pages)
 Response.CacheControl property, 545
 Response.Expires property, 544–545
 Response.ExpiresAbsolute property, 544
printer and file sharing (disabling), 610–612
 See also security
 Network dialog box, *611*
printing XHTML Web pages, 261–263
 See also XHTML
 CSS @media rule, 263
 CSS page-break-before and page-break-after
  properties, 261–263
progression option, graphics, 288–289
progressive mode, JPEG files, 284, *285*
protocol attribute, JavaScript links arrays, 400
proxy servers
 IP address determination, 514–516
 performance and Web-caching devices, 630, *631*
public key encryption, 598–599
 See also encryption; security
 finding public keys, 599
 overview, 598

public keys, downloading and installing, 600
publishing ASP (Active Server Pages), 527
publishing Web pages, PWS (Personal Web Server), 18–21
PWS (Personal Web Server), 16–21
 ASP (Active Server Pages) and, 527
 downloading, 16–17
 installing, 17–18
 IP addresses and, 19–21
 managing and publishing Web pages, 18–21
 Personal Web Manager, 18, *19*

Q

<q> (quotation) tags, character formatting tags, 42
quality attribute, Flash animation, 345
query results, displaying SQL in HTML tables on
 Web pages, 504–506
QueryString collection, retrieving form results from ASP,
 553–556
quick-loading tables, 103–104
 See also tables
QuickTime, sound and, 327
quotation tags. *See* <q> tags
quotes, PetQuotes.class (Java applets), 443–444

R

radio broadcasts, 327, 348–349
 See also broadcasting streaming audio and video; sound
radio buttons, 126–129
 See also forms
 <input> tags and type attribute, 126–127
 parsing and extracting form results via PHP4, 489–490
 validating group selections, 128–129
RAM
 CPU processing speed and, 630
 monitoring Web server performance, 632–633
random passwords via PHP4, 507–509
 See also PHP4
 mt_rand( ) function, 507
 script, 508
 usernames table, 508–509
readonly attribute, <input> tags, 120
RealAudio, sound, 326
RealNetworks server, broadcasting streaming audio and
 video, 350
RealPix format, SMIL (Synchronized Multimedia
 Integration Language), 356
RealPlayer, SMIL (Synchronized Multimedia Integration
 Language) and, 354, *355*, 357
RealText format, SMIL (Synchronized Multimedia
 Integration Language), 356
recordPageHit( ) function, tracking visitors via PHP4 and
 MySQL, 514
REDIRECT keyword, Ad Rotator, 574
redirecting Web browsers, 545–547
 See also ASP (Active Server Pages)
 Response.Redirect method, 545–547

redirector file
    Ad Rotator, 573
    tracking impressions and click-throughs, 579–580
referrer property, JavaScript document objects, 396
relative and absolute values for dimensioning
    cells, 85–86
    <table> tags, 84–85
relative pathnames, absolute pathnames comparison, 14–16
relative positioning, overlapping text, 178
release forms, copyright issues for Web graphics, 271–272
ReloadForever.html, denying access to systems, 594
remote services (disabling), 620–623
    See also security
    call-back systems, 622–623
    finger command, 623
    whois command, 623
removing cookies from cookie files, 407–409
    See also cookies; JavaScript
    CookieName parameter, 408
    deleteCookie( ) function, 408–409
    expiration dates, 407–408
repetitive and conditional processing
    JavaScript, 369–370
    PHP4, 478–484
replacing Submit and Reset buttons with images, 141–143
    See also forms
    action attribute, 141–142
    href attribute, 142
    name attribute, 142
Request.Cookies collection, cookies collection, 547–549
Request.Cookies method, cookies collection, 549–550
Request.Form collection
    Count property, 552
    Item method, 552
    Key method, 552
    retrieving form results from ASP Form collection,
        551–552
Request.QueryString collection, 554–556
    See also retrieving form results from ASP QueryString
        collection
    Count property, 555–556
    Item method, 556
    Key method, 556
Request.Server Variables collection, retrieving information
    from Server Variables collection, 556–557, *558*
reserved words, JavaScript, 365
Reset buttons, 138–140
    See also forms
    <input> tags and type attribute, 138
    onReset attribute, 139
    PreResetProc( ) function, 140
    preventing accidental clearings, 139–140
    replacing with images, 141–143
reset event, JavaScript events, *379*
resize values, cursor types, *214*
Response objects, SQL queries and results via ASP, 568
Response.Buffer property, ASP (Active Server Pages), 539–541

Response.CacheControl property, preventing Web browsers
    from displaying "stale" ASP, 545
Response.Clear method, ASP (Active Server Pages), 542–543
Response.End method, ASP (Active Server Pages), 543
Response.Expires property, preventing Web browsers from
    displaying "stale" ASP, 544–545
Response.ExpiresAbsolute property, preventing Web
    browsers from displaying "stale" ASP, 544
Response.Flush method, ASP (Active Server Pages), 541–542
Response.Redirect method
    Ad Rotator, 576
    redirecting Web browsers, 545–547
Response.Write method, 529, 532–539
    See also ASP (Active Server Pages)
    Ad Rotator, 575, 577
    chr( ) function, 534, 535
    Dim keyword, 536–537
    now( ) function, 535
    SQL queries and results via ASP, 568, 572
    tracking impressions and click-throughs, 577
    variables display, 536–539
    With keyword, 535–536
    writing double quote (") characters on Web pages,
        533–535
results
    displaying SQL query in HTML tables on Web pages,
        504–506
    form. *See* parsing and extracting form results via
        PHP4; retrieving form results from ASP...
    SQL queries and results via ASP, 568–573
retrieving form results from ASP Form collection, 550–552
    See also ASP (Active Server Pages); parsing and
        extracting form results via PHP4
    action attribute, 550
    <form> tags, 550–551
    GET method, 551
    method attribute, 550–551
    Request.Form collection, 551–552
retrieving form results from ASP QueryString collection,
    553–556
    See also ASP (Active Server Pages); parsing and
        extracting form results via PHP4
    action attribute, 553–554
    <form> tags, 553–554
    GET method, 553–554
    method attribute, 553
    POST method, 553
    Request.QueryString collection, 554–556
retrieving information from Server Variables collection,
    556–558
    See also ASP (Active Server Pages)
    Request.Server Variables collection, 556–557, *558*
retrieving values from cookie files, 406–407
    See also cookies; JavaScript
    cookie property, 406
    CookieName parameter, 406
    cookieValue( ) function, 406–407

getCookieValue( ) function, 406–407
unescape( ) function, 406
RLE (Run Length Encoding) compression, GIF files, 286
rotateBanner( ) function, self-changing banner ads
   (JavaScript), 412–413
rotator schedule file, Ad Rotator, 573–574
rows attribute, <textarea> tags, 121
rowspan attribute
   <td> (table data) tags, 72–74
   <tr> (table row) tags, 72–74
rsOrderDetail.EOF, SQL queries and results via ASP, 571
rsOrderInfo object, SQL queries and results via ASP, 572
rsOrderItems object, SQL queries and results via ASP, 572
rsOrderStatus object, SQL queries and results via ASP, 572
rules
   CSS (Cascading Style Sheets), 159, 160, 162, 163–164
   CSS for adding color to XHTML tables, 247–249
   CSS for embedding fonts within XHTML Web pages,
      249–251
   XHTML, 222–230

S

SATAN (Security Administrator Tool for Analyzing
   Networks), 623–624
   Courtney program for detecting, 624
   Gabriel program for detecting, 624
Save For Web dialog box, Photoshop, 289, 305, *306*
saving clip art. *See* GIF (Graphics Interchange Format) files
scanners, 292–294
   See also graphics
<script> tags
   calling user-defined JavaScript functions, 383
   external scripts, 409–410
   JavaScript, 360–361
   PHP4, 470
   validating data, 123
scripts
   ASP (Active Server Pages) and, 525–527
   CGI script attacks, 594–595
   external JavaScript, 409–410
   hiding from Web browsers without JavaScript support,
      361–362
   hiding via CDATA section (XHTML), 231–232
   JavaScript, 358–417
   sending data from HTML forms to PHP, 484–488
scrolling, <marquee> tags, 416–417
scrolling attribute, <iframe> tags, 253
search attribute, JavaScript links arrays, 400
section tags, HTML, 4–5
Secure Communications dialog box, server IDs, 602, *603*
secure keyword, storing cookies on visitors' hard drives,
   403–404
security, 586–625
   See also certificates; digital signatures
   ActiveX objects, 424

analyzing system vulnerabilities, 623–624
auditing system events to detect intruders, 614–616
client certificates, 612–613
credit card processing, 625
disabling remote services, 620–623
downloading and installing public keys, digital
   signatures, and server IDs, 600, *601*
encryption and, 597–599
firewalls, 595–597, 603–607
hacker threats, 587–595
Java applets, 422
NTFS (NT file system), 617–620
overview, 587
printer and file sharing (disabling), 610–612
server IDs, 600, 601–602, *603*
virus-detection software, 607–609, *610*
security settings, auditing system events to detect intruders,
   615–616
Security Settings dialog box, Java applets and ActiveX
   objects, 435–437
<select> tags
   drop-down lists, 129–131, 132
   id attribute, 131
   multiple attribute, 131, 132–133, 134
   name attribute, 131
   size attribute, 130
select event, JavaScript events, *379*
SELECT statements
   accessing Web sites via ASP, 563
   MySQL databases and tables, 504
selected attribute, <option> tags, 132
SelectedByDefault parameter, selection list items
   availability, 136
selectedIndex property, validating selection list choices, 133
SelectedWhenAdded parameter, selection list items
   availability, 136
selection list items, grouping XHTML. *See* <optgroup> tags
selection list items availability, 134–136
   See also forms
   addToList( ) function, 134–135, 136
   newOption( ) function, 136
   <select> tags and multiple attribute, 134
   SelectedByDefault parameter, 136
   SelectedWhenAdded parameter, 136
selection list values and hidden fields, 136–137
   See also forms
   prepFormResults( ) function, 137
selector {rule} statements, CSS (Cascading Style Sheets), 163
selectScheme( ) function, JavaScript document object color
   properties, 401
self-changing banner ads (JavaScript), 411–413
   See also banner ads; JavaScript
   onLoad event handler, 412
   rotateBanner( ) function, 412–413
   setTimeout( ) function, 412–413

semicolon (;) statement terminator, PHP4, 472
sending data from HTML forms to PHP scripts, 484–488
   See also forms; PHP4
   action attribute, 484–485, 486, 487
   <form> tags, 484–485, 486, 487
   GET method, 485–487
   method attribute, 485
   name attribute, 486
   POST method, 486–487
sending e-mail messages via PHP4, 491–493
   hyperlinks, 491
   mail( ) function, 491–493
sending form results via e-mail, 143–144
   See also forms
   action attribute, 143, 144
   enctype attribute, 144
   mailto:, 144
   name attribute, 143
<seq> tags, SMIL (Synchronized Multimedia Integration
   Language), 356
server applications and operating systems, performance and, 630
server IDs, 601–602, *603*
   See also certificates; digital signatures; security
   downloading and installing, 600
   Secure Communications dialog box, 602, *603*
Server Variables collection, retrieving information from,
   556–558
Server.CreateObject method
   accessing Web sites via ASP, 563–564
   Ad Rotator, 575
   SQL queries and results via ASP, 568
Session object, sessions via ASP, 566–567
sessions via ASP, 565–568
   See also ASP (Active Server Pages)
   ID cookies, 565–566, 568
   isEmpty( ) function, 568
   Nothing session variables, 567
   Session object, 566–567
   Session.Timeout property, 567
sessions via PHP4, 499–502
   See also PHP4
   "Accept Cookie" message box, *501*
   cookies, 500
   preventing masquerading, 516–517
   session_register( ) function, 501, 502
   session_start( ) function, 500–501
session_start( ) function, preventing session masquerading, 516
Session.Timeout property, sessions via ASP, 567
Set statements, connecting to MySQL DBMS via MyODBC
   driver, 561
setCookie( ) function
   cookies acceptance (determining via PHP4), 495
   formatting cookie data, 404, 405
setTimeout( ) function, self-changing banner ads (JavaScript),
   412–413
shadow property, filter properties, *205, 206*
shadows, drop-shadow effect, 192–194

Shockwave animation, 324–325
   See also animation
   <embed> tags, 325
   Web sites, *325*
shortcut keys, <label> tags and form, 148–149
ShowOrderStatus.asp, SQL queries and results via ASP, 571
sidebars, navigation, 97–98
signatures. *See* digital signatures
sine wave animation, SinLogo.class (Java applets), 450–451
single-line input fields, 119–120
   See also forms
   <input> tags, 119–120
SinLogo.class (Java applets), sine wave animation, 450–451
size attribute
   <font> tags, 32–33
   <hr> (horizontal rule) tags, 46
   <input> tags, 120
   <select> tags, 130
slicing images for quick loading, 102, *103*
   See also tables
   JPEG files, 102
small keyword, text size keywords for XHTML, 242
smaller keyword, text size keywords for XHTML, 244
SMIL (Synchronized Multimedia Integration Language),
   354–357
   See also animation; sound; video
   <par> tags, 355–356
   RealPix format, 356
   RealPlayer and, 354, *355*, 357
   RealText format, 356
   <seq> tags, 356
social-engineering attacks, breaking into systems, 593–594
software-based firewalls, 603–605
   See also firewalls; security
   Norton Personal Firewall, *605*
   Symantec Security Check program, 604
sound, 326–328
   See also animation
   adding to Web pages, 328
   <bgsound> tag, 328
   broadcasting streaming, 348–351
   capturing, 327
   <embed> tags, 328
   file formats, 327
   guidelines for using, 327
   <object> tags, 328
   QuickTime, 327
   radio broadcasts, 327
   RealAudio, 326
   SMIL (Synchronized Multimedia Integration
      Language), 354–357
   streaming, 351–352
   Web sites, *328*
source code, hiding ASP from Web site visitors, 531
source files, editing Java source code, 452
spaghetti graphics, tiled backgrounds, 302
<span> tags, form elements and CSS, 207–209

special characters. *See* character formatting tags; symbols and special characters

splash screens, adding Flash animation to Web sites, 342–345

SQL CREATE DATABASE statements, MySQL databases and tables, 503

SQL CREATE statements, accessing Web sites via PHP4, 509–510

SQL CREATE TABLE statements
    accessing Web sites via ASP, 563
    MySQL databases and tables, 503
    tracking visitors via PHP4 and MySQL, 512–513

SQL INSERT statements
    accessing Web sites via ASP, 563
    accessing Web sites via PHP4, 510
    MySQL databases and tables, 503–504

SQL queries and results via ASP, 568–573
    See also ASP (Active Server Pages)
    action attribute, 570
    Connection objects, 568, 571
    ConnectionString property, 569
    Execute method, 571
    GetOrderNumber.asp, 569–570
    Open method, 569
    Response objects, 568
    Response.Write method, 568, 572
    rsOrderDetail.EOF, 571
    rsOrderInfo object, 572
    rsOrderItems object, 572
    rsOrderStatus object, 572
    Server.CreateObject method, 568
    ShowOrderStatus.asp, 571
    Status item, 569

SQL queries and results via PHP4, 504–506
    if statements, 505
    mysql_connect( ) function, 504, 505
    mysql_fetch_array( ) function, 504, 506
    mysql_query( ) function, 504, 505–506

SQL query results, displaying in HTML tables on Web pages, 504–506

SQL SELECT statements
    accessing Web sites via ASP, 563
    MySQL databases and tables, 504

src attribute
    animation and onLoad events, 411
    <embed> tags, 325
    Flash animation, 345
    <frame> tags, 58
    GIF animation, 322, 336
    <iframe> tags, 253
    image-editing programs, 291
    images and links in cells, 98
    <img> (image) tags, 36, 269
    JavaScript images arrays, 398

SSL (Secure Socket Layer) protocol
    accessing Web sites via ASP, 565
    accessing Web sites via PHP4, 498
    client certificates, 612

start attribute, <ol> (ordered list) tags, 50

start and end tags
    ASP (Active Server Pages), 525, 528–531
    PHP4, 469–472

"Status: 404 not found" errors, 580–585
    See also ASP (Active Server Pages)
    BadURL( ) function, 582–583
    IIS (Internet Information Server), 583–585
    overview, 580–581
    replacing, 581–585

Status item, SQL queries and results via ASP, 569

storing cookies on visitors' hard drives, 402–404
    See also cookies; JavaScript
    domain keyword, 403
    expires keyword, 403
    overview, 402–403
    path keyword, 403
    secure keyword, 403–404

streaming audio and video, 351–352
    See also animation
    broadcasting, 348–351
    Cool Edit, 351–352

streaming vs. downloading video, 331–332
    See also broadcasting streaming audio and video

<strong> tags, character formatting tags, 42

<style> tags, 159–160, 162, 164
    See also CSS (Cascading Style Sheets)
    type attribute, 167

style attribute, 77–78
    See also <table> tags
    background images and colors, 81
    background-color property, 81
    background-image property, 81
    border-color properties, 77–78
    CSS (Cascading Style Sheets), 169–170
    list-style-type property, 202
    text size keywords for XHTML, 243

style sheets. *See* CSS (Cascading Style Sheets)

<sub> (subscript) tags, character formatting tags, 42

Submit buttons, 140–143
    See also forms
    name attribute, 141
    onSubmit attribute, 141
    replacing with images, 141–143
    value attribute, 141

submit event, JavaScript events, *379*

summary attribute, <table> tags, 70

<sup> (superscript) tags, character formatting tags, 42

switch statements, PHP4, 481

Symantec Security Check program, software-based firewalls, 604

symbols and special characters, 42–44
    See also character formatting tags
    copyright symbol, 43, *44*

Synchronized Multimedia Integration Language. *See* SMIL

T

tabindex attribute, <input> tags, 120
<table> tags, 67–68
    See also tables
    absolute and relative values for dimensioning, 84–85
    background attribute, 80–81
    bgcolor attribute, 80–81
    border attribute, 70, 72, 75–76
    bordercolor attribute, 76–77
    bordercolordark attribute, 76–77
    bordercolorlight attribute, 76–77
    cellpadding attribute, 83–84
    cellspacing attribute, 83–84
    height attribute, 84–85
    hexadecimal color values, 81–83
    images and links in cells, 98
    relative and absolute values for dimensioning, 84–85
    style attribute, 77–78
    summary attribute, 70
    width attribute, 84–85
table heading tags. *See* <th> tags
table selector, CSS (Cascading Style Sheets), 164
tables, 62–111
    aligning cell content horizontally and vertically, 86–88
    aligning Web page content via borders, 108–110
    aligning on Web pages, 89
    background images and colors, 78–81
    border attribute, 69–70, 75–78
    <caption> tags, 70
    cell background colors, 107–108
    cell padding and cell spacing, 83–84
    cells spanning multiple columns or rows, 72–74
    CSS rules for adding color to XHTML, 247–249
    displaying SQL query results on Web pages, 504–506
    form layout and, 145–147
    frames simulation, 104–107
    heading tags. *See* <th> tags
    hexadecimal color values, 81–83
    image map simulation, 100–101
    image maps and, 65–66
    images and links in cells, 98
    lists and bullets, 96–97
    MySQL databases and, 502–504
    navigation sidebars, 97–98
    nesting to control borders, 99, *100*
    overview, 63–66
    page layout and, 72
    quick loading, 103–104
    setting cell dimensions via relative or absolute values, 85–86
    setting dimensions via relative or absolute values, 84–85
    slicing images for quick loading, 102, *103*
    <table> tags, 67–68
    tags for creating, 67–72
    <td> (table data) tags, 67–69
    <th> (table heading) tags, 70–71

thumbnail images within, 93–95
    <tr> (table row) tags, 67–69, 71
    transparent GIFs, 89–91
    Web page gutter size and margin width, 110–111
    wrapping text around images, 91–93
tables and form layout, 145–147
    See also forms
    border attribute, 147
    height attribute, 145–146
    valign attribute, 145
tags
    See also under specific tag names
    character formatting, 41–42
    container, 4
    empty, 5
    section, 4–5
    table, 67–72
    XHTML, 222
target attribute
    <a> (anchor) tags, 58, 59
    <form> tags, 118
    <iframe> tags, 254
    JavaScript links arrays, 400
    multiple <iframe> tags, 256, 257
targetWindow parameter, navigation menus (Java applets), 446
<tbody> tags, CSS rules for adding color to XHTML tables, 247–248
<td> (table data) tags, 67–69
    See also tables
    background attribute, 80–81
    background images and colors, 78–81
    bgcolor attribute, 80
    bordercolor attribute, 78
    colspan attribute, 72, 74
    CSS rules for adding color to XHTML tables, 248
    height attribute, 85
    images and links in cells, 98
    rowspan attribute, 72–74
    width attribute, 85
templates, Web page, 517–519
text
    aligning, 37–39
    aligning Web page. *See* text-align property
    balancing text and graphics on Web pages, 272–274
    floating images and, 199–200
    formatting, 6–8
    overlapping, 177–179
    wrapping around images, 91–93
text editors, creating Web pages, 11–12
text flow, <p> (paragraph) and
 (line break) tags, 27–31
text size keywords for XHTML, 242–245
    See also XHTML
    CSS (Cascading Style Sheets), 242–244
    font-size property, 243
    large keyword, *243*
    larger keyword, 244

medium keyword, *242*
small keyword, *242*
smaller keyword, 244
style attribute, 243
x-large keyword, *243*
x-small keyword, *242*
xx-large keyword, *243*
xx-small keyword, *242*
text value, cursor types, *214*
text-align property
    class attribute and, 180
    CSS (Cascading Style Sheets), 179–181
    "justify" option, 180
text-only viewers, alt attribute and <img> (image) tags, 278–281
<textarea> tags, 120–122
    See also forms
    cols attribute, 121, 122
    id attribute, 121
    multiline input fields, 120–122
    name attribute, 121
    rows attribute, 121
    type attribute, 122
<tfoot> tags, CSS rules for adding color to XHTML tables, 247–248
<th> (table heading) tags, 70–71
    See also tables
    CSS rules for adding color to XHTML tables, 249
    height attribute, 86
    width attribute, 86
<thead> tags, CSS rules for adding color to XHTML tables, 247–248
thumbnail images within tables, 93–95
    See also tables
    <a> (anchor) tags and href attribute, 93–95
thumbnails with captions, 209–212
    See also CSS (Cascading Style Sheets)
    <div> tags, 210–212
    fLeft class, 210–211
    padding properties, 211
thumbnails and retrieving full size images, 307–309
    See also graphics
    href attribute, 307, 308–309
Tidy Configuration dialog box, HTML Tidy (converting HTML to XHTML), *235*
Tidy Output dialog box, HTML Tidy (converting HTML to XHTML), *236*
TidyGUI.exe, HTML Tidy (converting HTML to XHTML), 234–235
tiled backgrounds, 301–304
    See also graphics; images
    background attribute, 301–302
    spaghetti graphics, 302
tiles
    border graphics, 194–196
    positioning background images and watermarks, 196
<title> tags, 21–23
    XHTML, 229–230

title attribute
    cursor types, 212
    <form> tags, 119
title attribute and tool tips, 281–282, *283*
    See also graphics; <img> (image) tags
title property, JavaScript document objects, 396
tool tips
    cursor types, 212, 213
    title attribute and, 281–282, *283*
tours, virtual, 332–334
<tr> (table row) tags, 67–69, 71
    See also tables
    colspan attribute, 72, 74
    CSS rules for adding color to XHTML tables, 247
    rowspan attribute, 72–74
tracert command, intercepting and changing network messages, 588–589
tracking impressions and click-throughs, 576–580
    See also Ad Rotator; ASP (Active Server Pages)
    DisplayRotatorAd( ) function, 578
    GetAdvertisement method, 577–579
    redirection file, 579–580
    Response.Write method, 577
tracking visitors via PHP4 and MySQL, 512–514
    See also MySQL databases and tables; PHP4
    log files, 512–513
    recordPageHit( ) function, 514
    SQL CREATE TABLE statements, 512–513
Transitional XHTML DTD, <!DOCTYPE> element, 238
transparent GIFs, 89–91, 304–307
    See also GIF (Graphics Interchange Format) files; graphics; tables
    bounding boxes and, 304
    Photoshop, 305–306
    width attribute, 91
tweening, GIF animation, 341–342
type attribute
    accessing Web sites via ASP, 564
    button objects, 154
    Flash animation, 345
    hiding input in password fields, 153
    <input> tags, 119, 124–127, 138
    <link> tags, 167
    <object> tags, 433
    <ol> (ordered list) tags, 50
    passing values via hidden fields, 151
    <style> tags, 167
    <textarea> tags, 122
    <ul> (unordered list) tags, 51
type attribute and <input> tags
    checkboxes, 124–126
    Reset buttons, 138
typefaces
    See also <font> tags
    face attribute, 26–27
    selecting via font-family property, 172–174

U

<u> (underline) tags
    character formatting tags, 42
    formatting text, 8
    hyperlinks caveat, 41
<ul> (unordered list) tags, 50–51
    CSS (Cascading Style Sheets), 164
    list-style-type property, 202, *203*
    lists and bullets, 96
    type attribute, 51
underline tags. *See* <u> tags
unescape( ) function, retrieving values from cookie files, 406
unload event, JavaScript events, *379*
unordered lists. *See* <ul> tags
upload file functionality via PHP4, 520–522
    See also PHP4
    FTP (file transfer protocol), 520
    mkdir( ) function, 520–521
    move_uploaded_file( ) function, 521–522
    opendir( ) function, 520–521
URL arguments, preventing visitors from changing variable
    values via, 511–512
url property, JavaScript document objects, 396
user-defined JavaScript functions, calling, 382–384
username/password pairs
    See also passwords
    accessing Web sites via ASP, 562–563
    accessing Web sites via PHP4, 509
    breaking into systems, 591–592
usernames
    accessing Web sites via ASP, 562–565
    accessing Web sites via PHP4, 496–498, 509–511
    preventing linking to Web pages via PHP4, 498–499
usernames table, random passwords via PHP4, 508–509

V

validateAndSubmit( ) function, passing values via hidden
    fields, 152
ValidateForm( ) function
    validating data, 123–124
    validating radio button group selections, 129
    validating selection list choices, 134
validating data, 122–124
    See also forms
    <script> tags, 123
    ValidateForm( ) function, 123–124
validating forms via onClick attribute, 149–150
    See also forms; parsing and extracting form results
        via PHP4
validating radio button group selections, 128–129
    See also forms; radio buttons
    checked property, 129
    countSelections( ) function, 129
    length property, 129
    name attribute, 128

onSubmit attribute, 129
    ValidateForm( ) function, 129
validating selection list choices, 132–134
    See also forms
    <form> tags and method attribute, 134
    <form> tags and onSubmit attribute, 134
    <select> tags and multiple attribute, 132–133
    selectedIndex property, 133
    ValidateForm( ) function, 134
validating XHTML, 238–242
    See also XHTML
    <!DOCTYPE> element, 239, 241
    DTD (Document Type Definition), 239, 241
    HTML Validation service, 239–242
validator, CSS (Cascading Style Sheets), 216–218
valign attribute
    aligning cell content horizontally and vertically, 87, *88*
    tables and form layout, 145
value attribute
    button objects, 154
    <input> tags, 120, 125, 127
    <option> tags, 132
    passing values via hidden fields, 151
    Submit buttons, 141
values
    maintaining between HTTP requests via cookies
        collection, 547–550
    passing between JavaScript functions, 364–365
    passing parameter to Java applets, 429–431
    passing via hidden fields, 151–152
    preventing visitors from changing via URL
        arguments, 511–512
    retrieving from cookie files, 406–407
    XHTML attribute enclosed in quotes, 227
variables
    declaring JavaScript, 367
    displaying via Response.Write method, 536–539
    maintaining values between HTTP requests via
        cookies collection, 547–550
    PHP4, 474–476
    preventing visitors from changing values via URL
        arguments, 511–512
    retrieving information from Server Variables
        collection, 556–558
VBScript engine, ASP (Active Server Pages) and, 525, *526*,
    529, 530
vector graphics, Flash animation, 322–323
video, 328–332
    See also animation
    <a> (anchor) tags, 332
    broadcasting streaming, 348–351
    compatibility issues, 331
    overview, 328–329
    production of, 329–332
    SMIL (Synchronized Multimedia Integration
        Language), 354–357

streaming, 351–352
streaming vs. downloading, 331–332
video-editing programs, 329
Web sites, *331*
virtual tours, 332–334
See also animation
Web sites, *333*
virus-detection software, 607–609, *610*
See also security
ActiveX objects and, 609
CERT Web site, *610*
firewalls and, 608
macro-based viruses, 607–608
Web sites, *609, 610*
visitorSignIn( ) function, formatting cookie data, 405
vlinkColor property
JavaScript document object color properties, *402*
JavaScript document objects, 396
vspace attribute, JavaScript images arrays, 398

W

wait value, cursor types, *214*
watermarks, positioning background images and, 196–199
wave property, filter properties, *205, 206*
Web browsers
ActiveX objects and, 422–424
ASP (Active Server Pages) and, 527
cookies acceptance (determining via PHP4), 493–495
defined, 1
Java applets and, 420–422
preventing from displaying "stale" ASP, 543–545
redirecting, 545–547
Web pages and, 2–3
Web cams, 352–354
See also animation
Web sites, *352*
Web design
animation and, 318
graphics and, 265–267
Web farms, 631, *632*
See also performance
Web layout applications, creating Web pages, 13, *14*
Web page gutter size and margin width, 110–111
See also tables
width attribute, 111
Web page templates, 517–519
See also PHP4
Web pages
adding CSS (Cascading Style Sheets) to, 166–170
aligning content via borders, 108–110
aligning text. *See* text-align property
animation, 316–357
balancing text and graphics on, 272–274
comments, 24–25
creating, 5–6, 11–13, *14*
CSS (Cascading Style Sheets), 158–218

CSS rules for embedding fonts within XHTML, 249–251
displaying multiple. *See* frames
displaying SQL query results in HTML tables on, 504–506
embedding ActiveX objects in, 432–435
graphics, 264–315
gutter size and margin width, 110–111
<img> (image) tags, 35–37
inserting graphics into, 269–270
inserting Java applets into, 424–432
layering elements, 214–215, *216*
naming objects, 392–393
placing graphics into, 269–270
preventing linking to via PHP4, 498–499
printing XHTML, 261–263
publishing via PWS (Personal Web Server), 18–21
redirecting Web browsers, 545–547
sessions via PHP4, 499–502
sound, 326–328
tables, 63–111
templates, 517–519
<title> tags, 21–23
upload file functionality via PHP4, 520–522
video, 328–332
virtual tours, 332–334
Web browsers and, 2–3
writing double quote (") characters on, 533–535
Web servers
ASP (Active Server Pages) and, 527
benchmark programs and Web sites, *627*
monitoring performance, 631–635
Web sites
accessing via ASP, 562–565
accessing via PHP4, 496–498, 509–511
broadcasting streaming audio and video, *349–350*
Flash animation, *323, 347*
GIF animation, *322*
monitoring Web server performance, *635*
performance, *627*
Shockwave animation, *325*
sound, *328*
video, *331*
virtual tours, *333*
virus-detection software, *609, 610*
Web cams, *352*
Web server benchmark programs, *627*
Web-caching devices and proxy servers, performance and, 630, *631*
Web-safe color palette, 298–300, 311–313
See also color; graphics
dithering techniques, 311–313
Photoshop, 299, *300*
while loops
JavaScript, 377–378
PHP4, 483–484
whois command, disabling remote services, 623

width attribute
>   alt attribute and text-only viewers, 279
>   <embed> tags, 325
>   Flash animation, 345
>   <hr> (horizontal rule) tags, 46
>   <iframe> tags, 253
>   <img> (image) tags, 37, 277–278
>   JavaScript images arrays, 398
>   <object> tags, 433
>   preloading and caching images, 309–310
>   <table> tags, 84–85
>   <td> (table data) tags, 85
>   <th> (table heading) tags, 86
>   transparent GIFs, 91
>   Web page gutter size and margin width, 111
WIDTH keyword, Ad Rotator, 574
width property
>   columns, 183–184
>   filter properties and, 204
Windows, cross-platform issues for graphics, 274–276
Windows Task Manager dialog box, monitoring Web server
>   performance, 632–633, *634*
With keyword, Response.Write method, 535–536
word processors, creating Web pages, 12–13
word spacing, CSS (Cascading Style Sheets), 188
wrapping text around images, 91–93
>   *See also* tables
write method, JavaScript, 380–381
writing double quote (") characters on Web pages,
>   Response.Write method, 533–535

X

x-large keyword, text size keywords for XHTML, *243*
x-small keyword, text size keywords for XHTML, *242*
XHTML, 220–263
>   *See also* HTML (HyperText Markup Language)
>   attribute values enclosed in quotes, 227
>   <body> tags, 224
>   case sensitivity of, 225

CDATA section, 231–232
"container" elements, 226–227
converting HTML to. *See* HTML Tidy
CSS rules for adding color to tables, 247–249
CSS rules for embedding fonts within Web pages,
>   249–251
<!DOCTYPE> element, 228–229, 237–238
DTD (Document Type Definition), 225, 228–229,
>   237–238
empty tags, 226–227
grouping selection list items. *See* <optgroup> tags
<head> tags, 224
<html> tags, 223–224
HTML Tidy (converting HTML to XHTML), 233–237
<img> (image) tags, 269
inline frames, 251–257
media attributes, 257–260
nesting elements, 224–225
<optgroup> tags (grouping selection list items), 245–247
overlapping tags caveat, 224–225
overview, 221–222
printing Web pages, 261–263
requirements for creating valid, 222–230
rules, 222–230
tags, 222
text size keywords for, 242–245
<title> tags, 229–230
Transitional DTD and <!DOCTYPE> element, 238
validating, 238–242
"well-formed" requirement, 263–264
XML and, 221, 222
xray property, filter properties, *205*, *206*
xx-large keyword, text size keywords for XHTML, *243*
xx-small keyword, text size keywords for XHTML, *242*

Z

z-index property, layering Web page elements, 215, *216*

INTERNATIONAL CONTACT INFORMATION

AUSTRALIA
McGraw-Hill Book Company Australia Pty. Ltd.
TEL +61-2-9417-9899
FAX +61-2-9417-5687
http://www.mcgraw-hill.com.au
books-it_sydney@mcgraw-hill.com

CANADA
McGraw-Hill Ryerson Ltd.
TEL +905-430-5000
FAX +905-430-5020
http://www.mcgrawhill.ca

GREECE, MIDDLE EAST,
NORTHERN AFRICA
McGraw-Hill Hellas
TEL +30-1-656-0990-3-4
FAX +30-1-654-5525

MEXICO (Also serving Latin America)
McGraw-Hill Interamericana Editores S.A. de C.V.
TEL +525-117-1583
FAX +525-117-1589
http://www.mcgraw-hill.com.mx
fernando_castellanos@mcgraw-hill.com

SINGAPORE (Serving Asia)
McGraw-Hill Book Company
TEL +65-863-1580
FAX +65-862-3354
http://www.mcgraw-hill.com.sg
mghasia@mcgraw-hill.com

SOUTH AFRICA
McGraw-Hill South Africa
TEL +27-11-622-7512
FAX +27-11-622-9045
robyn_swanepoel@mcgraw-hill.com

UNITED KINGDOM & EUROPE
(Excluding Southern Europe)
McGraw-Hill Education Europe
TEL +44-1-628-502500
FAX +44-1-628-770224
http://www.mcgraw-hill.co.uk
computing_neurope@mcgraw-hill.com

ALL OTHER INQUIRIES Contact:
Osborne/McGraw-Hill
TEL +1-510-549-6600
FAX +1-510-883-7600
http://www.osborne.com
omg_international@mcgraw-hill.com